PRINCIPLES OF
ACCOUNTING

FIRST EDITION EDITED BY

STANLEY W. ROWLAND, LL.B., F.C.A.

FIFTH EDITION

REVISED BY

R. GLYNNE WILLIAMS, F.C.A.

THE DONNINGTON PRESS
40-42 ST. PETER'S STREET
ST. ALBANS

CASSELL & COMPANY, LTD.
37-38 ST. ANDREW'S HILL
LONDON, E.C.4

FIFTH EDITION 1956

Made and Printed in Great Britain by Butler & Tanner Ltd., Frome and London

CONTENTS

TABLE OF CASES CITED

EDITOR'S INTRODUCTION TO THE
FIRST EDITION

The first word in a book such as this may fittingly be addressed to the student who, by its aid, is about to enter on a course of serious study. The beginner whose opportunities for contact with the practical operations of commerce are restricted or non-existent may be pardoned if he is tempted to resign an unfamiliar field to the possession of technical specialists. One of the purposes of this book is to banish such timidity. This is an age when all problems, political, social, and even moral, bear an economic complexion, and every man of enquiring mind who moves in the world must necessarily form a personal judgment or suffer intellectual extinction. If economics is the study of wealth, the practical recording of quantitative values which we call accountancy cannot be dissociated from a complete view of the economic world. The student will therefore realise that a grasp of the principles which are about to be enunciated will furnish him with a potent instrument for the elucidation of economic truth.

Commerce is the economic contact of one man with another, and the possibility of developing a healthy commercial community rests on the expectation that bargains made will be honoured by mutual performance. The fundamental function of book-keeping is the systematic recording of those bargains and performances. In the strict use of language, accountancy includes book-keeping, but by common consent accountancy is usually understood as occupying itself with the proper summarisation, interpretation and use of the records provided by book-keeping. One first piece of counsel to the beginner is that he should reflect on the immense variety of the phenomena which are to be brought within the purview both of book-keeping and of accountancy. General rules must be framed to cover cases so different as those of the professional man, the manufacturer, the departmental store, the executor administering an estate, the stockbroker, the hospital, the bank, the railway company, the Government department and the life assurance institution. A list so compiled at random should remind the student both of the danger of too much theorising and of the interest which springs from perpetual variety. No text-book can be more than a finger-post which points the way ; the intelligent traveller casts his eye around at the unfolding of the landscape ; so the student of accounting is advised to check his reading at every point by relating his knowledge to the most diverse circumstances his imagination can conjure up.

The modern significance of correct accountancy has been emphasised by several important circumstances. Apart from the statutory provisions relating to bankruptcies and to companies, it must be remembered that the Income Tax Acts have constituted the British Treasury, in effect, a sleeping partner in every trading undertaking, and that the proper share of that partner can be ascertained only by careful account keeping. Further, the overwhelming importance of the joint stock principle in the field we are considering cannot be overstated. At a time when individual merchants adventured their own capital, the consequences of accounting error may not have been serious ; but the mark of modern commerce is the administration of capital by persons who do not own it. Where numerous small capitalists contribute to a common fund, committing the conduct of a given business to the care of directors, a liability to account immediately arises, and it is small wonder that a host of problems, legal and ethical, some of which await final solution, should have appeared. It is in connection with company accountancy that the distinction between capital and revenue assumes urgent importance. The privilege of incorporation confers on a company a continuing existence independent of that of the individuals who compose it ; the separation of the company's permanent fund of capital from accretions thereto which, in proper circumstances, are the property of the individual members, is a necessary corollary. In this field inaccuracy of accounting may easily lead to the gravest disasters.

The emergence of costing as a branch of modern accounting is a matter which may provoke the student's reflection. In essence, cost accounting is an attempt to associate expenditures of all kinds with the individual units of production which result therefrom. This attempt to ascertain "cost of production" has led to important developments. Few manufacturers are in the happy position of being able to fix their prices so as to yield a margin of profit over and above their costs. In the modern world it is becoming increasingly necessary to begin at the other end and to reduce costs as far as possible below an externally imposed selling price. The result is that cost accounting has become an instrument whereby wastage and inefficiency may be detected and corrected. The accountant has thus been promoted, in a sense, to a position of control and responsibility. The ledger is no longer the history of a voyage ; it is the chart whereby the ship is navigated.

Attention has above been called to the dependence of accountancy on correct book-keeping. The relation between the two may be likened to that between ability to read and the formation of good literary style. Illiterate poets have occasionally appeared, but they are remarkable exceptions. So the accountant must almost necessarily begin by grounding himself firmly in the ruling ideas of book-keeping. The balance sheet and revenue account, with the contemplation of which the accountant is so largely occupied, are transcripts of records made by book-keeping in books of account, and their significance cannot be fully present to the mind unless the mechanical process by which they are produced is reasonably well understood. So far is this true that the experienced accountant finds that chains of events and their resultant state of facts present themselves to his mind as pictures of ledger accounts rather than as verbal descriptions. The forms of book-keeping thus become the symbols of thought, and serve the accountant very much as x and y serve the mathematician.

It is necessary to view all trading as a stream of separable transactions. It is the business of the book-keeper to take every single transaction and separately to record its effect, without any reference to transactions which he may know have gone before or which he may have reason to believe will come after. It is fundamentally true that every transaction must have a double effect. That is to say, it is impossible for a business to receive anything without setting up a corresponding accountability therefor, either to an external party or to the proprietor on whose behalf the business is being carried on. Similarly, and on the other hand, it is impossible for the business to part with any values unless either a corresponding indebtedness against an external party is set up or unless a previously existing state of accountability to the proprietor is released or discharged. The universal rule of the equality of debit and credit is thus not an artificial creation of theory but is a reflection of natural fact. So-called " single entry " book-keeping, whatever form it may take, cannot be a logical system because it lacks the complete record of the double-sided transferring of value which is a necessary characteristic of every transaction. The trial balance is thus a characteristic feature of double entry book-keeping, because its agreement (subject to certain exceptional circumstances mentioned in Chapter I) is evidence of the complete reflection of the transactions recorded.

One special aspect of the trial balance must be mentioned because of its extreme importance in practical accountancy. The ability to produce a balanced trial balance is one of the fundamental safeguards against fraud. Every transaction results in a debit in one account and an equal credit in another (or others). It follows that the draughtsman of a scheme of book-keeping may arrange that the duty of making a debit and a credit shall fall on different parties. A person fraudulently minded must secure that the wrongful record shall appear both on the debit and credit side, for if he does not the disagreement of the trial balance will inevitably discover him. Such a division of responsibility necessitates collusion if fraud is to be concealed, and the difficulties thus placed in the way of a thief are too obvious to need further explanation.

While it is important to understand that balance sheets and revenue accounts are derived, in the mechanical sense, from accounts existing in the ledger, it is necessary also to observe that the accountant must take a broader view and must relate his figures to the events and facts which they purport to reflect. It has often been stated in text-books that the agreement of the result shown by a profit and loss account with that displayed by a balance sheet is proof of the correctness of the book-keeping. Such an assertion is dangerous in the extreme. The agreement referred to may be proof that the book-keeper's pen has effected correspondence between debit and credit, but it does not exclude the possibility that the book-keeper's mind may not have appreciated correctly the significance of the transaction presented for record. Notably, he may have confused the distinction between capital and revenue or, to use accounting language, he may have recorded in real accounts items which are proper to nominal accounts or *vice versa*. The accountant who remembers this does not fail to check his documents against the facts; especially will he be alert to discover whether the assets on a balance sheet represent existing values and whether liabilities may exist which are not disclosed.

This essential relation of documents to facts is worth dwelling upon. The two sides of a balance sheet certainly agree, because they summarise balances which book-keeping has automatically made equal; but there is another way of explaining the equality. The assets side of a balance sheet is a review of the total fund of wealth under administration, described in terms of the concrete form it happens to take at a selected moment. The liabilities side of the balance sheet is nothing but another view of exactly the same thing, for it is a statement of the sources from which the same gross fund of wealth was derived or (what is the same thing) of the accountabilities which naturally arise in respect of its possession. The assets are held partly because the proprietors contributed an original fund of

capital, partly because profits have subsequently accrued
in their favour, and partly because external parties have
made advances, whether by way of cash, services or goods.
From this point of view the balance sheet is not *made* to
balance ; it *does* balance. A similar mode of thought may
be applied to the revenue account. This describes on the
one side the successive accretions of wealth, viewed as
events occurring over a period, and on the other successive
diminutions of that wealth necessitated by the incurring
of expenses. The net result is the amount of profit for
which the business has become accountable to its proprietors during the period, and it is a matter of natural
necessity, as well as of book-keeping, that this amount
should be the same as that which is displayed on the liabilities
side of the balance sheet.

When the student has thoroughly assimilated Chapter I
in the light of the comments now made (and he will be
wise not to proceed too fast), he will be in a position to
commence the study of accountancy proper. It is not the
function of an introduction such as this to summarise what
is contained in later chapters ; but the importance of certain
vital points may well be stressed. It is often erroneously
thought, for example, that a balance sheet is a kind of
mathematical proposition capable of exact proof. Those
who hold this view have not realised that every balance
sheet of a trading concern must be partly a statement of
fact, and partly a statement of opinion. It is a statement
of fact in so far as the assets and the liabilities have tangible
existence, but wherever a valuation is assigned opinion is
at once imported. In this connection, it is extremely significant that an auditor under the Companies Act, 1929,
is not required to " certify " that a balance sheet is correct :
on the other hand, he " reports " his personal opinion whether
it is " properly drawn up so as to exhibit a true and correct
view ". There is a world of difference between the two
positions. The point in mind is exemplified chiefly in connection with the fixed assets. Their existence is a matter
of fact; their value is a matter of opinion. And " value " is
one of the most ambiguous words in the language. For

purposes of accounts, and in this connection, "value" must not be taken to mean something which could be realised on sale. It is merely that proportion of past expenditure the effectiveness of which has not yet expired. To take an extreme case, it is hardly conceivable that a railway tunnel could be sold apart from the railway, and in this case the only possible measure of "value" is the original cost of construction. It is a value in use as distinct from a value in exchange.

The gradual and inevitable expiry of the expenditure incurred in the provision of fixed assets is the subject matter of the study of depreciation, and the student's most careful attention should be directed to Chapter VII, which contains a detailed discussion of this very important matter. Incidentally the student should clearly understand that the making of depreciation entries, *per se*, has the effect of reducing the apparent amount of profit available for distribution as dividend : the amount so withheld exists within the business, although its identity is usually merged with the general assets of the undertaking. The earmarking of the amount, that is to say, its isolation as a tangible and available fund, is an operation separate from, though parallel to, the making of pure depreciation entries. It is this additional operation which distinguishes the sinking fund and insurance policy methods of depreciation, and the student cannot direct his attention too carefully to the distinctions involved. It may be remarked incidentally that the annuity method is often found a stumbling-block by students, and attention should be given to the exposition thereof, particularly to the explanation why the apparently irrelevant factor of interest is not so artificial as, at first blush, it might appear.

The amounts by which fixed assets depreciate are proper debits to profit and loss account before the profit of a period can be ascertained ; but to this general statement there is one prominent exception. The *financial* reason why depreciation entries are made springs from the fact that ultimately the time will arrive when the relative fixed assets will have to be replaced, and unless cash has been retained in the

business (or is otherwise available) the business will be unable
to effect renewal and will come to an end.   There is, however,
one peculiar asset to which this statement does not apply.
Goodwill is acquired when more is given for the purchase
of an existing business than the intrinsic value of its assets
would justify.   In this sense the price given is an " asset ".
But though this particular asset may depreciate (and modern
writers have given good reasons to believe that it does) it
stands in a class by itself for the reason that no necessity
will ever arise for renewal of the asset by expenditure of cash.
Accordingly, the depreciation of goodwill is an optional
matter, and if the option is exercised the proper entry is a
debit in appropriation account as distinct from profit and
loss.   The element of free choice is thereby expressed.   The
student will understand that the writing down of goodwill
in this way strengthens the financial position of a business
because it retains therein a portion of the liquid assets which
accrue through the process of profit-making.   It is, in fact,
a favourite means of building up a strong position.

It is in connection with depreciation that the double
account system becomes prominent.   In studying Chapter XI
the student should most carefully understand that the
system finds its application in connection with " public
utility " undertakings, where day-to-day maintenance is a
necessary condition of public safety, and where the idea of
ultimate winding-up (necessitating repayment of the original capital) cannot arise.   In such cases, accordingly, the
expense of maintenance is theoretically assumed to take the
place of provision for depreciation.   The ordinary commercial
undertaking keeps its capital intact by reflecting the gradual
effluxion of capital expenditure.   The double account undertaking keeps its capital intact in another sense : that is to
say, it uses its revenue for maintaining and renewing the
objects originally acquired in return for capital expenditure.
The double account balance sheet is accordingly rather an
account of what has been done with the original capital
than an attempt to assign a " value " to the objects which
now represent it.   The student must be most careful not to
forget that the obligation to maintain the assets is evidenced

(*e.g.*, in the case of railways) by a certificate to be given by the responsible officials to the effect that working efficiency has been maintained during the year.

The liabilities side of a commercial balance sheet usually contains matters of even greater interest to the accountant than does the assets side. It is, in fact, the side which is distinctly more difficult to criticise. The credit balances of which it is composed may represent definite liabilities to external parties, or accountabilities to proprietors either in respect of their capital contributions, or in respect of surpluses accrued through the operations of profit-making. Further, there may in practice be balances which represent mere diminutions of the values assigned to assets on the other side. It is not very often that there is any doubt about capital contributions, but the student will readily understand that any confusion between surplus, external liability and asset diminution may lead to serious error in the interpretation of the balance sheet. Two important comments arise. The merging of proprietors' surplus, or any part thereof, with external liability conceals from the proprietors the true extent of their interest in the undertaking, and this is a favourite means of creating a hidden reserve. The ethical and legal considerations which arise should be carefully studied.

There is an equally serious cause of error which arises from confusion between surplus and asset diminution, and only a person well versed in accounting is in a position to understand this important matter. A sinking fund is always a credit balance, whether it be raised for the purpose of the future extinction of an asset or for the purpose of providing funds for the amortisation of a liability ; but there is all the difference in the world between the two funds. The first must be treated as merely diminishing an asset ; the second will remain as a credit balance even after the relative liability is extinguished, and it is consequently a true part of proprietors' surplus, though possibly not immediately available for distribution.

The subject of inner reserves is closely allied to the degree

of disclosure which ought to be practised in the publication of
profit and loss accounts. Statute affords very little guidance,
but public opinion is steadily moving in advance of law.
The famous *Royal Mail* case produced a negative result in
law, but it profoundly affected the thinking of commercial
men. It is now generally recognised that non-recurring
or " extraneous " items of income ought not to be brought
to the credit of profit and loss account without specific
disclosure, especially in cases where their inclusion has the
effect of materially altering the opinion formed by the reader
as to the trend of trading results.

Something must finally be said about the wide and
difficult subject of holding companies. These afford a
device whereby companies may control large bodies of
trading assets without technically " owning " them. Ownership is effected, as it were, at second-hand by the means of
acquiring the shares of the company which has the legal
ownership. The result is that the profits or losses accruing
from the relative trading find no place (apart from dividends
declared) in the accounts of the holding company. There
is, in fact, nothing in law to prevent the holding company
bringing the dividends received from profitable subsidiaries
to the credit of its own profit and loss account while ignoring
altogether the losses made by others. It is obvious that in
such a state of affairs the view presented to the shareholders
of the holding company of the trading results of the economic
group may be ludicrously inaccurate.

The famous decision in *Verner* v. *General and Commercial
Investment Trust, Ltd.* (1894) has been wrongly adduced in
defence of this situation, but it should hardly be necessary
to point out that while (subject to Articles) that judgment
permits investment companies to ignore the depreciation
of their investments, it emphatically does not justify the
presentation of a misleading balance sheet. Further, there
is a great difference between a company formed to make
stock exchange investments and one formed to control the
whole conduct of the companies whose shares it acquires.
The Companies Act, 1929, has proceeded in true British
fashion by enacting an experimental compromise. In

effect, it requires only a "statement" by the directors of the holding company as to the action taken by them in regard to the profits and losses of subsidiaries. No figures whatever need be stated. Many far-sighted accountants are of opinion that such a solution can have no real permanence, and they foresee the advent of the principle of consolidation which is so largely practised in the United States. This subject is thickly bestrewn with practical difficulties, but the student may be reasonably certain that developments will sooner or later occur in British practice. He will therefore be well advised to pay particular attention to the sections of this book devoted to the matter.

STANLEY W. ROWLAND.

LONDON, *September*, 1934.

PREFACE TO THE FIFTH EDITION

In the preparation of the fifth edition of this work the opportunity has been taken to extend the text to cover the revised requirements of the professional examining bodies and to illustrate the effect of the provisions of the Companies Act, 1948, in relation to modern accounting practice. Further examples have been included throughout the text, and the exercises in Appendix III have been revised and extended to provide the reader with adequate practice in the solution of current examination problems.

Most of the exercises at the end of this work have been selected from examination papers set by the Institute of Bankers and the University of London, to whom acknowledgement is due and is here accorded.

R. G. W.

LONDON, *March,* 1956.

CHAPTER I

GENERAL PRINCIPLES

Book-keeping is so closely related to accounting that it is necessary to show how they differ. If A sells goods to B, the only accounting principle involved is the fundamental one that two aspects of the matter must be considered and recorded, if a true picture of the transaction is to be obtained. On the one hand, A has lost one asset, goods, for the legal property in these has passed to B, but on the other hand he has acquired another asset, which is either a debt due from B or cash, according to whether the transaction was a credit sale or a cash sale. As a matter of book-keeping this is recorded in A's books by debiting B's Account or Cash Account as the case may be and crediting Sales Account.

At the end of the year, A will probably have a stock of goods, which must be valued and brought into account before he can ascertain the results of trading. The principles to be followed in valuing stock in trade and the many other adjustments which must be made before a set of books can be closed for the year are matters of accounting; the methods by which they are recorded in the books so that these can be balanced off in preparation for the next period are matters of book-keeping.

Provided the book-keeper is properly instructed at the beginning of his duties, he can record routine transactions quite efficiently although he may know little or nothing of the principles of accounting. In point of fact, a business of any magnitude must employ a large number of book-keepers to do work of a routine nature. If these men are willing to remain book-keepers for the whole of their working lives, there is no imperative need for them to study the principles of accounting at all, although to do so would make their work understandable and therefore more interesting.

There must be at least one man, however, who is capable of directing the work of the book-keeping staff and of correlating the detailed records and preparing the final accounts. This man is the accountant.

To many people, the terms " accountant " and " auditor " are almost synonymous. This view is quite wrong, for an auditor is a person who checks and verifies accounts which have already been completed, and reports on their accuracy to the proprietors or other persons by whom he is engaged. An auditor must be well qualified in accounting, and for this reason he is usually a person who is in public practice as a professional accountant and auditor. Many small firms cannot employ a full-time book-keeper or accountant who is competent to complete the annual accounts ; so that, in practice, the auditor may be called upon to do this work. It should be clearly understood that in such circumstances the auditor is acting in a dual capacity and that his work as accountant is quite distinct from his work as auditor.

The distinction between the work of the accountant and that of the book-keeper has been emphasised in recent years by the introduction of mechanised methods of book-keeping. While this has revolutionised the routine of book-keeping, the principles of accounting have not been affected by it at all. The machine has replaced the clerk in such matters as casting columns of figures, copying amounts from one book into another and extracting balances from ledger accounts ; but it has not altered the fundamental rule that every credit entry in a ledger account must be compensated by an equivalent debit entry in another account and *vice versa*.

The purpose of this book is to consider the principles of accounting, but as, for the purpose of illustration and argument, it is frequently necessary to apply these principles to concrete facts, some knowledge of the methods of book-keeping is essential. In this Chapter, the recording of simple commercial transactions and the preparation of accounts to show the results of trading and the financial position of a concern at the end of a period will be considered in broad outline in order to show how the principles of accounting govern the routine matters of book-keeping.

Business Transactions.

Before the methods employed to record the transactions of a trader in his books of account, and the principles underlying the preparation of his accounts, can be studied, something must be known of the nature of these transactions. Accounts are usually expressed in terms of money but they are not, for that reason, restricted to recording transactions involving receipts and payments of cash. In any trading concern, assets or property of many different kinds besides cash are involved, and these must be reflected in the accounts, which must also record liabilities incurred. These assets and liabilities must be represented by money values, but it is essential to remember that these money values are symbolic of the assets and liabilities, which are " the facts behind the figures ". Thus, an item " Stock, £200 " appearing in a Balance Sheet does not represent 200 paper pounds but simply the cost, or the estimated value, of certain tangible articles of merchandise.

COMMENCING BUSINESS. Few businesses can be carried on without the aid of equipment and stocks of goods, and the acquisition of such essentials will be the first transaction in the establishment of a business. If the trader is commencing an entirely new venture, he will acquire his equipment through the usual trade sources ; if he is taking over an existing business, he may pay a lump sum for the business transferred to him, and will probably pay more than the market value of the net assets, i.e., the tangible assets less the outside liabilities, because he is acquiring the " goodwill " of the business. Sometimes two or more persons begin to trade in partnership or a limited company may be formed. Before the assets with which trading is to be commenced can be acquired, capital must usually be subscribed and a banking account opened. All these matters must be recorded in the books of account and the records will provide the " opening entries ".

BANK ACCOUNT. Sooner or later, there will be a receipt or payment of cash. In the days when debts were settled in coin or bullion, a trader could keep his store of gold and silver under lock and key and could ascertain the amount at any time by physical inspection and counting. With the growth of joint stock banking the bank account has come into general use in this country and it is the exception for any large payment to be made in cash or for large balances to be kept on business premises.

The balance due from banker to customer (or, in the case of an overdraft, from customer to banker) can be ascertained only by keeping accounts. Although a trader might conceivably rely on the statement of account (his Pass Book*) periodically presented to him by his bank, he would be very unwise to do so for the following reasons :—

(1) The Pass Book shows the balance according to the bank's books alone. On the average, several days will elapse between the drawing of a cheque and its presentation for payment. It may be necessary to send it by post to a creditor at a distance, and even if the latter pays it into his own account at once, another day or two will be occupied in passing it through the Bankers' Clearing House. Thus when the Pass Book is received, there may be several cheques outstanding and these must be taken into account before the available balance can be ascertained. On the other hand, cheques paid in by the trader during the last day or two may not have been credited to his account if they have not been cleared.

(2) The inconvenience caused by sending for the Pass Book every time the trader desired to know his balance would be considerable, and at the best the Pass Book could be obtained only during banking hours.

(3) Mistakes on the part of banks, although very rare, are not unknown.

* The term " Pass Book " is used to include the modern form of loose-leaf bank statement.

Thus the trader himself is practically forced to keep an account, in the form of a Cash Book,* showing on the one side the amounts paid in to the bank and on the other the cheques drawn. The balance shown by this account may differ considerably from that shown by the Pass Book and it will be necessary from time to time to prepare a Reconciliation Statement. When the Cash Book has been completed by the entry of all charges for cheque books, interest, commission, etc., made by the bank, the Reconciliation Statement will bring the two books into agreement.

PETTY CASH. When all important payments are made by cheque, it is usual to keep in the office a small amount of cash for minor day-to-day disbursements. This is known as " petty cash " and the person who keeps it as the " petty cashier ". Here again it is essential that an account should be kept ; not, as in the case of the Cash Book, in order to ascertain the balance in hand, for this can be found by counting the cash in the petty cash box, but as a check on the honesty and accuracy of the petty cashier, by recording the amount which should be on hand.

One of the best means of controlling petty cash expenditure is provided by the use of the imprest system. A fixed sum, or " imprest ", or " float ", is handed to the petty cashier when he commences his duties. At regular intervals, say weekly, his expenditure is totalled, and this amount is drawn from the bank and handed to the petty cashier in exchange for vouchers surrendered by him, so that his balance is restored to the amount of the original imprest. A voucher must be obtained for each petty cash disbursement. This system limits the amount of cash in the hands of the petty cashier to a reasonable sum and at regular intervals brings the amount actually expended to the notice of those in authority.

If the system is properly worked there is no risk that

* Throughout this book, unless the context otherwise requires, the expressions " Cash " and " Cash Book " will be applied to cash at bank which, in the strictest sense, is not cash at all, but a debt due to the trader. The modern practice is to bank all takings and make all but the smallest payments by cheque. The " Cash Book " is therefore the equivalent of an account, recording the transactions with the Bank from the trader's point of view.

a large balance may be accumulated which exists " on paper " only, and thus the area of any possible fraud is restricted. A great practical advantage of the plan is that the amount in hand may be checked very easily, for, obviously, it should be possible for the petty cashier to produce at a moment's notice the amount of his imprest either in cash or in cash and current unsurrendered vouchers taken together. Under any other scheme a check of the petty cash would involve going right back to the time when the cash was last counted, tracing all cheques drawn to the debit of the petty cash, comparing payments with vouchers, checking additions on both sides and finally subtracting credits from debits and ascertaining whether this balance exists in fact.

Goods. Most trading is done on credit terms. Supplies are obtained from day to day, according to requirements, but are usually paid for at monthly or longer intervals. It is customary for a creditor to render " statements " to his debtors as their accounts become due for payment, giving details of the amounts owing. A statement is a copy of a ledger account ; and it is obvious that a trader who sells goods on credit must keep such accounts as will enable him to ascertain the amount due from each of his debtors and to substantiate his claim if it becomes necessary for him to take steps to enforce payment. On the other hand, it is no less necessary that the business man who buys goods on credit should keep accounts in order to check the accuracy of the statements rendered to him.*

Expenditure. The purchase of goods for resale is only one item of expenditure in a trading business. Wages must be paid, premises bought or rented, lighted and heated, goods insured, the means of communication—stationery, telephone, etc.—obtained or installed, and many other matters attended to. True accounts must be kept of all these things if the trader is to be well informed as to the progress and financial position of his business.

---

* In law, a debtor is obliged to seek his creditor and pay the amount he owes him. If he does not do so he may be sued and will have to pay costs as well as the debt. A creditor is under no legal obligation to render statements of account and does so in practice as a matter of convenience.

Profit and Loss.

It is reasonable to assume that the object of the trader (the term " trader " is used in this Chapter to cover the various forms of business enterprise and includes sole traders, partnerships and limited companies) is the acquisition of profit. A trading concern earns profits by selling goods at a higher price than it pays for them, while a manufacturing concern endeavours to sell its products at a price which is greater than the total cost of production. In the process of trading, certain assets will be realised and others will be acquired. Thus stock may be sold and give place to a book debt ; the debtor may settle his account by giving a bill of exchange due at some future date, and if this bill is duly met it will in turn produce cash. In due course the cash will be used to purchase more goods and so the cycle is completed. It may be noted that at every stage except the first, the assets are converted into others of equal value. The first operation, however, results in the exchange of stock valued at cost price for a book debt equal in amount to its selling price, *i.e.*, a profit is made by exchanging one asset for another of greater value. This conception of profit is important for it shows that it can be computed in two ways, *viz.* :—

(1) By collecting in one account—

(a) The proceeds of sale of all goods sold and any miscellaneous items of income, and

(b) The cost of the goods sold and all expenses incurred in connection with their sale.

The balance of this account will indicate the net profit or loss for the period. Such an account is known as a Profit and Loss Account.

(2) By comparing the value of the net assets of the business (*i.e.*, the excess of its assets over its liabilities) at the end of the period with the corresponding value at its commencement. The net profit is represented by the increase in the net assets, subject to adjustment in respect of any

further capital introduced or withdrawn or amounts withdrawn on account of profits during the period. Conversely, the net loss is represented by the decrease in the net assets, subject to variations in the amount of capital.

The value of the net assets is found by examination of the Balance Sheet, and it is important to realise that the Balance Sheet (or, strictly, a comparison of successive Balance Sheets) reflects the results of the period just as the Profit and Loss Account does. The Profit and Loss Account shows how the profit or loss has arisen, whereas the Balance Sheet shows the form in which it exists.

Capital and Revenue.

It has been seen that the preparation of a trader's Profit and Loss Account involves the recording and summarisation of all expenses incurred in handling and selling goods. Some items of expenditure do not fall under this heading. Thus if a new machine is purchased during the course of the year, it would clearly be wrong to charge the whole of its cost as an expense of that year. Many years of useful service may reasonably be expected from the machine and at the most a proportion only of its cost should be charged in the Profit and Loss Account in any one year. In the first year of operation, when a great deal of equipment will have been purchased and possibly little business done, the distinction is seen to be vital. Thus one of the first essentials of an accounting system is that it should distinguish between *capital* expenditure and *revenue* expenditure.

CAPITAL EXPENDITURE is incurred in purchasing or constructing new property which is intended to assist in the production of profit, or in permanently improving, enlarging or extending existing property, in order to increase its profit-earning capacity. It is expenditure the direct benefit of which will extend over several trading periods and which replaces cash by a permanent asset. Examples are :— Purchase of new buildings, motor lorries, plant and machinery.

REVENUE EXPENDITURE is expenditure the direct benefit

of which is exhausted in the trading period under review and it includes—

(1) Expenditure incurred in maintaining the value of any existing asset, such as repairs, replacements and insurance.

(2) The cost of everything consumed in the process of manufacture and distribution, such as raw materials and labour.

(3) All expenses incidental to the working of the business, such as depreciation, interest, rent, salaries, etc.

Revenue expenditure includes all expenditure which cannot properly be debited to an asset account of a permanent nature.

The distinction between capital and revenue expenditure is extremely important from the point of view of the final accounts, because the former results in the acquisition of assets which must appear in the Balance Sheet, while the latter represents the expenses incurred in the business and is shown in the Profit and Loss Account.

Fixed and Current Assets.

While capital expenditure results in the acquisition of a permanent asset, revenue expenditure may result in the acquisition of a temporary one. It is necessary to recognise the essential difference between permanent or "fixed" assets and temporary or "current" assets.*

FIXED ASSETS are those which are intended to be held permanently for the purposes and benefit of the business. They may become worn out in service so that over a period of years it will be necessary to regard their cost as an essential part of the expense of running the business, or circumstances may make it expedient to sell them earlier than was anticipated and before the end of their useful life, but they are not acquired with a view to resale.

---

* Prior to the Companies Act, 1948, "current" assets were generally termed "floating" assets.

B*

CURRENT ASSETS are those which are intended for resale or which in the ordinary course of business will be converted into other assets. Consider the trading cycle discussed on page 133. Stock, book debts, bills receivable and cash are all current assets and their composition and amount is constantly changed in the process of trading.

The distinction between these and other classes of assets will be considered in greater detail in Chapter IV.

The Double Entry System.

Definitions of " Book-keeping " are numerous, but it is difficult to explain in a few words the exact meaning of a term which has such a wide and varied significance.

A modern English dictionary defines " Book-keeping " as " the art of recording pecuniary or business transactions in a regular and systematic manner ", but the term as understood by the practical man of business involves much more than the simple recording of transactions in a systematic manner ; it pre-supposes that such record shall be in a permanent form, and that the details concerning the transactions shall be so arranged that the monetary aspect of—

(1) Each separate transaction,

(2) Each group of similar transactions, *and*

(3) The whole of the transactions,

entered into during a given period, may be ascertained with the minimum of trouble and delay.

In order to accomplish this result, it has been found necessary to enter the transactions in specially ruled books, which facilitate the classification and aggregation of similar items, without impeding reference to any particular entry.

The system of " Double Entry " book-keeping, which is believed to have originated with the Venetian merchants of the fifteenth century, is the only system of recording the twofold aspect of every transaction. The result of applying this principle in practice may be usefully summarised in the axiom : " Every debit requires a credit and *vice versa*." These words express the fact that, in recording a transaction in accordance with the principles of double entry book-keeping—

(1) The receiver is charged or *debited* with the pecuniary value of whatever he (or it) receives; while

(2) The giver is *credited* with the same amount, this being the value of what he (or it) gives.

It is important to observe that double entry is not an artificial or merely mathematical rule, but is designed to reflect the essential nature of transactions regarded as " passings across " of money or money's worth from the viewpoint of one party to each business transaction.

The main book of account, called the Ledger, is composed of pages (or " folios ") divided vertically into two parts, each part containing a cash column; the left-hand side is called the " debit " side, and the right-hand side is called the " credit " side. An item which is entered on the left-hand (debit) side is accordingly said to be debited, and makes that account a debtor as far as the item debited is concerned. Conversely an item entered on the right-hand (credit) side is said to be credited, and makes that account a creditor as far as the item credited is concerned.

In the original and simplest form of account keeping, only two books are required, *viz.* :—

(1) A Journal, and (2) A Ledger.

The name of the former comes from the French word *journal*, which means a diary, day-book, or log-book. In it is written a complete daily list of the trader's transactions, entered in the order in which they occur. The labour of recording transactions in a Journal, or *journalising*, is undertaken in order to obtain a complete and reliable chronological record of the transactions. The items are arranged so as to show clearly the account to be debited or credited, as the case may be, thus facilitating the transfer, or *posting*, of the items to appropriate accounts in the *Ledger*.

To take a simple example, a sale of goods by *A* to *B* for £200 is journalised thus in *A*'s books :—

Date.	B		Dr.	£ 200	£
	To Sales				200
	Being sale of goods to B.				

Day Books.

Now in the course of a year or even of a month, many hundreds of sales will be recorded in the books, and if they are journalised in the above manner, each sale will be separately recorded and credited to Sales Account in the Ledger. It is clear that if a separate book or subsidiary journal is kept for recording sales alone—

(1) The second line, which consists only of the words " To Sales " and the repetition of the value of the sale shown in the first line, can be omitted, since the title of the book will indicate that each transaction is a sale and the amount of each sale has already been recorded ; and

(2) The double entry can be completed by totalling the entries for a given period and posting that *total* to the credit of Sales Account.

The Sales Account is thus credited with exactly the same amount as if each sale had been journalised in the ordinary way. If the Sales Journal (or Sales Day Book, as it is sometimes called) is totalled monthly, only twelve items will appear in the Sales Account instead of many hundreds, but the total amount credited will be the same. There will also be an economy of almost fifty per cent. in the number of entries in the Ledger.

Similar considerations apply to the other common transactions of a business. Purchases, Sales Returns and Allowances, Purchases Returns and Allowances, and (where they are used to any considerable extent) Bills Payable and Receivable may each be recorded in subsidiary journals. This does not involve any great departure from principle, however, for the transactions *are* journalised although in a special way and in special subsidiary journals.

Where the trader is accountable for the Purchase Tax charged to customers it is necessary to incorporate an additional column in the Sales Journal in which to record the Purchase Tax, the periodic total of which will be posted to the credit of an account for the Commissioners of Customs and Excise. The amounts paid quarterly to the Commissioners will be debited to this account.

Cash Book.

The practical recording of cash transactions, however, involves a more pronounced departure from principle. A ledger account must be provided for cash as for any other asset ; and in strict theory each transaction involving cash should be journalised. For example, when B pays A the £200 he owes him for goods supplied, A will enter in his Journal :—

Date.				£	£
	Cash		Dr.	200	
	To B				200
	Being cash received from B.				

It would, of course, be possible to adopt a similar method to that employed for recording Sales and Purchases and to use separate subsidiary journals for cash received and cash paid respectively, posting the totals periodically to a Cash Account in the Ledger, which would then reflect the balance of cash in hand. This method is in fact adopted in some cases and it has some advantages as compared with the usual method of recording the detailed cash transactions in one account. If written in the Ledger itself this cash account would occupy a great many pages, so it is usual to open a special form of separate ledger known as a Cash Book. It is then possible to dispense with the Journal altogether for recording cash transactions, which are entered in the Cash Book directly. The double entry is completed by posting from the Cash Book to the other account affected and the Cash Book thus serves the double purpose—

(1) Of acting as a Journal, or book of prime entry ;

(2) Of acting as a ledger account.

Discount.

In most businesses where credit terms are allowed to customers, a small discount is allowed for prompt payment. This is known as " cash discount ". It must not be confused with " trade discount ", which is an allowance made from the full invoice price to customers who purchase goods in the ordinary course of trade (*e.g.*, a wholesaler may invoice goods to a retailer at the full retail selling price less $33\frac{1}{3}$ per cent., which represents the retailer's gross profit). Trade discount should not be reflected in the books at all, although it may be shown in the detailed narration of the Day Books, and in the supplier's books the customer should be debited with the net trade price of the goods while the reverse entries will appear in the customer's books. Cash discount, on the other hand, is not earned until the relative account is paid, and many traders, through lack of liquid resources, are unable to take full advantage of the cash discount terms offered to them. For this reason, it is entered in the books at the time of payment and special columns in the Cash Book are very convenient for such entries. The discount column on the debit side records the amount of discount allowed to customers when they pay the cash which is entered in the debit bank column. Discount deducted on payment of a supplier's account, on the other hand, is shown in the credit discount column, against the net amount of cash paid, thus,

Dr.					CASH BOOK					*Cr.*
Date.	Name.	Fo.	Discount allowed.	Bank.	Date.	Name.	Fo.	Discount received.	Bank.	
19.. Jan. 1	To H. Jones	S.L. 23	£ s. d. 1 9	£ s. d. 3 8 3	19.. Jan. 3	By T. Smith	B.L. 51	£ s. d. 1 2 3	£ s. d. 21 2 9	

This treatment enables the book-keeper to credit H. Jones with a total of £3 10s. 0d., and to debit T. Smith with a total of £22 5s. 0d., thus showing that indebtedness between the parties, of the gross amounts stated, has been settled. The discount columns of the Cash Book are, however, nothing but a note of items which must subsequently be passed into Discount Account in the Ledger. The *total* of the " Discount Allowed " column must, at the end of a period, be *debited* to Discount Allowed Account, and the *total* of the " Discount Received " column must be *credited* to Discount Received Account. Alternatively one discount account may be used to record both items, but where this is done the totals of Discount Allowed and Discount Received should be kept separate, and not offset against each other (see example on page 24).

Classification of Transactions.

The classification of entries, or the collection of transactions of a similar nature, into appropriate accounts, demands care on the part of the book-keeper, but provided that a few simple rules are observed, the work presents no difficulties which cannot easily be overcome. Thus, the whole of a trader's transactions with another person are recorded in an account bearing that person's name ; whilst the trader's dealings in property and his items of expenditure are entered in accounts headed with the names of such property and class of expenditure respectively. Accounts which stand in the names of persons, firms or companies are called " Personal Accounts " ; all others are " Impersonal Accounts ".*

Impersonal Accounts may be sub-divided into two classes, *viz.* :—

    (1) *Real Accounts*, recording transactions in property, articles or commodities ; and

    (2) *Nominal Accounts*, recording items of income and expenditure due to intangible things.

The following list indicates a few of the more usual accounts coming under each heading :—

PERSONAL ACCOUNTS	IMPERSONAL ACCOUNTS	
	Real.	*Nominal.*
A. Anderson (a customer).	Land.	Rent.
Brotherton & Co. (a supplier of goods).	Buildings.	Wages.
Mr. Carter. (Capital account.)	Machinery.	Discounts.
(The last-named is an account showing	Stock in Trade.	Interest.
the proprietor's personal relations	Cash.	Insurance.
with his business.)		

If the fundamental distinction between capital and revenue is to be effected, transactions must be classified. It is essential that the necessary distinctions should be correctly made when the transactions are first recorded, for, as will

* An alternative classification of accounts is into (1) Real Accounts and (2) Nominal Accounts, assigning Personal Accounts to a sub-class under Real Accounts. This classification is based on the fact that a claim against a person is an asset just as much as are the tangible objects classified as " Real". The only difference is in the mode of enforcement.

be seen later, the Trial Balance, whilst affording a most valuable check on the accuracy of the book-keeper's work, does nothing to disclose errors of principle.

The risk of error can be greatly reduced by a carefully designed system of book-keeping. Personal accounts of customers and suppliers should be segregated in separate ledgers known as Sales (or Debtors) Ledgers and Purchases (or Creditors) Ledgers respectively. All other accounts may be contained in a General (or Impersonal) Ledger. Sometimes the place of the General Ledger is taken by a Nominal Ledger (containing the nominal accounts) and a Private Ledger containing the accounts of the assets of the business and of such matters as are deemed to be of a confidential nature, *e.g.*, Capital Account, Profit and Loss Account, etc. ; it is also usual to include a copy of the Balance Sheet, for memorandum purposes, in the Private Ledger. The entries in the Sales Day Book and Purchases Day Book should be restricted to goods sold and bought on credit terms in the ordinary course of business. Where a capital asset is acquired either the amount paid therefor should be posted direct from the Cash Book to the debit of the appropriate real account in the General Ledger or, if it is desired to record the personal aspect of the transaction (and this is essential when assets are purchased on long credit or instalment terms), an entry should be passed through the Journal proper, which should be retained for such exceptional transactions. Similarly, on the realisation of a fixed asset, care must be taken to exclude the transaction from the Sales Day Book and the Sales Ledger.

The Trial Balance.

It is obvious that if the transactions have been completely recorded in their two-fold aspect, that is to say, if every credit entry in the ledger is counterbalanced by a corresponding debit entry, the totals of the amounts posted to the debit of ledger accounts during a given period must agree with the total of the credit postings for the same period. Many accounts will contain postings to both the debit and the credit ; in some cases the accounts will show a balance (*i.e.*, the debit postings will exceed the credit postings, giving rise to a debit balance, or *vice versa*) ; while others will have been settled, the debit and credit postings being equal in total. It will be clear that, if a list of balances is extracted, care being taken to keep debits quite distinct from credits, the total of the debit balances must equal the total of the credit balances. The truth of this statement can quite easily be established by considering one account alone. It has been shown that the totals of the postings to all the accounts, if taken out and listed in two columns, must themselves agree in total. If the balance of an account is substituted for the whole of the postings thereto, the net result is to reduce the grand total by an equal amount on each side, since the balance is ascertained by deducting the smaller of the totals in that account from the larger. This can be done to every account without affecting the accuracy of the final agreement of totals. The final list of balances, totalled and agreed, is known as a Trial Balance.

The most useful property of the Trial Balance is the way in which, within certain limits, it proves the accuracy of the postings to the Ledger and of the balances extracted. If the Trial Balance does not agree, it is certain that errors have been committed either in posting the ledgers or in extracting the balances. On the other hand, if it does agree or when, by carefully searching for errors, it has been brought into agreement, it cannot be taken as absolute proof of the accuracy of the books. Obviously, if a transaction has been omitted from the books altogether, or has been entered at the wrong value, or has been duplicated, the Trial Balance will not thereby be thrown out of balance. In the absence of fraud, however, such errors and omissions are not likely to remain long undiscovered ; for most transactions are reflected sooner or later by a receipt or payment of cash and the balances of the Cash Book should be capable of agreement with the actual amounts of cash in hand and at the bank respectively. The most serious error that is not disclosed by the Trial Balance is, therefore, that which arises from the posting of an amount to the wrong account in the Ledger. Two balances will thus be shown incorrectly in the Trial Balance although the totals of the latter will be in agreement. The posting may be to another account of the *same class*, *e.g.*, a sale of goods to Smithson Brothers for

£100 may be debited to the account of Smith Brothers
in the Sales Ledger. Such an error—generally referred to
as an "error of commission"—is likely to be discovered
in the ordinary course of business; and even if it is not
discovered before the end of the year it will not vitiate
the accuracy of the final accounts, for the total of sundry
debtors will be correct. These arguments are not put forward in condonation of the errors but to show them in
proper relation to those of another type which are not disclosed by the Trial Balance and which may have a far-
reaching effect on the accuracy of the final accounts. This
type consists in the posting of a transaction to the *wrong
class* of account, and is particularly serious when an item of
profit or loss, instead of being posted to the appropriate
nominal ledger account, is posted either to a real account
or a personal account, or *vice versa*, *e.g.*, expenditure on
repairs to plant posted to the asset account. This is an
"error of principle" which can only be avoided by the
maintenance of a proper distinction between capital and
revenue and the strict classification of entries at every stage
of the book-keeper's work.

It is hardly necessary to add that if compensating errors
are made, that is to say, if two or more errors happen by
coincidence to offset one another, the Trial Balance will
not reveal the existence of any error at all; but with this
exception, the agreement of the Trial Balance can be taken
as *prima facie* evidence of the *arithmetical* accuracy of the
postings, additions and balances for the accounting period.

The Adjustment of the Nominal Ledger.

The preparation of a Trial Balance provides an additional
benefit in the form of a convenient summary of the balances
appearing in the ledgers at the date on which it is taken out.
This information is the groundwork on which the final
accounts are built up, but many adjustments must be made
before the Balance Sheet can show the true position of the
concern or the Profit and Loss Account show the true
profit or loss for the year. The following are the most
typical and important adjustments to be considered :—

EXPENSES. The usual practice is to record expenses in

the books when they are paid, the credit entry appearing in the Cash Book and the debit entry appearing in the Nominal Ledger. Most expenses are paid at more or less regular intervals and refer to periods of varying lengths. (Wages may be payable weekly, salaries monthly, rent quarterly, rates half-yearly and insurances yearly.) It is most improbable that they will all have been paid in respect of the exact period for which accounts are being prepared. They may be divided into two classes :—

(1) Those payable in advance, which may have been paid up to some date in the ensuing period, and

(2) Those payable in arrear, which may have been paid only up to some date in the past.

The proportions respectively paid in advance and accrued due must be brought into account for the following reasons :—

(a) So that the amounts charged in the Profit and Loss Account represent a proper proportionate charge for the period covered by the account, and

(b) So that the Balance Sheet properly reflects the true state of affairs at the end of the period.

Before the Nominal Ledger can be balanced off, it must be brought into agreement with the figures finally inserted in the accounts. This is effected in practice by bringing down the amounts accrued or paid in advance as credit or debit balances respectively.

EXAMPLE

X started business on 1st January, 1955. The rent of his business premises is £500 per annum, payable at the end of March, June, September and December. The rates on the premises, which are payable in advance, amount to £100 for the period from 1st January to 31st March, 1955; £200 each for the half-years to 30th September, 1955, and 31st March, 1956. Ignoring Income Tax, and assuming that the following payments were made for rent and rates, write up the nominal accounts involved, and close the accounts as at 31st December, 1955.

PAYMENTS FOR RENT			PAYMENTS FOR RATES		
1955			1955		
April 1.	3 mos. to 31st March, 1955 . . .	£125	Jan. 4.	3 mos. to 31st March, 1955 . . .	£100
July 4.	3 mos. to 30th June, 1955 . . .	125	April 13.	6 mos. to 30th Sept., 1955 . . .	200
Oct. 5.	3 mos. to 30th Sept., 1955 . . .	125	Oct. 4.	6 mos. to 31st March, 1956 . . .	200
1956					
Jan. 2.	3 mos. to 31st Dec., 1955 . . .	125			

It will be seen that, while the rent of X's premises is £500 per annum, he has actually paid during the year 1955 only £375, and a full quarter's rent, amounting to £125, was outstanding on 31st December, 1955. This liability is reflected by the credit balance of £125 brought down on Rent Account, which is then closed for the year by the transfer of £500 to Profit and Loss Account.

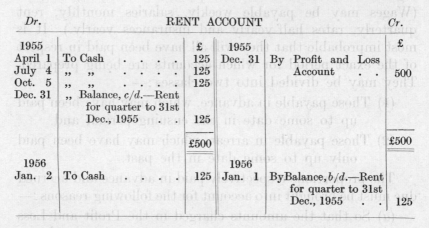

Dr.   RENT ACCOUNT   *Cr.*

1955		£	1955		£
April 1	To Cash	125	Dec. 31	By Profit and Loss	
July 4	,, ,, ...	125		Account . .	500
Oct. 5	,, ,, ...	125			
Dec. 31	,, Balance, c/d.—Rent				
	for quarter to 31st				
	Dec., 1955 . .	125			
		———			———
		£500			£500
1956			1956		
Jan. 2	To Cash	125	Jan. 1	By Balance, b/d.—Rent	
				for quarter to 31st	
				Dec., 1955 . .	125

In the case of the amount paid in respect of rates, the position is reversed as £500 has been paid during 1955, thus a sum representing the rates for the first three months of 1956 has been paid in advance. It is therefore necessary, on closing the books at 31st December, 1955, to reduce the charge to Profit and Loss Account and to show the amount paid in advance as an asset. The Rates Account appears as follows, with the £100 brought down as a debit balance at the commencement of the next period, thus :—

Dr.   RATES ACCOUNT   *Cr.*

1955		£	1955		£
Jan. 4	To Cash	100	Dec. 31	By Balance, c/d.—	
Apr. 13	,, ,, ...	200		Rates in advance	
Oct. 4	,, ,, ...	200		to 31st March, 1956	100
				,, Profit and Loss	
				Account . .	400
		———			———
		£500			£500
1956					
Jan. 1	To Balance, b/d.—Rates				
	in advance to 31st				
	March, 1956 . . .	100			

The adjustments for rent and rates will appear in the Balance Sheet as follows:—

BALANCE SHEET *
AS AT 31ST DECEMBER, 1955

	£		£
Accrued Expenses—Rent .	125	Prepayments—Rates . .	100

INCOME. In order that the true profit or loss for the accounting period may be ascertained, similar adjustments must be made for :—

(1) Income which applies to the current period but which has not yet been received, e.g., interest accrued on loans made by the business, and

(2) Income received during the current period which is applicable to a later period, e.g., rent received in advance from sub-let premises.

Adjustments under (1) will appear as an asset (Accrued Income) in the Balance Sheet (but such adjustments should not be made where there is any doubt whether the income will be received), while those under (2) will appear as a liability (Income Received in Advance) in the Balance Sheet.

STOCKS. It is unusual for the books to reflect the value of closing stock at the Trial Balance stage, although methods by which this can be effected will be considered in Chapter II. A Stock Account will have been opened in the General Ledger and a debit balance representing the value of the asset " Stock " at the beginning of the year will have been brought forward therein. No further entry will be made in this account before the end of the year, so that the Trial Balance will show the value of the opening stock as a debit balance. The closing stock must then be ascertained by a physical stocktaking. As it must appear as a credit item in the Trading Account and must be carried forward to the next period as a debit balance, the Stock Account is adjusted in the following way :—

* In accordance with modern practice, the use of general headings for a Balance Sheet, such as " liabilities " and " assets ", is considered inappropriate and unnecessary.

Dr.   STOCK ACCOUNT   *Cr.*

1955		£	1955		£
Jan. 1	To Balance, *b/d.* .	4,324	Dec. 31	By Trading Account	4,324
Dec. 31	„ Trading Account	5,927		„ Balance, *c/d.*	5,927
		£10,251			£10,251
1956					
Jan. 1	To Balance, *b/d.* .	5,927			

Thus the current period is relieved of the burden of expenditure on materials which it has not used up, while the succeeding period is charged up with the value of the stock transferred to it ; and so on from year to year. Conversely, the opening stock is eliminated from the Stock Account in the succeeding period by a credit to that account and a debit to Trading Account.

BAD DEBTS. When a customer is unable to pay all or any part of the amount due from him, a debit balance will remain on his account in the Sales Ledger. Debit balances in the Sales Ledger ordinarily represent assets and are shown in total in the Balance Sheet as " Sundry Debtors " or " Trade Debtors ". If a balance is known to be irrecoverable it is clearly wrong to regard it as an asset ; ascertained bad debts are therefore written off by transfer out of the relative accounts in the Sales Ledger to the debit of Bad Debts Account and appear as such in the Trial Balance ; subsequently the balance on Bad Debts Account is transferred to the debit of Profit and Loss Account. At the end of the year, however, it will usually be found that certain bad debts are expected although they cannot at that date be written off as irrecoverable, while other debts which appear to be good at that date, may never be received. Allowance is made for these expected losses by creating a Provision for Bad Debts and, in the absence of any more reliable indication of the loss likely to be suffered under this head, it usually takes the form of a percentage on the total value of Sundry Debtors. It would be impracticable and indeed wrong (for the fact that a bad debt is feared, does not reduce the amount legally due from the debtor) to write this percentage off each Sales Ledger Account and the necessary provision is made in the General Ledger, either in the Bad Debts Account or in a separate Provision for Bad Debts Account (see example on page 24).

While, in a normal business, the method of fixing the provision for bad debts is to take a percentage (according to experience) on the outstanding debtors, it must be observed that dangers attend this course if any of the debts are of exceptionally large amount or if special circumstances affect particular debts. In a small business it is sometimes possible to assess the risk separately for each debt, and in *all* cases it is advisable to combine an examination, as far as possible, of each account with the percentage method. Occasionally, as a further alternative, a small percentage on the credit sales of the period is taken. This plan has the merit of loading the expense of bad debts on to the period which receives the benefit of the initial sale.

DISCOUNTS. Although cash discounts are not entered in a trader's books until the relative accounts have been received or paid, some adjustment may be made at the end of the year for the amounts appropriate to the balances outstanding at that date. If a percentage on the amount of Sundry Debtors is provided, representing the discount which would be allowed if all the customers paid their accounts on the due date in the new year, it is not unreasonable to take credit for the corresponding percentage on Sundry Creditors, representing the discount which might be earned if all accounts owing were paid by the trader on the due date in the new year. Many traders, however, adopt the prudent course of providing for discounts allowable but ignoring discounts receivable, on the principle that losses should always be anticipated but profits should be ignored until they have been earned.

When the Provision for Discounts Allowable is calculated as a percentage on Sundry Debtors, any Provision for Bad or Doubtful Debts should be deducted first, for if a debt is bad there can be no question of allowing cash discount on payment. The following example shows the two methods commonly employed for recording Provisions for Bad Debts and Discounts.

EXAMPLE

At 31st December, 1955, X's Discount Account showed discounts allowed to debtors and discounts received from creditors amounting to £548 and £196 respectively. The total amount owing by Sundry Debtors at that date, after writing off bad debts, was £12,500, whilst £8,400 was owing to Sundry Creditors. It is desired to make a provision for doubtful debts of 5 per cent. on the total debtors, and provisions of 2½ per cent. for cash discounts on debtors and creditors. The bad debts written off during the year amounted to £342. Write up the Bad Debts and Discounts Accounts.

Method I.

Dr.			BAD DEBTS ACCOUNT			*Cr.*
1955		£ s. d.	1955		£	s. d.
—	To Sundries	342 0 0	Dec. 31	By Profit and Loss Account	342	0 0
		£342 0 0			£342	0 0

Dr.	PROVISION FOR BAD DEBTS ACCOUNT			*Cr.*
	1955		£	s. d.
	Dec. 31	By Profit and Loss Account (5% on £12,500)	625	0 0

Dr.			DISCOUNTS ACCOUNT			*Cr.*
1955		£ s. d.	1955		£	s. d.
—	To Discounts Allowed	548 0 0	—	By Discounts Received	196	0 0
Dec. 31	„ Profit and Loss Account	196 0 0	Dec. 31	„ Profit and Loss Account	548	0 0
		£744 0 0			£744	0 0

NOTE.—Two accounts are usually kept in practice, one for Discounts Received and one for Discounts Allowed.

Dr.	PROVISION FOR DISCOUNTS ON CREDITORS			*Cr.*
1955		£ s. d.		
Dec. 31	To Profit and Loss Account (2½% on £8,400)	210 0 0		

Dr.	PROVISION FOR DISCOUNTS ON DEBTORS			*Cr.*
			1955	£ s. d.
			Dec. 31	By Profit and Loss Account (2½% on £12,500— £625)	296 17 6

Method II.

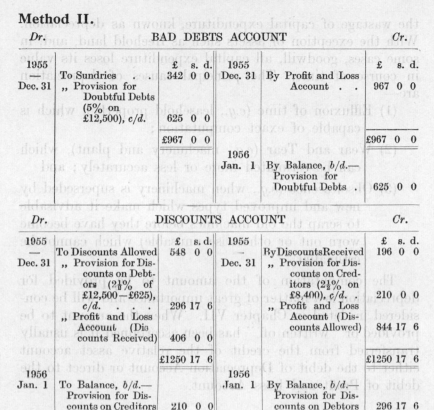

Dr.   BAD DEBTS ACCOUNT   *Cr.*

1955		£	s.	d.	1955		£	s.	d.
—	To Sundries	342	0	0	Dec. 31	By Profit and Loss			
Dec. 31	„ Provision for Doubtful Debts (5% on £12,500), c/d.	625	0	0		Account	967	0	0
		£967	0	0			£967	0	0
					1956 Jan. 1	By Balance, b/d.— Provision for Doubtful Debts	625	0	0

Dr.   DISCOUNTS ACCOUNT   *Cr.*

1955		£	s.	d.	1955		£	s.	d.
—	To Discounts Allowed	548	0	0	—	By Discounts Received	196	0	0
Dec. 31	„ Provision for Discounts on Debtors (2½% of £12,500—£625), c/d.	296	17	6	Dec. 31	„ Provision for Discounts on Creditors (2½% on £8,400), c/d.	210	0	0
	„ Profit and Loss Account (Discounts Received)	406	0	0		„ Profit and Loss Account (Discounts Allowed)	844	17	6
		£1250	17	6			£1250	17	6
1956 Jan. 1	To Balance, b/d.— Provision for Discounts on Creditors	210	0	0	1956 Jan. 1	By Balance, b/d.— Provision for Discounts on Debtors	296	17	6

NOTE.—Instead of posting to Profit and Loss Account the separate balances of discounts received and discounts allowed, the net balance of the Discounts Account (£438 17s. 6d.) may be posted to the debit of the Profit and Loss Account.

The latter course is not, however, to be recommended, as discounts allowed and discounts received relate to entirely different sets of transactions, and it is desirable that the totals be shown separately on their respective sides of the Profit and Loss Account.

The Sundry Creditors and Sundry Debtors will appear in the Balance Sheet as follows :—

BALANCE SHEET
AS AT 31ST DECEMBER, 1955

	£	s.	d.	£	s.	d.		£	s.	d.	£	s.	d.	£	s.	d.
Sundry Creditors	8,400	0	0				Sundry Debtors				12,500	0	0			
Less Provision for Discounts.	210	0	0	8,190	0	0	*Less* Provision for Bad Debts	625	0	0						
							Less Provision for Discounts	296	17	6	921	17	6	11,578	2	6

DEPRECIATION. The true net profit for a period can be ascertained only when due allowance has been made for the wastage of capital expenditure, known as depreciation. With the exception of assets such as freehold land, and, in some cases, goodwill, all capital expenditure loses its value in course of time. The principal causes of depreciation are—

(1) Effluxion of time (*e.g.*, leasehold property), which is capable of exact computation ;

(2) Wear and Tear (*e.g.*, machinery and plant), which can be estimated more or less accurately ; and

(3) Obsolescence (*e.g.*, when machinery is superseded by new and improved types which make it advisable to scrap the old machines before they have become worn out or otherwise unusable) which cannot be estimated.

The computation of the amount to be provided for depreciation is a matter of great importance and will be considered in detail in Chapter VII. When the amount to be provided or " written off " has been ascertained it is usually transferred from the credit of the relative asset account either to the debit of Depreciation Account or direct to the debit of Profit and Loss Account.

The Profit and Loss Account.

When the Trial Balance has been extracted and the adjustments outlined in the preceding section have been made, all the information is available for the preparation of the Profit and Loss Account. This is itself a ledger account, summarising all the information contained in the other nominal accounts, and if the adjustments have been made correctly the Profit and Loss Account shows the net profit or loss for the period. The *amount* of the profit or loss could, however, be ascertained by reference to Balance Sheets at the beginning and end of the period (due allowance being made for capital introduced or withdrawn during the period), and the Profit and Loss Account will achieve its true mission of showing *how* the profit or loss has occurred only if the following conditions are fulfilled :—

(1) The nominal ledger accounts must be chosen in such a

way that the income and expenditure will be shown in sufficient detail. Such income and expenditure must also be so classified as to afford the best possible material for criticising intelligently the administration of the business. For example, wages and certain salaries may be drawn from the bank in one sum weekly, but it is not for that reason necessary to post the total to a combined wages and salaries account. The sub-totals of wages and salaries can be ascertained from the Wages Book and entered " inset " in the Cash Book, to afford the information for posting to separate wages and salaries accounts. As will be seen in Chapter II, wages are frequently grouped in a different class of expenditure from salaries and this distinction will be of some importance. Nominal ledger accounts must therefore be opened with due regard to the form of the Profit and Loss Account which will ultimately be prepared from the information they contain.

(2) The Profit and Loss Account should itself be arranged in such a way that the items of expense will appear in logical sequence. It should be subdivided so that the gross profit or loss on trading or manufacture is shown, in addition to the net profit available for distribution, while appropriations or distributions of profit should be shown in a special Appropriation Account. The usual divisions of the Profit and Loss Account are—

    (a) Manufacturing and/or Trading Account.

    (b) Profit and Loss Account proper.

    (c) Profit and Loss Appropriation Account.

The form of a Profit and Loss Account and the information it contains depend on the nature of the business carried on and to a certain extent on the constitution of the business (i.e., whether it is a sole trader, partnership or limited company). Thus the Profit and Loss Account of a limited company carrying on a certain business will not differ greatly

from that of a sole trader carrying on a similar business ;
but certain items of expenditure, such as debenture interest
and directors' fees, will be found only in the accounts of
limited companies. When the disposition of the net profit
is considered, however, considerable differences of principle
are apparent. The profit made by a sole trader automatically swells his capital ; this is recognised by the
transfer of the balance of Profit and Loss Account to his
Capital Account. In a partnership, the partners have a
mutual interest in the property and assets of the firm and
each partner's share of the profit automatically increases the
amount due to him from the firm. The shares of profit are
therefore transferred either to the credit of the partners'
Capital Accounts or (preferably) to separate Current Accounts,
so that the net amount of capital contributed by each partner
may be readily ascertained (and also, where appropriate, to
facilitate the calculation of interest on capital).

On the other hand, the shareholders in a limited company
have no claim to receive any portion of the profits until
dividends have been declared in the manner provided by
the Articles of Association. Undistributed profits form a
fund which, although it will ultimately be applied for the
benefit of the shareholders, is quite distinct from their capital,
which is in shares of fixed denomination. Thus the balance
of the Profit and Loss Account of a limited company is not
transferred to Capital Account but is carried forward as a
running balance, being augmented by the profits made each
year and diminished by losses and by any dividends paid
or other appropriations of profit.

The Balance Sheet.

When the Profit and Loss Account has been completed
the balances remaining in the books can represent only
capital, assets, liabilities, provisions and reserves with the
addition of the balance of the Profit and Loss Account in
the case of a limited company. These balances are not
transferred to any other account but are carried forward in
the books to the new period. It is usual, however, to prepare a summary of these balances in a form similar to that

of an account. This summary is known as a Balance Sheet and shows the financial position of the concern at the end of the period. The Balance Sheet is not an account and is not an integral part of the double entry system although the ability to prepare a Balance Sheet from the balances shown in the books is one of the great advantages of the system. It shows the amount of capital invested in the business by the proprietor(s) and the disposition of that capital. It does not purport to be a Statement of Affairs, showing the realisable or break-up value of the assets, but it should show the position of the business as a " going concern ". The principles followed in attaining this end and the manner in which it is customary to present the figures will be considered in greater detail in Chapters IV and V.

Receipts and Payments Accounts.

A non-trading concern cannot prepare a Profit and Loss Account in the proper sense of the term. Small clubs and similar institutions frequently present their accounts in the form of a Receipts and Payments Account. This is merely a classified summary of the cash transactions for a period. Where it is proposed to present the annual accounts in this form, the Cash Book is usually provided with analytical columns to facilitate the dissection and totalling of the various classes of receipts and payments. The opening and closing balances of cash, both in hand and at the bank, must be brought into account to make the two sides of the account balance.

It would be wrong to assume that accounts of this nature have no merit. Income from donations and subscriptions is frequently of an uncertain nature and the amount actually received during a year may afford a better guide to the fortunes of the concern than the amount which, though it may be expected, is not legally due from the members for the same period. On the other hand, it is unlikely that the whole of the expenses will have been defrayed before the end of the year and a Receipts and Payments Account ignores the amounts outstanding. Credit may also be taken for subscriptions received in advance in respect of the next period and if stocks are carried (*e.g.*, the bar stocks of a social or athletic club) their value will not be shown. Further, it is obvious that some of the cash transactions may have been of a capital nature, *e.g.*, for the purchase of a permanent asset. Thus in all but the simplest cases, a Receipts and Payments Account falls far short of the ideal.

A partial remedy is to prepare a " Receipts and Expenditure Account " in which credit is taken only for income received, but provision is made for all accrued expenditure.

Income and Expenditure Accounts.

When the adjustments necessary to show the true results of the period, on a strict accounting basis, have been made as indicated in the preceding paragraphs, the result cannot be described as a Receipts and Payments Account, for it includes many items which have not been received or paid during the period which it covers and it could not be balanced by inserting the opening and closing cash balances. It does reflect the true income and expenditure of the concern, however, and for this reason it is known as an Income and Expenditure Account. Such an account is strictly comparable with the Profit and Loss Account of a trading concern, and when a proper set of books is kept on double entry principles (a course always to be recommended) the method of preparation is similar.

An Income and Expenditure Account should always be accompanied by a Balance Sheet, which will reflect the adjustments in respect of accrued income and expenditure, stocks, cash at bank and in hand, and any fixed assets. On the liabilities side will be shown the accumulated balance on Income and Expenditure Account and any capital funds that may have been contributed or set aside.

The treatment of entrance fees and life membership subscriptions raises some interesting points of principle.

ENTRANCE FEES are in a peculiar position because they do not create any liability towards the members from whom they are received but, on the other hand, they cannot be looked upon as a recurring source of income. If they are included in the Income and Expenditure Account of the year of receipt, they will cause the ordinary income of the year to be inflated and a false impression of success is likely to be given. It is therefore recommended that they should be credited direct to the accumulated balance of Income and Expenditure in the Balance Sheet, which will then reflect the true state of affairs, while the revenue for the year will not have been overstated. On the other hand, there are many cases where the entrance fee is a mere compensation for the expense entailed in the admission of a new member. In such cases no real objection can be taken to the inclusion of the entrance fees in the income of the year (separately stated), for the relative expenses are included on the other side.

Where the admissions of new members remain fairly constant from year to year, e.g., in the case of certain professional bodies, it is usual to take credit for entrance fees in the Income and Expenditure Account of each year.

LIFE MEMBERSHIP SUBSCRIPTIONS require different treatment because there is a liability to the members concerned to provide them with the benefits of membership free of charge for the remainder of their lives. Such subscriptions should not be merged with annual subscriptions, but should be carried to the credit of a separate account and appear as a special reserve or fund on the liabilities side of the Balance Sheet. A portion of this fund, based on the estimated number of years during which the liability will continue, can be transferred to the Income and Expenditure Account each year, or to the accumulated balance thereof, thus reducing the liability shown in the Balance Sheet.

When a proper set of books has not been kept, it will be possible to prepare only a Receipts and Payments Account in the first instance, but this can be converted into an Income and Expenditure Account and Balance Sheet as shown in the following example :—

EXAMPLE

The undernoted "Receipts and Payments Account" of the "Albany Athletic Society " is for the year ended 31st December, 1955. Other ledger balances of the Society are :—

	£	s.	d.
Capital Account (Donations, etc.) . . .	3,025	0	0
Club House and Grounds (as per valuation) .	2,000	0	0
Investments at cost	962	0	0
Furniture and Fixtures	320	0	0
Income and Expenditure Account (*Cr.* Balance brought forward)	296	10	0

RECEIPTS AND PAYMENTS ACCOUNT

Dr.   FOR THE YEAR ENDED 31ST DECEMBER, 1955   *Cr.*

	£	s.	d.		£	s.	d.
To Opening Balance in hand	74	10	0	By Upkeep of Grounds (*a*)	475	0	0
„ Annual Sub., Albany Mfg. Co. .	210	0	0	„ Wages of Grounds-men	468	0	0
„ Subscriptions . .	470	0	0	„ Ground Rent . . .	10	10	0
„ Entrance Fees . .	26	5	0	„ Printing and Sta-tionery (*b*) . .	46	10	0
„ Interest on Invest-ments				„ Postages and Sundries	9	10	0
£ s. d.				„ Closing Balance in hand	72	0	0
60 0 0							
Less Tax 27 0 0							
	33	0	0				
„ Proceeds of Lec-tures, Concerts, etc.	267	15	0				
	£1,081	10	0		£1,081	10	0

(*a*) This item includes £25 applicable to the previous year.

(*b*)   „   „   „   £10   „   „   „   „

The outstanding items at 31st December, 1955, are :—

Printing and Stationery, £8 ; the Delta Literary Association owed £10 10s. for the use of the Society's Hall ; two members' subscriptions of £5 each were in arrear.

Charge 10% for depreciation on Furniture and Fixtures.

Construct the Income and Expenditure Account for the year, and Balance Sheet as at 31st December, 1955. Entrance Fees should be capitalised.

INCOME AND EXPENDITURE ACCOUNT

Dr.   FOR THE YEAR ENDED 31ST DECEMBER, 1955   Cr.

Expenditure.	£	s.	d.	Income.	£	s.	d.
To Upkeep of Grounds .	450	0	0	By Annual Sub.,			
„ Wages	468	0	0	Albany Mfg. Co. . .	210	0	0
„ Ground Rent . . .	10	10	0	„ Subscriptions . . .	480	0	0
„ Postages and Sundries.	9	10	0	„ Interest on In-			
„ Printing and Stationery	44	10	0	vestments—			
„ Depreciation on Furni-				£ s. d.			
ture and Fixtures .	32	0	0	60 0 0			
				Less Tax . 27 0 0			
					33	0	0
				„ Lectures, Concerts, etc.	267	15	0
				„ Letting of Hall . .	10	10	0
				„ Balance—Excess of Ex-			
				penditure over Income	13	5	0
	£1,014	10	0		£1,014	10	0

BALANCE SHEET OF THE ALBANY ATHLETIC SOCIETY

AS AT 31ST DECEMBER, 1955

	£	s.	d.		£	s.	d.
Capital Account . . .	3,025	0	0	Balance at Bank . . .	72	0	0
Add Entrance Fees . .	26	5	0	Investments at cost . .	962	0	0
				Sundry Debtors . . .	10	10	0
	3,051	5	0	Debtors for Subscriptions	10	0	0
Income and Expenditure				Furniture and £ s. d.			
Account—				Fixtures— 320 0 0			
Brought for- £ s.				Less Depn. 32 0 0			
ward . 296 10					288	0	0
Less Deficit							
for 1955 . 13 5				Club House and Grounds			
	283	5	0	(as valued)	2,000	0	0
	3,334	10	0				
Sundry Creditors . . .	8	0	0				
	£3,342	10	0		£3,342	10	0

The society has apparently adopted the practice of keeping a Capital Account which is quite distinct from the
accumulated balance of income on Income and Expenditure
Account. The opening balance on Capital Account will have
been built up by crediting Entrance Fees and other receipts
of a capital nature in earlier years. If the alternative
practice of merging the two balances in one Accumulated

c

Fund had been adopted, the left side of the Balance Sheet
would have appeared as follows :—

	£	s.	d.	£	s.	d.
Accumulated Fund :—						
Balance at 31st December, 1954	3,321	10	0			
Add Entrance Fees . . .	26	5	0			
	3,347	15	0			
Less Deficit for 1955 . .	13	5	0			
				3,334	10	0
Sundry Creditors				8	0	0
				£3,342	10	0

Revenue Accounts.

In the widest sense, the term " Revenue Account " covers
any account dealing with income, profits or revenue, so that
Profit and Loss Accounts and Income and Expenditure
Accounts both fall under this heading.   It is quite usual to
talk of " writing off to revenue " in reference to an amount
debited to Profit and Loss Account or any of its subdivisions.
In a more restricted sense, however, the term " Revenue
Account " is applied to annual accounts of revenue and
expenditure prepared by certain concerns, either by custom
or in conformity with statute.

In general, the principles involved in the preparation of
Revenue Accounts do not differ from those involved in the
preparation of Profit and Loss Accounts.   Consideration of
the points of difference which arise in connection with various
specialised types of concerns will be discussed later in this
work.

The Canons of Accounting.

This Chapter will be concluded with a summary of the
main principles or canons of accounting which have emerged
from the foregoing outline.   They are as follows :—

(1) Every transaction has a two-fold aspect and each
aspect must be recorded in the books.

(2) The fundamental distinction between capital and
revenue must be observed meticulously.

(3) Expenditure must be reflected on an accrual basis.

(4) Profits may be brought into account when they have been earned ; it is not necessary to wait until they have been realised in cash, but if a loss is feared full provision should be made therefor.

(5) As a corollary to the last rule, current assets are usually valued at cost or market price, whichever is the lower in each case.

These rules represent the fruit of many years' experience and may be said to indicate the best accounting practice. They are scarcely open to argument or difference of opinion. On the other hand, there are other matters upon which opinion is divided and upon which it is unwise to dogmatise. It is also necessary to consider certain important statutory provisions which affect the accounts of some concerns. The most important (in the sense that they are of the most general application) of these are found in the Companies Act, 1948, and they affect the accounts of all limited companies. Other provisions, more limited in their application but none the less important to the concerns affected, are found in such Acts as the Assurance Companies Acts, 1909 and 1946, the Building Societies Acts, 1874 to 1894, and the Friendly Societies Acts, 1896 to 1929.

CHAPTER II

THE PROFIT AND LOSS ACCOUNT (1)

It has been seen that the object of the Profit and Loss Account is to show *how* the profit or loss has been made, as distinct from the *amount* of profit or loss, which is reflected by an increase or decrease in the net assets revealed by successive Balance Sheets. The Profit and Loss Account achieves this object by summarising on the credit side all the items of profit or gain and on the debit side all the items of loss or expense. It is obvious that the fact that a net profit is revealed does not prove that each transaction entered into has resulted in a profit, and it is quite impossible, from the information contained in the Profit and Loss Account, to ascertain the amount of profit or loss on single transactions. In some cases this is not a very serious disadvantage. Retail traders, for example, usually fix their selling prices at a certain percentage above cost price, and a fairly constant rate of gross profit is thus assured. On the other hand, fixed or overhead charges of quite considerable amount will be incurred in the course of a year and must be defrayed without reference to the volume of sales actually made. Thus an account which shows on the one hand the total value of goods sold and on the other hand the cost of those goods and the expenses of running the business presents the truest possible picture of the results of trading.

Subdivision of the Profit and Loss Account.

The fact that the Profit and Loss Account (and its subdivisions) is made to represent the operations of the year in total and does not reflect the results of the separate jobs or contracts undertaken does not prevent its being made as informative as possible. In most businesses there is a vital distinction between expenses which are incurred specially for particular contracts and those which relate to the business as a whole and which cannot be specifically allocated. The

36

distinction between the processes of manufacturing and selling is also important. Finally, it is always advisable to distinguish between expenditure incurred in earning profits and expenditure which represents the appropriation or division of profits already made. These distinctions are made by subdividing the Profit and Loss Account in the following manner, according to whether the operations carried on are of a manufacturing or merchanting nature, or both :—

(1) Manufacturing Account, showing the cost of manufacturing the product of the concern for the period ;

(2) Trading Account, showing the gross profit or loss on trading ;

(3) Profit and Loss Account, showing the net profit or loss for the period ; *and*

(4) Profit and Loss Appropriation Account, showing the disposition of the divisible profits.

In each subdivision, due regard is paid to the presentation of detail and the marshalling of information, so that the accounts may be rendered as informative as possible.

THE MANUFACTURING ACCOUNT

A Manufacturing Account, or Production or Working Account as it is frequently called, should be confined to ascertaining the cost of producing the goods made by the manufacturer.

It should include on the debit side all the prime costs and overhead expenses of manufacture such as—

(1) Stock of raw materials and of unfinished work at the commencement of the trading period ;

(2) Raw materials purchased ;

(3) Manufacturing wages ;

(4) Carriage on raw materials ;

(5) Factory expenses, such as rent, rates, lighting, etc., of the factory ;

(6) Power.

Subject to remarks made below, it should include on the credit side the stock of raw materials and unfinished work at the end of the trading period. The balance of the Manufacturing Account will then show the factory cost of manufacture, which is carried to the Trading Account.

MANUFACTURING ACCOUNT

Dr.   FOR THE YEAR ENDED 31ST DECEMBER, 1955   *Cr.*

	£		£
To Stock of Raw Materials, 1st Jan., 1955 . .	2,460	By Stock of Raw Materials, 31st Dec., 1955 . .	2,600
„ Unfinished Work, 1st Jan., 1955	1,200	„ Unfinished Work, 31st Dec., 1955. . . .	1,500
„ Materials Purchased. .	9,500	„ Balance, being Cost of Production transferred to Trading Account .	16,270
„ Carriage Inwards . .	350		
„ Factory Wages . . .	5,400		
„ Factory Rent . . .	200		
„ Fuel, Light and Power .	260		
„ Depreciation of Plant, etc.	1,000		
	£20,370		£20,370

The above form illustrates the general principles, but is capable of considerable modification to enable the maximum amount of information to be ascertained from the figures. Thus :—

(1) The opening and closing stocks of raw materials may be adjusted on the debit side of the account as in the next example, to show the amount of " Materials Consumed ", which, in relation to the cost of production, is more significant than purchases ;

(2) Unfinished work (alternatively termed " work-in-progress ") at the beginning and end of the period might be adjusted similarly, as the last items on the debit side of the account, so as to show the cost of producing the goods *completed* during the year in relation to the total cost of finished and unfinished work, as in the following specimen :—

MANUFACTURING ACCOUNT

Dr.	FOR THE YEAR ENDED 31ST DECEMBER, 1955		Cr.

	£	£		£
To Materials Consumed :—			By Balance, being Factory	
Stock, 1st Jan., 1955	2,460		Cost of Goods Completed	
Purchases . . .	9,500		during the year carried	
	———		to Trading Account .	16,270
	11,960			
Less Stock,				
31st Dec., 1955	2,600			
	———	9,360		
„ Carriage Inwards* . . .		350		
„ Factory Rent		200		
„ Factory Wages . . .		5,400		
„ Fuel, Light and Power .		260		
„ Depreciation of Plant,				
etc.		1,000		
COST OF PRODUCTION . .		16,570		
Unfinished Work, 1st Jan.,				
1955		1,200		
		17,770		
Less Unfinished Work,				
31st Dec., 1955 . .		1,500		
		£16,270		£16,270

(3) The Manufacturing Account may be charged with all the prime costs and factory costs of production as above and credited with the current market value of the goods produced. The balance thus shown represents the factory profit or loss on the basis of current market prices. The factory selling price of the goods is then transferred to the Trading Account as though the finished goods had been purchased from an outside source. In the above example, if the factory selling price of the goods produced was £20,000 the Manufacturing Account could be constructed as shown on page 40.

Where a gross profit on manufacture is shown, as a result of crediting the Manufacturing Account with the current market value of the goods produced, the valuation of finished

* Alternatively the amount of carriage inwards may be added to purchases in ascertaining the cost of materials consumed.

MANUFACTURING ACCOUNT

Dr.   FOR THE YEAR ENDED 31ST DECEMBER, 1955   *Cr.*

	£	£		£
To Materials Consumed :—			By Factory Selling Price of	
Stock, 1st Jan., 1955	2,460		Goods Completed dur-	
Purchases . . .	9,500		ing the year, transferred	
	11,960		to Trading Account . .	20,000
Less Stock,				
31st Dec., 1955	2,600			
		9,360		
„ Carriage Inwards . . .		350		
„ Factory Rent		200		
„ Factory Wages . . .		5,400		
„ Fuel, Light and Power .		260		
„ Depreciation of Plant, etc.		1,000		
FACTORY COST OF PRODUCTION		16,570		
Unfinished Work, 1st Jan., 1955		1,200		
		17,770		
Less Unfinished Work, 31st Dec. 1955		1,500		
FACTORY COST OF GOODS COM-PLETED DURING THE YEAR		16,270		
FACTORY PROFIT transferred to Profit and Loss Account .		3,730		
		£20,000		£20,000

stock in the Trading Account will exceed cost price. This unrealised profit must be eliminated in order to reduce the unsold stock to cost price ; the adjustment is usually made in the Profit and Loss Account—debit Profit and Loss Account with the " profit loading " on the stock and deduct this amount from the value of the stock in the Balance Sheet—so that the Trading Account will show the true gross profit based on cost of production.

The form of account must be decided by the manufacturer himself to conform to the requirements of his business.

There is some difference of opinion regarding the items of expenditure which should be charged to the Manufacturing Account. Some authorities contend that such items as Depreciation of Plant and Machinery should be charged to the Profit and Loss Account, but others are of the opinion that such depreciation (which is a loss incurred in actual production) is properly chargeable to the Manufacturing Account as a constituent of the cost of manufacture. The latter view appears to be reasonable, and is consistent with the general principles upon which a Manufacturing Account is compiled.

It is advisable at this point to consider briefly the elements of cost, as by this means much confusion may be avoided at later stages.

The Elements of Cost.

The three principal elements of cost are :—

    (1) Materials ;

    (2) Labour ;

    (3) Expenses ;

and for the purpose of analysing costs each item of expenditure must be classified into one of these three groups.

Each of these groups may be again divided into :—

    (1) Direct items ;

    (2) Indirect items.

Direct Items are those which can be directly charged to the particular unit (job, contract or process to which expenditure is allocated for the purpose of computing costs) on which they were expended, while *Indirect Items* (also termed *Establishment Charges* or *Overhead Charges*) are those which for any reason cannot be definitely allocated to particular units. For example, direct labour would include the wages of operatives engaged directly on the particular job or contract ; direct materials would include special purchases and goods drawn from store and used solely on one job ; while expenses incurred by operatives in travelling to a job away from the works, or the cost of hiring special plant for use on the job, would be direct expenses. Indirect labour may include the wages of foremen and shop cleaners ; indirect materials may include solder, oil, waste and similar items which cannot be apportioned ; while maintenance of plant and machinery, power and lighting, etc., are normally examples of indirect expenses.

c*

It must be appreciated, however, that items which are "direct" in one business may be "indirect" in another. A building contractor can allocate the wages of a foreman engaged on a particular contract to that contract (his wages are therefore *direct*), but a foreman in an engineering works may supervise the manufacture of many different articles, and his wages will be *indirect*.

The Total Cost of each unit may, therefore, be analysed as follows :—

$$
\left.
\begin{array}{l}
\left.
\begin{array}{l}
\left.
\begin{array}{l}
\text{Direct Labour} \\
\text{Direct Materials} \\
\text{Direct Expenses}
\end{array}
\right\} = \left\{
\begin{array}{l}
\text{Prime} \\
\text{Cost.}
\end{array}
\right. \\
\begin{array}{l}
\text{Factory (or Works) Overhead} \\
\quad \text{Charges embracing :—} \\
\quad \text{Indirect Labour} \\
\quad \text{Indirect Materials} \\
\quad \text{Indirect Expenses}
\end{array}
\end{array}
\right\} = \left\{
\begin{array}{l}
\text{Factory} \\
\text{Cost} \\
\text{(or} \\
\text{Works} \\
\text{Cost).}
\end{array}
\right. \\
\text{Administration Expenses} \\
\text{Selling and Distribution Expenses}
\end{array}
\right\} = \left\{
\begin{array}{l}
\text{Total} \\
\text{Cost} \\
\text{(or Cost} \\
\text{of Sales).}
\end{array}
\right.
$$

The Total Cost plus profit (or minus loss) gives the *Selling Price.*

FACTORY OVERHEAD CHARGES include, *inter alia* :—

Rent and Rates

$$
\text{Power} \left\{
\begin{array}{l}
\text{Coal} \\
\text{Gas or} \\
\text{Electricity}
\end{array}
\right\} \text{of Factory.}
$$

Heating and Lighting

Repairs to Plant and Machinery and Factory Buildings.

Insurance of   ,,   ,,   ,,   ,,

Depreciation of   ,,   ,,   ,,   ,,

Factory Wages not chargeable direct, *e.g.*, wages of store-keepers, foremen and of labour in the boiler-house and engine-house.

Drawing Office Salaries and Expenses.

In dealing with the remaining indirect expenses it is usually advisable to distinguish between Administration Expenses and Selling and Distribution Expenses, as follows :—

ADMINISTRATION EXPENSES.

Salary of General Manager.
Proportion of Office Salaries.
Salaries and Expenses of Directors.*
Proportion of Office Rent, Rates, Lighting, etc.

SELLING AND DISTRIBUTION EXPENSES.

Proportion of Office Salaries.
Proportion of Office Rent, Rates, Lighting, etc.
Advertising.
Travellers' Salaries and Expenses.
Commissions and Discount.
Bad Debts.
Carriage Outwards.

The overhead expenses debited in the financial accounts are, of course, the *actual* expenses incurred (adjusted as regards any outstandings or payments in advance), but the overhead expenses charged to jobs in the cost accounts are necessarily *estimates,* since it is usually necessary to close off many job accounts before the total overhead expenses for the period are known. There are various methods of charging up these indirect items in the cost accounts to the jobs in respect of which they were incurred. Thus, in the case of a contractor, Works Overhead Charges may be charged up as a percentage on the direct wages expended on that job, this percentage being based on the percentage of *total* overhead expenses to *total* wages for the previous year, adjusted where necessary to bring it into line with current conditions. Administration, Selling and Distribution Expenses may be similarly recovered as a percentage on Works Cost. The fixing and periodical checking of these percentages is made possible by classifying the same types of expenses under the headings of Factory, Administration, Selling and Distribution in both cost and financial accounts.

* The remuneration of a director employed, for example, as works engineer or sales manager, may be charged to factory overheads or selling expenses, as appropriate.

The connection between the broad classifications of the various elements of cost (as set out above) and the form of the Manufacturing Account and the subdivisions of the Profit and Loss Account should be apparent. Thus, the Manufacturing Account will include those items of expenditure which comprise the Factory Cost (*i.e.*, Prime Cost and Factory Overhead Charges), and, by the suitable sub-grouping of items, will disclose the Prime Cost and the Factory Cost of Production. Administration, Distribution and Selling Expenses, being additional to the Factory Cost, will be properly allocated to the Profit and Loss Account.

A typical example of the Manufacturing Account, where the total expenses are analysed in accordance with the above classification, is shown below.

MANUFACTURING ACCOUNT

Dr.   FOR THE YEAR ENDED 31ST DECEMBER, 1955   *Cr.*

	£	£		£
To Materials Consumed:—			By Factory Cost of	
Stock of Raw Materials,			Goods Completed	
1st Jan., 1955 . . .			during the year,	
Purchases			transferred to	
			Trading Account .	
Less Stock, 31st Dec., 1955 .				
„ Direct Wages				
„ Direct Expenses				
PRIME COST OF PRODUCTION .				
„ Indirect Materials				
„ Indirect Labour				
„ Indirect Expenses:—				
Factory Rent				
Power				
Heating, etc.				
Repairs to Plant . . .				
Depreciation of Plant . .				
FACTORY COST OF PRODUCTION				
Unfinished Work, 1st Jan., 1955				
Less Unfinished Work,				
31st Dec., 1955				
		£		£

It cannot be too strongly emphasised that whatever form of account is adopted or in whatever groups expenditure is collected, the treatment from year to year should be consistent. Otherwise, the accuracy of inferences from the figures will be seriously vitiated.

Working or Production Accounts.

In many concerns of a highly technical or specialised character, a " Working " or " Production " Account is constructed as a type of manufacturing account relating to a specific product. Such accounts may be used where :—

(1) The process is subsidiary to the main operation of the concern, *e.g.*, production of sand from a sand pit owned by a brick manufacturer, so that the Production Account is used to ascertain the cost of one or more types of raw material used in the principal manufacturing process.

(2) There are two or more distinct manufactures, all sold through a common trading organisation, so that the Production Accounts will show the separate costs of production, which will be transferred to the debit of Trading Account or alternatively each product can be transferred at the current buying price of similar manufactured goods so that the efficiency of each producing department can be gauged.

The following is an illustration of a Production Account used by an iron and steel company.

PIG IRON PRODUCTION ACCOUNT
Dr.   FOR THE YEAR ENDED 31ST DECEMBER, 1955   Cr.

	£		£
To Materials Consumed (in-cluding carriage there-on) :—		By Sales of Slag . .	5,200
Coal	8,500	„ Cost of Pig Iron pro-duced transferred	
Coke	12,600	to Trading Ac-	
Limestone . . .	3,400	count. . . .	41,700
Ironstone . . .	7,960		
Sundry Materials .	340		
	32,800		
„ Direct Wages . . .	9,200		
„ Direct Expenses . .	500		
	9,700		
„ Indirect Production Ex-penses	4,400		
	£46,900		£46,900

THE TRADING ACCOUNT

In a non-manufacturing concern, where goods are pur-chased for resale, the first account in which items of income and expenditure are summarised is the Trading Account. This account is confined to ascertaining the gross profit or loss made on the purchase and sale of goods, *i.e.*, the mer-chanting profit. It will therefore contain on the debit side—

(1) Stock of goods at the commencement of the trading period ;

(2) Goods purchased, less returns outwards ; and

(3) Any expenses incurred in bringing the goods into a merchantable state, *e.g.*, warehousing charges, but not expenses incurred in selling the goods.

On the credit side there will be—

(1) Goods sold, less returns inwards ; and

(2) Stock of goods at the end of the trading period.

The balance represents the gross profit or gross loss, as the case may be, and is carried to the Profit and Loss Account.

There is considerable diversity of opinion with regard to the items of expenditure which are properly chargeable to

the Trading Account. The divergence of views is similar
to that already indicated in respect of the Manufacturing
Account. The nature of the business will largely determine
which account should contain any particular item of expenditure. Thus, lighting, in the case of a merchanting business
(*i.e.*, a business which buys its goods in a finished state for
sale to customers), will be a proper charge to the Profit and
Loss Account, since no question of production costs can
arise. Even so, there is still room for alternative treatment
of certain items of expenditure. It is considered that in
the case of a non-manufacturing business, the Trading
Account should be confined to ascertaining the gross profit
on merchanting and that such items of expenditure as wages
incurred in selling and delivering the goods, discounts, etc.,
should be charged to the Profit and Loss Account. An
account compiled on these lines would take the following
form :—

TRADING ACCOUNT
Dr.   FOR THE YEAR ENDED 31ST DECEMBER, 1955   *Cr.*

	£			£
To Stock, 1st Jan., 1955 .		By Sales (*less* Returns) .		
„ Purchases (*less* Returns)		„ Stock, 31st Dec., 1955		
„ Carriage on Purchases .				
„ Warehousing Charges .				
„ Balance—Gross Profit transferred to Profit and Loss Account . . .				
	£			£

In the case of a manufacturing business, if a Manufacturing Account is prepared in the forms suggested in the
preceding pages, the Trading Account (sometimes referred
to in these cases as a " Warehouse Account ") will be confined
to ascertaining the gross profit on the sale of the goods completed during the trading period, and will take the same form
as above with the substitution of " cost of production " for
" purchases ". Stock, of course, will be confined to the stock
of finished goods, for the stocks of raw materials and work
in progress will already have been shown in the Manufacturing Account.

It is always advisable, if the necessary information (*i.e.*, the market value of goods produced) is available, to prepare the Manufacturing Account in the form illustrated on page 44. This is particularly desirable where it is also the practice of the business to purchase finished goods for resale from other sources, in order to facilitate comparison between the cost of manufacture and the cost of similar goods purchased. Note, however, that it is not possible to separate the gross profit on trading from the factory profit on manufacture unless the following information is available :—

(1) The stocks of finished goods (including both finished goods purchased and goods manufactured), as distinct from the stock of raw materials and work in progress ; *and*

(2) The market value of goods manufactured.

In the absence of this information, it is better not to prepare separate Manufacturing and Trading Accounts. A combined account, prepared on the following lines, may be presented.

TRADING ACCOUNT

Dr.   FOR THE YEAR ENDED 31ST DECEMBER, 1955   *Cr.*

	£		£
To Stock and Work in Progress at 1st Jan., 1955		By Sales (*less* Returns) .	
„ Purchases (*less* Returns).		„ Stock and Work in Progress at 31st Dec., 1955	
„ Carriage Inwards . .			
„ Wages			
„ Factory Expenses . .			
„ Depreciation of Plant .			
„ Gross Profit—transferred to Profit and Loss Account.			
	£		£

The Significance of Gross Profit.

Gross profit is represented by the credit balance of the Trading Account, *i.e.*, it is the excess of the credit side over the debit side ; but it is something more than a mere residue —the remainder after deducting from the total proceeds of sale the total cost price of the goods sold. Gross profit on trading is a result which bears a *definite relationship to sales.*

In most trading concerns, selling prices are fixed in the first instance to show a certain rate of profit on cost prices and the goods are priced or " ticketed " on this basis. If these prices are realised, each sale shows the same rate of profit and the total gross profit should bear this percentage to the total sales. In practice, however, there are many factors which will operate to prevent such an exact agreement. The more important are as follows :—

(1) There may be different " lines " which do not all realise the same rate of profit. The rate of gross profit shown by the Trading Account is thus the average rate earned on all the transactions entered into by the business, and its chief value as a check on the accuracy of the figures is lost. If the rate of gross profit is to have any useful meaning, the accounts must be *departmentalised* (see page 59). Lines of goods selling at different rates of profit must be regarded as separate departments, even though they are under the same management and control. The gross profits shown by the departmental Trading Accounts should then present a true picture of the trading results of each department, subject always to the incidence of any of the factors mentioned below, which may operate whether or not the accounts are departmentalised.

(2) Deterioration of goods, the accumulation of " slow-moving lines ", bargain sales and similar factors may make it necessary to reduce prices. This will have a twofold effect :—

    (a) The total gross profit will include the reduced profits on such goods as are sold in these circumstances, and will therefore show a lower percentage than the normal one ; and

    (b) In so far as it is necessary to write down the value of the unsold goods remaining in stock, the gross profit will not be a true total, but will represent—

(i) The sum of the gross profits on all the transactions, less any losses,

less (ii) The amount written off the unsold stock.

Thus the Trading Account is bound to show a rate of gross profit less than the " anticipated " profit ; but a comparison of the two percentages serves a useful purpose in showing up the undesirable features which cause the difference to exist.

(3) Misappropriations of stock and errors in charging out goods to customers will obviously throw out the rate of gross profit.

(4) Errors or fraudulent manipulations in the value of closing stock will also have an effect on the gross profit. This will be considered in detail later in this Chapter.

The gross profit provides the fund out of which the fixed or overhead charges will be met and thus determines the amount (if any) which will ultimately be available for distribution. If selling prices are fixed at such a low level that the prime costs are not covered, there will be no gross profit and consequently no net profit (except in the rare cases where extraneous income, *e.g.*, interest on investments, exceeds the total of gross loss and overhead expenses and thus converts a gross loss into a net profit). Thus, generally speaking, if a gross profit cannot be earned, it is better for a business to cease trading until conditions improve, for the net loss will then be kept down to the irreducible minimum represented by fixed charges. If trading is continued every sale will result in an increase in the net loss for the year— a most unsatisfactory state of affairs.

On the other hand, if a rate of gross profit, however small, can be secured, every sale is of benefit to the concern. The total gross profit may not be sufficient to cover the fixed charges but it at least reduces the net loss.* If the gross profit is sufficient to cover the fixed charges, any further increase results in a net profit.

Thus, if a retailer makes a gross profit of 20 per cent. on sales and his fixed expenses are £1,000, then, as long as his sales reach £5,000, the expenses are covered. Beyond this stage, any increase in turnover will yield an increase alike in gross and net profits, subject to any slight increase in the supplementary costs due to the increased turnover. If, therefore, the sales are doubled, the gross profit will be increased by £1,000 and the net profit by a like amount. This assumes, of course, that the fixed expenses of £1,000 remain constant, and in a merchanting business this may quite easily be so.

The significance of gross profit expressed in terms of sales is therefore very important and unless this is clearly realised the true value and object of the Trading Account is overlooked.

The relationship between gross profit and sales is well understood by Inspectors of Taxes, who rely on the percentage of gross profit to sales as a rough test of the validity of the profit shown by accounts supplied for the purpose of income tax assessment. Thus, a trader in a certain type of business may be expected to make a gross profit varying between 25 per cent. and 30 per cent. of his sales, and any percentage well outside this range may cause enquiry as to the reasons therefor.

Percentage and Comparative Trading Accounts.

Much useful information can be gleaned from a Trading Account which is compiled so as to express as a percentage the ratio which each item of expenditure bears to sales. By the insertion of additional columns, comparison may be made

* The purist may demand that where the Trading Account and the Profit and Loss Account each show losses, the greater should be known as the gross loss and the smaller as the net loss. This would lead to some confusion when comparing results for different periods or of different businesses, or where the Trading Account shows a profit which is converted into a loss in the Profit and Loss Account. Thus, a " gross " loss is taken to mean a loss revealed by the Trading Account and is the alternative of a gross profit, while a " net " loss is the final balance of the Profit and Loss Account for the period.

with the figures for other trading periods and the trend of operations and results noted.

Percentages are undoubtedly helpful if rightly understood, but they may be misleading. Thus, items which vary with turnover should show a fairly constant percentage. Where, however, the percentage of materials consumed has fallen, this may be due to cheaper material, and, if so, it may be a satisfactory sign. The possibility of stock manipulations should, however, not be overlooked for this may be the true explanation of the percentage variation.

When dealing with percentages, the following matters are important :—

(1) Percentage purchases are misleading, for a large purchase of goods may have been made towards the end of the trading period and thus no opportunity will have arisen for the conversion of such goods into sales. For this reason stocks of raw materials should be adjusted with purchases to give a figure for materials consumed in the case of a manufacturing business; and in the case of a trading concern, stocks of finished goods should be adjusted with purchases to give the cost price of goods sold.

(2) An increase in the monetary value of sales does not necessarily imply an increase in *output* or in the *volume* of sales, for prices may have risen (*e.g.*, by the imposition of the purchase tax or other duty), while items of expenditure which normally vary with output may remain constant and therefore be a lower percentage of the higher sales figure. Conversely, a decrease in the monetary value of sales does not necessarily imply a decrease in output or in the volume of sales, for prices may have fallen. Thus, where a duty has been imposed on the goods sold by a trader, if the old rate of gross profit was $33\frac{1}{3}$ per cent. on selling price and the new duty is one of 50 per cent., then, assuming that the trader passes on the duty to the consumer without any alteration to the amount of gross profit per unit sold. the following position will arise :—

	Cost price.	Gross profit.	Selling price.	% of gross profit to selling price.
	£	£	£	£
(a) Before imposition of duty	100	50	150	33⅓
(b) After imposition of duty .	150	50	200	25

In the year during which the duty is imposed, the Trading Account may be expected to show a gross profit of between 25 and 33⅓ per cent. Subsequently, unless further alterations in the rate of duty are made, a steady 25 per cent. may be expected.

(3) The holding up of stocks where trade is seasonal or subject to booms may have a detrimental effect on the percentage of expenditure including the percentage of those items which vary with *output* although such holding may be good sales policy.

(4) Some percentages may move directly and others inversely as a result of changed conditions of production or different business policies. Thus, if components which were formerly manufactured by the business itself are now purchased outside it would be reasonable to expect an increase in the percentage of Materials, and a decrease in Wages and Power.

(5) The presence of consignments outwards is likely to vitiate the accuracy of the percentages unless proper precautions are taken. The credit balance on Goods sent on Consignment Account, which is transferred to Trading Account at the end of the year, represents the cost price of goods sent on consignment. It should, therefore, be deducted from Purchases, so that the percentage of Gross Profit represents the true gross profit on goods sold.

The interpretation of results is more fully dealt with under that heading in Chapter III.

While percentage accounts for a single year yield much useful information, the accounts of two or more periods arranged comparatively in columnar form will be more useful than if they are shown separately, for the relative importance of each item can be more readily and fully appreciated. Examples of comparative Trading Accounts are given below.

Example 1.

Dr.   COMPARATIVE TRADING ACCOUNT   Cr.

	Year ended 31st Dec., 1954.		Year ended 31st Dec., 1955.			Year ended 31st Dec., 1954.		Year ended 31st Dec., 1955.	
	%	£	%	£		%	£	%	£
To Materials Used .	48·68	18,500	48·89	22,000	By Sales .	100·00	38,000	100·00	45,000
„ Wages .	32·90	12,500	32·44	14,600					
„ Coal and Coke .	1·32	500	1·38	620					
„ Gross Profit c/d.	17·10	6,500	17·29	7,780					
	100·00	£38,000	100·00	£45,000		100·00	£38,000	100·00	£45,000

It will be seen from the above example that the percentage of gross profit is fairly constant and this is only to be expected in view of the consistency in the percentages of the various items of cost.

Example 2.

Dr.   COMPARATIVE TRADING ACCOUNT   Cr.

	Year ended 31st Dec., 1954.		Year ended 31st Dec., 1955.			Year ended 31st Dec., 1954.		Year ended 31st Dec., 1955.	
	%	£	%	£		%	£	%	£
To Materials Used .	48·68	18,500	52·18	23,480	By Sales .	100·00	38,000	100·00	45,000
„ Wages .	32·90	12,500	32·44	14,600					
„ Coal and Coke .	1·32	500	1·38	620					
„ Gross Profit c/d.	17·10	6,500	14·00	6,300					
	100·00	£38,000	100·00	£45,000		100·00	£38,000	100·00	£45,000

It will be seen from the above example that the percentage of gross profit shows a considerable reduction as compared with the previous year and this reduction is explained by the fact that the percentage of cost of materials used has

increased.   These facts are clearly brought out by the use of
percentages.

Comparative or columnar accounts may also be used
where, for any reason, it is desirable to split accounts, *e.g.*,
where a partner retires and it is desired to show the results
of the business before and after his retirement, or where a
business is sold and it is required to ascertain the results of
trading for the period elapsing between the agreed date of
sale and the date on which the business was actually taken
over by the purchaser.

Turnover and Rate of Turnover.

The expression *turnover* is applied to the net sales of a
business for a given period, usually one year, as shown by
the Trading Account.   Rate of Turnover (or Velocity of
Stock or Turnover of Stock), however, is measured by reference to the *cost* of goods sold during the period and the
average stock held during the same period.   An example
will make this clear :—

TRADING ACCOUNT

Dr.   FOR THE YEAR ENDED 31ST DECEMBER, 1955   *Cr.*

		£			£
To Stock, 1st Jan., 1955 .		8,000	By Sales		60,000
„ Purchases		44,000	„ Stock, 31st Dec., 1955		12,000
„ Gross Profit		20,000			
		£72,000			£72,000

In this case the *turnover* is £60,000.

The *average stock* is £$\dfrac{8,000 + 12,000}{2}$ or £10,000.

The *cost of goods sold* (obtained *either* by deducting gross
profit from sales *or* by deducting the increase in stock
from purchases) is £40,000.

The *rate of turnover* is thus $\dfrac{40,000}{10,000}$ or 4 times per annum.

When examining comparative Trading Accounts for a number of years, the calculation of the rate of turnover for each year may provide a useful indication of the trend of the business. The accumulation of unsaleable stocks will almost certainly result in a drop in the rate of turnover.

While a given rate of turnover, say four times per annum, indicates that, on the average, the stock is held for a period of three months, it is essential to bear in mind that the rate is an average one and that the presence of a line of quickly moving goods may cloak the presence of a certain amount of unsaleable stock. This is one reason why comparison of one year with another is likely to give more reliable information than the examination of one year's accounts.

It is obviously to the advantage of a trader for his rate of turnover to be as high as possible, for he then secures a higher rate of profit on the average capital locked up in stock in trade. Moreover, the slower the turnover the greater the risk of loss through deterioration (where stock is subject to that form of waste); and the greater the amount of storage charges and other expenses of warehousing.

Owner-Occupied Premises.

Where a business concern is the owner-occupier of its business premises and consequently does not pay any rent, it is frequently found that in order to show the correct cost of manufacture and/or trading, gross profit or loss, and net profit or loss, a debit entry in lieu of rent is shown in the financial accounts of the business. Usually the debit entry is equivalent to the amount of the assessment of the premises for taxation or rating purposes.

The debit entry is normally shown either in the Manufacturing or Trading Account, and is offset by a corresponding credit entry, shown separately, either in :—

(i) the Profit and Loss Account ; or

(ii) the Profit and Loss Appropriation Account ; or

(iii) (in the case of a sole trader) the Capital Account.

The main object of these calculations is to enable more

accurate percentage calculations to be made in order to guide the owners of the business in determining the separate results of manufacture or trading, as distinct from the combined results of their trading and general financial policy (*e.g.*, the benefits resulting from the purchase of their own premises).

THE PROFIT AND LOSS ACCOUNT

The trader gathers together the various expenses and losses incurred during the year's trading by transferring them to the debit of the Profit and Loss Account, while to the credit of this account he places the gross profit and any items of gain which have accrued to him during the period from sources other than trading. The final balance remaining on the account shows whether he has made a net profit or sustained a net loss in respect of the whole of the year's operations.

Where the nominal accounts are suitably classified their relative importance can be seen, and excessive expenditure in any direction can be identified.

The Profit and Loss Account cannot be made so uniform in its contents as the Trading Account, as the items are bound to vary from business to business, and in the same business from year to year, but nevertheless much valuable information can be obtained from a comparison of successive Profit and Loss Accounts.

If the utmost advantage is to be derived from the account, the contents must be arranged in a logical order.* There are no hard and fast rules, but the following is an arrangement which affords the maximum amount of information with the minimum of effort on the part of the reader:—

(1) Establishment Charges, such as rent, rates, lighting and heating.

(2) Administration Expenses, such as clerical wages, salaries and directors' fees.

* Reference should be made to the recommendations of the Council of the Institute of Chartered Accountants with regard to the form and contents of the Profit and Loss Account (see Appendix II); these recommendations, however, are subject to the provisions of the Companies Act, 1948.

(3) Selling and Distribution Expenses, such as travellers' salaries and commissions, carriage outwards and packing materials.

(4) Finance Charges, such as loans and bank interest.

(5) Extraordinary Losses, such as loss by defalcation.

Certain items of expenditure may require to be apportioned, part as a charge to Manufacturing or Trading Account and part to the Profit and Loss Account. Thus, rent is capable of division into factory rent, warehouse rent and office rent. The portion properly due to the factory should be charged to the Manufacturing Account ; the warehouse rent should be charged to the Trading Account (if one is prepared) and the remainder will be charged to the Profit and Loss Account.

There is some difference of opinion about the treatment of discounts on purchases and on sales. As far as these discounts represent *trade* discounts they should be deducted from the relative purchase or sale in the books of original entry. Thus, although the amounts of trade discount received and allowed will not be shown in the accounts, they will be reflected either in the Manufacturing Account or in the Trading Account, because the *net* amounts of purchases and sales will be shown. On the other hand, *cash* discounts represent a financial charge or gain and as such should be shown separately in the Profit and Loss Account. Sometimes the balance alone is shown, either as a debit or as a credit according to whether the discounts allowed exceed the discounts received or *vice versa*, but this practice is not to be recommended. Some writers contend that where the separate amounts of cash discounts allowed and received are known, they should be shown as deductions from the amounts of purchases and sales appearing in the Trading Account. When special cash discounts are allowed in order to secure business there may be some justification for this view, but in ordinary cases, where comparatively small discounts (say $2\frac{1}{2}$ per cent.) are allowed as an inducement to secure the prompt payment of accounts, they should be regarded as financial charges or gains.

The following illustrates a *pro forma* Profit and Loss Account.

PROFIT AND LOSS ACCOUNT

Dr.   FOR THE YEAR ENDED 31ST DECEMBER, 19..   Cr.

	£	£			£	£
To Establishment Charges :—			By Gross Profit . .			
Rent and Rates . . .			,, Incidental Gains :			
Lighting and Heating .			Income from In-			
,, Administrative Expenses :			vestments .			
Office Salaries. . . .			Discounts			
Office Expenses . . .			Received .			
Sundry Expenses. . .			Bank Interest .			
,, Selling and Distribution Ex-						
penses : —						
Advertising						
Travellers' Salaries and						
Commissions . . .						
Travelling Expenses . .						
Salesroom Expenses . .						
,, Loan Interest						
,, Discounts Allowed . . .						
,, Bad Debts						
,, Staff Bonuses						
,, Depreciation of Furniture,						
etc.						
,, Net Profit						
		£				£

DEPARTMENTAL ACCOUNTS

Where a business consists of several different departments it is advisable to calculate the trading results achieved by each department, especially where they are under separate management.

In exceptional cases, each department is conducted as though it were a distinct business, and, accordingly, it has its own sales, purchases and impersonal ledgers, in which are recorded all transactions which relate specifically to it as a department. At the end of the trading period, stock-taking is carried out on a departmental basis, and separate Trading and Profit and Loss Accounts are compiled, the final figures being combined and transferred to the private ledger.

This method, however, may involve a certain amount of duplication of clerical work in keeping separate personal ledgers, as some customers of one department may be customers of other departments ; and the same duplication may occur with the accounts of suppliers. It is much more convenient to have the whole of the transactions with one person or firm concentrated in one personal account, and, therefore, the common practice is to keep one set of personal accounts for the business as a whole. This method will be assumed in the following discussion.

Apart from the exceptional case mentioned above, departmental accounts may be broadly divided into two classes :—

(1) Those designed to show the departmental gross profits only ;

(2) Those designed to show the departmental net profits as well as the departmental gross profits.

For both purposes it is necessary for the purchases and sales journals, returns books, etc., to contain additional columns for each department. The wages book must similarly be made out in columnar form and, of course, it is necessary to take stock separately for each department. Separate accounts may be opened in the general ledger for sales, purchases, wages, etc., to which the periodical totals of these items are posted. Alternatively the general ledger itself may be provided with extra columns to record separately the figures applicable to each department. Examples of columnar impersonal ledger accounts for two departments, A and B, are shown below.

Dr.   SALES   *Cr.*

Date.		Fo.	A.	B.	Total.	Date.		Fo.	A.	B.	Total.
			£	£	£				£	£	£
19.. Jan. 31	To Sundries	S.R.B. 5	51	12	63	19.. Jan. 31	By Sundries	S.D.B. 21	520	258	778
Feb. 28	,, ,,	10	25		25	Feb. 28	,, ,,	51	455	136	591

Dr.   WAGES   *Cr.*

Date.		Fo.	A.	B.	Total.	Date.		Fo.	A.	B.	Total
			£	£	£				£	£	£
19.. Jan. 5	To Cash .	C.B. 3	85	33	118						
,, 12	,, ,, . .	11	85	33	118						

Goods transferred from one department to another should not be merged in the purchases and sales of the departments concerned (for the inclusion of transfers at *cost* or at less than the normal selling price in the turnover would distort the gross profit ratio), but should be recorded in special accounts and shown separately at cost on both the debit and credit sides of the departmental Trading Account.

Alternatively the cost of the goods transferred may be credited to the Purchases Account of the transferor department (so that that account shows a net balance representing the cost of goods actually used in that department) and debited to the Purchases Account of the transferee department. The alternative methods are reflected in the Departmental Trading Accounts in the following way:—

Method I.*

TRADING ACCOUNTS

Dr. FOR THE YEAR ENDED 31ST DECEMBER, 1955 Cr.

	Dept. A.	Dept. B.		Dept. A.	Dept. B.
	£	£		£	£
To Stock at 1st Jan., 1955 . . .	6,000	10,000	By Sales . . .	35,000	80,000
,, Purchases . .	24,000	22,000	,, Transfers to Dept. B . .	10,000	
,, Transfers from Dept. A . .		10,000	,, Stock at 31st Dec., 1955 . .	5,000	8,000
,, Wages . . .	10,000	25,000			
,, Gross Profit, c/d.	10,000	21,000			
	£50,000	£88,000		£50,000	£88,000

Method II.

TRADING ACCOUNTS

Dr. FOR THE YEAR ENDED 31ST DECEMBER, 1955 Cr.

	Dept. A.	Dept. B.		Dept. A.	Dept. B.
	£	£		£	£
To Stock at 1st Jan., 1955 .	6,000	10,000	By Sales . . .	35,000	80,000
,, Purchases .	14,000(A)	32,000(B)	,, Stock at 31st Dec., 1955 . .	5,000	8,000
,, Wages . .	10,000	25,000			
,, Gross Profit, c/d. . .	10,000	21,000			
	£40,000	£88,000		£40,000	£88,000

* This method should be adopted where the goods are transferred at a price in excess of cost.

Notes :

(A) This might be shown in detail thus:—

	£	£
Purchases	24,000	
Less Transfers to Dept. *B* . . .	10,000	14,000

(B) This might be described as " Purchases, including transfers from Dept. *A*."

When it is desired to ascertain the net profit for each department, it is necessary to dissect the various items of gain and expenditure which are credited and debited to the Profit and Loss Account. If the exact amount of expenditure for each department is known, a columnar ledger will conveniently record the desired information. In many cases, however, the exact figures of the expenditure for each department are not available, and it is sometimes difficult to determine the most accurate and equitable method of apportioning the fixed overhead charges. Very often the apportionment is made upon an arbitrary basis (*e.g.*, one-half to department *A* and one-fourth each to departments *B* and *C*). Sometimes expenses are allocated in proportion to turnover (*e.g.*, assuming the total turnover to be £100,000 and the separate amounts for departments *A* and *B* to be £60,000 and £40,000 respectively, the proportion of, say, office expenses, for department *A* will be 60 per cent., and the proportion for department *B* 40 per cent.). But either of these methods may be inequitable in certain circumstances, and each item should be considered on its own merits before a method of apportionment is adopted for it. For example, it may be more equitable to apportion the charge for rent and rates on the basis of floor space occupied, while fire insurance may be fairly apportioned on the average value of the stock of each department. Direct selling expenses, *e.g.*, travellers' expenses, might be best apportioned in the ratio of departmental turnover.

Such departmental accounts as are considered here are best shown in columnar form (as illustrated in the following example) with the various items of expenditure for each department, and the totals, side by side. The departmental figures can easily be compared if the accounts are prepared in this way, and, to make the comparison still easier, the gross and net profits can also be shown as percentages of turnover.

EXAMPLE

The General Engineering Co., Ltd., of Birmingham, has two departments—(1) a Manufacturing Department, and (2) a Retail Department for the sale of general engineering sundries.

The following balances were extracted from the books of the company at 31st December, 1955. Prepare therefrom Trading and Profit and Loss Accounts of the two departments, and General Profit and Loss Account for the year ended 31st December, 1955, showing the percentages which the gross and net profits bear to the turnover of each department and the total :—

		£
Stock in Trade (Retail), at 1st January, 1955 . .		5,000
Do. (Works), do.		6,000
Rents, Rates and Insurance (Works) . . .		480
Purchases (do.)		8,000
Carriage and Freight (Inwards) (do.) . . .		500
Wages (do.)		6,500
Office Salaries (do.)		300
Office Expenses (do.)		120
Sales (do.)		19,800
Sales (Retail) . . .		35,000
Purchases (do.)		28,000
Carriage (Outwards) (do.)		1,000
Wages (do.)		800
Office Salaries (do.)		300
Office Expenses (do.)		300
Rent, Rates and Insurance (do.)		250
Interest on Investments		150
Bank Interest, less Commission		200
Profit and Loss Account (Credit balance) . . .		1,200
Directors' Fees		1,550

At 31st December, 1955, the value of the Stock-in-Trade of the Retail Department, as taken and certified by the manager, was £5,200, and of the Works Department, £6,150.

TRADING AND PROFIT AND LOSS ACCOUNTS

Dr.   FOR THE YEAR ENDED 31ST DECEMBER, 1955   *Cr.*

	Works Dept.	Retail Dept.	Total.		Works Dept.	Retail Dept.	Total.
	£	£	£		£	£	£
To Stock at 1st Jan.,1955	6,000	5,000	11,000	By Sales	19,800	35,000	54,800
„ Purchases . . .	8,000	28,000	36,000	„ Stock at 31st Dec.,			
„ Wages	6,500	800	7,300	1955	6,150	5,200	11,350
„ Carriage (Inwards)	500		500				
„ Balance, being Gross Profit, *c/d.* . .	4,950	6,400	11,350				
Percentage of Gross Profit to Turnover . . .	*25·00%*	*18·29%*	*20·71%*				
	£25,950	£40,200	£66,150		£25,950	£40,200	£66,150
	£	£	£		£	£	£
To Carriage (Outwards)		1,000	1,000	By Gross Profit, *b/d.* .	4,950	6,400	11,350
„ Rent, Rates and Insurance . . .	480	250	730				
„ Office Salaries . .	300	300	600				
„ Office Expenses .	120	300	420				
„ Departmental Net Profit, *c/d.* . .	4,050	4,550	8,600				
Percentage of Net Profit to Turnover .	*20·45%*	*13·00%*	*15·69%*				
	£4,950	£6,400	£11,350		£4,950	£6,400	£11,350

GENERAL PROFIT AND LOSS ACCOUNT

Dr.   FOR THE YEAR ENDED 31ST DECEMBER, 1955   *Cr.*

		£			£	£
To Directors' Fees. . . .		1,550	By Net Profit, *b/d* :—			
„ Balance, *c/d.*		7,400	Works Department .		4,050	
			Retail „ . .		4,550	
						8,600
			„ Bank Interest (less Commission)			200
			„ Interest on Investments			150
		£8,950				£8,950
		£				£
To Balance, *c/f.*		8,600	By Balance, *b/d.*			7,400
			„ Balance brought forward from previous year .			1,200
		£8,600				£8,600

Stock and Store Accounts.

Large manufacturing businesses usually maintain (as part of their system of Cost Accounts) a perpetual inventory of materials received into store and of issues made to jobs or processes. A Stores Ledger is opened with a Stock Account for each class of material, which is debited with the invoice price of materials received. As issues are made from stock, the relative Stock Account is credited with the value of the materials and at any date the stock on hand of that material can therefore be ascertained by balancing the Stock Account.

It is impossible to keep accurate Stock Accounts if a proper system of stores control is not in operation. The

Dr.   STOCK ACCOUNT   Cr.

Class of Material *Cast Iron Bars*   Store Room Bin No. *K.27*
Minimum Stock *10 tons*

Date.	Supplier.	Quan.	Price.	G.R. Book Fo.	£	s.	d.	Date.	Details.	Quan.	Price.	G.I. Book Fo.	£	s.	d.
1956 Jan. 3	Brown, Ltd.	20 tons	53/9 per ton	27	53	15	0	1956 Jan. 6	J. B.'s contract	1 t. 10 c.	53/9 per ton	12	4	0	8
								31	Balance, c/d.	18 t. 10 c.	,,		49	14	4
					£53	15	0						£53	15	0
Jan. 31	Balance, b/d.	18 t. 10 c.			49	14	4								

stores should be under the control of a storekeeper, who will only issue them on receipt of a duly authorised Stores Requisition, such as the following :—

No. 187.   STORES REQUISITION

Date, *19th Jan., 19..*   Dept. No. *2.*
                      Job No. *18B.*

Description of Material.	Count or Volume.	Weight. t. c. q. lbs.	Rate.	£	s.	d.
5″ Rings	70		1/-	3	10	0

Authorised by *A. B.*   Supplied from Bin No. *17.*
Materials received by *C. D.*   Storekeeper's Signature, *R. J.*
Entered : Bin Card..*E. F.*..Stores Ledger..*G. H.*...Job..*X. Y.*

The information contained in these forms will be entered in a Goods Issued Book, from which it will be posted to the credit of the relative Stock Account. The debit side of the Stock Accounts will be posted from a Goods Received Book, in which the storekeeper will have entered particulars

D

of all goods taken into store. As a matter of internal check, he should also make out a Goods Received Note, which will be passed through to the Counting House to enable the invoices received from suppliers to be checked before they are entered in the Purchases Day Book.

A Bin Card should also be made out in respect of each class of material and attached to the bin in which it is stored, showing receipts and issues, together with the balance in hand after each receipt or issue. Money values are not inserted on these cards. Since the Bin Cards and Stock Accounts are independently written up by the storekeeper and the Cost Department respectively, a valuable internal check is maintained on these records.

It is possible to " take stock " at the end of a period by extracting the balances of all the Stock Accounts, and the necessity for closing down the works in order to make an inventory of all the stocks on hand is thus avoided. The accuracy of the Stock Accounts should be checked from time to time by a comparison with the Bin Cards and a physical stocktaking, undertaken as a matter of systematic routine, but it is not necessary to check all the accounts on the same day. Small differences may be expected for reasons such as the following :—

(1) Through " breaking bulk ", *i.e.*, weighing or measuring small quantities (if 1 cwt. of material has to be weighed out in 1-lb. lots and the scale is turned on each occasion, it will not be possible to obtain 112 lots from the original parcel) ;

(2) Some materials alter in quantity or value while lying in store : thus tobacco loses moisture and therefore weighs less, while cotton absorbs moisture and gains in weight ; spirits evaporate and thus decrease both in value and quantity.

The stock-taker must satisfy himself that such differences are reasonable and must adjust the balances of the Stock Accounts so that they reflect the actual amounts in hand.

Although the detailed Stock Accounts will appear in the costing records and the duty of keeping them will devolve on the staff of the Cost Accountant, the total value of stock in hand can be reflected in the financial books by means of total accounts. The monthly total of stores purchased will be posted from the Purchases Day Book to the debit of Stores Account in the Nominal Ledger. A separate account will be opened for Materials Consumed and the monthly totals of goods issued less goods returned to store as shown by the storekeeper's Stores Issued Book will be debited to Materials Consumed Account and credited to Stores Account. The following are specimen accounts :—

Dr.			STORES			Cr.
19..			£	19..		£
Jan. 1	To Balance .	b/d.	2,613	Jan. 31	By Materials	
31	„ Purchases	B.J.	861		Issued J.	725
Feb. 28	„ do.	B.J.	619	Feb. 28	„ do. do. J.	791
Mar. 31	„ do.	B.J.	526	Mar. 31	„ do. do. J.	683
Apr. 30	„ do.	B.J.	795	Apr. 30	„ do. do. J.	542
May 31	„ do.	B.J.	913	May 31	„ do. do. J.	597
June 30	„ do.	B.J.	428	June 30	„ do. do. J.	621
					„ Balance. . c/d.	2,796
			£6,755			£6,755
July 1	To Balance .	b/d.	2,796			

Dr.			MATERIALS CONSUMED			Cr.
19..			£	19..		£
Jan. 31	To Stores Issued	J.	725	June 30	By Manufactur-	
Feb. 28	„ do. do.	J.	791		ing Account J.	3,959
Mar. 31	„ do. do.	J.	683			
Apr. 30	„ do. do.	J.	542			
May 31	„ do. do.	J.	597			
June 30	„ do. do.	J.	621			
			£3,959			£3,959

Stock Book Control.

The Stock and Store Accounts already considered are designed primarily to check or indicate (pending a physical stock-taking) the value of stock on hand, and they presuppose that the values of goods added to, and taken from, stock during the period are known. A similar method may be used to check the *takings* of a business for a given period, the opening and closing stock being taken by physical inventory and a strict record being kept of goods purchased and added to stock.

EXAMPLE

A licensed victualler had 28 bottles of Algerian wine in stock on 1st January. During the month 60 bottles were purchased and on 31st January the stock amounted to 32 bottles.

The number of bottles sold is obviously found by a simple calculation:

Number in stock at 1st January	28
Number purchased	60
	88
Number in stock at 31st January	32
Number sold	56

If the selling-price is known to be 12s. 6d. a bottle, it is obvious that the takings for the month must include £35 from this source alone ; and by making similar calculations for all the items in stock, the total value of goods sold during the period can be ascertained. This figure should agree with the actual takings within fairly close limits.

This method of control is restricted to those businesses in which the selling prices of the products are fixed, and is extensively used in the wine and spirit trade. Stock is taken by independent valuers at fairly frequent intervals, and a very close check is thus obtained on the honesty and efficiency of the manager. The calculations are usually made in books specially ruled for the purpose (see specimen below).

Stock Errors.

Where no detailed stock records are kept, it is difficult to detect errors, or fraudulent manipulations of stock, except by noticing the effect on the gross profit. It is important that this effect should be thoroughly understood.

STOCK BOOK

January, 19..

Description.		Stock b/f.	Pur-chases.	Total.	Stock c/f.	Sales.		
						No.	Price.	Amount.
								£ s. d.
Algerian Wine.	Bot.	28	60	88	32	56	12s. 6d.	35 0 0
,, ,,	½ Bot.	15	36	51	21	30	6s. 6d.	9 ,15 0
etc., etc.								

This ruling gives the bare essentials : columns are sometimes added to show the cost price as well as the selling price of goods sold ; and the estimated gross profit can then be obtained by deducting the total cost from the total sales.

A genuine error in taking stock has a twofold effect, for the reason that the closing stock of one period is the opening stock of the next. Thus, if the stock is valued at too low a figure, the profit for the past year will be understated, but the profit for the next year will be overstated by the same amount.

The following Trading Accounts show the results of a business for the two years ended 31st December, 1955 : stocks have been correctly valued and a steady gross profit of 20 per cent. on sales is revealed.

Dr.   Cr.

	1954.	1955.		1954.	1955.
	£	£		£	£
To Opening Stock .	10,000	12,000	By Sales . . .	25,000	30,000
„ Purchases . .	22,000	27,000	„ Closing Stock .	12,000	15,000
„ Gross Profit .	5,000	6,000			
	£37,000	£45,000		£37,000	£45,000

Now suppose that the stock at 31st December, 1954, had been overvalued by £2,000 ; the following results would have been shown :—

Dr.   Cr.

	1954.	1955.		1954.	1955.
	£	£		£	£
To Opening Stock .	10,000	14,000	By Sales . . .	25,000	30,000
„ Purchases . .	22,000	27,000	„ Closing Stock .	14,000	15,000
„ Gross Profit .	7,000	4,000			
	£39,000	£45,000		£39,000	£45,000

The incorrect gross profit of £7,000 for 1954 is 28 per cent. of the turnover of £25,000 for that year ; for 1955 the corresponding percentage is $13\frac{1}{3}$. Thus the errors in the stock have caused errors in the rate of gross profit of 8 per cent. and $6\frac{2}{3}$ per cent. for successive years and the total " swing " in the gross profit is $14\frac{2}{3}$ per cent. While the *amount* of the error is the same each year—£2,000, the percentage differs because it is based on a turnover of £25,000 in 1954 and on one of £30,000 in 1955.

When the rate of gross profit of a business, after being relatively steady for several years, suddenly fluctuates in this way, it is very reasonable to ascribe the cause to errors in stocktaking. These errors are of two kinds :—

(1) *Errors of commission.*—Mistakes in counting or measuring the stock, pricing it, calculating values or casting the stock sheets.

(2) *Errors of principle.*—The inclusion of goods in stock which have not been entered as purchases for the year just ended and other errors of this type. These spring from breaches of the fundamental rule that—

    (*a*) Goods which have been bought (*i.e.*, become the legal property of the trader) during the period, and no others, should have been—

        (i) Entered in the books as purchases, and

        (ii) Included in the closing stock unless previously sold ;

    (*b*) The closing stock is restricted to goods which fall within (i) above and all goods which have actually been sold during the period (whether delivered to the customer or not) should have been—

        (i) Entered in the books as purchases, unless they were included in the opening stock ; and

        (ii) Excluded from the closing stock.

The question of stock valuation will be considered in Chapter IV : from what has been said above it should be clear that, although the physical inventory of stock may be correct, the final accounts will be wrong if the books themselves have not been properly written up, and the resulting

	1954.	1955.		1954.	1955.
	£	£		£	£
To Opening Stock .	10,000	12,000	By Sales . . .	25,000	30,000
„ Purchases . .	20,000	29,000	„ Closing Stock	12,000	15,000
„ Gross Profit .	7,000	4,000			
	£37,000	£45,000		£37,000	£45,000

Dr.   *Cr.*

errors have the same effect as errors in stocktaking. Thus, in the example considered on page 69, if the stock at 31st December, 1954, had been correctly valued at £12,000 but £2,000 of the purchases for the year 1954 had been omitted from the records of that year and entered in January, 1955, the errors in the gross profit would have been the same as if the stock had been overvalued by £2,000 (see page 70).

Fraudulent errors or manipulations of stock have the same effect as genuine errors if they are restricted to one stock-taking and are allowed to " work themselves out " in the next year. It is probable, however, that such manipulations will not be restricted to one year's stocktaking but will be applied systematically during a series of years. In such circumstances, it is difficult to draw any reliable inferences from the Trading Accounts, and the only effective check is that which is afforded by a reliable system of Stock Accounts (see pages 64 *et seq.*).

Interim Stock Accounts.

In the case of departmental stores and multiple shops, where the average gross profit on sales of each department or shop is fixed at a standard rate, it is usual to keep a weekly statistical record of estimated stock accounts and to take stock at irregular intervals, so that a comparison of the actual and estimated stock can be made, and a general check maintained upon the departmental managers and shop managers.

The method is similar to that already considered on page 67 except in one important particular. There will be no available record of the actual cost price of goods sold (*i.e.*, taken from stock) as there is where detailed stock accounts are kept for costing purposes. By deducting the expected rate of profit from the selling value of goods sold, however, a *close approximation* to the cost price can be obtained.

The form of the weekly statistical stock account (which is purely a memorandum account and quite distinct from the ordinary accounts) is as follows :—

STATEMENT OF STOCK

FOR THE WEEK ENDING 8TH JANUARY, 19..

	A. DEPARTMENT. Average Rate of Profit = 25% on S.P.		B. DEPARTMENT. Average Rate of Profit = 20% on S.P.	
	£	£	£	£
Commencing Stock at C.P.. .		3,200		2,100
Purchases		790		540
		3,990		2,640
Sales at S.P..	900		820	
Less Estimated Profit . .	225	675	164	656
Estimated Stock at C.P. . .		£3,315		£1,984

The estimated closing stock is carried forward as the commencing stock of the next week and so on from week to week, until the next occasion on which stock is actually taken by physical inventory, when any difference is adjusted. Small differences are probably due to slight variations in the rate of profit actually earned, but the reason for any large discrepancy should be ascertained and steps taken to eliminate the causes thereof.

It should be noted, however, that this system can be satisfactorily applied only when—

(1) The rate of profit does not vary, or varies only within narrow limits ;

(2) Stock is taken at frequent intervals; and

(3) Wastage, or loss from damage, is small, and accurate records are taken of such losses.

Moreover, the accuracy of the estimated stock is entirely dependent upon the accuracy of the figures for the respective items in the statistical stock account. Any error in the figures of the component items must necessarily be repeated in the final figure for the estimated stock.

In the case of retail shops where the goods are charged

out by Head Office at selling price, the statistical stock account is compiled wholly on the basis of sale price.

An important advantage of maintaining these stock accounts is that the proprietors of the business are enabled to watch closely the value of stock held, with the twofold object of preventing any undue increase or decrease, and of seeing that the stock carried at all times is fully covered by insurance.

Loss of Stock by Fire.

When stock is lost by fire and no detailed records are available to show the amount or value of the goods which have been lost, it is necessary to adopt similar methods to those outlined in the preceding paragraphs. The statement prepared will cover the period since the latest date on which the value of stock is known (usually the date of the last Balance Sheet).

Where the percentage of gross profit is subject to some variation, an average percentage must be ascertained by reference to the trading results of recent years. This average percentage is then used as the basis for making the claim.

EXAMPLE

On 14th April, 1956, a fire destroyed the greater part of the premises of a Company. Stock to the value of £1,860, and the books, were saved from the fire. From the information available the following details were extracted :—

				Sales. £	Gross Profit. £
Year to December 31st,	1951	.	. .	85,872	21,468
,,	,,	,, 1952	. . .	71,234	21,370
,,	,,	,, 1953	. . .	60,122	19,640
,,	,,	,, 1954	. . .	53,930	18,336
,,	,,	,, 1955	. . .	48,762	16,254

The Stock on 31st December, 1955, was valued at £9,860.

For the period from 1st January, 1956, to the date of the fire, Sales amounted to £15,900, Purchases to £7,816 and Productive Wages to £1,924.

Prepare a statement in support of a claim for loss of stock to be made on the Insurance Company.

D*

BLANK CO., LTD.
STATEMENT OF CLAIM FOR LOSS OF STOCK
AS AT 14TH APRIL, 1956

	£	£
Stock as at 1st January, 1956		9,860
Add Purchases from 1st January, 1956, to 14th April, 1956 .	7,816	
Productive Wages do. do.	1,924	
		9,740
		19,600
Deduct Sales do. do.	15,900	
Less Estimated Gross Profit (33⅓ per cent., see below) .	5,300	
		10,600
		9,000
Deduct Stock salvaged from fire		1,860
Amount of Claim for Loss of Stock . . .		£7,140

The approximate ratios of gross profit to turnover during the five years ended 31st December, 1955, are as follows:—

	%
1951	25
1952	30
1953	32⅓
1954	34
1955	33⅓
Average (say) . .	31

The average of 31 per cent. is the average of the percentages and not the true average gross profit for the five years ended 31st December, 1955. The true average would be found by expressing the total of the gross profits, £97,068, as a percentage of the total sales, £319,920, which gives a result equal to 30·3 per cent.

Assuming that there are no reasons for thinking that the ratio of gross profit for 1956 would differ considerably from that for 1955, it is considered that the ratio of 33⅓ per cent. for the year 1955 should be taken as the basis for the claim. The ratios have tended to increase over the period and have, in fact, averaged 33⅓ per cent. during the last three years, and it is thought that this basis is more equitable than the five years' average of 31 per cent.

The above is a relatively simple and straightforward claim, but other considerations might influence the compilation of the claim, e.g. :—

(1) Any variation in the basis of valuation of stock over the whole period, e.g., excessive undervaluation in 1951 or overvaluation in 1955 ;

(2) Any variation in the nature of the trade conducted by the company over the period, e.g., the purchase of "job lots" during 1954 and 1955 showing a higher rate of gross profit ;

(3) Seasonal trade, which may make it not strictly correct to base the estimated gross profit for the period 1st January, 1956, to 14th April, 1956, on percentages obtained from figures relating to complete years : in the absence of accurate accounts covering exactly similar periods in the earlier years, however, these percentages would probably be accepted ;

(4) Any change in the treatment of prime cost items over the period, *e.g.*, the charging of productive wages or other direct expenses (or part thereof) to Profit and Loss Account in place of Trading Account during any year ;

(5) The insurance policy might contain an " average " clause, providing that if the value of the stock insured is greater than the amount insured, the claim must be restricted to that proportion of the loss which the amount insured against bears to the value of the stock. If, therefore, the Company had only insured against a loss of £7,500, it could only receive from the Insurance Company :—

$$\frac{7,500}{9,000} \times £7,140 = £5,950$$

and would be deemed to be its own insurer for the balance.

Apart from the above factors relating to the component items of the Trading Account, the terms of the insurance contract may affect the computation of the claim, for the policy may stipulate the basis for computing the claim.

Approximate Profit and Loss Accounts.

The statistical stock accounts discussed in the preceding paragraphs really form approximate Trading Accounts, and in a similar way, estimated Profit and Loss Accounts may be compiled periodically, with the object of watching the progress of the business closely, and supervising the ratio of the expenses to profits.

The approximate Profit and Loss Account, which is compiled, say, weekly, should show the figures for the week and the totals from the beginning of the year, and should also contain columns in which both these sets of figures are expressed as percentages of the turnover for the corresponding periods. For certain items, weekly amounts must be calculated, for example, rent, rates, insurance, directors' fees, etc.

The following example shows the appearance of an approximate Profit and Loss Account :—

APPROXIMATE PROFIT AND LOSS STATEMENT
WEEK ENDING 14TH JANUARY, 1956

	Per-centage.	WEEK ENDING 14th January, 1956	Per-centage.	TOTAL TO DATE, 14th January, 1956
		£	£	£	£
Sales		1,800		3,400
Estimated Gross Profit	25%	£ 450	25%	£ 850
Rent and Rates . .	2·00	36	2·12	72
Wages	7·33	132	7·91	269
Salaries	2·50	45	2·65	90
Discounts	3·50	63	3·50	119
Expenses	3·00	54	3·29	112
	18·33	330	19·47	662
Estimated Net Profit	6·67	£120	5·53	£188
	25·00		25·00	

At the close of each trading period, the figures given in these approximate statements should be compared with those given in the actual final accounts, and any discrepancy examined with a view to ascertaining its cause and making, as far as possible, future approximate accounts more accurate.

Percentages in Profit and Loss Accounts are not of the same importance as percentages in Trading Accounts. Thus, since rent is constant, a change in its percentage value probably indicates a change in turnover alone, which is already evident from the figure for turnover itself. It may be useful to know the percentage which each item of direct expense bears to the total of these expenses. This total can then be expressed as a percentage on turnover.

Unrealised Profits in Stock-in-Trade.

Where finished stocks of manufactured goods are included in the Trading Account at a value in excess of cost price as a result of crediting the Manufacturing Account with the current market value of the goods produced, the unrealised profit (which may be regarded as an " inter-departmental profit ") must be eliminated from the final accounts in order to reduce the unsold stock to cost price ; the appropriate adjustment has already been explained on page 40. If, however, the stock of manufactured goods is correctly valued at market price, which is lower than cost price (this will be apparent from the fact that a loss was incurred on manufacture), no adjustment is necessary.

Similarly, in chemical and other industries in which raw materials pass through various processes before finally emerging as the finished product, it is a fairly common practice to transfer the output of one process to the next process at a figure based on the estimated cost of obtaining similar materials from outside sources. In most cases, this figure will be in excess of actual cost, provided that the concern is working efficiently. The stocks in the various stages of manufacture at the end of the accounting period will therefore include a certain amount of unrealised " inter-process profit ", which must be excluded from the stock valuation in the final accounts.

EXAMPLE

At the commencement of the year 1955 a manufacturing company was engaged in making an article (A) which it sold direct to consumers without the intervention of a warehouse.

During the year it decided to operate another factory for the purpose of turning out another article (B) which could be made by the simple application of labour (not material) to article A. Thereafter, it sold article A and article B direct to the public from the respective factories.

At the end of the year 1955 the company's accountant prepared from the books the subjoined accounts. You are required to study these accounts and to state carefully :—

(a) Whether (with reasons) you consider £10,000 is the true profit for the year ; and

(b) If not, what is the true profit ; and

(c) What entry you would propose to make in the books to effect any necessary correction of the profit.

MANUFACTURING ACCOUNT (FACTORY A)

Dr.   FOR YEAR TO 31ST DECEMBER, 1955   *Cr.*

	£		£
To Stock of Raw Materials at 1st Jan., 1955 (at cost) .	1,000	By Sales to Public, 3,000 Articles	15,000
„ Raw Materials Purchased	18,000	„ Transfer to Factory B, 6,000 Articles (at cost	
	19,000	plus 5%)	26,460
Less Stock of Raw Materials at 31st Dec., 1955 (at cost).	1,500	„ Stock of 1,000 Finished A Articles at 31st Dec., 1955 (at cost plus 5%)	4,410
	17,500		
„ Productive Wages . . .	20,000		
„ Factory Overhead Expenses	4,500		
Total Cost of Producing 10,000 Articles . . .	42,000		
„ Factory A Profit to Profit and Loss Account . .	3,870		
	£45,870		£45,870

MANUFACTURING ACCOUNT (FACTORY B)

Dr.   FOR YEAR TO 31ST DECEMBER, 1955   *Cr.*

	£		£
To Transfer from Factory A, 6,000 Articles as above .	26,460	By Sales to Public, 4,000 Articles	28,000
„ Productive Wages . . .	5,000	„ Stock of 2,000 Finished B Articles at 31st Dec., 1955 (at cost plus 5%) .	11,361
„ Factory Overhead Expenses	1,000		
Total Cost of Producing 6,000 Articles . . .	32,460		
„ Factory B Profit to Profit and Loss Account . .	6,901		
	£39,361		£39,361

PROFIT AND LOSS ACCOUNT

Dr.   FOR YEAR TO 31ST DECEMBER, 1955   *Cr.*

	£		£
To Selling Expenses . . .	771	By Profit transferred from	
,, Net Profit, *c/d.* . . .	10,000	Factory *A*	3,870
		Factory *B*	6,901
	£10,771		£10,771
		By Net Profit, *b/d.* . . .	10,000

(*a*) The net profit of £10,000 that is shown in the Profit and Loss Account is not the true profit for the year, for it includes the following unrealised profits :—

(i) The profit margin added to the closing stock in Factory *A*.

(ii) The double profit margin added to the closing stock in Factory *B*.

(*b*) The true profit is ascertained as follows :—

$$
\begin{array}{lrrr}
 & £ & £ & £ \\
\text{Net Profit as per Profit and Loss Account} & . & . & 10,000 \\
\text{\textit{Deduct}: Unrealised profits on stocks:---} & & & \\
\end{array}
$$

Factory *A*, $\dfrac{5}{105} \times £4,410$ 210

Factory *B*,

(1) $\dfrac{5}{105} \times £11,361$ 541

(2) Proportion of Factory *A*'s profit in closing stock of Factory *B*.

$\dfrac{5}{105} \times £8,820$

$\left[\dfrac{2,000}{6,000} \times £26,460 \right]$ . . . 420
— 961
—— 1,171

£8,829

(*c*) The entry necessary to correct the net profit is :—

	£	£
Profit and Loss Account . . . . *Dr.*	1,171	
To Provision for Unrealised Profits on Stocks		1,171

Being provision for unrealised factory profits on stocks at Factory A and Factory B at 31st December, 1955.

The provision will appear in the Balance Sheet as a deduction from the book value of the stocks of finished goods, *viz.* :—

	£	£
Stocks of Finished Goods	15,771	
Less Provision for Unrealised Profits	1,171	
		14,600

CHAPTER III

THE PROFIT AND LOSS ACCOUNT (2)

In the case of a sole trader, the Profit and Loss Account has achieved its object when it has shown how the profit or loss for the period has been made. The balance of the account, representing net profit or loss, is transferred to Capital Account, for profits automatically swell the capital while losses reduce it, subject to the introduction or withdrawal of capital. The functions of the Profit and Loss Account are restricted to—

(a) Closing the nominal ledger accounts in the trader's books so that the transactions of successive periods are kept distinct.

(b) Providing information, both for the personal use of the proprietor and as evidence to third parties (*e.g.*, Inspector of Taxes, prospective purchasers of the business, etc.), of the results of carrying on the business.

When business is carried on in partnership or through the medium of a limited company, however, other and perhaps more important considerations arise. The Profit and Loss Account is then prepared primarily for the benefit of the *proprietors* of the business and shows them how they have benefited or lost as the result of the year's operations. It is in the nature of an account presented by an agent to his principal. Finally, when the profits have been distributed, it records their disposition.

Partnership.

Partnership is defined by Section 1 of the Partnership Act, 1890, as " the relation which subsists between persons carrying on a business in common with a view of profit ", but the relation of agent and principal which exists between partners is explained by Sir Frederick Pollock's definition : " Partnership is the relation which subsists between persons who have agreed to share the profits of a business, carried on by all or any of them for the benefit of all of them." Thus the essential features of a partnership are—

(1) There must be a *business,* and for this purpose " business " means any trade, occupation or profession.

(2) It must be carried on *in common—i.e.,* it must be carried on by some or all of them for the benefit of all of them.

(3) It must be *with a view of profit* ; therefore the members of a club, which is not carried on for the purpose of making profits, are not partners.

Subject to five statutory exceptions,* the sharing in the profits of the partnership business is very strong evidence of the existence of a partnership, and, unless it is rebutted, gives rise to a presumption that a partnership in fact exists. The doctrine that the sole test of partnership was participation in profits was destroyed by the judgment in *Cox* v. *Hickman,* 1860. It was decided there that the true test of partnership was not merely participation in profits, but participation in profits in such a way as to create a relation of *agency* between the participators.

Rights of Partners.

Business may be carried on in a " firm name ", but, in English law, a firm has no separate entity apart from its members. Each partner is an agent for the firm and his

---

* By Section 2 (3) of the Partnership Act, 1890.
The following do not of themselves render a person a partner or liable as such : —
  (i) The receipt by a person of a debt out of accruing profits.
  (ii) The receipt by a servant or agent of a share of the profits of a business.
  (iii) The receipt by the widow or child of a deceased partner of an annuity payable out of the profits.
  (iv) The advance of money by way of loan, on a contract that the lender shall receive a rate of interest varying with the profits arising from carrying on the business, provided that the contract is in writing, and signed by or on behalf of all the parties thereto. (The object of the contract in writing is to afford proof that no partnership exists.)
  (v) The receipt of an annuity or a portion of the profits of a business, in consideration of the sale of the goodwill of the business.

co-partners for the purpose of the business of the partnership, and the acts of every partner who does any act for carrying on, in the usual way, business of the kind carried on by the firm of which he is a member, bind the firm and his partners. Nevertheless, the remedies of creditors are against the partners *personally*, and each partner is jointly liable for all the debts of the firm, while the estate of a deceased partner is jointly and severally liable for debts contracted during the lifetime of the deceased.* The personal liability of the partners and the power of each to bind the others are the essential features of partnership, as distinct from other associations (*e.g.*, limited companies) for carrying on business.

All property and rights and interests in property originally brought into the partnership stock or acquired, whether by purchase or otherwise, on account of the firm or for the purposes and in the course of the partnership business, are called *partnership property* and must be held and applied by the partners exclusively for the purposes of the partnership and in accordance with the partnership agreement. Thus, although a partnership has no separate entity, partnership property is quite distinct from the private property of the partners and forms a separate estate or fund, out of which the liabilities of the firm are primarily payable. It is essential that accounts should be kept to record the property of the firm and the rights and interests of the partners in it. Monetary disputes between partners can be settled only on the basis of an account, which will always be ordered by the Court.

When two or more persons commence a business in partnership, it is usual for them to agree among themselves on such matters as the proportions and amounts of capital to be contributed by each, and the basis on which profits

---

* The difference between being " jointly " and " jointly and severally " liable is that in the former case there is only one cause of action, and therefore when a plaintiff has sued one or some of the partners, and obtained judgment, he cannot bring a subsequent action against any of the others if the judgment remains unsatisfied ; whereas in the latter case a plaintiff may first obtain judgment against one or more of the partners and subsequently sue other partners, one or more at a time, and obtain judgment against them, until all the partners have been sued, or the amount due has been paid.

or losses are to be shared. If profits are not to be shared in the same proportions as those in which capital is contributed, it is quite usual for interest to be paid on capital before arriving at the balance of profit available for distribution. Similarly, if a partner makes an advance to the firm in excess of his agreed capital, provision will usually be made for interest to be paid to him at a certain rate ; while if some of the partners devote the whole of their time to the business of the firm and others are not actively engaged in it, provision may be made for salaries to be paid to the active partners. Agreement on these matters may be expressed (*i.e.*, by deed, in writing or even verbally) or implied from the conduct of the partners. In the absence of any agreement at all, the Partnership Act (Section 24) provides—

(1) All the partners are entitled to share equally in the capital and profits of the business, and must contribute equally towards the losses whether of capital or otherwise sustained by the firm.

(2) The firm must indemnify every partner in respect of payments made and personal liabilities incurred by him—

  (*a*) In the ordinary and proper conduct of the business of the firm ; or

  (*b*) In or about anything necessarily done for the preservation of the business or property of the firm.

(3) A partner making, for the purpose of the partnership, any actual payment or advance beyond the amount of capital which he has agreed to subscribe, is entitled to interest at the rate of 5 per cent. per annum from the date of the payment or advance.

(4) A partner is not entitled, before the ascertainment of profits, to interest on capital subscribed by him.

(5) Every partner may take part in the management of the partnership business.

(6) No partner shall be entitled to remuneration for acting in the partnership business.

(7) No person may be introduced as a partner without the consent of all existing partners.

(8) Any difference arising as to ordinary matters connected with the partnership business may be decided by a majority of the partners, but no change may be made in the nature of the partnership business without the consent of all existing partners.

(9) The partnership books are to be kept at the place of business of the partnership (or the principal place, if there is more than one), and every partner may, when he thinks fit, have access to and inspect and copy any of them.

Partnership Accounts.

It has been seen that the sharing of profit is an essential object of partnership. The recording of the profits or losses actually made and the way in which they are shared among the partners is therefore an essential feature of partnership accounts. The Profit and Loss Appropriation Account shows

A, B AND CO.
PROFIT AND LOSS APPROPRIATION ACCOUNT

Dr.   FOR THE YEAR ENDED 31ST DECEMBER, 1955   Cr.

	£	£			£	£
To Salaries :			By Net Profit, *brought down*			6,980
B	600		„ Interest on Drawings :			
C	400				£	
		1,000	A		25	
„ Interest on Capital :	£		B		20	
A	400		C		15	
B	100					60
C	50					
		550				
„ Balance, Divisible Profit :						
	£					
A, $\frac{4}{9}$	2,440					
B, $\frac{3}{9}$	1,830					
C, $\frac{2}{9}$	1,220					
		5,490				
		£7,040				£7,040

on the credit side the amount of net profit brought down from the Profit and Loss Account and any amounts due from partners in respect of interest on drawings (if the Partnership Agreement so provides), and on the debit side the amounts of any partnership salaries, interest on capital, and the balance finally available for distribution divided in the agreed proportions. If a loss is incurred, it will, of course, be debited to the Appropriation Account, and the amount chargeable to each partner will be credited. An example of such an account is given on page 84.

Interest on loans made to or by the partners should appear in the Profit and Loss Account.

Limited Partnerships.

A limited partnership is one formed and registered under the Limited Partnership Act, 1907,* having one or more general partners liable for all the debts and obligations of the firm, and one or more limited partners, who at the time of entering into the partnership contribute thereto as capital a sum or sums of money or property valued at a stated amount, and who are not liable for the debts or obligations of the firm beyond the amount so contributed. A limited partner may not, during the existence of the partnership, draw out or receive back any part of his contribution. If he does so he is liable for the debts and obligations of the firm up to the amount withdrawn.

A limited partner may not take part in the management of the firm ; and if he does so, he becomes liable as a general partner for all debts and obligations of the firm incurred while he so takes part in the management. He cannot bind the firm, but he can demand production of the accounts, inspect the books, either personally or by his agent, and advise on the management of the business.

With the consent of the general partners, a limited partner may assign his share in the partnership, and upon

* Owing to the passing of the Companies Act, 1907, which has since been incorporated in later Companies Acts, and the subsequent popularity of the private limited company, with a minimum membership of two, the provisions of the Limited Partnership Act have not been utilised to a very great extent.

such assignment, the assignee becomes a limited partner with all the rights of the assignor.

Neither the death, bankruptcy nor lunacy of a limited partner dissolves the partnership. In the event of dissolution, limited partnerships are wound up by the general partners.

Limited Companies.

The unrestricted liability of partners and the difficulty of conducting partnerships with a large number of active partners (each capable of binding the firm in contracts with third parties) were the principal factors which led to the development of the joint-stock company system. The formation and regulation of limited companies are now governed by the Companies Act, 1948.* Section 434 of that Act prohibits the formation of partnerships of more than twenty persons (ten in the case of a banking business), so that nearly all large-scale commercial enterprises are now operated by limited companies. On the other hand, private limited companies can be formed with only two members, so that limited companies are not confined to large enterprises alone.

A *private company* is one which, by its Articles of Association—

(*a*) Restricts the right to transfer its shares ; and

(*b*) Limits the number of its members to fifty, not including persons who are in the employment of the company and persons who, having been formerly in the employment of the company, were while in that employment, and have continued after the determination of that employment to be, members of the company ; and

(*c*) Prohibits any invitation to the public to subscribe for any shares or debentures of the company.

Any company which is not a private company, as defined above, is a *public company*.

* It may be noted that the following classes of companies are governed by the Companies Act, 1948 : (*a*) Companies limited by shares ; (*b*) Companies limited by guarantee ; and (*c*) Unlimited companies. Only those falling within the first class will be considered in this book.

The characteristics of a limited company which distinguish it from a partnership are :—

(1) The company is a distinct legal entity apart from its members, and this separate legal entity is not affected by changes in its membership. It can contract, sue and be sued in its corporate name and capacity ;

(2) The duty of conducting the company's business is delegated to a comparatively small number of directors (who may or may not also be shareholders) ;

(3) The liability of the shareholders is limited to the amount which each has agreed to subscribe in the form of shares : *i.e.*, when a shareholder has paid for the agreed number of shares, he cannot be made liable to contribute any further amount towards the liabilities of the company ;

(4) The constitution of a company (*i.e.*, the objects with which it is formed, its name and domicile and the nominal amount of its share capital) is set out in a Memorandum of Association which can only be altered in certain special ways. The regulations or bye-laws of the company which lay down the rights and duties of the members as between themselves and the company are set out in the Articles of Association. Both these documents must be filed with the Registrar of Companies * when a company is incorporated, and are open to inspection by the public ;

(5) The profits of a company do not at once accrue to the members in proportion to their interests in the company. The shareholders can only receive profits in the form of dividends on their shares, and such dividends must be duly declared in accordance with the provisions of the company's Articles before they become due to the shareholders ;

(6) An annual audit is compulsory in the case of a limited company.

* At the Companies Registration Office, Bush House, London, W.C.1.

A private company, as compared with a public company, enjoys, *inter alia*, the following privileges :—

(1) Only two members are necessary to enable the company to carry on business.

(2) The company is not liable to be wound up because it has less than *seven* members, but it is a ground for winding up if the number of members falls below *two*.

(3) No statutory report need be filed, nor need a statutory meeting be held.

(4) The directors may act without having filed their consents to act in that capacity or signed the Memorandum of Association or a contract for their qualification shares.

(5) No statement in lieu of prospectus need be filed.

(6) No minimum subscription is required before proceeding to allot shares or commence business.

The Companies Act, 1948, introduced a new form of private company which, having satisfied certain conditions prescribed by Section 129 and the Seventh Schedule, is exempt from filing accounts with the annual returns ; a company which satisfies such conditions is referred to as an "*exempt private company*". The principal conditions are :—

(1) No body corporate (unless itself an exempt private company) holds any directorship, shares or debentures in the company.

(2) No person other than the holder has any interest in the shares or debentures.

(3) Not more than fifty persons hold debentures.

(4) Neither the company nor the directors are parties to any arrangement whereby the policy of the company is determined by persons other than the directors, members or debenture holders.

The intention of these conditions is to restrict the privileges of an exempt private company (see below) to companies of a family nature, and to exclude from such privileges subsidiaries of public companies.

If a company is an exempt private company, it enjoys, *inter alia*, the following additional privileges :—

(1) The annual returns (filed with the Registrar of Companies and open to inspection by the public) need not include a copy of the last annual accounts and auditor's and directors' reports.

(2) The auditor need not be a member of a recognised body of accountants or otherwise authorised by the Board of Trade.

(3) A partner or employee of an officer is not debarred from appointment as auditor.

(4) The prohibition on loans to directors, except in certain circumstances, does not apply.

The Appropriation Account.

The disposition of the profit made by a limited company is recorded in the Profit and Loss Appropriation Account, but this differs from the Appropriation Account of a partnership in that the whole of the profit is not necessarily disposed of. Any balance of profit, after dividends actually declared and other appropriations have been debited, is carried forward to the next year and forms part of the balance which will then be available for distribution. Thus the Profit and Loss Account is not closed each year but is continuous. If losses are made in excess of the balance of profits brought forward the Profit and Loss Account will be thrown into debit and will appear as a deduction from share capital in the Balance Sheet.

The legal rules for determining the amount of profit available for distribution to the shareholders of a company and the provisions of the Companies Act, 1948, regarding the preparation and publication of annual accounts are of such importance that they will be considered in detail in Chapters VIII and X. At this stage it may be useful to illustrate the general form of the Profit and Loss Appropriation Account which, as a matter of book-keeping, shows how the available balance for the year has been disposed of.

X.Y. CO., LTD.

PROFIT AND LOSS APPROPRIATION ACCOUNT

Dr.		FOR THE YEAR ENDED 31ST DECEMBER, 1955		Cr.

	£			£
To United Kingdom Taxation :—		By Balance, brought forward from last year .		24,730
£		„ Net Profit for year,		
Profits Tax, 1955 . 3,000		brought down. . .		37,860
Income Tax—				
Balance of 1955–56				
liability . . 1,250				
————				
4,250				
Reserve towards				
1956–57 liability 14,060				
————	18,310			
„ Transfer to General Reserve	4,500			
„ Interim Dividends (after deduction of Income Tax) for the year ended 31st December, 1955 :—				
Preference . . 3,520				
Ordinary . . 2,530				
————	6,050			
„ Provision for Proposed Final Dividends (after deduction of Income Tax) for the year ended 31st December, 1955 :—				
Preference . . 3,520				
Ordinary . . 5,060				
————	8,580			
„ Balance carried forward .	25,150			
	£62,590			£62,590

In theory, proposed appropriations of profit, *e.g.*, dividends, should not be recorded in the books until after the necessary ratification—usually a resolution of shareholders—has been obtained.

In recent years, however, it has become usual for com-

panies to include proposed dividends and other appropriations of profit in the Profit and Loss Appropriation Account
so that the Balance Sheet will give a clear view as to the
effect of the proposed dividends, etc., upon the surplus of
current assets over current liabilities. Although this practice may be theoretically incorrect as a liability (the proposed
dividend) will be included which may not become a debt on
the refusal of the members to sanction the proposed dividend,
it has received statutory authority in the Companies Act,
1948, which requires the amount of proposed dividends to be
shown in the published accounts.*

The inclusion of all appropriations in the accounts shows
the amount which will be required for distribution to the
shareholders and completes the accounts for the financial
year by showing the results of trading and their application
in one account, and avoids the inclusion in the accounts of
the next period of appropriations which were set out in the
directors' report for the previous period, and which have
already been dealt with and disposed of. Furthermore, the
practice facilitates the linking up of the accounts from one
period to another, the balance carried forward to the following period being clearly shown in the accounts of that
year.

Taxation.

Although most business men regard Income Tax as an
unavoidable expense, for accounting purposes it should be
treated as an appropriation of profits. That Income Tax
is an appropriation of profits—the Government's share—is
supported by the nature of the tax and the way in which it
is computed. When Income Tax is payable on the profits
of a business, any tax charged in the Profit and Loss Account
is added to the profit shown in order to arrive at the amount
of profit for the assessment.

One of the characteristic features of the British taxation system is the principle of deduction of tax at the

---

* Reference should be made to the recommendations of the Council of the Institute
of Chartered Accountants with regard to the inclusion in accounts of proposed profit
appropriations (see Appendix II).

source. Income which is in the nature of annual interest,*
i.e., debenture interest, loan interest, ground rent, etc., is
usually paid to the recipient under deduction of tax. The
payer retains tax at the standard rate for the time being
in force and must account to the Inland Revenue authorities
for the amount so deducted unless he can show that the
payment was made out of income which has already suffered
tax at the standard rate. Thus the Income Tax deducted
from such annual interest is in effect assessed and collected
from the payer.

A company must deduct tax from " annual payments ",*
such as debenture or loan interest and ground rent, and the
amount of tax actually paid by the company in respect of
the assessment on its profits will include the amount so
deducted. The amounts which are paid "less tax" will
probably appear "net" in the company's books and a
transfer must be made to adjust the accounts affected. This
is illustrated by the following journal entries :—

1956			£	£
Mar. 31	Debenture Interest . . . . *Dr.*		2,875	
	To Cash			2,875
	Being payment of interest for 6 months to date on £200,000			
	5% Debentures, less Income Tax at 8s. 6d. in the £.			
	Debenture Interest . . . . *Dr.*		2,125	
	To Income Tax			2,125
	Being adjustment of Income Tax deducted as above.			

It will be seen that as a result of these entries, Cash is
credited with the amount actually paid, £2,875, while Debenture Interest Account is debited with the full amount of
interest for the half year, £5,000. The tax deducted, £2,125,
is credited to Income Tax Account where it cancels an equivalent amount of the tax paid by the company, leaving the
net balance of tax actually suffered to be debited to Profit

---

* The exact interpretation of the terms " annual interest " or " annual payments " or " annual charges " is one of the most difficult matters in income tax law
and practice. It may be noted, however, that the term " annual " does not necessarily mean paid yearly but there must be some degree of permanence about the
transaction. Thus interest on bank overdrafts and other short loan or trade interest
is paid without deduction of tax and is allowed as a deduction in computing the
assessable profits of the payer.

and Loss Account (or preferably the Profit and Loss Appropriation Account).

It is essential that tax on annual charges should be adjusted as above, so that the *gross* amount of the interest, ground rent, etc., may be shown in the Profit and Loss Account. Similarly, where income (*e.g.*, dividends, interest, etc.) is received under deduction of tax, such income should be grossed-up in order that the *gross* amount, before deduction of tax, may be shown in the Profit and Loss Account.

The payment of a dividend to its shareholders, on the other hand, does not affect the amount of Income Tax payable by a company (although a company may deduct tax at the standard rate from such dividends) for the assessment is made on the amount of the company's adjusted profits before the appropriation of dividends therefrom. Thus it is recommended that where dividends are described as " less Income Tax " or " free of Income Tax " the amounts shown in respect thereof should be the *net* amounts payable.

The principle of deducting tax at the source is not affected by the practice of some companies of paying dividends " free of tax " for this is merely a different way of expressing the rate of dividend. Thus, when Income Tax is 8s. 6d. in the £, a dividend of 20 per cent. gives the shareholders a net return of 11·5 per cent., and a dividend of 11·5 per cent. " free of tax " is exactly the same as a dividend of 20 per cent. less tax.

Some companies still follow the practice of *grossing-up* the dividends and crediting the tax deducted on payment of the dividends to Income Tax Account where it may be offset against the tax actually paid by the company under direct assessment on its profits and which is debited to Income Tax Account. The result is, in theory, that only the tax actually suffered by the company is transferred from Income Tax Account to Profit and Loss Appropriation Account. Nevertheless, the former method by which the net amount of dividends is included in the accounts is favoured by modern authoritative opinion and supported by statutory recognition in the Companies Act, 1948.

Dividends and Income Tax are both appropriations of

profit so that the final balance of Profit and Loss Appropriation Account will be the same, whether dividends are shown "gross" or "net".*

The following is the summarised Appropriation Account of the *A.B. Co., Ltd.*, for the year ended 31st March, 1956, dividends being charged "net".

Dr.	£	Cr.	£
To Interim Dividend for year ended 31.3.56, less tax	1,725	By Balance, brought forward	4,653
„ Final Dividend for year ended 31.3.56, less tax	3,450	„ Net Profit for the year .	9,210
„ Income Tax	5,000		
„ Balance, carried forward	3,688		
	£13,863		£13,863

If the gross dividends are to be shown, the following adjustment must be made :—

1956		£	£
Mar. 31	Dividend Account . . . . *Dr.*	3,825	
	To Income Tax Account		3,825
	Being adjustment of tax deducted from dividends paid for year to date.		

and the summarised Appropriation Account will then appear as follows :—

Dr.	£	Cr.	£
To Interim Dividend (gross) for year ended 31.3.56	3,000	By Balance, brought forward	4,653
„ Final Dividend (gross) for year ended 31.3.56 .	6,000	„ Net Profit for the year .	9,210
„ Income Tax	1,175		
„ Balance, carried forward	3,688		
	£13,863		£13,863

The incidence of taxation and its effect on profits and on the financial position disclosed by the Balance Sheet, together with the extent to which the Inland Revenue on the one hand and the shareholders on the other have participated in profits, are matters which should be made clear to shareholders.

The assessment of liability to Profits Tax is based on

* Reference should also be made to the recommendations of the Council of the Institute of Chartered Accountants with regard to the treatment of taxation and dividends in accounts (see Appendix II).

the profits of the accounting period under review. The assessment of liability to Income Tax is, however, for the fiscal year ended 5th April and is normally based on the profits of the immediately preceding accounting period. The minimum or legal amount to be provided for taxation is thus the aggregate of taxes assessable on these bases, apportioned, as regards Income Tax, according to the period covered by the accounts under review. Thus, assuming a company's accounting year terminates on 31st December, the amount to be included in respect of taxation for the year ended 31st December, 1955, would be computed as follows :—

Profits Tax.—The estimated liability on the profits for the year to 31st December, 1955 (this will be payable one month after assessment).

Income Tax.—Last quarter of the assessed liability for the fiscal year 1954–55 (based on the adjusted profits to 31st December, 1953, and payable on 1st January, 1955) plus three-quarters of the assessed liability for the fiscal year 1955–56 (based on the adjusted profits to 31st December, 1954, and payable on 1st January, 1956).

Income Tax so apportioned takes no account, however, either of the balance of the liability assessable for the current fiscal year (remaining one-quarter of the assessed liability for 1955–56 in the above example), or of the liability which, in normal circumstances, will arise in respect of profits included in the accounts but not assessable until the following fiscal year (profits of 1955 assessable in 1956–57 in the above example). Further, unless provision be made year by year for Income Tax based on each year's results, the trend of net available profits will not be apparent, and cases will arise where the profits earned in a succeeding period will bear a disproportionate charge for taxation—indeed, they may even be insufficient to meet it. Thus modern opinion recommends that :—

(1) The charge for all forms of taxation should be stated in the accounts.

(2) The charge for Income Tax should be based on the profits earned during the period covered by the accounts. Where it has been the practice to charge only the minimum or legal liability, it may be necessary to build up the reserve for future taxation on current profits by appropriations over several years, which will be made in addition to the charge in respect of the current liability during those years. Whatever method is adopted the basis of the charge and of any supplemental provision made for Income Tax should be disclosed. Income Tax on revenue taxed before receipt should be included as part of the taxation charge for the year and the relative income should be credited gross in the Profit and Loss Account.

(3) Taxation charges may be affected by losses in the current period, deficiencies or losses brought forward or adjustments of taxation in respect of previous periods, the effect of which, if material, should be disclosed. Any provision made in excess of the amount required to cover the estimated future liability on profits earned to date should, if material, be similarly disclosed.

(4) Any provision for (or in excess of) the estimated future liability to Income Tax in respect of the fiscal year commencing after the date of the Balance Sheet should not be included with current liabilities but should be grouped with *reserves* and suitably described.*

The Companies Act, 1948, provides that the amount of the charge for taxation assessable on profits should be separately stated in the Profit and Loss Account, distinguishing, where practicable, between Income Tax and other forms of taxation. The basis on which the charge for Income Tax is computed should also be stated.

* Reference should also be made to the recommendations of the Council of the Institute of Chartered Accountants with regard to the treatment of taxation in accounts (see Appendix II).

Directors' Fees.

When the remuneration of the directors is fixed by the Articles, either at a fixed sum per annum per director or at a total sum which the directors may divide as they please, it should be regarded as an expense incurred in operating the company and not as an appropriation of profits. The debit for directors' fees (which will include any amount accrued due but unpaid at the date of the Balance Sheet) will then be found in the Profit and Loss Account.

It is not uncommon, however, for the Articles to provide that the remuneration of the directors shall be fixed by the shareholders at the Annual General Meeting of the company. In such a case it should be regarded as an appropriation of profits, and the amount actually paid during the year (normally the remuneration for the previous year) should be debited to the Appropriation Account. Where, however, it is the practice to include proposed appropriations of profits in the accounts, the proposed remuneration for the current year should be debited to the Appropriation Account.

In addition to the fixed or other fees payable to the directors as such, it will usually be found that some of them devote the whole of their time to the company's affairs and accordingly receive special remuneration, which may be in addition to or in substitution for the ordinary fees. These salaries are definitely incurred in operating the company and should be charged either to the Profit and Loss Account, or, in the case of a works manager, to Manufacturing Account.

Since 1st July, 1948, it is illegal to pay directors' remunerations " free of tax " unless it is payable under a contract which was in force on 18th July, 1945, providing expressly, and not merely by reference in the Articles, for payment " free of tax ".

The Companies Act, 1948, requires full disclosure of the aggregate of directors' emoluments in the published accounts (see Chapter X).

Commission on Net Profits.

The remuneration of the directors or of the managing

E

director may take the form of a commission on net profits. The calculation of the amount due requires careful consideration of the Article or Agreement under which the commission is payable. This Article or Agreement must be most carefully drawn if disputes are to be avoided and it is desirable that " net profit " should be defined as clearly as possible. It was decided in *Johnston* v. *Chestergate Hat Manufacturing Co. Ltd.* (1915), and upheld in *Edwards* v. *Saunton Hotel Co. Ltd.* (1943), that in the absence of agreement Income Tax is not to be charged in arriving at the amount of the net profit.

When the amount of net profit has been ascertained, the calculation of the commission does not present much difficulty. The Article or Agreement may provide, however, that the commission is to be calculated on the net profit remaining *after charging the commission* itself. A simple calculation is then involved. Suppose that the profit before charging the commission amounts to £1,000 and that the rate of commission is 7 per cent. If the correct amount of commission is £x, the balance of profit after charging the commission will be £(1,000 — x).

The commission is 7 per cent. of £(1,000—x)

$$x = \frac{7}{100}(1,000 - x)$$

$$= 70 - \frac{7x}{100}$$

$$\therefore \frac{107x}{100} = 70$$

$$\therefore x = \frac{7,000}{107} = £65 \text{ 8s. 5d.}$$

The amount of the commission is £65 8s. 5d., which is 7 per cent. of the balance of profit after charging the commission, £934 11s. 7d.

A rule of thumb method of arriving at the same result is—

(1) Express the rate per cent. to be paid to the directors as a fraction ($\frac{7}{100}$ in the above example) ;

(2) Increase the denominator by adding to it the numerator (in the above example this gives $\frac{7}{107}$).

This fraction applied to the profits balance before the commission has been charged will give the commission.

Appropriations for the Repayment of Liabilities.

In the case of limited companies, a special type of appropriation of profits is encountered, which has for its object the repayment of liabilities. Similar considerations apply to the redemption of Redeemable Preference Shares under the provisions of Section 58 of the Companies Act, 1948.*

It might be thought that the repayment of a liability is not a matter which affects profits at all. The immediate effect of the repayment is to reduce the assets and liabilities by the same amount. Thus if Debentures amounting to £10,000 are repaid, the transaction may be recorded by the following journal entry :—

Date			£	£
	Debentures	Dr.	10,000	
	To Cash			10,000

and the effect of the repayment can be seen by considering the following skeleton Balance Sheets which show the positions before and after the repayment.

BALANCE SHEETS

	(a) Before repayment.	(b) After repayment.		(a) Before repayment.	(b) After repayment.
	£	£		£	£
Capital	50,000	50,000	Assets, including		
Debentures . . .	10,000	—	Cash . . .	110,000	100,000
Other Liabilities .	20,000	20,000			
Profit and Loss Account balance .	30,000	30,000			
	£110,000	£100,000		£110,000	£100,000

* *Vide* Chapter VI.

Both before and after the repayment, the company had a share capital of £50,000 and undivided profits amounting to £30,000, so that the total interest of the shareholders in the company was £80,000 represented by—

	(a) Before repayment of debentures.	(b) After repayment of debentures.
	£	£
Assets	110,000	100,000
Less Liabilities	30,000*	20,000
(*Including Debentures)		
	£80,000	£80,000

Nevertheless, it is nearly always considered advisable to transfer an amount equal to the sum applied in repayment of the debentures, £10,000, in this case, from Profit and Loss Appropriation Account to the credit of a Reserve Account, so that the balance of profits available for distribution is reduced. It has already been shown that profits must be represented by an increase in net assets and that the increase in net assets over a period is the true measure of profits for that period. Thus the net assets of £80,000 before the debentures were repaid represented £50,000 capital and £30,000 profits. The assets which represent the capital may be regarded as permanent, whereas the profits should be in a liquid form and the money applied to the repayment of the debentures necessarily comes out of the fund of liquid assets. Thus, although the repayment of the debentures does not involve any loss in the ordinary sense, it reduces the fund of cash out of which profits may be distributed.

If the whole of the £30,000 standing to the credit of Profit and Loss Account were to be paid out in dividend immediately after the repayment of the debentures, it would obviously be necessary to encroach on the capital assets to the extent of £10,000 and this might seriously affect the future profits of the company. To avoid the distribution of the whole of the profits in this way, a transfer should be made to General Reserve, thus—

Date	Profit and Loss Appropriation Account	£	£
	Dr.	10,000	
	To General Reserve		10,000

The Balance Sheet will then show the following position :—

BALANCE SHEET

	£		£
Capital	50,000	Assets	100,000
Liabilities	20,000		
General Reserve . . .	10,000		
Profit and Loss Account .	20,000		
	£100,000		£100,000

The transfer to General Reserve recognises that £10,000 of the shareholders' money has been applied for a capital purpose, instead of being paid out in dividend. If it is desired to make permanent recognition of this fact, the General Reserve might be used to pay up *bonus shares* to be issued to the present shareholders in the proportion of one new share for every five held at present.

When the whole issue of Debentures is repaid in one year, as in the foregoing illustration, to transfer an amount to General Reserve equal to the total amount repaid would result in a very serious diminution of the available profits for the year. To avoid this it is usual to build up the Reserve by annual allocations of profit for a period of years preceding the repayment, thus equalising the charge against revenue. This aspect of the matter is dealt with in Chapter VI.

Capital Profits and Losses.

Fixed assets have been defined as those which are intended to be held permanently for the purposes and benefit of the business. The *intention* to earn profits by their use in the business instead of re-selling them at a profit is the essential feature which distinguishes them from current* assets. Over a period of years, most fixed assets will lose value or *depreciate,* in the service of the business. Provision for depreciation is a necessary charge in arriving at the profits, but when the methods for calculating the provision necessary are considered in detail, it will be seen that they

* Prior to the Companies Act, 1948, the term " floating assets " was applied to those assets now regarded, under modern practice, as " current assets ".

are nearly always in the nature of estimates. Thus, when a fixed asset is realised, either at the end of its useful life, or at any other time and for any reason, it is most unlikely that the amount received will be exactly equal to the value at which the asset stands in the books.

Inasmuch as the realisation of an asset at a figure above or below its book value results in an increase or decrease respectively in the total net assets, a profit or loss is incurred, for this is the simplest conception of profit and loss. If the sale takes place at the end of the useful life, so that what is disposed of is a mere shell or residue, the profit or loss is not likely to be very large and represents an adjustment of the total charge for depreciation. As such, it may properly be brought into the Profit and Loss Account for the year of sale.

On the other hand, circumstances may arise which make it necessary to realise fixed assets much sooner than was originally intended. The expansion of a business, for example, may necessitate removal to more commodious premises and it may be decided to sell much of the old equipment instead of removing it. In such circumstances, it is unlikely that the provision already made for depreciation will prove adequate, for it is well recognised that second-hand equipment can only be sold for a very small sum.* This does not prove that the annual provision for depreciation has been too low. The balances in the books at the end of a year, or the Balance Sheet which summarises those balances, do not purport to show the *realisable* value of the fixed assets. They should be shown at cost less such part of that cost as has been deemed to be recovered. Thus the loss which is almost certain to be incurred when an asset is sold before it has actually become useless should not be regarded as an ordinary trading loss for the year but as a special *capital loss*. Similarly, if more than the book value is obtained (this might happen in the case of the more permanent assets such as freehold land), the resulting profit is exceptional. It does not arise from the ordinary trading operations of the

* This statement is subject to qualification in times of rising price levels when second-hand equipment may be saleable at inflated prices.

concern, but from an extraneous cause such as a favourable movement in the general price level. It is a *capital profit*.

From an accounting point of view, it is clearly desirable that the special nature of capital profits and losses should be recognised. The transaction cannot be ignored, for a balance will remain on the asset account and this must be disposed of. If a profit on sale is made, a credit balance will remain, but it does not represent a liability ; while if the asset is sold at a loss, the remaining (reduced) debit balance can no longer be said to represent an asset.

In the case of a capital profit, the resulting credit balance may be—

(1) Transferred to Profit and Loss Account. The profit for the year will then be overstated and an illegal dividend might be paid.*

(2) Transferred to Capital Account or Capital Reserve. Where sole traders or partners are concerned, it is perhaps immaterial whether the profit is transferred to Capital Account through the Profit and Loss Account or directly. The latter course is to be preferred if the accounts are likely to be brought to the notice of third parties (*e.g.*, in connection with a sale of the business to a limited company).

The share capital of a limited company is fixed, however, and may only be altered in the manner prescribed in the Companies Act, 1948. Capital profits should therefore be transferred to a special account which will be called " Capital Reserve ".† This has most of the qualities of a capital account, for it represents part of the shareholders' interest in the company and it cannot be distributed in dividends. It will be seen later that one of the most important principles of company accounting is the rule that dividends may not be paid out of

* The legal position in regard to the payment of dividends out of capital profits will be considered in Chapter VIII.

† It will be seen in Chapter VIII that under certain conditions, it is permissible to distribute capital profits in dividends ; if the profit is one which complies with these conditions it might alternatively be credited to " General Reserve".

capital. Further, under the Companies Act, 1948, the expression " capital reserve " is restricted to a reserve " not regarded as free for distribution through the Profit and Loss Account ".

(3) Transferred to the credit of another asset account. If this course is adopted the usual practice is to write down an intangible asset such as goodwill, for to write down a tangible asset beyond the reasonable requirements of ordinary depreciation would be to create an additional reserve which under the requirements of the Companies Act, 1948, would require separate disclosure in the published Balance Sheet.

The debit balance resulting from a capital loss may be—

(1) Transferred to Profit and Loss Account. Where, however, the loss is a very heavy one, it may be permissible to write it off over a limited number of years, showing the remaining balance under a distinctive heading in the Balance Sheet in the meantime.

(2) Transferred to Capital Account (in the case of a sole trader or a partnership). The reason for this treatment is the same as in the case of a capital profit [see (2) on previous page].

In the case of a limited company, capital losses cannot be debited to the Share Capital Account any more than profits can be credited thereto. The question of the treatment of capital losses of a limited company is so bound up with the question of the availability of profits for dividend that full consideration is deferred until Chapter VIII. Under the Companies Act, 1948, all material gains or losses arising from causes " of an exceptional or non-recurrent nature " (this will include capital profits and losses) must be shown separately in the published Profit and Loss Account.

Capital Appreciation and Depreciation.

It would not be proper to take credit for a capital profit on the sale of one asset without considering the values of the others. A profit must be represented by an increase in the value of the net assets ; and this involves a valuation of all the assets on a going concern basis. If any depreciation is disclosed, in excess of that for which provision has been made in the usual way, the capital profit should be applied in writing down the value of the assets concerned, as indicated in the preceding paragraph.

Except in the above circumstances, it is not usually considered necessary to provide for exceptional depreciation of fixed assets. A fair annual charge for depreciation, such as will spread the cost of the asset (less any residual value) over its estimated working life, is computed, and if provision is made to this extent each year, any extraordinary fluctuations in value can be ignored. If any provision is made for exceptional depreciation, or, under present conditions, for increased costs of replacement, it may be regarded as a matter of prudence or conservatism : an appropriation of profits rather than a loss incurred in earning them.

In any case, it would be most imprudent to take credit for an unrealised capital appreciation, for this does not result in any increase in the balance of circulating capital available for distribution. The following examples illustrate the essential difference between a realised capital profit and an unrealised capital appreciation.

Example I : Where a fixed asset valued at £2,000 in the books is sold for £2,500.

BALANCE SHEET

	(a) Before realisation.	(b) After realisation.		(a) Before realisation.	(b) After realisation.
	£	£		£	£
Capital . . .	10,000	10,000	Fixed Assets . .	6,000	6,000
Creditors . .	6,000	6,000	Fixed Asset sold in		
Profit on Sale of			(b)	2,000	—
Capital Asset. .	—	500	Circulating Capital (Stock, Debtors, etc.)	8,000	10,500
	£16,000	£16,500		£16,000	£16,500

E*

Example II : Where the same asset is not sold but is *revalued* at £2,500.

BALANCE SHEET

	(a)	(b)		(a)	(b)
	£	£		£	£
Capital	10,000	10,000	Fixed Assets . .	6,000	6,000
Creditors . . .	6,000	6,000	Fixed Asset appre-		
Appreciation in value			ciated in (b) .	2,000	2,500
of Capital Asset .	—	500	Circulating Capital	8,000	8,000
	£16,000	£16,500		£16,000	£16,500

In the first illustration the £500 exists in actual distributable form, but in the second illustration it does not.

Somewhat different considerations apply when the appreciation or depreciation of current assets is considered. The general rule that current assets are brought into account at cost or market value, whichever is the lower, makes it essential to provide for depreciation of such assets but, as a general rule, appreciation must be ignored until it has been realised. As a general rule, current assets are not likely to remain unconverted for more than a few months and the question of bringing into account depreciation or appreciation merely determines which of two periods shall receive a profit or bear a loss. The only exception to the general rule is found when current assets are of a nature which will make it necessary to hold them for a considerable time. Good examples may be found in new wines and timber, which may take many years to mature and season respectively, during which time they should increase steadily in value. When such stocks are essential to the business, it is permissible to take credit for some portion of the increased value each year although it may not be prudent to bring them into account at the full market value, for this may never be realised. This practice might be looked upon as the equivalent of charging the ultimate year of sale with reasonable interest on the money invested originally in the stocks available for the year of sale.

Dividends Received.

When the assets of a company include investments in other companies, it may be expected that dividends will be received and will appear as items of income. It is usual to credit to Profit and Loss Account the dividends received during the trading period, but to take no account of amounts which have accrued due, unless a further dividend has actually been declared since the date of the Balance Sheet and before the books are closed for the year. This is prudent, and is a course to be recommended for dividends on ordinary shares. Dividends on preference shares in sound concerns may be anticipated if there are no reasons to suspect that the dividend will not ultimately be paid. Dividends and interest in respect of Government and like securities may be apportioned to bring into the current accounts the due proportion of dividend or interest accrued but not paid.

As already stated on page 93, it is usual to credit to Profit and Loss Account the gross amount of the dividend or interest, *i.e.*, the amount before income tax has been deducted by the payers, and to debit the amount of tax deducted to the Income Tax Account. This amount will represent the tax which has been paid (by deduction) on part of the company's income. The company will not again be taxed on this income : on the other hand certain circumstances may arise leading to a refund of the whole or part of the tax so borne.*

Transfer Fees.

The amounts received by a limited company for effecting a transfer of shares (usually 2s. 6d. per deed of transfer) are an item of revenue gain. The total amount received during the trading period will be credited to Profit and Loss Account.

Deferred Revenue Expenditure.

In the early years of a business it may be necessary to spend a considerable sum in advertising and other publicity work. There is usually a " lag " between the expenditure

* Reference should also be made to the recommendations of the Council of the Institute of Chartered Accountants with regard to the treatment of taxation and dividends in accounts (see Appendix II).

and the income which it produces. In such cases it is proper to charge only a part of the total cost of such publicity to the current year's Profit and Loss Account, and to carry the balance forward as deferred revenue expenditure which will be charged to revenue by degrees over the period during which benefit is expected to be derived from it.

Similar principles may be applied in farm accounts where the cost of fertilisers may be apportioned over, say, four years, in the proportion of 5 : 4 : 3 : 2, or otherwise according to the known effects of fertilisers on the soil in the years following the application of them.

Thus the object of adopting a deferred treatment of expenditure is to allocate the charge against the revenues of successive years in respect of items of an extraordinary (see below), non-recurring or partly capital nature.

Extraordinary Revenue Expenditure.

These are items which are not repeated annually, *e.g.*, heavy repairs to plant and machinery at fairly long intervals, say, three or four years. It would be unfair to charge the whole of the cost of the repairs to the period in which the repairs are effected, because the revenues of preceding years are benefited by the wear and tear now made good.

The recurrent expenditure should preferably be provided for by the creation of a Provision for Maintenance Account, a sum equal to one-third (where the repairs are necessary every three years) of the estimated cost of such repairs and replacements being charged annually to Profit and Loss Account and credited to the Provision for Maintenance Account, to which the expenditure will be debited as and when incurred.

The adoption of this method will equalise the charge over the periods, will enable the true profits to be shown in each period, and will stabilise the rate of dividend, so far as it is affected by this kind of fluctuation. As it is important that the necessary cash should be available at the time the repairs are effected, it is advisable that the profits thus set aside should be earmarked either by placing cash on deposit at the bank or by an investment in gilt-edged securities.

Alternative methods of treating this expenditure are :—

(a) The institution of an Equalisation of Dividends Reserve.* This method is satisfactory in effect ; but as the reserve is an appropriation of profits the figure for net profit is misleading when this method is adopted.

(b) The treatment of the expenditure as Deferred Revenue Expenditure. This method is not strictly correct, as the expenditure is not incurred for the benefit of the future, but to make good the ravages of the past.

The decision as to which method is to be adopted is ultimately a matter for the proprietors to decide for themselves.

Development Expenditure.

Certain unproductive expenditure may be necessary before the business is finally in a profit earning position, e.g., colliery workings require to be opened before a new mine can be worked, and in the case of a clay pit it is necessary to remove the overburden (soil and sod) before the clay can be extracted. It would be inequitable to regard all such expenditure, which may be heavy, as recoverable from the production of the year in which the development work took place. The expenditure is, accordingly, debited to a Development Account and is usually written off over a period of years. It is important that expenditure of this kind should not be permanently capitalised because as the valuable deposit is extracted, the mine becomes worth less and less, until, when it is completely exhausted, its value becomes nil and any asset under the name of Development Expenditure becomes fictitious.

Any miscellaneous sources of income obtained during the period of development, e.g., grazing of cattle on land awaiting development, sale of stone, etc., advertisements on hoardings, should be set off against the cost of development.

* *Vide* Chapter VI.

Obsolete Capital Expenditure.

It has been shown in the preceding paragraph that expenditure in certain circumstances may be regarded as being temporarily of a capital nature. This view may also be applied to capital which has been sunk and is now of no value or is worth only a scrap value. The necessity for prudent accounting in respect of obsolete or unrepresented capital expenditure has already been indicated. Since the loss is an extraordinary one there are valid grounds for regarding it as being capable of deferred treatment. If the balance of the loss is shown in the accounts from year to year as a loss, and not as the original asset, there is nothing to be said against this treatment.

Where the loss is occasioned by the substitution of a new or improved type, there are definite reasons for adopting a deferred treatment of the loss due to obsolescence. Future years may be expected to benefit from the substitution or replacement, and in so far as this benefit is not absorbed by an increased depreciation charge, the loss on the old asset is properly recoverable from the yield of the new one. It is therefore equitable to write off the loss over the years following its occurrence.

In certain circumstances the loss may be so great that the earning capacity of the concern as a whole is irretrievably impaired. If so, the losses must be met immediately ; and if there are no reserves to draw upon, then a capital reduction scheme to eliminate the loss will be necessary.

Where free reserves exist, all that is necessary is a book entry to transfer the capital loss to the account for the reserve, and this would be the prudent course to take. A concern is usually capitalised in accordance with its estimated earning capacity, so that there is a fairly definite relationship between the capital employed and the profits earned. This relationship is not, however, constant, for there is a degree of capitalisation at which the maximum rate of return is obtainable. Capitalisation above or below this point will yield a less than proportionate amount of profit. The effect of this on capital losses is important and may be advanced as a reason for writing off the loss immediately, unless replacement is contemplated, *e.g.*, since part of the capital has been sunk and lost, the profit earning capacity of the remaining capital may be impaired. It is for this reason that heavy capital losses require an immediate capital reorganisation or reduction and even moderate capital losses may require reinstatement if profits are to be maintained at their previous level in relation to the capital employed.

Capitalisation of Expenses.

There are certain items of expenditure which although not usually of a capital nature, may become so in certain circumstances. Such items of expenditure as wages of workmen employed on the erection of new machinery, legal charges in connection with the purchase of land, etc., should clearly be charged to the accounts for the resulting assets and not to Profit and Loss Account.

The Interpretation of Results.

The final figures enable us to form a judgment of the efficiency displayed in the conduct of the business whose results are under review. Results show the fruits of policy and may be used as a basis of criticism.

The results of different periods and of different concerns may be considered in columnar form to facilitate comparison and then a process of detailed analysis may be undertaken. Increases in overhead charges may indicate the advisability of closing a particular department, or replacing an obsolete machine. In association with technical experts, the production policy can be reviewed in the light of the running costs of the machines and the amount of capital invested therein, and suitable recommendations advanced for consideration. The accumulation of stocks may point to the need for investigation not only into the sales policy of the business, but also into the purchasing policy.

Variations in gross profit may be due to differences in local markets for raw materials, injudicious buying, differences in inwards freight charges, differences in labour charges, wasteful methods of production, varying selling prices, differing methods of allocating wages and overhead charges, relative efficiency of plants, leakages or all or any of these, or they may be due to one firm being on full time while other firms are on short time.

Enquiry will chiefly take the form of a close scrutiny of the respective costing methods as regards allocations of wages, power and overheads : *e.g.*, general yard labour may be treated as an overhead or as a charge of handling raw materials ; power charges may include or exclude a charge for depreciation and repairs. Buying prices, stocks carried and selling prices will be compared, care being taken that as far as possible the comparison is on a basis of uniform quality. Stock records of raw materials and finished products will be examined for signs of leakage. Attention should then be given to relative weights of material consumed per unit of output to discover waste in manufacture, and to costs of power generation, where an obsolete plant may add heavily to costs of manufacture.

The Significance of Percentage Relationship.

The general significance of percentages has already been discussed in Chapter II. The following illustration will serve to show the manner in which figures may be interpreted and the importance which may be attached to percentage relationships.

EXAMPLE

Mr. X, who is seeking to purchase a share in a sound partnership, asks you to investigate the accounts of a private firm requiring additional capital. The accounts of the firm for the past three years are submitted to you, showing the following trading results :—

TRADING AND PROFIT AND LOSS ACCOUNTS

	1953.	1954.	1955.			1953.	1954.	1955.
	£	£	£			£	£	£
Stock, 1st Jan. .	40,800	30,880	36,560	Sales . £90,000				
Purchases £42,400				Returns. . 6,800		83,200		
Returns . . 2,400								
40,000				Sales . . 57,600				
Purchases . 42,170				Returns. . 7,000			50,600	
Returns . . 3,600								
38,570				Sales . 96,800				
Purchases . 56,972				Returns . . 3,200				93,600
Returns . . 2,100								33,400
54,872				Stock, 31st Dec. .		30,880	36,560	
Gross Profit, c/d . .	33,280	17,710	35,568					
	£114,080	£87,160	£127,000			£114,080	£87,160	£127,000
Trade Charges, including Rent, Rates, Lighting, Heating, Advertising, etc.	14,440	7,280	17,395	Gross Profit, b/d . .		33,280	17,710	35,568
Bad Debts . . .	880	422	210	Dividends on Investments . .		—	576	825
Depreciation . .	1,320	970	1,940					
Net Profit . . .	16,640	9,614	16,848					
	£33,280	£18,286	£36,393			£33,280	£18,286	£36,393

What (if any) special investigation do the above figures demand ? Enumerate in detail the special points which occur to you as calling for attention.

Before giving advice as to the advisability or otherwise of investing capital in the firm, an investigation should be made in connection with the following points arising out of the accounts supplied :—

(1) The percentage of gross profit to turnover has fluctuated over the period, being approximately 40 per cent., 35 per cent. and 38 per cent. respectively for the three years under review. In view of the increase in the gross profit percentage during the third year, particular attention should be paid to the closing stock, and tests should be made to ascertain whether this has been correctly valued. In addition, the ratio of returns inward to sales for the third year is considerably lower than for either of the previous years ; the returns inward book should therefore be examined for the opening weeks of 1956, and tested with the goods inward book (if kept) and correspondence with debtors, to ascertain whether returns have been dealt with in the correct accounting period.

(2) The wide fluctuations in sales during the three years should be investigated : the firm's selling policy may have been altered in 1954, and concentrated on cheaper lines yielding a lower rate of gross profit, or an unprofitable branch may have been closed during that year, or a new branch may have been opened in 1955. (See also (3) below.)

(3) Wide fluctuations occur in Trade Charges over the three years. As many of these, such as Rent and Rates, are more or less fixed, the reason for the big drop in 1954 should be investigated ; the closing down of an unsuccessful branch in that year may be the explanation. The reason for the increased ratio of Trade Charges for 1955 as compared with 1953 and 1954 should be investigated.

(4) The firm's policy with regard to Bad Debts should be examined. The practice may be to write off debts only as and when they are definitely considered bad, and an insufficient provision, or none at all, may have been made for doubtful debts in the later years. Individual sales ledger balances should therefore be scrutinised.

(5) Explanations should be sought as to the wide variations in the depreciation charge. Was the 1954 provision adequate ? Does the 1955 charge include any charges for obsolescence or for losses on sale of assets ? On what class or classes of assets is the charge made ?

(6) The reason for requiring additional capital should be ascertained (*e.g.*, the financing of an important contract, or the acquisition of a new branch). Explanations should be obtained as to the reason for locking up a considerable portion of the firm's capital in investments.

(7) Finally, advice should not be given on the strength of the information derived from the Trading and Profit and Loss Accounts alone. Balance Sheets should be obtained for the three years in question and the trend of the assets and liabilities noted. Such points as adequacy of depreciation of fixed assets, contingent liabilities, extent of working capital, etc., must all be taken into consideration.

Past Results as a Guide to Future Policy.

The possibilities of the future can be judged only in the light of what has happened in the past. It is important, therefore, when policy is under consideration, that past results be reviewed and that any outstanding points be seen in their proper perspective.

The following points require careful consideration before future obligations, contracts and financial commitments can be undertaken :—

(1) The available stock. Past results may indicate the unwarranted piling up of stocks. Future production policy should therefore be determined in the light of the effective sales during the previous year.

(2) Forward contracts may exist in respect of raw materials so that future production policy and sales policy must be such as will at least absorb the subject matter of these contracts.

(3) The cost *tendencies* should be studied, for certain trends may have a marked effect upon the costs of the coming year. Thus results may indicate that a particular machine is nearing the stage when replacement will be imperative.

An increase in the scale of output might yield a more than proportionate increase in net profits owing to the fact that the volume of gross profit which suffices to cover the fixed overhead charges (as explained on page 51) has been passed ;

but it might give a less than proportionate increase in net profits owing to the fact that the cost of getting further orders and of executing them by overtime work at a rate above normal has reached a point at which it is so high that it absorbs too much of the gross profit.

CHAPTER IV

THE BALANCE SHEET (1)

A Balance Sheet has been defined as " a classified summary of the balances remaining open in a set of books after the collection of the nominal balances into one account (the Profit and Loss Account) and including the balance of that account, and so arranged as to show the assets on the right-hand side, and the liabilities on the left ".

It is instructive to examine this definition in detail, in order to ascertain the nature and qualities of a Balance Sheet.

(1) The Balance Sheet summarises the balances remaining in the books after all nominal balances have been transferred to the Profit and Loss Account. Just as the agreement of the Trial Balance proves the arithmetical accuracy of the entries in the books *before* the Profit and Loss Account has been prepared, so the agreement of the Balance Sheet proves the arithmetical accuracy of those adjustments and transfers which are necessary for the preparation of the Profit and Loss Account.

(2) The assets are shown on the right-hand side, and the liabilities on the left. This is purely a convention, and it should be observed that a Balance Sheet shows balances on the side opposite to that on which they appear in the ledger. (Assets, represented by debit balances in the ledger, appear on the right-hand or " credit " side of the Balance Sheet and liabilities, represented by credit balances in the ledger, appear on the left-hand or " debit " side.*)

* It is contended, in modern practice, that the use of general headings for a Balance Sheet, such as " assets " and " liabilities ", is inappropriate and unnecessary ; but the respective sides of the Balance Sheet are still referred to as the " assets side " and " liabilities side " despite the fact that many items included in the Balance Sheet represent neither assets nor liabilities but merely outstanding debit and credit balances.

It may be noted that in the U.S.A. and some continental countries, the sides of the Balance Sheet are reversed, as compared with British practice.

(3) The items in the Balance Sheet are presented in the form of a classified summary. If all the balances were shown in detail, as in a Trial Balance, the Balance Sheet would do little more than prove the arithmetical accuracy of the books, for the information it contained would be lost in a maze of detail. The first essential is that all items which are of a similar nature should be shown in total. One item " Sundry Debtors " will be shown instead of the many—perhaps thousands—of individual balances in the Sales Ledger, and " Sundry Creditors " must be totalled in the same way. The process of summarisation (which is known as " grouping ") must not be carried too far, however, for the Balance Sheet might then become misleading. Thus, it would not be correct to include loans and book debts under the heading " Sundry Debtors " and the position is not greatly improved by calling the total " Sundry Loans and Debtors ", for though the reader is then put on his guard, he is not given the relative amounts of the two distinct kinds of indebtedness.

When the headings under which the assets and liabilities are to be shown have been fixed, they must be arranged in a logical sequence. This process is known as " marshalling " the assets and liabilities and will be considered in greater detail hereafter.* In the case of limited companies, certain classifications are obligatory by the Companies Act, 1948 ; these are set out in Chapter X.

(4) The balance of the Profit and Loss Account is included in one form or another. It has already been shown that there is a vital distinction between the accounts

* Reference should be made to the recommendations of the Council of the Institute of Chartered Accountants with regard to the form of the Balance Sheet (see Appendix II).

of sole traders and partnerships on the one hand
and limited companies on the other, and that, in
the case of the former, profits are evidenced by an
increase in capital and the Profit and Loss Account
is closed each year by transfer to Capital (or Current) Account or Accounts. Limited Companies,
on the other hand, have fixed share capitals and
the balance of undistributed profits *does* appear as
a separate item in the Balance Sheet, as an addition
to (in the case of a credit balance) or a deduction
from (in the case of a debit balance) issued share
capital and reserves.

(5) The Balance Sheet summarises the accounts remaining
open in the books : it is not an account in itself
and does not enter into the double entry system of
ledger accounts. It is a statement which summarises the information contained in the books themselves, and though it is conventionally shown in
account form this is not essential.* The headings
" Dr." and " Cr." and the prefixes " To " and
" By ", although occasionally encountered in practice, are not necessary, and the descriptive headings
" Capital and Liabilities " and " Assets " are considered to be inappropriate and unnecessary. It
should scarcely be necessary to add that a Balance
Sheet shows the position *as at* a given date and
cannot be properly described as *for the year ended*
on that date. It has been said that " A Balance
Sheet is like an instantaneous photograph and—
like most instantaneous photographs—sometimes
catches people in awkward positions ".

The two sides of a Balance Sheet are in fact nothing but
two views of the same thing. The " assets side " is a description of the concrete items which make up the total fund
of wealth adventured in profit earning. The " liabilities
side ", on the other hand, is a statement of the sources from
which the gross fund of profit-earning assets has been derived,

---

* Alternative ways in which a Balance Sheet might be presented will be considered
later.

or of the accountabilities under which the administrators of the assets stand in respect of the assets committed to their charge.

Apart from the introduction of further capital, this fund of assets can only be increased in either or both of the following ways :—

(1) By buying assets on credit, when there will be a corresponding increase in the accountability of the business to outside creditors, shown on the left-hand side of the Balance Sheet. When these liabilities are discharged, the totals will be restored to their former amounts, and the only effect of the transaction is a reshuffling of the right-hand side, cash having been reduced and other assets increased.

(2) By earning profits, when there will be a corresponding increase in the accountability of the business to the proprietors, which will be reflected as an increased balance on Capital Account(s) in the case of a sole trader or partnership, or on Profit and Loss Account in the case of a limited company. In this case the increase in the totals of the two sides of the Balance Sheet remains until the proprietors withdraw their profits.

The elementary but none the less important point brought out by this argument is that the Balance Sheet always shows on the one hand the fund of assets for which the business is accountable, and on the other hand the nature and extent of its accountabilities therefor (*i.e.*, to outside creditors and to the proprietors).

The Relation between Balance Sheets and Profit and Loss Accounts.

In Chapter I it was shown that there are two conceptions of profit or loss :—

(1) The Profit and Loss Account view, obtained by summarising all the items of income and expenditure (*i.e.*, the nominal accounts) in one account and striking a balance ; and

(2) The Balance Sheet view, obtained by comparing successive Balance Sheets and calculating the increase or decrease in the net assets of the business, due allowance being made for capital introduced or withdrawn during the period.

Whereas the Profit and Loss Account shows how the profit (or loss) has been made, the Balance Sheet shows how the capital invested in the business at the beginning of the period has been augmented by the profit made (or decreased by the loss incurred). Since the same figure—the net profit (or loss)—is reflected in both the Balance Sheet and the Profit and Loss Account, there must be a very close connection between them, in spite of obvious differences of form and structure. This connection is seen to originate from the facts that—

(1) The Profit and Loss Account summarises the entries in the books during a period, and

(2) The Balance Sheet summarises the balances remaining at the end of that period.

They can be linked together in a chain of alternate Balance Sheets and Profit and Loss Accounts, thus :—

Balance Sheet as at 31st December, 1953,

Profit and Loss Account for the year ended 31st December, 1954,

Balance Sheet as at 31st December, 1954,

Profit and Loss Account for the year ended 31st December, 1955,

Balance Sheet as at 31st December, 1955,

and so on, throughout the life of the business.

It has also been shown that profits result from the sale or conversion of assets and that in arriving at the net profit or loss for the year, as distinct from that on one completed transaction, the valuation of the assets is of the greatest importance. The question arises—

(1) Are the entries made in the books primarily with the object of preparing a Profit and Loss Account of

which the Balance Sheet is a corollary (a mere summary of the remaining balances) ; or

(2) Is the Balance Sheet the primary object and the Profit and Loss Account merely a subsidiary statement showing how the profit determined by the Balance Sheet has in fact been earned ; or

(3) Are the Profit and Loss Account and the Balance Sheet co-ordinate in importance, not dependent on each other, though mutually explanatory, but arising independently from the accounts which together they represent ?

The answer is not as simple as might be thought, and it depends on the nature of the items which appear in the Balance Sheet.

Current assets—those which are intended for resale, or which in the ordinary course of business will be converted into other assets—must be valued at cost or market value, whichever may be the lower in each case. This is necessary to ensure that no credit is taken for a profit until it has been realised and that full provision is made for any anticipated loss ; and it will be seen that, so far as current assets are concerned, the Profit and Loss Account depends on the Balance Sheet.

On the other hand, fixed assets—those which are intended to be held permanently for the purposes and benefit of the business and which are subject to waste—are valued at cost, less depreciation. Now depreciation is not charged with the object of reducing the book value of the asset to its realisable value but for the purpose of charging its cost against the profits earned during its working life and providing the necessary funds for its replacement. In other words, the Balance Sheet value of wasting assets is fixed by the consideration of the annual charges for depreciation which are necessary for the accurate determination of the profit or loss on the year's working. Thus, so far as wasting assets are concerned, the Balance Sheet depends on the Profit and Loss Account.

Fixed assets that are not subject to waste are retained in the books at cost until they are sold, when the resultant profit or loss may be taken to Profit and Loss Appropriation Account or, preferably, to Capital Reserve as it is of a capital nature. So far as these assets are concerned and also as regards liabilities, which by their nature do not give rise to profit or loss when they are discharged, the Balance Sheet is independent of the Profit and Loss Account.

The complementary relation between the Balance Sheet and the Profit and Loss Account is important, for it reflects the vital distinction between capital and revenue. This distinction must be made at every stage of the accountant's work; and when the revenue element of any transaction has been eliminated and taken to Profit and Loss Account, what remains must be capital, and *vice versa*. A transaction may be wholly of a revenue nature, or wholly capital, or it may be composite so that an apportionment is necessary, but the following rule emerges. Whereas the Profit and Loss Account reflects the revenue transactions of the year, or so much of all the transactions as may properly be ascribed to revenue, the Balance Sheet prepared at the end of the year reflects the capital transactions or so much of all the transactions as may properly be capitalised.

The Classification of Assets.

Assets may be classified into the following main groups :—

(1) *Fixed* or *Capital Assets** by means of which the business operations are carried on, *e.g.*, Buildings, Plant and Machinery. The successful continuance of the business depends upon the maintenance of the fixed or capital assets. Those fixed assets which, by their nature, are consumed in the service of the business by effluxion of time (*e.g.*, leases), or by wear and tear (*e.g.*, machinery), or by consumption (*e.g.*, mines), are known as *Wasting Assets*. It is seen that the adjective " fixed " is used in a relative sense : there must be an element of continuity, which is not present in the case of—

---

* Assets which would be fixed assets in one business may be current assets in another—the determining factor is the purpose with which the asset is held. Compare furniture in the case of a hotel with furniture in the case of a furniture dealer.

(2) *Current, Floating, Circulating* or *Trading Assets* which
are used in the process of trading or production or
are a result of such operations, *e.g.*, stock-in-trade,
work-in-progress, debtors, cash ;

(3) *Liquid Assets*—a subdivision of (2) comprising cash
and the more realisable of the current assets such
as gilt-edged investments and bills of exchange ; and

(4) *Fictitious Assets, e.g.*, Deferred Revenue Expenditure
and other items of expenditure which are really of
a " loss " nature.

Assets are sometimes classed as either tangible or intangible. Thus goodwill is intangible because it is not
evidenced by anything material ; nevertheless it may be of
great value and if the business is disposed of as a going
concern the goodwill may actually be sold. All fictitious
assets are obviously intangible but it must be emphasised
that the terms " intangible " and " fictitious " are not
synonymous. The division of assets into tangible and intangible is not of great practical importance and as it is sometimes difficult to draw a clear distinction between the two
classes the terms should not be used if they can be avoided.

Marshalling the Assets.

To maintain itself in good repute and to work economic-
ally, a business must be able to pay its debts as they fall due
without resorting to expensive borrowing. Hence one question that might easily form in the mind of the reader of a
Balance Sheet would be whether liquid assets were reasonably
commensurate with immediate liabilities. This consideration suggests one reason for care in the arrangement of the
various items shown in a Balance Sheet. It is clear that
there must be at least a rough relation between the assets
and liabilities, for out of the former the latter must be met.

There are two common ways in which assets are arranged :
one is the order of decreasing realisability, the other is the
order of decreasing permanence. The sorting out of assets
into a special order, whatever it may be, is called " Marshalling the Assets ".

A typical marshalling in order of permanence would be—

1. Goodwill.
2. Patents and Trade Marks.
3. Freehold Land and Buildings.
4. Leasehold Land and Buildings.
5. Plant and Machinery.
6. Fittings and Fixtures.
7. Motor Vehicles.
8. Stock:
    (a) Raw Materials.
    (b) Work-in-Progress.
    (c) Finished Goods.
9. Sundry Debtors:
    (a) On open accounts.
    (b) On bills receivable.
10. Cash at Bank:
    (a) On deposit account.
    (b) On current account.
11. Cash in Hand.
12. Fictitious Assets and Adjustments.

Obviously, goodwill is the most unrealisable form of asset, as it can be disposed of only in the event of the business being sold as a " going concern ". Freehold land and buildings are of a more permanent nature than leasehold land and buildings, and the latter are more permanent than plant and machinery. Fittings and fixtures are less permanent than plant, but obviously take precedence over motor vehicles. Stock-in-trade has to be sold before it can become a " book debt ", hence sundry debtors follow after stock-in-trade. Similarly, cash ranks after book debts, while fictitious assets and adjustments are shown last.

Included in fictitious assets are such items as Advertising Suspense Account and Obsolete Plant Suspense Account, where it is desired to spread the cost of advertising or the loss through obsolescence over a few years.

It should be added, however, that the method of arranging the assets in order of realisability has obvious advantages for certain classes of undertakings, such as Banks and Investment companies, in which cases it is almost universally adopted in order to emphasise the liquid position. But, nevertheless, the method of showing the assets in the order of permanence is more suitable for commercial undertakings generally, and it is usually adopted by firms and companies of this class.

Realisability and permanence would, of course, give very similar orders, except that the one is the reverse of the other. The Balance Sheet of a bank will afford an example of the order of realisability. Thus—

1. Coin, Notes and Balances with the Bank of England.
2. Balances with, and cheques on, other Banks.
3. Money at Call and Short Notice.
4. Bills Discounted.
5. Investments.
6. Loans and Advances to Customers.
7. Liabilities of Customers for Acceptances.
8. Bank Premises.

The matter of marshalling the assets, and the requirements of the Companies Act, 1948, in regard thereto, are discussed in Chapter X.

Valuation of Fixed Assets.

When an asset is first purchased it is obvious that the only possible value that can be given in the Balance Sheet is its cost. Later on, however, the valuation will be affected by any changes in the earning capacity of the asset, and sound financial policy will usually dictate a reduction in the book value. The commonest form of such a reduction is the writing off of " depreciation " by annual charges in some methodical way. This will be fully explained and discussed in Chapter VII, but it is advisable at this stage to consider some typical assets in the aspect of their values.

Goodwill.

In a case which came before the courts in 1810, Goodwill was defined as " nothing more than the probability that the old customers will resort to the old place " ; but this is felt to be a rather narrow view. The following much more comprehensive definition is due to Lord Lindley :—

" The term goodwill can hardly be said to have any precise signification. It is generally used to denote the benefit arising from connection and reputation, and its value is what can be got for the chance of being able to keep that connection and improve it. Upon the sale of an established business its goodwill has a marketable value, whether the business is that of a professional man or of any other person. But it is plain that goodwill has no meaning except in connection with a continuing business, and the value of the goodwill of any business to a purchaser depends, in some cases entirely, and in all very much, on the absence of competition on the part of those by whom the business has been previously carried on."

There are four principal classes of goodwill, *viz.* :—

(1) *Local*, arising from the situation of the trader's premises, *e.g.*, a retail shopkeeper in a busy market centre ;

(2) *The Personal Reputation* of the individual, arising through his skill, influence and personality, as in the case of a professional man, *e.g.*, an accountant or a doctor ;

(3) *The Reputation of the Goods Sold*, arising from the high standard of quality of the goods themselves, *e.g.*, a well-advertised brand of proprietary goods.

(4) *The Absence of Competition*, or the existence of an absolute or partial monopoly.

Other sources of goodwill may exist in the possession of loyal, contented and efficient employees, or favourable long-term contracts.

On the purchase of a business the excess of the purchase price over the total value of the assets, less liabilities taken over, represents the amount paid for goodwill. This is debited to Goodwill Account, which usually remains at this original figure, being neither depreciated nor written up in value until a change takes place in the ownership of the business through sale or through the death or retirement of one of the partners or the admission of a new partner. In the case of a limited company, goodwill is not usually depreciated except as a result of financial prudence which may allocate profits for this purpose. The personal element of the goodwill of a company is reduced to a minimum so that there is little or no alteration in its value with changes in the personnel of the company's membership.

The goodwill of a partnership business may belong to one partner only, or it may be shared by some or all of the partners in certain proportions according to the terms of the Partnership Agreement. In the event of there being no special agreement upon the matter, goodwill belongs to all the partners in the proportions in which they share profits or losses.

At one time the value of goodwill was generally based on the purchase of a certain number of years' average profits, e.g., three to five years' purchase, but it is now usual to adopt the " super profits " basis of computing the value of goodwill.*

If the average profits of a business are greater than those normally earned in similar businesses, the excess is deemed to be due to goodwill, which is thus taken as the capitalised value of profits in excess of the investment yield of the net capital actually employed.

For example, if the average profits of a business over an agreed period amount to £17,000 per annum, and the normal commercial yield on capital invested in such a business is deemed to be 8 per cent. per annum, then, assuming the net capital employed in the business to be £100,000, the excess of

* In the case of a professional practice, it is usual to value goodwill on the basis of a certain number of years' gross recurring fees.

the average profits (£17,000) over the normal profits (£8,000, *i.e.*, 8 per cent. on £100,000) represents the " goodwill " or " super " profits. Thus, in this case, the super profits amount to £9,000 per annum and this figure would be taken as the basis of the computation of goodwill.

The amount of money which would be required to be invested at 8 per cent. to yield £9,000 per annum would be $£\dfrac{100}{8} \times 9{,}000$ or £112,500. If the future super profits could be regarded as fixed at £9,000 in perpetuity, £112,500 might be regarded as a fair price to pay for the right to enjoy them, but in practice it is most unlikely that such a large amount would be paid. Competition and other factors will all tend to reduce the profits to the common level enjoyed by other concerns. The most scientific method of valuing goodwill is that which is known as the *terminable annuity* method, under which the value of goodwill is taken as being equivalent to the present value of the right to receive an annual sum, equal to the ascertained amount of super profits, for an agreed number of years, discounted at an agreed rate per cent. If ten years is taken as a reasonable period, the value of an annuity of £9,000 per annum, taking compound interest at 8 per cent., is found to be £60,391.*

Alternatively, goodwill might be valued at a certain number of years' purchase of the super profits, without introducing the complication of an annuity calculation. Thus at five years' purchase its value would be £45,000; at six years' purchase, £54,000 and at seven years' purchase, £63,000. The proper basis of calculation is a highly technical matter, depending on the nature of the business concerned, the locality in which it is carried on, the current condition of the investment market and many other factors : and it is quite possible for the most scientific calculation to be upset by individual circumstances which cannot readily be

* Either by reference to Annuity Tables or from first principles by evaluating the expression—

$$£9{,}000 \left(\frac{1 - \dfrac{1}{1 \cdot 08^{10}}}{\cdot 08} \right)$$

expressed in figures. At such a time, goodwill can be valued only at the amount the purchaser is prepared to pay for it.

The accountant is primarily concerned with recording the actual cost of goodwill, and the basis on which that amount was actually calculated is a matter of only secondary importance to him. Nevertheless it is often useful to be able to check the value at which goodwill stands in the books after an interval of some years, when the actual profit record may have proved very different from that of the earlier period on which the calculation was originally based.

Goodwill should not be written up, because credit should not be taken for an unrealised appreciation. Neither should goodwill even be recorded unless it is necessary in order to adjust the rights of partners when the constitution of a firm is changed or to explain the difference between the net assets acquired and the price paid when a business is purchased.

It will be seen, therefore, that goodwill will normally be valued at cost and will usually remain at that figure. Since goodwill must, by definition, vary with profits, it is, for this reason, impracticable to record its fluctuating value. The fact that a company is in a position to write down goodwill is evidence of the value of the goodwill, and any writing down will have the effect of conserving the liquid resources, as well as creating a valuable reserve.

Investments.

These are fixed assets when the intention is to hold them more or less permanently as a form of reserve fund or for the sake of the dividends or interest they yield. Thus, in the case of a holding company,* the investments in subsidiary companies may be classed as fixed assets, and in the case of an investment trust company, the various holdings will be in the nature of fixed assets.

The usual basis of valuation (that is to say, cost less an allowance for depreciation) will apply except that any depreciation may be capable of exact determination, e.g., by

* *Vide* Chapter IX.

F

the fluctuations in market quotations. Temporary fluctuations may be ignored, but since it is frequently difficult or altogether impossible to distinguish temporary fluctuations from long-period market trends it is usually advisable to compute the value of the holdings according to the prices ruling at the date of the Balance Sheet, and to create an Investment Reserve Account in respect of any decrease in the total current market value of the investments compared with cost. Appreciations in value should, in accordance with the canons of accounting expressed on page 34, be ignored.

If investments are held for resale on the appreciation of market values, as in the case of finance companies, they are current assets and should be valued at the lower of cost or current market value.

In all cases (whether the investments are fixed or current assets) it is desirable that a note of the current market value (if different from book value) should be appended to the Balance Sheet.

Land, Buildings, Plant, etc.

These assets all conform to the general principles laid down in the preceding pages and no modifications in treatment are called for.

In the case of leasehold land and buildings the depreciation will be measurable by reference to the period of the lease, and allowance should be made for the estimated cost of dilapidations (if any) at the end of the lease. In the case of plant and similar assets of uncertain life, the depreciation charge must be calculated according to the best estimate of the period of usefulness that can be made. The main thing is not to overestimate this period. When the estimate of the useful life of plant takes the form of an expected number of working hours or units of output, it may be argued that the depreciation charge for a year should be based on the output of that period rather than on a strict time basis. While it is clearly desirable that when overtime is being worked plant should be depreciated at more than the normal rate, a method which resulted in no provision being made during idle periods would be fallacious. Even with the best attention, idle plant is likely to depreciate almost as quickly as that which is in normal operation and the risk of obsolescence is often greater.

In the case of mines, quarries and similar wasting assets, however, where the freehold is owned, the depreciation can reasonably be based on the actual output for the year, expressed as a fraction of the estimated total output. If leasehold property is concerned, a double calculation is necessary: the depreciation may be based primarily on the output but it must be seen that this results in a balance which is not greater than that which would be revealed if the cost had been written off on a time basis, fixed by reference to the length of the lease.

Assets of very short effective life, such as loose tools, jigs and patterns, may frequently be dealt with by periodical re-valuation, which in no case should exceed cost price.

The Valuation of Current Assets.

It has been stated as a general rule that current or floating assets must be valued at cost or market price, whichever is the lower. This rule requires closer examination, for " cost " and " market value " are terms which are not of general application. Cash, which is the first and last form of working or circulating capital, has, for example, a very definite market value : can it be said to have a cost price ? It is true that, if a furniture dealer sells a table for £5 which he receives in cash at once, what really happens is an exchange of one asset for another, and in that sense the cost of the £5 note received from the customer is one table ; but on the other hand, it was shown at the commencement of this book that the study of accounting requires all assets and transactions to be expressed in a monetary unit. Thus, although an economist might describe the transaction as the exchange of a table for a £5 note, the accountant must regard it as the exchange of a table which cost (say) £4, and therefore is valued at that price, for £5 in cash. In this sense the cost of the £5 received is the £4 originally expended on the table, i.e., a profit of £1 has been *made and realised*. It is clearly ridiculous to consider cash as having any other value than its face value, for it is the unit in which all other assets and all transactions and liabilities are expressed.

The consideration of book debts arising out of trading transactions carries the examination a stage further. If the table which cost £4 had been sold on credit for £5 it is much more pertinent to enquire whether the cost of the book debt is not £4 and whether, following the general rule, the debt should not be brought into the books at that value. Practical considerations overrule this argument, for clearly the debtor owes £5 and this must be recorded in the books. A profit of £1 has been *made* although it has not yet been *realised*. Unless there is any reason to doubt that it will ultimately be realised, the rules of accounting permit credit to be taken for such a profit in the period during which the sale was made and require, as a necessary corollary, that the debt shall be brought into the Balance Sheet at its face value.

Perhaps the best way of looking at the problem is to say that where any profit-making transaction results in the acquisition of any current asset other than cash (*e.g.*, book debts, bills receivable) the cost of that asset is the cash which might have been received instead ; in other words, part of the potential cash resources of the business have been *temporarily invested* in other current assets. If, however, there is any doubt regarding the ultimate realisation of these assets, then they are brought in at their estimated realisable value by the deduction from their face value of a reasonable provision for bad debts or doubtful bills, which satisfies the " market price " restriction in the general rule.

Stock-in-trade is, of course, the current asset *par excellence* and the terms " cost " and " market value " are quite clear in their application to it.

Profits and Circulating Assets.

At the commencement of business, the circulating assets represent the amount of capital expended in their acquisition, *i.e.*, the circulating assets (practically restricted to stock at this stage) are stated at cost. At a subsequent stage in the business cycle an element of profit begins to attach to the fund of circulating assets. This profit accrues between the purchase of stock and the sale of it. During any of the subsequent stages up to the ultimate conversion into cash, no further profits will accrue, but losses may be incurred, *e.g.*, bad debts. Thus, at any date the fund of circulating assets represents a rather heterogeneous mass comprising costs, costs plus profits, and costs plus profits minus losses. An illustration will make this clear :—

STAGE 1.		Cost.	Profit.	
		£	£	£
Circulating Capital absorbed in Stock . .		6,000		
Less Stock sold		4,000	500	4,500 Debtors
Stock on hand at cost		£2,000		

STAGE 2.	Book value representing cost plus profit.	Cost equivalent.	Profit.		
	£	£	£		£
Debtors outstanding .	4,500	4,000	500	Profit realised	
Less realised . . .	2,700	2,400	300	in cash . .	300
Remaining Debtors. .	1,800	1,600	200	Profit unrealised	
				in cash . .	200
				Total Profit .	500
STAGE 3.					
Bad Debts incurred .	450	[400]	[50]	Absolute loss .	450
Book Value of Debtors	1,350			Net Profit . .	50

NOTE.

The cost equivalent and profit included in the debtors written off as bad is immaterial, for since profits realised and unrealised are taken into account, an absolute loss of £450 has been incurred (the profit of £50 previously having been included in the profit of £500 on realisation of the stock). The circulating assets will then appear in the Balance Sheet at the following values :—

		£
Stock (at cost)		2,000
		£
Sundry Debtors (cost + profit) . . .	1,800	
Less Bad Debts	450	
(cost + profit − loss)	1,350	1,350
Cash (cost of stock sold and paid for + profit). .		2,700
		£6,050

representing the original circulating capital of £6,000 plus the net profit of £50.

It may be necessary to emphasise that, in this paragraph, the way in which profits and losses are *represented* by current assets has been considered: the principles involved in the *valuation* of current assets are not at issue. In fact, as was seen earlier in this Chapter, it is the valuation of the current assets which determines the net profit or loss for the year and, to this extent, the Profit and Loss Account depends on the Balance Sheet for its values instead of the Balance Sheet depending on the Profit and Loss Account, as in the case of wasting assets.

The special factors affecting the valuation of various types of current assets will now be considered in detail.

Stock-in-Trade.

Stock-in-trade may consist of—

(1) *Raw materials*, *i.e.*, materials which will eventually be converted into the saleable products of the concern ; and

(2) *Finished Stock*, *i.e.*, goods which are in a saleable condition but which have not yet been disposed of to a customer.

In the case of a concern which buys its goods in a saleable condition, the question of stock of raw materials does not arise, but the stock of a manufacturing concern will probably comprise both raw materials and finished goods, in addition to materials which are at an intermediate stage, *i.e.*, Work-in-Progress, which will be considered later in this Chapter. So far as stock-in-trade is concerned, it is highly advisable to show Raw Materials and Finished Stock separately in the Balance Sheet.

Following the general rule as to the valuation of current assets, Raw Materials should be valued at cost, or current market price, if lower. The only occasion upon which it is permissible to value stock above cost is where such stock exhibits any inherent tendency to increase in value with the passage of time, *e.g.*, timber, wines, etc., which season or mature with age. In such cases stocks are, in practice, frequently valued at cost plus interest thereon at, say, 5 per cent. per annum ; but where this method is adopted, the value should never exceed that at which stocks of a similar stage of maturity could be purchased in the open market.

Finished Stock should similarly be valued at the lower of cost or current market price. Where the firm has manufactured its own stock, " cost " will be represented by the direct materials, wages and expenses incurred in producing the goods, together with an addition to cover works and administration overhead expenses restricted to such expenditure as has been incurred to bring the stock to its existing condition and location. Since selling and distribution overhead expenses are, strictly speaking, only attachable to goods which have been *sold*, it is considered sound practice to exclude them when valuing Finished Stock.

The following are bases usually adopted in practice for calculating *cost* in connection with the valuation of stock-in-trade :—

(1) " *Unit* " *cost*, by which each article, batch or parcel is valued at its individual cost. In certain cases, such as bulk stocks, this method is not always capable of application and records, including the allocation of expenses, may become unduly complicated. Further, it may not be practicable to apply the method to partly processed stocks or finished products where the individual units lose their identity.

(2) " *First in, first out* " (F.I.F.O.), which assumes that goods sold or consumed were those which had been longest on hand and that the quantity in stock represents the latest purchases. It has the effect of valuing unsold stock in a reasonably close relation to replacement price. In certain manufacturing or producing businesses, however, it is difficult to apply accurately through the various stages of manufacture or production.

(3) " *Average* " *cost*, which entails averaging the book value of stock at the commencement of a period with the cost of goods added during the period

after deducting consumption at the average price,
the periodical rests for calculating the average being
as frequent as possible having regard to the nature
of the business. It has the effect of smoothing out
distortion of results arising from excessive, and often
fortuitous, fluctuations in purchase price and production costs and is particularly suitable to manufacturing businesses where several processes are
involved.

The bases referred to above are founded on the principle
that " cost " is an historical fact. In some cases, however,
their application is unsuitable or impracticable owing to the
nature of the business and stock-in-trade is taken at a cost
estimated by one of the following methods :—

(4) " *Standard* " *cost*, which entails valuing stock at a
pre-determined or budgeted cost per unit. It is
coming more into use, particularly in manufacturing or processing industries where several operations
are involved or where goods are produced on mass-
production lines.

(5) " *Adjusted selling price* ", where an estimated cost is
obtained by pricing stock at current selling prices
and deducting an amount equivalent to the normal
profit margin and the estimated cost of disposal.

Other methods of stock valuation are the " base stock "
method, which retains permanently certain basic stock at
a fixed price not exceeding its original cost, and that known
as " last in, first out " (L.I.F.O.), which is based on the
principle that profit and loss in trading is the difference
between the price at which goods are sold and their replacement cost. There is, however, only limited application of
either of these methods in this country.

Market value is commonly interpreted as the price at
which it is estimated that the stock can be realised either
in its existing condition or as incorporated in the product
normally sold after allowing for expenditure to be incurred
before disposal ; or the cost of replacing the stock in bulk
at the accounting date.

Whatever basis is adopted for ascertaining cost or calculating market value, it should be such as will not distort the view of the real trend of trading results and should be applied consistently, regardless of the amount of profits available or losses sustained.

The correct valuation of stock at the close of the trading period is most important, as upon it will depend the accuracy of the gross profit shown in the Trading Account, and consequently of the net profit shown in the Profit and Loss Account. Moreover, it is necessary that both aspects of any transaction relating to stock (the liability as well as the asset) be taken into account in the same trading period ; obviously, if goods received during the last few days of a trading period are included in the closing stock credited to Trading Account but the invoice is not entered in the Purchases Day Book until the beginning of the next period, the gross and the net profit would be inflated by the amount of that invoice.

The invoices for all goods received during a trading period must therefore be passed through the Purchases Day Book during that period. Where an invoice cannot be obtained (*e.g.*, for goods received from abroad) an estimated amount must be passed through the books to cover the liability. Conversely, where an invoice has been entered in the books, but the goods have not yet been received, they should be included in stock at cost as if they had been received.

Similarly, all goods sold and delivered during the same period must be charged out to the customer through the Sales Day Book. It sometimes happens, however, that goods sold during one trading period are not delivered until the next period. Two diverse methods of dealing with such transactions are met with in practice, *viz.* :—

(1) The goods are debited to the debtor through the Sales Day Book and credited to the Sales Account at the time of sale. In this case, the goods must not be included in the stock on hand at the close of the trading period.

F*

(2) The goods are not charged out to the customer until delivery is effected ; in this case the goods are properly included in the stock on hand at their cost price, but no entry is made in the Sales Day Book in respect of the sale.

It is sometimes difficult to determine which method should be adopted, but the circumstances of each individual case must receive consideration. From a legal view-point, where it is the intention of the parties that the property in the goods (*i.e.*, the absolute right of ownership) passes to the buyer at the time of sale, the first method may be correctly adopted, since the goods are the customer's property. But where it is the intention that the ownership of the goods shall not pass until delivery is effected, the second method is the right one to pursue.*

It may seem almost superfluous to add that only the trader's own property should be included in stock on hand, but where a trader customarily handles goods as agent for others, or receives goods on consignment, the warning is not out of place.

Obsolete and unsaleable stock, and damaged goods (if any), must be entered at a suitable valuation.†

Where goods have been purchased forward and are not covered by forward sales, provision should be made for the excess, if any, of the purchase price over the market value and should be shown as such in the accounts. Similarly, where goods have been sold forward and are not covered by stocks and forward purchases, provision should be made for the excess, if any, of the anticipated cost over sales value.

Stock at Branches.

In the case of concerns which carry on their business through a number of branch establishments, it is necessary

---

* These distinctions assume the greatest importance in the case of goods which are subject to a hire-purchase agreement. Consideration of the methods adopted to record such transactions in the books of both " vendor " and purchaser (or hirer) is beyond the scope of this volume.

† Reference should be made to the recommendations of the Council of the Institute of Chartered Accountants with regard to the valuation of stock-in-trade (see Appendix II).

to take stock at each branch at the end of the trading period, in order that the entire stock-in-trade of the concern may be shown in its annual accounts. Similarly, any stock which is in transit from head office to branches at the date of the Balance Sheet must be taken into account and shown, either by inclusion in the general stock-in-trade or separately as " Goods in Transit ".

Where goods are sold at fixed prices (*e.g.*, in the case of a multiple-shop tobacconist), they are frequently charged out from head office to branches *at selling prices*. A close degree of control is thereby maintained over the branches, since, at any time, they must account for the value of the goods received, either as unsold stock, book debts or cash (or a combination of the three). Unsold stock at branches must not, however, be brought into the final accounts at the prices at which it has been charged out to the branches ; from the point of view of the concern as a whole, the profit included in the stock at branches has not yet been realised and must be excluded for the purpose of the final accounts.

Goods out on Consignment.

In certain trades, it is a common practice for an exporter to send out goods to an agent in a foreign country, to be sold there on his (the exporter's) behalf. This type of export transaction is known as a Consignment and the exporter and the foreign agent are respectively designated the Consignor and the Consignee. The relationship between the two parties is one of principal and agent, not of seller and buyer ; the consignee does not become the debtor of the consignor until he has sold the whole or a portion of the consignment, when he becomes responsible for remitting the proceeds of sale, after deducting any expenses incurred by him in respect of the consignment (*e.g.*, landing charges) and also his commission, which usually takes the form of an agreed percentage of the gross proceeds. Until, therefore, the consignment has been completely disposed of, the unsold portion must appear in the consignor's accounts as " Stock on Consignment " and should be valued at the lower of—

(1) Cost, plus a proportionate part of the expenses incurred in respect of the whole consignment; or

(2) Current *local* market price (*i.e.*, in the consignee's country).

Where the consignment is of a speculative nature, it may be prudent to make a provision to cover any possible loss on the balance of the consignment.

If goods have been invoiced out to the consignee at selling prices, care must be taken to ensure that unsold stocks are reduced to cost for the purpose of the final accounts, as in the case of " Stock at Branches " discussed above.

Bad debts in respect of goods consigned are borne by the consignor, unless the agent expressly assumes liability for such losses. In such a case, he is known as a *del credere* agent, and usually receives an extra rate of commission for the risk involved.

Goods on Sale or Return.

In some trades it is customary to send goods out on sale or return (*i.e.*, on approval). There is no sale, in the strict sense, until the customer has signified his intention to keep the goods either by a specific acceptance or by retaining them for a longer period than that specified in the agreement under which they were sent to him.* Thus goods which, at the date of a Balance Sheet, have been sent out on sale or return but have neither been accepted nor returned within the period allowed, should be treated as stock-in-trade and valued accordingly, subject to any allowance for wear and tear in transit, etc., that experience may dictate.

In practice, a Balance Sheet is rarely completed until several weeks after the date " as at " which it is said to be

* Many firms adopt the practice of printing on the " Appro. Note " or " Pro Forma Invoice " sent with the goods a notification that they will be charged for if not returned within (say) seven days.

drawn up. During the period most of the " sale or return transactions " open at the end of the year will have been completed and it might be argued that, if it is known that a sale did eventually transpire,* credit could be taken for it in the period in which the goods were sent out. The answer is found in the maxim that a Balance Sheet should always reflect the legal position as at a certain date. Although *possession* of the goods passes to the customer when they are delivered to him, the *legal property* in them does not pass until he has accepted them and the sale actually occurs on the later date.

If goods " on approval " or " on sale or return " are passed through the Sales Day Book and charged out to the prospective buyers, returns being recorded by a credit note, it will be seen that the tracing of goods still on approval will be difficult and tedious and accompanied by grave risks of inaccuracy through the overlooking of entries. The system adopted in practice, where goods are so charged out, is to forward to the prospective purchaser a *pro forma* invoice, a copy of which is placed in a special file marked "Goods on Approval ", to be removed when the goods are finally accepted or returned. Although this system is theoretically adequate, and enables the quantity of goods on approval to be ascertained by an inspection of the *pro forma* invoices in the file at the date of closing the accounts, it will not commend itself to the accountant ; for it involves many steps, each of which adds to the labour and the risk of error.

A much better system is the use of a special Journal known as a Sale or Return Day Book ruled in the following way :—

* The question of " after-acquired information " is one of the greatest practical importance. It may well be asked, " How far is the accountant (a) entitled, (b) required, to take note of facts which have occurred between the close of the financial year and the completion of the final accounts ? Furthermore, how far is the auditor entitled, or required, to take any such facts as may be brought to his notice into consideration before reporting on the accounts ? " It is difficult to give an answer which would cover all possible cases, but if the safe rule of—

   (i) Taking notice of anything which operates to reduce profits but

   (ii) Ignoring anything which would operate to increase them

is applied, the result is unlikely to offend against the principles of good accounting.

GOODS ON SALE OR RETURN BOOK

Date.	Particulars.	Cash Details.	Total of Pro Forma Invoice.	Date sold or re-turned.	Sales Ledger Folio.	Goods sold.	Goods re-turned.
19..		£ s. d. *	£ s. d.	19..		£ s. d.	£ s. d.

* This column is unnecessary if duplicate invoices are filed.

This book is both a memorandum book and a special sales day book. When goods are despatched, the selling price is entered in the " Cash Details " and " Total of Invoice " memorandum columns, and no further entry is made until it is known that the goods have been accepted or returned. In the latter case they are entered in the " Goods returned " memorandum column, and neither the entries made when the goods were despatched nor those made upon their return affect the double entry. If the goods are sold they are extended to the " Goods sold " column and posted to the debit of the customer's account in the Sales Ledger. The total of this column is subsequently posted to the credit of Sales Account.

The difference between the total of the " Pro Forma Invoice " column and the combined totals of the " Goods sold " and " Goods returned " columns represents the goods out on approval at any given date. For stocktaking purposes these goods outstanding must be reduced from selling price to cost price, and treated as ordinary stock for valuation purposes.

The advantages of a special Sale or Return Day Book are :—

   (1) At stocktaking, goods out " on approval " cannot be treated as ordinary sales, and thus cause the gross profit shown to be fictitious ;

(2) A duplication of the work of invoicing and passing goods on sale or return through the books and of crediting and passing goods returned through the books is avoided.

Where the number of sale or return transactions is considerable it may be necessary to extend the above ruling, in order to avoid unnecessary labour in bringing forward the details of outstanding goods ; this can be achieved by increasing the size of the book and arranging sections which will enable the balance to be carried forward to a succeeding period on the same page as the original entries.

Work-in-Progress.

Work-in-Progress must be carefully distinguished from Raw Materials or Finished Stock. In a manufacturing concern it represents goods which are partly manufactured at the date of the Balance Sheet, and it should be recorded in a separate account in the ledger.

The valuation to be placed upon work-in-progress differs somewhat from that of finished stock, and it is necessary to determine the amount of raw material, labour and other expenses which has been incurred to date in its manufacture. A reasonable charge may be added to cover works and administration overhead expenses, but no charge should be included in respect of selling and distribution overhead expenses, as these are only incurred when the goods are sold. In any case, care must be taken to see that the valuation does not exceed the market value (*i.e.*, the expected selling price) of the goods, due allowance being made for the additional cost which will be incurred before they can be sold.

Any cash received on account of work-in-progress * should be shown in the Balance Sheet as a deduction from the latter. Such cash receipts will appear in the books as credit balances on the customers' accounts in the Sales or Contracts Ledger.

The rule that the valuation of work-in-progress must not exceed cost may be relaxed in the case of comparatively long

---

* Builders or engineers who perform work under contract usually receive payment by instalments, the architect or civil engineer who acts for the customer giving certificates from time to time as stated portions of the work are finished.

contracts which are nearing completion at the date of the Balance Sheet. In such circumstances it is permissible to take credit for a proportion, not exceeding (say) two-thirds, of the profit in respect of work completed. Such profit is the difference between the contract price of that work, as shown by the architect's or engineer's certificates, and the actual cost. If, however, the full amount certified has not been received in cash, it is advisable to refrain from adding profit in respect of any part which, though certified, has not been paid for. This is particularly necessary where the terms of the contract provide that a certain percentage of the amount certified shall be retained until completion.

It should scarcely be necessary to add that if there is any reason to anticipate that the cost of finishing the contract will exceed the balance of the contract price, full provision must be made for the estimated loss.

EXAMPLE

The Constructional Company, Ltd., is engaged upon a large contract for the North West Stores, Ltd. The contract price is £200,000, and at 31st March, when the Constructional Company, Ltd., prepares its Balance Sheet, the expenditure on the contract had been as under:—

	£
Materials	50,000
Wages and Salaries	65,000
Other expenses directly attributable to the contract	800

Overhead expenses are estimated to amount to 2 per cent. of the cost of materials.

The whole of the work done (with the exception of that completed during the previous month—estimated cost £4,000) has been certified, the contract price being £115,800. Of this amount, 80 per cent. has been paid, the remainder being retained until completion of the contract.

It is required to compute the value (including a fair addition for profit) of the work-in-progress.

Profit can only be computed on work certified, and the cost of this section of the work may be arrived at as follows:—

	£
Materials	50,000
Wages and Salaries	65,000
Direct Expenses	800
Overheads, 2 per cent. on £50,000	1,000
	116,800
Less cost of work not certified	4,000
Cost of work certified	£112,800

The contract price of such work is £115,800 so that a profit of £3,000 is disclosed on the work certified. The amount to credit in the current Profit and Loss Account should not be more than :—

		£
Two-thirds of profit	=	2,000
Less reserve in respect of retention moneys		
$\frac{20}{100}$ of £2,000		400
Profit taken		£1,600

The work-in-progress will, therefore, be valued as under :—

	£	£
Cost of work certified	112,800	
Profit thereon	1,600	
		114,400
Cost of work not certified		4,000
		£118,400

and will appear in the Balance Sheet—

	£	£
Work-in-Progress	118,400	
Less Cash on account	92,640	
		25,760

Stores-in-Hand.

Stores-in-hand are those materials which are used in connection with the upkeep and maintenance of plant and machinery and other assets employed in the process of manufacture, *e.g.*, fuel, oils, cleaning materials, packing materials, etc. The item should be valued separately and not included with the general stock-in-trade. By this means it is ensured that the amount charged against revenue will represent the actual value consumed during the trading period, the amount of the valuation being credited to the expenditure account and brought down as a balance.

Investments.

When one of the main objects of a business is the buying and selling of stocks and shares (*e.g.*, a stockjobber or a finance company), investments held at the date of a Balance Sheet should be treated as current assets and valued as such. Investments held by a trading or manufacturing company will usually be regarded as current assets if they take the form of a temporary investment of surplus liquid resources.

Depreciation of investments held as current assets will be provided for by writing them down to market value when this is lower than the value at which they appear in the books. On the other hand, an unrealised appreciation will be ignored.* Market value will usually be ascertainable by reference to a Stock Exchange quotation. This takes the form of a double price, *e.g.*, 101–101½, the lower figure being the price at which the jobbers are willing to buy stocks or shares from members of the public who wish to sell them, and the higher that at which they will dispose of their own holdings. As stockjobbers are not allowed to deal directly with members of the public, the purchase or sale must be effected through the agency of a stockbroker, who charges a commission for his services. This commission, and the contract stamp and transfer stamp duty which are also payable by a purchaser, increase the amount payable and may be capitalised and taken into account when valuing the investments at cost. For purposes of valuation, market value may be taken at the mean of the two quoted prices, *i.e.*, 101¼ in the case quoted above.

Investment Accounts.

The purchase and sale of investments and the receipt of interest or dividends thereon present some interesting and important considerations of capital and income. Investments are unique in that they produce an income which is usually fixed at a certain percentage per annum on the nominal value of the stocks or shares. This income may be considered to accrue from day to day † and it is obvious that where an investment is held for less than a whole year, the interest credited to Profit and Loss Account should be an amount which is strictly comparable with the period during which the investment has been held.

At the end of the year, a certain amount of interest will have accrued, unless the interest happens to have been paid on and up to that date. Where first-class securities are

* If investments have been written down in the past, it may be permissible to write them up again to their original cost, if the market value returns to that or a higher value.

† Section 2 of the Apportionment Act, 1870, provides that all rents, annuities, dividends, and other periodical payments in the nature of income (whether reserved or made payable under an instrument in writing or otherwise) shall, like interest on money lent, be considered as accruing from day to day, and shall be apportionable in respect of time accordingly.

concerned, it is quite in order to take credit for such accrued interest. The Investment Account will appear as follows :—

3½ PER CENT. WAR LOAN

Dr. *Cr.*

Date.		Nom.	Income.	Capital.	Date.		Nom.	Income.	Capital.
1955		£	£	£	1955		£	£	£
Jan. 1	To Balance, *b/d.*	12,000	35	11,160	June 1	By Cash . .		210	
Dec. 31	„ P. & L. A/c.		420		Dec. 1	„ do.		210	
					31	„ Balance, *c/d.* : Int. accrued		35	
						Capital .	12,000		11,160
			£12,000	£455	£11,160			£12,000	£455	£11,160
1956									
Jan. 1	To Balance, *b/d.*	12,000	35	11,160					

It will be noted that it is usual to provide three money columns on each side of an Investment Account. The first of these shows the nominal value of the holding, on which interest will be received at the specified rate ; this column is in the nature of a memorandum, and does not enter into the double entry system. The second and third columns record the income and capital transactions respectively in the stock. As interest is paid on 3½ per cent. War Loan every six months, on 1st June and 1st December, there will always be one month's interest accrued on 31st December. This is recorded by bringing down a debit balance on the income column (in this case £35). As the stock has been held throughout the year, a similar opening balance appears and the net result is a transfer of £420 to Profit and Loss Account representing a full year's interest. In the capital column, the stock is brought down at cost, both at the beginning and at the end of the period.

Except in the case of a new issue, when application will be made direct to the Bank of England in the case of most British Government Stocks or to the issuing house or the company itself in the case of an industrial flotation, stocks and shares are usually purchased through the medium of a Stock Exchange. It is the universal practice to pay interest or dividends to those persons who are registered as the holders of the stock or shares on the day when the transfer books are closed for the purpose of preparing the dividend warrants. Thus a purchaser of stocks or shares on the Stock Exchange (which amounts to a purchase from some other person who wants to sell all or part of his holding) ordinarily takes the whole of the next payment of dividend or interest. This is reflected in the quotation of the stocks or shares which, other things being equal, increases slightly from day to day throughout the period of (say) six months in respect of which interest is paid. The quotation is said to be " cum dividend " (cum div.) and part of the purchase price may be regarded as a payment by the purchaser to the vendor of interest from the last preceding interest date to the date of transfer. The purchaser is reimbursed for this payment when he receives the next full instalment of interest and the balance of the latter represents his interest for the period during which he has actually held the stock.

The necessary adjustments in the purchaser's books are shown in the following example.

£1,000 3½ per cent. War Stock is purchased on 1st March, 1955, when the quotation is 84–84½. Brokerage and contract stamp amount to £2 13s. 0d. The total amount paid for the stock will be :—

£1,000 stock at 84½ .	.	.	. £845 0 0
Brokerage and Contract Stamp.	.	.	2 13 0
			£847 13 0

Dr. 3½ PER CENT. WAR LOAN *Cr.*

Date.		Nom.	Income.	Capital.	Date.		Nom.	Income.	Capital.
		£	£ s. d.	£ s. d.			£	£ s. d.	£ s.
1955 Mar. 1	To Cash .	1,000		847 13 0	1955 June 1	By Cash .		8 15 0	8 15
Dec. 31	„ P. & L. A/c. .		29 3 4		Dec. 1 31	„ do. . „ Balance, c/d. .	1,000	17 10 0 2 18 4	838 18
		£1,000	£29 3 4	£847 13 0			£1,000	£29 3 4	£847 13
1956 Jan. 1	To Balance, b/d. .	1,000	2 18 4	838 18 0					

On 1st June, 1955, the purchaser received a full six months' interest on the holding, but as he had only held it for three months, one half of the amount received is regarded as a capital receipt and is entered in the capital column. It will be seen that when allowance has been made for the one month's interest accrued due on 31st December, 1955, the balance of the income column available for transfer to Profit and Loss Account amounts to £29 3s. 4d., which is equivalent to 3½ per cent. on £1,000 for ten months, the period during which the stock has been held.

Similar considerations apply when stocks or shares are sold cum div. In this case, part of the sale price represents interest from the last regular date of payment.

Thus, continuing the last example, if £500 of the stock is sold on 1st September, 1956, and the net proceeds amount to £432, the investment account will be written up as follows:—

Dr. 3½ PER CENT. WAR LOAN *Cr.*

Date.		Nom.	Income.	Capital.	Date.		Nom.	Income.	Capital.
		£	£ s. d.	£ s. d.			£	£ s. d.	£ s. d.
1956 Jan. 1	To Balance, b/d. .	1,000	2 18 4	838 18 0	1956 June 1 Sept. 1	By Cash . ,, do. .	500	17 10 0 4 7 6	427 12 6
Dec. 31	,, P. & L. A/c. :				Dec. 1	,, do. .		8 15 0	
	Interest :		29 3 4		31	,, Balance, c/d. .	500	1 9 2	419 9 0
	Profit on Sale .			8 3 6					
		£1,000	£32 1 8	£847 1 6			£1,000	£32 1 8	£847 1 6
1957 Jan. 1	To Balance, b/d. .	500	1 9 2	419 9 0					

It will be noted that—

(1) On 1st September, 1956, £4 7s. 6d. has accrued due as interest on the £500 stock sold on that date, so that amount out of the total net proceeds of £432 is credited in the Income column.

(2) On 31st December, 1956, the unsold portion of stock, which represents one half of the original holding, is carried down at cost. The Capital column then shows a credit balance of £8 3s. 6d. which is the profit on sale of £500 stock. This may be transferred to Profit and Loss Account where the purchase and sale of securities is part of the ordinary business of the concern; otherwise it would be better to transfer it to Capital Reserve or to apply it in writing down the book value of other investments which have depreciated. Alternatively, the profit on the sale of part of a holding can be ignored until the entire holding has been realised; whereas a loss on sale of part of a holding should be written off, the balance remaining being brought down at original cost price or reduced to current market price.

(3) The £29 3s. 4d. transferred to Profit and Loss Account from the income column represents:—

	£ s. d.
3½ per cent. on £500 for 1 year . .	17 10 0
3½ per cent. on £500 for 8 months .	11 13 4
	£29 3 4

As transfer books must usually be closed for the preparation of dividend warrants about one month before a dividend or payment of interest falls due, it follows that when a holding of stock or shares changes hands while the transfer books are closed, the next dividend or interest will be paid to the vendor. This is recognised by an " ex dividend "

3½ PER CENT. WAR LOAN

Dr.

Date.		Nom.	Income.	Capital.
		£	£	£ s. d.
1955				
May 1	To Cash:— Purchase of £12,000 Stock at 83 ex div. £9,960 0 0 Add Brokerage and Contract Stamp . . 30 12 0	12,000		9,990 12 0
June 1	" Transfer to Income, Interest for 1 month . . .		210	
Dec. 31	" Transfer to Profit and Loss A/c.:— Income Profit on Realisation .			178 14 0
		£12,000	£210	£10,204 6 0

Cr.

Date.		Nom.	Income.	Capital.
		£	£	£ s. d.
1955				
June 1	By Transfer from Capital, per contra . . .		35	
Nov. 1	" Cash:— Sale of £12,000 Stock at 85 ex div. £10,200 0 0 Less Brokerage and Contract Stamp . . 30 14 0	12,000		10,169 6 0
Dec. 1	" Cash, Interest for 6 months : Income, 5 months Capital, 1 month . .		175	35 0 0
		£12,000	£210	£10,204 6 0

NOTES.—(1) The sum of £210 transferred to Profit and Loss A/c. from the Income column represents 3½ per cent. on £12,000 for six months.

(2) The profit on realisation, £178 14s. 0d., represents the difference of 2 per cent. between the purchase and sale prices on £12,000 Stock (i.e., £240) less two sets of brokerage and contract stamps, £61 6s. 0d.

(ex div.) quotation : about one month (3½ per cent. War Loan five weeks) before a dividend is due, Stock Exchange dealings in the shares change from a cum div. to an ex div. basis. The practical result of this is that the quotation falls by the net amount of the next dividend, for whereas a purchaser on one day, when the quotation is cum div., is going to receive the whole of the next dividend, a purchaser on the next day, when the quotation is ex div., is not going to receive any portion of it. The necessary adjustments are shown in the example on page 150, where £12,000 3½ per cent. War Loan is purchased on 1st May, 1955, at 82½–83 ex div. (brokerage and contract stamp £30 12s. 0d.) and is sold on 1st November, 1955, at 85–85½ ex div. (brokerage and contract stamp £30 14s. 0d.).

Investment Accounts have been considered in some detail because no other transactions afford a better or more exact distinction between capital and revenue. It should be noted that where the investments are held in trust, although the distinction between income (payable to the life tenant) and capital (held in trust for the ultimate benefit of the remainder-man) is very important, the law does not require an apportionment either of the purchase price or of the proceeds of realisation.

CHAPTER V

THE BALANCE SHEET (2)

One of the most important functions of the Balance Sheet is to show how the total interest of the proprietors—their capital and any undistributed profits—is represented by assets. These amounts will rarely agree in total, however, because of the existence of liabilities. In one sense, capital itself may be regarded as a liability—the amount due from the business to its proprietors—but for the purpose of this Chapter a clear distinction will be maintained between the terms capital and liability. Thus, in the majority of cases, the total assets shown on the right-hand side of the Balance Sheet represent a mixed fund of capital (including undistributed profits) and liabilities. Alternatively, the capital may be regarded as represented by a net balance of assets less liabilities.

The Classification of Liabilities.

The important distinction between fixed and current assets can be extended and applied to liabilities. In the course of trading, liabilities will be incurred for goods supplied and other expenses. Bills payable may be given, but sooner or later the liabilities, either on the debts themselves or on the bills, must be discharged out of the liquid resources of the business. If the latter are not sufficient, recourse may be had to a bank overdraft, which may be secured on fixed assets but will nevertheless be discharged in the ordinary course of business out of the fund of current assets. All the liabilities thus noted have the following characteristics :—

(1) They fluctuate from day to day according to the commitments of the business ; and

(2) They are due for payment immediately or within a comparatively short time.

152

They, and any others of a similar nature, are therefore classified as *current liabilities* and, as stated above, they will be discharged, in the ordinary course of business, out of the fund of *current assets*. Other liabilities have a degree of permanence which places them in a different category ; they are known as *fixed liabilities*. Some writers use the alternative terms " short term " liabilities and " long term " or " funded " liabilities.

Liabilities, whether fixed or current, are sometimes regarded as a form of capital. In such a case, the " capital " of a business, or the total fund available for the purchase of assets, would include—

(1) The Capital proper, *e.g.*, the share capital and reserves of a limited company or the capital (and current) accounts of partners or a sole trader ;

(2) Loan Capital, *i.e.*, fixed liabilities : this term is frequently applied to debentures issued by limited companies ;

(3) Circulating Capital, *i.e.*, current liabilities.

On the other hand, the terms " capital " and " assets " are sometimes regarded as interchangeable in their generic sense, " capital " being thus interpreted as meaning the assets representing the results of the expenditure of capital. Circulating capital may, therefore, mean either the amount of trade creditors outstanding plus other fluctuating credit balances, or the fund of circulating assets used in the cycle of business operations. The context will usually indicate which meaning is intended, but the twofold interpretation should be constantly borne in mind.

Unless a clear distinction is made in the Balance Sheet between fixed and current liabilities, it will be impossible to judge the adequacy or otherwise of the financial resources of the business. The current liabilities will require to be discharged at an early date, and for this reason alone the immediate liability should be ascertainable. Furthermore, resort will have to be had to the fund of circulating assets for the necessary money with which to effect payment. The Balance Sheet should, therefore, show the respective amounts of circulating assets and current liabilities so that the adequacy of the former to meet the latter may be judged and steps taken, if necessary, to place the business on a better financial footing.

Fixed liabilities, on the other hand, will not require to be discharged until such time as the stipulated currency of the liability shall have expired, or upon a stipulated date. There is, therefore, no significance in the relationship of the respective amounts of fixed liabilities and circulating assets. Nevertheless, the fixed liabilities must be repaid at some date,* and must, therefore, be covered by assets. These assets are primarily the fixed assets which, as a general rule, cannot be realised until the business comes to an end. Where fixed liabilities have to be repaid without resort to the process of selling fixed assets, the repayment must be effected out of fresh borrowing or out of profits as already indicated in Chapter III.

The Capital Account.

The statement of the capital contributed by the proprietors of the business is usually placed at the head of the liabilities side of the Balance Sheet, although in the case of sole traders and partnerships it is not infrequently placed as the last item on the liabilities side, *i.e.*, representing the amount which is payable *after* creditors and other claims, in the event of the winding up of the business.

It is usual to restrict the application of the term " Capital Account " to the account which records the amount contributed by the proprietors (*e.g.*, in the case of a limited company, the Share Capital Account, but in this case, as will be seen later, the practice is determined by statutory rules), although loans raised may sometimes be classed as capital (not, of course, *share* capital). Loan Capital will be separately considered later in this Chapter.

The Capital Account of a sole trader or partner may be varied by undrawn profits and losses not made good by further introduction of capital. In the case of a limited

---

* Except in the case of Irredeemable Debentures, which are sometimes issued.

company, however, the Capital Account must remain intact at the full amount contributed by the shareholders, adjustments in respect of neither profits nor losses being permitted therein. At any date, therefore, the balance on the Capital Account will indicate the indebtedness of the company to its shareholders.* Profits and losses are collected together in the Profit and Loss Account, which is a continuing account running from year to year. The balance, therefore, is carried forward to the next year and not transferred to the Capital Account.

The Capital Account is of considerable interest to the investor in shares, for it represents the amount of his and his co-investors' claims on the assets of the business after the prior claims of creditors have been met. Capital, however, is only the key to the true position, for the divisible fund really consists of the assets. Although the capital fund may appear in the Balance Sheet as intact, this may not really be the case. Losses will result in a diminution of the fund of assets with the result that part of the capital will be unrepresented. The shareholders must, in such cases, suffer a loss *pro rata* to their holdings.

The creditor views the Balance Sheet in a somewhat different light. He recognises that the capital fund may not be intact and he therefore pays more attention to the realisable value of the assets. He is not so much concerned with the continuity of the business as the shareholder : as long as there are sufficient assets available to satisfy his claims, he is content, for if the business was disposed of the next day, his claim would be paid off.

The Capital of a sole trader exists as one fund without any subdivision into smaller units and is, of course, represented by the assets of the business. The accounting in respect thereof is a relatively simple matter, which need not be enlarged upon.

* The same distinction between capital indebtedness and amount available to satisfy the indebtedness, as was noted above, will apply here. Thus, it does not necessarily follow that the amount of capital indebtedness will be repayable on a liquidation of the company. There may be losses (evidenced by a debit balance on the Profit and Loss Account) which will have to be met out of capital. The amount due to each shareholder will, therefore, be reduced *pro rata*.

The Capital of Partners.

A Partnership Agreement usually provides for the contribution of the necessary capital in stated amounts or proportions which may or may not be the same proportions as those in which the profits are to be shared. In the absence of agreement, Section 24 of the Partnership Act, 1890, provides that the partners are entitled to share *equally* in the capital and profits of the firm ; but this does not mean that they are entitled to have the assets divided in equal shares, irrespective of the amount of capital actually contributed by each. It means that in the absence of agreement, each partner can be called upon to contribute his fair proportion of the capital required. If the partners do not contribute in equal proportions it would seem that there is at once an implied agreement to the contrary and the capital of each partner is fixed by the amount he has contributed, either in cash or in assets taken over at an agreed valuation.

The capital of a partner does not necessarily remain fixed at the amount originally contributed. It may be augmented by profits, items such as salaries and interest on capital (if not withdrawn in cash) and any further capital contributed, and it may be reduced by drawings and losses. For accounting purposes the capital may sometimes be regarded as fixed (subject, of course, to any express withdrawals or additions), and profits, drawings and similar items may be recorded in separate Current Accounts. These will be shown in the extracts from the Balance Sheet on the next page, the partners being *A*, *B* and *C*.

Alternatively, the Capital and Current Accounts may be combined, but Loan Accounts must always be kept distinct, for on dissolution they must be settled before any claims on account of capital can be met.

The Share Capital of Companies Incorporated under the Companies Act, 1948.

A share is a fixed proportion or fraction (aliquot part) of the company's share capital. From a legal point of view, however, a share may be defined as the interest which a

	£	£	£	£
Loan Account, *A* *				2,000
Capital Accounts :—				
A			8,000	
B			2,000	
C			1,000	
				11,000
Current Accounts :—				
A. Balance at 1st January, 19.. . .		1,000		
Add Interest on Capital		400		
Share of Profits		2,440		
		3,840		
Less Drawings	2,000			
Interest on Drawings . . .	25			
		2,025		
			1,815	
B. Balance at 1st January, 19.. . .		500		
Add Interest on Capital		100		
Share of Profits		1,830		
		2,430		
Less Drawings	1,300			
Interest on Drawings	20			
		1,320		
			1,110	
C. Balance at 1st January, 19.. . .		400		
Add Interest on Capital		50		
Share of Profits		1,220		
		1,670		
Less Drawings	1,000			
Interest on Drawings	15			
		1,015		
			655	
				3,580

shareholder has in a company, and it is measured by a sum of money for the purpose of (1) computing the shareholder's liability, (2) ascertaining the amount of the shareholder's dividend, *i.e.*, his proportionate part of the profits, and (3) reckoning his share in the surplus assets of the company in the event of winding up. The issue of a share certificate is *prima facie* evidence that the person named thereon is the owner of the shares set out in the certificate. Under Section 26 of the Companies Act, 1948, the *legal* basis of the title is the entry of the member's name in the company's Register of Members.

* If the liabilities are marshalled in the order of permanence, the Loan Account will follow the Capital and Current Accounts.

A shareholder is liable to contribute to the company, whether for the purchase of assets or the discharge of liabilities, only such part of the nominal value of the shares held by him as he has not already paid.   Once this amount has been paid, the shareholder is under no further liability, and even if the assets of the company are insufficient to discharge its liabilities, the shareholder is not responsible for any deficiency. This is known as *the principle of limited liability*.

The various terms used in connection with share capital are—

(1) *Nominal, Authorised or Registered Capital, i.e.*, the amount which a company takes power, in its Memorandum of Association, to issue. A stamp duty of 10s. per cent. must be paid on the original nominal capital of a company and on any subsequent increase thereof irrespective of the amount actually issued.

(2) *Subscribed or Issued Capital, i.e.*, the total nominal value of the shares allotted to members.

(3) *Called-up Capital, i.e.*, the total amount of the subscribed capital which has actually been called up by the directors.

(4) *Paid-up Capital, i.e.*, the total amount paid up, or credited as paid up, on the issued share capital.

(5) *Uncalled Capital, i.e.*, the total amount which has not been called up on the issued share capital.

(6) *Unissued Capital, i.e.*, that portion of the nominal capital which has not been allotted to members.

(7) *Reserve Capital, i.e.*, uncalled capital which a company, by special resolution, has declared capable of being called up only in the event of liquidation.*

It is not necessary that the whole of the nominal or

---

* Under Section 60 of the Companies Act, 1948, " a limited company may by special resolution determine that any portion of its share capital which has not been already called up shall not be capable of being called up, except in the event and for the purposes of the company being wound up, and thereupon that portion of its share capital shall not be capable of being called up except in the event and for the purposes aforesaid ".   This power does not depend on the Articles.   The marginal note in the Act refers to such earmarked capital as " Reserve Liability ".   Refer also to Section 60, Companies Act, 1948, reproduced in Appendix I to this work.

authorised capital shall be issued, or that the whole amount of each share shall be paid up.

The three principal classes of shares are Preference, Ordinary and Deferred, but there are many variations of these ; the following list includes the kinds most frequently encountered :—

(1) Preference.   (6) Preferred Ordinary.

(2) Cumulative Preference.   (7) Deferred Ordinary.

(3) Participating Preference.   (8) Deferred.

(4) Redeemable Preference.   (9) Founders'.

(5) Ordinary.

The respective rights and privileges attaching to each class of share of any company are determined by the provisions of its Memorandum and Articles of Association, but the more usual features of the above classes of shares may be summarised thus :—

(1) PREFERENCE SHARES are those which confer some preferential right over other classes of shares, usually the right to a fixed dividend before any dividend is paid to the holders of ordinary shares. In many cases, the additional right to a return of capital in priority to other classes is also given, but this priority as regards capital requires an express provision in the company's regulations.

The favourable position of the preference shareholders is frequently exaggerated, for not only will they suffer in respect of income when profits are inadequate even to meet their prior claims to dividend or when losses are sustained, but they may also suffer in respect of capital when losses are such as to render a drastic reduction of capital essential. Thus, where a company has been through a bad period, making heavy losses, and has at last reached a point where profitable trading is again possible, it is often to the benefit of all concerned to face facts and reduce the issued capital so as to bring it into line with the actual capital (i.e., available net assets). By this means an earlier return to dividend paying is made possible. In such cases it is nowadays regarded as inevitable that the preference shareholders as well as the ordinary shareholders should be called upon to make sacrifices, which usually take the form of a reduction in their capital. The preference shareholders may be compensated to some extent either by an increase in their rate of dividend, or by the grant of participating rights, or by the issue of a proportion of the ordinary shares in the reconstructed company.

It cannot be too strongly emphasised that where any writing down of capital is necessary, the preferential status of the preference shareholders should be retained, *e.g.*, they should not bear the brunt of the loss, but only a fair proportion, having regard to the other classes of shareholders.

(2) CUMULATIVE PREFERENCE SHARES entitle the holder, when profits are divided, to a dividend at a fixed rate, such dividend being payable out of future profits when the current year's profits are insufficient. All arrears of dividend on these shares must be paid before the other shareholders can participate in the profits. Unpaid cumulative preference dividends are not liabilities in the ordinary sense ; the liability is contingent upon the earning of sufficient profits to pay the dividends *and* upon the declaration of the dividend. Moreover, the directors are usually authorised by the Articles to transfer a part or even the whole of the profits to reserve before the payment of any dividends.

Preference shares are assumed to be cumulative if the contrary is not clearly stated in the Memorandum or Articles of Association.

The Companies Act, 1948, provides that the published accounts of a company must disclose the amount of any arrears of fixed cumulative dividends and the period for which the dividends are in arrear ; the amount must be stated before deduction of tax, except that, in the case of tax-free dividends, the amount must be stated as free of tax.

(3) PARTICIPATING PREFERENCE SHARES usually confer the right, when profits are divided, to a fixed dividend, and, in addition, entitle the holder to participate in surplus profits (if any) after the ordinary shareholders have received a dividend at a stated rate.

(4) REDEEMABLE PREFERENCE SHARES may be issued by a limited company if authorised by its Articles. Such shares may be cumulative, non-cumulative, or participating, according to the terms of issue, but the power of redemption is subject to the conditions laid down in Section 58 of the Companies Act, 1948 (see page 230).

Every Balance Sheet of a company which has issued redeemable preference shares must contain a statement specifying what part of the issued capital of the company consists of such shares and the earliest date on which the company has power to redeem the shares.*

Where, on a winding up, the surplus assets are more than sufficient to repay to all the shareholders in full the capital due to them, the question of the participation of the preference shareholders in the excess arises. In every case, the question depends upon the provisions in the Memorandum and Articles of Association of the company defining the rights of the various classes of shareholders. Where such provisions do not deal either expressly or by implication with the respective rights of preference and ordinary shareholders in cases where assets are more than sufficient to repay the capital, the preference shareholders are entitled to participate in the excess assets *pari passu* with the ordinary shareholders (*Re Madame Tussaud and Sons*, 1927). A provision giving preference shareholders priority for *repayment of capital* in a winding up does not necessarily, by implication, negative their ordinary right to participate in surplus assets (*Re Fraser and Chalmers, Ltd.*, 1919), but this is mainly a matter of construction of the appropriate clause in the Memorandum (*Collaroy* v. *Giffard*, 1928).

(5) ORDINARY SHARES are those which, as a general rule, are entitled to the whole of the surplus profits after satisfaction of the rights of preference shareholders. Except where Participating Preference or Deferred Shares are issued, no fixed rate of dividend on Ordinary Shares is stated.

(6) and (7). The Ordinary Shares are sometimes split

* Refer also to Section 58, Companies Act, 1948, reproduced in Appendix I to this work.

G

into two sub-classes, PREFERRED ORDINARY and DEFERRED
ORDINARY. The holders of the former class of share have
a prior right to a fixed non-cumulative dividend, and until
this dividend is paid the holders of Deferred Ordinary Shares
do not participate in the distribution of profits.

Obviously, where both Preference and Ordinary Shares
are in existence, the relative merits of the two classes of
shares as a possible investment will depend not only on their
dividend rights, but also on their rights as to capital repayment. Thus, if in addition to a priority as to dividend, the
Preference Shares also carry a preference as to capital repayment, the Ordinary Shares must usually be regarded as a
speculative investment, and to make them attractive to
investors it will be necessary for the company to show a
good profit and dividend record.

(8) and (9). DEFERRED or FOUNDERS' SHARES are those
which rank for dividend after all the other classes have
received fixed rates of dividend. They are usually issued
as fully paid to the original vendors or their nominees in
satisfaction of part of the purchase price of the business, or
for services rendered in the formation of the company.
These shares are usually of small nominal value, for as the
shares come in for all the surplus rights in the company,
i.e., all the residue of profits distributed, and may carry extensive voting powers, their nominal value is irrelevant to
their real value, and the lower it is the less the company
has to pay in the form of capital duty.

It has already been shown that goodwill may be regarded
as the capitalised value of an annuity of the average super
profits earned by the business. It will be clear, therefore,
that the Deferred Shares will reap the benefit of the existence
of goodwill, for they receive by way of dividend the whole,
or practically the whole, of the super profits. Frequently,
when an existing business is acquired and a substantial price
is paid for goodwill, that part of the purchase price is satisfied
by means of an issue of Deferred Shares. Thus, the somewhat anomalous position arises of a person who purports to
sell goodwill yet retains for himself the benefit derived there-

from.   This fact has led to a considerable amount of criticism of the method of finance by means of which goodwill is purchased in this way.   On the other hand, it might be argued that the risk of loss of goodwill is not taken by the company.

Shares which carry the right to the whole of the profits remaining after the payment of dividends on Preference Shares and other fixed dividend shares are sometimes referred to as *equity shares* ; this is a descriptive term and not a class of share, and is generally applicable to Ordinary Shares excepting where Deferred or Founders' Shares are entitled to the residual profits.

Stock.

When a company is formed its capital must be expressed in shares, each of which is numbered * and capable of identification for the purpose of determining liability for calls, etc. As soon as the shares have become fully paid, however, the company, if it wishes and its Articles permit, may convert the shares or any class of them into stock.   The holding of a member is then expressed in terms of its nominal value, *e.g.*, £100 stock instead of a number of shares of a given value, *e.g.*, 100 shares of £1 each.

In many respects stock and shares are similar ; each confers upon the holder exactly the same rights and privileges, and in fact, stock has been legally defined as " a set of shares put together in a bundle ".   Shares, however, may be partly paid, while stock must be fully paid ; again, each share must possess a distinctive number, while stock cannot be so numbered.

Stock cannot be issued in the first instance except by certain Statutory Companies (see Chapter XI) which are governed by their own special Acts of Parliament.

Shares and stock are ordinarily transferable in the same manner, but while fractions of a share cannot be transferred, stock may be transferred in any amount, from 1d. upwards, subject to any restrictions imposed by the company's regulations.   Public companies usually stipulate that stock shall

---

* Distinctive numbers may be dispensed with where all the shares of that class are fully paid and rank *pari passu*.

be transferable only in multiples of a stated amount, *e.g.*, 5s. or £1.

Stock may be subdivided into several classes in the same way as shares.

Issue of Share Capital.

After the Memorandum and Articles of Association have been filed with the Registrar of Companies and the company has been registered, the next important step is to obtain the share capital with which the company will commence trading. In the case of private companies, this is usually subscribed by the proposed directors and their relatives and friends. For public companies, however, the more general method is to issue a prospectus inviting the public to take up the shares, although the directors and their friends often subscribe for a large proportion of the shares offered for subscription.

The prospectus sets forth particulars of the company, its directors and other officials, its business, an estimate of its future prospects, and the amount and nature of the capital offered for subscription. In addition to much other information, it further states the amount of deposit payable upon application for shares, the amount payable upon allotment, and whether further instalments are payable on stated dates or when " called " by the directors. An application form is attached, usually with directions that it should be forwarded with the application money direct to the company's bankers.

Where the company has been in existence for some time, and capital is then issued, an auditor's report of the company's profits or losses must also be set out in respect of *each* of the five financial years immediately preceding the issue of the prospectus, and of the rate of dividends paid in respect of each class of shares during the said five years, and of the assets and liabilities at the date of the last accounts ; and, if the proceeds or any part thereof are to be applied in the purchase of a business or of shares in a company so that the latter will become a subsidiary, an accountant's report of the profits or losses of such business or company during each of the five years immediately preceding the issue of its prospectus, and of its assets and liabilities.

In the case of a company which has been carrying on business, or of a business which has been carried on for less than five years, the above particulars must be given for the maximum period possible.*

In the case of a public company, no shares may be allotted unless a prospectus has been filed with the Registrar of Companies and the minimum amount (see page 183) has been subscribed and at least 5 per cent. of the nominal value of each share applied for has been paid in cash or by cheque. In calculating these amounts, shares payable otherwise than in cash are excluded.

If a public company does not issue a prospectus, it may not allot any shares unless at least three days previously it has filed a statement in lieu of prospectus, giving much the same information as is required to be disclosed in a prospectus.

If the minimum subscription is not obtained within 40 days of the issue of the prospectus, the application moneys must be returned to the senders; if not returned within 48 days, the directors are liable to repay the money with interest at 5 per cent. per annum from the expiration of the 48th day.

So that intending subscribers may have an opportunity of examining the prospectus, no allotment may be made until the third day after the opening of the lists. Where the prospectus states that application will be made to a Stock Exchange for permission to deal in the shares, the application moneys must be kept in a separate bank account, and must be returned within eight days if application for such permission is not made or refused; otherwise the directors are liable as stated above.

It seems hardly necessary to add that a private company is unable to issue a prospectus, for such an action would amount to an invitation to the public to subscribe for shares.

Although a contract to take shares in a company is a contract to contribute a certain limited sum to the resources of the company, it is not essential that the contribution should take the form of a cash payment or payments. Shares

---

* Refer also to Part II, Fourth Schedule, Companies Act, 1948, reproduced in Appendix I to this work.

may be allotted for any *bonâ fide* consideration in money or money's worth, but when they are allotted as either partly or fully paid up for a consideration other than cash the contract under which they are so allotted must be filed with the Registrar of Companies. If there is no written contract, then a statement containing particulars of the transaction and bearing a revenue stamp of the same value as would have been borne by a written contract (with certain exceptions a transfer or conveyance of property attracts an *ad valorem* duty of two pounds per cent.) must be filed in lieu thereof.

When a company is formed to take over an existing business, it is quite usual for part of the purchase price to be discharged by the allotment of shares. Such shares are, of course, allotted for a consideration other than cash and, as stated above, the stamped contract for sale or a statement in lieu thereof must be filed with the Registrar. The book-keeping entries necessary to record such a transaction are illustrated by the following Journal entries :—

JOURNAL

19.. Jan. 1.			£	£
	Goodwill	Dr.	12,000	
	Land and Buildings	,,	15,000	
	Plant and Machinery	,,	5,000	
	Stock-in-trade	,,	7,500	
	Sundry Debtors	,,	11,500	
	Cash	,,	1,000	
	To Sundry Creditors			8,000
	,, Brown & Jones			44,000
	Being assets acquired, liabilities taken over, and consideration for the purchase of the business of Brown & Jones, in accordance with the contract dated..........19..			
10.	Brown & Jones	Dr.	44,000	
	To Ordinary Share Capital Account			35,000
	,, Cash			9,000
	Being nominal value of Ordinary Shares of £1 each credited as fully paid, allotted to :—			
	Alfred Brown £20,000			
	Arthur Jones 15,000			
	and cash paid in settlement of purchase price of the business as per contract dated........19.., and resolution of the directors dated..........19..			

In order to minimise the nominal value of property taken over by the company (with consequent economy in stamp duty) it is a common practice for the company to collect debts and pay creditors as *agents for the vendor*, instead of taking these balances into its own books. For this service a commission is usually payable to the company.

Calls.

Calls are instalments of the purchase price of shares which are payable in accordance with the terms of issue or as determined by the directors.

Shareholders sometimes pay up the whole or a part of the nominal value of their shares in advance of the date upon which the calls have become due. Such *calls paid in advance* are not part of the share capital and on winding-up take preference over called-up capital. They are, in effect, loans to the company, and carry interest (less Income Tax at the standard rate in force at the date of payment) against the company in accordance with the provisions of the Articles. Such interest is a charge against profits, and is debited to a special Interest on Calls in Advance Account, the balance of which is transferred to the debit of Profit and Loss Account.*

Calls in arrear (*i.e.*, sums which have become payable on the shares but which have not yet been paid by certain shareholders) should appear in the Balance Sheet as a deduction from the particular class of share capital to which they relate. The amount of interest (less Income Tax) received may be credited to Profit and Loss Account by transfer from a special Interest on Calls in Arrear Account.† When such interest has accrued at the date of the Balance Sheet, but has not been received by the company, it is considered advisable, from the viewpoint of prudence, to credit the amount concerned to a Reserve Account, and to defer the transfer to Profit and Loss Account until the interest is actually received.

Table A (a model set of Articles appended to the

---

* If interest paid on calls in advance is regarded as " annual interest " (see page 92), the gross amount thereof should be debited to Profit and Loss Account.

† If interest received on calls in arrear is regarded as " investment " income (see page 93), the gross amount thereof should be credited to Profit and Loss Account.

Companies Act, 1948) provides for a charge of 5 per cent. per annum in respect of calls in arrear and an allowance of 5 per cent. per annum in respect of calls in advance, although the company may have its own Articles which may provide otherwise.

Premiums on Shares.

The real or " intrinsic " value of shares largely depends upon the success (or otherwise) of a company as evidenced by the amount of dividends paid and the strength of the financial position disclosed in its Balance Sheets. Thus, a successful company making a further issue of shares is often able to obtain for such shares a higher price than their nominal or face value ; in other words they are issued " at a premium ". The premium is usually included in the amount payable on allotment.

Section 56 of the Companies Act, 1948, requires that premiums on shares shall be credited to a " Share Premium Account " to be shown separately in every Balance Sheet. The balance to the credit of such account may be applied in :—

(1) Paying up unissued shares to be issued as bonus shares ;

(2) Writing off preliminary expenses, share issue expenses or commissions or discounts on shares or debentures ; or

(3) Providing any premium payable on the redemption of redeemable preference shares or debentures ; but it cannot be applied in any other manner.*

Such premiums must not be credited to Share Capital Account as they do not form part of the capital of the company, and it is illegal to credit them to Profit and Loss Account.

EXAMPLE

The Newcome Company, Limited, issued, on 1st March, a prospectus inviting applications for 25,000 Ordinary Shares of £1 each at a premium of 5s. per share,

---

* Refer also to Section 56, Companies Act, 1948, reproduced in Appendix I to this work.

payable as to 2s. 6d. on application, 7s. 6d. on allotment (including the premium), and the balance as and when required. The issue was fully subscribed and the company went to allotment on 10th March. Show the journal entry, recording the application and allotment.

JOURNAL

19—		£	£
Mar. 10	Application and Allotment Account . . *Dr.*	12,500	
	To Ordinary Share Capital Account . . .		6,250
	,, Share Premium Account		6,250
	Being total amount payable on application (2s. 6d.		
	per share) and allotment (7s. 6d., including the		
	premium, 5s. per share) on 25,000 Ordinary		
	Shares of £1 each, numbered 1 to 25,000, allotted		
	this day. (Vide Minute Book, Resolution No.		
	. . .)		

Issue of Shares at a Discount.

By Section 57 of the Companies Act, 1948, a company is allowed to issue at a discount shares of a class already issued, provided that:—

(1) The issue is authorised by a resolution passed at a general meeting of the company and sanctioned by the Court ;

(2) The resolution specifies the maximum rate of discount at which the shares are to be issued ;

(3) At the date of issue at least one year has elapsed since the date on which the company was entitled to commence business ; and

(4) The shares are issued within one month after the date on which the issue was sanctioned by the Court or within any extended time allowed by the Court.

Particulars of any discount allowed on such shares, and not yet written off, must be disclosed in every annual return, and in every prospectus relating to the issue of the shares, and in every Balance Sheet issued subsequently to the issue of the shares.*

The discount must be brought into the books when the shares are allotted, since the statutory necessity to disclose the discount in the Balance Sheet arises when the shares are issued.

* Refer also to Section 57, Companies Act, 1948, reproduced in Appendix I to this work.

G*

The shares must appear in the Balance Sheet at their full nominal value, for this is the true amount of indebtedness of the company to its shareholders. The discount will appear in the Balance Sheet as a fictitious asset until it has been written off.

EXAMPLE

Bad Way, Ltd., made an issue of 70,000 Ordinary Shares of £1 each at a discount of 5s. per share. The cash was duly received. Show the entries in the company's journal and the position in the Balance Sheet after the shares had been issued.

JOURNAL

	£	£
Application and Allotment (Sundry Shareholders) A/c. . . . . *Dr.*	52,500	
Discount on Shares Account . . . . . „	17,500	
To Ordinary Share Capital Account . . .		70,000
Being issue of 70,000 Ordinary Shares of £1 each at a discount of 5s. per share as per resolution dated....................and duly confirmed by the Court.		

Extract from BALANCE SHEET

Issued Share Capital:—	£		£
70,000 Ordinary Shares, £1 each, fully called . .	70,000	Discount on Ordinary Shares	17,500

NOTE.—The discount should be written off to Profit and Loss Account over a short period of years, although there is no legal compulsion to do this.

The power to issue shares at a discount is useful when a company requires further capital at a time when its shares are quoted on the Stock Exchange below their nominal value, since the public would normally not be willing to pay the full nominal value for new shares under such circumstances, but might be quite willing to subscribe at a price below the nominal value of the shares.

Forfeiture and Reissue of Shares.

Where the amount due upon shares is payable by instalments, it occasionally happens that a shareholder fails to pay one of the instalments. The Articles of Association of most companies authorise the directors, after certain formalities have been observed, to " forfeit " such shares. The usual procedure, and its effects, are as follows :—

(1) Directors may, at any time after failure to pay a call or instalment, serve the defaulting member with a notice requiring payment of the amount due, with any accrued interest.

(2) The notice must give at least fourteen days for payment, and must state that the shares will be forfeited in the event of non-payment.

(3) If default is made, the directors may resolve to forfeit the shares.

(4) Forfeited shares may be sold or otherwise disposed of, but until this happens the forfeiture may be cancelled.

(5) The defaulter ceases to be a member of the company, but remains liable to pay to the company all moneys due at the date of forfeiture until the company shall have received payment of such moneys.

(6) A statutory declaration of a director stating that certain shares have been forfeited, and a receipt for the amount paid, form a good title to the shares.

(7) Calls, instalments and premiums on the shares are included in the above provisions.

Forfeiture can be carried out only where the directors possess the necessary powers and the procedure set forth in the Articles must be followed to the letter.

When shares are forfeited the entries required in the company's financial books are—

(a) Debit the Share Capital Account and credit Forfeited Shares Account with the whole amount previously credited to the former account in respect of the shares forfeited (i.e., the amount called-up on the shares).

(b) Debit the Forfeited Shares Account and credit the Call Account or Accounts with the instalment(s) owing but unpaid by the shareholder at the time of forfeiture.

Where the shares were originally issued at a premium, the

premium credited to Share Premium Account in respect of
the shares forfeited should also be transferred to Forfeited
Shares Account.

Unless or until the shares are reissued, the balance on the
Forfeited Shares Account (representing the amount already
received from the defaulting member) will be shown as a
separate item on the liabilities side of the Balance Sheet.

EXAMPLE

The *X.Y.Z.* Co., Ltd., has a nominal capital of £20,000, divided into 20,000
Ordinary Shares of £1 each. The whole of the capital has been issued at par
on the following terms :—

Payable on Application	2s. 6d.	per share.
Payable on Allotment	2s. 6d.	per share.
First Call	10s.	per share.
Second Call	5s.	per share.

The calls have been made and paid in full by the members with the exception
of A. Jackson, who has failed to pay the first and second calls on the 100 shares
allotted to him. On 1st December the directors resolve to forfeit the shares.

Show the journal entries recording the forfeiture, the Call Accounts, Ordinary
Share Capital Account, and Forfeited Shares Account, and show how the above
items will appear in a Balance Sheet prepared immediately after the forfeiture.

JOURNAL

		£	£
19.. Dec. 1	Ordinary Share Capital Account . . . .*Dr.* To Forfeited Shares Account . . . . . . *Being forfeiture of 100 shares allotted to A. Jackson, for* *non-payment of the first and second calls of 10s. and 5s.* *per share respectively, as per Resolution of this date.*	100	100
	Forfeited Shares Account . . . .*Dr.* To First Call Account . . . . „ Second Call Account . . . . *Being transfer of calls unpaid on forfeiture of the above* *shares.*	75	50 25

Dr.	ORDINARY SHARE CAPITAL ACCOUNT			*Cr.*

19..		£	19..		£
Dec. 1	To Forfeited Shares Account . . . „ Balance, c/d. . .	100 19,900		By Application and Allotment Ac- count . . . „ First Call Account „ Second Call Ac- count . . .	5,000 10,000 5,000
		£20,000			£20,000
			19.. Dec. 1	By Balance, b/d. . .	19,900

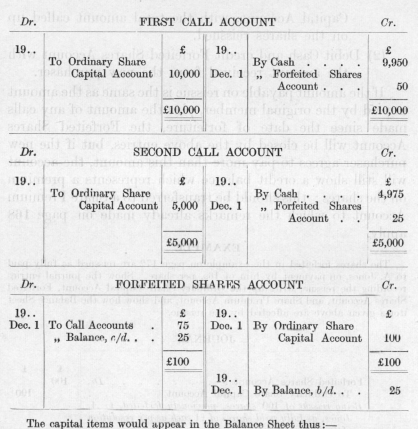

Dr.   FIRST CALL ACCOUNT   Cr.

19..		£	19..		£
	To Ordinary Share			By Cash	9,950
	Capital Account	10,000	Dec. 1	„ Forfeited Shares	
				Account . . .	50
		£10,000			£10,000

Dr.   SECOND CALL ACCOUNT   Cr.

19..		£	19..		£
	To Ordinary Share			By Cash	4,975
	Capital Account	5,000	Dec. 1	„ Forfeited Shares	
				Account . .	25
		£5,000			£5,000

Dr.   FORFEITED SHARES ACCOUNT   Cr.

19..		£	19..		£
Dec. 1	To Call Accounts .	75	Dec. 1	By Ordinary Share	
	„ Balance, c/d. . .	25		Capital Account	100
		£100			£100
			19..		
			Dec. 1	By Balance, b/d. . .	25

The capital items would appear in the Balance Sheet thus :—

                                         £   £

AUTHORISED CAPITAL :—
   20,000 Ordinary Shares of £1 each   .   .   20,000

ISSUED CAPITAL :—
   20,000 Ordinary Shares of £1 each, fully called .   20,000
   Less Shares forfeited   100
                                           19,900
FORFEITED SHARES ACCOUNT   25

If, as is usual, the directors have power to reissue the forfeited shares, they may do so by selling them to a new purchaser for any sum they can obtain which, together with the amount previously received from the original holder, is not less than the called-up value of the shares on the date when they are reissued. The liability to pay future calls is taken by the purchaser.

Upon reissue the necessary entries are—

(1) Debit Forfeited Shares Account and credit Share

Capital Account, with the total amount called up on the shares reissued.

(2) Debit Cash and credit Forfeited Shares Account with the amount received from the new purchaser.

If the amount payable on reissue is the same as the amount unpaid by the original member, plus the amount of any calls made since the date of forfeiture, the Forfeited Shares Account will be closed by the above entries, but if the new purchaser agrees to pay more than this amount, the account will still show a credit balance which represents a premium on the shares ; this should be transferred to a Share Premium Account to which the remarks already made on page 168 apply.

EXAMPLE

The shares forfeited in the example on page 172 are reissued as fully paid to A. Jones, on payment by him of 16s. per share. Show the journal entries recording the reissue, write up the Ordinary Share Capital Account, Forfeited Shares Account, and Share Premium Account, and show how the Balance Sheet items given above are affected by the reissue.

JOURNAL

	£	£
Forfeited Shares Account . . . . Dr.	100	
To Ordinary Share Capital Account		100
Being reissue of 100 shares, previously forfeited, to A. Jones, as fully paid shares of £1 each as per resolution of the directors dated . . . , 19 . .		
Cash . . . . Dr.	80	
To Forfeited Shares Account		80
Being cash paid by A. Jones in respect of the above 100 shares, issued at 16s. per share.		
Forfeited Shares Account . . . . Dr.	5	
To Share Premium Account		5
Being transfer of premium of 1s. per share, payable on reissue of the above shares.		

Dr.	ORDINARY SHARE CAPITAL ACCOUNT		Cr.
	£		£
To Balance, c/d.	20,000	By Balance, b/d. . . .	19,900
		„ Forfeited Shares Account	100
	£20,000		£20,000
		By Balance, b/d . . .	20,000

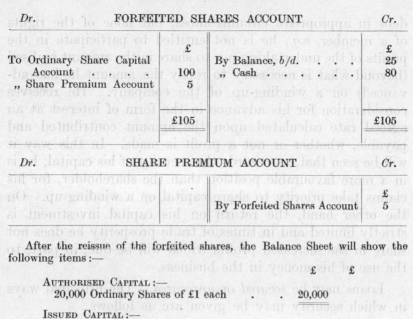

Dr. FORFEITED SHARES ACCOUNT *Cr.*

	£		£
To Ordinary Share Capital Account	100	By Balance, *b/d.* . . .	25
„ Share Premium Account	5	„ Cash	80
	£105		£105

Dr. SHARE PREMIUM ACCOUNT *Cr.*

			£
		By Forfeited Shares Account	5

After the reissue of the forfeited shares, the Balance Sheet will show the following items :—

	£	£
AUTHORISED CAPITAL :—		
20,000 Ordinary Shares of £1 each . .	20,000	
ISSUED CAPITAL :—		
20,000 Ordinary Shares of £1 each, fully paid	20,000	
SHARE PREMIUM ACCOUNT		5

Marshalling the Liabilities.

There are two recognised methods of arranging the entries on the " liabilities " side of the Balance Sheet. In the first method the liabilities are shown in the order in which they rank for payment, Capital being placed last of all. The second method shows the liabilities in order of permanence, Capital being placed first, followed by long-term liabilities, and showing current liabilities last. Sole traders and partnerships usually adopt the first method, although sometimes the second method is followed. Limited companies almost invariably adopt the second method.

Fixed Liabilities.

The balance of the contributed capital, in all kinds of businesses, is supplied from outside sources in the form of loans. A person who advances money to a company in this way does not thereby constitute himself a member of the company. His status is that of a creditor ; and as such he acquires all the rights of a creditor, *e.g.*, to sue for his debt in appropriate circumstances, but none of the rights of a member, *e.g.*, he is not entitled to participate in the profits of the undertaking nor to share in the amount realised (beyond what is necessary to repay the amount he has advanced) on a winding-up of the company. He receives consideration for his advance in the form of interest at an agreed rate calculated upon the amount contributed and payable, whether or not a profit is made. In this way it will be seen that, as regards the security of his capital, he is in a more favourable position than the shareholder, for his claims take priority to share capital on a winding-up. On the other hand, the return on his capital investment is strictly limited and in times of trade prosperity he does not share in the increased profits which will be due, in part, to the use of his money in the business.

Loans may be *secured* or *unsecured*. The principal ways in which security may be given are as follows :—

(1) *A Fixed Charge* on an asset or assets belonging to the borrower.

The characteristic of a fixed charge is that a specific and identified property is charged and the rights of the lender are rights over that particular property. Consequently, any right or charge subsequently given over that property will be subject to the prior right conferred by the fixed charge. The manner of creating a fixed charge differs according to the property charged. In the case of land the charge is created by a legal or equitable mortgage, whereby the lender as mortgagee is granted a legal estate or equitable interest in the property charged, though subject to that the property remains vested in the borrower ; in the case of choses in action,* *e.g.*, shares, the fixed charge takes the form of a transfer, subject to the borrower's right to redeem. Though the effect of a fixed charge is generally to leave the borrower in beneficial enjoyment of the property, he cannot

* A legal term used to embrace rights enforceable by action and not by physical possession.

waste the property or do any act calculated to reduce the security, and though he can sell the property he can only sell it subject to the charge. If the charge is created by a legal mortgage of land the mortgagee is entitled to go into possession. The Law of Property Act, 1925, confers a number of remedies upon mortgagees and states the events upon which the remedies become exercisable. The instrument of charge frequently modifies the statutory provisions. Generally, the result is that on the borrower falling into arrear with his payment of interest for a specified time, or on his failure to repay the loan within a certain time after a demand for repayment has been made, the lender can sell the property charged or appoint a receiver thereof in order to recover the moneys lent. Where the lender sells the property under the mortgage he recoups the principal, interest and costs owing and holds any balance of the proceeds upon trust for the borrower.

(2) *A Floating Charge* on all the assets, or a particular class of assets, for the time being of a company.

The main characteristic of a floating charge is that, notwithstanding the charge, the company is able to deal freely with the assets charged in the ordinary course of business, so that, for example, it may create a fixed charge over a certain specific asset or assets even though such assets are already comprised in a floating charge, and the fixed charge may have priority over the floating charge. The rights of a lender who takes a floating charge are not rights in any defined or specific assets, for when his rights become exercisable, although they will extend to all the assets generally described in the charge, the assets may have altered considerably in form and detail. A floating charge is a useful manner of charging those assets which from their nature are not conveniently made the subject of a fixed charge, *e.g.*, stock-in-trade and book debts.

When it becomes necessary for the lender to enforce his security [*e.g.*, when a winding-up order is made against the company, or when the company defaults in payment of interest, or when, for any other reason (as specified in the instrument of charge) the security of the lender is jeopardised] the charge is said to *crystallise*. It then becomes a fixed charge on all the assets charged, *i.e.*, on all the assets of the company, or on those particular assets which fall within the description of the class charged, as the case may be, at the moment of crystallisation, and whether the individual assets were in existence or not when the charge was created. Thus, a floating charge is a method of charging future property as well as existing property and it may even be made to extend to uncalled capital. The usual manner of enforcing the security is by the appointment of a receiver to act on behalf of the lender. Such appointment is made either by the lender himself (under powers given by the instrument of charge) or by the Court on the application of the lender. On the appointment of a receiver the company loses its right to deal with the assets. Frequently, a receiver is empowered by the terms of his appointment to perform acts of management—as carrying on the business—in which case he is a " Receiver and Manager ". In this event, the powers of the directors cease, the company loses its rights to deal with the assets and the whole conduct of affairs devolves on the receiver and manager.*

(3) The property of third parties may, by arrangement, be charged on behalf of the borrower or the debt may be guaranteed by a third party. Thus the directors of a company may deposit their own investments with a bank as security for an advance

* The terms " fixed " and " floating " as applied to assets and charges respectively must not be confused. Fixed charges nearly always attach to fixed assets but floating charges are by no means restricted to floating (or current) assets—they nearly always cover *all* the assets, subject to any prior fixed charges on some or all of the fixed assets.

to the company, or they may guarantee the account, *i.e.*, give the lender recourse to them for the amount of the advance if the company should default. This may be the only security given or it may be in addition to such security as the borrower is able to give. In the latter event it is known as *collateral security*, because it " runs side by side " with the main obligation of the principal debtor.

An unsecured loan ranks *pari passu* with the ordinary trade creditors and enjoys no priority, except over the shareholders of a limited company, who can receive no return in the event of liquidation until all the creditors, secured and unsecured, have been repaid.

Debentures.

A debenture is a bond, usually under the company's seal and secured by a charge on the company's property or undertaking, bearing a fixed rate of interest, and being either repayable within a specified period or on a specified date, or irredeemable during the existence of the company.

Where an issue of debentures is made to the public, it is usual for a *Trust Deed* to be drawn up, appointing certain persons to act as trustees for the debenture holders. The deed conveys to the trustees the legal estate in those assets which are the subject of a fixed charge and, in addition, usually gives the trustees power to appoint a receiver in the event of a breach of certain covenants in the deed, and to summon meetings of debenture holders. The creation of a Trust Deed strengthens the position of the debenture holders, since the trustees are appointed to protect their interests and, should the security of the holders be in jeopardy, can take action more promptly than the body of debenture holders could.

Since a company might, by charging all its assets as security for debentures or other loans, seriously prejudice the position of unsecured creditors, particulars of all charges created by a company must within twenty-one days be registered at Bush House, where they are open to inspection. In default of registration, the charge is void against the liquidator and any creditor of the company.

Although debentures are usually issued in consideration of a cash payment made to the company at the time of issue (or a series of payments as in a public issue of shares) they may be issued in satisfaction of any existing claim against the company, *e.g.*, a creditor who cannot obtain immediate payment of his debt may agree to take debentures instead. In this connection, however, the provisions of Section 322 of the Companies Act, 1948, must be noted :—

"Where a company is being wound up, a floating charge on the undertaking or property of the company created within twelve months of the commencement of the winding up shall, unless it is proved that the company immediately after the creation of the charge was solvent, be invalid, except to the amount of any cash paid to the company at the time of or subsequently to the creation of, and in consideration for, the charge, together with interest on that amount at the rate of five per cent. per annum or such other rate as may for the time being be prescribed by order of the Treasury."

Thus a company cannot fraudulently prefer one class of creditors at the expense of the general body of unsecured creditors by issuing debentures when it is on the point of going into liquidation. Debentures nearly always give a floating charge on all the assets of the company and, in addition, a fixed charge may be given on some or all of the more permanent assets such as freehold land and buildings. This leaves the company free to deal with its current assets in the ordinary course of business but prevents it from realising, or giving any prior charge on, the assets which have been specifically charged in favour of the debenture holders. Debentures may also be issued in the form of stock, the main difference between debentures and debenture stock being that a debenture must be transferred in its entirety while debenture stock may be transferred in whole or in part ; but the Articles often provide that any transfer of stock must not involve a fraction of a specified amount.

Debentures may be—

(1) Payable to a registered holder (with or without interest coupons payable to bearer) ; or

(2) Payable to bearer simply (with or without power for the bearer to be registered as holder).*

The practical effect of issuing debentures is that the holders—

(a) Receive their interest whether or not profits are made ; and

(b) In the event of liquidation or when the company can no longer pay the interest without realising its fixed assets, have a first claim on the proceeds of the assets charged in their favour, ranking before the ordinary unsecured trade creditors.

A public issue of debentures is made in a way that is very similar to the procedure in an issue of shares. A prospectus is prepared and issued, application and allotment sheets are compiled, allotment letters are issued, and so on, in the same way as for an issue of shares. Any premiums received on an issue of debentures should be treated in a similar manner to premiums on shares, although this is not compulsory under the Companies Act, 1948.

Debentures may be issued at a price below their face value, that is, at a discount, but the liability of the company is for the full amount of the debentures, and, therefore, the full amount must be shown as a liability in the company's books and accounts. The amount of the discount is debited to a Debenture Discount Account, and must be shown, separately, as a fictitious asset in the Balance Sheet until written off. This discount is usually written off out of profits during the life of the debentures, e.g., when debentures are to be redeemed at the end of, say, ten years, then one-tenth of the discount might be written off annually.†

Interest accrued on debentures or other secured loans is generally shown in the Balance Sheet as an addition to the principal ; alternatively it may be merged with the other provisions for accrued expenses. The former treatment

---

* The exchange control regulations now in force require all bearer securities (including share warrants) to be deposited with an authorised depositary, e.g., a bank.

† The redemption of debentures and an alternative treatment of discount on debentures will be considered in Chapter VI.

reflects the fact that the security given covers principal and interest; thus the liability will be shown in the following way :—

	£	£
10,000 5% Debentures of £10 each . .	100,000	
Add Interest accrued	1,250	
		101,250

Current Liabilities.

The presentation of current liabilities in a Balance Sheet does not raise any important question of principle. The accountant will be chiefly concerned to see that the grouping and description of the items are not misleading. Thus, trade creditors (*i.e.*, open balances on the Purchases Ledger) will be shown separately from a bank overdraft, which in turn should not be grouped with other temporary loans. Composite items such as " Sundry Creditors, Provisions, Loans, and Credit Balances " should be avoided and in the case of a limited company are now illegal.

Current liabilities may be secured in any of the ways applicable to fixed liabilities : bank overdrafts, in particular, will nearly always be secured. Quite a common method of securing bank overdrafts is to issue debentures of a face value in excess of the limit of the advance. In such cases, the measure of the company's liability at any given date is the amount due to the bank on the overdrawn account and *not* the nominal value of the debentures issued as collateral security. The transaction will be shown in the Balance Sheet by means of a note, thus—

	£
Bank Overdraft	5,963

(Secured by the issue of 10,000 Debentures of £1 each)

Taxation.

Modern opinion recommends that the amounts set aside in respect of taxation should be disclosed in the Balance Sheet as follows :—

(1) The amount of Income Tax payable in respect of the liability for the current fiscal year (based on the profits of the preceding accounting year) will be shown as a current liability provided that the amount can be determined with substantial accur-

acy ; if the amount cannot be so determined, the sum set aside will be classified as a provision.

(2) The amount of Income Tax payable for the following fiscal year (based on the profits of the current accounting year) will be shown as or included in the amount of the " Reserve for Future Income Tax ".

(3) The amount of Profits Tax payable in respect of the profits of the current accounting year will be shown as a current liability if the amount can be determined with substantial accuracy, otherwise it will be shown as a provision. The amount may be included with the current liability or provision, as the case may be, for Income Tax, or it may preferably be shown as a separate figure.*

Working Capital.

If the current assets of a concern exceed its current liabilities, it is able to meet its debts as they become due for payment and is therefore solvent. A company is solvent if it can pay its liabilities to outside creditors, although a considerable proportion of the shareholders' capital may have been lost and may be represented by a debit balance on Profit and Loss Account. This question of solvency is relatively of more importance to a prospective creditor than a consideration of the Balance Sheet as a whole. The excess of current assets over current liabilities is known as *working capital* and it may be regarded as a first essential for every business to have adequate liquid resources and, therefore, working capital.

The importance of working capital receives statutory recognition in the Companies Act, 1948, which provides that where shares are offered to the public for subscription, particulars must be given in the prospectus as to—

(1) The minimum amount which, in the opinion of the directors, must be raised by the issue of those shares in order to provide the sums, or, if any part

* The distinction between the terms " provision " and " reserve " is discussed in Chapter VI.

thereof is to be defrayed in any other manner,* the balance of the sums, required to be provided in respect of each of the following matters :—

(*a*) The purchase price of any property purchased or to be purchased which is to be defrayed in whole or in part out of the proceeds of the issue;

(*b*) Any preliminary expenses payable by the company and any commission so payable to any person in consideration of his agreeing to subscribe for, or of his procuring or agreeing to procure subscriptions for, any shares in the company;

(*c*) The repayment of any moneys borrowed by the company in respect of the foregoing matters ;

(*d*) *Working capital* ; and

(2) The amounts to be provided in respect of the matters aforesaid otherwise than out of the proceeds of the issue and the sources out of which those amounts are to be provided (Section 4, Part I, Fourth Schedule, Companies Act, 1948).

Furthermore, it is provided that no allotment of shares shall be made until applications have been received equal at least to the " minimum subscription " mentioned in the prospectus (Section 47).

Computation of Working Capital.

The most important factors to be taken into consideration when computing the amount of working capital necessary in a new business are as follows :—

(*a*) The period occupied in producing or manufacturing goods before sales can commence and the period of credit allowed to customers before cash will be received in respect of the initial sales.

(*b*) The cost of raw materials, wages and fluctuating

---

* For example, the company may have been formed to take over an existing business, part of the consideration being an allotment of shares to the vendors.

overhead expenses estimated as likely to be incurred during the above periods.

(c) The fixed expenses of the business for the same periods.

(d) Any payments which have to be made in advance, e.g., insurance ;

(e) The amount of selling and distributive expenses for the same periods ; and

(f) The amount of stock-in-trade which must ordinarily be carried.

The amount thus ascertained may be reduced by the amount of credit which will be allowed by suppliers to the business ; but, on the other hand, some addition should be made to allow for contingencies and reasonable expansion.

When the necessary capital has been raised, the amount of working capital ceases to be an estimate, and is the actual amount of cash and other current assets available when all the fixed assets necessary for the purpose of the business have been acquired.

The working capital of a business is continually fluctuating, being increased by transactions which involve the receipt of money by the company, and being reduced by transactions which involve the payment of money.

The factors operating to *increase* working capital include :—

(1) The earning of profits.

(2) The raising of fresh capital or loans.

(3) The sale of fixed assets.

The factors operating to *reduce* working capital include :—

(1) The incurring of losses.

(2) Capital expenditure on fixed assets.

(3) The redemption of preference shares, debentures or loans.

(4) Making long-term investments or granting loans.

(5) The payment of dividends.

(6) The payment of taxation liabilities.

The amount of working capital is not affected by transactions which are represented by transfers between ledger accounts and which do not involve the payment of money, such as writing off preliminary expenses or providing for depreciation out of profits, or transferring an amount out of Profit and Loss Account or General Reserve to Capital Redemption Reserve Fund upon the redemption of preference shares.

At any given date, the amount of working capital should be ascertainable from a Balance Sheet drawn up on that date. When the Balance Sheet is presented in the customary form, some additions and subtractions may be necessary. If it is desired to show the working capital at a glance, however, the following arrangement may be adopted :—

MANUFACTURING COMPANY, LTD.
BALANCE SHEET
AS AT 31ST DECEMBER, 19..

	£	£
Fixed Assets :—		
Goodwill at cost		10,000
Freehold Property at cost	16,000	
Less Depreciation	2,500	
		13,500
Machinery and Plant at cost	4,320	
Less Depreciation	1,320	
		3,000
Investments in Subsidiary Companies :—		
Shares in *K*. Ltd. at cost	850	
Shares in *X*. Ltd. at cost	1,050	
		1,900
TOTAL FIXED ASSETS		28,400
Deduct Mortgage on Freehold Property	10,000	
Interest accrued on Mortgage	500	
		10,500
FREE FIXED ASSETS		17,900
	7,000	
Liquid and Other Current Assets :—	12,000	
Stock in Trade at cost	1,600	
Sundry Debtors	70	
Cash at Bank		
Cash in Hand	20,670	
£		
Deduct Sundry Creditors 4,670		
Provision for Bad Debts 500		
	5,170	
WORKING CAPITAL		15,500
Total Net Assets		**£33,400**
Represented by Capital and Undistributed Profits as follows:—		
Share Capital, Authorised and Issued :—		
10,000 6% Preference Shares of £1 each fully paid . . .		10,000
150,000 Ordinary Shares of 2s. each, fully paid. . . .		15,000
		25,000
General Reserve		5,000
Profit and Loss Account :—		
Balance as at 1st January, 19.	2,040	
Net Profit for the Year	1,360	
		3,400
		£33,400

The above form is worthy of close study as it is now
followed in general outline by many public companies (see
Chapter X) : it was suggested, as long ago as 1932, by

the late Lord Plender, a past President of the Institute of
Chartered Accountants in England and Wales.

A steadily increasing amount of working capital is generally indicative of successful trading whereas a decreasing
amount *may* be indicative of losses but may, alternatively,
be due to expansion of the business (*i.e.*, increase in fixed
assets) without a corresponding increase in share or loan
capital.

It has already been stated on page 183 that the measurement of working capital is a test of solvency.   If current
assets exceed current liabilities by a reasonable margin, a
concern should have little difficulty in meeting its current
liabilities as they fall due for payment.   In this connection
it may be observed that there is an important distinction
between the *absolute* amount of working capital and its
relative amount : the distinction is illustrated by the following example :—

	Business X.	Business Y.
	£	£
Stock	60,000	100,000
Cash and Debtors	20,000	20,000
	80,000	120,000
Creditors	60,000	100,000
Working Capital	£20,000	£20,000

The absolute amount of working capital is £20,000 in each
case but *X* is in a relatively much sounder position than *Y*.
A fall of 20 per cent. in the price level of the commodities
dealt in by *Y* will eliminate its working capital and it will
almost certainly find itself in financial difficulties.   *X*, on
the other hand, can experience a fall of $33\frac{1}{3}$ per cent. before
its working capital is absorbed and (except over a comparatively long period) such a catastrophe is a very rare
occurrence.

The unsatisfactory state of affairs disclosed by *Y* may
usually be ascribed to *overtrading*.   That is to say, a concern
commences with a working capital which is satisfactory both
as to amount and ratio to current liabilities.   Business and

the concern's credit are both good and it finds it can increase its sales considerably. This necessitates the purchase of a considerable quantity of raw materials, and as there is a "time lag" between the purchase of the raw materials and the sale of the finished product, the immediate effect is a large increase in creditors and a corresponding increase in stock and work-in-progress. The absolute amount of working capital is not affected but its ratio to current liabilities probably falls to a dangerous level. When the boom has spent itself there is a sudden drop in values and insolvency results, i.e., technical insolvency in that the concern is unable to meet its commitments as they fall due out of its liquid resources.

Overtrading is always likely to lead to this unsatisfactory position because of the well-known tendency of prices to fluctuate down more rapidly than up. In normal times prices of an article tend to rise slowly until they reach the point where competition is attracted. There is a sudden burst of activity in which all the concerns manufacturing the article produce to the limit of their capacity in order to make the most of the boom while it lasts. As a result the market is flooded and prices fall precipitously.

Contingent Liabilities.

Certain transactions may result in liabilities which are not directly represented by credit balances in the books. The best example is afforded by discounted bills of exchange. When a trader discounts a bill receivable either with his bank or with some other person, he parts with one asset—a bill— and receives another—cash—in its place. If the bill is duly met on maturity by the acceptor the transaction is finally closed ; but if it is dishonoured the trader will immediately become liable on it as drawer or endorser. It is true that if he meets this liability his right against prior parties will be revived, so that the additional liability is (on paper) balanced by an additional asset, but the very fact that the bill has been dishonoured is direct evidence that the full discharge of the bill is, at the least, doubtful. The trader clearly cannot rely on the revival of the debt as sufficient protection against his own possible liability and must always bear in mind the chance that he may have to meet the bill himself without effective remedy. Such a liability is known as a *contingent liability*.

It is usual to refer to contingent liabilities in a note placed at the foot of the Balance Sheet, thus :—

(There is a contingent liability in respect of bills discounted amounting to £. . .)

In the Balance Sheets of banks, however, any possible liability of the bank on bills which it has endorsed or accepted * is shown on the liabilities side of the Balance Sheet, the corresponding liability of customers to the bank being shown among the assets, thus :—

	£			£
Acceptances and Endorsements on account of Customers, *per contra* .	. 250,613		Liability of Customers on Acceptances and Endorsements, *per contra* † .	. 250,613

Other examples of contingent liabilities are :—

(1) *Calls on Partly Paid Shares*. Some authorities consider that the contingent liability to meet future calls on investments held is indicated sufficiently by describing the investments as partly paid, thus :

£

1,000 Ordinary Shares of £1 each in *A.B.* Ltd., 10s. per share paid up, at cost 500

Others consider that a footnote should also be made thus :—

(There is a contingent liability of £500 in respect of calls on partly paid shares.)

(2) *Maintenance and Repair Agreements*. Some manufacturing concerns sell their products under an agreement which provides for free maintenance and repair for a certain period. Full provision should be made for the expected cost of completing the agreements outstanding at the date of the Balance Sheet, on the basis of past experience, and, to this extent, the liability may be regarded as an actual

---

* Bills which have been discounted for customers and are still held by the bank are assets and are shown as such.

† Any provision for bad or doubtful debts that may be considered necessary will be included with other items on the liabilities side.

one. The possible or contingent liability, however, is obviously greater than any reasonable estimate of the probable or actual liability ; this should be recognised by a general footnote, thus :—

> (There is a contingent liability in respect of maintenance and repair agreements outstanding at the above date. Full provision has been made for the estimated amount of such liability.)

(3) *Actions at Law.* If the concern is known to be involved in litigation at the date of the Balance Sheet and there is a possibility that costs or damages will be incurred, it is advisable to add a note to that effect.

Apart from contingent liabilities, other classes of liabilities of an uncertain nature which it is advisable to indicate by a note on the Balance Sheet are :—

(1) Commitments in respect of purchases for future delivery, made some considerable time before the goods are required ; and

(2) Contracts in respect of forward sales of goods not yet manufactured.

In the case of exceptional contracts for future delivery, it is suggested that the note on the Balance Sheet should include details of the volume of such commitments and the potential profit or loss arising therefrom (*Rex* v. *Bishirgian and Others*, 1936).

Under the Companies Act, 1948, the general nature of any contingent liabilities *and* commitments for capital expenditure and, if material, their amount or estimated amount, must be noted on the Balance Sheet.

Contingent Assets.

Although it is customary to make a note of contingent liabilities on the Balance Sheet of a concern, it is less common, probably for reasons of conservatism, to find that similar disclosure has been made of contingent assets, *e.g.*, an option to apply for shares in another company on favourable terms. Strictly speaking, however, disclosure should be made of both contingent liabilities *and* contingent assets, as the omission of the latter may, in certain circumstances, result in the Balance Sheet giving a materially misleading impression as to the prosperity or otherwise of the concern.

Insolvency.

When a trader is unable to meet his debts as they become due, he is insolvent and may, either on his own petition or on that of a creditor, be made bankrupt. Alternatively, if the creditors consent, he may enter into a Deed of Arrangement and convey his property to a trustee for the benefit of his creditors, the expense and stigma of bankruptcy thus being avoided. A detailed consideration of the law of insolvency is beyond the scope of this book, but its effect, as regards the claims of creditors, will be considered.

While a business is being carried on, liabilities will be discharged in the ordinary course of trading, and the question of priority does not arise. In bankruptcy, however, each claim, or " proof ", must be considered on its merits and while some debts are preferred to those of ordinary trade creditors, others are deferred.

The following debts enjoy statutory priority and must be paid in full (or *pari passu* among themselves if the assets are deficient) before any distribution is made to the general body of unsecured creditors.

(1) Local rates (for the twelve months preceding the Receiving Order).

(2) Assessed taxes (*e.g.*, Income Tax, Sur-Tax and Profits Tax). (But not for more than one year of assessment which must end not later than the 5th April preceding the date of the Receiving Order. If more than one year's assessment is in arrear, the Inland Revenue may choose which one shall be treated as preferential.)

(3) Wages and salaries of any clerk, workman, etc., for a period not exceeding four months prior to the Receiving Order, and to an amount not exceeding £200 for any employee.

(4) Contributions payable under the National Insurance Acts (for the twelve months preceding the Receiving Order).

(5) The amount of Purchase Tax becoming due to the Crown during the twelve months preceding the Receiving Order.

Certain debts rank even before the above : these are known as " pre-preferential debts " and include the following :—

(1) Any funds of a Trustee Savings Bank or Friendly Society in the hands of the debtor as a trustee or officer of the bank or society.

(2) The proportionate part of the premium paid by an apprentice or articled clerk where the period of service is terminated by the bankruptcy.

(3) The funeral and testamentary expenses of a deceased insolvent.

(4) The expenses of a trustee under a Deed of Arrangement which has been set aside by a subsequent bankruptcy.

The landlord usually receives preferential treatment by virtue of his power to distrain on furniture and goods found on the debtor's premises—this right is not lost on bankruptcy but is restricted to six months' rent accrued due before the adjudication.

Secured creditors rely primarily on their security, and if that is sufficient they receive payment in full. If the security is insufficient they are known as partly secured creditors and may prove with the unsecured creditors for the balance of their debt.

Deferred creditors include the following :—

(1) Persons who have advanced money to the debtor in return for a rate of interest varying with the profits.

(2) The vendor of the goodwill of a business who is to receive as consideration a share in the profits of the business.

H

(3) A wife who has advanced money to her husband for use in his business or trade, or *vice versa.*

The first duty of a debtor against whom a Receiving Order has been made is to prepare a Statement of Affairs in proper form, which is filed with the Official Receiver and circulated to all known creditors. The Statement of Affairs is, in some respects, similar to a Balance Sheet, since it sets out the assets and liabilities of the debtor on a given date. Assets, however, are shown at their estimated realisable value while liabilities are so arranged that those having priority or security are shown separately. The final balance of the Statement shows the estimated deficiency of assets to meet the claims of unsecured creditors, or, in some cases, the estimated surplus. The deficiency or surplus is explained in a separate Deficiency (or Surplus) Account.

Liquidation.

Limited companies are " wound up " when they are unable to pay their debts or when they have completed their purpose and the members wish to realise the assets. There are three types of *liquidation* :—

(1) Voluntary (*i.e.*, by resolution of the company itself) ;

(2) Compulsory (*i.e.*, by Order of the Court) ;

(3) Under supervision of the Court (*i.e.*, commencing as a voluntary liquidation but continuing under the supervision of the Court).

Voluntary liquidation may take the form of—

(a) A members' voluntary winding up, if the directors make a statutory declaration that the company will be able to pay its debts in full within twelve months from the commencement of the winding up.

(b) A creditors' voluntary winding up.

In the first case, a " liquidator " is appointed by the members ; in the second his appointment is under the control of the creditors.

Preferential debts in liquidation are similar to those in bankruptcy ; and there are no deferred debts. Where debentures carrying a floating charge have been issued, the debenture holders will have a prior claim on the assets, after preferential debts and specific charges, *e.g.*, mortgages, have been satisfied.

The directors of a company which is being wound up compulsorily must submit a Statement of Affairs in the prescribed form. The prescribed form of statement shows the assets at their estimated realisable values, distinguishing between assets charged and not charged, and classifies the liabilities under the headings of secured, preferential, debenture-holders and unsecured; the statement thus distinguishes between the deficiency (or surplus) as regards creditors and the deficiency (or surplus) as regards members.

A company which is being wound up voluntarily is under no statutory obligation to submit a Statement of Affairs to the members or the creditors, but it is usual to prepare one, following the official form used in compulsory liquidation as closely as may be possible.

The total deficiency is explained in a Deficiency Account, as in the case of bankruptcy. In compulsory liquidation, the Deficiency Account must cover a period of three years preceding the date of the winding-up order, or, where the company has been incorporated for less than three years, from the date of incorporation.

Reduction of Capital.

It has already been shown in this Chapter that the Capital Account of a limited company must remain intact at the amount subscribed by its shareholders, and cannot be reduced by being debited with losses incurred. Where, however, heavy losses have been suffered, so that a considerable portion of the shareholders' capital has been irretrievably lost, the company may, subject to the conditions outlined below, apply to the Court for permission to reduce its share capital, and utilise the amount thus made available in extinguishing any debit balance on Profit and Loss Account, and in writing down any assets which are considered to be shown in the books in excess of present going concern values.

The procedure to be adopted in such circumstances is outlined in Sections 66 to 71 of the Companies Act, 1948, and may be summarised in the following manner :—

(1) A scheme showing the amounts to be written off the company's capital (distinguishing the amount to be written off shares of different classes), and the manner in which the reduction is to be applied to the various assets is prepared and submitted to the shareholders, who must approve the scheme by means of a special resolution.

(2) After the special resolution has been passed, a petition is made to the Court for sanction of the scheme.

(3) If satisfied that all creditors entitled to object to the reduction have either consented or been paid or secured, the Court may make an order confirming the reduction on such terms as it thinks fit.

(4) After sanction by the Court, a copy of the order, with particulars of the reduction and accompanied by copies of the special resolution as passed and confirmed by the shareholders, must be filed with the Registrar of Companies.

(5) The old share certificates must be called in from the shareholders and endorsed with particulars of the reduction, or alternatively, the old certificates must be cancelled and new ones issued.

(6) Particulars of the reduction should be endorsed on each member's account in the Share Register.

The rights of the different classes of shareholders among themselves must be considered in determining the amount to be written off each class of share. Thus, if the preference shares have a right, in the event of a winding-up, to a return of capital in priority to the ordinary shares, then the whole or the major portion of the loss is frequently borne by the holders of the ordinary and the deferred shares (if any).

Where, as in most cases, it is equitable that the ordinary shares shall bear the loss, they should never be entirely eliminated, though they may have to be reduced to a very small nominal value (*e.g.*, 1s. 0d.). By this means the ordinary shareholders retain some interest in the business and can thus reap some benefit from a future improvement in the profit-earning capacity of the business. Where part of the loss is borne by the preference shareholders, it is usual to compensate them by increasing their dividend rights or by the allotment of ordinary shares (as reduced in value), thus enabling the preference shareholders to participate in any surplus profits. Otherwise the ordinary shares retain the whole of the " equity " (*i.e.*, the right to receive surplus profits) and do not suffer any effective loss under the capital reduction scheme, for the reduction of the nominal paid-up value of these shares merely gives effect to losses which have already taken place, and does not make the position of the ordinary shareholders any worse than it was before the reduction took place. In fact, the position of the ordinary shareholders is usually improved after a capital reduction scheme in that the amount of the prior ranking preference capital may be reduced and arrears of cumulative preference dividends reduced (or capitalised), while the reduction in the value of fixed assets may result in lower depreciation charges in future.

These, however, are only the general principles, and in practice any scheme which does not appear to bear too hardly on any particular class or classes of shareholders will receive the sanction of the Court.

The method of treatment in the financial books is to credit a Capital Reduction Account with the total amount of the reduction, the capital account of each class of share affected being debited with the portion of the reduction relative thereto. The debit balance of the Profit and Loss Account and any amounts written off assets are debited to the Capital Reduction Account, the respective assets accounts being credited.

EXAMPLE

The Balance Sheet of Manufacturers, Ltd., shows the following position :—

BALANCE SHEET AS AT —— 19..

	£		£
Authorised Capital :—		Freehold Premises at cost.	4,500
20,000 5% Preference		Plant and Machinery at	
Shares of £1 each . .	20,000	cost	4,500
20,000 Ordinary Shares of		Stock-in-Trade	9,400
£1 each	20,000	Sundry Debtors . . .	3,600
		Cash at Bank	4,375
	£40,000	Profit and Loss Account .	5,025
Issued Capital :—			
10,000 5% Preference			
Shares of £1 each, fully			
paid	10,000		
15,000 Ordinary Shares of			
£1 each, fully paid . .	15,000		
	25,000		
Sundry Creditors . . .	6,400		
	£31,400		£31,400

The Preference Shares are preferential as to return of capital on winding-up. Resolutions are passed and sanctioned by the Court :—

"That the Preference and Ordinary Shares be reduced by 2s. 6d. and 7s. 6d. per share respectively, to be applied as follows—

Profit and Loss Account	.	.	.	.	£5,025
Freehold Premises	.	.	.	.	500
Plant and Machinery	.	.	.	.	1,350."

Make the entries necessary to give effect to the above, and prepare the new Balance Sheet.

JOURNAL

			£	£
19..	Sundries	Dr.		
	To Capital Reduction Account			6,875
	Preference Share Capital Account		1,250	
	Ordinary Share Capital Account		5,625	
	Being reduction of 2s. 6d. per share on 10,000 5% Preference Shares of £1 each and 7s. 6d. per share on 15,000 Ordinary Shares of £1 each in accordance with special resolution passed on —— 19– and sanctioned by Order of the Court dated —— 19–.			
	Capital Reduction Account . . . . . . Dr.		6,875	
	To Sundries			
	Profit and Loss Account			5,025
	Freehold Premises Account			500
	Plant and Machinery Account			1,350
	Being amounts written off in accordance with special resolution passed on —— 19– and sanctioned by Order of the Court dated —— 19–.			

Dr.   CAPITAL REDUCTION ACCOUNT   Cr.

19–		£	19–		£
	To Profit and Loss Account	5,025		By Preference Share Capital Account.	1,250
	,, Freehold Premises Account	500		,, Ordinary Share Capital Account.	5,625
	,, Plant and Machinery Account . .	1,350			
		£6,875			£6,875

Dr.   5% PREFERENCE SHARE CAPITAL ACCOUNT   Cr.

19–		£	19–		£
	To Capital Reduction Account . .	1,250		By Balance, b/d. . .	10,000
	,, Balance, c/d. . .	8,750			
		£10,000			£10,000
				By Balance, b/d. . .	8,750

Dr.   ORDINARY SHARE CAPITAL ACCOUNT   Cr.

19–		£	19–		£
	To Capital Reduction Account . . .	5,625		By Balance, b/d. . .	15,000
	,, Balance, c/d. . .	9,375			
		£15,000			£15,000
				By Balance, b/d. . .	9,375

ADJUSTED BALANCE SHEET AS AT —— 19–

	£			£	£
Authorised Capital :—			Freehold Premises		
20,000 5% Preference Shares of £1 each reduced, by Order of the Court, to 17s. 6d. each .	17,500		at cost	4,500	
			Less Amount written off . . .	500	4,000
20,000 Ordinary Shares of £1 each reduced, by Order of the Court, to 12s. 6d. each	12,500		Plant and Machinery at cost	4,500	
			Less Amount written off . . .	1,350	
	£30,000				3,150
			Stock-in-Trade		9,400
Issued Capital :—			Sundry Debtors		3,600
10,000 5% Preference Shares of £1 each reduced, by Order of the Court, to 17s. 6d. each .	8,750		Cash at Bank . . .		4,375
			Profit and Loss Account	5,025	
15,000 Ordinary Shares of £1 each reduced, by Order of the Court, to 12s. 6d. each	9,375		Less Amount written off . . .	5,025	—
	18,125				
Sundry Creditors	6,400				
	£24,525				£24,525

NOTE.—The Court may order the Company to add the words "and reduced" to its name for a specified period.

Where a company's capital is in excess of its requirements it may, either with or without extinguishing or reducing the liability on any of its shares, pay off any excess of unemployed share capital (Section 66, Companies Act). In this case Share Capital Account is debited with the amount returned to the shareholders and Cash Account credited, the necessary alterations being also made in the Share Register.

Capital Reconstructions.

Reconstruction is a term used in a very wide sense to express any material alteration in the constitution of a company or in the rights or interests of shareholders, debenture-holders or other creditors. Amalgamations and absorptions (see page 202) as such do not necessarily involve reconstruction but are frequently encountered in reconstruction schemes.

Reconstructions may be found necessary for a number of reasons. A company may be burdened with an accumulation of losses which it is desirable to clear off in order to place the company in a favourable position for the earning of profits and the distribution of dividends (see page 195) ; it may be desirable to raise further capital from existing shareholders by forming a new company and allotting to them partly-paid shares therein ; the company may wish to extend the scope of its Memorandum ; and so on.

Apart from the matters already mentioned in the preceding pages under " Reduction of Capital ", the following points, where appropriate, should be considered in drafting a reconstruction scheme :—

(1) The maintenance of adequate liquid capital. For this purpose a further issue of shares by the new or reconstructed company may be necessary if external liabilities of the old company are to be discharged.

(2) The preservation of the equities of the shareholders. This will depend upon the reasons for the reconstruction. Any accumulated losses will seriously affect the equity of the ordinary shareholders in cases where preference shares are preferential as to capital. In other cases the relative equities of ordinary and

preference shareholders as they existed in the old company should, as far as possible, be maintained in the new company.

(3) Debentures should be satisfied either by repayment or by exchange for a new issue of debentures at a lower rate of interest with a capital compensation, or partly for debentures and partly for shares.

(4) The claims of creditors must be given careful consideration.

(5) The effect on the taxation liability of the company should always be considered. Reconstructions are often necessary when losses have been incurred for several years. For income tax purposes, losses can be carried forward and may substantially reduce the future liability of the company. If the reconstruction scheme involves the liquidation of the old company, this benefit will be lost, as for income tax purposes accumulated losses cannot be carried forward from one company to another.

EXAMPLE

The following is the Balance Sheet of a limited company :—

	£		£
Authorised and Issued Share Capital :—		Goodwill at cost	30,000
100,000 7½% Preference Shares of £1 each, fully paid	100,000	Patents and Trade Marks at cost (£14,000) less depreciation	10,000
200,000 Ordinary Shares of £1 each, fully paid .	200,000	Property, Plant, etc., at cost (£180,000) less depreciation	140,000
	300,000	Stock-in-Trade	12,000
£10,000 6% Debentures . .	10,000	Trade Debtors	15,000
Bank Loan (Secured) . .	23,000	Profit and Loss Account .	138,600
Trade Creditors	12,600		
	£345,600		£345,600

The directors are desirous of reconstructing the company to avoid the weight of interest charges, and to apportion the losses equitably over the various classes of persons concerned.

If consulted by the directors, to what points would you pay particular attention in formulating a scheme ?

Particular attention should be paid to the following points in drafting a scheme for the reconstruction of the company :—

H*

(1) The desirability or otherwise of winding up the existing company. If a new company was formed it would lose the benefit, from a taxation point of view, of the large accumulated losses. On the other hand, a new company would probably be more favourably placed towards obtaining additional capital. The choice of method would obviously depend upon the actual facts, details of which are not given.

(2) The rights of the different classes of shareholders as determined in the Memorandum and Articles of Association, e.g. :—

(a) Are there any arrears of Preference dividends ? (Preference dividends are cumulative unless the Articles provide to the contrary.)

(b) Are the Preference Shares preferential as to capital ? If so, the whole or the greater part of the loss should be borne by the Ordinary Share-holders.

The Articles may contain special provisions as to the rights of shareholders on a winding-up or reorganisation, although any such provisions could be varied by a special resolution.

(3) The rights of the Debenture-holders and whether they are secured or unsecured. Before a scheme could finally be formulated it would be necessary to call a meeting of the Debenture-holders in order to ascertain their attitude towards a reconstruction, the amount of sacrifice (if any) they would be prepared to make, and the satisfaction which they would most readily accept for their debt.

(4) The same considerations would apply to the Bank Loan although, as this is secured, the Bank would probably not be prepared to make any sacrifice. It should be ascertained whether the Bank would be willing to look to the new company or to the reconstructed company for the ultimate repayment of the Loan. Otherwise the scheme would have to be framed with a view to replenish-ing the liquid resources of the company, depleted by repayment of the Bank Loan.

(5) The general attitude of Creditors towards the reconstruction and the composition they would be prepared to accept.

(6) The valuation of assets ; presumably Goodwill is of no value and the other assets should be revalued with a view to ascertaining the full amount of the loss of capital to be written off under the reorganisation.

(7) The state of the money and share markets and the general trade outlook. This would determine whether an issue of capital in the form of shares or deben-tures would be likely to meet with any success and whether any such issue would be advisable from the point of view of possible future profits.

Amalgamations and Absorptions.

Where two or more companies sell their assets to a new company formed for the purpose, the process is generally termed Amalgamation, while where one company is pur-chased by another, the process is generally termed Absorp-tion. In practice, however, the two terms are often used rather loosely when referring to the joining together of two business enterprises.

A Realisation Account should be opened in the books of the business being absorbed or amalgamated (i.e., the transferor company) in order to determine any profit or loss on realisation, thus this account will be debited with the assets taken over by the transferee company and credited with the liabilities acquired by such company and the amount of the purchase price. The remaining balances in the old company's books (*e.g.*, Share Capital Account, General Reserve, Profit and Loss Account, etc.) will be transferred to Sundry Shareholders Account in order to close off such accounts and the amount of the purchase price will be debited to Sundry Shareholders Account. Alternatively, the purchase price can be recorded in a Purchasing Company's Account as a link between the corresponding entries in Realisation Account and Sundry Shareholders Account. The balance on Realisation Account, representing the profit or loss on realisation, is then transferred to Sundry Shareholders Account to complete the closing off of the books of the absorbed or amalgamated company.*

The acquisition of the transferred business will be recorded in the books of the absorbing company (or the new company in the case of an amalgamation) by debiting the acquired assets (as revalued, if necessary) to their appropriate accounts, crediting the liabilities taken over to their respective accounts and crediting the vendors with the amount of the purchase price. The vendors are then debited, and cash, share capital, etc., credited with the settlement of the purchase price. The excess of the purchase price over the net value of the assets acquired (*i.e.*, total assets acquired as revalued less liabilities assumed) represents the amount paid for Goodwill. Where, however, the net value of the assets acquired exceeds the purchase price the difference represents Capital Reserve ; this should be shown separately in the purchasing company's books or used to write down the value of any of the fixed assets, or goodwill (where the balance on that account has been included in the net assets taken over), acquired.

EXAMPLE

With the object of eliminating competition and also of effecting economy in working, Large, Ltd., took over the business of Small, Ltd., on the following terms :—

---

* Where the business being absorbed is that of a sole trader or partnership the appropriate entries will be made in the Capital Account(s) in place of Sundry Shareholders Account.

(a) Large, Ltd., to pay the shareholders in Small, Ltd., 10s. 0d. per share, and to give three 10s. 0d. Ordinary Shares in the former company for every £1 share in the latter company. The 10s. 0d. shares were considered as being at par.

(b) Large, Ltd., to take over the assets (including goodwill) at book values, and to assume the liabilities (issuing its own 5 per cent. Mortgage Debentures in place of those taken over) of Small, Ltd.

The transaction was to be carried out on 1st January, 19–, on which date the Balance Sheet of Small, Ltd., was as follows :—

	£		£
Authorised Share Capital :—		Goodwill at cost	140,000
200,000 Ordinary Shares		Freehold Land and Build-	
of £1 each	200,000	ings at cost	60,430
		Plant and Machinery at cost	
Issued Share Capital :—		(£30,000) less depreciation	14,210
190,000 Ordinary Shares		Fixtures and Fittings at	
of £1 each, fully paid . .	190,000	cost (£7,000) less depre-	
General Reserve	60,000	ciation	4,200
Profit and Loss Account .	19,840	Stock-in-Trade	16,250
		Trade Debtors . . .	44,860
	269,840	Investments in Government	
5% Mortgage Debentures .	48,000	Securities	59,000
Trade Creditors	30,600	Cash at Bank	9,490
	£348,440		£348,440

Give the entries in the Ledger to close off the books of Small, Ltd., and show how Large, Ltd., would record the purchase of the business in its Journal.

SMALL, LTD.

Dr. REALISATION ACCOUNT *Cr.*

19–		£	19–		£
Jan. 1	To Sundry Assets—		Jan. 1	By Sundry Liabili-	
	Goodwill . .	140,000		ties—	
	Freehold Land			5% Mortgage	
	and Buildings	60,430		Debentures .	48,000
	Plant and			Trade Creditors	30,600
	Machinery .	14,210		„ Large, Ltd., Pur-	
	Fixtures and			chase Price . .	380,000
	Fittings . .	4,200			
	Stock-in-Trade .	16,250			
	Trade Debtors .	44,860			
	Investments .	59,000			
	Cash at Bank .	9,490			
	„ Sundry Share-				
	holders Account				
	—Profit on				
	Realisation . .	110,160			
		£458,600			£458,600

Dr.   SUNDRY SHAREHOLDERS ACCOUNT   *Cr.*

19–		£	19–		£
Jan. 1	To Large, Ltd.—Purchase Price—		Jan. 1	By Ordinary Share Capital . . .	190,000
	Cash	95,000		„ General Reserve .	60,000
	Ordinary Shares in Large, Ltd.—570,000 Shares of			„ Profit and Loss Account . .	19,840
				„ Realisation Account—Profit	
	10s. 0d. each .	285,000		on Realisation .	110,160
		£380,000			£380,000

Dr.   LARGE, LTD.   *Cr.*

19–		£	19–		£
Jan. 1	To Realisation Account—Purchase Price . .	380,000	Jan. 1	By Sundry Shareholders Account—Cash	95,000
				Ordinary Shares .	285,000
		£380,000			£380,000

LARGE, LTD.
JOURNAL

19–			£	£
Jan. 1	Sundries	*Dr.*		
	To Sundries			
	Freehold Land and Buildings		60,430	
	Plant and Machinery		14,210	
	Fixtures and Fittings		4,200	
	Stock-in-Trade		16,250	
	Trade Debtors		44,860	
	Investments		59,000	
	Cash at Bank		9,490	
	Goodwill		250,160	
	5% Mortgage Debentures			48,000
	Trade Creditors			30,600
	Small, Ltd. (Vendors)			380,000
			£458,600	£458,600
	Being assets and liabilities taken over from Small, Ltd., and purchase consideration as per agreement dated . . .			
		Dr.		
Jan. 1	Small, Ltd. (Vendors)		380,000	
	To Sundries			
	Cash			95,000
	Ordinary Share Capital Account . . .			285,000
	Being discharge of purchase consideration by payment of £95,000 in cash and allotment of 570,000 Ordinary Shares of 10s. 0d. each, fully paid.			

NOTE.—" Goodwill, £250,160 " is a " balancing item " and represents the goodwill previously appearing in the books of Small, Ltd. (£140,000) *plus* the excess (£110,160) of the purchase consideration (£380,000) over the net assets (including Goodwill £140,000) taken over (£269,840). It will be seen that, where the purchasing company does not revalue any of the assets and liabilities taken over, the goodwill *arising out of the purchase* is numerically equivalent to the profit on realisation as shown in the vendor's books.

The amalgamation of business interests can take the form of :—

(*a*) A horizontal amalgamation in which concerns carrying on the same trade or stage of production combine in order to eliminate competition and economise in expenses of management and operation.

(*b*) A vertical amalgamation in which concerns combine with or absorb other concerns upon which they previously relied for the supply of their own raw materials or as consumers or distributors of their own products.

(*c*) A combination of both these types, horizontal amalgamation occurring at one or more stages of a vertical amalgamation.

The amalgamation can be achieved in various ways according to the degree of co-operation desired. From an accountancy point of view, amalgamation of limited company enterprises may be broadly divided into the two following classes :—

(1) Amalgamation by the purchase of assets, for a consideration expressed in cash and/or shares of the purchasing company. This method is frequently used when it is found desirable for the businesses of one or more small concerns to be taken over by a larger concern or an entirely new company. The principal advantages that may be expected are economy in expenses of management and production, elimination or reduction of competition, and greater opportunity of expansion. Shareholders will also benefit from the increased marketability of shares in a larger company and the fact that Stock Exchange quotations may often be obtained. One of the disadvantages of this type of amalgamation is that it is sometimes found necessary to pay

an inflated price to dissentient members of the vendor companies in order to acquire their shareholdings. It should be noted, however, that Section 209 of the Companies Act, 1948, enables a company to acquire compulsorily the shares of members dissenting from a scheme of amalgamation, on the same terms as those offered to approving shareholders (subject to the order of the Court), provided that the scheme has been approved by the holders of at least nine-tenths in value of the shares or class of shares affected.

The ownership of each vendor company's assets is transferred to the purchasing company, and these assets (revalued, if desired) appear in any subsequent Balance Sheets of the latter company. Correspondingly, the assets disappear from the Balance Sheets of the vendor company and in their place appear the cash and/or shares received in consideration therefor. As a rule, the vendor company will then go into liquidation and distribute the cash and the shares in the purchasing company amongst its members.

(2) Amalgamation by the purchase of shares (this is the holding company type of amalgamation, to which more detailed reference will be made in Chapter IX). The point that it is desired to emphasise here is that, in contrast to method (1) above, the legal ownership of the assets belonging to the company whose shares have been acquired (say, Company A) remains vested in that company—the change is merely one of shareholdings, the purchasing company (say, Company B) becoming a shareholder in the place of the shareholders whose holdings have been acquired. This transaction will not be reflected in the Balance Sheet of Company A. Subsequent Balance Sheets of Company B will, however, contain a new asset " Shares in Subsidiary Company, at cost ", while the issued share capital will be increased or cash will be reduced, according

to whether the shares in Company *A* were purchased for shares in Company *B* or for cash.

This method of amalgamation lends itself to arrangements for concentration of production, division of markets, standardisation of output and sharing of technical knowledge and research.

EXAMPLE 1

At 31st December, 19–, the summarised Balance Sheets of three companies, *A*, Ltd., *B*, Ltd., and *C*, Ltd., were as follows:—

A, LTD.

	£		£
Nominal Capital—		Leasehold Premises at cost,	
Ordinary Shares of £1 each	300,000	less depreciation . . .	40,000
		Machinery at cost, less de-	
Issued Capital—		preciation	40,000
Ordinary Shares of £1		Stock-in-Trade	20,000
each, fully paid . . .	100,000	Debtors	5,000
Profit and Loss Account .	10,000	Bank Balance	25,000
	110,000		
Creditors	20,000		
	£130,000		£130,000

B, LTD.

	£		£
Nominal and Issued Capital—		Freehold Premises at cost .	10,000
Ordinary Shares of £1		Machinery at cost, less de-	
each, fully paid . . .	30,000	preciation	12,000
Less Profit and Loss Account	5,000	Stock-in-Trade	7,000
		Debtors	4,000
	25,000	Bank Balance	2,000
Creditors	10,000		
	£35,000		£35,000

C, LTD.

	£		£
Nominal and Issued Capital—		Goodwill at cost . . .	6,000
5% Preference Shares of		Freehold Premises at cost .	10,000
£1 each, fully paid . .	5,000	Machinery at cost, less de-	
Ordinary Shares of £1		preciation	16,000
each, fully paid . . .	20,000	Stock-in-Trade	10,000
		Debtors	8,000
	25,000	Bank Balance	10,000
Profit and Loss Account .	14,000		
	39,000		
5% Debentures (Secured) .	15,000		
Creditors	6,000		
	£60,000		£60,000

The advantages of close trading union having become apparent, a scheme is agreed of which the following are the salient points:—

(a) Company D is formed with a capital of 200,000 Ordinary Shares of £1 each of which 50,000 are at once issued to the public for cash at a premium of 2s. 0d. per share.

(b) All parties agree that the Goodwill of A, Ltd., is worth £20,000 and that its other assets are as stated. A, Ltd., sells the whole of its assets (except Bank Balance, but including Goodwill) to D, Ltd., taking as consideration £48,000 in cash and the balance in D Shares at a premium of 2s. 0d. each. The liability to the Creditors of A, Ltd., is not transferred.

(c) An arrangement is also made whereby D, Ltd., acquires 18,000 of the issued Ordinary Shares in B, Ltd. The value of B's Machinery is agreed at £9,000, but otherwise the values in the Balance Sheet of B, Ltd., are taken by all parties as being correctly stated. The value of the 18,000 Shares is accordingly arrived at from the Balance Sheet and an appropriate number of Ordinary Shares in D, Ltd., is issued in exchange at a premium of 2s. 0d. per share.

(d) The Ordinary Shares in C, Ltd., are agreed, after negotiation, to be worth 33s. 0d. each, and the holders of 14,000 of these agree to exchange their holdings against an appropriate number of shares in D, Ltd., valued at 22s. 0d. each.

You are required to ignore all costs and to prepare the Balance Sheet of D, Ltd., as it would appear when all the transactions are complete.

D, LTD.

	£			£
Nominal Share Capital—		Goodwill at cost. . . .		20,000
200,000 Ordinary Shares		Leasehold Premises at cost.		40,000
of £1 each	200,000	Machinery at cost . . .		40,000
		Investments in Sub-		
Issued Share Capital		sidiary Com-		
153,000 Ordinary Shares		panies at cost—	£	
of £1 each, fully paid .	153,000	18,000 Ordinary		
Share Premium Account .	15,300	Shares of £1		
		each, fully paid,		
		in B, Ltd. . . 13,200		
		14,000 Ordinary		
		Shares of £1		
		each, fully paid,		
		in C, Ltd. . . 23,100		
				36,300
		Stock-in-Trade		20,000
		Debtors		5,000
		Bank Balance		7,000
	£168,300			£168,300

NOTES.—(1) Purchase of Assets in A, Ltd.:—

	£
Assets (other than Bank Balance) as per Balance Sheet	105,000
Goodwill (agreed valuation)	20,000
	£125,000

	£	£
Purchase Consideration—		
Cash	48,000	
70,000 (77,000 × $\frac{20}{22}$) Ordinary Shares in D, Ltd., at 2s. 0d. premium	77,000	
		125,000

(2) Purchase of Shares in B, Ltd.:—

	£
Value of 30,000 Ordinary Shares as per Balance Sheet (£35,000 less £10,000) . . .	25,000
Less Agreed reduction in value of Machinery	3,000
	£22,000

$$\text{Value of 18,000 Shares} = £22,000 \times \frac{18,000}{30,000} \quad . \qquad \begin{array}{c} £ \\ 13,200 \end{array}$$

Purchased for 12,000 (13,200 × $\frac{20}{22}$) Ordinary Shares in D, Ltd., at 2s. 0d. premium.

(3) Purchase of Shares in C, Ltd.:—

	£
Value of 14,000 Ordinary Shares at 33s. 0d. .	23,100

Purchased for 21,000 (23,100 × $\frac{20}{22}$) Ordinary Shares in D, Ltd., at 2s. 0d. premium.

(4) Section 149 of the Companies Act, 1948 (see Chapter X), requires the method of arriving at the amount of fixed assets to be disclosed in the Balance Sheet. From the point of view of the new company, Leasehold Premises and Machinery are correctly described as being valued " at cost ", despite the fact that, in the old company's books, they were valued on a basis of original cost to that company less depreciation written off.

(5) As will be appreciated when Chapter IX is reached, D, Ltd., holds a sufficient number of shares in both B, Ltd., and C, Ltd., to constitute each of those companies a subsidiary company of D, Ltd., within the meaning of Section 154, Companies Act, 1948, and the latter company is therefore under a statutory obligation to show its investments in subsidiary companies separately in its published accounts. These provisions (which relate to disclosure in the Balance Sheet) do not affect the book-keeping entries necessary to record the purchase of the shares.

(6) Although it is outside the scope of the question, it will be of interest to consider the entries required in the books of A, Ltd., B, Ltd., and C, Ltd. These are as follows:—

A, LTD.

This company will probably go into liquidation, and, after discharging its creditors, distribute to its shareholders its remaining cash and the shares in D, Ltd., acquired in part satisfaction of the sale of its assets. The principal ledger accounts will appear, in summarised form, as follows:—

REALISATION ACCOUNT

	£		£
To Sundry Assets (other than Bank Balance) per Balance Sheet . . .	105,000	By D, Ltd., Purchase Consideration	125,000
„ Sundry Shareholders Account— Profit on Realisation	20,000		
	£125,000		£125,000

SUNDRY SHAREHOLDERS ACCOUNT

	£		£
To Ordinary Shares in D, Ltd., 70,000 Shares of £1 each at 2s. 0d. premium	77,000	By Share Capital Account .	100,000
		„ Profit and Loss Account .	10,000
„ Cash	53,000	„ Realisation Account . .	20,000
	£130,000		£130,000

D, LTD.

	£		£
To Realisation Account . .	125,000	By Ordinary Shares in D, Ltd.	77,000
		„ Cash	48,000
	£125,000		£125,000

ORDINARY SHARES IN D, LTD.

	£		£
To D, Ltd.	77,000	By Sundry Shareholders Account	77,000

CASH

	£		£
To Balance per Balance Sheet	25,000	By Creditors	20,000
„ D, Ltd.	48,000	„ Sundry Shareholders Account	53,000
	£73,000		£73,000

The shareholders in A, Ltd., will therefore receive 10s. 7·2d. in cash for every share held in A, Ltd., and 7 Ordinary Shares in D, Ltd. (valued at 22s. 0d. per share) for every 10 shares held in A, Ltd.

B, LTD., AND C, LTD.

Each of these companies retains its separate existence, and no record of the transactions appears in its financial books, for the transactions take place between D, Ltd., and certain shareholders in B, Ltd., and C, Ltd. These latter companies will, however, require to record in certain statutory books (e.g., Register of Members) the fact that D, Ltd., is now a shareholder in the place of those holders who have transferred their shares to that company.

EXAMPLE 2

The two companies whose Balance Sheets are shown below are to amalgamate and a new company is to be formed to take over their businesses as they stand. What settlement is equitable as regards the shareholders ? Assume that the book values of the assets have been specially valued on the same basis in each case, for the purpose of the amalgamation, and that the shares in the new company will be of one class only and of £1 nominal value each.

NORTH, LTD.

	£		£
Nominal Capital—		Goodwill	2,000
30,000 Shares of £1 each .	30,000	Leasehold Premises . . .	2,500
		Machinery	9,036
Issued Capital—		Office Furniture	219
20,000 Shares of £1 each,		Stock-in-Trade	3,060
12s. 6d. per share, paid-		Debtors	4,592
up	12,500	Cash at Bank	1,211
Creditors	8,018		
Bank Loan	2,000		
Profit and Loss Account .	100		
	£22,618		£22,618

SOUTH, LTD.

	£		£
Nominal and Issued Capi-		Patents	2,700
tal—		Freehold Land and Build-	
50,000 Shares of £1 each,		ings	9,700
fully paid	50,000	Machinery	15,980
Creditors	10,093	Stock-in-Trade	11,420
General Reserve . . .	9,000	Debtors	26,971
Profit and Loss Account .	1,000	Cash at Bank	3,322
	£70,093		£70,093

Such a problem as this merely resolves itself into a valuation of the shares in the respective companies, so as to arrive at the number of shares in the new company that ought to be allotted to the existing shareholders in order to preserve their relative positions.

Value of Shares in North, Ltd. :—

	£
Paid-up Capital	12,500
Profit and Loss Account	100
	£12,600

Therefore each £1 share (12s. 6d. paid-up) is worth £$\frac{12,600}{20,000}$ = 12s. 7·2d.

Value of Shares in South, Ltd. :—

	£
Paid-up Capital	50,000
General Reserve	9,000
Profit and Loss Account	1,000
	£60,000

Therefore each £1 share (fully paid) is worth $£\dfrac{60,000}{50,000} = £1$ 4s. 0d.

If, then, the new company satisfies the members of the old company with 72,600 shares of £1 each, fully paid, the members of North, Ltd., will receive 12,600 shares for 20,000 original shares, and the members of South, Ltd., will receive 60,000 shares for 50,000 original shares, that is :—

North, Ltd., shareholders will receive 63 new shares for 100 old shares ; and South, Ltd., shareholders will receive 6 new shares for 5 old shares.

Since the members of the two original companies will not often hold shares in exact multiples of 100 or 5, the number of new shares that they are entitled to will often contain a fraction. These fractional shares may be allotted to the liquidators of the old companies, who will get the best price they can for them and divide the proceeds amongst the shareholders for whom they are acting, or a cash equivalent may be determined to enable the liquidators to deal with the fractional shares.

The reconstruction and amalgamation of companies have been facilitated by the exemption from stamp duties afforded by various Finance Acts. Where a company is registered or an existing company has its share capital increased for the purpose of acquiring the undertaking of, or not less than 90 per cent. of the shares in, another company and the consideration consists, as to at least 90 per cent. thereof, in shares of the purchasing company, then—

(a) the sale agreement is exempt from *ad valorem* duty, and

(b) the new capital created for the purpose (with certain limitations) is exempt from capital duty.

The detailed provisions are complicated but their general effect is to make possible reconstruction schemes involving exchanges of shares between two companies without payment of duty.

CHAPTER VI

PROVISIONS, RESERVES AND SINKING FUNDS

The definition of a Balance Sheet given at the beginning of Chapter IV might be thought to imply that the preparation of annual Profit and Loss Accounts and Balance Sheets was a mere matter of book-keeping, involving only the transfer and summarisation of the balances in the books. Obviously, this is true only in the simplest cases ; in others the adoption of the double entry system automatically provides the groundwork of " raw material " which forms the basis of the annual accounts, but many adjustments are necessary. These adjustments are ultimately entered in the books to bring the latter into line with the draft accounts. Thus the entries in the books fall into two main classes :—

(1) Those which arise as a direct result of specific transactions entered into during the year. They are made at or about the time when the transactions occur, primarily with the object of recording those transactions themselves ; the fact that they will ultimately be summarised and reflected in the Profit and Loss Account or in the Balance Sheet is only a secondary consideration.

(2) Those which are made at the end of the year and are directly connected with the preparation of the annual accounts. The most important of these are—

    (a) Provisions for accrued expenses or payments in advance.

    (b) Provision for the depreciation of fixed assets.

    (c) Provisions for—

        (i) Known losses—*e.g.*, bad debts.

214

(ii) Expected losses—*e.g.*, doubtful debts.

(iii) Possible or contingent losses—*e.g.*, bills receivable discounted.

(*d*) Appropriations of profit to facilitate the repayment of liabilities or capital.

(*e*) Appropriations of profit for prudential purposes—*e.g.*, reserves for the equalisation of dividends and general reserves.

Transfers which fall into the last two categories are known as *reserves*. The essential feature which distinguishes them from other entries in the books is the element of choice which is present. With the exception of reserves for known losses, which are preferably regarded as provisions, or actual liabilities, the proprietors of the concern are free to make their own appropriations. In a business of any magnitude or complexity, the creation of adequate reserves is a matter which calls for the greatest care and foresight on the part of those who frame the accounts.

The present trend of authoritative opinion with regard to the uses of the terms " provision " and " reserve " has received statutory recognition in the Eighth Schedule of the Companies Act, 1948, which provides, in relation to matters required to be disclosed in the published Profit and Loss Accounts and Balance Sheets of companies, that :—

(1) (*a*) The expression " provision " shall, subject to (2) below, mean any amount written off or retained by way of providing for depreciation, renewals or diminution in value of assets or retained by way of providing for any known liability of which the amount cannot be determined with substantial accuracy ;

(*b*) The expression " reserve " shall not, subject to (2) below, include any amount written off or retained by way of providing for depreciation, renewals or diminution in value of assets or retained by way of providing for any known liability (and the expression " liability " shall

include all liabilities in respect of expenditure
contracted for and all disputed or contingent
liabilities) ;

(c) The expression " capital reserve " shall not include
any amount regarded as free for distribution
through the Profit and Loss Account, and the
expression " revenue reserve " shall mean any
reserve other than a capital reserve.

(2) Where—

(a) any amount written off or retained by way of
providing for depreciation, renewals or diminution in value of assets, not being an amount
written off in relation to fixed assets before
1st July, 1948 ; or

(b) any amount retained by way of providing for any
known liability ;

is in excess of that which in the opinion of the
directors is reasonably necessary for the purpose,
the excess shall be treated as a reserve and not as
a provision.*

Thus, for the purposes of the Companies Act, 1948, the
term " provision " is employed to indicate known depreciation or diminution in the value of assets and known liabilities,
the amount of which, however, cannot be estimated with
reasonable accuracy, whereas if the amount of a known
liability can be estimated with substantial accuracy, it must
be classified as a liability, and not as a provision. Where
the amount set aside as a provision is greater than the amount
reasonably necessary for the purpose, the excess must be
classified as a reserve and not as a provision.

The fact that the disposition of the available balance of
profits is a matter which must ultimately be decided by the
proprietors themselves does not remove it from the province
of the accountant, who should be regarded as an expert
whose advice will, in most cases, be accepted by them.

* Reference should also be made to the recommendations of the Council of the
Institute of Chartered Accountants with regard to the significance and accounting
treatment of provisions and reserves (see Appendix II), and to the requirements of
Part IV, Eighth Schedule, Companies Act, 1948 (see Appendix I).

Thus the consideration of provisions and reserves is an important item in the study of accounting. For this reason it is regrettable that there should be considerable differences in practice in the use of the common terms such as " provision ", " reserve " and " reserve fund ".

The consensus of opinion favours the following interpretations :—

(1) Provisions for specific purposes (*e.g.*, Provisions for Bad Debts, Depreciation or Accrued Expenses) should be sufficiently described to indicate their purpose. Several of such provisions may, however, be included in one item in the Balance Sheet under the heading " *Sundry Creditors and Provisions* ", where provisions for accrued expenses are included with trade creditors. Provisions for the reduction in value of assets, such as provisions for depreciation and bad debts, should, however, be deducted from the appropriate asset. All classes of provisions are created by a charge against Profit and Loss Account.

(2) " *Reserve* " or " *General Reserve* ", standing alone, signifies undistributed profits available for distribution at a later date. Such revenue reserves represent appropriations of profits.

(3) " *Capital Reserve* " signifies capital profits or other profits which are, either by law or by the will of the proprietors or their delegates, not distributable as dividends (*e.g.*, profits prior to incorporation). This class of Reserve is fully dealt with in Chapter VIII on " Divisible Profits and Dividends ".

(4) The word " *Fund* " should be used only when represented by specific investments outside the business. Such investments should be shown separately in the Balance Sheet and their purpose indicated (*e.g.*, Investments of Sinking Fund for Redemption of Debentures *per contra*, or Leasehold Redemption Policy). An exception to this rule must be made in the case of a Capital Redemption Reserve Fund created in accordance with Section 58 of the

Companies Act, 1948. Such a fund need not be invested outside the business, but it must be given its statutory title.

(5) The expression *Sinking Fund* should be used only when certain amounts are set aside annually in accordance with some obligation or preconceived intention to do so (*e.g.*, under the terms of a Debenture Deed), or where annual provision is made, on a scientific basis, by means of fixed instalments calculated so as to take into account compound interest over the period of accumulation (*e.g.*, for amortisation of leaseholds by annual premiums on a Capital Redemption Policy or otherwise).

Provisions for Specific Purposes (charges against profits).

A specific provision may be made in respect of such items as the following :—

(1) An expense or loss of uncertain amount, *e.g.*, provision for possible bad debts, or an accrued expense or loss of certain amount.

(2) A future expense, a portion of which should prudently be charged against the period under review, *e.g.*, a provision for leasehold dilapidations.

(3) An equalisation of periodical expenditure, *e.g.*, a provision for repairs equalisation.

(4) A reduction in the value of an asset through use or age (not a decrease in the fund of assets merely as a result of the incidence of trading losses) : *e.g.*, a provision for depreciation.

(5) Any possible contingency which would affect the profits or the valuation of assets : *e.g.*, a provision in respect of possible losses on forward purchases, owing to falls in market prices ; or a fall in value of investments, owing to a possible diminution in the income derived therefrom.

(1) PROVISIONS FOR FUTURE LOSSES AND ACCRUED EXPENSES. In so far as a future loss cannot be determined with substantial accuracy, the estimated amount should be

provided. This is achieved by debiting Profit and Loss Account and crediting a Provision Account, suitably described, with the estimated amount. A provision of this kind is not *essential* to the correct statement of current profits, since the loss or expense is a *future* liability. The adjustment is made in accordance with the canons of accounting (*i.e.*, if a loss is feared, provision should be made therefor—see page 35) as a matter of prudence, and not as a matter of the strictly correct determination of *current* profits. Where, however, the amount of expenditure accrued due can be calculated with a fair degree of accuracy, *e.g.*, accrued rent, an adjustment will be made on the relevant expense account, the amount outstanding being included in the Balance Sheet as a current liability.

Where the future loss or expense is of uncertain amount a fair estimate must be made after a consideration of all the relevant facts. It will usually be possible, where the loss or expense is a normal one which usually accrues in the particular business, *c.g.*, bad debts, to estimate from past experience what the future loss is likely to be. Where the loss or expense is of an exceptional kind, however, *e.g.*, contingencies arising during process of contracts, a fair estimate of the loss must be made from whatever facts are available. Any error in the original estimate may be adjusted when the ultimate loss is determined, although it should be realised that any over-estimate has the effect of creating a secret reserve.

(2) PROVISIONS FOR FUTURE EXPENSES. Provisions of this type may be in the nature of a provision for a contingent liability, in that the future expense may or may not be incurred. It is usually possible to determine whether or not a claim will ultimately lie against the concern, *e.g.*, the dilapidation of leasehold property. Although the amount of such a claim may be unascertainable, the fact that a liability for repairs or reconditioning will arise should be recognised. It is only prudent to regard the loss as accruing throughout the period of the lease, or throughout a portion of that period, and, therefore, a yearly provision should be made for it.

(3) Provisions for the Equalisation of Expenditure. These were considered in Chapter III under the heading " Extraordinary Revenue Expenditure ". The principle involved is that of equalising as far as may be possible the annual debits to Profit and Loss Account in respect of items of expenditure which, by their nature, are incurred in irregular amounts or at irregular intervals (although the benefit to the business is, within limits, continuous). If the expenditure is incurred after the benefit has been received (expenditure on repairs, for example, is incurred to make good the ravages of the past), it is necessary to provide by annual charges to Profit and Loss Account an amount equal to the estimated average cost over a period of years. On the other hand, when the expenditure is incurred in advance (*e.g.*, advertising), the process of equalisation does not involve the creation of a provision. A *debit balance* representing " Deferred Revenue Expenditure " (see Chapter III) is carried forward, being reduced each year by the amount written off to revenue.

(4) Provisions for Depreciation. The methods by which the annual charge for depreciation can be computed will be considered in detail in the next Chapter, but it may be noted here that as an alternative to writing down an asset by the amount of depreciation suffered during a period, a provision of a like amount may be created. The asset then remains in the books at cost until it is scrapped or replaced when the balance on the provision account should be sufficient to eliminate the balance on the asset account. At any intermediate date, the Balance Sheet shows both the original cost of the asset and the total amount provided for depreciation up to that date. The provision may be shown either as a separate item on the liabilities side of the Balance Sheet or, preferably, as a deduction from the relative asset.

(5) Provisions for Contingencies. When it is necessary to note the existence of a contingent liability, consideration should also be given to the *probable* loss as distinct from the *possible* loss which is evidenced by the note on the Balance Sheet. If bills receivable have been discounted, the possible or contingent liability is the face value of the bills ; the

probable liability depends on the standing of the party from whom the bill was originally received (probably, but not necessarily, the acceptor). A provision to cover the probable loss, which will not necessarily be the same as the liability, for something may be recovered from the person from whom the bill was received, should be created but, as the corresponding asset (bills receivable) no longer appears in the Balance Sheet, the provision should appear on the left-hand side of the Balance Sheet, unlike the Provision for Bad and Doubtful Debts which appears as a deduction from the appropriate asset.

Reserves for Repayment of Liabilities or Capital.

It was shown in Chapter III that the repayment of a fixed liability such as debentures results in a diminution of the fund of working capital unless profits have been set aside or reserved for the purpose of the redemption. Exactly similar principles apply when a company has issued, and proposes to redeem, Redeemable Preference Shares ; and in this case, the necessity to set aside profits has been recognised by the legislature, in the provisions of Section 58 of the Companies Act, 1948, relating to the creation of a Capital Redemption Reserve Fund. As mentioned on page 218, the profits set aside for the latter fund are not necessarily invested outside the business, but the word " fund " is included in the statutory title.

Such redemptions will now be considered in detail.

Redemption of Debentures.

Debentures, unless stated to be irredeemable, are redeemed according to the terms of issue, e.g., by periodical drawings, or by repayment either on the fixed date or subject to the necessary notice being given to the debenture-holders, at the option of the company. The requisite funds for the repayment of the debentures may be obtained—

(a) From a new issue of shares or debentures ;

(b) Out of the liquid resources of the company.

When the first method is adopted and the funds required are obtained from a new issue, it is not necessary to create a reserve of profits, for the fund of working capital has not

been depleted. It is more usual, however, for the terms of
issue to provide that redemption shall be effected, either—

(1) By annual drawings, out of profits ; or

(2) By purchase in the open market, if the price is favourable and funds are available ; or

(3) In a lump sum, either on a fixed date or subject to
the necessary notice being given to the debenture-
holders, at the option of the company ; the necessary
sum to be provided by the accumulation of a
sinking fund.

(1) REDEMPTION BY ANNUAL DRAWINGS.

The actual redemption will be recorded by debiting
Debenture Account with the amount of cash paid out, any
premium on redemption being transferred to the debit of a
special Premium on Redemption of Debentures Account.

It was shown on page 99 that the process of redemption
depletes the working capital of the company and it is
advisable, therefore, to effect a corresponding reduction in
the balance of undistributed profits. The premium, if any,
may be regarded as additional interest or consideration for
the use of the debenture-holders' money and should be
treated as a charge against profits, or alternatively may be
debited to Share Premium Account (if any). If, in addition,
a sum equal to the nominal value of the debentures redeemed
is transferred from Profit and Loss Appropriation Account to
the credit of a Debenture Redemption Reserve Account, the
total amount withdrawn from profits available for distribution will be equal to the amount actually paid out (*i.e.*, the
nominal value plus the premium) on redemption. When the
whole issue of debentures has been redeemed, the balance
on the Debenture Redemption Reserve Account should be
transferred to the credit of General Reserve (for it represents
a form of undistributed profits).

If debentures which are to be redeemed by annual
drawings were originally issued at a discount, it is necessary
to write off the discount to Profit and Loss Account during
the currency of the debentures. This discount is really in
the nature of *capitalised interest*, for it represents an additional

EXAMPLE

The terms of issue of a series of £10,000 6 per cent. Debenture Stock provide for the redemption of one-tenth of the original issue by annual drawings at 105. The entries in the ledger for the first three years will appear as follows :—

Dr.		6 PER CENT. DEBENTURE STOCK			Cr.
1st Year.			£	1st Year.		£
31st Dec.	To Cash . . .	1,050	1st Jan.	By Cash . . .	10,000
	„ Balance, c/d. .	9,000	31st Dec.	„ Premium on Redemption of Deb. Stock A/c. . . .	50
		£10,050			£10,050
2nd Year.				2nd Year.	
31st Dec.	To Cash . . .	1,050	1st Jan.	By Balance, b/d. .	9,000
	„ Balance, c/d. .	8,000	31st Dec.	„ Premium on Redemption of Deb. Stock A/c. . . .	50
		£9,050			£9,050
3rd Year.				3rd Year.	
31st Dec.	To Cash . . .	1,050	1st Jan.	By Balance, b/d. .	8,000
	„ Balance, c/d. .	7,000	31st Dec.	„ Premium on Redemption of Deb. Stock A/c. . . .	50
		£8,050			£8,050
				4th Year.	
				1st Jan. By Balance, b/d. .	7,000

Dr.	PREMIUM ON REDEMPTION OF DEBENTURE STOCK				Cr.
1st Year.		£	1st Year.		£
31st Dec.	To 6% Deb. Stock .	50	31st Dec.	By Profit and Loss A/c.	50
2nd Year.			2nd Year.		
31st Dec.	To 6% Deb. Stock .	50	31st Dec.	By Profit and Loss A/c.	50
3rd Year.			3rd Year.		
31st Dec.	To 6% Deb. Stock .	50	31st Dec.	By Profit and Loss A/c.	50

Dr. DEBENTURE REDEMPTION RESERVE ACCOUNT Cr.

		£			£
1st Year.			1st Year.		
31st Dec.	To Balance, c/d. .	1,000	31st Dec.	By Appropriation A/c. . . .	1,000
		£1,000			1,000
2nd Year.			2nd Year.		
31st Dec.	To Balance, c/d. .	2,000	31st Dec.	By Balance, b/d. .	1,000
				„ Appropriation A/c. . . .	1,000
		£2,000			£2,000
3rd Year.			3rd Year.		
31st Dec.	To Balance, c/d. .	3,000	31st Dec.	By Balance, b/d. .	2,000
				„ Appropriation A/c. . . .	1,000
		£3,000			£3,000
			4th Year.		
			1st Jan.	By Balance, b/d. .	3,000

NOTE.—The debit balance on Premium on Redemption of Debenture Stock Account may be written off against any credit balance on Share Premium Account (see page 168).

consideration to the investor, while from the company's point of view it may be regarded as a part of the total cost of obtaining the use of the debenture-holders' money. The most equitable method of treating this discount therefore regards it as interest paid in a lump sum and charges it to revenue in yearly instalments proportionate to the benefit obtained, which is represented by the nominal value of the debentures outstanding at the beginning of each year.

Thus, in a simple case where an issue of 5,000 £1 Debentures is repayable by five equal annual drawings of 1,000 Debentures, the amounts outstanding at the commencement of each of the five years are :—

		£
1st Year	. . . .	5,000
2nd „	. . . .	4,000
3rd „	. . . .	3,000
4th „	. . . .	2,000
5th „	. . . .	1,000

If the total discount was £500, it should be written off in proportion to the above amounts, i.e., in the first year, $\dfrac{5,000}{15,000}$

or $\frac{5}{15}$ ths, in the second year, $\frac{4,000}{15,000}$ or $\frac{4}{15}$ ths, and so on. The total of £500 will thus be written off in the following sums :—

									£	s.	d.
1st Year.	$\frac{5}{15}$ ths of £500	.	.	.	.	.	=		166	13	4
2nd Year.	$\frac{4}{15}$ ths	,,	.	.	.	.	=		133	6	8
3rd Year.	$\frac{3}{15}$ ths	,,	.	.	.	.	=		100	0	0
4th Year.	$\frac{2}{15}$ ths	,,	.	.	.	.	=		66	13	4
5th Year.	$\frac{1}{15}$ th	,,	.	.	.	.	=		33	6	8
									£500	0	0

(2) REDEMPTION BY PURCHASE IN THE OPEN MARKET.

The terms of issue of debentures frequently give the directors of the company power to redeem them by purchase in the open market, usually as an alternative to redemption by drawings or at a fixed date. This option may prove of considerable benefit to the company when the debentures can be purchased on the market at a price which is below that at which they would otherwise be redeemable, and since the purchases will themselves tend to raise the market price or at least prevent it falling any further, the debenture holders as a body may themselves benefit from such a provision.

As the purchase of the debentures depletes the company's working capital, a sum equal to the amount expended in the purchase of the debentures should be transferred from Profit and Loss Appropriation Account to the credit of Debenture Redemption Reserve Account.

If the debentures when purchased are immediately cancelled the entries in the books will be similar to those shown above in connection with a redemption by annual drawings, so that the actual amount of debentures outstanding appears as a liability in the Balance Sheet. Any premium (or loss) on purchase is dealt with as already illustrated in the case of a redemption by annual drawings, whereas any discount (or profit) on purchase will appear on the left-hand side of the Balance Sheet as, say, " Profit on Purchase of Debentures ", the balance on which may be utilised to offset any subsequent losses on purchase of further debentures.

I

On the other hand, the debentures may not be cancelled immediately, but may be held as investments by trustees acting for the company. In that case they will appear in the books and in the annual Balance Sheets at their cost to the company. Sooner or later they will be cancelled and any difference between their book value as an investment and the nominal value at which they appear as a liability can be transferred to the Debenture Redemption Reserve Account.

(3) REDEMPTION IN A LUMP SUM.

When an issue of debentures is expressed to be redeemable on or before a given date, without any provision for annual drawings or purchases on the market, it is incumbent on the company to accumulate sufficient liquid assets to provide for the redemption. The only way in which this can be assured is—

(a) To withdraw annual sums from Profit and Loss Appropriation Account and thus establish a Reserve for Redemption of Debentures sufficient to cover the liability ; and

(b) To invest the amounts thus appropriated in gilt-edged securities or an insurance policy.

The creation of a Reserve is not sufficient in itself, for the working capital which should accumulate as a result may easily become locked up in capital expansion or be dissipated by losses incurred in later years. Frequently the terms of issue make the investment of the annual instalments obligatory and in any case it is always advisable that such a *sinking fund*, as it is called, should be created.

The following example illustrates a redemption of debentures in these circumstances :—

EXAMPLE

The Suburban Company, Limited, showed in their accounts on 31st December, 19. ., a Debenture Redemption Reserve Fund of £100,000, which was represented by an investment in 3½ per cent. War Loan of £128,775 (nominal). On the following 30th June the company's bank balance was £12,000, and the War Loan having been sold at 80 net, the proceeds were paid into the bank, and Debentures, amounting to £100,000, were paid off. Show by means of ledger accounts the entries in the books of the company in respect of the above transactions.

Dr.		DEBENTURE ACCOUNT			*Cr.*
19..		£	19..		£
June 30	To Cash . . .	100,000	June 30	By Balance, *b/d.* .	100,000

Dr.		DEBENTURE REDEMPTION RESERVE FUND			*Cr.*
19..		£	19..		£
June 30	To General Reserve	100,000	June 30	By Balance, *b/d.* .	100,000

Dr.		INVESTMENT ACCOUNT—3½% WAR LOAN			*Cr.*
19..		£	19..		£
June 30	To Balance, *b/d.* .	100,000	June 30	By Cash . . .	103,020
	„ Profit transferred to General Reserve . . .	3,020			
		£103,020			£103,020

Dr.		GENERAL RESERVE			*Cr.*
19..		£	19..		£
June 30	To Balance, *c/d.* .	103,020	June 30	By Debenture Redemption Reserve Fund .	100,000
				„ Investment Account . . .	3,020
		£103,020			£103,020
			19..		
			July 1	By Balance, *b/d.* .	103,020

Dr.		CASH ACCOUNT			*Cr.*
19..		£	19..		£
June 30	To Balance, *b/d.* .	12,000	June 30	By Debenture Account . .	100,000
	„ Realisation of Investments .	103,020		„ Balance, *c/d.* .	15,020
		£115,020			£115,020
19..					
July 1	To Balance, *b/d.* .	15,020			

It will be observed that the profit on realisation of the sinking fund investment has been carried to the credit of General Reserve. An alternative method, identical in its ultimate effect, is to transfer the profit on realisation to Debenture Redemption Reserve Fund, before the balance of the latter account is transferred to General Reserve.

Alternatively, the amounts appropriated and invested outside the business may be utilised in paying the premiums on an endowment insurance policy which is taken out for the amount required to redeem the debentures so that the policy will mature on or shortly before the date when the debentures are to be redeemed. Such a form of endowment policy is generally termed a " Capital Redemption Policy ".

The main advantage of this method over the method of investing in gilt-edged securities is that the full amount of the policy will be received at its maturity, whereas with securities there is always the risk of loss on realisation. Furthermore, no expenses are attached to the payment of the annual premium, whereas expenses in the form of brokerage and contract stamps are incurred when investing in securities. On the other hand, the annual charge, as represented by the premium, will be greater, because the insurance company will necessarily require to make a profit out of the transaction in addition to paying its own expenses.

EXAMPLE

A company issued £2,000 5 per cent. Debenture Stock at par on 1st January, 1946. The Stock was to be redeemed at the end of ten years. To provide for redemption a ten years' capital redemption policy was taken out, also on 1st January, 1946. Assume the annual premium to be £180, and reckon the surrender value at the amount of premiums paid, plus 2 per cent. compound interest. Write up the necessary accounts in the company's books for the years 1946, 1947 and 1948, and show the entries necessary when the Debenture Stock is redeemed at the end of the tenth year, assuming that the books of the company then showed the surrender value of the policy as being £1,931.

Dr.		DEBENTURE STOCK ACCOUNT					Cr.	
1956			£ s. d.	1946			£ s. d.	
Jan. 1	To Cash . .		2,000 0 0	Jan. 1	By Cash . .		2,000 0 0	

Dr.   DEBENTURE REDEMPTION RESERVE FUND   *Cr.*

1946		£	s.	d.	1946		£	s.	d.
Dec. 31	To Balance, *c/d*	183	12	0	Dec. 31	By Profit and Loss Appropriation A/c.	180	0	0
						„ Policy A/c., Interest .	3	12	0
		£183	12	0			£183	12	0
1947					1947				
Dec. 10	To Balance, *c/d.*	370	17	5	Jan. 1	By Balance, *b/d.*	183	12	0
					Dec. 31	„ Profit and Loss Appropriation A/c.	180	0	0
						„ Policy A/c., Interest .	7	5	5
		£370	17	5			£370	17	5
1948					1948				
Dec. 31	To Balance, *c/d.*	561	17	9	Jan. 1	By Balance, *b/d.*	370	17	5
					Dec. 31	„ Profit and Loss Appropriation A/c.	180	0	0
						„ Policy A/c., Interest .	11	0	4
		£561	17	9			£561	17	9
					1949				
					Jan. 1	By Balance, *b/d.*	561	17	9
	*	*				*			
1956					1956				
Jan. 1	To General Reserve	2,000	0	0	Jan. 1	By Balance, *b/d.*	1,931	0	0
						„ Policy A/c.	69	0	0
		£2,000	0	0			£2,000	0	0

Dr.   GENERAL RESERVE   *Cr.*

					1956		£	s.	d.
					Jan. 1	By Debenture Redemption Reserve Fund .	2,000	0	0

Dr.   POLICY ACCOUNT   *Cr.*

		£	s.	d.			£	s.	d.
1946					1946				
Jan. 1	To Cash . .	180	0	0	Dec. 31	By Balance, *c/d.*	183	12	0
Dec. 31	,, Debenture Redemption Reserve Fund .	3	12	0					
		£183	12	0			£183	12	0
1947					1947				
Jan. 1	To Balance, *b/d.*	183	12	0	Dec. 31	By Balance, *c/d.*	370	17	5
	,, Cash . .	180	0	0					
Dec. 31	,, Debenture Redemption Reserve Fund .	7	5	5					
		£370	17	5			£370	17	5
1948					1948				
Jan. 1	To Balance, *b/d.*	370	17	5	Dec. 31	By Balance, *c/d.*	561	17	9
	,, Cash . .	180	0	0					
Dec. 31	,, Debenture Redemption Reserve Fund .	11	0	4					
		£561	17	9			£561	17	9
1949									
Jan. 1	To Balance, *b/d.*	561	17	9					
	*				*		*		
1956					1956				
Jan. 1	To Balance, *b/d.*	1,931	0	0	Jan. 1	By Cash . .	2,000	0	0
	,, Debenture Redemption Reserve Fund .	69	0	0					
		£2,000	0	0			£2,000	0	0

Redeemable Preference Shares.

By Section 58 of the Companies Act, 1948, a company limited by shares may, if so authorised by its Articles, issue preference shares which are, at the option of the company, capable of being redeemed.

This is a novel provision (first introduced in the Companies Act, 1929) which had no counterpart in any of the earlier

Acts and in many ways it may be regarded as a breach with tradition. Formerly it was an accepted principle that the share capital of a company was irredeemable and formed a fund which, subject to the incidence of losses, was always available to meet the claims of creditors.

For this reason, the interest of creditors has been protected by the statutory provision that redemption must be effected either—

(a) Out of profits which would be available for dividend; or

(b) Out of the proceeds of a fresh issue of shares made for the purposes of the redemption,

and at the date of the redemption the shares redeemed must be fully paid.

Where any such redemption is made out of profits available for dividends, the company must transfer out of such profits to the credit of a " Capital Redemption Reserve Fund ", a sum equivalent to the nominal amount of the shares redeemed. Thus the principle that when profits are applied for a capital purpose, a transfer to a Reserve Account should be made in order to preserve the working capital and safeguard the rights of creditors has received statutory recognition. Section 58 applies, however, only in the case of a redemption of redeemable preference shares ; in other cases, e.g., when debentures are redeemed out of liquid assets, a transfer to reserve is made as a matter of conservative financial policy and not under statutory compulsion.

This Capital Redemption Reserve Fund can be reduced only in accordance with the rules relating to the reduction of capital (see page 195), except that the Fund may be used in paying up unissued shares of the company to be issued to members as fully paid bonus shares.

Where a company has redeemed or is about to redeem any preference shares, it may issue shares up to the nominal value of the shares redeemed or to be redeemed and such an issue is not to be deemed to be an increase of share capital for the purpose of stamp duty unless the issue is made before the contemplated redemption and the redemption does not take place within one month after the issue of the shares.

Any balance on Share Premium Account (see page 168), whether arising in connection with the fresh issue of shares made for the purposes of redemption or any other issue, may be applied in providing the premium, if any, on the redemption of redeemable preference shares. The statutory provision in this regard is permissive and not obligatory ; there is no compulsion to utilise the Share Premium Account for this purpose although generally it would be wise to take advantage of the opportunity to do so.

Particulars of all redeemable preference shares must be included in every Balance Sheet of the company, specifying—

(a) What part of the issued capital consists of such shares ; and

(b) The earliest date on which the company has power to redeem those shares.

Notice of any redemption of redeemable preference shares, specifying the shares redeemed, must be given to the Registrar of Companies within one month after the date of the redemption.*

EXAMPLE

1. Redemption out of Profits :

The Progressive Company, Ltd., made an issue of 60,000 Redeemable Preference Shares of £1 each and 100,000 Ordinary Shares of £1 each. On 30th June, 19.., the Redeemable Preference Shares were redeemed out of profits at a premium of 5s. a share. Show by means of Journal entries the records in the company's books and draft the Balance Sheet, after the redemption.

JOURNAL

19..		£	£
June 30	Profit and Loss Appropriation Account . . *Dr.*	75,000	
	To Capital Redemption Reserve Fund		60,000
	,, Premium on Redemption of Redeemable Preference Shares Account		15,000
	Being profits appropriated to effect redemption of 60,000 Redeemable Preference Shares of £1 each, at a premium of 5s. a share as per resolution of directors dated		
	Redeemable Preference Share Capital A/c. . . *Dr.*	60,000	
	Premium on Redemption of Redeemable Preference Shares . . . . *Dr.*	15,000	
	To Cash		75,000
	Being redemption of Redeemable Preference Shares in accordance with the above terms.		

* Refer also to Section 58, Companies Act, 1948, reproduced in Appendix I of this work.

EXTRACT FROM BALANCE SHEET (liabilities side)

	£
Authorised Share Capital (say):—	
60,000 Redeemable Preference Shares of £1 each . . .	60,000
200,000 Ordinary Shares of £1 each	200,000
Issued Share Capital:—	
100,000 Ordinary Shares of £1 each	100,000
Capital Redemption Reserve Fund	60,000

It will be seen that the entries are analogous to those necessary when debentures are redeemed out of profits.

2. Redemption out of Proceeds of a New Issue of Shares :

Assume the same particulars as before, but the shares are redeemed out of the proceeds of an issue of 60,000 Ordinary Shares issued at par for this purpose.

JOURNAL

19..		£	£
June 30	Cash . . . . *Dr.*	60,000	
	To Ordinary Share Capital		60,000
	Issue of 60,000 Ordinary Shares of £1 each, fully paid		
	up as per resolution dated		
	Profit and Loss Appropriation Account . . . *Dr.*	15,000	
	To Premium on Redemption of Redeemable		
	Preference Shares		15,000
	Provision of premium payable on the redemption of		
	60,000 Redeemable Preference Shares of £1 each at a		
	premium of 5s. a share.		
	Redeemable Preference Share Capital Account . *Dr.*	60,000	
	Premium on Redemption of Redeemable Preference		
	Shares . . . . *Dr.*	15,000	
	To Cash		75,000
	Being redemption of Redeemable Preference Shares in		
	accordance with the above terms as per resolution dated		
	. . . .		

EXTRACT FROM BALANCE SHEET (liabilities side)

	£
Authorised Share Capital (say):—	
60,000 Redeemable Preference Shares of £1 each . . .	60,000
200,000 Ordinary Shares of £1 each	200,000
Issued Share Capital :—	
160,000 Ordinary Shares of £1 each, fully paid . . .	160,000

The compulsory creation of a Capital Redemption Reserve Fund may be effected by a series of transfers over the period of years during which the Redeemable Preference Shares are outstanding, instead of by a lump sum transfer when the shares are redeemed. In such circumstances it may also be advisable to create a sinking fund investing annual sums outside the business in order that funds may be

I*

available for redemption purposes when required. The accounting entries required for the creation and maintenance of such a fund are similar to those described elsewhere in this Chapter in connection with the redemption of debentures.

General Reserves.

All the reserves (and provisions) considered in the preceding paragraphs have had as their principal object the setting aside of profits to cover some known liability or contingency. Quite apart from such reserves, however, profits may be set aside as a measure of prudence with the objects—

(a) Of equalising the amount available for distribution in successive years, profits being set aside in periods of prosperity to create a reserve which will be available to augment the Profit and Loss Account balance in later years or to meet any unexpected contingency or catastrophic loss, or

(b) Of conserving the liquid resources of the business and providing for capital expansion without the issue of further share or loan capital.

In the first case, the creation of the reserve does not of itself represent any locking up of current assets and the fund of working capital which is available for distribution is not

BALANCE SHEETS
AS AT 30TH JUNE, 19..

	Before transfer.	After transfer.		Before transfer.	After transfer.
	£	£		£	£
Share Capital . .	50,000	50,000	Fixed Assets . .	40,000	40,000
General Reserve .		10,000	Working Capital at commencement		
Profit and Loss Account . . .	20,000	10,000	of year . . .	10,000	10,000
			Additional Current Assets representing profits for year . . .	20,000	20,000
	£70,000	£70,000		£70,000	£70,000

thereby affected. This is shown by the Balance Sheets (page 234) which reflect the position of a company before and after transferring £10,000 from Profit and Loss Account.

The company has made a profit of £20,000 during the year and its net current assets must have increased by that amount. Although £10,000 has been taken out of the balance on Profit and Loss Account and transferred to General Reserve, this is only a book-keeping entry : the assets which represent the profits remain in the same form as before.

On the other hand, if £10,000 of additional capital expenditure had been incurred during the year, the following position would result :—

BALANCE SHEET

AS AT 30TH JUNE, 19..

	£		£	£
Share Capital . . .	50,000	Fixed Assets at commencement of year . .	40,000	
General Reserve . .	10,000			
Profit and Loss Account	10,000	Add Additions during year	10,000	50,000
		Working Capital at commencement of year . .	10,000	
		Add Profit for the year .	20,000	
			30,000	
		Less Amount expended on additions to fixed assets	10,000	20,000
	£70,000			£70,000

Assuming that the £10,000 working capital in hand at the commencement of the year is the amount which is necessary for the ordinary trading purposes of the business, the liquid assets available for distribution amount to only £20,000 — £10,000 = £10,000. The position is in fact very similar to that illustrated on page 100 in connection with the redemption of liabilities, and as a matter of prudent finance it might be advisable to capitalise the General Reserve in the form of a bonus issue of shares, thus preventing its distribution to shareholders in the form of a cash dividend.

These considerations should show quite conclusively that

a General Reserve is something more than a mere transfer from Profit and Loss Account. Just as a profit is itself, in the truest sense, an increase in the net assets of a business, so a General Reserve is a surplus of assets over liabilities, capital and the undistributed balance of Profit and Loss Account. Such a surplus is itself a profit and a General Reserve is only another form of undistributed profits ; thus it is usually classified as a Revenue Reserve. It follows that where a General Reserve has been created out of the profits of past years, and losses which have had the effect of throwing the Profit and Loss Account into debit have then been incurred, the General Reserve no longer exists in its entirety. Consider the following example :—

BALANCE SHEETS

	(*a*) £	(*b*) £		(*a*) £	(*b*) £
Capital	10,000	10,000	Fixed Assets . .	9,000	9,000
General Reserve .	4,000	4,000	Current Assets .	5,000	4,000
			Loss for the year .		1,000
	£14,000	£14,000		£14,000	£14,000

In (*a*) there is a *bona fide* surplus of £4,000, representing accumulated profits, and it will be seen that this is reflected on the assets side of the Balance Sheet by assets to the extent of £14,000 available as against capital of £10,000.

In (*b*) a loss of £1,000 has been sustained, with the result that the current assets have been reduced to this extent. It would clearly be incorrect to say that there is still a surplus of £4,000 available to the proprietors, for as against the capital of £10,000 there are assets of £13,000, *i.e.*, there is a surplus of only £3,000. This demonstrates convincingly that the General Reserve cannot exist intact unless trading profits are being made. As soon as a loss is incurred, the reserve in fact is *automatically* reduced, and it would be quite illogical to show a General Reserve and a debit balance on Profit and Loss Account in the same Balance Sheet.

Capital Reserves.

It has been explained in Chapter III that certain profits are of a capital nature and in Chapter VIII it will be shown that, save in exceptional circumstances, such profits are not available for distribution as dividends. A limited company cannot transfer profits to Share Capital Account, which remains fixed at the paid-up value of the shares issued to the members and can be increased only by an additional allotment of shares. Capital profits must therefore be transferred to a Capital Reserve which is similar to a General Reserve in that it represents a surplus of assets over liabilities but differs from it in that this surplus may not be a profit available for distribution in dividends. On a scheme for increasing the share capital the balance of a Capital Reserve could be used for paying up bonus shares.

The following items, which usually appear in a Balance Sheet under separate headings, are really in the nature of a Capital Reserve :

(1) Share Premium Account, *i.e.*, where a company has issued its own shares at a price in excess of their nominal value and has thus become possessed of net assets in excess of its capital liability ;

(2) Forfeited Shares Account, *i.e.*, amounts received originally as share capital on shares subsequently forfeited in respect of which there is now no liability to the shareholders.

Reserve Funds.

It should be clearly realised that a fund may be built up in association with any type of provision or reserve. Thus a provision for depreciation may be accompanied by the setting aside of definite funds for replacement, and a reserve for the redemption of debentures may likewise be represented by a fund of assets set aside for the purpose.

Where, as in the former case, a fund is built up to provide for a future loss, the annual allocation is, in accordance with the general principle enunciated at the beginning of this Chapter, a charge against profits, for the amounts transferred to the Depreciation Fund will never again become available for distribution. When the time comes for the fund to be applied for the purpose for which it was created, it disappears from the books. Thus, suppose that a lease which cost £5,000 has been allowed to remain in the books at that figure, depreciation having been provided for by the accumulation of a Depreciation Fund of £5,000, represented by gilt-edged investments of the same amount. If £5,000 is now required to obtain a renewal of the lease on similar terms the investments will be sold to provide the necessary funds and the credit balance on the Depreciation Fund will be used to extinguish the debit balance on the old lease account.

Dr.	DEPRECIATION FUND		*Cr.*
	£		£
To Transfer to Old Lease Account	5,000	By Balance, *b/f.*	5,000

Dr.	INVESTMENTS OF DEPRECIATION FUND		*Cr.*
	£		£
To Balance, *b/f.*	5,000	By Cash	5,000

(The possibility of a profit or loss on realisation has been ignored ; if the investments have been suitably chosen, there is likely to be only a small balance which should be transferred to Profit and Loss Account.)

Dr.	OLD LEASE ACCOUNT		*Cr.*
	£		£
To Balance, *b/f.*	5,000	By Transfer from Depreciation Fund	5,000

Dr.	NEW LEASE ACCOUNT		*Cr.*
	£		
To Cash	5,000		

Where the Reserve Fund is built up to provide for the redemption of a liability or to strengthen the financial position of the business, it is an appropriation of profits. The realisation of the investments which constitute the fund provides the liquid resources necessary to accomplish its object (*e.g.*, the redemption of debentures) : the fund remains as a credit balance in the books and is not required to extinguish a debit balance as in the preceding paragraph. Profits have been set aside to prevent the withdrawal of current assets required for a capital purpose ; they are profits which could have been distributed in dividends but have been applied inside the business for some other purpose which enhances the value of the shareholders' interest in the company. This is recognised by transferring the balance of the fund to the credit of General Reserve, as in the example on page 229.

Sinking Funds.

The term " sinking fund " was first used in reference to proposals to pay off or " sink " the National Debt. It is now applied to any fund which is created by the regular investment of such an amount as, with compound interest earned thereon, will accumulate to a given sum at the end of a stated period. Sinking funds are much favoured by Governments and Local Authorities as a method of providing for the repayment of debt, and many public loans are issued on terms that a sinking fund is to be operated. Strictly, the repayment of a loan (*e.g.*, debentures) by instalments is a form of sinking fund, but for accounting purposes the term is usually restricted to *accumulative* sinking funds, which are formed by investment in securities for the purpose of—

(1) *Replacing a wasting asset* at the expiration of its expected life, or

(2) *Repaying a liability* on its due date.

So far as the building up of the sinking fund is concerned, what is required is the provision of a sum of money on a given date some years ahead : the ultimate use to which that sum of money is to be put is immaterial.

In practice the investment of sinking fund instalments is nearly always restricted to gilt-edged securities,* in order to ensure, as far as may reasonably be possible—

(1) Safety of capital, and

(2) A constant rate of interest.

---

* Alternatively the instalments may be used to pay the premiums on a capital redemption policy (see page 228).

As Income Tax will be deducted from, or payable on, the interest received from the investment in securities, the calculation must be based on the estimated *net* rate. The fact that compound interest is allowed for in the calculation of the annual * instalment presupposes that all interest received will be reinvested with the next instalment of the sinking fund and on the same terms. The amount of the annual instalment is found from compound interest (annuity) tables, the use of which is explained in Chapter VII.

Thus, to take a simple example, if it is required to accumulate a sum of £100 at the end of 5 years and a net rate of interest of 5 per cent. per annum is expected, annuity tables will show that at that rate of interest £1 per annum will amount in 5 years to £5·5256.

If £5·5256 can be obtained by the annual investment of £1, then, by simple proportion, £100 can be obtained by the annual investment of $£\dfrac{100}{5 \cdot 5256} = £18 \cdot 0976$ or £18 1s. 11d.

The fund will accumulate in the following manner:—

		£	s.	d.	£	s.	d.
1st Year.	Amount invested (at end of year)				18	1	11
2nd Year.	Interest		18	1			
	Annual instalment	18	1	11			
	Total amount invested				19	0	0
					37	1	11
3rd Year.	Interest	1	17	1			
	Annual instalment	18	1	11			
					19	19	0
					57	0	11
4th Year.	Interest	2	17	1			
	Annual instalment	18	1	11			
					20	19	0
					77	19	11
5th Year.	Interest	3	18	0			
	Annual instalment †	18	2	1			
					22	0	1
					£100	0	0

* For convenience, the appropriations and investment will be assumed to be made annually—actually they might be made half-yearly or at other regular intervals.

† The final instalment is adjusted to £18 2s. 1d. to cover the fractional pence over the period.

From the point of view of the accountant, the accumulation of a sinking fund presents two distinct features—

(1) The fund itself is built up either by annual appropriations of profit, as in the case of a Reserve for Redemption of Debentures considered on page 226, or by annual charges to Profit and Loss Account where the purpose of the fund is to provide against a loss which should properly fall on revenue, as in the case of a Depreciation Sinking Fund. These appropriations or charges remain constant; they are not affected by the interest earned on the investments.

(2) The investments representing the fund are acquired by annual payments of cash. After the first year, interest is received on the amounts already invested; the annual payment therefore increases, for it includes—

    (a) The fixed annual payment, and

    (b) The reinvestment of the interest received.

The accumulation of the fund illustrated in the example on page 240 will be recorded in the accounts on pages 243 and 244.

The disposition of the ultimate balance on the Sinking Fund Account will depend on the purpose of the fund. If it has been created for the redemption of a liability, it represents undistributed profits and will be transferred to General Reserve. On the other hand, if it has been created to provide for a loss, such as depreciation, it will be used to extinguish the debit balance remaining on the asset account, as in the example on page 238.

The following example illustrates the effect on the entries in a Balance Sheet on the redemption of a liability and the replacement of an asset, assuming the investments realised their par value :—

(a) *Balance Sheet immediately before redemption and replacement :—*

	£		£
5 per cent. Debentures . .	10,000	Machinery at cost	7,000
		Debenture Sinking Fund	
Debenture Sinking Fund . .	10,000	Investments	10,000
Depreciation Sinking Fund		Depreciation Sinking Fund	
(Machinery)	7,000	Investments	7,000

(b) *Balance Sheet immediately after redemption and replacement :—*

	£	£		£	£
5 per cent. Debentures	10,000		Machinery at cost .	7,000	
Less : Cash Repayment . . .	10,000		*Less :* Transfer from Depreciation Sinking Fund . .	7,000	
General Reserve		10,000	New Machinery at cost. . .		7,000
Debenture Sinking Fund . . .	10,000		Debenture Sinking Fund Investments	10,000	
Less : Transfer to General Reserve	10,000		*Less :* Cash on Sale	10,000	
Depreciation Sinking Fund . . .	7,000		Depreciation Sinking Fund Investments	7,000	
Less : Transfer to Machinery Account	7,000		*Less :* Cash on Sale	7,000	
			Cash (Realisation of Investments) .	17,000	
			Less : New Machinery . . £7,000 Repayment of Debentures £10,000	17,000	

Any profit on realisation of the investments should preferably be transferred to General Reserve. On the other hand, if a loss is incurred it is advisable to make it good out of revenue, for, to the extent of the loss, the redemption of the liability or the replacement of the asset will deplete the working capital by a correspondingly greater amount than was expected.

The risk of loss on realisation may be minimised by a careful selection of investments, and securities should be chosen which have a redemption date approximating to the time when the funds will be required (*i.e.*, short-dated securities), thus eliminating any loss on realisation and avoiding the brokerage on the sale of the investments.

Dr.   SINKING FUND ACCOUNT   *Cr.*

		£	s.	d.			£	s.	d.
1st Year.					1st Year.				
31st Dec.	To Balance, *c/d.*	18	1	11	31st Dec.	By Profit and Loss Appropriation A/c.*	18	1	11
2nd Year.					2nd Year.				
31st Dec.	To Balance, *c/d.*	37	1	11	1st Jan.	By Balance, *b/d.*	18	1	11
					31st Dec.	„ Cash—Interest received		18	1
						„ Profit and Loss Appropriation A/c.	18	1	11
		£37	1	11			£37	1	11
3rd Year.					3rd Year.				
31st Dec.	To Balance, *c/d.*	57	0	11	1st Jan.	By Balance, *b/d.*	37	1	11
					31st Dec.	„ Cash—Interest received	1	17	1
						„ Profit and Loss Appropriation A/c.	18	1	11
		£57	0	11			£57	0	11
4th Year.					4th Year.				
31st Dec.	To Balance, *c/d.*	77	19	11	1st Jan.	By Balance, *b/d.*	57	0	11
					31st Dec.	„ Cash—Interest received	2	17	1
						„ Profit and Loss Appropriation A/c.	18	1	11
		£77	19	11			£77	19	11
5th Year.					5th Year.				
31st Dec.	To Balance, *c/d.*	100	0	0	1st Jan.	By Balance, *b/d.*	77	19	11
					31st Dec.	„ Cash—Interest received	3	18	0
						„ Profit and Loss Appropriation A/c.	18	2	1
		£100	0	0			£100	0	0
					6th Year.				
					1st Jan.	By Balance, *b/d.*	100	0	0

Secret Reserves.

The reserves considered so far deal only with adjustments, charges and appropriations from profit which are made in the books of account and are shown in the final accounts. There

* When the fund is accumulated for the replacement of an asset the annual charge appears in Profit and Loss Account.

Dr.   SINKING FUND INVESTMENTS   *Cr.*

		£	s.	d.			£	s.	d.
1st Year.					1st Year.				
31st Dec.	To Cash . .	18	1	11	31st Dec.	By Balance, *c/d.*	18	1	11
2nd Year.					2nd Year.				
1st Jan.	To Balance, *b/d.*	18	1	11	31st Dec.	By Balance, *c/d.*	37	1	11
31st Dec.	,, Cash . .	19	0	0					
		£37	1	11			£37	1	11
3rd Year.					3rd Year.				
1st Jan.	To Balance, *b/d.*	37	1	11	31st Dec.	By Balance, *c/d.*	57	0	11
31st Dec.	,, Cash . .	19	19	0					
		£57	0	11			£57	0	11
4th Year.					4th Year.				
1st Jan.	To Balance, *b/d.*	57	0	11	31st Dec.	By Balance, *c/d.*	77	19	11
31st Dec.	,, Cash . .	20	19	0					
		£77	19	11			£77	19	11
5th Year.					5th Year.				
1st Jan.	To Balance, *b/d.*	77	19	11	31st Dec.	By Balance, *c/d.*	100	0	0
31st Dec.	,, Cash* . .	22	0	1					
		£100	0	0			£100	0	0
6th Year.									
1st Jan.	To Balance, *b/d.*	100	0	0					

are, however, certain adjustments for which no entry evi-
dencing their creation appears in the final accounts. These
reserves are known as secret, hidden or inner reserves and
although their *existence* may sometimes be inferred from an
intelligent perusal of the accounts, their *amount* is not ascertainable in this way.

Like other forms of reserves, they are created either to
increase the financial stability of the company or to provide
for contingencies. The more usual methods by which they
are created are—

(1) Charging capital expenditure to revenue ; *e.g.*, im-
     provements and additions to buildings, machinery
     and plant, which in the ordinary way are capitalised,
     are charged against the current year's profits.

(2) The undervaluation of assets ; *e.g.*, fixed assets, in-

* In practice this instalment would not be invested, but the cash would be earmarked, with the proceeds of sale of the £77 19s. 11d. investments already made,
for the purpose of the Fund.

vestments or stock-in-trade are valued much below cost or market price, while some very prosperous concerns value " Goodwill ", in their balance sheets, at a purely nominal figure or write it off altogether.

(3) The creation of specific provisions in excess of actual requirements, *e.g.*, excessive provisions for depreciation or for bad debts.

(4) Grouping unrelated items on the liabilities side of the Balance Sheet, *e.g.*, Reserves and Creditors under a general heading such as " Sundry Creditors and other Credit Balances ".

The foregoing remarks indicate the position prior to 1st July, 1948, for the provisions of the Companies Act, 1948, require considerable disclosure with regard to provisions and reserves, thus the existence, creation and utilisation of secret reserves will now be apparent from an inspection of the published accounts of companies.

Although there was much to be said against the creation of secret reserves, it was commonly held that there was no harm in understating a company's financial position in its Balance Sheet, whereas in no circumstances should the Balance Sheet overstate the financial position.

The following arguments were advanced for and against the creation and utilisation of secret reserves :—

Advantages.

(1) They facilitate trade expansion by keeping in the business current assets which might otherwise be distributed as dividends.

(2) They serve to equalise the apparent balance of profits and the dividends paid therefrom.

(3) Public confidence is fostered in the company.

(4) They help to assure a stable market price for the shares.

Where financial stability is very important, as in the case of banking and assurance companies, these arguments acquire special significance.*

* This fact is recognised in the exempting provisions with regard to disclosure contained in Part III, Eighth Schedule, Companies Act, 1948 (see Appendix I).

Disadvantages.

(1) Extensive creation of such reserves will cause the annual balance sheets to present an entirely false view of the state of the company's affairs.

(2) Declaration of dividends is vested in the shareholders (subject to the recommendations of the directors), and when secret reserves are created they are not in possession of all the information which has a bearing on the amounts of dividend which might be declared.

(3) The creation of secret reserves may operate unfairly between the different classes of shareholders. Preference shareholders nearly always stand to benefit, for while the reserves are only likely to be created in years when the profits are amply sufficient to cover the preference dividends, they may be drawn on to help pay these dividends when times are not so good. Ordinary shareholders, on the other hand, although they benefit from the provision of reasonable reserves which will be available to equalise the fund of divisible profits, stand to lose if the profits are systematically and regularly understated by the creation of secret reserves.

(4) If excessive secret reserves are created the market value of the shares may be permanently depressed.

(5) Unscrupulous directors may use secret reserves to manipulate prices of shares on the open market.

The trend of public and judicial opinion, prior to the Companies Act, 1948, with regard to secret reserves may be illustrated by reference to *Newton* v. *Birmingham Small Arms Co., Ltd.*, 1906, and *Rex* v. *Kylsant*, 1931, and it is advisable to refer to these two cases before considering the relevant provisions of the Companies Act, 1948.

The *creation* of secret reserves was considered in *Newton* v. *Birmingham Small Arms Co., Ltd.*, 1906, and as this is the only High Court decision which has any direct bearing on the subject it is worthy of close study. Special

resolutions had been passed altering the company's Articles
to enable the directors to accumulate an " internal reserve
fund " " for any purpose which the directors in their absolute
discretion may consider will serve, protect or advance the
interests of the company ". The auditors were to have all
the facts relating to the fund disclosed to them, and it was to
be their duty to see that it was applied for the purposes of
the company in accordance with the provisions of the Articles ;
but they " were not to disclose any information in regard
to the same to the shareholders or otherwise ". Although
these alterations of the Articles were held to be *ultra vires*,
the creation of secret reserves as an ordinary matter of
business routine was not condemned but, on the whole, received the approval of the learned Judge. In the course
of the judgment it was stated that " The purpose of the Balance Sheet is primarily to show that the financial position
of the company is at least as good as there stated, not to
show that it is not or may not be better ". The company lost
its case, not because it sought to take power to create secret
reserves, but because it sought to fetter the auditors in the
discharge of their duty to report to the members, by making
it impossible for them to refer to the secret reserves even if
they wished to do so.

The *utilisation* of secret reserves was considered in *Rex* v.
Kylsant, in which the chairman and auditor of the Royal Mail
Steam Packet Company were tried on a criminal charge of
issuing false accounts with intent to deceive the shareholders.
Although the charges failed and it was shown in the course
of the trial that what at first appeared to be a manipulation
of secret reserves over a period of years resolved itself into
the release of specific provisions for taxation liabilities which
were no longer necessary, it was inevitable that the question
of secret reserves should attain considerable prominence.
In this case, the bringing into account without disclosure of
" special credits " had materially altered the state of affairs
shown by the annual Profit and Loss Accounts and in some
years, when the company had traded at a loss, it had been
made to appear comparatively prosperous. Not only had
dividends been paid out of the credit balances thus made

available but the "net profits" had been incorporated in a prospectus for the issue of debenture stock.*

The extract from Mr. Justice Wright's summing up quoted below shows that the question is mainly one of degree.

"We have heard a great deal about the keeping of secret reserves, and we have heard a great deal about the commercial troubles which may flow from that practice. We have heard a great deal about what is often done in practice, and it may be reasonably and properly done, but the question may arise some day, and possibly will arise, in some appropriate proceeding in order to find out and elucidate these very special matters. It was said by a very learned judge on one occasion, by way of observation and not by judgment, that a company, that is to say the shareholders, could not complain if the position of the finances of the company was better than the accounts disclosed. That has been quoted from time to time as a justification for this method of keeping reserves secret. But there may be very great evils if those who have the control and management of the companies, and who control and manage companies for the benefit of the shareholders who entrust their moneys to companies, have very large portions of the company's assets left in the secret disposition of the managing authority. It may work very well in many cases ; no doubt it does ; it is a practice which is being followed, no doubt, by many concerns of the highest standing. On the other hand, it may be the subject of almost intolerable abuse. Such a system may be used to cover up negligences, irregularities, and almost breaches of faith. It is said to be a matter of domestic concern between the company and the shareholders, but if shareholders do not know and cannot know what the position is, how can they form any view about it at all ? How can they consider whether it is something which they are satisfied with or which they are not satisfied with ? "

Although the Royal Mail case presented several novel features (*e.g.*, the company was not registered under the Companies Acts) and in spite of the acquittal of the auditor and the chairman on the charge relating to the accounts, the very fact that the case was brought and was very strongly presented by the law officers of the Crown has been of the greatest benefit in strengthening the hands of auditors. In this connection it may be noted that the Judge said :

"If the accounts from which dividends and expenses are paid are being fed by undisclosed reserves, it seems difficult to see how an auditor can possibly discharge his duty of giving a true and accurate view of the company's affairs without mentioning and drawing attention to the fact, which may be almost of vital importance as indicating the state of the company's affairs."

Before the Royal Mail case was brought, it was thought that, inasmuch as the balance of the Profit and Loss Account

---

* It was in regard to the issue of this prospectus that the chairman of the Royal Mail Steam Packet Company, Lord Kylsant, was convicted on a separate charge.

is itself one item in the Balance Sheet, the auditor's duty was restricted to verifying that this balance was in fact available for distribution in dividends. The matter has been placed beyond all doubt by the Companies Act, 1948, and the auditor must pay careful attention to the wording of the Profit and Loss Account which accompanies the Balance Sheet. It is seen that the *creation* and *use* of secret reserves are two entirely distinct matters, and while the one may often be commended, the other requires the greatest care and, save in the most exceptional circumstances, should be disclosed.

The possibility of the abuses inherent in the creation and utilisation of secret reserves has resulted in provisions being included in the Eighth Schedule to the Companies Act, 1948, making it compulsory to disclose all reserves and provisions created by a company in its published accounts, together with details of amounts transferred thereto or withdrawn therefrom during the accounting period. In addition, the Act requires disclosure in the Profit and Loss Account of any material respects in which it is affected by transactions of an exceptional or non-recurrent nature ; thus any secret reserves which would escape detection under the first-mentioned provision are brought to light by this requirement.

It should be noted, however, that the provisions of the Act do not prevent the creation of reserves and provisions in the manner described in (1) to (3) on pages 244 and 245, but simply require that such reserves and provisions must be disclosed in the accounts.

The general provisions of the Companies Act, 1948, with regard to disclosure of the creation and utilisation of secret reserves are not applicable, in their entirety, to banking and insurance companies as it is recognised that, in the case of such companies, their continued success is largely dependent upon the retention of public confidence, and in these circumstances secret reserves serve a useful purpose.

CHAPTER VII

DEPRECIATION

The word " depreciation " is used in more than one sense, and unless its meanings are clearly explained, confusion is likely to result. Once these different meanings have been distinguished, the context will always make the word quite definite.

The primary meaning of the word " depreciation " is loss of value through wear and tear or some other form of material deterioration. In this sense the word describes a fact and has no reference to any accounting process. Depreciation must take place whether it is reflected in the books of account or not. Machines wear out, leases come to an end, and these and similar things are therefore said to depreciate.

The secondary sense of the word " depreciation " is the operation of adjusting the book values of assets. As machines or other assets get old, it is the practice of accountants to reduce their values in the books of account, and it is usual to call this " depreciating the machines " and the resulting charge to Profit and Loss Account, " Depreciation ". There are many influences that go to decide the fact and the extent of depreciation in this sense, and wear and tear and other forms of actual loss of utility are not the only factors to be considered. To take an extreme case, Goodwill may be written off rapidly if a business is prosperous : yet this very prosperity is an indication that Goodwill is at least as valuable as it ever was. Thus an asset that is actually increasing in value may be written down in the books of account, and the term " depreciation " is sometimes extended to cover even such an instance as this.

Depreciation takes place irrespective of repairs and maintenance ; thus the fact that an asset is maintained out of revenue by a substantial expenditure on repairs does not render a provision for depreciation unnecessary.

The book-keeping entries involved in writing down assets are quite simple, as the examples will show, and the main object of this Chapter is to discuss the systems that are followed in reducing book values over a series of years. The merits and demerits of these systems will be considered, and the factors that determine the amounts by which book values should be adjusted will be indicated.

It is essential to realise that the chief concern of accounting is to discover and indicate how much and in what manner capital increases or decreases ; and that all the arguments and devices that are about to be detailed are directed towards a proper distinction between capital and revenue—*i.e.*, towards an accurate calculation of profit or loss, the accepted names for capital fluctuations.

Before examining the systems of depreciation that are commonly in use, it is as well to consider the effect of making a charge for depreciation against revenue. The typical entry is a debit in Profit and Loss Account and a credit in the account of the asset that is being depreciated. The latter entry is intended to reduce the book value of the asset to what is considered a fair statement of its value to the business as a going concern. There is no attempt to arrive at the market value of the asset—the amount it would be likely to realise if it were sold secondhand.

The debit entry in Profit and Loss Account makes the balance of that account—the amount that remains disposable as dividends—less than it otherwise would have been. Now the greater part of the debits in Profit and Loss Account represent actual expenses, for which cash has been or will be paid out. But a charge for depreciation is different. No cash has been expended, and the effect is to prevent cash from being paid out and thus to preserve the working capital of the business from being depleted. If the depreciation had not been charged a corresponding amount might have been distributed, and when the asset required renewing new capital would have had to be found.

The following Balance Sheet shows the position of a company before the commencement of a year's trading :—

BALANCE SHEET
AS AT 1ST JANUARY, 1955

	£		£
Issued Share Capital :—		Goodwill at cost	20,000
50,000 Ordinary Shares of		Plant at cost	30,000
£1 each	50,000	Stock	15,000
Profit and Loss Account . .	5,000	Debtors	8,000
		Cash	2,000
	55,000		
Creditors	20,000		
	£75,000		£75,000

During the ensuing year a profit of £10,000, before making provision for depreciation of plant, was earned. The Balance Sheet at the end of the year shows the following position :—

BALANCE SHEET
AS AT 31ST DECEMBER, 1955

	£		£
Share Capital :—		Goodwill at cost	20,000
50,000 Ordinary Shares of		Plant at cost	30,000
£1 each	50,000	Stock	14,000
Profit and Loss Account :—		Debtors	6,000
£		Cash	13,000
Balance, *b/f.* . . 5,000			
Profit for Year . . 10,000			
	15,000		
	65,000		
Creditors	18,000		
	£83,000		£83,000

Finally, if the necessary provision for depreciation of plant is £3,000 and the balance of the profit for the year, £7,000, is distributed as dividend, leaving the same balance to be carried forward on Profit and Loss Account at the end of the year as was brought in at the beginning of it, the second Balance Sheet must be adjusted as follows :—

BALANCE SHEET
AS AT 31ST DECEMBER, 1955

	£			£
Share Capital :—		Goodwill at cost		20,000
50,000 Ordinary Shares of			£	
£1 each	50,000	Plant at cost . . .	30,000	
Profit and Loss Account :—		*Less* Depreciation .	3,000	
£				27,000
Balance, *b/f.* . . 5,000		Stock		14,000
Profit for Year . . 7,000		Debtors		6,000
		Cash		6,000
12,000				
Less Dividend . . 7,000				
	5,000			
	55,000			
Creditors	18,000			
	£73,000			£73,000

It is seen that although the whole of the net profit has been distributed, the working capital has increased by £3,000, which is the amount of depreciation written off plant. The working capital is calculated as follows :—

	1st Jan., 1955.	31st Dec., 1955.
	£	£
Stock	15,000	14,000
Debtors	8,000	6,000
Cash	2,000	6,000
	25,000	26,000
Less Creditors	20,000	18,000
	£5,000	£8,000

Every asset in a business is expected to yield a profit, and it cannot do so until it has paid for itself. Hence the charges for depreciation that are made annually in respect of it are properly deducted from the revenue of the business in order to recover the original capital expenditure on the asset.

The time over which the depreciation charges are spread should not be greater than the estimated life of the asset, as they are needed to build up the sum that will be necessary for its renewal.

It may be thought advisable, under present conditions, to provide by means of " depreciation " for an amount greater than the cost of the asset, on the ground that the cost of replacement may be greater than that of the original. In such a case we are not merely recovering money spent : in addition we are accumulating further capital ; and theoretically a depreciation charge which is based on an increased cost of renewal should be divided into two portions. The part which would suffice to recover cost over the estimated period is a proper cost or expense of the business, to be provided for before net profit is ascertained ; but the remainder is a gift of present profits to future years, and is a part of net profits—not the cost of production—and thus should be debited (as a transfer to reserve) to Appropriation Account.*

The increase in the general level of prices has caused other accounting problems such as the question as to whether materials consumed should be charged in the accounts at their original historical cost, or at their current replacement value. Moreover, distortion may appear in the interrelationship of fixed assets appearing in the Balance Sheet at original cost (which may have been pre-war in the case of land and buildings) to current assets at recent prices, and some authorities advocate the revaluation of fixed assets. If fixed assets are revalued at an amount exceeding their original cost price the following entries must be made in the books :—

(a) The amount of past depreciation provisions no longer required will be transferred to revenue reserve.

(b) The amount by which the current valuation exceeds original cost must be transferred to capital reserve, and is not available for dividend.

The future annual provisions for depreciation must be based

---

* Reference should be made to the recommendations of the Council of the Institute of Chartered Accountants with regard to depreciation of fixed assets and on the matter of rising price levels in relation to accounts (see Appendix II).

on the revised valuation, and consequently the charges against profits will be heavier than previously was the case.

A charge for depreciation is in no way dependent upon the existence of profits. Depreciation is as much a charge against profits as wages, and should be made without regard to the amount of profit available. It would savour of doubtful finance if a necessary provision for depreciation was waived, particularly if the waiver had the effect of showing a small profit when actually a loss had been made. The Companies Act, 1948, provides that, where practicable, fixed assets must be shown in the Balance Sheet at cost or valuation, the aggregate amount of depreciation being deducted therefrom. The amount charged for depreciation during the current accounting period must also be disclosed in the Profit and Loss Account. The shareholders will therefore be able to obtain some indication as to the adequacy or otherwise of the amount charged for depreciation in the accounts of a company. The temptation encountered by directors in times of bad trade to reduce or omit the normal provision for depreciation is restricted, for such a variation from the former practice would constitute a change in the basis of accounting, and the Companies Act, 1948, requires the effect of any such change to be disclosed by way of note, whilst if no provision for depreciation is made, a note to that effect must be made in the accounts.

The main methods of providing for depreciation are six in number. They are as follows :—

1. RE-VALUATION. This is simply the examination of the asset by a competent person who gives a certificate of what he considers to be the true value of the asset.

2. FIXED INSTALMENT METHOD. The cost, less anticipated break-up value, is divided by the number of years of estimated life, to ascertain the sum to be written off annually. This method is also known as the " Fixed Charge " Method or the " Straight Line " Method.

3. REDUCING BALANCE METHOD. A rate per cent. is decided, such that if it is applied to the balance

of the book value at the end of each year it will reduce that value to the approximate equivalent of break-up value by the time the estimated period of life has passed. This is known also as the " Reducing Instalment " Method.

4. ANNUITY METHOD. For the moment it is enough to say that this method is based on the assumption that when money is retained in a business by way of a depreciation provision, it begins to earn interest. Hence any annual sum written off really provides for its own original amount *plus* the interest earned by it as time goes on. This interest is taken into consideration.

5. SINKING FUND. This is also known as the " Depreciation Fund " Method. No entries on account of depreciation are made in the asset account, but annual investments are made, which, being allowed to accumulate at compound interest, will reach the book value of the asset (or any other estimated cost of replacement) by the time the asset is expected to go out of use. It will be seen that interest is taken into account in this method, as it is in the Annuity Method, but the form of calculation is different.

6. CAPITAL REDEMPTION POLICY. This is a modification of the last-mentioned method.

In addition, the *Depreciation Provision* (previously termed " Depreciation Reserve ") Method may be noted as a method of book-keeping rather than as a method of calculating the amount to be provided for depreciation. Thus, under any of the first four methods outlined above, an amount to be provided out of revenue is calculated and is actually written off the value of the asset as shown in the books. Instead of this, the annual provision can be carried to a separate Provision for Depreciation Account, the asset being allowed to remain at cost : thus both the original cost of the asset and the total provision for depreciation to date are shown in the Balance Sheet.

In general it may be stated that the assessment of depreciation involves the consideration of three factors : the cost of the asset, which is known, the probable value realisable on ultimate disposal, which can generally only be estimated within fairly wide limits, and the length of time during which the asset will be commercially useful to the undertaking. In most cases, this last factor is not capable of precise calculation. Provisions for depreciation are therefore in most cases matters of estimation, based upon the available experience and knowledge, rather than of accurate determination. They require adjustment from time to time in the light of changes in experience and knowledge, including prolongation of useful life due to exceptional maintenance expenditure, curtailment due to excessive use, or obsolescence not allowed for in the original estimate of the commercially useful life of the asset.

Revaluation.

A typical example of revaluation is the stock-taking that is regularly done in all businesses where stocks are held. It is the only way to deal with certain kinds of assets with a view to obtaining a fair statement of profit or loss. The method of treating stock in hand is already known and it is obvious that any changes of valuation, as they will affect the gross profit as shown by the Trading Account, must also affect the net profit in the Profit and Loss Account to the same extent.

Other assets such as farmers' live stock, packages, loose tools, patterns, etc., may be written down expressly, by carrying the difference between the book value and the revaluation to Profit and Loss Account, or (in the case of loose tools) may be treated in a Manufacturing Account as stock is treated.

It is evident that this method is rough and ready in that it takes into consideration *fluctuation* in value as well as *depreciation*. An asset may change in value because of, *e.g.*, market fluctuations as soon as it has been acquired, and such a change would be reflected in a revaluation. The only limit set to this is the practical rule that assets should not be written *up* above cost price.

K

When a more systematic method can be applied, revaluation should not be adopted, if only because it makes very unequal charges year by year in respect of the same asset, although the services rendered by the asset are probably about the same year by year.

Revaluation has a value as a rough check that can be applied from time to time on the results of other methods.

Fixed Instalment Method.

Suppose that machinery has been purchased at a cost of £1,000, that its life is estimated at five years and that its break-up value will be about £40. The amount that has to be written off in five years is £1,000 — £40 = £960. This can be done by writing off £$\frac{960}{5}$ or £192 per annum, if no account is taken of interest.

The principle is simple and the entries are merely an annual :—

	£	s.	d.	£	s.	d.
Depreciation . . . . *Dr.*	192	0	0			
To Machinery				192	0	0
Being annual provision for depreciation.						

It is sometimes contended that under this method the annual *cost of the service of the machinery* is not as uniform as appears at first sight, since charges for repairs and maintenance will tend to increase towards the end of the effective life of the asset. This objection may be overruled on two grounds, *viz.* :—

(1) Although the argument may be true when applied to a single machine, it loses its significance when a number of machines, of varying ages and effective lives, are involved.

(2) Maintenance and depreciation are two entirely different heads of expenses, arising from separate causes. The annual charge for depreciation is computed upon the very assumption that the machines will be properly maintained.

Nevertheless, it is sometimes the practice to create a combined provision for repairs, maintenance and depreciation, as in the example given on page 260.

A disadvantage that deserves more attention is that when additions are made to the machinery in the written down account a fresh calculation of the amount to be written off annually has to be made. This may be remedied by the raising of a separate depreciation account which is *credited* with the sums provided for depreciation each year. The accounts are summarised below, assuming a five-year life and residual value nil.

Dr.		MACHINERY ACCOUNT			Cr.
Year.			£		£
1	To Cash		1,000		
2	„ „ (Additions)		100		
3	„ „ „ .		160		

Dr.	DEPRECIATION (MACHINERY) ACCOUNT				Cr.
		£	Year.		£
			1	By P. and L. A/c.— 20% . . .	200
			2	„ do. do.	220
			3	„ do. do.	252

Depreciation has been calculated on the additions for the whole of the year during which they were acquired. This is, of course, the safest method to adopt when no further information is available ; but if the Profit and Loss Account is to show a strictly accurate debit for the year, a proportionate charge should be made.

If it were thought that repairs and renewals would amount on the average to about 5 per cent. per annum of the original cost, a combined charge could be made as in the following example :—

Dr.		MACHINERY ACCOUNT			Cr.
			£		
Year 1	To Cash		1,000		
Year 2	„ „ (Additions)		100		
Year 3	„ „ „ .		160		

Dr.   DEPRECIATION (MACHINERY) ACCOUNT   *Cr.*

		£			£
Year 1	To Cash, Repairs and		Year 1.		
	Renewals . .	30	Dec. 31	By P. and L. A/c.—	
Dec. 31	„ Balance, *c/d.* . .	220		25% of £1,000 .	250
		£250			£250
Year 2	To Cash, Repairs and		Year 2	By Balance, *b/d.* . .	220
	Renewals . .	25	Dec. 31	„ P. and L. A/c.—	
Dec. 31	„ Balance, *c/d.* . .	470		25% of £1,100 .	275
		£495			£495
Year 3	To Cash, Repairs and		Year 3	By Balance, *b/d.* . .	470
	Renewals . .	60	Dec. 31	„ P. and L. A/c.—	
Dec. 31	„ Balance, *c/d.* . .	725		25% of £1,260 .	315
		£785			£785
			Year 4	By Balance, *b/d.* . .	725

As before, the additions are kept in the Machinery Account, the balance of which is readily referred to for the calculation of the annual charge.

It sometimes happens that, in consequence of abnormal expenditure during any one period, the Depreciation and Maintenance Account (if kept) may show a debit balance. If this is likely to be recouped out of subsequent provisions it may be allowed to stand (being in effect a form of Deferred Revenue Expenditure), but such a balance may indicate inadequacy of the annual provision, which should then be revised as necessary.

An objection to the above may be seen in the fact that there is no safeguard against the continued provision for depreciation in respect of items which have been completely written off. There is thus a serious risk of making imaginary and totally unnecessary charges against revenue ; and no further elaboration of accounts can eliminate this possibility without a great deal of trouble. In fact, nothing less than a detailed plant register or plant ledger, containing a complete record of data relating to each item of plant purchased and used in the business, will suffice. A ruling of a book suitable for this purpose is shown on page 261. This may have great advantages quite apart from the safeguard provided against

PLANT REGISTER.

Particulars of Machine: *Slasher Sizer.*
Erected in: *Preparation Room.*

Date Purchased: *January 3rd, 19..*
Expected life: *Twenty years.*

Makers: *Howard & Bullough, Ltd.*
Estimated Scrap Value: *£100.*

Date.	Particulars.	Folio.	Original Cost and Additions.			Repairs.			Renewals.			Depreciation written off. 19..			Book Value. 19..			Depreciation written off. 19..			Book Value. 19..			Etc.	
			£	s.	d.	£	s.	d.	£	s.	d.	£	s.	d.	£	s.	d.	£	s.	d.	£	s.	d.	£	s.
19.. Jan. 3	Cost of machine purchased on this date		2,500									120		·	2,380		·								

NOTES.—(1) The repairs and renewals columns are memorandum columns only and do not affect the book value of the machine.
(2) If necessary, additional columns may be inserted for costing data, *e.g.*, running hours, fuel consumption, etc., and for taxation capital allowances.

fictitious depreciation, and if so it will perfect the Fixed Instalment Method of depreciation so far as that is possible. It will show, for example, the detailed cost of keeping up every item of plant and machinery, and add much valuable knowledge of the relative merits of the various types in use.

It may be noted that there has been some conflict of opinion about the treatment of additions *in the first year* of their existence. The following methods have been advocated. They do not introduce any real difficulty.

(1) The additions are ignored by the calculation of depreciation on the *opening* balance of the account ;

(2) They are included, by basing the calculation on the *closing* balance ;

(3) They are depreciated at half-rate, on the assumption that they were acquired half-way through the year.

(4) They are depreciated proportionately, by applying to them that fraction of the normal rate which is equal to that fraction of the year during which they have been in possession.

Reducing Balance Method.

Suppose an asset costs £1,000 and is estimated to reach a break-up value of £240 in four years. To adjust its value by the Reducing Balance Method, a fixed rate per cent. of each year's balance is deducted from that balance, and the rate must be calculated so as to leave the estimated residual value in the estimated time. It will be found that a rate of 30 per cent. achieves this result, as is shown by the account on page 263.

If the Fixed Instalment Method had been used it would have been necessary to write off £190 $\left(i.e., £\dfrac{1,000 - 240}{4} \right)$ during each of the four years ; it is interesting to compare the amounts of the annual debits to Profit and Loss Account under the two methods. [See " Comparative Table " on page 263.]

Dr. MACHINERY ACCOUNT *Cr.*

		£			£
Year 1	To Cash	1,000	Year 1	By Depreciation, 30%	300
				„ Balance . . .	700
		£1,000			£1,000
Year 2	To Balance (B₁)*. .	700	Year 2	By Depreciation, 30%	210
				„ Balance . . .	490
		£700			£700
Year 3	To Balance (B₂) . .	490	Year 3	By Depreciation, 30%	147
				„ Balance . . .	343
		£490			£490
Year 4	To Balance (B₃) . .	343	Year 4	By Depreciation, 30%	
				(nearest unit) .	103
				„ Balance . . .	240
		£343			£343
Year 5	To Balance (B₄) . .	240			

COMPARATIVE TABLE

Year.	(1) Reducing Balance Method.	(2) Fixed Instalment Method.
	£	£
1 . . .	300	190
2 . . .	210	190
3 . . .	147	190
4 . . .	103	190
	£760	£760

It is seen at once that, although the *ultimate object* of charging £760 to Revenue over a period of four years is secured in both cases, the methods and their effect are very different. Thus :—

(1) *The Fixed Instalment Method* requires an annual charge of 19 per cent. on the original balance of

* See "Calculation of the Rate of Depreciation" on page 268.

£1,000 ; this remains constant for each of the four years ;

(2) *The Reducing Balance Method* requires an annual charge of 30 per cent. on the balance remaining each year after all the previous years' provisions have been credited. Thus the amounts written off each year decrease progressively (in this example, considerably) so that although the charges for the early years exceed the corresponding charges under the Fixed Instalment Method, those for later years are less.

This is admittedly an extreme example, and when a longer period is considered the difference will not be so marked. Nevertheless there will always be differences and they will be of the same kind.

It is interesting to compare the results obtained by writing off the same percentage under the two methods. For this purpose 5 per cent. has been chosen, for this rate has been widely used in practice for many different purposes.* By the Fixed Instalment Method, an annual provision of 5 per cent. will write off an asset completely in 20 years.

If the fixed instalment charge of £50 per annum is correct, *i.e.*, if the asset actually has a life of 20 years and no scrap value, to charge depreciation by the Reducing Balance Method at 5 per cent. per annum is clearly inadequate. In the first year, the amounts written off are the same ; thereafter they fall steadily under the Reducing Balance Method, and in the 14th year the charge of £25 13s. 4d. is approximately half the fixed charge of £50. At the end of 20 years, when the cost of the asset should have been completely written off, a balance of £358 9s. 9d. remains in the books (*i.e.*, about 36 per cent. of the cost) and only £641 10s. 3d. (64 per cent. of the cost) has been written off.

---

* It is the rate (applied to the reducing balance) allowed by the Inland Revenue authorities for calculating the depreciation ("Annual Allowance" or "Wear and Tear") of many types of plant and machinery ; although a claim may be made so that the depreciation allowance, for taxation purposes, is computed on the Fixed Instalment Method.

The following table can be constructed :—

COMPARATIVE TABLE

Year.	Fixed Instalment Method.		Reducing Instalment Method.	
	Depreciation for Year.	Balance on Asset A/c.	Depreciation for Year.	Balance on Asset A/c.
	£	£	£ s. d.	£ s. d.
1	50	950	50 0 0	950 0 0
2	50	900	47 10 0	902 10 0
3	50	850	45 2 6	857 7 6
4	50	800	42 17 4	814 10 2
5	50	750	40 14 6	773 15 8
6	50	700	38 13 9	735 1 11
7	50	650	36 15 1	698 6 10
8	50	600	34 18 4	663 8 6
9	50	550	33 3 5	630 5 1
10	50	500	31 10 3	598 14 10
11	50	450	29 18 9	568 16 1
12	50	400	28 8 10	540 7 3
13	50	350	27 0 4	513 6 11
14	50	300	25 13 4	487 13 7
15	50	250	24 7 8	463 5 11
16	50	200	23 3 4	440 2 7
17	50	150	22 0 2	418 2 5
18	50	100	20 18 1	397 4 4
19	50	50	19 17 3	377 7 1
20	50	—	18 17 4	358 9 9
	£1,000		£641 10 3	

It is obvious that the Reducing Balance Method entails a higher percentage charge than the Fixed Instalment Method ; the calculation of this rate will be considered later.

At this stage it will also be obvious that, unless a residual value is decided upon, the calculation of a depreciation rate by the Reducing Balance Method is impossible ; for no rate less than 100 per cent. can reduce any balance to zero, however small that balance may be, and a rate of 100 per cent. would charge the whole of the cost of the asset to revenue in the first year. On the other hand, any rate will reduce the book value much more rapidly at the start than in the

K*

later years, and so a large range of rates will bring any amount down to a *negligible* quantity in about the same time.

The graph shown on page 267 has been prepared to show the effect of applying various rates of depreciation by the Reducing Balance Method to an asset which originally cost £1,000.

It is evident that the effect on the annual charge of a difference between two rates of depreciation is greatest during the earlier years and that it becomes quite small after about ten years for any rates that are likely to be used in practice.

The effect of increasing the rate per cent. is to increase the amount of depreciation that is written off during the earlier years. Thus at the end of the second year £440 has been written off at 25 per cent., and £640 at 40 per cent. ; but at the end of the ninth year, when £925 has been written off at 25 per cent., only £990 has been written off at 40 per cent. The ratio in the first place is 11 : 16, or roughly $\frac{2}{3}$, and in the second it is about $\frac{14}{15}$. These figures are quite rough, as near as can be read from the graph, but a more exact calculation would give substantially the same result.

It might be argued that the choice of rate per cent. could conveniently be made subject to the normal increase in repair expenditure for the type of asset according to experience and expert advice, so as to make repairs plus depreciation yield an approximately straight line graph, which would indicate equal cost for equal service. But it is a question whether any such accuracy of fitting is possible, particularly for a number of machines of varying estimated lives.

At the higher rates the curves begin to approach a horizontal direction in the neighbourhood of the ninth year, and it is clear that here the reducing effect of the rate is becoming useless.

The main advantage of the method lies in the simplicity of the necessary calculations and entries once a rate has been fixed. Whether or not it gives a true picture of the physical facts of depreciation is a very doubtful question. Where it is used in conjunction with Cost Accounts it will

GRAPH SHOWING THE EFFECT OF THE REDUCING BALANCE METHOD
OF DEPRECIATION.

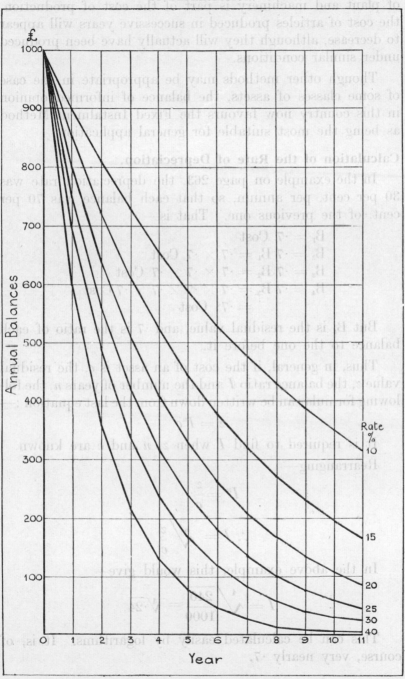

obviously lead to inconsistent results, for, since depreciation of plant and machinery is part of the cost of production, the cost of articles produced in successive years will appear to decrease, although they will actually have been produced under similar conditions.

Though other methods may be appropriate in the case of some classes of assets, the balance of informed opinion in this country now favours the Fixed Instalment Method as being the most suitable for general application.

Calculation of the Rate of Depreciation.

In the example on page 263, the depreciation rate was 30 per cent. per annum, so that each balance was 70 per cent. of the previous one. That is—

$$B_1 = \cdot7 \text{ Cost}$$
$$B_2 = \cdot7\, B_1 = \cdot7 \times \cdot7 \text{ Cost}$$
$$B_3 = \cdot7\, B_2 = \cdot7 \times \cdot7 \times \cdot7 \text{ Cost}$$
$$B_4 = \cdot7\, B_3 = \cdot7 \times \cdot7 \times \cdot7 \times \cdot7 \text{ Cost}$$
$$= \cdot7^4 \text{ Cost}$$

But B_4 is the residual value, and $\cdot7$ is the ratio of each balance to the one before it.

Thus, in general, if the cost of an asset is c, the residual value z, the balance ratio I and the number of years n, the following formula can be written down from the last equation :—

$$z = I^n c$$

It is required to find I when z, n and c are known.

Rearranging—

$$I^n = \frac{z}{c}$$

$$\therefore I = \sqrt[n]{\frac{z}{c}}$$

In the above example, this would give—

$$I = \sqrt[4]{\frac{240}{1000}} = \sqrt[4]{\cdot24}$$

This can be calculated easily by logarithms. It is, of course, very nearly $\cdot7$.

The *depreciation rate* corresponding to this balance ratio is found immediately from the relation $r = 100 (1 - I)$ where r is the rate per cent. per annum at which the asset depreciates. This gives $r = 100 (1 - \cdot7) = 100 \times \cdot3 = 30$.

Alternatively, tables such as the one presented on page 265 are available, showing the balances remaining at the end of successive years when depreciation is calculated at a given percentage rate. By examining several tables at different rates of depreciation a rate may be found which will reduce the cost to residual value at the end of the expected life of the asset.

Interest.

Before examining the remaining systems of depreciation it is necessary to consider generally the effect of interest on transactions which are more or less protracted and which are therefore affected by the element of *waiting*.

Money can always earn interest ; and if a business brought its proprietor no more than the amount he had invested would yield in gilt-edged securities, he would be well advised to transfer his capital from the business to the securities and so minimise the risk of loss. The idea of the earning power of money is in the mind of every business man consciously or unconsciously, and whenever he makes a purchase one of the elements that go to decide the price he is willing to pay is the time he must wait to realise the return he is to obtain.

In the case of raw material for manufacture, purchases are made frequently and each lot is used quickly, so that in each purchase the question of interest is as nearly absent as it can well be, yet even in this type of transaction time is a consideration. Discounts are given for prompt payment, and every effort is made to avoid " locking up " capital in excessive stocks.

Now a piece of raw material diminishes, as such, in quantity as it yields the service we get from it. Its " depreciation " takes the form of actual disappearance as raw material. Only when quantities large enough to last a longer time than usual are acquired can depreciation in the form of deterioration enter ; and such large purchases are made only when the market is advantageous for buying, so that there is a speculative element in the transaction. But in this instance the purchase is partly a financial adventure and not purely a purchase of material, as such, for production. Hence, as the element of depreciation enters, so does the element of interest on money invested ; for if no more than current interest was likely to be derived from a purchase in excess of normal requirements, it would be safer and easier to use the normal financial channels for the disposal of surplus funds.

It may be taken as a fact that any business man would definitely allow for loss of interest in any such transaction as we have described.

When a mine, a leasehold property or a machine is purchased, a store of service is taken that is very much in excess of immediate requirements. A lease may be taken for a term of twenty years, but the property can only be used for a day at a time. Thus although a lump sum, or premium, may be paid at the outset, the benefit of the lease can only be enjoyed in equal annual amounts over the period of its life and at any intermediate date it has a residual value which is approximately equal to the cost of a shorter lease for the remainder of the term.

When a mine or a quarry is bought the investment is exactly comparable with the purchase of an amount of stock by a merchant in excess of the requirements of the immediate future. Every ton of material extracted from a mine reduces the value of the asset as a whole, although it does not reduce the value of the residue per unit. Hence every unit extracted should bear the same charge for depreciation. Although it may be difficult to estimate the value of the contents of an unworked mine, such an estimate must have been made when the purchase of it took place ; and so long as this was not too high the element of cost recovery in each unit extracted will not be too low.

It therefore appears logical to depreciate such assets as mines by writing off the cost in proportion to the output.

If a mine closes down, it cannot depreciate in the material sense. If output is abnormal it must be wasting rapidly.*

But the remaining material in a partly exhausted mine is not being used at all, and much of it may not be used for years. Hence the money that will ultimately be received for its contents must be waited for ; and the present value of that money is represented in the purchase price by a smaller sum which differs from the expected return by the discount on that return for the estimated time of waiting. To write off equal amounts per ton extracted on account of depreciation is clearly not the way to allow for this. The calculation of depreciation should have some reference to the calculation of purchase price; for the total charge for depreciation is intended to recover the purchase price, and, from the opposite point of view, the purchase price is a concentration of the depreciation charges as foreseen at the time of the purchase.

Let it be assumed for the purpose of this argument that it is expected to extract the same amount of material from the mine during each year of its life. The purchase price can then be considered to represent—

(1) The cost of a certain number of tons of material available for sale during the first year, *plus*

(2) The cost of the same number of tons of material available during the second year, *plus*

(3) The same for the third year, and so on throughout the expected life of the mine.

Now a ton of material which can be obtained at once, or during the year, is obviously worth more than a ton of the same material obtainable in two years' time, which, in turn, is worth more than a similar quantity only obtainable in the third year, and so on. To find the value at the present time of a sum of money payable at some future date it is necessary to apply the principle of discounting, just as a banker discounts a bill when he buys it from the holder before it is due for payment. The same principle must be applied

* This fact was recognised by the Inland Revenue authorities in their allowance for exceptional war-time depreciation.

to find the present value (and hence the cost) of the output of the mine, which can only be enjoyed over an extended period. In other words, when a lasting asset is bought, the purchaser expects to get interest on the money he pays immediately for a service which is bound to be spread over a future period.

This argument can be applied to machines as well as to mines. If one machine would give ten years' service and could be bought for £200, while another would give the same annual service for five years only and could be bought for £100, it would obviously be cheaper to buy two successive machines for £100 each than to buy the £200 machine ; for we should have the use of £100 while the first machine purchased was in use, and the interest on that £100 would go to swell our profits.   Hence, because of the interest factor, a machine lasting ten years is not worth twice as much as a machine giving the same annual output for five years only. The straight line method of depreciation would make the same annual charge for both kinds of machine.

Depreciation and interest, then, are physically inseparable. They are both introduced by time, and although they are not identical it is impossible to provide for one exactly without allowing for the other.

The best example to take is clearly one in which depreciation is wholly and solely due to the passage of time, so that there is no qualitative deterioration to fog the relation between depreciation and interest, which also depends entirely on the passage of time.   Such an example is afforded by a lease.

Imagine a property of land and buildings which can be let at a fair rent of £100 per annum, and suppose that money can safely earn 5 per cent. per annum, paid yearly, by way of interest.   A 20-year lease of the property is bought for £1,246 and the property is let for £100 per annum.   The published tables show that £1,246 is the Present Value (at 5 per cent.) of £100 per annum for 20 years.

If the price of the lease is calculated fairly on the basis of the rent receivable, these two things must be exactly equivalent. In other words, if a business man paid £100 rent for the property to use in his business, he would have made just as much profit by the end of the 20 years as if he had paid £1,246 in a lump sum at the beginning of that period.*

Now the first £100 rent (assumed payable at the end of the first year) represents one-twentieth of the service the property is to render to the business. It is, in fact, the cost of that service. But the owner of the lease expects interest on all the money he has invested in it, and therefore looks upon 5 per cent. of £1,246, or £62·3, as revenue, and the remainder, £37·7, as a recovery of capital. And having recovered £37·7 of his £1,246, and knowing that he only has £1,208·3 to come, he *depreciates* his lease by £37·7, writing it down to £1,208·3.

At the end of the next year the £100 rent will consist of interest on £1,208·3 only, or £60·415, the balance of £39·585 being capital. It would seem from this that the investor's income from interest was decreasing, but it must be remembered that he would reinvest each recovery of capital at once and thus his income from interest would be constant so long as the rate of interest he could obtain remained the same.

The Annuity Method.

The principles outlined above are those which underlie this method of depreciation. An annual amount equivalent to a rent is debited as a charge against revenue and interest is added to the debit balance of the asset account. The debit to revenue will always be greater than the interest, and the difference will be the net charge. The debit to revenue, or " rent " charge, is called " depreciation ", but in reality it is interest *plus* depreciation ; and the true provision for depreciation is brought about by the opposition in the Profit and Loss Account of this so-called " depreciation " debit and the interest credit.

Consider the following example of the working of an

---

* This conclusion disregards the taxation angle as lump sum payments for leases are disallowable while regular rent payments are allowable against profits for taxation purposes.

account for a five years' lease costing £2,000, interest being
allowed at 5 per cent. per annum :—

Dr.   LEASE ACCOUNT   *Cr.*

		£	s.	d.			£	s.	d.
1st year	To Cash . .	2,000	0	0	1st year	By Depreciation * .	461	19	0
	„ Interest at 5% per annum .	100	0	0		„ Balance, c/d. .	1,638	1	0
		£2,100	0	0			£2,100	0	0
2nd year	To Balance, b/d.	1,638	1	0	2nd year	By Depreciation . .	461	19	0
	„ Interest at 5% per annum .	81	18	1		„ Balance, c/d. . .	1,258	0	1
		£1,719	19	1			£1,719	19	1
3rd year	To Balance, b/d.	1,258	0	1	3rd year	By Depreciation . .	461	19	0
	„ Interest at 5% per annum .	62	18	0		„ Balance, c/d. . .	858	19	1
		£1,320	18	1			£1,320	18	1
4th year	To Balance, b/d.	858	19	1	4th year	By Depreciation . .	461	19	0
	„ Interest at 5% per annum .	42	19	0		„ Balance, c/d. . .	439	19	1
		£901	18	1			£901	18	1
5th year	To Balance, b/d.	439	19	1	5th year	By Depreciation* .	461	19	1
	„ Interest at 5% per annum .	22	0	0					
		£461	19	1			£461	19	1

(* The amount of £461 19s. 0d. is ascertained from Annuity Tables and,
owing to the approximation to the nearest penny, a small error has to be adjusted
in the last Depreciation charge.)

The Profit and Loss Account for the corresponding years
will show entries similar to the following :—

Dr.   PROFIT AND LOSS ACCOUNT (YEAR 1)   *Cr.*

	£	s.	d.		£	s.	d.
To Depreciation :— Lease	461	19	0	By Interest :— Lease	100	0	0

and the actual depreciation charge is evidently the difference
between these entries, *viz.* :—

	£	s.	d.
	461	19	0
	100	0	0
	£361	19	0

which reduces the cost of £2,000 to £1,638 1s. 0d., the opening
balance of the second year.

It is fairly obvious that the entries for interest are not
essential to this method. The crediting of the interest on
the balance of the Lease Account is a purely fictitious entry,
for every farthing that is due to the lease must already have
been included in the other items credited to revenue, and
the interest on the lease is thus a repetition of income already
brought in. It is necessary, however, to correct the fixed
annual " depreciation " charge on the debit side of the
Profit and Loss Account.

The crediting of interest, however, simplifies the keeping
of the Lease Account. Once the uniform annual amount
(£461 19s. in the example given above) has been ascertained,
there is nothing left to do but calculate the 5 (or other rate)
per cent. on the opening balance for the year. This is the
simplest way to arrive at the net charge, and it might as
well be done in the account where the procedure stands clear
for inspection as on separate sheets of paper, in which case
the resulting figures would not be self-explanatory.

The following table puts the whole process in a nutshell :—

DEPRECIATION OF A LEASE COSTING £2,000, INTEREST AT 5 PER CENT. P.A.

Year.	P. and L. Debit for Depreciation.	P. and L. Credit for Interest.	Net Charge.	Annual Increase of Net Charge.	Balance of Cost.
1	461·950	100·000	361·950	—	1,638·050
2	461·950	81·903	380·047	18·097	1,258·003
3	461·950	62·900	399·050	19·003	858·953
4	461·950	42·948	419·002	19·952	439·951
5	461·950	21·998	439·952	20·950	—

The column " Net Charge " shows the amounts actually provided each year to make good the cost in the end. The last item in this column is too great by 0·001, but this cannot be avoided when the results are approximated to three decimal places and it is left uncorrected so that all the calculations can be followed.

It will be observed that the net charge increases as the years go on, though not so violently as the charges under the Reducing Balance Method *decrease*. This gives the impression that the cost of renewal is not fairly distributed over the years of use. But money would not be hoarded in a business unless it was likely to yield a return ; and if this is granted it will be understood that the profits of the business will be increased by the earnings of the sums retained by means of the net charges.

Now each item in the " Annual Increase of Net Charge " column is the interest at 5 per cent. on the item in the " Net Charge " for the previous year. It therefore represents the earnings of the previous year's net charge, or the theoretical increase of profits due to that net charge. Hence, as the net charge increases the net profits theoretically increase correspondingly and the burden of depreciation is exactly equal for all the years, always assuming that the rate of interest used is the same as that which the business itself can yield on capital invested therein.

It will be observed that on the correctness of the estimate of the rate of interest employed in the calculation depends the accuracy of the result. If this is chosen without reference to the actual circumstances, if, for example, the current interest rate on gilt-edged securities is taken, it may be far from correct, for the earnings of money in the business may be different. Hence the argument that the net charges should be considered to earn the same rate of interest as if they had been invested outside the business is not beyond criticism, since as the amounts set aside for depreciation are retained in the business and utilised as additional working capital, they may be considered as earning the rate of interest which the business itself can earn on its own capital.

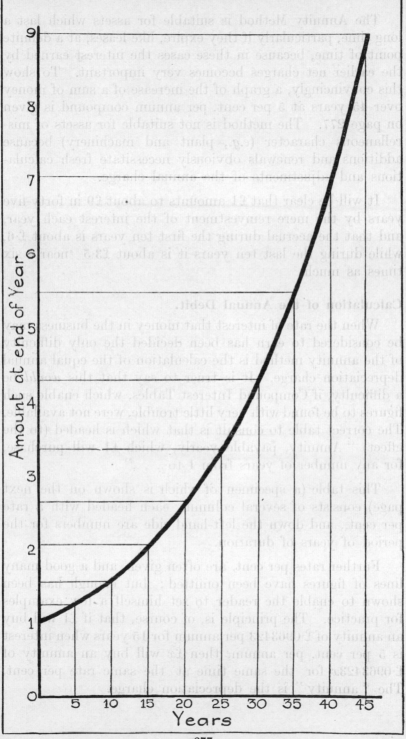

The Annuity Method is suitable for assets which last a long time, particularly if they expire, like leases, at a definite point of time, because in these cases the interest earned by the earlier net charges becomes very important. To show this convincingly, a graph of the increase of a sum of money over 45 years at 5 per cent. per annum compound is given on page 277. The method is not suitable for assets of miscellaneous character (*e.g.*, plant and machinery) because additions and renewals obviously necessitate fresh calculations and adjustments of the annual charge.

It will be clear that £1 amounts to about £9 in forty-five years by the mere reinvestment of the interest each year, and that the accrual during the first ten years is about £·6, while during the last ten years it is about £3·5—nearly six times as much.

Calculation of the Annual Debit.

When the rate of interest that money in the business may be considered to earn has been decided the only difficulty of the annuity method is the calculation of the equal annual depreciation charge. It is truer to say that this *would* be a difficulty, if Compound Interest Tables, which enable such figures to be found with very little trouble, were not available. The correct table to consult is that which is headed (to the effect) " Annuity, payable yearly, which £1 will purchase, for any number of years from 1 to . . ."

This table (a specimen of which is shown on the next page) consists of several columns, each headed with a rate per cent., and down the left-hand side are numbers for the period of years of duration.

Further rates per cent. are often given, and a good many lines of figures have been omitted ; but enough has been shown to enable the reader to set himself a few examples for practice. The principle is, of course, that if £1 will buy an annuity of £·0963423 per annum for 15 years when interest is 5 per cent. per annum, then £x will buy an annuity of £·0963423x for the same time at the same rate per cent. The " annuity " is the depreciation charge.

TABLE

SHOWING THE ANNUITY, PAYABLE YEARLY, WHICH £1 WILL PURCHASE, FOR ANY NUMBER OF YEARS FROM 1 TO 50

Years.	3 per cent.	3½ per cent.	4 per cent.	4½ per cent.	5 per cent.
1	1·0300000	1·0350000	1·0400000	1·0450000	1·0500000
2	·5226108	·5264005	·5302961	·5340976	·5378049
3	·3535304	·3569342	·3603485	·3637734	·3672086
4	·2690270	·2722511	·2754900	·2787436	·2820118
5	·2183546	·2214814	·2246271	·2277916	·2309748
10	·1172305	·1202414	·1232909	·1263788	·1295046
15	·0837666	·0868250	·0899411	·0931138	·0963423
20	·0672157	·0703611	·0735817	·0768761	·0802426

EXAMPLE: Required the depreciation charge for writing off a machine costing £500, estimated to last 15 years, with interest at 4½ per cent. per annum. Scrap value nil.

£1 will purchase an annuity for 15 years of £·0931138

Multiply by 500

46·5569

∴ Depreciation charge = £46 11s. 2d. (approximately).

In some sets of tables called " Depreciation Tables ", which are compound interest tables under another name, the heading of the table given above would be to the effect " Amount required to write off £1 by the Annuity Method ".

The Depreciation (or Sinking) Fund Method.

When the Annuity Method is followed, although money is accumulated in the business it is not kept in the form of cash. If it were it would not earn the rate of interest it is assumed to earn (unless that rate was fixed at the level of bank interest on deposits, which would be unreasonable). Hence a difficulty arises in taking the money out of the business again when it is wanted, as it may probably have become locked up in non-readily realisable assets. This would be very inconvenient, and might cripple the business if the amount were large.

In consequence of this feature, it is common to institute what is known as a Sinking Fund Investment, which is increased annually by a fixed amount and which consists of safe and readily realisable securities that bear interest. When the asset in respect of which the investment is made requires renewal, the securities are sold, and cash is available for the replacement of the asset.

The fact that interest is earned on the securities should not be unduly emphasised as an advantage of this method, for the interest will certainly be at a low rate and will probably be less than the interest earned by the business on its own capital. There is thus a loss of interest in taking funds outside the business for investment, but this loss (or diminution) is compensated by the fact that when the asset in respect of which the investment is made requires renewal, the securities may be sold and the funds obtained without any adverse effect on the business.

The book-keeping scheme consists of the raising of two accounts :—

(1) A Depreciation Fund Account, which may also be known as an " Amortisation Fund Account ", a " Sinking Fund Account ", or a " Redemption Fund Account ", though the name adopted here is the best description when the object of the account is to replace a wasting asset ;

(2) A Depreciation Fund Investment Account, which also may have other names corresponding with those given above.

The asset account is kept in its original state, *i.e.*, the cost of the asset is not written down at all.

The Sinking Fund Method is particularly useful for leases where replacement on a known date will be absolutely inevitable. By heavy expenditure on repairs, worn-out plant may be kept in use for years after the point has been reached where it would be really more economical to replace it, if financial conditions do not warrant its immediate replacement. This latitude is not available where leases are concerned, for a substantial premium will usually be charged for any extension of the original terms.

The working of the accounts is best explained by means of an example. Suppose that a seven-year lease has been bought for £5,000 and that the cost is to be recovered by the Depreciation Fund Method at 4 per cent. compound interest.

The proper table of Annual Sinking Fund Instalments must be consulted for the amount to be charged in the Profit and Loss Account each year. This table is different from the one already quoted. As a Compound Interest table it would be headed (to the effect) " The Annuity, payable yearly, which will amount to £1 for any number of years from 1 to . . .". In a set of depreciation tables it might be headed " Annual Sinking Fund Instalments to provide £1 ". In some tables this particular table is omitted, and a table showing " The Sum to which an Annuity of £1 (or a Sinking Fund Instalment of £1), accumulating at Compound Interest will amount in any number of years from 1 to . . ." must be used.

Specimens of these two tables are here given.

SINKING FUND TABLE I
OF ANNUAL SINKING FUND INSTALMENTS TO PROVIDE £1

Years.	3 per cent.	3½ per cent.	4 per cent.	4½ per cent.	5 per cent.
3	·323530	·321934	·320349	·318773	·317209
4	·239027	·237251	·235490	·233744	·232012
5	·188356	·186481	·184627	·182792	·180975
6	·154598	·152668	·150762	·148878	·147017
7	·130506	·128544	·126610	·124701	·122820
10	·087231	·085241	·083291	·081379	·079505
15	·053767	·051825	·049941	·048114	·046342
20	·037216	·035361	·033582	·031876	·030243

SINKING FUND TABLE II

OF SUMS TO WHICH AN ANNUITY OF £1, PAYABLE YEARLY, AT COMPOUND INTEREST, WILL AMOUNT IN 1 TO 50 YEARS

Years.	3 per cent.	3½ per cent.	4 per cent.	4½ per cent.	5 per cent.
3	3·090900	3·106226	3·121600	3·137025	3·152500
4	4·183627	4·214943	4·246464	4·278191	4·310125
5	5·309136	5·362466	5·416323	5·470710	5·525631
6	6·468410	6·550152	6·632975	6·716892	6·801923
7	7·662462	7·779407	7·898294	8·019152	8·142008
10	11·463879	11·731393	12·006107	12·288209	12·577892
15	18·598914	19·295681	20·023588	20·784054	21·578564
20	26·870374	28·279682	29·778079	31·371423	33·065954

It is necessary to find what annual investment at compound interest will accumulate to £5,000 in seven years at 4 per cent. By Table I, £·12661 will amount to £1,

$$\therefore \text{ £·12661} \times 5000 \text{ will amount to £5,000}$$

$\therefore$ The annual instalment is £633·05
or about £633 1s.

Or, by Table II, £1 will amount to £7·898294.

Let the required instalment be £x

Then £x will amount to £5,000

$$\therefore \text{£}x = \text{£}\frac{5000}{7·898294}$$

$$= \text{£}633·048$$

or about £633 0s. 11½d.

The slight difference is due to the approximation of the last decimal figure in the tables.

If the instalment is taken as being £633·048, the following entries will be made in the books. (Decimals are used to facilitate the calculation but in practice the amounts would be converted into £ s. d.)

Assuming the asset appears in the books at cost, the entries at the end of the first year will be—

JOURNAL

Year.		£	£
Dec. 31	Profit and Loss Account . . . . . *Dr.*	633·048	
	To Depreciation Fund		633·048
	Being annual provision for depreciation.		

This entry will be repeated at the end of each of the seven years.

CASH BOOK
(Credit Side)

		Bank. £
Dec. 31	By Depreciation Fund Investment	633·048

During the second year this investment will earn interest at 4 per cent., and this will be invested in turn. The entries will, therefore, be (in addition to a Journal entry precisely the same as before)—

CASH BOOK
(Debit Side)

		Bank. £
Dec. 31	To Depreciation Fund (*interest on first year's investment*) .	25·322

(Credit Side)

		Bank. £
Dec. 31	By Depreciation Fund Investment	658·370
	(*Instalment plus interest on first year's investment.*)	

and there will be similar entries increasing in amount for the following years.

The accounts will finally appear as shown on pages 285 and 286.

In the last charge to the Profit and Loss Account an adjustment of £·018 has to be made. This is due to the three-place approximation.

The last item of cash on the debit side of the Depreciation Fund Investment Account, £801·006 (representing the annual instalment £633·030 and interest received during the seventh year, £167·976) will not actually be invested but will be earmarked for the purpose of the Fund.

In the Balance Sheet, the Depreciation Fund will appear most properly as a deduction from the cost price of the Lease, while the Investments will also appear on the same side of the Balance Sheet.

It is quite possible to make the first investment of a Sinking Fund at the beginning of the first year : in that case the annual instalment will earn a year's interest by the time it would otherwise have been invested ; and the same applies to all the subsequent instalments. It follows that when investments are made at the beginnings of years they should be less than those made at the ends of years, other things being equal, by the interest they earn during the first year of their investment. The tables given in this Chapter apply to funds built up by investments at the ends of years, and to calculate the necessary sums for investment at the beginnings of years, the figures given must be divided by $(1 + i)$, where i is the interest on £1 for one year at the rate selected.

In working examples, the student must be very careful to see whether investments are made at the beginning or the end of the year, for a mistake about this will make all his work incorrect.

Where the investments are made at the beginning of each year, the first re-investment of interest will be made at the beginning of the second year and not at the end of that year (see page 287), as is the case in the accounts illustrated on the following pages.

Dr.		LEASE			Cr.
Year 1 Jan. 1	To Cash	£ 5,000	Year 7 Dec. 31	By Depreciation Fund	£ 5,000

Dr.		DEPRECIATION FUND			Cr.
Year. 1 Dec. 31	To Balance, c/d.	£ 633·048	Year. 1 Dec. 31	By P. and L. A/c.	£ 633·048
2 Dec. 31	To Balance, c/d.	1,291·418	2 Jan. 1 Dec. 31	By Balance, b/d. „ Cash (Interest) . . „ P. and L. A/c.	633·048 25·322 633·048
		£1,291·418			£1,291·418
3 Dec. 31	To Balance, c/d.	1,976·123	3 Jan. 1 Dec. 31	By Balance, b/d. „ Cash (Interest). . . „ P. and L. A/c.	1,291·418 51·657 633·048
		£1,976·123			£1,976·123
4 Dec. 31	To Balance, c/d.	2,688·216	4 Jan. 1 Dec. 31	By Balance, b/d. „ Cash (Interest) . . „ P. and L. A/c.	1,976·123 79·045 633·048
		£2,688·216			£2,688·216
5 Dec. 31	To Balance, c/d.	3,428·794	5 Jan. 1 Dec. 31	By Balance, b/d. „ Cash (Interest) . . „ P. and L. A/c.	2,688·216 107·530 633·048
		£3,428·794			£3,428·794
6 Dec. 31	To Balance, c/d.	4,198·994	6 Jan. 1 Dec. 31	By Balance, b/d. „ Cash (Interest) . . „ P. and L. A/c.	3,428·794 137·152 633·048
		£4,198·994			£4,198·994
7 Dec. 31	To Transfer to Lease Account	5,000·000	7 Jan. 1 Dec. 31	By Balance, b/d. „ Cash (Interest) . . „ P. and L. A/c.	4,198·994 167·976 633·030
		£5,000·000			£5,000·000

Dr. **DEPRECIATION FUND INVESTMENT** Cr.

Year.		£	Year.		£
1			1		
Dec. 31	To Cash . . .	633·048	Dec. 31	By Balance, c/d.	633·048
2			2		
Jan. 1	To Balance, b/d.	633·048	Dec. 31	By Balance, c/d.	1,291·418
Dec. 31	„ Cash (Interest and Instalment) . .	658·370			
		£1,291·418			£1,291·418
3			3		
Jan. 1	To Balance, b/d.	1,291·418	Dec. 31	By Balance, c/d.	1,976·123
Dec. 31	„ Cash . . .	684·705			
		£1,976·123			£1,976·123
4			4		
Jan. 1	To Balance, b/d.	1,976·123	Dec. 31	By Balance, c/d.	2,688·216
Dec. 31	„ Cash . . .	712·093			
		£2,688·216			£2,688·216
5			5		
Jan. 1	To Balance, b/d.	2,688·216	Dec. 31	By Balance, c/d.	3,428·794
Dec. 31	„ Cash . . .	740·578			
		£3,428·794			£3,428·794
6			6		
Jan. 1	To Balance, b/d.	3,428·794	Dec. 31	By Balance, c/d.	4,198·994
Dec. 31	„ Cash . . .	770·200			
		£4,198·994			£4,198·994
7			7		
Jan. 1	To Balance, b/d.	4,198·994	Dec. 31	By Cash (proceeds of investments)	5,000·000
Dec. 31	„ Cash . . .	801·006			
		£5,000·000			£5,000·000

NOTE.—In the above example Income Tax has been ignored and it has been assumed that the instalments and interest are invested at par ; also that, at maturity, the investments are realised at par.

The first investment would be

$$\frac{£633 \cdot 048}{1 \cdot 04} \text{ or } £608 \cdot 700$$

and the Depreciation Fund Account would appear as follows:—

Dr.			DEPRECIATION FUND			Cr.
Year. 1		£	Year. 1			£
Dec. 31	To Balance, *c/d*.	633·048	Jan. 1	By P. and L. . (or temporary A/c.)		608·700
			Dec. 31	„ Interest .		24·348
		£633·048				£633·048
2			2			
Dec. 31	To Balance, *c/d*.	1,291·418	Jan. 1	By Balance, *b/d*.		633·048
				„ P. and L. A/c.		608·700
			Dec. 31	„ Interest .		49·670
		£1,291·418				£1,291·418

and so on.

The Investment Account would be correspondingly modified.

It will be observed that the balance of the Depreciation Fund Account is always the same as that of the Investment Account and on the opposite side. This must be so, and if any difference appears there must be an error in the work. If care is taken to maintain this agreement, there should not be much difficulty in the book-keeping.

As more than one security would probably be utilised for investment, there would very likely be more than one Depreciation Fund Investment Account.

It will be noticed that at the end of the period the Depreciation Fund Account is transferred to the asset account, closing it. The Investment Account is closed by the cash realised. The cash for the purchase of a new asset is now in hand. In the example the investments are assumed to realise their book value exactly: in practice they would yield more or less than that value, and the excess or deficit would have to be adjusted by a credit or debit to Profit and Loss Account according to circumstances.

This last point introduces the outstanding weakness of the system. If very stable securities are selected for investment, in order to ensure the exact working out of the calculation on which the fund is based, then low rates of interest must be accepted and (as the tables show) large annual instalments must be set aside. If a reasonably high rate of interest is aimed at, the expectations which the tables evoke will not be fulfilled, because the securities will be more subject to fluctuations. Hence the calculation of the annual instalment is more or less a fiction.

This difficulty is overcome by the use of short-dated redeemable securities, the guaranteed redemption dates approximating to the anticipated dates of asset replacement, or alternatively by the use of insurance policies as a means of investment.

Furthermore, it should be borne in mind that expenses are incurred, e.g., brokerage and stamp duties, when buying and selling investments, and unless such expenses are charged to revenue the calculation of the capital fund invested will be affected.

Some authorities contend that where it is foreseen that the cost of replacement will be higher than the cost of the old asset (consider the replacement of a building erected 50 years ago), it may be considered prudent to base the depreciation calculation on the higher figure. But it should be remembered that where this policy is adopted, only the provision for depreciation of the old asset should be charged against profits in the Profit and Loss Account. The additional amount to meet higher replacement cost cannot be regarded as a charge against the current year's profit because it is made solely for the benefit of the years when the new asset is in use, and must therefore be regarded as an appropriation of profit, i.e., a reserve, to be entered in the Profit and Loss Appropriation Account.

The Capital Redemption Policy Method.

The only theoretical difference between this and the foregoing system is that the cash, instead of being used to buy securities, is paid in the form of premiums to an insurance company.*

This makes the calculation of the annual instalment an exact forecast of what will happen, and although the rate of interest earned is not high it is better than could be obtained from other investments that approach an insurance policy in stability. In particular, the risk of *loss* on realisation is practically eliminated, for nothing less than the failure of the insurance company could cause a loss.

There are two ways of keeping the accounts for the Capital Redemption Policy Method :—

(1) Where a Policy Account is opened ;

(2) Where no Policy Account is opened.

When a Policy Account is opened, the annual premium is debited to it and interest is added yearly until the maturity of the policy at such a rate as to make the balance agree ultimately with the amount received from the insurance company. The entries (assuming a 20-year policy for £5,000, interest being calculated at 3 per cent. giving an annual premium of £180·658) would be—

CASH BOOK
(Credit Side)

Year.		Bank. £
Jan. 1	By Lease	5,000
	(*For the purchase of the Lease.*)	
1 to 20		
Jan. 1	„ Capital Redemption Policy	180·658
	(*For the premiums every year.*)	

* Most insurance companies, in conjunction with their life assurance business, issue a type of Endowment Policy known as a Sinking Fund or Capital Redemption Policy, under which the sum assured is payable at the end of a given period in return for an annual premium. Such policies are similar to Life Assurance Endowment Policies, but the life risk is absent. The premiums are usually calculated so that the sum assured represents the premiums plus compound interest at (say) 3 per cent., the company making its profit by earning a higher rate of interest on its invested funds.

L

JOURNAL

Year.		£	£
1	Profit and Loss Account . . . . *Dr.*	180·658	
and so on	To Lease Redemption Fund		180·658
	(*For the annual charge against Revenue.*)		
		£	£
1	Capital Redemption Policy . . . . *Dr.*	5·420	
and so on	To Lease Redemption Fund		5·420
	(*For the interest on the balance of the Capital Redemption Policy for the first year.*)		

If the actual accounts are raised on the lines indicated here, it will be seen that they are very similar to those involved in a depreciation fund where investments are made at the beginning of the year. The debit to Profit and Loss Account should be observed. The effect of this is, of course, to prevent the distribution in dividends of the money required for the insurance premium.

It will be noted that the first premium is paid at the beginning of the first year, whereas under the Sinking Fund Method, the first investment is usually made at the end of the first year. In consequence, interest is earned as from the commencement of the first year when an assurance policy is taken out and an entry for interest is made at the end of the first year. Under the Sinking Fund method, however, the first interest is earned during the second year, and the first entry in respect of interest is made at the end of the second year.

Some accountants advocate the maintenance of the Capital Redemption Policy Account at its surrender value in case there should be occasion to realise the policy before maturity. If this is done the surrender values in successive years must be ascertained from the insurance company, which probably supplies tables from which the surrender value for each year can be found.

The book-keeping for the maintenance of the Policy Account at the surrender value of the policy consists of an adjustment at the end of each accounting period. No entries will be made for interest. Suppose, for example, a premium of £150 has been paid at the beginning of the first year of assurance and that at the end of the year the surrender value of the policy is found to be £135. As in the previous example the first entry will be :—

			£	£
Profit and Loss Account	. . . . .	*Dr.*	150	
To Lease Redemption Fund	. . . . .			150
Being annual provision for Lease Redemption.				

and the adjusting entry will be :—

			£	£
Lease Redemption Fund	. . . . . .	*Dr.*	15	
To Capital Redemption Policy	. . . .			15
Being adjustment of Capital Redemption Policy to surrender value.				

This will make the Fund Account agree with the Policy Account. When the policy is nearing maturity, the increase in the surrender value for a particular year will probably exceed the premium for that year, and the adjusting entry will consist of—

			£	£
Capital Redemption Policy	. . . . .	*Dr.*	—	
To Lease Redemption Fund	. . . . .			—
Being adjustment of Capital Redemption Policy to surrender value.				

But surrender values are complicated by factors other than interest, and for this reason it is common to find that no Policy Account at all is kept, in which case the premiums are charged direct to revenue by transfer from an Insurance Premium Account which is first of all debited with the cash paid for the premiums. There is thus no allowance *in the books* for interest, and the depreciation, at any particular time, of the asset cannot be seen. Either the surrender value of the policy would have to be specially ascertained for this purpose, or the value of the premiums on a sinking-fund basis would have to be found in tables. As there will be no balance to include in the Balance Sheet in respect of the policy, it is proper to annotate the item " Lease " to the effect that it is covered by an insurance policy. When the policy is realised at maturity, the account to be credited with the proceeds is the Lease Account, which is thus closed.

Relation of Annuity and Depreciation Fund Methods.

As the reader will suspect, there is a very close relation between these two methods, for they both take into account compound interest, they both have to provide for the cost of an asset, and they both operate by equal annual charges to revenue. The following table, which shows the writing down of an asset costing £1,000, with a working life of 10 years and a scrap value of Nil, interest being taken into account at 5 per cent. per annum, should make it clear that the two methods are in fact *exactly the same*, except in the manner of keeping the accounts. It will soon be realised, also, that this *book-keeping* difference is due solely to the fact that when the Annuity Method is employed the annual charges are invested in the business, whereas when the Depreciation Fund Method is employed the annual instalments are invested outside.

A study of this table will show that, since the two methods are mathematically the same, the first Net Charge under the Annuity Method is the Annual Instalment under the Depreciation Fund Method; the Total Investment under the Depreciation Fund Method is the sum of the Net Charges to the same date under the Annuity Method; and that the " Net Charge " Column is the sum of the " Annual Instalment " and " Interest on Accumulation " columns.

COMPARATIVE TABLE

Year.	Annuity Method.				Depreciation Fund Method.			
	Depreciation Charge.	Interest on Balance of Asset.	Net Charge.	Depreciated Value.	Annual Instalment.	Interest on Accumulation.	Total Investment.	Depreciated Value.
1	129·505	50	79·505	920·495	79·505		79·505	920·495
2	129·505	46·025	83·480	837·015	79·505	3·975	162·985	837·015
3	129·505	41·851	87·654	749·361	79·505	8·179	250·639	749·361
4	129·505	37·468	92·037	657·324	79·505	12·532	342·676	657·324
5	129·505	32·866	96·639	560·685	79·505	17·134	439·305	560·685
6	129·505	28·034	101·471	459·214	79·505	21·966	540·986	459·214
7	129·505	22·961	106·544	352·670	79·505	27·039	647·330	352·670
8	129·505	17·634	111·871	240·799	79·505	32·307	759·202	240·798
9	129·505	12·040	117·465	123·334	79·505	37·960	876·667	123·333
10	129·500 (adjusted)	6·166	123·334	—	79·500 (adjusted)	43·833	1,000·000	—

CHAPTER VIII

DIVISIBLE PROFITS AND DIVIDENDS

Ubi jus ibi remedium—where there is a right there is a remedy. Thus, where a person has a right to the profits of a business or a share of those profits, he has a legal remedy should any dispute arise in regard thereto. It is inevitable, therefore, that in the course of various cases it should have been necessary for the Courts of this country to consider the meaning of the word " profits".

A number of these cases have arisen from appeals against income tax and other taxes based on profits (*e.g.*, sur-tax, profits tax, etc.) where the conception of profit is to a certain extent defined and restricted by statute. A consideration of the law of income tax is outside the scope of this volume, but it is interesting to note that, even in this specialised field, the Courts will look primarily to ordinary commercial practice. Thus :

" Profits and gains must be ascertained on ordinary principles of commercial trading " (Lord Halsbury, L.C., in *Gresham Life Assurance Society* v. *Styles*, 1892).

" Profits are ascertained by setting against the income earned the cost of earning it " (Lord Herschell in the same case).

" . . . . In computing the balance of profits and gains for the purposes of income tax . . . two general and fundamental commonplaces have always to be kept in mind. In the first place, the profits of any particular year or accounting period must be taken to consist of the difference between the receipts from the trade or business *during such year or accounting period* and the expenditure laid out to *earn those receipts*. In the second place, the account of profit and loss to be made up for the purpose of *ascertaining that difference* must be framed consistently with the ordinary principles of commercial accounting, so far as applicable, and in conformity with the rules of the Income Tax Act. . . . For example, the ordinary principles of commercial accounting require that in the profit and loss account of a merchant's or manufacturer's business the values of the stock-in-trade at the beginning and at the end of the period covered by the account should be entered at cost or market price, whichever is the lower ; although there

293

is nothing about this in the taxing statutes " (*Whimster & Co.* v. *C. of I.R.*, 1926).

Other cases have arisen out of disputes regarding shares of profit or commissions on net profits payable under service or other agreements, as, for example, in *Johnston* v. *Chestergate Hat Manufacturing Co., Ltd.*, 1915 (*vide* page 98) ; but these are of limited application, depending on the construction of the particular agreement in each case. In *re Spanish Prospecting Company, Ltd.*, 1910, however, the claim of two persons who were entitled to salaries, subject to the proviso that they should not be entitled to draw them " except only out of profits ", was considered and the illuminating judgment of Lord Justice Fletcher Moulton is worthy of close study.

" The word ' profits ' has, in my opinion, a well-defined meaning, and this meaning coincides with the fundamental conception of ' profits ' in general parlance, although in mercantile phraseology the word may at times bear meanings indicated by the special context, which deviate in some respects from the fundamental signification. ' Profits ' implies comparison between the state of a business at two specific dates, usually separated by an interval of a year. The fundamental meaning is the amount of gain made by the business during the year. This can only be ascertained by a comparison of the assets of the business at the two dates.

" We start, therefore, with this fundamental definition of ' profits ', viz., if the total assets of the business at the two dates be compared, the increase which they show at the later date as compared with the earlier date (due allowance, of course, being made for any capital introduced into or taken out of the business in the meanwhile) represents in strictness the profits of the business during the period in question.

" But the periodical ascertainment of profits in a business is an operation of such practical importance as to be essential to the safe conduct of the business itself. To follow out the strict consequence of the legal conception in making out the accounts of the year would often be very difficult in practice. Hence the strict meaning of the word ' profit ' is rarely observed in drawing up the accounts of firms or companies. These are domestic documents designed for the practical guidance of those interested, and, so long as the principle on which they are drawn up is clear, their value is diminished little, if at all, by certain departures from this strict definition which lessen greatly the difficulty of making them out. Hence certain assumptions have become so customary in drawing up Balance Sheets and Profit and Loss Accounts that it may almost be said to require special circumstances to induce parties to depart from them. For instance, it is usual to exclude gains and losses arising from causes not directly connected with the business of the company—such, for instance, as a rise in the market value of land occupied by the company. The value assigned to trade buildings and plant is usually fixed according to an arbitrary rule, by which they are originally taken at their actual cost and are assumed to have depreciated by a certain percentage each year, though it cannot be pretended that any such calculation necessarily gives their true value either in use or in exchange. These, however, are merely variations of practice by individuals. They rest on no settled principle. They mainly arise from the sound business view that it is better to underrate than to overrate the profits, since it is impossible for you to foresee all the risks to which a business may in future be exposed. For instance, there are many sound business men who would feel bound to take account of depreciation in the value of business premises, or in the value of plant especially designed for the production of a particular article, although they would not take account of appreciation in the same arising from like causes.

" To render the ascertainment of the profits of a business of practical use it is convenient that the assets, of whatever nature they be, must be represented by their money value. But as a rule these assets exist in the shape of rights, and not in the shape of money. The debts owed to the company may be good, bad, or doubtful. The figure inserted to represent stock-in-trade must be arrived at by a valuation of the actual articles. Property, of whatever nature it be, acquired in the course of business has a value varying with the condition of the market. It will be seen, therefore, that in almost every item of the account a question of valuation must come in. In the case of a company like that with which we have to deal in the present case, the process of valuation is often exceedingly difficult, because the property to be valued may be such that there are no market quotations and no contemporaneous sales or purchases to afford a guide to its value. It is not to be wondered at, therefore, that in many cases companies that are managed in a conservative manner avoid the difficulty thus presented, and content themselves by referring to assets of a speculative type without attempting to affix any specific value to them. But this does not in any way prevent the necessity of regarding them as forming a part of the assets of the company which must be included in the calculations by which *de facto* profits are arrived at. Profits may exist in kind as well as in cash. For instance, if the business is, so far as assets and liabilities are concerned, in the same position that it was the year before, with the exception that it has contrived during the year to acquire some property, say mining rights, which it had not previously possessed, it follows that those mining rights represent the profits of the year, and this whether or not they are specifically valued in the accounts.

" But though there is a wide field for variation of practice in these estimations of profit in the domestic documents of a firm or company, this liberty ceases at once when the rights of third persons intervene. For instance, the Inland Revenue has a right to a certain percentage of the profits of a company by way of income tax. The actual Profit and Loss Accounts of the company do not in any way bind the Crown in arriving at the tax to be paid. A company may wisely write off liberally under the head of depreciation, but they will be only allowed to deduct the sum representing actual depreciation for the purpose of calculating the profits for the purpose of income tax. The same would be the case if a person had a right to receive a certain percentage of the profits made by the company. In the absence of special stipulations to the contrary, ' profits ', in cases where the rights of third parties come in, mean actual profits, and they must be calculated as closely as possible in accordance with the fundamental conception, or definition to which I have referred. I would have it clearly understood that these remarks have no bearing upon the vexed question of the fund out of which dividends may legally be paid in limited companies."

This judgment shows clearly that the legal interpretation of profit does not differ greatly from the accounting view which has been considered in the preceding Chapters of this

book, and it may be said that the determination of profits
is a matter of accountancy rather than of law. When the
disposition of profits is considered, however,—and it must
be borne in mind that the primary object in running a business
for the acquisition of profit is to provide a fund which will
be available for distribution among the proprietors—considerations of law necessarily override those of accountancy.
The accountant may ascertain the true profits of a business ;
he cannot dictate to the proprietors when they are considering
the disposition of those profits (although he might, of course,
advise as to the effect of any project and express an opinion
about its financial prudence).   When sole traders or partnerships are concerned, the question is not one of great importance.   The firm has no separate entity, as distinct from
its members, and the withdrawal of profits (or of capital)
does not affect the legal remedy of third parties who have a
personal right of action against a sole trader or every member
of a partnership.

Where a limited company is concerned, the distribution
of profits is still a matter primarily for the shareholders :

" The profits of an undertaking are not such sums as may
remain after payment of every debt, but are the excess of
revenue receipts over expenses properly chargeable to revenue
account.   As to what expenses are properly chargeable to
capital, and what to revenue, it is necessarily impossible to
lay down any general rule.   In many cases, it may be for the
shareholders to determine this for themselves, provided the
determination be honest and within legal limits " (Buckley
on Companies).   Other important issues do arise, however.
If profits are withdrawn, the fund available to meet the
claims of trade creditors and debenture-holders is reduced
but the members are not personally liable to make good any
deficiency which may result.   Where the shares are divided
into different classes, the payment of dividends on the
Ordinary or Deferred Shares may prejudice the rights of
the holders of other classes of shares enjoying cumulative
preferential rights.   On the other hand, if the Preference
shareholders' rights are not cumulative, the Ordinary shareholders may object to the payment of the Preference dividend

when the profits are only just sufficient for that purpose and the liquid resources of the company may be strained as a result.

Disputes arising out of the payment or non-payment of dividends have from time to time been brought before the Courts. The rules which have emerged from the results of these disputes will be considered in detail.

Divisible Profits.

Those legal decisions which largely determine what is, and what is not, divisible profit, have primarily been designed to prevent a contravention of law and certainly not to confound and confuse the business man, or to attempt to interfere in matters which are of a purely domestic nature. The Courts have taken pains to make this clear, *e.g.* :—

> " Subject to any provisions to the contrary contained in the Articles, the disposition of the revenue is entirely in the hands and under the control of the company . . . is a matter of internal arrangement " (*Lee* v. *Neuchatel Asphalte Co., Ltd.*, 1889).

This is definite enough, but the determination of what is revenue and what is not revenue for the purposes of distribution is, unfortunately, not so clear, thus—

> " The mode and manner in which a business is carried on, and what is usual or the reverse, may have a considerable influence in determining the question of what may be treated as profits and what is capital. . . . It is easy to lay down as an abstract proposition that you must not pay dividends out of capital, but the application of that very plain proposition may raise questions of the utmost difficulty in their solution. What are profits and what is capital may be a difficult and sometimes an almost impossible problem to solve " (*Dovey and Others* v. *Cory*, 1901).

A company has, therefore, considerable liberty in the disposition of its revenue balances, and the Articles, as long as they do not override general principles of law, may deal comprehensively and conclusively with this matter.

It is possible to lay down two broad and general principles which hold good in all cases and which cannot in any circumstances be violated, *i.e.* :—

(1) The shareholders' capital may not be used for the payment of a dividend ; and

L*

(2) A dividend may only be paid out of a *bona fide* surplus or profit.

It will be seen that the second rule is really a corollary of the first.

The first rule is prohibitive, and because of its wide and sweeping assertion is not, of itself, adequate as a guide in many of the particular cases that may arise in practice. The second rule is positive but it involves the same difficulties of definition as have previously been noted, *e.g.*, What is profit ? Further rules with a more specific application have, therefore, been evolved. These rules deal more particularly with the computation of profits available for distribution by considering, on the one hand, the necessary charges against revenue (more particularly, depreciation), and, on the other hand, by an analysis of certain credit items which fall into the category of capital profits and which have been discussed in Chapter III.

It has already been stated, but it will bear repetition, that the general attitude of the Courts in the matter of dividends leans against interfering with the domestic affairs of a company : that is to say, the onus is on a complainant to show that the directors have contravened the general law or the provisions of the company's Articles or that they have acted in a dishonest manner or in a manner in which no reasonable business man would act. Each case must be treated on its merits, but the provisions of the Articles are always of the greatest importance. In this, as in other matters, they may *restrict* the general rules of law but they cannot extend them. Thus, any Article which restricts the fund of divisible profits (*e.g.*, by providing that depreciation of fixed assets shall be calculated on a certain basis) would have the utmost bearing on the problem, but one which purported to provide that dividends could, if necessary, be paid out of capital would be *ultra vires* and of no effect.

Depreciation and Loss of Capital.

Two of the leading cases under this heading are *Lee* v. *Neuchatel Asphalte Co.*, 1889, and *Verner* v. *General and*

Commercial Trust, 1894. In each it was held that in declaring dividends without first writing down the book values of certain fixed assets, the company had not exceeded its powers. In the case of *Verner* v. *General and Commercial Trust* the company's business was that of an investment trust ; the interest and dividends received on its investments were carried to the credit of revenue, and it was proposed to distribute the balance of the Revenue Account as dividends without providing for depreciation of the capital value of the company's investments although the market value of some of them was greatly reduced. In the course of the judgment it was stated that—

"Fixed capital may be sunk and lost, and yet the excess of current receipts over current payments may be divided ; but floating or circulating capital must be kept up, as otherwise it will enter into and form part of such excess, in which case to divide such excess without deducting the capital which forms part of it will be contrary to law."—Lindley, L.J., in *Verner* v. *The General and Commercial Investment Trust, Ltd.*, 1894.

It should be added, however, that in the cases referred to, the company's Articles contained no clauses requiring the directors to make good capital losses out of revenue ; in fact, in the *Neuchatel* case the Articles provided that dividends *could* be paid before providing for depreciation of fixed assets. Of course, it must be understood that any provisions in a company's Articles requiring such losses to be made good are valid and binding and that effect must be given to them.

While the legal position is that losses of fixed assets need not necessarily be provided for, yet from a commercial point of view such provision is absolutely essential to the prosperity and success of a *continuing* undertaking. Accordingly, the business practice is to make good the losses or wastage of such fixed assets as land and buildings, plant and machinery, etc., and ample provisions are made either by writing off the losses, or by raising sinking funds for their replacement, out of profits. On the other hand, when the fixed capital of a company is represented by such an inherently wasting asset as a gold mine, it is rarely found that any provision is made for the replacement of the capital by the time the mine is worked to exhaustion and is, therefore, valueless.

The reason for this is that such a company is usually

formed for the specific purpose of exploiting the asset, and that the intention is to wind up when the asset is worked out. The appropriation of profits in order to provide for depreciation would simply result in the accumulation of a fund which would be returned to members on the dissolution of the company, and it is considered more equitable and convenient to pay a higher rate of dividend over the period of the company's existence. It must be understood that, from the point of view of the shareholders, dividends paid in these circumstances include a portion of the capital originally subscribed. If all the members are aware of the true facts, and the regulations of the company contain no provisions to the contrary, the law will not interfere ; and, indeed, there is no reason why it should do so.

> " If the company retains assets sufficient to pay its debts, any excess of money, obtained by working the property over the cost of working it, may be divided amongst the shareholders ; and this is true, although some portion of the property itself is sold, and in one sense the capital is thereby diminished " (*Lee* v. *Neuchatel Asphalte Co., Ltd.*, 1889).

The law, therefore, does not require that fixed capital should be maintained intact, and as long as there are sufficient assets to pay creditors (*i.e.*, the company is not insolvent as regards creditors), and the provisions of the Articles or of law are not contravened, a profit shown by the accounts may be divided.* Nor does the law require any provision to be made for replacement, *e.g.* :—

> " I know of no obligation imposed by law or statute to create a reserve fund out of revenue to recoup the wasting nature of capital " (*Lee* v. *Neuchatel Asphalte Co., Ltd.*, 1889).

> " The Companies Act does not require the capital to be made up if lost, and it does not prohibit payment of dividends so long as the assets are of less value than the capital called up, nor does it make loss of capital a ground for winding-up " (Ibid.).

In cases of capital loss or depreciation, however, a distinction must be drawn between losses of fixed capital and losses of floating capital. It has already been shown that floating capital is that which has been used directly in the earning of profits, *e.g.*, profit is earned by the use of floating

---

* This statement applies primarily to *revenue* profits. The disposition of capital profits will be considered later in this Chapter.

capital in the cycle of trade (stock is converted into book debts, and the latter into cash). Any fall in the value of floating assets will, therefore, alter the measure of profit attaching to the transaction at that particular stage in the conversion into cash, *e.g.*, a fall in the value of stock resulting in a fall in selling prices will cause a reduction in the profit attaching from the conversion of stock into debtors and also in the ultimate fund of cash.* This fact has been recognised by the Court in its ruling on the necessity of providing for capital losses, as will be apparent from the passage from *Verner* v. *The General and Commercial Investment Trust, Ltd.*, 1894, cited on page 299.

What is fixed capital and what is floating capital will be left to the Courts to decide with due regard to the facts of the case, *i.e.*, the use to which the capital is put and the purposes for which it is held. Thus, where a company purchased mines to supply raw material for its main manufacture, such mines were to be regarded as floating assets and depreciation accordingly provided :—

> " I think that the money invested in those items (mining leases) is properly regarded as circulating capital. Suppose the company had bought enormous stocks of ore sufficient to last for ten years, it could hardly be said that the true value of so much of this as remained from time to time ought not to be brought into the Balance Sheet, and I can see no difference for the purpose of the account between ore in situ and ore so bought in advance " (*Bond* v. *The Barrow Hæmatite Steel Co., Ltd.*, 1902).

The above principles give the *legal* position, but besides the law there are the dictates of financial prudence. These are a matter for the company itself and the law will only interfere in matters of law, not of discretion. This is very important and the distinction has been well emphasised in the cases dealing with divisible profits, thus—

> " The broad question raised by this appeal is whether a limited company which has lost part of its capital can lawfully declare or pay a dividend without first making good the capital which has been lost. I have no doubt it can—that is to say, there is no law which prevents it in all cases and under all circumstances. Such a proceeding may sometimes be very imprudent, but a proceeding may be perfectly legal and may yet be opposed

---

* The Companies Act, 1948, refers to " current assets " as a term synonymous with floating assets, but, in view of the use of the term " floating assets " in case law, the latter term is retained in this Chapter. Similarly, the term " floating or circulating capital " may be interpreted as the fund represented by current assets, *e.g.*, stocks, debtors, cash, etc.

to sound commercial principles. We, however, have only to consider the legality or illegality of what is complained of."—Lindley, L.J., in *Verner* v. *The General and Commercial Investment Trust, Ltd.*, 1894.

Of course, the Balance Sheet must always show the *true position*.

"It is obvious that capital lost must not appear in the Balance Sheet as intact: the accounts must show the truth and not be misleading or fraudulent" (Lindley, L.J., in the same case).

This means that, if fixed assets have depreciated in value, although it is not essential that *provisions* should be made for this depreciation, the accounts must not be drafted in such a way that its *existence* will be concealed from the shareholders. Investment trust companies, relying on the authority of the *Verner* case, usually retain their investments at cost but state the current market value as a note, so that both the existence and amount of any capital depreciation are at once obvious.

It may be desirable to add that this rule has no application to finance companies, which may possess considerable holdings of investments but are not for that reason to be confused with investment trusts. A finance company is one which endeavours to make profits by *dealing* in investments, although in the process of so doing it may hold investments for a time and, in the ordinary course of events, will receive dividends thereon. Further, it may undertake to float new companies and may underwrite the whole or part of a public issue of shares ; if the issue is unsuccessful, it may be left with large blocks of the shares on its hands which cannot be unloaded on to the market for a long time. Any holding like this is clearly in the nature of stock in trade—*i.e.*, a floating asset. The extract from Lord Justice Lindley's judgment in the *Verner* case, quoted on page 299, shows clearly that it is essential that a finance company should provide for the depreciation of its investments.

Capital Appreciation and Capital Profits.

An appreciation in the total value of capital assets, *if duly realised* by sale or by the getting in of some portion of such assets, may in a proper case be treated as available for purposes of dividend (*Foster* v. *The New Trinidad Lake Asphalte Co., Ltd.*, 1901).

Moreover, such a profit on sale of *part* of an undertaking must remain after taking into consideration the result of the *whole* accounts, *e.g.*, a realised accretion to the estimated value of one item of the capital assets can be deemed to be profit divisible amongst the shareholders only after deducting therefrom any losses whether of capital or revenue.

In such instances, the Articles of Association of the company must not forbid the distribution of capital profits (*Lubbock* v. *The British Bank of South America*, 1892).

This gives the strictly legal view, but from the *financial* point of view the following factors would be taken into consideration before it was decided to distribute capital profits which legally might be distributed as dividends :—

(1) The future financial policy of the company, and in particular, any financial commitments already made which in the future will draw upon the company's liquid resources : *e.g.*, capital profits may be used for capital extensions and expansion of business, and may therefore be conserved as working capital.

(2) The amount of working capital available at the moment ; a distribution should not be made if it will reduce this below the amount required for current trading purposes.

As a general rule, capital appreciation which has not been realised is not available for distribution as a dividend. This is sound in law and in finance because the appreciation does not result in any increase in the fund of circulating assets. Where, however, the " appreciation " is really in the nature of an adjustment of a secret reserve originally created by providing excessively for depreciation, the amount by which the asset is written up, being the measure of profits previously written off in excess of true requirements, may be credited back to Profit and Loss Account and is available for dividend. Thus—

" Where a company, although it has written down goodwill out of profits, has not done so *intending for all time* and in all circumstances to waive the

right to distribute these profits ; and where the company has decided to
write back such profits on the ground that the goodwill is worth more than
its then book value, the company is not thereby precluded from treating
such appropriated profit, written back, as available for distribution, providing
that there is nothing in the Memorandum or Articles to prohibit its so doing "
(*Stapley* v. *Read Bros., Ltd.*, 1924).

This ruling supports the contention that *excess* depreciation is not in the nature of a charge against revenue but is
an appropriation of profits which may, as long as a surplus
still exists, be transferred back to profits.

Revaluation of Fixed Assets.

The increase in the general level of prices in recent years
has resulted, in many cases, in the market value of certain
fixed assets such as land and buildings being considerably in
excess of their original cost or valuation as shown in the
Balance Sheet.   Leading authorities consider that as a general
rule such assets should continue to be shown in the Balance
Sheet at historical cost, but in particular cases there may be
special circumstances which justify the writing up of the
assets concerned, *e.g.*, where the company is about to offer
further shares to the public.   In such cases it is necessary to
apportion the amount by which the book value is written
up ; the amount by which the revised value exceeds original
cost represents an unrealised capital profit, whereas past provisions for depreciation no longer required are of a revenue
nature and may be transferred back to Profit and Loss
Account, although it is considered preferable to credit them
to General Reserve.

When the book value of fixed assets is written up on
a revaluation it is necessary to review the annual provisions
for depreciation.   Each case depends on its merits, in the
case of freehold properties it may be considered that a reduced
amount or even nothing should be charged in future years ;
in the case of leaseholds or assets such as plant and machinery, the burden of depreciation charges in future years will
generally be increased.

Another problem resulting from the increase in the general
level of prices is the question of replacement of fixed assets.
The charging of depreciation provisions based on historical

cost results in the retention of funds equivalent to the original cost of the asset at the expiration of its life, but in the majority of cases these funds will be insufficient to finance the replacement of the asset at current higher prices. Unless measures are taken to build up the necessary funds within the business the company will find itself short of liquid resources and obliged to seek further capital merely to maintain its present earning capacity. Where this problem is likely to arise it is considered sound financial policy to make annual appropriations out of divisible profits to a Reserve for Fixed Assets Replacement sufficient to cover the anticipated increase in the cost of replacement; such transfers from Profit and Loss Appropriation Account are in addition to the normal depreciation provisions based on historical cost charged in the Profit and Loss Account.

Past Losses.

The legal position with regard to past losses (shown in the accounts as a debit balance on Profit and Loss Account), and particularly the effect thereof on the divisibility of current profits, is by no means clear. It was stated in *Ammonia Soda Co., Ltd.* v. *Chamberlain*, 1918, that—

(1) The contention that no dividends can be properly paid out of profits, so long as there are losses previously incurred and not made good, has no foundation in law.

(2) It could not be said in all such cases that dividends can be properly paid without making good the previous loss, for the nature of the business and the amount of the loss may be such that no honest and reasonable man of business would think of paying dividends without providing for it.

In such circumstances it is quite likely that the Court would take the view that a payment could not be properly made by the directors. Furthermore, it is necessary to consider the old debit balance of the Profit and Loss Account, to see whether it represents a loss of fixed or circulating capital. For practical purposes, however, it is difficult to see how a loss shown by an account can be distinguished as a loss of fixed or circulating capital or as a combination of both. Thus, depreciation of a fixed asset is a loss of fixed capital, but where a loss is shown over the whole business it is not possible to say that the whole loss thus shown, with the exception of the amount charged by way of depreciation of fixed assets, is a loss of floating capital, for it is impossible to apportion specific items of gains over specific losses.

The effect of any profit distribution where there are also existing losses needs to be carefully considered. Clearly, if a dividend is paid before the company has reached the stage when its receipts on trading exceed its outgoings, such a payment is a reduction of the paid-up capital and is *ultra vires*. But, where a company has made past losses and then makes a profit out of which it pays a dividend, the question is a different one. Legally such a dividend is not paid out of paid-up capital. In fact, the assets which represent the paid-up capital remain at the same value as before the payment of dividend. Possibly the balance to the credit of Profit and Loss Account should be applied in making up lost capital ; but if it is not so applied, but is applied in paying a dividend, such a payment does not involve a reduction of capital : what it does involve is failure to make good capital which has already been lost. In so far as such a capital loss represents a loss of fixed capital, there is no legal obligation to provide therefor, although the practical difficulty of tracing the incidence of losses of fixed and circulating capital, noted above, applies.

One other consideration, in addition to the question of the making good of past losses out of current profits, arose in the *Ammonia Soda* case. That consideration was whether or not an appreciation of capital could be applied in wiping out the past losses to enable the current profit to be divided. On this point the following extract from the judgment of Mr. Justice Peterson is important.

" I am not satisfied that the proposition that it is contrary to all principles of commercial accountancy to utilise an increase in the value of fixed assets for the purpose of getting rid of a debit which represents loss of paid-up capital is not too wide. It may be a *precept of prudence* and yet be far removed from the sphere of the categorical imperative. Assuming that a company ought to keep the value of its assets up to the amount of the liabilities and paid-up capital, or, in other words, to see that its paid-up capital is intact, why should it be absolutely precluded from stating the true value of its assets ? If it is necessary and proper that a company shall maintain its assets at the amount of its paid-up capital and liabilities, there would not appear to be anything illegitimate in showing that the assets are equal to the paid-up capital and liabilities. Nor for this purpose can it matter that the increased value is due to the fixed assets. The paid-up capital is represented by both fixed and circulating capital, and it seems somewhat arbitrary that circulating capital may be shown at its true value while fixed capital must not."

The above ruling is considered by many authorities to be at variance with strict accountancy principles, but in so far as a loss represents a deficiency in the paid-up capital it is permissible by law, when considering whether there is a deficiency in paid-up capital owing to past losses which ought to be made good out of future profits, to ascertain the real value of assets with the object of discovering if, in fact, there is a deficiency in the paid-up capital. This was the final view expressed in the *Ammonia Soda* case, and as a result it may be taken that a *bona fide* capital appreciation may be applied in extinguishing past losses to enable current profits to be divided. The capital appreciation must be *bona fide*, *i.e.*, the paid-up capital must be intact and the directors must have acted honestly.

General Summary.

The rules discussed above may be conveniently summarised as follows :—

(1) The shareholders' capital may, in no case, be used for the payment of a dividend ;

(2) Dividends can only be paid out of a *bona fide* surplus or profit, but in certain cases this may include profits of a capital nature ;

(3) A dividend must not be paid which will, in any way, jeopardise the security of the creditors of the company ;

(4) The legal decisions bearing on this subject are in all cases subject to the provisions of the company's Memorandum and Articles of Association, which can restrict the power of the company to declare dividends but which cannot extend them so as to contravene general rules of law ;

(5) A dividend can be paid out of current profits without making good a loss of fixed capital, provided the assets are sufficient to cover the liabilities, but depreciation of floating or current assets must always be provided for (*Verner* v. *General and Commercial Investment Trust, Ltd.*, 1894) ;

(6) Depreciation of fixed assets need not be charged in the calculation of current profits (*Lee* v. *Neuchatel Asphalte Co., Ltd.*, 1889 * ; *Verner* v. *General and Commercial Investment Trust, Ltd.*, 1894);

(7) Capital profits are available for distribution if they have been realised, if a surplus remains after a *bona fide* revaluation of all the company's assets, and if the company's Articles of Association do not forbid the distribution of capital profits (*Foster* v. *New Trinidad Lake Asphalte Co., Ltd.*, 1901) ;

(8) It is not always necessary to make good a debit balance on Profit and Loss Account out of current profits before paying a dividend, but regard must be had to the way in which such a debit balance has been incurred (*Ammonia Soda Co., Ltd.* v. *Chamberlain*, 1918) ;

(9) When goodwill has been excessively depreciated in the past, a *bona fide* revaluation can be made and any excess depreciation written off credited back to Profit and Loss Account (*Stapley* v. *Read Bros., Ltd.*, 1924);

(10) The Court will decide each case on its own merits, and will also decide which assets are fixed and which are floating or current, having regard to all the circumstances and to the provisions of the Memorandum and Articles of Association (*Bond* v. *Barrow Hæmatite Steel Co., Ltd.*, 1902).

---

* The value of this case as an authority on this point is lessened by the provision in the company's Articles which *permitted* the payment of dividends before providing for depreciation of fixed assets. Nevertheless, the observations of the learned Judges in this case and the subsequent decision in the *Verner* case would appear to place the matter beyond question.

Surplus.

It may be convenient, at this stage, to describe what is meant by a " surplus ".

In the accounting sense, a " surplus " is the amount by which the net book value of the assets exceeds the total of paid-up capital plus liabilities to external creditors. A surplus can only arise if profits have been earned, for when a new company is floated, the total of its assets (including goodwill) must be equal to the combined totals of share capital and creditors. It would therefore be proper to define " surplus " in another form of words, and to say that it is a credit balance, or series of credit balances, denoting the existence within the undertaking of profits which have not yet been distributed to its proprietors.

Any credit balance on Profit and Loss Account is clearly part of the surplus at that date, and it is not difficult to see that General Reserves fall into the same category. Other balances entering into the determination of profits are :—

(1) CAPITAL RESERVES. Although these may not normally be distributed in dividends, they cannot be regarded as liabilities and on liquidation they will increase the amount returnable to the shareholders. A credit balance on Forfeited Shares Account falls into this class.* In certain circumstances, however, a balance on Capital Reserve Account is merely a credit balance which offsets an excessive valuation placed upon fixed assets, e.g., a Capital Reserve Account which is created on the purchase of another business as a going concern, and accordingly it would be ignored in ascertaining any surplus.

(2) APPROPRIATION OF PROFITS. Reserves built up by appropriation of profits in order to accumulate working capital, e.g., Reserves for Redemption of Debentures remain as a credit balance when the debentures have been repaid. Even at an intermediate date such a reserve represents profits intentionally withheld from distribution and should

* Special considerations apply in the case of the credit balance on Share Premium Account (see page 168).

be taken into account in determining the value of the shareholders' interest in the company at any given date.

On the other hand, reserves built up for replacements of assets and provisions to cover specific losses (*e.g.*, bad debts) do not enter into the calculation of surplus. It is true that they are not liabilities in the ordinary sense, but for this purpose they should be regarded as diminutions of asset values (*e.g.*, if a Provision for Depreciation of £60,000 has been built up against Leasehold Properties standing in the Balance Sheet at cost, £100,000, this is only an alternative of stating them at cost less depreciation, £40,000).

The Distribution of Profits.

There are no provisions in the Companies Act relating to the distribution of the profits of a company, the only regulations applicable being those contained in each company's Articles of Association. In Table A * there are clauses relating to dividends, and although special Articles may extend or vary these provisions, the principal clauses of Table A are usually retained.

The Articles customarily provide that—

(1) No dividend shall be paid otherwise than out of profits (Table A, § 116) ;

(2) The right to declare dividends shall be vested in the members in general meeting, but no dividend may be declared at a rate exceeding that recommended by the directors (Table A, § 114) ;

(3) The directors may pay such interim dividends as appear to be justified by the profits (Table A, § 115) ; and

(4) Before recommending any dividend the directors may transfer to reserve such sums as they deem desirable (Table A, § 117).

It will be seen, therefore, that the responsibility for the

---

* Table A is a model set of Articles contained in the Companies Act, 1948, which applies (1) to all companies which do not register their own Articles and (2) to companies registering their own Articles in so far as the Articles do not exclude or modify its provisions.

distribution of profits among the members rests primarily with the directors.

The phrase " otherwise than out of profits " which is used in § 116 of Table A should be noted carefully, for it is generally agreed that it does not exclude the distribution of capital profits. " Otherwise than out of profits " is, of course, not quite equivalent to " out of capital ".

Where the Articles give the directors the discretion indicated in (4) above it is not open to any shareholder, even if he is a Preference shareholder, to object to the exercise of this right and to insist on the payment of a dividend (*Bond* v. *Barrow Hæmatite Steel Co., Ltd.*, 1902).

Shareholders are entitled to have a dividend paid in cash, unless there is an express agreement to accept shares, debentures, or specific assets (*Hoole* v. *The Great Western Railway Co.*, 1868).

A dividend is a debt due by the company to the shareholders as from the date of declaration, but it does not carry interest. The company may be sued thereon if the amount remains unpaid, and the action is not barred until the expiration of twelve years after the cause of action first arose or after such longer period as may be stipulated in the Articles.

Interim Dividends.

When the Articles permit, the directors may pay interim dividends before the end of a company's financial year. Frequently the terms of issue provide that the fixed dividends on Preference Shares shall be paid at half-yearly intervals. These dividends, when paid, are in the nature of interim dividends and are subject to declaration by the directors.

Before any interim dividends are declared, the following matters should receive careful consideration :—

(1) *The nature of the trade.* The trade may be seasonal, as in the case of a seaside hotel.

(2) *The available profits.* Interim accounts should be prepared in order that the amount of profit available for distribution may be accurately determined.

(3) *The cash resources of the company.* Although a cash fund does not necessarily imply an equivalent

amount of divisible profit, it is essential that profits earned should be largely represented by cash to enable a dividend to be paid without unduly depleting the working capital.

(4) *The future financial commitments of the business.* Obviously, it will be impracticable to distribute profits by way of dividend if the funds are required to finance expansion.

(5) *The possibility of subsequent losses.* A fair margin should be left after deducting the amount of the proposed interim dividend from the profits shown by the accounts, for any subsequent loss that exceeds the margin allowed for the remainder of the financial period must fall on capital.

Power to pay interim dividends must be expressly conferred by the Articles. Unlike a final dividend, an interim dividend is declared by the directors without the sanction of the members in general meeting. Further, the declaration of an interim dividend does not give rise to a debt due from the company, and thus a shareholder cannot claim the payment of an interim dividend which has been declared (*Lagunas Nitrate Co.* v. *Schroeder*, 1901).

Payment of Interest out of Capital.

Section 65 of the Companies Act, 1948, provides that where shares are issued for the purpose of raising funds for the construction of works, buildings, etc., which will not become revenue-earning for some considerable time, the company may pay interest on such paid-up capital and charge the said interest to capital as part of the cost of construction. The payment is, however, subject to the following conditions :—

(1) It must be authorised by the company's Articles, or by special resolution ;

(2) It must be sanctioned by the Board of Trade ;

(3) The rate of interest must not exceed 4 per cent. per annum or such other rate as may for the time being be prescribed by Order of the Treasury ;

(4) The period for which it is paid must be such as the Board of Trade determines and must not in any case extend beyond the close of the half-year next after the half-year during which the works were actually completed ;

(5) The payment of the interest shall not operate as a reduction of the amount paid up on the shares in respect of which it is paid;

(6) The accounts of the company must clearly show the capital on which such interest is paid, and also the rate of interest.*

The Companies (Interest out of Capital) Order, 1929, provides that the maximum rate of interest to be paid in pursuance of the above section shall in no case exceed 6 per cent. per annum, in place of the maximum rate of 4 per cent. specified in Section 65. The Companies Act, 1948, provides that the 1929 Order shall have effect as if it was an Order of the Treasury.

The payment of interest on share capital under the provisions of Section 65 does not amount to the payment of a dividend out of capital ; for interest and dividends are essentially different in their nature. The interest is paid during a period in which the question of dividend payment could not arise, for before the works in course of construction became revenue-bearing there could be no fund of profits out of which a dividend could be paid.

Where loans (*e.g.*, debentures) have been raised for capital purposes, the interest thereon may be paid out of capital, and that fact may be recognised in the accounts, *i.e.*, by charging the interest so paid to the asset account. This interest is, of course, interest paid to a *creditor* and should be distinguished from interest paid to a *shareholder*, under Section 65.

Profits made Prior to Incorporation.

In many cases a company takes over a business from a date prior to its incorporation ; for example, a company regis-

---

* Refer also to Section 65, Companies Act, 1948, reproduced in Appendix I to this work.

tered on the 1st February may acquire the vendor's business as from the 31st December of the previous year, the date on which the vendor's last balance sheet and accounts were compiled. From a legal point of view a company cannot earn profits prior to its incorporation, *i.e.*, before it exists as a legal entity ; moreover, the vendor's price for his business is usually fixed at such a figure as to include the amount of the estimated profits for the intervening period.

Such profits are not available for distribution ; for to distribute them amongst shareholders would, in fact, amount to a payment of dividends out of capital, for it is to be presumed that the equivalent of those profits has already been paid to the vendor as part of the purchase price. Such profits should be placed to a special reserve, of a capital nature, and used for capital purposes only, *e.g.*, the reduction of goodwill.

Sometimes, however, the vendor stipulates that the price agreed upon shall be for the business as at the date from which it is taken over, and the contract further provides for the payment of interest on the purchase money until the completion of the purchase is effected. In such cases, the interest payable up to the date of incorporation may be charged against any profits accruing prior to incorporation. These may be ascertained by taking stock and drawing up accounts at the date of incorporation, or, if this method is inconvenient, they must be ascertained approximately by apportioning over the two periods the profits shown in the accounts at the end of the first trading period.

There are three principal methods of apportionment, *viz.*—

   (1) On the basis of turnover ;

   (2) On the basis of time; and

   (3) On the combined bases of turnover and time.

For example, a company was incorporated on the 1st February and took over a business as from the previous 31st December. The profits for the first year were £3,000, the turnover for January being £4,000, and for the remaining eleven months £46,000. The apportionment may be made as follows :—

On the Basis of Turnover.—This method gives the pre-incorporation profits as $\frac{4}{50}$ of £3,000 = £240, leaving £2,760 available for distribution.

On the Basis of Time.—By this method the pre-incorporation profits are $\frac{1}{12}$ of £3,000 = £250, leaving £2,750 available for distribution.

On the Combined Bases of Turnover and Time.—A further method which gives a much more accurate result and which should be used when the information is available is to apportion the gross profit according to the turnover during the respective periods, and the expenses according to time or other bases, the argument being that gross profits vary directly with the turnover, while expenses vary in response to other circumstances, irrespective of the turnover in those periods.

On this last basis the items in the Profit and Loss Account will be apportioned in accordance with the following rules :—

(1) Those items such as Directors' Fees, Debenture Interest, etc., which relate wholly to the period *after* incorporation must be charged thereto ;

(2) Those items applicable to the period *prior* to incorporation will be charged to that account, *e.g.*, Partners' Salaries, Interest on Partners' Capital, etc.;

(3) The remaining revenue items may be divided into two classes. The first embraces those that vary according to time, *e.g.*, Rent, Rates and other standing charges ; these may be apportioned on a time basis, *i.e.*, $\frac{1}{12}$ before and $\frac{11}{12}$ after incorporation in the above example. The other class covers those items that vary with the turnover, *e.g.*, Discounts Allowable, Salesmen's Commissions, etc., and these may be apportioned according to the amount of the sales before and after incorporation, *i.e.*, $\frac{4}{50}$ before and $\frac{46}{50}$ after incorporation in the above example.

(4) In some businesses certain expenses may be of a seasonal nature, *e.g.*, lighting, etc., and these may

be apportioned according to the time or turnover during the season they were actually incurred, *i.e.*, apportioned under methods (3) and (4) above, not over the whole year, but only over the season in which they are incurred.

EXAMPLE

Johnsons, Limited, was incorporated on 30th June, 1955, to acquire the business of D. Fletcher & Son. The company was to take over the business as from 1st January, 1955, on the basis of the Balance Sheet, dated 31st December, 1954.

The accounts for the year ended 31st December, 1955, disclosed the following :—

The Trading Account showed a Gross Profit of £80,000.

The sales for the year amounted to £400,000 (1st January to 30th June, £180,000 ; 1st July to 31st December, £220,000).

The following expenses were debited to the Profit and Loss Account :—

Preliminary Expenses ($\frac{1}{3}$), £2,000 ; Directors' Fees, £1,500 ; Bad Debts, £1,640 (1st January to 30th June, £780 ; 1st July to 31st December, £860) ; Advertising, £3,600 (under a contract amounting to £300 per month) ; Salaries, Depreciation, and General Expenses, £21,600 ; Underwriting Commission and Brokerage, £4,540.

The net profit for the year amounted to £45,120.

If, in your opinion, the whole of the above net profit was not available for distribution, prepare a statement showing how you would deal with it.

The amount of profits earned prior to incorporation are not available for distribution and should therefore be carried to a Capital Reserve Account and utilised for capital purposes, *e.g.*, reduction of goodwill.

	Prior to Incorporation. £	Subsequent to Incorporation. £
Gross Profit apportioned according to turnover .	36,000	44,000
Less Expenses :—		
Preliminary Expenses .		2,000
Directors' Fees .		1,500
Bad Debts .	780	860
Advertising .	1,800	1,800
Salaries, Depreciation, etc. .	10,800	10,800
Underwriting Commission, etc. .		4,540
	13,380	21,500
Net Profit .	22,620	22,500
	£36,000	£44,000

Therefore an amount of £22,620 should be transferred to Capital Reserve Account.

It should be noted that certain expenses obviously relate solely to the company, and are therefore charged entirely against profits subsequent to incorporation.

Where a *loss* is incurred prior to incorporation the effect is to increase the purchase price to a corresponding extent; thus such loss should be debited to Goodwill Account (since Goodwill in these cases is regarded as the residual asset, *i.e.*, the excess of the purchase price over the net assets acquired) and written off as soon as profits are available.

The Capitalisation of Profits.

If so desired, and subject to the Articles, profits may be capitalised instead of distributing them in the form of cash dividends. This may be effected in two ways:—

(1) By applying the profits in discharging *pro tanto* the liability of shareholders in respect of uncalled capital, *i.e.*, the amounts not yet called up from the shareholders in respect of the shares already issued to them.

(2) By issuing bonus shares and satisfying the issue price thereof out of profits available for distribution as dividend.

In the capitalisation of profits in this way there are legal difficulties. In the first method above, there is the point that the liability in respect of uncalled capital is a liability of the shareholders to the company and cannot properly be discharged by the company out of money belonging to it, even if that money does represent profit. The difficulty is met by declaring a dividend or bonus to the extent of the profits which it is desired shall be capitalised: this creates a debt due from the company to the shareholders which may be set off against the liability of the shareholders to the company in respect of uncalled capital.

In the issue of bonus shares, it has been suggested that when there is no option to receive cash, the shares are not fully paid *as against the company*. On the other hand, the declaration of a dividend or bonus constitutes the shareholders creditors of the company, and the release of their claims may be said to be good and valid consideration for regarding the shares as fully paid. To be on the safe side, it is wise to have an agreement made between the company and a trustee for the shareholders stipulating that the trustee shall receive the fully paid shares and that they shall be considered as fully paid, the bonus being applied for this purpose.

Where a company has already issued the whole of its authorised capital, the authorised capital must be increased in the manner provided by the Act. Unless the transaction is such as to give the members an unconditional option to take the bonus in shares or in cash it will be necessary to file a contract constituting the title to the shares " allotted for a consideration other than cash ".

There is no statutory authority for the capitalisation of profits by a limited company, and, as already observed, the shareholders are entitled to have their dividends paid in cash. Authority must, therefore, be included in the Memorandum or Articles of Association if it is likely that a bonus will ever be paid in shares ; otherwise a special resolution to alter the Articles will be necessary.

The payment of bonuses in fully paid shares does not *increase* working capital but it conserves it. Working capital is increased by profits and reduced by capital expenditure, and to the extent that additional capital expenditure has been incurred undivided profits will not be represented by working capital. The payment of a cash bonus in such circumstances would be legal but imprudent, whereas the payment of a share bonus will accurately reflect the company's position and bring the issued capital into closer relationship with the amount actually expended in the acquisition of capital assets. On the other hand the indiscriminate capitalisation of profits in excess of what is warranted by the expansion of the business results in " watered " capital and the accumulation of unnecessarily large liquid balances.

It is sometimes thought that bonus shares represent an increase in the intrinsic value of the company's capital, but this is not so. The real worth of the capital is represented by the earning capacity of the assets, and this is in no way affected by an issue of bonus shares. It has already been shown (see Chapter IV) that where profits are earned over and above the fair commercial return (having regard to the nature of the business) on the invested capital, the market value of shares in the company will stand at a premium.* This premium is to a large extent a measure of the goodwill of the business and also indicates the disproportion which exists between the nominal amount of the share capital and the value of the assets.

Thus, if a company has £25,000 capital in £1 shares and £25,000 in undivided profits, each £1 share is represented by net assets to the extent of £2 ; and if the profits earned represent a normal commercial yield for a business with net assets to the value of £50,000, the shares will stand in the open market at about £2 a share. If, now, an issue of bonus shares is made to the extent of £25,000, the net assets of the company are unchanged but each shareholder has two £1 shares instead of one as formerly. In other words, his total equity in the company is a capital equity measured by his shares which will be quoted at par and which will entitle him to share in an equivalent amount of the company's assets. Formerly his equity in the company was not entirely of a capital nature but represented a claim to capital of £1 and a claim to undivided profits of £1 for each share. A bonus, therefore, amounts to a conversion of equities and nothing more, and has the effect of bringing the return on the share capital more into line with the normal commercial rate of yield. Where bonus shares are issued on this basis, there is no danger of " watered " capital or over-capitalisation as indicated in the next section of this Chapter. It will be seen, therefore, that the objects of issuing bonus shares are as follows :—

(1) To bring the rate of dividend down to a more reasonable level (but see below as to the possible effect on future profits of retaining in the business the profits applied in giving effect to the bonus) ;

(2) Thereby to reduce the market value of the shares to a price which will be low enough to make them attractive as an investment ; and

* Other considerations enter into the market value of a company's shares, but they may be ignored for the present purpose.

(3) Where the profits retained in the business are used for trading expansion, to bring the issued capital into line with the amount of capital expenditure.

In so far as profits are retained in the business and utilised in purchasing additional capital equipment, it is quite reasonable to expect a proportionate or more than proportionate increase in the profits. This being so, an issue of bonus shares of an amount equivalent to the amount of capital expenditure will have the effect merely of preserving the same rate of return on the increased capital. It will be realised, however, that a permanent increase in future profits is not likely as a result of the retention of current profits in the business, unless such profits are used to increase the fixed assets by means of which future profits may be earned.

It is also doubtful finance to issue bonus shares merely because, on account of trade expansion, it is impracticable to pay a cash dividend. Apart from the above considerations, *increased* profits (which will be necessary to maintain an *equivalent* return on the increased capital, to that earned in the past) are not assured, and a distribution which will disturb the capital equities is best held over until the relationship between the contributed capital and the profit-earning capacity of the assets representing such capital has become stabilised. Then, and only then, is it possible to judge whether or not the profit earned by the capital equipment is more than a fair commercial return, so as to justify an issue of bonus shares.

The entries necessary in the books of account on an issue of bonus shares are as follows :—

EXAMPLE

The Alpha Company, Limited, had an issued and paid-up capital of 20,000 shares of £1 each, and a General Reserve of £7,000. Part of the reserve was distributed among the shareholders by declaring a bonus of one fully paid share for every five shares held by the members. Show the journal entries recording the bonus.

JOURNAL

19..		£	£
General Reserve . . . . *Dr.*		4,000	
To Bonus Account			4,000
Being transfer of amount required for the bonus payable in fully paid shares as per resolution dated ....19....			
Bonus Account . . . . *Dr.*		4,000	
To Share Capital Account			4,000
Being allotment and issue of 4,000 shares of £1 each credited as fully paid, in satisfaction of bonus declared on................19...., in the proportion of one share for every five shares held in this company.			

Where new shares are issued in place of Preference Shares redeemed, the Capital Redemption Reserve Fund may be applied, up to an amount equal to the nominal amount of the shares so issued, in paying up unissued shares to be issued to the members as fully paid bonus shares (see page 231).

Watered Capital and Over-capitalisation.

The indiscriminate capitalisation of profits by issuing bonus shares is known as " watering " the capital, and the capital so issued, as " watered " capital. As already indicated, the foundation of a bonus issue is the earning of profits in excess of the average. Clearly, if bonus shares are issued so that it is impossible to pay a fair rate of dividend on the increased capital, the issue has served no useful purpose. In fact, such an issue will defeat all the objects indicated above, *e.g.*, by reducing the profits to a lower level than the fair commercial return, the marketability of the company's shares except possibly as a speculation, will be seriously impaired.

Watered capital is the exact reversal of the state of affairs which exists before a justifiable issue of bonus shares is made, *e.g.*, where the profits earned are in excess of the average and the share capital consequently has too high a market value. It is to be doubted which state of affairs is the more disadvantageous to the company. Where capital is watered, discontent may be caused amongst the shareholders if their dividends are reduced, and the attractiveness of the shares

M

as an investment will be impaired. Furthermore, the conservation of liquid resources in such cases may be somewhat of an embarrassment, *e.g.*, where profitable employment therefor cannot be found.   On the other hand, before a bonus issue is made, discontent may be aroused amongst the workers who read in high dividends a justification for higher wages, and the share capital will, in most cases, be quoted at too large a premium to be regarded as a particularly attractive investment.

OVER-CAPITALISATION is similar to the watering of capital in that it also is brought about by an issue of capital in excess of the true requirements as measured by the earning capacity of assets.   Over-capitalisation usually arises from an erroneous estimate of financial requirements when a company is formed.   Thus over-capitalisation will occur in the following circumstances :—

(1) On the purchase of a business by a limited company if—

(*a*) A price is paid for goodwill which is not justified by profits ; or

(*b*) An inflated price is paid for fixed assets which have not been revalued in the light of current profit earning capacity.

(2) On the formation of a limited company if the capitalisation is fixed without due regard to the scale of production and the amount of working capital required, so that the company finds itself equipped with a superfluity of fixed assets or with an amount of working capital which it cannot use profitably.

When a company is over-capitalised it is hampered from the start by its inability to earn profits sufficient to yield a fair return on its capital.   On the other hand, if a company is capitalised on too low a scale, it may find itself short of fixed assets and consequently unable to avail itself of the benefits to be derived from operating at the most favourable scale of production without resorting to borrowing, and it may also find itself short of working capital and so suffer from the embarrassment of being unable to buy and sell on favourable terms.

In either event, the profits will usually be too low to yield a satisfactory return on the capital subscribed.

Since it is far easier to increase the capital than to reduce it, it is better to err on the side of under-capitalisation than on that of over-capitalisation.

CHAPTER IX

THE ACCOUNTS OF HOLDING COMPANIES

Companies holding shares in other companies may be divided into four main groups :—

(1) The first group consists of those companies whose main object is to invest their funds in the shares of other companies with a view to obtaining dividends from such investments. Such companies may be termed " *investment trust companies* ", as their investments are spread over a number of other companies in order to obtain a good return with reasonable safety upon the total capital invested. The investments are usually made in a variety of concerns, not necessarily engaged in the same or allied trades, with the object of spreading the risk as widely as is compatible with profitable investment. The holding in any one company may constitute a controlling interest, but since the main purpose of the trust is to derive revenue from its holdings rather than to control the operations of the company whose shares are held, and since the funds are widely spread over different holdings to minimise risk, this will not often occur.

However, the activities of such trusts have been somewhat extended of recent years, and it is now not uncommon to find them obtaining controlling interests, usually in companies engaged in the same trade or in the same chain of production, with the object of controlling a particular industry (see (3) below).

The holdings will be of the nature of fixed assets, as they are held mainly as income-producing assets and not for the purpose of resale.*

(2) The companies in this group undertake the promotion of other companies and buy up the shares of other companies for resale to the public with the object of making a profit

* See footnote on next page.

on the resale. These companies are termed "*finance companies*", and the shares held by them may be regarded as stock-in-trade, *i.e.*, current assets. At any particular date, the shares held will usually constitute a controlling interest (*e.g.*, the holding will represent a majority of the issued share capital or will carry a majority of the voting power) ; but this is not the purpose for which the shares are held : it is merely a state of affairs which is incidental to the company's business (*i.e.*, buying and selling shares, and the formation of companies), although control is not sought.

(3) The third group of companies acquire all or a working majority of the ordinary shares of other companies in order to control the activities of such " subsidiary " companies. The investments in such subsidiary companies will thus be regarded as fixed assets.

(4) The companies in the fourth group merely acquire a minority holding in the shares of other companies (control not being desired) to facilitate trade connections with such " associated " or " affiliated " companies, *e.g.*, several companies engaged in the same trade may hold, between them, the entire share capital of a company supplying them with raw materials. In no case will the holdings constitute a majority holding, but each company in the " group " will obtain its raw materials at a cheaper price than that which would be charged to an " outside " customer. The investments in such associated or affiliated companies are also fixed assets.

In view of its special legal recognition and regulation, the third type of company is particularly important. Although any company which holds shares in another

---

* Investment Trust Companies must not be confused with *Unit Trusts*, which are a comparatively modern innovation (which originated in the United States of America) and are not registered as limited companies. Although the main object of an investment trust company is to hold investments for the sake of dividends likely to be earned, the selection of the investments is in the hands of the directors, who are nearly always given power to change them at their discretion. The falls in the market value of the investments of some of these companies has undoubtedly stimulated the movement in favour of the unit trust, in which the available funds are invested in specified securities in stated proportions (although these conditions do not apply in certain " flexible "—as opposed to " fixed "—unit trusts). The holder of a " sub-unit " (which is the counterpart of a proportion of a block of shares in an investment trust) thus knows exactly what his investment represents and further security is usually given by the appointment of trustees (frequently one of the leading banks or insurance companies) in whose names the securities are registered.

concern, for whatever purpose, might be described as a holding company, that description is in law confined to companies which acquire holdings in " subsidiary " companies within the meaning of Section 154 of the Companies Act, 1948, and it will be so used in this book.*

Holding companies of this kind may be divided into two well-defined classes—those which, in addition to holding the controlling interest in and directing the affairs of other companies, are themselves actively engaged in a trade or business ; and those of a non-trading character which confine their activities to the control of the operations of other companies, and whose principal source of income is the dividends they derive from their subsidiaries.

The distinction between these two classes of holding companies will be apparent from an inspection of their individual published Balance Sheets, for that of the former will include the usual trading assets, e.g., plant and machinery, while the assets of the latter will be confined mainly to investments in, and amounts owing by, subsidiary companies.

The " Legal " Holding Company.

Section 154 of the Companies Act, 1948, defines a company as being the holding company of another if, and only if, that other company is its subsidiary company ; while a subsidiary company is defined as :—

(a) a company of which another company is a member and controls the composition of its board of directors ; or

(b) a company of which another company holds more than half in nominal value of its equity share capital (i.e., issued share capital excluding any part thereof which, neither as regards dividends nor as regards capital, carries any right to participate beyond a specified amount in a distribution) ;

(c) a company which is itself a subsidiary company of another subsidiary company (i.e., a sub-subsidiary company).*

* Refer also to Section 154, Companies Act, 1948, reproduced in Appendix I to this work.

The composition of the board of directors of a company is deemed to be controlled by another company if the latter has power to appoint or remove all or a majority of the directors. In this case, however, *some* shares must be held in order to constitute in law the relationship between holding company and subsidiary company.

A holding of any shares possessing fixed dividend rights will not be counted in determining whether or not a company is a holding company by virtue of the number of shares held. On the other hand, if "equity shares" are held by a nominee of a company on its behalf, such shares must be taken into account in determining the number of shares held; this provision was included in the Act in order to avoid the possibility of undisclosed control through nominees.

Section 154 also provides that in determining whether one company is a subsidiary of another no regard shall be taken of any shares held or power exercisable by the other company in a fiduciary capacity, *e.g.*, a bank holding shares in a company as trustee, *or*, any shares held or power exercisable by way of security for money lent in the ordinary course of business, *e.g.*, a bank holding shares in a company as security for money lent.

For the purposes of the above provisions the term company includes any body corporate and is not therefore confined to a company registered under the Companies Acts.

A company may own a substantial holding of shares in another company, but if none of the provisions of Section 154 brings the latter company within the definition of a subsidiary company the term affiliated (or associated) company should be used (see page 325).

The Development of Holding Companies.

The development of the holding company may be attributed to the desire of business men for consolidation and amalgamation without the disturbing elements of liquidation. Amalgamation by means of a holding company may be said to possess the following advantages :—

(1) The interests of several subsidiary companies may be consolidated without unnecessary interference with the existing organisation of such companies.

(2) It is not necessary to go to the expense of liquidation, nor to incur the expense of acquisition of an entire share capital (as would be necessary in an amalgamation by means of absorption or reconstruction).

(3) The method lends itself to arrangements for the restriction of output, the division of markets, the standardisation of output and the pooling of technical knowledge and research work (which are so often the reasons behind an amalgamation) more readily than any other method of amalgamation.

(4) Since less cash will be required to purchase a controlling interest (when purchase is effected by a cash payment) than to purchase the entire undertaking, the stamp duty on any increase of capital which may be necessary for the purpose, will be correspondingly lighter.

(5) Stamp duty on the conveyance and transfer of assets will be avoided.

Originally the holding company was designed to acquire an interest in a single company or a small group of companies engaged in the same trade, a process known as horizontal amalgamation. By degrees, however, as the facility by which unification and control could be achieved by this means was recognised, the system of subsidiary companies was extended to the vertical amalgamation (e.g., in which concerns combine with other concerns upon which they have relied for the supply of their raw materials or as consumers or distributors of their products). With this growth, the control became more and more complex until at the present time the ramifications of a holding company may extend by means of holdings through a chain of subsidiary and sub-subsidiary companies to very remote concerns. The complexity of holdings, particularly when there are cross holdings (*e.g.*, of subsidiary in subsidiary or subsidiary in holding company),* has caused the question of finance and the intelligible presentation of accounts to be exceedingly difficult. Not infrequently the holding company itself is a trading concern, so that the element of inter-company indebtedness has been added to this difficulty.

Amalgamation by means of a holding company is not without its disadvantages and difficulties. The interests of the minority shareholders (*i.e.*, the persons holding the shares which are not purchased by the holding company) may not be identical with the interests of the majority—the holding company—with the result that the interests of the former will probably be sacrificed to the interests of the latter.

The Acquisition of Control.

Control can be acquired in the following ways :—

(1) By the formation of a new company to acquire, on a predetermined basis of valuation, the shares of several existing companies, in exchange for shares in the new company. Future profits of the subsidiaries are paid by way of dividend to the holding company, which, in turn, distributes them amongst its shareholders, thereby giving to each individual member of any of the old companies who has exchanged his shares for shares in the holding company an interest in the profits of all the companies involved in the amalgamation. The subsidiary companies are the revenue-earning units, so that, although the shareholder looks to the holding company for the security of his capital, he is really dependent upon the subsidiary companies ; unless, of course, the holding company is a trading company, in which case his security is divided between holding and subsidiary companies.

The effect of such an arrangement is that, whereas before the transfer each subsidiary company had a number of shareholders (small or large according to whether it is a private company or a public company), after the transfer it has,

* Section 27 of the Companies Act, 1948, provides that it is illegal for a subsidiary company to acquire shares in its holding company except shares acquired before 1st July, 1948, and any shares so held are deprived of all voting rights.

M*

in effect, one only,* while the holding company has a list of members equivalent to the combined former membership of all the subsidiaries.

As a matter of book-keeping, the exchange of shares will be recorded in the books of the holding company by the following Journal entry :—

> Investments in Subsidiary Companies . . Dr.   —
> To Share Capital Account . . . . . .   —
> *Being allotment of . . . shares of . . . each as con-
> sideration for transfer to this company of . . .
> shares in X Ltd., as per Resolution of Directors
> . . .*

This entry should be compared with that shown on page 166 in connection with the issue of shares to the vendor of a business. It is essential that the clearest distinction should be maintained between the acquisition of the *assets* of a business (whether sole trader, partnership or another limited company is immaterial) and the acquisition of *shares* in order to secure the control of another company.

(2) As above, except that the holding company may acquire the shares by a payment in cash to the shareholders in the subsidiary companies, in which case such shareholders lose all rights in the combined organisation. The holding company may acquire the whole of the shares in such sub-sidiaries or merely sufficient shares to ensure effective control by means of voting power. When the holding company does not acquire the whole of the shares, shareholders who do not sell become " outside " or " minority " shareholders.

(3) One of the existing companies which are to be amalga-mated (usually the one with sufficient unissued share capital or with adequate liquid resources) may be constituted as the holding company to purchase the whole of the share capital of the subsidiary companies or to acquire sufficient shares in each subsidiary to ensure effective control of it. The

---

* The legal objection which would arise if all the shares became registered in one name—that of the holding company—so that the number of members of the subsidiary company thus fell below two or seven, in the case of a private company or a public company respectively, is surmounted by allotting, say, one share each to the requisite number of *nominees* who hold those shares on behalf of the holding company and pay over to it any dividends they may receive.

shares may be acquired by either of the methods indicated in (1) and (2) above. The method to be chosen will be that which is most acceptable to the majority of the shareholders in the subsidiary companies.

In practice, it is usually found necessary to reorganise the boards of directors of the holding company and the various subsidiary companies, and this is usually effected by giving each subsidiary company a representative on the directorate of the holding company. This reorganised board of directors controls the policy of the whole of the consolidated undertaking. The boards of the subsidiary companies will also require reorganisation by the election of nominees of the holding company to the various boards, thus making the subsidiary companies integral parts of the organisation of the holding company, and yet retaining the legal fiction of separate entity. It should be noted, however, that this arrangement is not common to all holding companies : the method of reorganisation adopted depends on the circumstances of each particular case.

The Accounts of Holding Companies.

Where a company is interested at the date of its annual accounts in a subsidiary company within the definition set out in Section 154, it must comply with the general provisions of the Companies Act, 1948, which are applicable to all companies with regard to disclosure in their published accounts, and also with the special provisions of Part II of the Eighth Schedule of the Act with regard to information concerning its relationship to its subsidiary companies. The general provisions of the Act with regard to disclosure in published accounts are more fully dealt with in Chapter X.*

It may, however, be noted at this stage that the Eighth Schedule provides that the Balance Sheet of a holding company must disclose, under separate headings, the aggregate amount of each of the following items :—

(1) Shares held in subsidiary companies ;

(2) Debts due from subsidiary companies ;

(3) Debts due to subsidiary companies.

* Refer also to Parts I and II, Eighth Schedule, Companies Act, 1948, reproduced in Appendix I to this work.

In each case totals only need be disclosed. Thus, where a holding company has more than one subsidiary company, only the totals of each of the above items need be disclosed, and not the individual amounts applicable to each company.

The items, " debts due to subsidiary companies ", and " debts due from subsidiary companies ", include general indebtedness whether on account of ordinary trading transactions (*i.e.*, purchase and sale of goods), loans or debentures. Thus, where any debentures are held in subsidiary companies, they may be included in the item " debts due from subsidiary companies ", but in practice it is desirable to show such debentures as a distinct item, as they differ in nature from trade debts and loans. Provided that the aggregate indebtedness of subsidiary companies to the holding company and the aggregate indebtedness of the holding company to its subsidiary companies are separately shown, there is no legal or practical objection to the deduction of one item from another, but the mere disclosure of the net difference without the two aggregate totals is a definite contravention of the provisions of the Act. In any event, these items must not be merged in the general items of sundry debtors and creditors in the Balance Sheet of the holding company.

It is also provided that there must be shown by way of note to the Balance Sheet or in a statement or report annexed thereto, the number, description and amount of any shares and/or debentures held by any of the subsidiary companies in the holding company, excluding shares or debentures held as personal representative or trustee and in which no beneficial interest is maintained by the company or any subsidiary otherwise than as security for a loan made in the ordinary course of business.

Sections 150 to 153 of the Companies Act, 1948, contain provisions regarding the form of accounts to be submitted to the members of a holding company in general meeting. Section 150 places an obligation on the holding company to lay before the company in general meeting *group accounts* dealing with the state of affairs and profit or loss of the company and its subsidiaries, except where :—

(1) the company is, at the end of its financial year, a wholly owned subsidiary of another body corporate incorporated in Great Britain (*i.e.*, has no members except the holding company and its wholly owned subsidiaries or nominees).

(2) in relation to any subsidiary company the directors are of opinion that :—

(*a*) it would be impracticable (*e.g.*, a foreign subsidiary) or of no real value to the members (*e.g.*, where the amounts involved are insignificant) ; or

(*b*) the result would be misleading, or disclosure harmful to the business of the company or any of its subsidiaries ; or

(*c*) the business of the holding company and that of the subsidiary are so different that they cannot reasonably be treated as a single undertaking.

In the above circumstances group accounts need not deal with any such subsidiaries, and where the directors are of the same opinion regarding all subsidiaries of the company group accounts will not be required.

The approval of the Board of Trade is required for not dealing in the group accounts with a subsidiary on account of the circumstances mentioned in (*c*) above, or in (*b*) above where it is considered harmful.

Section 151 provides that the group accounts to be laid before the members of the holding company must be consolidated accounts comprising :—

(1) a *Consolidated Balance Sheet* dealing with the state of affairs of the company and all the subsidiaries to be dealt with in the group accounts ; and

(2) a *Consolidated Profit and Loss Account* dealing with the profit or loss of the company and those subsidiaries ;

except that where the directors of the company are of the opinion that the same or equivalent information could be better presented to, and more readily appreciated by, the members in some other form, the group accounts may be prepared in a form other than that indicated in (1) and (2) above.

Section 151 also outlines alternative methods for submission of group accounts indicating that separate sets of consolidated accounts may be prepared in respect of the holding company and separate groups of subsidiaries or that separate accounts may be prepared dealing with each subsidiary.

It should be observed, however, that the same or equivalent information must be given as would be shown if consolidated accounts were prepared in the manner stated in (1) and (2) above. Thus the directors of a company cannot escape their obligation under the Act to give full information merely by preparing the group accounts in a different form.

The normal method of preparing consolidated accounts will be dealt with later in this Chapter.

Section 151 (3) provides that the group accounts may be wholly or partly incorporated in the holding company's own Balance Sheet and Profit and Loss Account. Thus it would appear that the directors of a holding company could fulfil the requirements of the Act by submitting to the members in general meeting the group accounts covering its own accounts and those of its subsidiaries without submitting a separate Balance Sheet and Profit and Loss Account of its own activities. There is, however, some difficulty in reconciling this provision with Section 148, which provides that every company shall lay before its members in general meeting a Balance Sheet and Profit and Loss Account once in each calendar year, and with Section 150 (1) which provides that a holding company shall submit group accounts along with its *own* Balance Sheet and Profit and Loss Account. Section 149 (5) does, however, specifically provide that the Profit and Loss Account *may* be framed as a Consolidated Profit and Loss Account. In the circumstances, it is considered that it is advisable to prepare the accounts of the holding company in the normal manner and to prepare also consolidated accounts showing the position of the group as a separate document. In any event it will be necessary to prepare separate accounts in respect of the holding company for taxation purposes.*

The financial year of each of the subsidiary companies must coincide with the financial year of the holding company except where, in the opinion of the directors of the holding company, there are good reasons against it (Section 153 (1)). Where the financial year of any subsidiary does not coincide with that of the holding company, the accounts of the subsidiary at the last financial year of the subsidiary ending prior to the financial year of the holding company must be included in the group accounts unless the Board of Trade directs otherwise (Section 152 (2)).

The group accounts, if prepared as consolidated accounts, must comply with the requirements of the Eighth Schedule of the Act regarding disclosure to be made in the published accounts of companies (see Chapter X), so far as applicable thereto, and if prepared in some other form must give the same or equivalent information, unless the Board of Trade modifies these requirements.

The main object of the legislation enacted in the prescribed Sections of the Companies Act, 1948, is to make it compulsory for all holding companies to prepare and publish consolidated accounts except in special circumstances which are covered by the exceptions stated.†

The Accounts of Subsidiary Companies.

Part II of the Eighth Schedule of the Companies Act, 1948, provides that the following information must be disclosed in the Balance Sheet of a subsidiary company :—

(a) The aggregate amount due from the holding company and fellow subsidiary companies ; and

(b) The aggregate amount due to the holding company and fellow subsidiary companies.

* The general consensus of opinion is that a holding company must publish its own Balance Sheet as well as a Consolidated Balance Sheet (or Group Accounts in some other form) ; but if a Consolidated Profit and Loss Account is published it is not necessary to publish also its own Profit and Loss Account, provided that the Consolidated Profit and Loss Account complies with the requirements of the Act, and shows how much of the consolidated profit or loss for the financial year is dealt with in the accounts of the holding company.

† Refer also to Sections 151 to 153 of the Companies Act, 1948, reproduced in Appendix I to this work.

The term " fellow subsidiary companies " is defined as companies which are subsidiaries of the same holding company but which are not subsidiaries of each other. This information corresponds with that required to be disclosed by a holding company under items (2) and (3) on page 331, but in this case it is legally necessary to distinguish between indebtedness in respect of debentures and otherwise.

Profits and Losses of Subsidiary Companies.

Before considering the preparation of consolidated accounts, it will be necessary to understand the treatment of profits and losses of subsidiary companies and the manner in which they affect the holding company as a separate entity.

Where the holding company holds the entire issued share capital of a subsidiary it will, obviously, be entitled to the whole of the profits earned by that subsidiary. Where, however, the holding company holds only a portion of the share capital of its subsidiary, it will be entitled to a share of the profits of that subsidiary proportionate to its holding. Thus, if the issued share capital of a subsidiary company is £100,000 and the holding company holds shares to the nominal value of £80,000, it will be entitled to eight-tenths of any profits earned by that subsidiary. The right to profits accrues by virtue of the shares held and although it is dependent upon the distribution of profits by way of dividend, the holding company is usually in a position to control such distribution. Thus, if the whole of the profits earned in any year are not distributed as dividend, but a portion thereof is allocated to general reserve, the holding company still has its *proportionate* claim on the profits of the subsidiary so set aside.

Similarly, a loss sustained by a subsidiary company will fall, in whole or in part according to the extent and nature of the holding, upon the holding company. To some extent the loss may be regarded purely as a loss of capital (*i.e.*, the diminution in the value of an investment) since the trading results of the holding company (where a trade is carried on) may not be affected by the subsidiary's loss. Where, however, the subsidiary has consistently earned profits which have been duly received by the holding company, any loss sustained will undoubtedly reduce the revenue of the holding company, and, in such an event, the loss of the subsidiary becomes, in reality, a revenue loss of the holding company.

Profits of a subsidiary company, in so far as they are applicable to the shares held by the holding company, augment the holding company's fund of divisible profits, whereas losses, in so far as they fall upon the holding company, diminish this fund, and prudent accounting practice recognises this.*   In addition, it is usually considered wise to restrict the amount of a subsidiary company's profit taken into the holding company's own Profit and Loss Account to those profits which have actually been received by the holding company as a dividend from the subsidiary or which will be received from dividends already declared by the subsidiary.

As, however, a subsidiary company which has earned a profit may be temporarily deprived of the liquid resources out of which a dividend would have been paid, by reason of capital development, and may therefore be unable to pay a dividend, or may be placed in funds by the holding company to enable a dividend to be paid, it is necessary to look to the reasons for the non-declaration of a dividend, or to the facts behind the declaration of a dividend, as the case may be, before finally deciding upon the manner in which the holding company's share of the profits of the subsidiary shall be dealt with in the holding company's accounts.

In law there is nothing to prevent a holding company from using the dividend received from profit-making subsidiaries in order to pay a dividend on its own shares without taking into account its share of losses suffered by other subsidiaries.   This practice is unsound, for the holding company may be paying a dividend at a time when the combined results of the companies show a loss on the year's working. The best practice is for the holding company to make full provision in its own accounts for its proportionate share of the losses of its subsidiary companies, and, as indicated

---

* As will be seen later in this Chapter, this statement is not without qualification in respect of profits or losses of a subsidiary company earned or sustained prior to the date of acquisition of the shares by the holding company.

above, to take credit in its own accounts only for dividends actually received from or declared by profit-earning subsidiary companies.

The treatment of inter-company profits (*i.e.*, profits arising out of transactions between holding company and subsidiaries) entails special considerations which are dealt with under a separate heading later in this Chapter.

Those profits (and losses) of a subsidiary company which do not belong to the holding company (*e.g.*, the proportion due to the outside shareholders) also require special treatment where a Consolidated Balance Sheet is prepared and are separately dealt with under the heading of " Minority, or Outside, Shareholders " (see page 350).

Treatment of Profits and Losses of Subsidiaries in the Accounts of the Holding Company.

Quite irrespective of the manner in which the final accounts of the holding company are presented (*e.g.*, whether or not a Consolidated Balance Sheet is prepared), the profits and losses of the subsidiary companies, in so far as they apply to the holding company, must be accounted for according to recognised accounting principles. The following entries illustrate the principles applied to effect this :—

(a) *Dividends declared by the subsidiary and duly received by the holding company.*

Cash . . . . *Dr.* —
  To Profit and Loss Account *
    (or Dividends from Subsidiaries Account) .   —

(b) *Dividends declared but not yet received.*

Subsidiary Company . . . . *Dr.* —
  (Current or Dividend Account)
  To Profit and Loss Account * . . . . .
    (or Dividends from Subsidiaries Account) .   —

This entry will be made only if there is no reason to doubt that the dividend will ultimately be paid.

(c) *Holding company's share of profits not yet declared as dividend by subsidiary.*

* But see the special considerations which arise where a period prior to acquisition of the shares is involved (pages 354 *et seq.*).

In accordance with the principles enunciated above, these are best left out of the holding company's accounts. If these profits are included in the holding company's accounts, the entry will be as follows :—

Subsidiary Company . . . . *Dr.*
  (Dividend Suspense Account)
To Profit and Loss Account . . . . . .
  (or Profits of Subsidiary Companies Account)   —

The ordinary Current Account of the subsidiary company must not be debited, for until the dividend is declared, the relation of debtor and creditor does not exist. The debit balance should be shown as a separate item on the right-hand side of the Balance Sheet of the holding company, thus—

Profits of Subsidiary Companies not yet declared in
  dividends   . . . .   —

and the credit entry in the Profit and Loss Account should be worded similarly.

It must be remembered that the payment of a dividend by the holding company entails the disbursement of liquid assets: in ordinary circumstances these are provided by the dividends received from subsidiary companies. In (*a*) the dividends have already been received and appear as cash in the Balance Sheet of the holding company, while in (*b*) the debt due from the subsidiary company in respect of a dividend already declared is in the nature of a current asset and it may be assumed that it will have been received in cash before the holding company pays its own dividend. On the other hand, when, as in (*c*), credit is taken for profits of a subsidiary company, *without any corresponding increase in current assets* due to the declaration of a dividend by that company, it may be financially impossible for the holding company to pay a dividend (except in so far as it may have other sources of income), although a considerable credit balance may appear on its Profit and Loss Account. In these circumstances, it would be better for the transfer to be made to the credit of General Reserve instead of to Profit and Loss Account ; or alternatively it might be credited to Profit and Loss Account in the first instance, an equivalent amount then being appropriated from profits and transferred to General Reserve thus—

Profit and Loss Account . . . . . *Dr.* | —
To General Reserve. . . . . | —

Being transfer to General Reserve of an amount equivalent to the profits of subsidiary companies not yet declared in dividends.

In both (*b*) and (*c*), when a dividend is ultimately received out of the profits which have already been taken to the credit of Profit and Loss Account, it must be credited to the Current, or Dividend, Account in the case of (*b*) and to the Dividend Suspense Account in the case of (*c*). Care must be taken not to credit the same profits *twice* to Profit and Loss Account—once before they are declared in dividend and again when the dividend is received.

(*d*) *Holding company's share of losses of subsidiary.*

The share of loss applicable to the holding company's interest in the subsidiary company may either be written off the book value of that investment or carried to a special Reserve Account which will be available for writing down the investment at a later date—

Profit and Loss Account * . . . . . *Dr.* | —
To Investments in Subsidiary Companies *or* Investment Reserve Account . . . . . . | —

This treatment reflects the fall in the intrinsic value of the holding of shares in the subsidiary company, which must necessarily be involved when losses are incurred and the resources of the subsidiary company are thus depleted. If profits are earned in subsequent years, the subsidiary company will probably make good the debit balance on its own Profit and Loss Account before declaring any dividends; and it will then be quite in order for the holding company to take credit for its share of those profits to the extent of previous provisions for losses by reversing the entry above—

---

* But see the special considerations which arise where a period prior to the acquisition of the shares is involved (page 354).

Investments in Subsidiary Companies *or* Investment
    Reserve Account . . . . *Dr.*
    To Profit and Loss Account . . . . .

By the time the subsidiary company has retrieved the losses of former years, the holding company will have written back the investment to its original value (or have eliminated the Investment Reserve Account) and thereafter the profits of the subsidiary company will be declared in dividends and treated as in (*a*) or (*b*).

Consolidated Accounts.

It has already been explained that, under the provisions of the Companies Act, 1948, it is legally necessary for a holding company to prepare group accounts comprising a Consolidated Balance Sheet and a Consolidated Profit and Loss Account combining the assets and liabilities and the profits and/or losses of the holding company and its subsidiary companies, unless some other form of group accounts is considered more desirable.

Under normal circumstances it is considered that a holding company will prepare consolidated accounts in the manner set out in this Chapter, although it must not be overlooked that companies have the option of preparing the group accounts in some other form provided that the same or equivalent information which would be supplied by consolidated accounts is given. As the alternatives to consolidation referred to in Section 151 of the Act, *e.g.*, preparing separate accounts in respect of each subsidiary or expanding the information regarding subsidiaries in the accounts of the holding company, will be practicable only in very few cases, it would appear that the group accounts will, in the majority of cases, involve some form of consolidation although, as regards large holding companies, a number of consolidated accounts may be prepared dealing separately with the interests of the holding company and different groups of subsidiary companies.

Consolidated Balance Sheets.

A Consolidated Balance Sheet is intended to exhibit in a single statement a bird's-eye view of the state of the financial

affairs of a group of associated companies, and it is designed
to overcome the limitations of the separate Balance Sheet
by showing the interest of the holding company's shareholders in the assets and liabilities of the group as a whole.

The several companies comprising a group are separate
entities, each keeping its own set of books and compiling
its own final accounts, but as a Consolidated Balance Sheet,
like the Balance Sheet of a single company, should set out
the position at a particular time, the Balance Sheet of the
holding company and the separate subsidiary Balance Sheets
from which the consolidated statement is prepared should all
be drawn up as at the same date and should be compiled on
a uniform basis as regards the classification and valuation of
items.*

Where, however, the Balance Sheets of the holding and
subsidiary companies are not prepared on the same date it
is incorrect to state that a Consolidated Balance Sheet cannot
be prepared. A Consolidated Balance Sheet showing with
a reasonable degree of accuracy the position of the group of
companies can be compiled in such cases by means of analysis
and schedules of adjustments.

A Consolidated Balance Sheet may be drawn up in respect
of *any* group of associated companies and is not necessarily
confined to the " legal " holding company and its subsidiaries.

Consolidated Balance Sheet where the Holding Company holds the entire Share Capital of the Subsidiary.

When a holding company owns all the shares of a subsidiary company, the assets and liabilities of the latter belong
in effect (though not in strict law) entirely to the holding
company, and a Consolidated Balance Sheet can be prepared
by combining the relative items in the Balance Sheets of the
holding and subsidiary companies. The item " Shares in
Subsidiary Company ", which appears in the holding company's own Balance Sheet, is replaced in the Consolidated
Balance Sheet by the assets and liabilities (including un-

* Reference should be made to the recommendations of the Council of the Institute
of Chartered Accountants with regard to consolidated accounts (see Appendix II).

distributed profits) which the holding company controls by reason of this shareholding. The Consolidated Balance Sheet thus ignores the separate legal entities of the two companies and shows the position of the group as a whole.

Any inter-company balances (*e.g.*, debts owing by a subsidiary company to the holding company, or *vice versa*) must be eliminated in preparing the Consolidated Balance Sheet. Thus if, at the date of the Balance Sheet, a subsidiary company owes £1,000 to the holding company, this debt will appear as an asset in the holding company's Balance Sheet under the heading of " Debts due from Subsidiary Company " and as a liability in the subsidiary company's Balance Sheet under the heading " Debts due to Holding Company ". But when a Consolidated Balance Sheet is prepared, the item, which is an asset of one member of the group, is neutralised by the corresponding liability of another member, and both asset and liability must be eliminated. A similar adjustment is made where debentures in the subsidiary company are held by the holding company, or *vice versa*.

Where bills of exchange are given by the holding company to its subsidiary company, or *vice versa*, the item " Bills Payable " in one Balance Sheet may be cancelled out against the corresponding item " Bills Receivable " in the other Balance Sheet, when the Consolidated Balance Sheet is being prepared. If the bills have been discounted it is not possible to cancel them out, because in the one Balance Sheet they will appear as " Bills Payable ", whereas in the other Balance Sheet the proceeds of discount will be included in " Balance at Bank ", and a note will be appended to show the contingent liability for bills discounted. In the Consolidated Balance Sheet the total of the bills discounted will appear as a liability under the heading of " Bills Payable " and the note as to the contingent liability in respect of the bills receivable discounted will not be necessary since the actual liability is shown instead.

Furthermore, where the holding company sells goods to the subsidiary, or *vice versa*, and the goods still remain unsold in the accounts of the buying company, any profit added by the selling company must be eliminated from stock-in-hand in the Consolidated Balance Sheet. From the point of view of the companies as separate legal entities it is perfectly correct to show stock at cost (unless this is above current market value) ; but from the point of view of the group as a whole, such a procedure would be equivalent to taking credit for a profit before it had been earned by actual resale of the goods to a person outside the group of companies. The adjustment in respect of unrealised profit on inter-company sales is effected by reducing the stock-in-trade of the buying company and the profit balance of the selling company in the Consolidated Balance Sheet. It should be clearly understood that this adjustment in respect of unrealised inter-company profits is *for the purposes of a Consolidated Balance Sheet only*. In the separate accounts of the selling company, as long as a *bona fide* sale has been effected to the buying company, it is immaterial whether or not the buying company has in turn sold the goods. As far as the selling company is concerned, the transaction is completed between itself and the buying company. Similarly, in the separate accounts of the buying company, the goods will appear at cost, which, in normal cases, is their legitimate valuation.

EXAMPLE

From the following Balance Sheets of Traders, Ltd., and its two subsidiaries, Traders (Southern Counties), Ltd., and Traders (Midlands), Ltd., drawn up as at 31st December, 19. ., prepare a Consolidated Balance Sheet to show the position of the group of companies as a whole. The stock-in-hand of Traders (Southern Counties), Ltd., includes £500 stock purchased from Traders, Ltd., upon which the latter company has taken credit for £100 profit. The bills receivable of Traders (Southern Counties), Ltd., include bills amounting to £300 accepted by Traders, Ltd., while bills to the extent of £100 received by Traders (Midlands), Ltd., from Traders, Ltd., have been discounted.

TRADERS, LTD.
BALANCE SHEET
AS AT 31ST DECEMBER, 19..

	£			£
Share Capital, Authorised and Issued:—		Freehold Property, at cost		10,000
20,000 Ordinary Shares of £1 each . . .	20,000	Plant and Machinery, at cost (£5,000), *Less* depreciation . . .		2,250
Profit and Loss Account .	4,000	Investments in Subsidiary Companies, at cost:—	£	
	24,000	Traders (S.C.), Ltd., 5,000 Ordinary Shares of £1 each . . .	5,000	
Sundry Creditors:— £		Traders (M.), Ltd., 2,500 Ordinary Shares of £1 each . . .	2,500	
General . . . 3,600				
Traders (S.C.), Ltd. 500				
	4,100			7,500
Bills Payable . . .	400	Stock, at cost . .		5,250
		Sundry Debtors:		
		General . . 2,500		
		Traders (M.), Ltd. 250		
				2,750
		Cash at Bank		750
	£28,500			£28,500

TRADERS (SOUTHERN COUNTIES), LTD.
BALANCE SHEET
AS AT 31ST DECEMBER, 19..

	£			£
Share Capital, Authorised and Issued:—		Plant and Machinery, at cost (£6,000), *Less* depreciation		2,500
5,000 Ordinary Shares of £1 each	5,000	Stock, at cost		2,500
Profit and Loss Account .	1,500	Sundry Debtors:— £		
	6,500	General . . . 1,000		
		Traders, Ltd. . . 500		
Sundry Creditors:— £				1,500
General . . . 800		Bills Receivable		500
Traders (M.), Ltd. 200		Cash at Bank		500
	1,000			
	£7,500			£7,500

TRADERS (*MIDLANDS*), *LTD.*
BALANCE SHEET
AS AT 31ST DECEMBER, 19..

	£			£
Share Capital, Authorised and Issued:—		Plant and Machinery at cost (£2,600), *Less* depreciation		1,500
2,500 Ordinary Shares of £1 each . . .	2,500	Stock, at cost		700
Less Profit and Loss Account.	50	Sundry Debtors:—	£	
	2,450	General . . .	700	
		Traders (S.C.), Ltd.	200	
Sundry Creditors:—	£			900
General . . .	500	Cash at Bank . . .		100
Traders, Ltd. .	250			
	750			
(There is a contingent liability of £100 in respect of bills receivable discounted.)				
	£3,200			£3,200

CONSOLIDATED BALANCE SHEET
AS AT 31ST DECEMBER, 19..

	£			£
Share Capital, Authorised and Issued:—		Freehold Property, at cost .		10,000
20,000 Ordinary Shares of £1 each . . .	20,000	Plant and Machinery, at cost (£13,600), *Less* depreciation:—		
Profit and Loss Account:—	£	[£2,250 + £2,500 + £1,500]		6,250
Traders, Ltd. .	4,000	Stock, at cost:—		
Less profit on unsold stock . .	100	[£5,250 + £2,500 + £700 − £100]		8,350
	3,900	Sundry Debtors:—		
Traders (S.C.), Ltd.	1,500	[£2,500 + £1,000 + £700]		4,200
	5,400	Bills Receivable:—		
Less Traders (M.), Ltd.—Loss . .	50	[£500 − £300] . . .		200
	5,350	Cash at Bank:—		
	25,350	[£750 + £500 + £100] .		1,350
Sundry Creditors :—				
[£3,600 + £800 + £500]	4,900			
Bills Payable :—				
[£400 − £300] . . .	100			
	£30,350			£30,350

NOTES.

(1) Traders (S.C.), Ltd., holds bills receivable amounting to £500, of which £300 represents bills drawn on Traders, Ltd. In the Consolidated Balance Sheet this latter item is a contra which cancels out, leaving bills payable of £100 (*i.e.*, £400 − £300) and bills receivable £200 (*i.e.*, £500 − £300).

(2) Since the whole of the bills payable of Traders, Ltd., are inter-company bills, the item would entirely disappear in the Consolidated Balance Sheet were it not for the fact that bills to the extent of £100 have been discounted by one of the subsidiaries. The amount of the bills discounted will therefore appear under the heading of " Bills Payable " representing the external liability (*i.e.*, to the bank) and, for this reason, the note as to the contingent liability on the Balance Sheet of Traders (M.), Ltd., is not necessary in the Consolidated Balance Sheet.

Consolidated Balance Sheet where the Shares are Acquired at a Premium or at a Discount.

In the above example it is assumed that the shares in the subsidiary companies have been acquired at par. When, however, a holding company acquires the shares of a subsidiary company at a premium or at a discount, certain adjustments become necessary when preparing the Consolidated Balance Sheet.

If the shares are acquired at a premium, the sum paid by the holding company will exceed the nominal paid-up value of the shares acquired. This sum represents the valuation attached by the holding company, at the time of the purchase, to the excess of assets over liabilities in the subsidiary company's Balance Sheet, as far as that excess relates to the shares acquired. Consequently, when these assets and liabilities are substituted for the investment in the subsidiary company in the Consolidated Balance Sheet, there will be a difference which represents the excess of the purchase price paid over the nominal paid-up value of the shares acquired. This difference represents an undisclosed asset which must be brought into the Consolidated Balance Sheet as " Goodwill " (or " Excess of cost of shares in subsidiary over their nominal value " or " Cost of Control ") in addition to any Goodwill of the holding and/or subsidiary company which may already appear in their respective Balance Sheets.

Where shares in a subsidiary company are acquired at a discount, the cost of such shares is less than the value of the holding, based upon the net assets appearing in the books of the subsidiary company. The difference in this case must be shown as " Capital Reserve " on the liabilities side of the Consolidated Balance Sheet.

Where the shares in one subsidiary company have been acquired at a premium and those in a second company have been acquired at a discount, the premium should be set-off against the discount, and the net difference shown as Goodwill or Capital Reserve (as the case may be) in the Consolidated Balance Sheet.

EXAMPLE

From the Balance Sheets given below prepare a Consolidated Balance Sheet of Bishop, Ltd., and its subsidiary companies, Dean, Ltd., and Curate, Ltd., to show the position of the group of companies as a whole. The shares in the subsidiary companies were acquired many years previously and the balances on General Reserve and Profit and Loss Account have been created subsequent to the acquisition of the shares by Bishop, Ltd.

BISHOP, LTD.

BALANCE SHEET

AS AT 31ST DECEMBER, 19..

	£		£
Share Capital :—		Freehold Property, at cost .	32,000
Authorised—		Plant and Machinery, at	
20,000 5% Preference		cost (£40,000), *Less* de-	
Shares of £1 each .	20,000	preciation	30,000
100,000 Ordinary Shares		Investments in Subsidiary	
of £1 each . . .	100,000	Companies, at cost :—	
		Dean, Ltd., 20,000 Ordin-	
Issued—	£120,000	ary Shares of £1 each .	25,000
20,000 5% Preference		Curate, Ltd., 10,000	
Shares of £1 each,		Ordinary Shares of £1	
fully paid . . .	20,000	each	8,000
60,000 Ordinary Shares		Stock on hand, at cost . .	10,000
of £1 each, fully paid	60,000	Sundry Debtors	19,000
		Debts due from Subsidiary	
	80,000	Companies . . .	3,000
General Reserve. . . .	25,000	Bank Balance	5,000
Profit and Loss Account .	12,000		
	117,000		
Sundry Creditors . . .	13,000		
Debts due to Subsidiary			
Companies	2,000		
	£132,000		£132,000

DEAN, LTD.

BALANCE SHEET

AS AT 31ST DECEMBER, 19..

	£		£
Share Capital :—		Leasehold Property, at cost	
Authorised and Issued—		(£25,000), *Less* depreciation	15,000
20,000 Ordinary Shares		Plant and Machinery at	
of £1 each, fully paid	20,000	cost (£16,000), *Less* depre-	
General Reserve . . .	6,000	ciation	10,000
Profit and Loss Account .	9,000	Stock on hand, at cost .	3,000
		Sundry Debtors . . .	6,500
	35,000	Debt due by Holding Com-	
Sundry Creditors . . .	3,000	pany	500
Debt due to Holding Com-		Bank Balance	5,000
pany	2,000		
	£40,000		£40,000

CURATE, LTD.

BALANCE SHEET

AS AT 31ST DECEMBER, 19..

		£
Share Capital :—		
Authorised—		Freehold Property, at cost	3,000
12,000 Ordinary Shares		Stock on hand, at cost . .	3,000
of £1 each . . .	12,000	Sundry Debtors . . .	6,500
		Debt due to Holding Com-	
Issued—		pany	1,500
10,000 Ordinary Shares		Investments in Government	
of £1 each, fully paid	10,000	Securities	4,000
Profit and Loss Account .	2,000		
	12,000		
Sundry Creditors . . .	4,000		
Debt due to Holding Com-			
pany	1,000		
Bank Balance (overdrawn)	1,000		
	£18,000		£18,000

CONSOLIDATED BALANCE SHEET
AS AT 31ST DECEMBER, 19..

	£			£
Share Capital :—		Goodwill—		
Authorised—		£5,000 — £2,000 . . .		3,000
20,000 5% Preference		Freehold Property, at cost—		
Shares of £1 each .	20,000	£32,000 + £3,000 . .		35,000
100,000 Ordinary Shares		Leasehold Property, at cost		
of £1 each . . .	100,000	(£25,000), *Less* deprecia-		
		tion		15,000
	£120,000	Plant and Machinery, at cost		
Issued—		(£56,000), *Less* deprecia-		
20,000 5% Preference		tion—		
Shares of £1 each,		£30,000 + £10,000 . .		40,000
fully paid . . .	20,000	Stock on hand, at cost—		
60,000 Ordinary Shares		£10,000+£3,000+£3,000		16,000
of £1 each, fully paid	60,000	Sundry Debtors—		
		£19,000 + £6,500 + £6,500		32,000
	80,000			
General Reserve—		Investments in Government		
£25,000 + £6,000 . .	31,000	Securities		4,000
Profit and Loss Account—		Bank Balances—		
£12,000+£9,000+£2,000	23,000	£5,000+£5,000−£1,000 .		9,000
	134,000			
Sundry Creditors—				
£13,000 + £3,000 + £4,000	20,000			
	£154,000			£154,000

NOTES : (1) The amount of Goodwill is arrived at as follows :—

	£
Premium on acquisition of shares in Dean, Ltd. . .	5,000
Less Discount on acquisition of shares in Curate, Ltd. .	2,000
	£3,000

(2) The inter-company debts cancel out and do not appear in the Consolidated Balance Sheet.

Minority, or Outside, Shareholders.

Up to this point it has been assumed that the holding company acquires the whole of the issued share capital of the subsidiary company, but in practice this is not always the case. The holding company may acquire only sufficient shares to give it a majority of the voting power or to enable it to appoint the majority of the directors of the subsidiary company, and the shareholders owning the remainder of the shares are usually referred to as Minority or Outside Shareholders. The preference shareholders are often included in this term, for, where the preference shares carry voting rights only when the dividend is in arrear, the holding company may not trouble to acquire any.

Since the Consolidated Balance Sheet is drawn up to show the position of the group as a whole, it is evident that, where there are minority or outside shareholders in the subsidiary company, it is incorrect to bring in the whole of the assets and liabilities of the subsidiary without any further amendment. For example, if the capital of a company consists of 1,000 shares of the same class, then each share gives the holder an interest which is equal in value to a one-thousandth part of the net assets of the company or, in other words, to a one-thousandth part of the share capital plus any undistributed profits. Consequently, where the holding company holds, say, 800 shares, the share of the net assets attributable to the holding of the outside shareholders (the owners of the remaining 200 shares) must be taken into consideration when preparing the Consolidated Balance Sheet. This may be done by including :—

(1) Only such proportion of each asset and liability as is attributable to the holding company (four-fifths, in the above example) ; *or*

(2) The whole of the assets and liabilities, showing the value of the outside shareholders' interest in the " equity " of the subsidiary company as a separate item on the liabilities side, *i.e.*, as an offset against the total assets and liabilities of the subsidiary which have been taken into the Consolidated Balance Sheet although the holding company is entitled only to a part thereof.

The second method presents a much truer picture of the facts and is nearly always used in preference to the first method, which will not be considered any further in this book.

Where the outside shareholders hold the whole or part of the preference shares in the subsidiary company, their proportionate share of unpaid cumulative dividends should be provided for in the Consolidated Balance Sheet but no such provision should be made for unpaid cumulative dividends on the holding company's own holding of preference shares. In other words, full provision should be made in the Consolidated Balance Sheet for the maximum liability to outside shareholders. Where a debit balance is shown on the Profit and Loss Account of the subsidiary company, a deduction should be made from the interests of outside shareholders for their proportionate share of such loss.

The total interests of outside or minority shareholders will be represented by the amount of their paid-up capital plus their proportionate share of *all* undistributed profits of their company (*e.g.*, Profit and Loss Account, and General Reserve), less their proportionate share of any losses. The amount of such interests is unaffected by the consolidation adjustments for goodwill or capital reserve (see page 347), or for profit on unsold stocks (see page 343), which concern only the members of the holding company.

EXAMPLE

Finance, Ltd., holds 20,000 Ordinary Shares and 5,000 Preference Shares in Commerce, Ltd., whose summarised Balance Sheet is shown on page 353. No dividend has yet been paid or declared on the Preference Shares for the current year. These shares are preferential as regards dividends but have no right to share in any surplus on liquidation. Compute the value of the interests of the minority or outside shareholders in Commerce, Ltd.

COMMERCE, LTD.

BALANCE SHEET AS AT 31ST DECEMBER, 19..

	£		£
Share Capital :—		Sundry Assets	64,750
Authorised—			
10,000 5% Cumulative Preference Shares of £1 each	10,000		
40,000 Ordinary Shares of £1 each . . .	40,000		
	£50,000		
Issued—			
10,000 5% Cumulative Preference Shares of £1 each, fully paid .	10,000		
25,000 Ordinary Shares of £1 each, fully paid	25,000		
	35,000		
General Reserve . . .	15,000		
Profit and Loss Account .	4,750		
	54,750		
Sundry Creditors . . .	10,000		
	£64,750		£64,750

Value of Interests of Outside Shareholders :—

	£	£
Preference Shares	5,000	
Add Dividend thereon at 5 per cent. .	250	
		5,250
Ordinary Shares.	5,000	
Add Share of General Reserve ($\frac{5000}{25000}$ of £15,000) .	3,000	
Share of Profit and Loss Account less Pref. Div.* ($\frac{5000}{25000}$ of £4,250)	850	
		8,850
		£14,100

* For this calculation, the *whole* of the Preference dividend must be taken into account. Income Tax has been ignored.

NOTE.—Since the Preference Shares are not entitled to participate in any surplus on a winding up of the company, the whole of the General Reserve belongs to the Ordinary Shareholders.

N

Pre-acquisition Profits and Losses.

Where a holding company acquires some or all of the shares of a subsidiary company which, at the date of purchase of the shares, has a credit balance on Profit and Loss Account or a General Reserve, representing undistributed profits, these items must be specially treated both in the separate Balance Sheet of the holding company and in the Consolidated Balance Sheet of the group. The principles involved are similar to those which require the apportionment of the first dividend received after the purchase of an investment " cum-dividend ".*

(1) TREATMENT IN THE HOLDING COMPANY'S BALANCE SHEET.

From the point of view of the holding company alone, the price paid for the shares in the subsidiary company will include (in the absence of agreement to the contrary) the proportionate share of undistributed profits attaching to such shares, by way of either a premium or a cum dividend quotation. Any dividends received by the holding company, which have been declared out of these profits, are, in effect, a return of that part of the purchase price of the shares which represents undivided profits. As such, the dividend received should be credited against the cost of the investment to reduce the latter to its true ex-dividend cost or to eliminate the premium.

The first dividend received by the holding company will usually require to be apportioned by reference to the period of the Profit and Loss Account out of which it has been declared. Thus, if the shares were acquired on the 30th September, and the first dividend was received in respect of the year to the following 31st December, three-quarters of the dividend should be credited against the cost of the investment, the remaining one-quarter being credited to revenue. This is the general rule, and it assumes that the dividend has been declared out of profits *earned* during the year in respect of which the dividend is expressed to be payable. If, however, the divisible fund of profits has been

* *Vide* page 148.

augmented by transfers from reserves which existed at the date when the shares were acquired, the dividend should be regarded as payable out of current profits and out of reserves *pro rata*, the amount payable out of profits being apportioned as above, and the amount payable out of reserves being credited against the cost of the investment.

Losses existing at the date of acquisition of the shares by the holding company will not usually cause any adjustment to be made in the valuation of the holding, since the price paid for the shares will have taken into account any accumulated losses. The holding company's share of current losses shown by the first Profit and Loss Account will require to be apportioned on a time basis.

EXAMPLE

On the 30th September, 1955, Major, Ltd., acquired 20,000 Ordinary Shares of £1 each in Minor, Ltd., at a cost of £30,000, and 30,000 Ordinary Shares of £1 each in Petit, Ltd., at a cost of £26,000. Both Minor, Ltd., and Petit, Ltd., make up their accounts to the 31st December in each year, and on this date immediately following the acquisition of the shares by Major, Ltd., the Balance Sheets of the two companies were as follows:—

MINOR, LTD.

BALANCE SHEET

AS AT 31ST DECEMBER, 1955

	£		£
Authorised and Issued Share Capital :—		Sundry Assets	54,000
30,000 Ordinary Shares, £1 each, fully paid .	30,000		
General Reserve . . .	10,000		
Profit and Loss Account :— £			
Profit for year . 3,000			
Transfer from Reserve . . . 3,000			
	6,000		
	46,000		
Sundry Creditors . . .	8,000		
	£54,000		£54,000

PETIT, LTD.
BALANCE SHEET
AS AT 31ST DECEMBER, 1955

	£		£
Authorised and Issued Share Capital :—		Sundry Assets	40,000
40,000 Ordinary Shares, £1 each, fully paid. .	40,000		
Less Profit and Loss Account (loss for year)	8,000		
	32,000		
Sundry Creditors . . .	8,000		
	£40,000		£40,000

On 26th February, 1956, Minor, Ltd. declared a dividend of 20 per cent. for the year to 31st December, 1955, and this dividend was duly paid.

Show how the following would be dealt with in the accounts of Major, Ltd., drawn up as at 31st March, 1956—

(a) The dividend received from Minor, Ltd.
(b) The shares held in Minor, Ltd.
(c) The shares held in Petit, Ltd., having regard to the loss sustained by that company.

Income tax may be ignored.

		£
(a) Dividend received from Minor, Ltd.		4,000

Payable equally out of current profits and reserve and therefore apportioned as follows :—

	Capital. £		Income. £
Payable out of Reserve	2,000		
„ „ „ Profits . . .	($\frac{3}{4}$) 1,500	($\frac{1}{4}$)	500
	£3,500		£500

The entry in the books to record the dividend will, therefore, be :—

	£	£
Cash . . . . . *Dr.*	4,000	
To Profit and Loss Account . .		500
„ Investment in Subsidiary Company		3,500

(b) In the Balance Sheet, the Investment Account (ignoring for the time being the investment in Petit, Ltd.) will appear as follows :—

	£	£
Investment in Subsidiary Company at cost	30,000	
Less Pre-acquisition Profits . .	3,500	
		26,500

(c) Of the loss sustained by Petit, Ltd., the proportion attributable to the holding of Major, Ltd., accrued to 30th September, £4,500 (*i.e.*, three-fourths of three-fourths of £8,000) may be assumed (in the absence of information to the contrary) to be taken into account in the cost of the shares, so that at that date the shares are properly valued at cost, *i.e.*, £26,000.

When the accounts of the holding company are made up at 31st March, provision should be made for the balance of loss sustained from 1st October to 31st December, *i.e.*, £1,500, and, in addition, for any further loss which is known to have been sustained during the period 1st January to 31st March following.

The investment will appear in the Balance Sheet :—

	£	£
Investment in Subsidiary Company at cost	26,000	
Less proportion of loss	1,500	
		24,500

or alternatively the £1,500 may be credited to Investment Reserve Account.

(2) Treatment in the Consolidated Balance Sheet.

In the Consolidated Balance Sheet the holding company's share of any undistributed profits accumulated prior to acquisition of the shares should not therefore be included under General Reserve or Profit and Loss Account, as the case may be, but should be treated as a separate item, either as a Capital Reserve or as a deduction from any Goodwill item arising out of the excess of the purchase price of the shares over their nominal value. Conversely, the holding company's share of any pre-acquisition losses of a subsidiary company should be treated as an addition to Goodwill or as a deduction from Capital Reserve. It should be clearly realised that in the separate Balance Sheet of the holding company, the necessity for distinguishing between pre-acquisition profits and profits made after the date on which the shares are acquired only arises when dividends are received from or declared by the subsidiary company (since only to that extent are the profits of the subsidiary company taken into account by the holding company). In the case of the Consolidated Balance Sheet, however, it is necessary to maintain the distinction even if no dividends are paid or declared by the subsidiary out of the pre-acquisition profits, since the profits of the subsidiary company are taken into account in the Consolidated Balance Sheet even if they have not been distributed or declared as dividend. The illustrations which follow will make this point clear.

It will thus be observed that profits made by a subsidiary company prior to the date when its shares were acquired by a holding company must be kept separate from profits made after that date.

The proportion of profits (or losses) attributable to the outside shareholders is not affected by the date of acquisition of the shares by the holding company. Such profits (or losses) belong to the outside shareholders and appear under that heading as already indicated.

Where accounts of the subsidiary are not available at the date of acquisition of the shares, the profits of the subsidiary company during the year in which the shares are acquired should be apportioned on a time basis for the purpose of inclusion in the Consolidated Balance Sheet.

EXAMPLE I

Ascot, Ltd., acquired 10,000 shares in Sandown, Ltd., at a cost of £16,000, and 5,000 shares in Gatwick, Ltd., at a cost of £4,000 on 1st January, 19.., out of a total issued capital of 15,000 shares and 8,000 shares respectively. All the shares are of £1 denomination, fully paid, and neither of the subsidiary companies had issued any Preference Shares. At the date of acquisition the accounts of Sandown, Ltd., showed a General Reserve of £12,000 and a credit balance on Profit and Loss Account of £4,500, and the accounts of Gatwick, Ltd., showed a debit balance on Profit and Loss Account of £6,400. Show how these facts would be set out in the Consolidated Balance Sheet of Ascot, Ltd., and its subsidiary companies.

Shares in Sandown, Ltd.

	£
Shares acquired, 10,000 shares of £1 each, fully paid	10,000
Cost of acquisition	16,000
Excess of cost over paid-up value	6,000

Share of undistributed profits at date of acquisition attributable to the above holding :

	£	
General Reserve, $\frac{10000}{15000}$ of £12,000	8,000	
Profit and Loss Account, $\frac{10000}{15000}$ of £4,500 . .	3,000	
		11,000
Net amount to be credited to Capital Reserve . . .		£5,000

Shares in Gatwick, Ltd.

		£
Shares acquired, 5,000 shares of £1 each, fully paid . . .		5,000
Cost of acquisition		4,000
Excess of paid-up value over cost		1,000

Share of debit balance on Profit and Loss Account attributable to the above holding :—	
$\frac{5000}{8000}$ of £6,400	4,000
Net amount to be regarded as Goodwill	£3,000

In the Consolidated Balance Sheet, the £3,000 will be deducted from the £5,000 and a net amount of £2,000 will appear as Capital Reserve.

The reasons for this treatment may be clearer if the Balance Sheets of the two subsidiary companies are examined. The Balance Sheet of Sandown, Ltd., can be reconstructed (in skeleton form) from the information given and will appear as follows :—

SANDOWN, LTD.

BALANCE SHEET as at 1st January, 19..

	£		£
Share Capital . . .	15,000	Sundry Net Assets . .	31,500
General Reserve . . .	12,000		
Profit and Loss Account .	4,500		
	£31,500		£31,500

Ascot, Ltd., has acquired a two-thirds interest in this company, *i.e.*, for £16,000 it has acquired an interest in assets worth ⅔ of £31,500 or £21,000. The difference of £5,000 is in the nature of a capital profit and is carried to Capital Reserve.

Similarly, the Balance Sheet of Gatwick, Ltd., would show the following position :—

GATWICK, LTD.
BALANCE SHEET as at 1st January, 19..

	£		£
Share Capital	8,000	Sundry Net Assets . . .	1,600
Less Profit and Loss Account.	6,400		
	£1,600		£1,600

In this case Ascot, Ltd., has acquired a five-eighths interest in net assets of £1,600 (*i.e.*, £1,000) for £4,000. Hence it has paid £3,000 for Goodwill.

EXAMPLE II

From the following Balance Sheets of Major Co., Ltd., and its subsidiary company, Minor Co., Ltd., drawn up at 31st December, 19.., prepare a Consolidated Balance Sheet as at that date. The interests of the minority shareholders of Minor Co., Ltd., are to be shown as a separate item. At the date of acquisition of the shares the General Reserve of Minor Co., Ltd., amounted to £2,000, and the Profit and Loss Account to £4,000.

MAJOR CO., LTD.
BALANCE SHEET as at 31st December, 19..

	£		£
Share Capital, Authorised and Issued—		Freehold Property, at cost	20,000
100,000 Shares of £1 each	100,000	Plant and Machinery, at cost (£35,000), *Less* depreciation	25,000
General Reserve . . .	10,000		
Profit and Loss Account .	15,000		
	125,000	Shares in Minor Co., Ltd., at cost—	
Sundry Creditors . . .	15,000	30,000 Shares of £1 each	40,000
		Stock, at cost	15,000
		Sundry Debtors	20,000
		Bank Balance	20,000
	£140,000		£140,000

MINOR CO., LTD.
BALANCE SHEET as at 31st December, 19..

	£		£
Share Capital, Authorised and Issued—		Plant and Machinery, at cost (£20,000), *Less* depreciation	12,000
40,000 Shares of £1 each	40,000		
General Reserve . . .	2,000	Stock, at cost	20,000
Profit and Loss Account .	6,000	Sundry Debtors . . .	10,000
	48,000	Bank Balance	10,000
Sundry Creditors . . .	4,000		
	£52,000		£52,000

CONSOLIDATED BALANCE SHEET
AS AT 31ST DECEMBER, 19..

	£	£	£	£
Share Capital, Authorised and Issued:—			Goodwill, at cost (Excess of cost of shares in subsidiary over their nominal value). . . 10,000	
100,000 Shares of £1 each . . .		100,000		
Capital Reserve:—	£		*Less* Capital Reserve *per contra* 4,500	
Proportion of General Reserve (see below) . . .	1,500			5,500
Proportion of Profit and Loss Account (see below)	3,000		Freehold Property, at cost	20,000
			Plant and Machinery, at cost (£55,000), *Less* depreciation . . .	37,000
Deducted from Goodwill, *contra*	£4,500		Stock, at cost . . .	35,000
General Reserve:—			Sundry Debtors . . .	30,000
Major Co., Ltd.	10,000		Bank Balance . . .	30,000
Minor Co., Ltd.—				
Minority Shareholders (see £ below) . . . 500				
Capital Reserve (see above) . . . 1,500				
£2,000	—			
		10,000		
Profit and Loss Account:—				
Major Co., Ltd. . . .	15,000			
Minor Co., Ltd. . . 6,000				
Less Capital Reserve (see above) . 3,000				
Minority Shareholders (see below) 1,500				
£4,500	1,500			
		16,500		
		126,500		
Minority Shareholders in Minor Co., Ltd.:—				
10,000 Shares of £1 each .	10,000			
Proportion of General Reserve (see above) . . .	500			
Proportion of Profit and Loss Account (see above)	1,500			
		12,000		
Sundry Creditors		19,000		
		£157,500		£157,500

NOTE—Alternatively, the net amount of £5,500 for Goodwill may be computed as follows:—

Paper value of 40,000 Shares (at date of acquisition) .	£46,000	
Paper value of 30,000 Shares (do.)	£34,500	
Price paid for 30,000 Shares	£40,000	
Excess	£5,500	

N*

EXAMPLE III

The Balance Sheets of Duke, Ltd., and its subsidiaries, Earl, Ltd., and Knight, Ltd., as at 31st May, 1956, were as follows :—

	DUKE. £	EARL. £	KNIGHT. £		DUKE. £	EARL. £	KNIGHT. £
Share Capital, Authorised and Issued (£1 shares) :				Goodwill . . .	6,000	—	2,000
				Property . . .	5,000	—	4,500
6% Preference				Plant and Machinery	5,000	1,000	3,700
Shares . .	30,000		5,000	Stock	3,500	3,500	7,000
Ordinary Shares	20,000	8,000	15,000	Debtors	6,500	4,000	6,500
				Bills Receivable .	—	1,000	500
				Investments at cost	45,000	—	4,600
	50,000	8,000	20,000	Bank Balance . .	3,000	200	2,000
General Reserve .	2,500	—	2,300				
Profit and Loss Acount . . .	8,500	—	4,000				
Do. (Debit) . .		800					
	61,000	7,200	26,300				
5% Debentures .	3,000	1,000					
Sundry Creditors .	8,000	1,500	3,500				
Bills Payable . .	2,000	—	1,000				
	£74,000	£9,700	£30,800		£74,000	£9,700	£30,800

The Shares in all companies are of £1 denomination, fully paid.

Duke, Ltd., acquired its holding of 6,000 Ordinary Shares in Earl, Ltd., on 1st June, 1955, for £4,500. At the date of acquisition the Profit and Loss Account was in debit to the extent of £1,000.

Duke, Ltd., holds all the Ordinary Shares of Knight, Ltd., this investment appearing in the books at £23,000. At the date of acquisition (1st June, 1953) there was a credit balance on Profit and Loss Account of £650 and on Reserve Account, Nil. No dividends have been declared on the Ordinary Shares in Knight, Ltd., previous to 31st May, 1955, but full dividends have been paid on the Preference Shares.

Earl, Ltd., owes Duke, Ltd., £750, and Knight, Ltd., £250, while Duke, Ltd., owes Knight, Ltd., £1,500.

Duke, Ltd., has given bills value £800 to Earl, Ltd., and these are still held by the latter company, while bills value £200 given by Duke, Ltd., to Knight, Ltd., have been discounted by the latter company.

Duke, Ltd., supplies the two subsidiaries with goods for resale at a profit to it of 25 per cent. on cost. Included in the Balance Sheet of Earl, Ltd., is stock invoiced to it by Duke, Ltd., at £500, and in the Balance Sheet of Knight, Ltd., similar stock invoiced at £2,000.

On 30th November, 1955, Knight, Ltd., declared an interim dividend out of current earnings of 4 per cent. for the year ending 31st May, 1956, but this has not yet been paid. In Knight, Ltd.'s books provision has been made for this debt, but no adjustment has been made in the books of Duke, Ltd. On 30th November, 1955, the full interim dividend was paid on the Preference Shares by Knight, Ltd., but no provision has yet been made for the final dividend on these shares for the year ending 31st May, 1956.

From the above information prepare a Consolidated Balance Sheet of Duke, Ltd., and its subsidiaries as at 31st May, 1956, showing full details of all adjustments and calculations. Income tax may be ignored.

NOTES ON CONSOLIDATED BALANCE SHEET (see pages 364 and 365) :—

(1) The gross profit of 25 per cent. on the cost of goods sold by Duke, Ltd., to its subsidiaries is equivalent to 20 per cent. on the selling price. The price at which Duke, Ltd., *sells* the goods is that at which the subsidiaries *buy* them. Therefore the unrealised inter-company profit is 20 per cent. of the price at which the goods stand in the Balance Sheets of the subsidiaries, *i.e.*—

$$\begin{array}{ll} & £ \\ \text{Earl, Ltd., 20\% of £500} & = 100 \\ \text{Knight, Ltd., 20\% of £2,000} & = 400 \\ \hline & £500 \end{array}$$

(2) As an intermediate step this could have been first transferred to Capital Reserve, and then offset *contra* against the computed value of goodwill.

(3) The Profit and Loss Account of Earl, Ltd., is apportioned as follows :—

	Total.	Proportions.	
		Duke, Ltd. ($\frac{3}{4}$).	Minority ($\frac{1}{4}$).
	£	£	£
Debit balance at date of acquisition by Duke, Ltd. (1.6.55)	1,000	750	250
Debit balance at date of Balance Sheet (31.5.56)	800	600	200
Profit for year ended 31.5.56 . . .	£200	£150	£50

The figure to be dealt with in the Consolidated Balance Sheet is the debit balance at 31st May, 1956—£800. £200 of this is attributable to the outside shareholders and is therefore deducted from the value of the minority interests. £150 is credited to Profit and Loss Account, representing the holding company's proportion of the profit for the year and £750 is added to Goodwill, representing the holding company's proportion of the debit balance at the date on which it acquired the shares.

(4) It is assumed that the Preference shareholders in Knight, Ltd., have no participating rights beyond their fixed dividend.

(5) The interim dividend declared by Knight, Ltd., but unpaid, is presumably included under the heading of Sundry Creditors in the Balance Sheet. If there is any reason to doubt that the dividend will be ultimately paid, a reserve should be made in respect thereof.

Consolidated Statement of Subsidiaries.

As an alternative to the presentation of a Consolidated Balance Sheet of the whole undertaking, *i.e.*, of the holding company and the subsidiary companies, the separate Balance Sheet of the holding company may be supplemented by a

	£	£	£
Authorised and Issued Share Capital :—			
30,000 6% Preference Shares of £1 each, fully paid			30,00
20,000 Ordinary Shares of £1 each, fully paid			20,0
			50,0
General Reserve :—			
Duke, Ltd.		2,500	
Knight, Ltd.		2,300	
			4,8
Profit and Loss Account :—			
Duke, Ltd.	8,500		
Less Inter-company profit on stocks held by Earl, Ltd., and Knight, Ltd. (see note 1)	500		
	8,000		
Add Interim dividend due from Knight, Ltd.	600		
		8,600	
Earl, Ltd.—Proportion of profit for year attributable to Duke, Ltd.'s holding (75% of £200, *i.e.* £1,000 — £800) .		150	
Knight, Ltd. . . . . £	4,000		
Less Balance at date of acquisition (see note 2) . 650			
Preference dividend for half-year to date . . 150			
	800		
		3,200	
			11,9
			66,7
Minority Interests of Outside Shareholders :—			
2,000 Ordinary Shares of £1 each in Earl, Ltd.	2,000		
Less Proportion of debit balance on Profit and Loss Account (25% of £800) (see note 3)	200		
		1,800	
5,000 6% Preference Shares in Knight, Ltd.	5,000		
Add Final dividend for half-year to date (see note 4) . .	150		
		5,150	
			6,9
5% Debentures :—			
Duke, Ltd.		3,000	
Earl, Ltd.		1,000	
			4,0
Sundry Creditors :—			
Duke, Ltd.	8,000		
Less Amount due to Knight, Ltd.	1,500		
		6,500	
Earl, Ltd. . . . . £	1,500		
Less Amount due to Duke, Ltd. 750			
Amount due to Knight, Ltd. . . . 250			
		1,000	
		500	
Knight, Ltd.	3,500		
Less Interim dividend due to Duke, Ltd. (see note 5) . .	600		
		2,900	
			9,9
Bills Payable :—			
Duke, Ltd.	2,000		
Less Bills held by Earl, Ltd.	800		
		1,200	
Knight, Ltd.		1,000	
			2,2
			£89,8

	£	£	£
odwill—			
Duke, Ltd.		6,000	
Knight, Ltd.		2,000	
Add Excess of cost of shares in Knight, Ltd., over nominal value (£23,000 — £15,000)		8,000	
Add Proportion of debit balance on Profit and Loss Account of Earl, Ltd., at date of acquisition of holding (75% of £1,000) (see note 3)		750	
		8,750	
Less Excess of nominal value of shares in Earl, Ltd., over cost (£6,000 — £4,500) £1,500			
Credit balance on Profit and Loss Account of Knight, Ltd., at date of acquisition of holding (see note 2) 650		2,150	
		6,600	14,600
operty :—			
Duke, Ltd.		5,000	
Knight, Ltd.		4,500	
			9,500
nt and Machinery :—			
Duke, Ltd.		5,000	
Earl, Ltd.		1,000	
Knight, Ltd.		3,700	
			9,700
ocks :—			
Duke, Ltd.		3,500	
Earl, Ltd. 3,500			
Less Inter-company profit (20% of £500) 100		3,400	
Knight, Ltd. 7,000			
Less Inter-company profit (20% of £2,000) 400		6,600	13,500
ndry Debtors :—			
Duke, Ltd.		6,500	
Less Amount due by Earl, Ltd.		750	
		5,750	
Earl, Ltd.		4,000	
Knight, Ltd. 6,500			
Less Amount due by Duke, Ltd. £1,500			
Amount due by Earl, Ltd. 250			
		1,750	
		4,750	14,500
ls Receivable :—			
Earl, Ltd. 1,000			
Less Bills from Duke, Ltd. 800			
		200	
Knight, Ltd.		500	
			700
estments :—			
Duke, Ltd. (£45,000 — £27,500)		17,500	
Knight, Ltd.		4,600	
			22,100
nk Balance :—			
Duke, Ltd.		3,000	
Earl, Ltd.		200	
Knight, Ltd.		2,000	
			5,200
			£89,800

separate schedule in the form of a Balance Sheet summarising the combined assets and liabilities of all the subsidiary companies. As in the case of the Consolidated Balance Sheet already described, the interests of outside shareholders in the subsidiary companies are shown as a liability in the consolidated statement. This method is not so effective as the Consolidated Balance Sheet of the whole undertaking, as it does not reveal the combined position of all the companies in the group. It is, however, a form of presentation permitted by the Companies Act, 1948, provided that the full requirements of the Act with regard to disclosure of information are satisfied by this method.

It will be seen that the Consolidated Statement of Subsidiaries does not present a true picture of the group as a whole, and in particular—

(1) It does not show the Goodwill or Capital Reserve representing the excess or deficiency of the purchase price of the shares over their nominal paid-up value ; and

(2) The balance of Profit and Loss Account is not necessarily available for distribution to the members of the holding company, for no adjustments have been made in respect of profits or losses prior to acquisition. This disadvantage can be overcome by the presentation of a Consolidated Profit and Loss Account to show the available balance.

EXAMPLE

From the Balance Sheets of Duke, Ltd., and its subsidiary companies and the information set out in the example on page 362, you are required to prepare a consolidated statement in the form of a Balance Sheet of the two subsidiary companies, Earl, Ltd., and Knight, Ltd. (See pages 368 and 369.)

Consolidated Profit and Loss Account.

A Consolidated Balance Sheet may be accompanied by a Consolidated Profit and Loss Account showing the combined results of the holding company and the subsidiary companies, in order to give a true and fair view of the profit or loss for the period of the holding company and of the subsidiaries dealt with thereby, so far as concerns the interest of the holding company in those subsidiaries. The final balance of the Consolidated Profit and Loss Account must represent profits which are distributable as regards the group, and thus the following adjustments will be necessary :—

(1) The due proportion of the profits or losses of sub-subsidiaries applicable to the minority interests must be deducted and transferred to Minority Interests to show what is available for distribution within the group.

(2) The holding company's proportion of pre-acquisition profits of subsidiaries must be transferred to Capital Reserve, while the corresponding proportion of pre-acquisition losses must be transferred to Goodwill.

(3) The holding company's proportion of any unrealised inter-company profits in respect of unsold stocks must be eliminated by a transfer to write down the stock values.

(4) Any inter-company dividends must be eliminated.

Care must be taken that the fund shown as the divisible fund consists solely of profits earned by the holding company and by subsidiaries since the date of acquisition of the shares by the holding company in so far as such profits may be attributed to the holding company's holding in the subsidiary companies.

EXAMPLE I

Red, Ltd., is interested in two subsidiary companies, White, Ltd., and Blue, Ltd. On 31st March, 1955, Red, Ltd., acquired 20,000 Ordinary Shares of £1 each in White, Ltd. (representing the entire share capital of that company) and on 31st May, 1955, 18,000 Ordinary Shares of £1 each in Blue, Ltd. (the issued share capital of which was 24,000 Ordinary Shares of £1 each). All the shares are fully paid up. On 10th July, 1955, White, Ltd., paid an interim dividend of 10 per cent. for the year ending 30th September, 1955, and

CONSOLIDATED STATEMENT

AS AT 3⟩

	£	£
Share Capital :—		
(Held by Holding Co.)		
6,000 Ordinary Shares of £1 each, fully paid, in Earl, Ltd. . .	6,000	
15,000 Ordinary Shares of £1 each, fully paid, in Knight, Ltd. .	15,000	
		21,00⟩
General Reserve—Knight, Ltd.		2,30⟩
Profit and Loss Account :—		
Knight, Ltd. (£4,000 − £150)	3,850	
Less Earl, Ltd.—Proportion of debit balance	600	
		3,25⟩
Minority Interests :—	£	26,55⟩
2,000 Ordinary Shares of £1 each, fully paid, in Earl, Ltd.	2,000	
Less Proportion of debit balance on Profit and Loss Account	200	
	1,800	
5,000 6% Preference Shares of £1 each, fully paid, in Knight, Ltd.	5,000	
Add Final dividend for half-year to date	150	
	5,150	
		6,95⟩
5% Debentures—Earl, Ltd.		1,00⟩
Sundry Creditors :—		
Earl, Ltd.	1,500	
Less Amount due to Knight, Ltd.	250	
	1,250	
Knight, Ltd.	3,500	
		4,75⟩
Bills Payable—Knight, Ltd.		1,0⟩
		£40,2⟩

JBSIDIARY COMPANIES

AY, 1956

	£	£
oodwill—Knight, Ltd.		2,000
roperty—Knight, Ltd.		4,500
lant and Machinery :—		
Earl, Ltd.	1,000	
Knight, Ltd.	3,700	
		4,700
tock :—		
Earl, Ltd.	3,500	
Knight, Ltd.	7,000	
		10,500
undry Debtors :—	£	
Earl, Ltd.		4,000
Knight, Ltd.	6,500	
Less Amount due by Earl, Ltd.	250	
	6,250	
		10,250
ills Receivable :—		
Earl, Ltd.	1,000	
Knight, Ltd.	500	
		1,500
vestments—Knight, Ltd.		4,600
ank Balance :—		
Earl, Ltd.	200	
Knight, Ltd.	2,000	
		2,200
		£40,250

on 15th July, 1955, Blue, Ltd., paid an interim dividend of 12 per cent. for a similar period.

Red, Ltd., supplies its subsidiaries with raw materials invoiced at cost plus 25 per cent. During the year ended 30th September, 1955, raw materials to the amount of £2,000 had been supplied to White, Ltd., and £3,000 to Blue, Ltd., of which £500 of the former and £1,000 of the latter were in stock at 30th September, 1955.

The Profit and Loss Accounts of the three companies for the year ended 30th September, 1955, were as follows:—

Dr.   *Cr.*

	RED, LTD. £	WHITE, LTD. £	BLUE, LTD. £		RED, LTD. £	WHITE, LTD. £	BLUE, LTD. £
To Administrative and Selling Expenses .	5,000	3,000	4,000	By Profit on Trading and Sundry Income . .	17,000	10,000	8,200
„ Interim Dividends paid .		2,000	2,880				
„ Balance available	12,000	5,000	1,320				
	£17,000	10,000	8,200		£17,000	10,000	8,200

Prepare a Consolidated Profit and Loss Account of Red, Ltd., and its subsidiary companies for the year ended 30th September, 1955. Ignore Income Tax.

CONSOLIDATED PROFIT AND LOSS ACCOUNT
OF RED, LTD., AND ITS SUBSIDIARIES
FOR THE YEAR ENDED 30TH SEPTEMBER, 1955.

Dr.   *Cr.*

	£			£
To Administrative and Selling Expenses . . .	12,000	By Profit on Trading:— £		
„ Minority Interests in Blue, Ltd.—		Red, Ltd. 17,000		
¼ of (£2,880 + £1,320)	1,050	*Less* Interim dividends from— £		
„ Pre-acquisition Profits :— White, Ltd.—		White, Ltd. 2,000		
½ of £7,000 . . .	3,500	Blue, Ltd. 2,160		
Blue, Ltd.,—		—— 4,160		
⅔ of (£4,200 − £1,050)	2,100	12,840		
„ Elimination of inter-company profit on stocks of White, Ltd. and Blue, Ltd. :—		White, Ltd. . . . 10,000		
£		Blue, Ltd. 8,200		
White, Ltd., 20% of £500 . . . 100		——		31,040
Blue, Ltd., 20% of £1,000 . . . 200				
—— 300				
„ Balance available . .	12,090			
	£31,040			£31,040

EXAMPLE II

The Profit and Loss Accounts of Arthur, Ltd., and its three subsidiary companies, Basil, Ltd., Claude, Ltd., and David, Ltd., for the year to 31st December, 1955, are as follows :—

Dr.	ARTHUR, LTD.			Cr.
	£			£
To Dividend for 1954 . .	16,000	By Balance, b/f . . .		16,000
„ Balance, c/f. . . .	37,100	„ Net Profit for 1955 .		28,300
		„ Dividends Received .		8,800
	£53,100			£53,100

Dr.	BASIL, LTD.		Cr.
	£		£
To Interim Preference Divi-		By Balance, b/f . . .	—
dend for 1955 . .	300	„ Net Profit for 1955. .	500
„ Balance, c/f. . . .	200		
	£500		£500

Dr.	CLAUDE, LTD.		Cr.
	£		£
To Interim Dividend for		By Balance, b/f . . .	13,000
1955	8,000	„ Net Profit for 1955 .	12,000
„ Balance, c/f. . . .	17,000		
	£25,000		£25,000

Dr.	DAVID, LTD.		Cr.
	£		£
To Final Dividend for 1954	2,800	By Balance, b/f . . .	3,600
„ Net Loss for 1955 .	3,300	„ Balance, c/f . . .	2,500
	£6,100		£6,100

The Issued Share Capital of the subsidiary companies is as follows :—

	BASIL, LTD.	CLAUDE, LTD.	DAVID, LTD.
Ordinary :—	£	£	£
Total	20,000	40,000	24,000
Held by Arthur, Ltd. .	16,000	30,000	24,000
6 per cent. Preference :—			
Total	10,000	—	—
Held by Arthur, Ltd. .	—	—	—

Arthur, Ltd., acquired the shares in Basil, Ltd., and David, Ltd., on 31st December, 1954. The shares in Claude, Ltd., were acquired on 31st December, 1953, when the credit balance on the Profit and Loss Account of Claude, Ltd., was £4,000. Claude, Ltd., paid no dividends in 1954.

In December, 1955, Arthur, Ltd., sold goods to David, Ltd., for £3,750, and

these goods were still held by David, Ltd., on 31st December, 1955. The cost
of these goods to Arthur, Ltd., was £3,000.

It is required to prepare a Consolidated Profit and Loss Account for the year
ended 31st December, 1955. Ignore Income Tax.

CONSOLIDATED PROFIT AND LOSS ACCOUNT
OF ARTHUR, LTD., AND ITS SUBSIDIARIES
FOR THE YEAR ENDED 31ST DECEMBER, 1955.

Dr.　　　　　　　　　　　　　　　　　　　　　　　　　　　　Cr.

	£			£	£
To Dividend for 1954 . .	16,000	By Balance, b/f—			
„ Interim Dividend on Pre-		Arthur, Ltd. . . .	16,000		
„ ference Shares in Sub-		Basil, Ltd. . . .	—		
sidiary—Basil, Ltd.	300		£		
„ Ordinary Dividends of		Claude, Ltd.	13,000		
Subsidiaries— £		Less to			
Claude, Ltd. 8,000		Minority			
Less to Minority		Interests (¼)	3,250		
Interests (¼) 2,000				9,750	
————		Less to Capital			
6,000		Reserve (¾th			
David, Ltd. 2,800		of £4,000)	3,000		
————				6,750	
Contra . . £8,800		David, Ltd. .	3,600		
		Less to Capital			
„ Balance, c/f	40,160	Reserve .	3,600	—	
					22,750
		„ Net Profit for 1955—	£		
		Arthur, Ltd. . . .	28,300		
		Basil, Ltd. .	500		
		Less to Minority			
		Interests (⅕th			
		of £200) .	40		
			—	460	
		Claude, Ltd.	12,000		
		Less to Minority			
		Interests (¼)	3,000		
			—	9,000	
				37,760	
		Less Net Loss for 1955—			
		David, Ltd. . .	3,300		
				34,460	
		Less Profit on Unsold			
		Stock	750		
					33,710
		„ Dividends received	8,800		
		Less Contra . .	8,800	—	
	£56,460				£56,460

NOTES.—(1) The dividend of £2,800 received by Arthur, Ltd., out of pre-acquisition profits of David, Ltd., should be credited to the Cost of Shares of David, Ltd., in the books of Arthur, Ltd., and not to Arthur, Ltd.'s Profit and Loss Account. As this dividend is cancelled for consolidation purposes, the Consolidated Profit and Loss Account is not affected by the treatment in the books of Arthur, Ltd.

(2) The Ordinary Dividends of Subsidiary Companies and Dividends Received would not appear in the final draft of the Consolidated Profit and Loss Account, but are shown above in order to explain the workings.

(3) The balance of consolidated profits carried forward may be reconciled as follows :—

	£	£
Balance carried forward—Arthur Ltd., ...	37,100	
Less Dividends received now excluded	8,800	
		28,300
Balance carried forward—Basil, Ltd.	200	
Less Proportion attributable to Minority Interests (⅕)	40	
		160
Balance carried forward—Claude, Ltd.	17,000	
Less Proportion attributable to Minority Interests (¼)	4,250	
	12,750	
Add Interim Dividend paid to Arthur, Ltd. . . .	6,000	
	18,750	
Less Transfer to Capital Reserve	3,000	
		15,750
		44,210
Less Net Loss of David, Ltd. (this is the only item in the Profit and Loss Account of David, Ltd., which relates to the period since acquisition)	3,300	
Profit on Unsold Stock	750	
		4,050
Consolidated Profits carried forward		£40,160

Examples of the published accounts of holding companies are given in Chapter X.

CHAPTER X

PUBLISHED ACCOUNTS

(In this Chapter, references are to the Companies Act, 1948, unless the context otherwise requires.)

The law does not oblige a sole trader or a partnership to publish any accounts at all nor even to keep any accounts.* In the case of a company incorporated under the Companies Acts, there are definite provisions relating to the keeping of proper accounts, the preparation of final accounts, and the presentation of these to the members of the company. Since the control of such companies may be practically divorced from the ownership of the shares, accurate accounts are necessary to enable the proprietors of a company to see the result of the activities of the directors whom they appoint to manage the business in which their funds are invested. The law has recognised this need, and has provided accordingly.

Those provisions of the Companies Act, 1948, which have any bearing on the preparation and presentation of the annual accounts of companies are reproduced in Appendix I to this work (see pages 475 *et seq.*). The interpretation and effect of these provisions will now be considered ; reference should be made to the detailed provisions of any section which is quoted.

Books of Account.

The provisions of the Act with regard to the keeping of books of account are contained in Sections 147 and 331, and

* Section 158 of the Bankruptcy Act, 1914, as amended by Section 7 of the Bankruptcy Act, 1926, imposes severe penalties upon a trader who, having been adjudged bankrupt, or against whom a Receiving Order has been made, had failed to keep books of account as specified in the amending section prior to the date of presentation of the bankruptcy petition. This provision has, to some extent, the effect of compelling a trader to keep *some* books of account. Similarly, the requirements of the Income Tax Acts with regard to the production of accounts for taxation purposes may compel traders and partners to keep adequate books of account.

it is interesting to observe the material differences between the requirements of these sections.

Section 147 applies to every company and provides that proper books of account shall be kept with respect to—

(a) All sums of money received and expended by the company and the matters in respect of which the receipt and expenditure takes place ;

(b) All sales and purchases of goods by the company ; and

(c) The assets and liabilities of the company.

The books must give a true and fair view of the state of the company's affairs and explain its transactions. Where books of account are kept at a place outside Great Britain adequate returns of the contents of such books (made out for periods of six months or less) must be sent to Great Britain ; such returns must be open to inspection by the directors and must contain all information material for the purpose of preparing the annual accounts of the company.

The books of account must be kept at the registered office of the company or at such other place as the directors think fit, and are to be open at all times to inspection by the directors.

Section 331, which applies only on liquidation of a company, imposes penalties if proper books of account have not been kept throughout the period of two years immediately preceding the commencement of the liquidation. For the purpose of this Section proper books of account include, in addition to the books required by Section 147, such books and accounts as are necessary to exhibit and explain the transactions and financial position of the trade or business of the company, including books containing—

(1) Entries from day to day in sufficient detail of all cash received and paid ;

(2) Statements of the annual stocktakings (where the business has involved dealings in goods) ; and (except in the case of goods sold by way of ordinary retail trade)

(3) Entries of all goods sold and purchased, showing the goods and the buyers and sellers thereof in sufficient detail to enable those goods and those buyers and sellers to be identified.

Sections 147 and 331 should be read together in determining what accounts and records should be kept.

It will be seen that the provisions of Section 331 are more comprehensive than those of Section 147, and in order to avoid liability on the liquidation of a company, the records kept should comply with the requirements of the former section throughout the existence of the company, *e.g.*, stock records should be compiled and the appropriate statements thereof filed with the documents of the company. Furthermore, Section 331 requires detailed day books, for here it is essential to identify the goods bought and sold, and the sellers and buyers thereof, except in regard to that part of a company's trade which is conducted on a purely retail basis.

Apart from any statutory provisions, however, practically all limited companies cause detailed records of their trading transactions to be kept, in order that the true profits may be ascertained periodically and the financial position of the concern shown clearly ; and in the Articles of Association of a company there may be particular directions as to accounts. The accountant is just as strictly bound to observe any such regulations as he is to observe those of the Act.

Presentation of Accounts.

Section 148 (1) provides that the directors of every company must *lay before the company in general meeting* a Profit and Loss Account (or, in the case of companies not trading for profit, an Income and Expenditure Account), not later than eighteen months after the incorporation of the company and, subsequently, once at least in every calendar year. The account must cover the period from the preceding account (or, in the case of the first account, since the incorporation of the company) to a date not earlier than nine months before the date of the meeting. In the case of a company having interests abroad, the account must be made up to a date not earlier than twelve months before the meeting.

Subsection (2) provides that once in every calendar year the directors must cause to be made out and to be *laid before the company in general meeting* a Balance Sheet, as at the date to which the Profit and Loss Account (or Income and Expenditure Account) is made up.

There must be attached to every such Balance Sheet a report by the directors with respect to the state of the company's affairs, the amount (if any) which they recommend should be paid by way of dividend, and the amount (if any) which they propose to carry to reserve. The report must also deal, so far as is material for the appreciation of the state of the company's affairs by its members and will not in the directors' opinion be harmful to the business of the company or of any of its subsidiaries, with any change during the financial year in the nature of the company's business, or in the company's subsidiaries, or in the classes of business in which the company has an interest, whether as member of another company or otherwise (Section 157).

It will be seen that the directors are responsible for the preparation of the Profit and Loss Account and Balance Sheet, and are subject to penalties if they fail to take all reasonable steps to comply with the foregoing provisions.

Section 158 provides that a copy of every Balance Sheet, including every document required by law to be annexed thereto (*i.e.*, Profit and Loss Account, and Group Accounts, if any), which is to be laid before the company in general meeting, together with a copy of the auditor's report, must, not less than twenty-one days before the date of the meeting, be sent to every member (whether entitled to receive notice of general meetings or not), every debenture-holder (whether so entitled or not), and to all other persons who are entitled to receive such notices.

Published Accounts.

Section 149 provides that every Profit and Loss Account must give a true and fair view of the profit or loss of the company for the financial year, and every Balance Sheet must give a true and fair view of the state of affairs of the company as at the end of its financial year.

The contents of the Profit and Loss Account and Balance Sheet must comply with the requirements of the Eighth Schedule to the Act, so far as applicable thereto, but the Board of Trade may, on the application or with the consent of a company's directors, modify any of the requirements of the Act as to the matters to be stated in the Profit and Loss Account and Balance Sheet, for the purpose of adapting them to the circumstances of the company.

The provisions of the Act as to the contents of the Profit and Loss Account do not apply if :—

(a) The company has subsidiaries ; and

(b) The Profit and Loss Account is framed as a Consolidated Profit and Loss Account dealing with all or any of the company's subsidiaries as well as the company and—

    (i) complies with the requirements of the Act relating to Consolidated Profit and Loss Accounts ; and

    (ii) shows how much of the consolidated profit and loss for the financial year is dealt with in the accounts of the company.

In the case of a company not trading for profit, the foregoing references to the Profit and Loss Account (and Consolidated Profit and Loss Account) apply equally to the Income and Expenditure Account.

The distinction between a Profit and Loss Account and a Profit and Loss Appropriation Account is an accounting concept which is not recognised by the Companies Act, 1948. It will generally be found necessary to prepare two accounts ; a detailed Profit and Loss Account with an Appropriation section for the information of the directors, and a Profit and Loss Account complying with the requirements of the Act for publication. Both accounts will show the same final balance, but the statutory Profit and Loss Account will disclose only certain items of expenditure not charged in arriving at the amount of profit or loss, and particulars of appropriations of profits. The matters to be disclosed in the statutory form of account are dealt with in the following paragraphs.

Disclosure in Profit and Loss Account.

Part I, Eighth Schedule of the Act, provides that the following information must be disclosed in the Profit and Loss Account :—

(1) (*a*) The amount charged to revenue by way of provision for depreciation, renewals or diminution in value of fixed assets.

(*b*) The amount of the interest on the company's debentures and other fixed loans.

(*c*) The amount of the charge for United Kingdom income tax and other United Kingdom taxation on profits, including, where practicable, as United Kingdom taxation any taxation imposed elsewhere to the extent of the relief, if any, from United Kingdom income tax, and distinguishing, where practicable, between income tax and other taxation.

(*d*) The amounts respectively provided for redemption of share capital and for redemption of loans.

(*e*) The amount, if material, set aside or proposed to be set aside to, or withdrawn from, reserves.

(*f*) The amount, if material, set aside to provisions other than provisions for depreciation, renewals or diminution in value of assets or, as the case may be, the amount, if material, withdrawn from such provisions and not applied for the purposes thereof.*

(*g*) The amount of income from investments, distinguishing between trade investments and other investments.

* The Board of Trade may direct that a company shall not be obliged to show an amount so set aside to provisions if the Board is satisfied that disclosure is not advisable in the public interest and would prejudice the company, but subject to the condition that any heading stating an amount arrived at after taking into account the amount so set aside to provisions shall indicate that fact.

PRO FORMA PROFIT

<small>Showing Requirements of Companies</small>

£

To DIRECTORS' REMUNERATION—   £

    Fees . . . .

    Managerial Salaries . . . .

,, PENSIONS OF PAST DIRECTORS . . .

,, COMPENSATION TO DIRECTORS FOR LOSS OF OFFICE

,, AUDITORS' FEES . . . .

    (*to be disclosed if not fixed by company in general meeting*)

,, DEPRECIATION, RENEWALS AND AMOUNTS WRITTEN

    OFF FIXED ASSETS . . . .

    (*basis of provision to be stated if other than by way of deprecia-*

    tion charges or renewals, and statement if no provision if such

    is the case)

,, INTEREST ON DEBENTURES AND FIXED LOANS (gross)

,, LOSSES OF A NON-RECURRENT NATURE . . .

    (*e.g., loss on sale of stock at reduced prices*)

,, TRANSFERS TO PROVISIONS . . . .

    (*the nature of the liability should be stated*)

,, PROFIT FOR THE YEAR SUBJECT TO TAXATION carried

    down . . . .

                                   £

                                         £

To TAXATION—

                    £

    Income Tax . . . .

    Profits Tax . . . .

    (*basis upon which the charge for Income Tax is computed to be*

    stated, and any adjustments, if material, in respect of under-

    or over-provision in previous years to be disclosed)

,, PROFIT FOR THE YEAR AFTER TAXATION carried down

                                    £

To TRANSFER TO CAPITAL REDEMPTION RESERVE FUND

,, TRANSFER TO RESERVE FOR REDEMPTION OF

    DEBENTURES AND OTHER LOANS . . . . .

,, TRANSFER TO GENERAL RESERVE . . . . . .

,, DIVIDENDS PAID OR PROPOSED . . . .

    (*statement to be made as to whether the dividends are subject to*

    deduction of tax)

,, BALANCE CARRIED FORWARD PER BALANCE SHEET

                                    £

Note.—Columns would be required in this account in which to record the corresponding figures for the previous year.

AND LOSS ACCOUNT

ACT, 1948, AS TO DISCLOSURE

£

By NET TRADING PROFIT FOR YEAR . . . . . .
„ INCOME FROM INVESTMENTS (gross)—

£

Trade Investments . . . .
Other Investments . . . .

„ AMOUNTS WITHDRAWN FROM PROVISIONS . . . .
„ PROFITS OF A NON-RECURRENT NATURE . . . . .

£

By PROFIT FOR THE YEAR SUBJECT TO TAXATION
brought down . . . .

£

By PROFIT FOR THE YEAR AFTER TAXATION brought
down . . . .
„ AMOUNTS WITHDRAWN FROM RESERVES . . . .
„ BALANCE BROUGHT FORWARD from previous year .

£

(*h*) The aggregate amount of the dividends paid and proposed.

(2) If the remuneration of the auditors is not fixed by the company in general meeting, the amount thereof (including any amount paid in respect of the auditors' expenses) must be shown under a separate heading.

(3) The following matters must be stated by way of note, if not otherwise shown—

(*a*) If depreciation or replacement of fixed assets is provided for by some method other than a depreciation charge or provision for renewals, or is not provided for, the method by which it is provided for or the fact that it is not provided for, as the case may be.

(*b*) The basis on which the charge for United Kingdom income tax is computed.

(*c*) Whether or not the amount stated for dividends paid and proposed is for dividends subject to deduction of income tax.

(*d*) Except in the case of the first Profit and Loss Account laid before the company after the commencement of the Act (*i.e.*, 1st July, 1948), the corresponding amounts for the immediately preceding financial year for all items shown in the Profit and Loss Account.

(*e*) Any material respects in which any items shown in the Profit and Loss Account are affected—

(i) by transactions of a sort not usually undertaken by the company or otherwise by circumstances of an exceptional or non-recurrent nature ; or

(ii) by any change in the basis of accounting.*

---

* Banking, discount and assurance companies are exempted from some of the requirements of Part I of the Eighth Schedule with regard to disclosure in published accounts (see Chapter XI).

Reference should also be made to the recommendations of the Council of the Institute of Chartered Accountants with regard to the form and contents of the published Profit and Loss Account (see Appendix II).

The amounts to be shown in respect of interest on debentures and fixed loans, and income received from investments, are gross amounts before deduction of Income Tax. Dividends paid or proposed may be shown gross or net, but a note must state which is the case ; in practice dividends paid or proposed are invariably shown net.

It is not necessary to disclose interest on a bank overdraft, as this is not a " fixed loan".

Examples of matters which would call for disclosure under (3) (e) above, if material, are (i) losses by fire or profits on sale of fixed assets, and (ii) a change in the basis of stock valuation.

DIRECTORS' EMOLUMENTS. Section 196 provides that the accounts laid before the company in general meeting (*i.e.*, the Profit and Loss Account *or* Balance Sheet) or a statement annexed thereto must disclose, so far as the information is contained in the company's books or papers or the company has the right to obtain it from the persons concerned, the aggregate amount of :—

(*a*) Directors' emoluments from the company and subsidiaries, including fees and percentages, expense allowances if subject to United Kingdom income tax, contributions to pension schemes and the estimated cash value of other benefits ;

(*b*) Directors' and past directors' pensions (including pensions payable to dependants and nominees), if not paid out of a pensions fund maintained by contributions ;

(*c*) Compensation to directors and past directors for loss of office as director or in connection with the management of a company or a subsidiary ;

distinguishing under each heading (i) the total paid in respect of services as director, and (ii) the total paid otherwise ; and in respect of (i) distinguishing between sums received from the company, its subsidiaries, and other persons. Sums accountable for to the company or a subsidiary, and compensation accountable for to the members under a scheme for the transfer of their shares, are to be excluded.

The amounts to be shown under Section 196 for any financial year are the sums receivable in respect of that year, whenever paid, or, in the case of sums not receivable in respect of a period, the sums paid during that year.

If the foregoing requirements are not complied with, the auditors must, as far as practicable, include them in their report.

EXAMPLE

During the year ended 31st December, 1955, Blank, Ltd., made the following payments (inclusive of all sums due for the year) to its directors :—

A. Director's Fee, £250.

B. Managing Director's Salary, £2,000 ; Expenses Allowance (subject to Income Tax), £500 ; Director's Fee, £250.

C. Director's Fee, £100 ; Salary as Secretary, £250.

During the year D resigned his position as director and was paid a sum of £1,000 by the company as compensation for loss of office as a director, and a pension amounting for the year to £200.

By virtue of his office as director, B was allowed the use of a house owned by the company rent free. The annual value of the house was £150.

A received a salary of £1,000 as managing director of Vague, Ltd., which is a subsidiary of Blank, Ltd.

The amounts may be disclosed in the Profit and Loss Account in the following manner :—

	Including from Subsidiary.	From Blank, Ltd.	
	£	£	£
To Directors' Remuneration :—			
Fees	750	750	
Management Salaries	3,750	2,750	
			3,500
	£4,500		
,, Pension to Past Director in respect of services as director.			200
,, Compensation paid to Past Director for Loss of Office as Director . . .			1,000

NOTES.—(1) The total amounts shown above are made up as follows :— Emoluments from Directorships : A—£250 ; B—£250 and £150 ; C— £100 = £750.

Emoluments from Management : B—£2,000 and £500 ; C—£250 = £2,750.

(2) Alternatively to the above method of disclosure the same information may be disclosed by way of note only inserted or attached to the Profit and Loss Account or Balance Sheet.

The pro-forma Profit and Loss Account on pages 380 and 381 summarises the requirements of the Companies Act, 1948, with regard to disclosure.

Disclosure in Balance Sheet.

Before the passing of the Companies Acts, 1929 and 1948,

a common fault of the usual form of published Balance Sheet was the paucity of the information disclosed therein. This fault was directly due to a certain amount of reticence in disclosing information which, it was feared, might prejudice the interests of a company engaged in a strictly competitive trade or industry. Although this fear was, to some extent, justified, it had given rise to a practice which, when carried to excessive lengths, resulted in a Balance Sheet which was so secretive that its main purpose (*i.e.*, to serve as an intelligible guide to the state of affairs of the company) was defeated. It was not uncommon, therefore, for a company to publish a Balance Sheet which, by means of the aggregation of balances of a similar and dissimilar nature, and by vague descriptions of the items, gave little indication of the true state of affairs of the company. The provisions of the Companies Act, 1948, have, to a considerable extent, succeeded in improving the marshalling and disclosure of information in Balance Sheets.

Part I, Eighth Schedule of the Act, provides that the following information must be disclosed in the Balance Sheet :—

(1) Summaries of the authorised share capital, issued share capital, liabilities and assets, with such particulars as are necessary to disclose the general nature of the assets and liabilities and there must be specified :—

    (*a*) Any part of the issued capital that consists of redeemable preference shares, and the earliest date on which the company has power to redeem those shares.

    (*b*) Any share capital on which interest has been paid out of capital during the financial year and the rate of such interest, so far as this information is not given in the Profit and Loss Account.

    (*c*) The amount of the share premium account.

    (*d*) Particulars of any redeemed debentures which the company has power to re-issue.

(2) There must be stated under separate headings, so far as they are not written off :—

    (*a*) The preliminary expenses.

    (*b*) Any expenses incurred in connection with any issue of share capital or debentures.

    (*c*) Any sums paid by way of commission in respect of any shares or debentures.

    (*d*) Any sums allowed by way of discount in respect of any debentures.

    (*e*) The amount of discount allowed on any issue of shares.

(3) The reserves, provisions, liabilities and fixed and current assets must be classified under headings appropriate to the company's business, and fixed assets must be distinguished from current assets, and the method of arriving at the amount of the fixed assets must be stated.* The amount of the fixed assets must, where practicable, be shown by stating :—

    (*a*) their cost or, in the case of assets standing in the company's books at a valuation, the amount of the valuation ; and

    (*b*) the aggregate amount provided or written off for depreciation or diminution in value since the date of acquisition or valuation, as the case may be. The book value of fixed assets as at 1st July, 1948, may be substituted for cost or valuation in cases where figures prior to that date cannot be ascertained without unreasonable expense or delay.

(4) The aggregate amounts respectively of capital reserves, revenue reserves and provisions (other than provisions for depreciation, renewals or diminution in

---

* The Board of Trade have intimated that no objection will be taken to an asset not being described as " fixed " or " current " if to do so would not be a true and fair description (*e.g.*, advances to subsidiary companies, expenditure on preliminary expenses, etc.), provided the nature of the asset is clearly stated.

value of assets) must be stated under separate headings if material and unless the Board of Trade directs otherwise.* There must also be shown (unless shown elsewhere or the amount involved is not material) the source of any increase in the amounts of capital reserves, revenue reserves and provisions (other than provisions for depreciation, etc.) and the application of any decrease since the end of the immediately preceding financial year.

(5) There must be shown under separate headings :—

(a) The aggregate amounts respectively of the company's trade investments, quoted (i.e., on a recognised stock exchange) investments other than trade investments, and unquoted investments other than trade investments.

(b) Such part of the goodwill, patents and trade marks as is shown in, or ascertainable from, the company's records, although the whole amount thereof may not be ascertainable.

(c) The aggregate amount of any outstanding loans made by the company for the purchase of its shares under the provisions of Section 54.

(d) The aggregate amount of bank loans and overdrafts.

(e) The net aggregate amount (after deduction of income tax) which is recommended for distribution by way of dividend.

(6) Where any liability of the company is secured otherwise than by operation of law on any assets of the company, the fact that that liability is so secured must be stated but it is not necessary to specify the assets on which the liability is secured.

* The Board of Trade may direct that a company shall not be obliged to show a separate statement of the amount of provisions if the Board is satisfied that disclosure is not advisable in the public interest and would prejudice the company, but subject to the condition that any heading stating an amount arrived at after taking into account a provision shall indicate that fact.

(7) The nominal amount and book value of any of the company's debentures held by a nominee or trustee for the company must be stated.

The following matters must be stated by way of note to the Balance Sheet, or in a statement or report annexed to the Balance Sheet, if not otherwise shown :—

(1) The number, description and amount of any shares in the company which any person has an option to subscribe for, together with the following particulars of the option :—

(a) the period during which it is exercisable ; and

(b) the price to be paid for shares subscribed for under it.

(2) The amount of any arrears of fixed cumulative dividends on the company's shares and the period for which the dividends or, if there is more than one class, each class of them, are in arrear, the amount to be stated before deduction of income tax or stated as free of tax if such is the case.

(3) Particulars of any charge on the assets of the company to secure the liabilities of any other person, including, where practicable, the amount secured.

(4) The general nature of any other contingent liabilities not provided for and, where practicable, the aggregate amount or estimated amount of those liabilities, if it is material.

(5) The aggregate amount or estimated amount, if it is material, of contracts for capital expenditure, as far as not provided for.

(6) If, in the opinion of the directors, any of the current assets have not a value, on realisation in the ordinary course of the company's business, at least equal to the amount at which they are stated, the fact that the directors are of that opinion.

(7) The aggregate market value of the company's quoted investments, other than trade investments, where it differs from the amount of the investments as stated.

(8) The bases on which foreign currencies have been converted into sterling where the amount of the assets or liabilities affected is material.

(9) The basis on which the amount, if any, set aside for United Kingdom taxation is computed.*

It is not essential to show goodwill as a distinct item from patents and trade marks, and these assets may be disclosed as a single item.

Where a company has more than one bank balance, it is normally necessary to disclose the aggregate amount of overdrafts. Overdrafts and credit balances should not be set off in order to show only the net balance unless the balances are with the same bank, and the bank would so treat the amounts by reason of some arrangement with the company.

Secured liabilities must be described as such in the Balance Sheet, but it is not legally necessary to specify the security. Furthermore, a liability may be secured by other means than an asset of the company, e.g., a private asset of a director, and in such cases it is not even necessary to disclose the fact of security.

FIXED ASSETS. The normal method of arriving at the amount of any fixed asset is to take the difference between :—

(a) its cost or, if it stands in the company's books at a valuation, the amount of the valuation ; and

(b) the aggregate amount provided or written off since the date of acquisition or valuation, as the case may be, for depreciation or diminution in value.

For assets under each heading whose amount is arrived at in this way, the aggregate of (a) and the aggregate of (b) must each be stated. This method is usually referred to as the " normal basis " and should not give rise to any special accounting difficulties where the requisite figures are readily ascertainable.

* Banking, discount and assurance companies are exempted from some of the requirements of Part I of the Eighth Schedule with regard to disclosure in published accounts (see Chapter XI).

Reference should also be made to the recommendations of the Council of the Institute of Chartered Accountants with regard to the form and contents of the published Balance Sheet (see Appendix II).

Where, however, the records do not enable the normal basis to be used, and the figures relating to the period before 1st July, 1948, cannot be obtained without unreasonable expense or delay, the net amount at which the assets stood in the company's books at 1st July, 1948 (after deduction of the amounts previously provided or written off for depreciation or diminution in value), can be regarded as a valuation of those assets on that date. This notional valuation method is usually referred to as the " net book amount basis ".

Accounting difficulties arise where the latter basis is necessary and particularly where an asset heading, such as plant and machinery, can be divided into :—

(a) assets of known cost (or valuation) during, say, the previous ten years, to which the normal basis could be applied ; and

(b) an earlier residue of assets that cannot be identified for the purpose of applying the normal basis.

The proper presentation in such circumstances is largely a matter of good accounting practice, so that the accounts show a true and fair view of the state of affairs.

It appears that the provisions of the Act may be observed if, under an asset heading with appropriate wording, one aggregate figure is shown embodying both cost and valuation (including " net book amount " where this has to be treated as a valuation) with one aggregate deduction for depreciation.

The following alternative suggestions are regarded as complying with the Act :—*

Suggestion A

	£	£
PLANT AND MACHINERY At cost † (and, where figures for cost or valuation are not reasonably obtainable, at the net amount standing in the company's books on 1st July, 1948, less sales)	825,000	
Less Depreciation	225,000	
		600,000

* These suggestions are based on the opinion of counsel obtained by the Council of the Institute of Chartered Accountants.

† Or " independent valuation in 19– " ; or " partly cost and partly independent valuation in 19– ", according to the circumstances.

Suggestion B

(Adapting *A* to circumstances where several fixed assets can be grouped conveniently under the same heading.)

	Cost, etc.	Depreciation.	Net.
	£	£	£
FREEHOLD AND LEASEHOLD LAND AND BUILDINGS, PLANT AND MACHINERY At cost * (and where figures for cost *or valuation* are not reasonably obtainable, at the net amount standing in the company's books on 1st July, 1948, less sales), less depreciation :—			
Freehold land and buildings . .	225,000	25,000	200,000
Leasehold land and buildings .	85,000	10,000	75,000
Plant, machinery and equipment	825,000	225,000	600,000
	£1,135,000	£260,000	875,000

* As in Suggestion *A* above.

Suggestion C

(Distinguishing the totals for items dealt with on the normal basis and items dealt with on the net book amount basis.)

	Cost, etc.	Depreciation.	
	£	£	£
PLANT AND MACHINERY			
At cost,† less depreciation	550,000	100,000	
At the net amount standing in the company's books on 1st July, 1948 (where figures for cost *or valuation* are not reasonably obtainable) less sales and depreciation	275,000	125,000	
	£825,000	£225,000	600,000

† As in Suggestion *A* above.

Suggestion D

(A variant of Suggestion C.)

	£	£	£
PLANT AND MACHINERY			
(a) At cost *	550,000		
(b) At the net amount standing in the company's books on 1st July, 1948 (where figures for cost or valuation are not reasonably obtainable less sales)	275,000		
		825,000	
Deduct Depreciation on amount stated at :—			
(a) above	100,000		
(b) above	125,000		
		225,000	
			600,000

* As in Suggestion A above.

The division of the totals between normal basis and net book amount basis (Suggestions C or D) will usually give a fairer view of the assets than is the case where one total only is shown and it approaches nearest to the intention behind the requirement to show cost less accumulated provisions.

It may be considered desirable for purposes of clarity and to enable the Balance Sheet to be read easily (particularly as the comparative figures for the previous year must be given) to show in the main part of the Balance Sheet an abbreviated description thus :—

PLANT AND MACHINERY
Per Schedule £600,000

the details, under whatever method of presentation is adopted, being shown in the separate schedule.

References in the foregoing suggestions to 1st July, 1948, will require to be amended to the company's prior accounting date in any case where it has been impossible to apply the statutory date.

LOANS TO OFFICERS, ETC.—Section 190 of the Act prohibits the making of loans to directors, and the giving of guarantees or security for such loans by other persons, unless :—

(1) The company is an exempt private company (see page 88) ; or

(2) The loan is made by a subsidiary where the director is its holding company ; or

(3) The ordinary business of the company includes the lending of money, and the loan is made in the ordinary course of business ; or

(4) The loan is to enable the director to meet expenses incurred for the purposes of the company or to enable him to perform his duties, and the loan is either made :—

      (i) with the prior approval of a general meeting of the purposes and amount ; or

      (ii) on condition that the loan shall be repaid, or the guarantee or security discharged, within six months after the next annual general meeting if not approved at that meeting.

The Act contains several provisions designed to secure the proper disclosure of loans made to officers (including directors) of the company.

Section 197 requires the accounts (*i.e.*, the Balance Sheet or by way of note to the Balance Sheet or Profit and Loss Account) which are laid before the company in general meeting to show :—

(*a*) The amount of any loans made during the financial year to any officer,* or to any person who after the making of the loan became an officer during the year, whether by the company or a subsidiary thereof (*i.e.*, a company which was a subsidiary at the end of the company's financial year), or by any other person under a guarantee or security provided by the company or a subsidiary.

(*b*) The amount of any such loans repaid during the year.†

---

* The term "officer of a company" is defined by Section 455 as including a director, manager or secretary. This definition, although giving some guidance, is not complete as although the term is said to include "a director, manager or secretary", other persons holding responsible positions with a company, *e.g.*, a chief accountant, may also be regarded as officers according to the circumstances of the case.

† Repayments made during the current year of loans advanced in *previous* years need not be shown, but repayments of loans made during the year under review must be shown.

o*

(c) The amount of any such loans made prior to the year and still outstanding at its expiration.

The above provisions as to disclosure of loans apply to both public and private companies (including exempt private companies), but do not apply where :—

(a) The ordinary business of the company or subsidiary includes the lending of money and the loan is made in the ordinary course of business, e.g., banking companies ; or

(b) The loan does not exceed £2,000 and is made to an employee, provided that such loan is certified by the directors as being in accordance with any practice adopted or about to be adopted by the company or subsidiary with respect to loans to employees ;

except where the loan is made by the company under the guarantee of or on a security provided by a subsidiary thereof or made by a subsidiary under a guarantee of or on a security provided by the company or another subsidiary.

Section 196 provides that if the foregoing requirements are not complied with, the auditors must, as far as practicable, disclose the information in their report.

Example

A limited company makes up its accounts to 31st December. At the commencement of the year the following loans to the Company were outstanding :—

		£
A—Manager		2,000
B—Secretary		3,500
C—Director		750

During the year, A repaid the whole of his loan and B repaid £1,000. A further loan of £1,000 was made to C, and D, another director, was advanced a sum of £1,500 which he repaid before the end of the year. A loan of £1,000 to A was made by a subsidiary company.

The information to be disclosed in the Balance Sheet of the company or by way of note thereto, at 31st December, would be as follows :—

Loans to Officers of the Company—	£	£	£
Made during year		2,500	
Less Repaid		1,500	
			1,000
Made prior to current year and still outstanding		3,250	
			4,250

(Note.—During the year a loan of £1,000 was made by a subsidiary company to an officer of the company and is still outstanding.)

NOTES.—(1) Although the amount of the loans made and repaid during the year must be disclosed, there is no necessity to specify the extent to which loans made prior to the current year have been repaid during the year. This information can, however, be ascertained by comparing the details set out in consecutive Balance Sheets.

(2) The total amounts shown above are made up as follows :—

Loans made during year : C—£1,000 ; D—£1,500 = £2,500.

Loans made prior to current year and still outstanding : B—£2,500 ; C—£750 = £3,250.

Part IV, Eighth Schedule of the Act, contains certain interpretations of expressions referred to in Part I and these may be conveniently summarised, at this stage, as follows :—

(a) " *Provision* ", subject to (e) below, means any amount written off or retained by way of providing for depreciation, renewals or diminution in value of assets, or retained by way of providing for any known liability of which the amount cannot be determined with substantial accuracy.

(b) " *Reserve* ", subject to (e) below, does not include any amount written off or retained by way of providing for depreciation, renewals or diminution in value of assets or retained by way of providing for any known liability.

(c) " *Capital Reserve* " does not include any amount regarded as free for distribution through the Profit and Loss Account, and the expression " Revenue Reserve " means any reserve other than a " Capital Reserve ".

(d) " *Liability* " includes all liabilities in respect of expenditure contracted for and all disputed or contingent liabilities.

(e) Where any amount written off or retained as in (a) above is in excess of the amount which, in the opinion of the directors, is reasonably necessary for the purpose, the excess should be treated as a " Reserve " and not as a " Provision ".

(f) " *Quoted Investment* " means an investment for which a quotation or permission to deal has been granted by a recognised stock exchange, and the term " *Unquoted Investment* " is construed accordingly.

The requirements of the Act with regard to disclosure in the published Balance Sheet are summarised in the pro forma Balance Sheet set out on pages 398 and 399.

In accordance with Section 155, the Balance Sheet must be signed on behalf of the board by two of the directors of the company, or, if there is only one director, by that director.

The Profit and Loss Account and, so far as not incorporated in the Balance Sheet or Profit and Loss Account, any Group Accounts laid before the company in general meeting, must be annexed to the Balance Sheet, and the auditors' report must be attached thereto.

Notes on Pro-forma Balance Sheet (pages 398 and 399) :—

(1) Goodwill, Patents and Trade Marks may alternatively be shown as a separate item under the heading of Fixed Assets.

(2) Fixed Assets must be classified according to their general nature, *e.g.*, Freehold Land and Buildings ; Leasehold Land and Buildings ; Plant and Machinery ; Fixtures and Fittings ; Motor Vehicles, etc.

(3) Amounts owing from subsidiary companies may alternatively be shown under Current Assets in appropriate circumstances. In the case of a Balance Sheet prepared for a subsidiary company, this heading will be replaced by one entitled " Amounts owing from Holding Company and Fellow Subsidiary Companies " and it will be necessary to distinguish between indebtedness in the form of debentures and otherwise. The same information must be disclosed in regard to amounts owing to such companies.

(4) Alternatively, Investments may be included separately as Fixed Assets or Current Assets according to the purpose for which they are held.

(5) Alternatively, the Amounts owing to Subsidiary Companies may be shown separately under the headings " Loan Capital " or " Current Liabilities " according to whether they are not currently repayable or otherwise. See also remarks under (3) above, where the company is itself a subsidiary company.

(6) The general nature of Current Liabilities must be disclosed ; the items Trade Creditors and Current Taxation are merely illustrative of the manner in which the disclosures would be made.

(7) These notes are merely illustrative. Notes on other matters would be included as appropriate.

Disclosure in Published Accounts of Holding Companies.

In addition to the foregoing provisions of the Companies Act, 1948, with regard to disclosure in the published accounts, a holding company must disclose the aggregate amount under separate headings of each of the following items :—

(1) Shares held in subsidiary companies.

(2) Debts due from subsidiary companies.

(3) Debts due to subsidiary companies (Part II, Eighth Schedule).

The items " Debts due from subsidiary companies " and
" Debts due to subsidiary companies ", include general indebtedness whether on account of ordinary trading transactions (*i.e.*, purchase and sale of goods), loans or debentures,
but where debentures are held in subsidiary companies, it
is advisable (though not legally essential) that the aggregate
amount thereof should appear as a separate item from other
debts due from subsidiary companies.

The provisions of Part I, Eighth Schedule of the Act
with regard to disclosure of investments and disclosure of
the cost or valuation and amounts written off for depreciation, etc., of fixed assets do not apply in relation to fixed
assets consisting of interests in the company's subsidiaries.

The required information would usually be disclosed in
the manner set out below, *e.g.*—

(1) Investments in and advances to subsidiary companies
at cost, *Less* amounts written off :—

Investments
Advances.

Where, however, the advances are in the nature of trading
transactions between the holding company and subsidiaries,
or otherwise are of the nature of *current* assets, they should
not be grouped with the amount of shares in subsidiary
companies but should be separately stated amongst the
current assets, *e.g.*—

(2) Investments in subsidiary companies at cost
(included with the *fixed* assets).

Advances to, and Current Accounts of subsidiary
companies
(included with the *current* assets).

(3) Debts due to subsidiary companies (shown separately
from other creditors).

There must also be shown, either by way of note to the
Balance Sheet of the holding company or in a statement or
report annexed thereto, the number, description and amounts
of any of the holding company's shares or debentures held
by its subsidiary companies, excluding shares or debentures

PRO FORMA

Showing Requirements of Com-

	£	£	£

I. AUTHORISED SHARE CAPITAL
   (*showing details of each class of share*)

II. ISSUED SHARE CAPITAL—
   Preference Shares . . . . .
   Redeemable Preference Shares . . .
      (*earliest date of redemption to be stated*)
   Ordinary Shares . . . . .
   Deferred Shares . . . . .
   Capital on which Interest is being paid pend-
      ing completion of construction . .
      (*rate of interest to be stated*)
      (*gross amount of arrears of fixed cumulative
      dividends to be stated on each class of share*)

III. CAPITAL RESERVES—
   Capital Redemption Reserve Fund . .
      (*equivalent to the nominal value of the shares
      redeemed*)
   Share Premium Account . . . .
   Capital Reserves . . . . .
      (*sources of increases and application of
      decreases to be stated, if not given else-
      where*)

IV. REVENUE RESERVES—
   General Reserve . . . . .
   Reserve for Future Income Tax . . .
      (*Income Tax liability based on current year's
      profits, subject to agreement*)
   Profit and Loss Account . . . .

V. LOAN CAPITAL—
   Mortgages, Mortgage Debentures and Secured
      Loans . . . . . .
      (*particulars required of redeemed debentures
      which the company has power to re-issue*)
   Other Long-term Liabilities . . .

VI. AMOUNTS OWING TO SUBSIDIARY
   COMPANIES (*see Note 5*)

VII. CURRENT LIABILITIES AND PROVISIONS—
   Trade Creditors } (*see Note 6*)
   Current Taxation }
   Bank Loans and Overdrafts . . .
   Provisions . . . . . .
      (*i.e., provision for any known liability of
      which the amount cannot be determined
      with substantial accuracy, e.g., provisions
      for Profits Tax and deferred repairs ;
      sources of increases and applications of
      decreases to be stated if not given elsewhere*)
   Proposed Dividends . . . . .
      (*dividends to be stated at net amounts, i.e.,
      after deduction of Income Tax*)

			£

Note.—Columns would be required in which to record

BALANCE SHEET

PANIES ACT, 1948, AS TO DISCLOSURE

<table>
<tr><td></td><td></td><td></td><td>£</td><td>£</td></tr>
<tr><td>I.</td><td>GOODWILL, PATENTS AND TRADE MARKS
(see Note 1)
(if ascertainable, and so far as not written off)</td><td></td><td></td><td></td></tr>
<tr><td>II.</td><td>FIXED ASSETS (see Note 2)
(these may be defined as assets not held for sale
or conversion into cash)</td><td>Cost or
Valuation
£</td><td>Deprecia-
tion.
£</td><td></td></tr>
<tr><td>III.</td><td>SUBSIDIARY COMPANIES—
Shares in Subsidiary Companies . .
Amounts owing from Subsidiary Companies
(see Note 3) . . . . .</td><td></td><td></td><td></td></tr>
<tr><td>IV.</td><td>INVESTMENTS (see Note 4)—
Trade Investments . . .
Other Quoted Investments . .
   (market value to be stated if different from
     book value)
Other Unquoted Investments . .</td><td></td><td></td><td></td></tr>
<tr><td>V.</td><td>CURRENT ASSETS
(these may be defined as cash and assets held for
conversion into cash)</td><td></td><td></td><td></td></tr>
<tr><td>VI.</td><td>LOANS TO EMPLOYEES
(in aggregate, for purchase of fully-paid shares
in the company)</td><td></td><td></td><td></td></tr>
<tr><td>VII.</td><td>LOANS TO DIRECTORS AND OFFICERS
(in aggregate, showing loans made and repaid
during period, and prior loans still outstand-
ing, with a note of loans made by subsidiary
or any other person under guarantee of the
company or subsidiary)</td><td></td><td></td><td></td></tr>
<tr><td>VIII.</td><td>CAPITAL AND ISSUE EXPENSES—
(so far as not yet written off)
Preliminary Expenses . .
Expenses on Issue of Shares or Debentures
Commission on Issue of Shares or Debentures
Discount on Issue of Shares . .
Discount on Issue of Debentures . .</td><td></td><td></td><td></td></tr>
</table>

NOTES : (1) Contingent Liabilities . .
        (2) Commitments for Capital Expen-
           diture

Balance Sheet to be signed by two Directors,
or if there is only one Director, by that
Director.

AUDITORS' REPORT to members to be
attached to Balance Sheet

£

the corresponding figures for the previous year.

£

To AUDITORS' FEES
    (*to be disclosed if not fixed by company in general meeting*)
  „ DEPRECIATION, RENEWALS AND AMOUNTS WRITTEN
    OFF FIXED ASSETS
    (*basis of provision to be stated if other than by way of depreciation
    charges or renewals, and statement of no provision if such is the
    case*)
  „ INTEREST ON DEBENTURES AND FIXED LOANS
  „ TRANSFER TO CAPITAL RESERVE
    (*proportion of profits earned by subsidiary companies prior to the
    acquisition of control, where such control was acquired during
    the year*)
  „ TRANSFER TO CAPITAL REDEMPTION RESERVE FUND
  „ TRANSFER TO RESERVE FOR REDEMPTION OF DEBEN-
    TURES AND LOANS
  „ TRANSFER TO GENERAL RESERVE
  „ PROVISIONS FOR SPECIAL CONTINGENCIES
  „ TAXATION—

£

Income Tax . . . .
Profits Tax . . . .

    (*basis upon which the charge for Income Tax is
    computed to be stated, and any adjustments, if
    material, in respect of under- or over-provisions
    in previous years to be disclosed*)
  „ LOSSES OF A NON-RECURRENT NATURE
    (*e.g., loss on sale of fixed assets*)
  „ BALANCE OF CONSOLIDATED INCOME FOR THE
    YEAR CARRIED DOWN—

£

Belonging to Minority Interests . . . .
Belonging to the Group . . . .

£

To PROVISION FOR DIVIDENDS PAID OR PROPOSED
    (*statement to be made as to whether the dividends are subject to
    deduction of tax*)
  „ BALANCE BEING UNDISTRIBUTED PROFITS CARRIED
    FORWARD TO NEXT YEAR—

£

Belonging to Minority Interests . . . .
Belonging to the Group . . . .

£

NOTE.—The sub-division into three sections may, alternatively, be adopted

PROFIT AND LOSS ACCOUNT

PANIES ACT, 1948, AS TO DISCLOSURE

£

By COMBINED NET TRADING PROFIT FOR YEAR

" INCOME FROM INVESTMENTS—

£

Trade Investments . . . .

Other Investments . . . .

" AMOUNTS WITHDRAWN FROM RESERVES

" AMOUNTS WITHDRAWN FROM PROVISIONS

" PROFITS OF A NON-RECURRENT NATURE
(e.g., *profit on sale of fixed assets*)

£

By BALANCE OF CONSOLIDATED INCOME FOR THE YEAR
BROUGHT DOWN—

£

Belonging to Minority Interests . . . . . .

Belonging to the Group . . . .

" BALANCE BROUGHT FORWARD FROM PREVIOUS YEAR

£

(see pages 380 and 381) in order to emphasise the profit before and after taxation.

PRO FORMA CONSOLIDATED

Showing Requirements of Companies

£   £   £

I. **AUTHORISED SHARE CAPITAL**
   (showing details of each class of share)

II. **ISSUED SHARE CAPITAL—**
   Preference Shares . . . .
   Redeemable Preference Shares . . . .
      (earliest date of redemption to be stated)
   Ordinary Shares . . . .
   Deferred Shares . . . .
   Capital on which Interest is being paid pending com-
     pletion of construction . . . .
       (rate of interest to be stated)
       (gross amount of arrears of fixed cumulative dividends
       on each class of share to be stated)

III. **CAPITAL RESERVES—**
   Capital Redemption Reserve Fund . . . . . .
      (equivalent to the nominal value of the shares redeemed)
   Share Premium Account . . . .
   Capital Reserves . . . .
      (sources of increases and application of decreases to be
      stated if not given elsewhere ; proportion of pre-
      acquisition profits and surplus over nominal value of
      shares in subsidiary companies to be included under
      this heading)

IV. **REVENUE RESERVES—**
   General Reserve . . . .
   Reserve for Future Income Tax . . . .
   Profit and Loss Account :—
     Amount attributable to the Group . . . . . .

V. **SHARE OF CAPITAL AND SURPLUS OF OUTSIDE
   SHAREHOLDERS IN SUBSIDIARY COMPANIES**

VI. **MORTGAGES, MORTGAGE DEBENTURES AND
   SECURED LOANS**
   *(particulars required of redeemed debentures which the
   company has power to reissue)*

VII. **AMOUNTS OWING TO SUBSIDIARY COMPANIES
   NOT CONSOLIDATED** (if any)

VIII. **PROVISIONS**
   *(i.e., provision for any known liability of which the amount
   cannot be determined with substantial accuracy, e.g.,
   provision for Profits Tax and deferred repairs ; sources
   of increases and application of decreases to be stated if
   not given elsewhere)*

IX. **CURRENT LIABILITIES**
   *(the aggregate amount of bank loans and overdrafts to be
   stated separately, whether secured or not)*

X. **DIVIDENDS RECOMMENDED FOR DISTRIBUTION—**
   (dividends to be stated at net amounts, after deduction of tax)
   1. Holding Company . . . .
   2. Outside Shareholders of Subsidiary Companies . .

£

Note.—The corresponding amounts for the immediately preceding financial year of all items

BALANCE SHEET

ACT, 1948, AS TO DISCLOSURE

£   £

I. GOODWILL, PATENTS AND TRADE MARKS
(if ascertainable, and so far as not written off ; excess of cost of shares in subsidiary companies over nominal value to be included under this heading)

II. FIXED ASSETS
(these may be defined as assets not held for sale or conversion into cash ; if practicable, these assets must be shown at cost or valuation, the aggregate amount of depreciation being deducted therefrom)

III. SUBSIDIARY COMPANIES NOT CONSOLIDATED (if any)—
Shares. . . . .
Amounts owing . . . .

IV. INVESTMENTS—
Trade Investments . . . .
Other Quoted Investments . . . .
(market value to be stated if different from book value)
Other Unquoted Investments. . . . .

V. CURRENT ASSETS
(these may be defined as cash, and assets held for conversion into cash)

VI. LOANS TO EMPLOYEES
(in aggregate, for purchase of fully-paid shares in the company)

VII. LOANS TO DIRECTORS AND OFFICERS
(in aggregate showing loans made and repaid during period and prior loans still outstanding)

VIII. CAPITAL AND ISSUE EXPENSES—
(so far as not yet written off)
Preliminary Expenses . . . .
Expenses of Issue of Shares or Debentures . . . . .
Commission on Issue of Shares or Debentures . . . .
Discount on Issue of Shares . . . .
Discount on Issue of Debentures . . . .

NOTES : (1) Contingent Liabilities.
(2) Commitments for Capital Expenditure.

Balance Sheet to be signed by two Directors, or if there is only one Director, by that Director.

AUDITORS' REPORT to Members to be attached to Balance Sheet.

£

shown in the foregoing Consolidated Profit and Loss Account and Balance Sheet must be given.

held as personal representative or trustee and in which no beneficial interest is maintained by the company or any subsidiary otherwise than as security for a loan made in the ordinary course of business.

Under Section 150 of the Act, the preparation of Group Accounts is excused in certain circumstances (see page 333), but when such Group Accounts are not published, there must be annexed to the holding company's own Balance Sheet, in order to comply with Part II, Eighth Schedule of the Act, a statement showing :—

(a) the reasons why subsidiaries are not dealt with in the Group Accounts ;

(b) the net aggregate amount (so far as it concerns members of the holding company and is not dealt with in the accounts of that company) of the subsidiaries' profits less losses (or *vice versa*), both in respect of the financial years of subsidiaries ending with or during the financial year of the holding company, and, in respect of their previous financial years since they became subsidiaries of that company ;

(c) the net aggregate amount (as in (b) above) so far as the resultant profits have been dealt with, or the resultant loss provided for, in the accounts of the holding company ;

(d) any qualifications contained in the auditors' reports of subsidiaries in respect of any of the respective financial years as above, and any note on the published accounts of such subsidiaries to call attention to a matter, which, but for such note, would have necessitated a qualification in the auditors' reports, in so far as such qualification or note is not covered by the holding company's own accounts and is material from the point of view of its members ; and

(e) in the case of any subsidiaries whose financial years did not end with that of the holding company, the reason why the directors of the holding company consider that the respective financial years should not coincide, and the concluding dates of the financial years of such subsidiaries ending next before that of the holding company, or, in the case of several such subsidiaries, the earliest and latest of such concluding dates.

The provisions of the Companies Act, 1948, with regard to Group Accounts have already been discussed in Chapter IX but reference should be made at this stage for purposes of revision to the *pro forma* Group Accounts (Consolidated Profit and Loss Account and Consolidated Balance Sheet) summarising the requirements of the Act with regard to disclosure, set out on pages 400 to 403.

Specimen Published Accounts.

The following specimens provide practical illustrations of the presentation of accounts in a form which complies with the requirements of the Companies Act, 1948 ; they are based on the actual published accounts of well-known companies and they illustrate the conventional " two-sided " or orthodox form of Profit and Loss Account and Balance Sheet (Illustration 1) and the same document prepared in the " vertical " form (which is growing in popularity) by which the information is presented in the form of financial statements (Illustration 2).

ILLUSTRATION 1

BLANK,

PROFIT AND LOSS ACCOUNT FOR THE

1954. £		£	£
22,823	Depreciation of Fixed Assets		26,532
	Remuneration of Directors:—		
1,500	For Services as Directors	1,988	
9,000	For Other Services.	11,099	
			13,087
315	Auditors' Fees and Expenses		315
	Balance of Profit before Taxation and Transfers		
123,525	to Reserves		124,968
£157,163			£164,902
	Taxation in the United Kingdom (based on profits of current year):—		
14,250	Profits Tax	15,500	
49,750	Income Tax, 1956–57	51,600	
			67,100
59,525	Balance of Profit after Taxation		57,868
£123,525			£124,968
22,823	Reserve for Replacement of Plant. . . .		25,000
20,000	Staff Pensions Reserve		25,000
	Proposed Dividend of 20 per cent. less Income		
8,250	Tax		8,625
18,800	Balance carried forward		18,043
£69,873			£76,668

LTD.

YEAR ENDED 31ST DECEMBER, 1955

1954. £		£
147,513	Trading Profit	150,202
9,650	Income from Trade Investments (gross)	14,700
£157,163		£164,902
123,525	Balance of Profit before Taxation and Transfers to Reserves	124,968
£123,525		£124,968
59,525	Balance of Profit after Taxation	57,868
10,348	Balance brought forward from 31st December, 1954 .	18,800
£69,873		£76,668

BALANCE SHEET AS AT

1954. £		£	£
	CAPITAL AND RESERVES		
	Share Capital—Authorised and Issued, 300,000 Ordinary Shares of 5s. 0d. each,		
75,000	fully paid		75,000
	Capital Reserves:—		
30,000	Share Premium Account		30,000
	Revenue Reserves:—		
100,000	General Reserve	100,000	
25,000	Plant Replacement	50,000	
30,000	Staff Pensions	55,000	
	Reserve for United Kingdom Income Tax,		
49,750	1956–57	51,600	
18,800	Profit and Loss Account	18,043	
			274,643
328,550			
			379,643
	CURRENT LIABILITIES AND PROVISIONS		
91,142	Creditors and Accrued Charges	62,769	
	United Kingdom Income Tax (other than		
23,640	tax on profits for the year)	27,500	
14,250	Profits Tax	15,500	
8,250	Proposed Dividend (net)	8,625	
137,282			114,394
£465,832			£494,037

SUMMARY OF FIXED ASSETS

1954.	Depreciation to date.		
£	£	£	
			Land and Buildings :—
40,000	2,000	38,000	At cost
23,170	1,258	21,912	At the net book amount at
80,320	37,150	43,170	Plant and Machinery at cost
17,596	4,400	13,196	Furniture, Fixtures, Fittings
£161,086	£44,808	£116,278	

NOTE.—The cost of replacement of Loose Tools

31st December, 1955

1954. £		£	£
	FIXED ASSETS		
	Land and Buildings, Plant and Machinery, Furniture, Fixtures, Fittings and Motor		
116,278	Vehicles (per Summary annexed) . . .		107,285
34,714	Trade Investments at cost		44,107
150,992			151,392
	CURRENT ASSETS		
	Stocks and Work in Progress as valued by		
134,752	the Directors	177,475	
81,312	Debtors and Payments in Advance . . .	97,842	
98,776	Cash at Bankers and in Hand	67,328	
			342,645
314,840			
	NOTE.—There were Capital Commitments at 31st December, 1955, estimated at £20,000 for which no provision had been made (31st December, 1954, £15,000).		
£465,832			£494,037

AT 31st December, 1955

	1955	Depre- ciation to date.	
	£	£	£
	50,000	2,800	47,200
1st July, 1954	23,170	1,522	21,648
	85,955	59,258	26,697
and Motor Vehicles at cost	19,500	7,760	11,740
	£178,625	£71,340	£107,285

and Equipment is charged direct to Revenue.

ILLUSTRATION 2

BLANK, LTD.

PROFIT AND LOSS ACCOUNT FOR THE YEAR ENDED 31ST DECEMBER, 1955

1954. £	1954. £		£	£
147,513		Trading Profit		150,202
9,650		Income from Trade Investments . .		14,700
	157,163			164,902
		TOTAL PROFIT SUBJECT TO :—		
22,823		Depreciation of Fixed Assets . . .	26,532	
		Remuneration of Directors :—		
		£		
1,500		For Services as Directors . 1,988		
9,000		For Other Services . . . 11,099		
			13,087	
315		Auditors' Fees and Expenses . . .	315	
	33,638			39,934
	123,525	NET PROFIT BEFORE TAXATION . . .		124,968
		Taxation in the United Kingdom (based on profits of current year) :—		
14,250		Profits Tax	15,500	
49,750		Income Tax, 1956–57	51,600	
	64,000			67,100
	59,525	LEAVING AN AVAILABLE BALANCE OF .		57,868
		Add Brought forward from 31st December, 1954		
	10,348			18,800
	69,873			76,668
		Deduct Appropriations—		
22,823		Reserve for Replacement of Plant .	25,000	
20,000		Staff Pensions Reserve	25,000	
		Proposed Dividend of 20 per cent. less		
8,250		Income Tax	8,625	
	51,073			58,625
	£18,800	BALANCE OF PROFIT UNAPPROPRIATED .		£18,043

BALANCE SHEET AS AT 31ST DECEMBER, 1955

1954.			1955	
£	£		£	£
		FIXED ASSETS—		
		Land and Buildings, Plant and Machinery, Furniture, Fixtures, Fittings and Motor Vehicles (per		
	116,278	Summary annexed *)		107,285
	34,714	Trade Investments at cost . . .		44,107
	150,992	TOTAL FIXED ASSETS.		151,392
		CURRENT ASSETS—		
		Stocks and Work in Progress as valued		
134,752		by the Directors	177,475	
81,312		Debtors and Payments in Advance .	97,842	
98,776		Cash at Bankers and in Hand . .	67,328	
£314,840		TOTAL CURRENT ASSETS	£342,645	
		CURRENT LIABILITIES AND PROVISIONS—		
91,142		Creditors and Accrued Charges . .	62,769	
		United Kingdom Income Tax (other		
23,640		than tax on profits for the year).	27,500	
14,250		Profits Tax	15,500	
8,250		Proposed Dividend (net)	8,625	
		TOTAL CURRENT LIABILITIES AND PRO		
£137,282		VISIONS	£114,394	
177,558		TOTAL NET CURRENT ASSETS . . .	228,251	
		RESERVE FOR UNITED KINGDOM INCOME		
49,750		TAX, 1956–57	51,600	
		TOTAL NET CURRENT ASSETS, after pro-		
	127,808	viding for Income Tax, 1956–57. .		176,651
	£278,800			£328,043
		SHARE CAPITAL—		
		Authorised and Issued :—		
		300,000 Ordinary Shares of 5s. 0d.		
	75,000	each, fully paid		75,000
		CAPITAL RESERVES—		
	30,000	Share Premium Account		30,000
	105,000			105,000
		REVENUE RESERVES :—		
100,000		General Reserve	100,000	
25,000		Plant Replacement	50,000	
30,000		Staff Pensions	55,000	
18,800		Profit and Loss Account	18,043	
	173,800			223,043
		NOTE.—There were Capital Commitments at 31st December, 1955, estimated at £20,000 for which no provision had been made (31st December, 1954, £15,000).		
	£278,800			£328,043

* The Summary of Fixed Assets will be similar in form to that given on pages 408 and 409.

Window Dressing in a Balance Sheet.

The very fact that a Balance Sheet is a statement which may be presented in many ways suggests that a way may be found which will show the affairs of the business in the most favourable light possible. This manipulation of the Balance Sheet so as to show a state of affairs more favourable than that which would be disclosed by a mere statement of the balances as they stand in the books, is known as " window dressing ".

Window dressing always involves manipulation in some way or another, but the manipulation is not necessarily fraudulent; neither is it necessarily wrong. Furthermore, window dressing does not mean that the Balance Sheet shows a better state of affairs than actually *exists*. What it does mean is that the Balance Sheet shows the existing affairs in the most favourable light possible.

Window dressing does not, as a rule, involve or require any adjustment in ledger accounts; it more usually takes the form of the grouping of items in the Balance Sheet, or it may be the result of a definite financial policy adopted during the last few weeks of a trading period. In the latter case the Balance Sheet shows the true state of affairs as at the date on which it is drawn up, but this state of affairs is not *typical* of that which subsisted during the year as a whole.

Although the operation of window dressing is a form of manipulation which has something in common with the creation of excessive reserves it usually has the opposite effect. The creation of excessive reserves makes a Balance Sheet show a state of affairs which is less favourable than that which actually exists. Window dressing, on the other hand, is designed to give the reader of a Balance Sheet a more favourable impression of the position and prospects of the company than he would otherwise receive.

The following are typical examples of window-dressing operations:—

(1) COLLECTION OF BOOK DEBTS. If a special effort is made to collect book debts just prior to the date of the Balance

Sheet in order to show a substantial balance of cash at bank, then legitimate " window dressing " has taken place, for the fact that the book debts are capable of easy collection proves that the business is in a strong liquid position.*

This type of " window dressing " was often adopted by the banks just prior to the Balance Sheet date, but the practice was somewhat severely condemned in the Report of the Committee on Finance and Industry (" The Macmillan Report ", issued in 1931).

(2) BORROWING. It may be difficult at first to realise that a concern may improve its financial position as shown by its Balance Sheets by borrowing money, even though such loans are reflected in the Balance Sheets. Nevertheless there are several ways in which this may be done :—

(a) By " borrowing from Peter to pay Paul " a bank overdraft may be paid off or reduced just before the date of the Balance Sheet and replaced, for example, by an increase in the aggregate amount owing to subsidiary companies (see also " Inter-Company Transactions " below). Although the existence of a bank overdraft may not in itself be a sign of weakness, an overdraft which is seen to be increasing from year to year is nearly always a danger signal and its disclosure may weaken the credit of the concern. By adopting the tactics already suggested it may be made to appear in the published accounts at a reasonable and steady level.

(b) If borrowed money is not used to repay other liabilities, it will exist in the form of cash or other liquid assets. Thus the very important ratio of current assets to current liabilities may be altered. Consider the position disclosed by the Balance Sheet below.

The company is technically insolvent, for the current liabilities exceed the current assets by £5,000, while the ratio of cash to current liabilities is as low as 1 : 40. But if £20,000 could have been borrowed during December

---

* Unless, of course, excessively generous discounts have been allowed as an inducement to debtors to pay more quickly than usual.

BALANCE SHEET
AS AT 31ST DECEMBER, 19..

	£			£
Authorised and Issued Share Capital:—		Fixed Assets		60,000
		Current Assets:—	£	
10,000 Shares of £5 each .	50,000	Stock . . .	25,000	
Less Profit and Loss		Debtors . . .	9,000	
Account	15,000	Cash	1,000	
	———			35,000
	35,000			
Debentures (secured) . .	20,000			
Sundry Creditors . . .	40,000			
	———			———
	£95,000			£95,000

under conditions that would give the transaction an appearance of permanence (*e.g.*, by the mortgage of fixed assets), the Balance Sheet would have shown the following state of affairs :—

BALANCE SHEET
AS AT 31ST DECEMBER, 19..

	£			£
Authorised and Issued Share Capital:—		Fixed Assets		60,000
		Current Assets:—	£	
10,000 Shares of £5 each .	50,000	Stock	25,000	
Less Profit and Loss		Debtors . . .	9,000	
Account	15,000	Cash	21,000	
	———			55,000
	35,000			
Debentures (secured) . .	20,000			
Loan (secured)	20,000			
Sundry Creditors . . .	40,000			
	———			———
	£115,000			£115,000

The company now appears to be solvent and the ratio of cash to current liabilities is in excess of 50 per cent.

(*c*) By entering into large contracts just before the end of its financial year, a concern may increase both its assets and its liabilities. The Balance Sheet will then give a flattering picture of the importance of the concern and the magnitude of its business.

(3) INTER-COMPANY TRANSACTIONS. When several companies are virtually under the same control, the opportunities
for window-dressing operations are many, particularly if the
companies do not all make up their accounts at the same
date. Thus a holding company may purport to sell goods
to its subsidiary companies just before the close of its own
financial year, on the understanding that the goods will be
returned early in the new year. Inter-company indebtedness
may be cancelled by means of accommodation bills drawn
on other subsidiary companies. After the date of the
Balance Sheet the bills are retired and the indebtedness is
thus reinstated.

When substantial sums are due on loan account from one
company in the group to another, interest may be charged
on such loans as a mere book entry, in the knowledge that it
can never be recovered and will be cancelled in the succeeding
period.

Transactions such as these are clearly fraudulent, and it
is perhaps a misuse of the term " window dressing " to include
them. Nevertheless, they illustrate the type of manipulation
which is available to those who control groups of companies ;
and it is undoubtedly possible to use this control for mani-
pulating the finance of the companies in a manner which,
although it is not illegal, is open to objection from the point
of view of honest and accurate accounting.

THE CRITICISM AND INTERPRETATION OF PUBLISHED ACCOUNTS

Many persons, other than the shareholders of a company,
are interested in its annual accounts. Stockbrokers and
prospective shareholders, creditors and prospective creditors
and the trade protection societies and Chambers of Trade
which exist for the protection of the trading community at
large are all concerned to know as much as possible about
the financial position of the more important concerns. Every
company, whether public or private, must send a copy of
every Balance Sheet, including every document required
to be annexed thereto (i.e., Profit and Loss Account and

Group Accounts, if any, together with a copy of the auditor's report (see page 432) to every shareholder and debenture-holder. In addition, every company must file an *annual return* with the Registrar of Companies, and the annual return of every company, other than an exempt private company, must include certified copies of the last audited Balance Sheet and Profit and Loss Account (and Group Accounts, if any) and of the directors' and auditor's reports. This return is available to inspection at the Companies Registration Office, Bush House, London, W.C.1, by any person on payment of a nominal fee. Thus all the information (except any that may be given orally at the annual general meeting) which is available to shareholders is also available to other interested parties. In practice the published accounts of the more important companies and a report of the proceedings at the annual general meeting are published in the financial press and given a wide measure of publicity.

However, published accounts are not necessarily as full and informative as they might be. The relative provisions of the Companies Act, 1948, are, of necessity, somewhat general in their terms, for it is manifestly impossible to lay down any hard and fast form of accounts that would be suitable for all the multifarious businesses which are carried on by companies registered under the Companies Acts. The provisions of the Eighth Schedule of the Companies Act, 1948, discussed earlier in this Chapter, have done a great deal to prevent the worst types of secretive and deceptive Balance Sheets, and if the shareholders are not satisfied with the amount of information they are given they can always ask questions at the annual general meeting and, in extreme cases, refuse to adopt the directors' report and accounts. The latter course is rarely taken in practice and most shareholders seem only too willing to receive without question the accounts presented to them.

Under Section 164 of the Act, inspectors may be appointed by the Board of Trade to investigate the affairs of a company and to report thereon in such manner as the Board may direct, upon the application either of not less than two hundred members or of members holding not less than one-tenth of the issued share capital. The power of the Board of Trade is discretionary, and applicants may be required to show good *prima facie* grounds for their action and to deposit security (not exceeding £100) to cover the costs of the inquiry.

In addition to the powers of the Board of Trade under Section 164, the Board *must* appoint inspectors if required to do so by the Court or by special resolution of the company (Section 165). The Board is also given discretionary power by Section 165 to appoint inspectors in circumstances where it appears that the business is being conducted fraudulently, or information is improperly withheld from the members.

Inspectors appointed under either section are empowered to examine all the books and documents of the company concerned, and of its holding or subsidiary company, and may require the officers and agents of any such company to give evidence upon oath. On the conclusion of the investigation, the inspectors must report their opinion to the Board of Trade, and a copy of the report must be forwarded to the registered office of the company. A further copy of the report must, at the request of the applicants for the investigation, be delivered to them and (where the investigation was made by order of the Court) to the Court. If the Board think fit, they may also forward a copy to any member or creditor of the company whose interests appear to the Board to be affected. The Board also has power to print and publish any report.

The points to which a person examining a set of accounts is likely to direct his attention will naturally depend on his relationship to the company. The point of view of a creditor or a prospective creditor is naturally different from that of a shareholder or a prospective shareholder, while a stockbroker or anybody else who is professionally interested in the finances of a company, may require to adopt the viewpoint of either debenture-holders (*i.e.*, creditors) or shareholders.

In all cases, however, it must be remembered that share-

holders and, indirectly, other interested parties, have the
protection of the auditor's report on the annual accounts of
the company. The auditor must state in his report, *inter
alia* :—" whether he has obtained all the information and
explanations he has required and whether, in his opinion,
the Balance Sheet is properly drawn up so as to exhibit a
true and fair view of the state of the company's affairs
according to the best of his information and the explanations
given to him and as shown by the books of the company ".
The chief value of this report lies in its check on the accuracy
of the figures presented ; it does not, in itself, add anything
to the information disclosed, except in the rare cases where,
for any reason, the auditor finds it necessary to " qualify "
his report.*

Creditors and Prospective Creditors.

(1) DEBENTURE-HOLDERS. Secured creditors, such as
debenture-holders, are primarily interested in the realisable
value of the assets on which their security is charged.
Although they may have been given a floating charge on
all assets, the current assets are realised or " turned over "
in the ordinary course of trade, and, if losses are incurred,
will be seriously depleted. Thus the fixed assets form the
backbone of the security and the debenture-holders are
concerned to see :—

(a) The basis on which they are or were originally valued
(*e.g.*, freehold property, although not subject to
depreciation in the usual sense, may suffer considerable fluctuations in value over a period of
years) ;

(b) The adequacy of any charge for depreciation ;

(c) Whether any provision has been made for replacement by a sinking fund or any other method.

Nevertheless the amount of the current assets (and thus
of the working capital) is not without importance to the
debenture-holder. Although debenture interest is due
whether profits are made or not, it cannot be paid if cash,

* The contents of the auditor's report are discussed at length on pages 432 to 434.

or the equivalent of cash, is not available for the purpose. Debenture-holders, like other investors, are primarily concerned with the regular receipt of their income, and although there may be valuable fixed assets which they can attach in the event of a default, they do not want to be obliged to take such a course. In the long run, the payment of debenture interest is dependent on the earning of profits and a prospectus which advertises a new issue of debentures will lay as much stress on the *profit record* (showing how many times the charge for interest is covered by annual profits) as on the value of the assets (which on such an occasion will usually be certified by competent valuers). Investors who propose to purchase debentures in the open market, and their professional advisers, must rely on the published accounts for the same purpose.

(2) BANKERS. If the directors of a public company approach its bankers for an overdraft, the bank manager will almost certainly examine the recent published accounts of the company, although he is, of course, in a position to call for any further information if he wants it.* In general, the point of view of a banker is similar to that of a debenture-holder or other secured creditor, in that he is primarily concerned with—

(*a*) The security available, and

(*b*) The ability of the company to pay interest on the due dates.

In addition, he will want to make sure that the early repayment of the advance will be possible, for a main essential of banking practice is the avoidance of " frozen " credits (*i.e.*, the locking-up of an advance in fixed assets which can only be realised at a ruinous loss and at the cost of destroying the company).

(3) TRADE CREDITORS. It is doubtful whether many persons who regularly supply or are asked to supply a company with goods or services in the ordinary course of business

---

* Where a large advance is involved, the bank would probably require an independent investigation by a reputable firm of accountants ; the consideration of such an investigation is beyond the scope of this work.

concern themselves with its published accounts when considering the amount of credit which can safely be given. They are more likely to rely on the credit reports which can be otained from certain trade protection societies. In general, it may be said that an established company is able to obtain all the trade credit it requires so long as it can give trade references from other suppliers and avoid getting "black-listed" in trade association circulars in respect of judgments obtained against it.

If an ordinary creditor does have occasion to examine the published accounts, he will be concerned as much with the existing liabilities as with the assets. He will want to know—

> (a) Whether there are any secured debts (*e.g.*, debentures or bank overdrafts) which will have a prior claim on the assets in the event of liquidation;
>
> (b) The net balance available for unsecured creditors; and
>
> (c) Whether there is any uncalled capital, and, if so, whether all or any portion of it has been reserved, *i.e.*, declared by special resolution to be incapable of being called up except in the event of a winding up.

Uncalled capital is a potential asset which might have great significance to a prospective creditor of a company, for although it is not a debt due to the company until the simple formality of a call has been effected, it becomes an immediately realisable debt once the call has been made.* If, however, the uncalled capital has been wholly or partly reserved, as it has been by many banking companies, the position is different. On the one hand, there can be no call until a winding up has begun, in which case the balance sheet valuations may be subject to considerable modification; and on the other hand, reserved capital cannot be subjected

---

* The possibility of bad debts, arising out of the inability of certain shareholders to pay the call moneys on their shares, must be borne in mind. The prospective creditor will do well to ascertain whether the share capital is spread over a large body of shareholders or whether it is concentrated in a comparatively small number of holders.

to any charge, so that its existence constitutes a strong protection for the ordinary creditor.

Profits are a matter of minor importance, but a series of losses might indicate that much of the shareholders' capital (which ranks after unsecured creditors) had been lost and that great care should be exercised.

Shareholders and Prospective Shareholders.

Generally speaking, while a company is reasonably successful, shareholders of all classes are concerned more with earning capacity and with the probability that the business will continue as a going concern than with the realisable value of the assets. Preference shareholders are concerned primarily with the cover for their fixed dividends and the maintenance of adequate reserves which will ensure the continual prosperity of the company. Ordinary shareholders, on the other hand, are concerned with the amount of the surplus profits, as this fixes the maximum dividend which can be paid to them. Those who, taking the shorter view that " a bird in the hand is worth two in the bush ", are anxious to receive the largest possible dividends and to let the future look after itself, may well criticise a too prudent policy which seems to them to benefit the Preference shareholders (by making possible the payment of preference dividends in years when trading losses are incurred) * much more than themselves. There is perhaps some justification for this view when the Preference dividends are non-cumulative. Other Ordinary shareholders take the longer view that the setting aside of ample reserves is of the greatest benefit to the company as a whole and thus, ultimately, to themselves. The fund of working capital will thus be conserved and increased and expansion will be possible without any corresponding increase in share or loan capital. The Ordinary shareholders own the " equity " of the company, and its prosperity and expansion ultimately redound to their advantage, either in increased dividends or in the issue of bonus shares.

* Companies frequently draw on reserves to pay the fixed preferential dividends, but hesitate to do so to pay a dividend on the Ordinary shares.

Earning Capacity of a Business.

The true value of a business depends almost entirely upon the earning capacity of that business, *i.e.*, the ability of the concern to make profits. To ascertain the earning power of a business, a thorough perusal of the published accounts will be of little assistance, as neither a Profit and Loss Account nor Balance Sheet affords very much information as to reasons for variations in profits, etc. The profits shown in the published accounts may not be normal, but may be attributable mainly to rising or falling markets. The mere interpretation of accounts will not enable the earning power of a business to be gauged ; thus it is necessary to consider, if possible, the various factors that determine earning capacity. These include, for example, the following :—

(1) Efficiency of works lay-out and management ;

(2) Efficiency of buying department ;

(3) Strength of general sales policy ; and

(4) Effectiveness of financial policy.

A knowledge of the above factors as applied to any particular business, together with a thorough and correct interpretation of the published accounts under review, will afford a reasonably sound guide as to the actual financial strength of the business.

Criticism of Published Accounts.

The criticism of published accounts is a wide subject embracing the whole field of accounting. In practice, criticism becomes necessary under various circumstances, among which are the following :—

(1) On the sale of a business or the admission of a new partner.

(2) On a company proposing to take over an existing undertaking.

(3) On an investor wishing to decide whether to purchase a certain commercial security.

(4) On a shareholder wishing to determine whether to increase or reduce his holding.

(5) On a creditor (or prospective creditor) wishing to determine the security for his claim.

In examining published accounts critically they must be considered from all points of view, and the examiner should at the outset ask himself such questions as the following :—

(1) Is the business carried on likely to be a permanent one ?

(2) Is it likely to continue as a going concern ?

(3) Is it working a wasting asset ?

(4) Is it working a novelty, the popularity of which is likely to wane ?

Criticism of Various Items in a Balance Sheet.

In the following paragraphs are set out the principal points that should arise in the mind of a person engaged in the criticism of a Balance Sheet as regards the items that are common to the majority of those published.

SHARE CAPITAL.

(1) Classes of share capital, their rights and priorities, and date of redemption of redeemable preference capital.

(2) Ratios of nominal, subscribed and paid-up capital.

(3) Amount of any uncalled capital and reserve capital.

(4) Calls in arrear, treatment thereof, and possibility of recovery.

(5) Arrears of dividends on cumulative preference shares.

(6) Amount of forfeited shares and treatment of any profit on reissue.

Of the above items (5) is of particular importance to a prospective investor in ordinary shares, as such arrears will normally have to be made good before a dividend can be declared on the ordinary shares.

RESERVES.

(1) Detailed composition of reserves and differentiation between capital reserves and revenue reserves.

(2) Manner in which reserves employed, whether locked up in plant, etc., or invested in marketable securities.

(3) Current market value of investments earmarked for reserves.

PROFIT AND LOSS ACCOUNT BALANCE.

(1) Details of balance brought forward, net profit or loss for current year, appropriations to reserves, etc., dividend payments.

(2) Ratio of net profit to capital employed in business.

(3) Ratio of net profit to average of preceding years.

DEBENTURES.

(1) Terms of issue and dates of redemption.

(2) Treatment of any premiums or discounts on issue.

(3) Nature of charge, fixed or floating.

(4) Margin of security and interest accrued but unpaid.

(5) Provision for repayment.

(6) Extent of collateral issues.

(7) Amount of redeemable debentures available for reissue.

SUNDRY CREDITORS AND PROVISIONS.

(1) Detailed composition of this item, specifying in particular loans from officers and subsidiary companies.

(2) Customary terms of credit.

(3) Nature of security (if any) held by creditors.

(4) Ratio of creditors to capital employed and to current assets.

(5) Amount of working capital, *i.e.*, excess of current assets over current external liabilities.

(6) Nature of provisions and adequacy for specific purposes.

BILLS PAYABLE.

(1) Unexpired term to run.

(2) Details of any " finance " bills.

BANK LOANS AND OVERDRAFTS.

(1) Provision for interest, repayment and limit available.

(2) Nature of security.

(3) Reason for obtaining loans.

GOODWILL.

(1) Origin, excess of purchase consideration over net assets acquired or specially computed.

(2) Basis of valuation.

(3) Ratio to average net profits and average " super " profits.

PATENTS, TRADE MARKS, ETC.

(1) Origin, created or acquired by assignment.

(2) Basis of valuation.

(3) Unexpired term.

LAND AND BUILDINGS.

(1) Detailed composition and general location.

(2) Basis of valuation.

(3) Terms of leases, provision for renewal and possible liability for dilapidations.

(4) Trend of values and degree of realisability.

PLANT AND MACHINERY.

(1) Detailed composition and probable term of utility.

(2) Basis of valuation.

(3) Provision for replacement, particularly in times of rising prices.

(4) Present degree of realisability.

P*

STOCK.

(1) Nature, raw materials, work-in-progress, finished goods.

(2) Basis of valuation and by whom valued.

(3) Ratio to cost of turnover.

SUNDRY DEBTORS.

(1) Detailed composition, trade debts, loans, payments in advance, etc.

(2) Provisions for bad and doubtful debts.

(3) Usual terms of credit.

(4) Ratio to turnover.

BILLS RECEIVABLE.

(1) Unexpired term to run.

(2) Stability of acceptor.

(3) Provision for doubtful bills.

(4) Contingent liability for discounted bills.

INVESTMENTS.

(1) Detailed composition of investments, whether in quoted or unquoted securities, associated and subsidiary companies, etc.

(2) Object of investment, sinking funds, trade purposes, etc.

(3) Basis of valuation, ratio of book value to current market value.

(4) Ratio of income yield.

(5) Contingent liability for uncalled amounts.

LOANS.

(1) Detailed composition, specifying in particular loans to directors and officers or subsidiary companies.

(2) Nature and margin of security.

(3) Rate of interest.

(4) Amount of accrued interest, specifying arrears.

(5) Reserves for possible losses where margin inadequate.

PRELIMINARY AND CAPITAL ISSUE EXPENSES.

(1) Detailed composition and date when incurred.

(2) Provisions for writing off.

Deductions from Comparative Balance Sheets.

The actual information obtainable from a detailed criticism of a single Balance Sheet is limited, and where possible the investigator should endeavour to draw his deductions from a series of Balance Sheets, *e.g.*, from the Balance Sheets of the last three to seven years. Where this comparative method is adopted, various deductions, among which are the following, can be made :—

(1) If share or loan capital is frequently increased without a corresponding increase in profits a weak financial position is indicated.

(2) If bank loans are retained for considerable periods, it is indicated that the revenue-earning capacity of the company is inadequate to justify an increase of share capital.

(3) If profits are comparatively stable over a period of years, and approximate to the average of such years, it is indicated that profits should not fluctuate provided normal conditions are maintained.

(4) If dividends are maintained and regular appropriations made to reserve, and the working capital remains stable, steady and satisfactory progress is evident.

(5) If profits are gradually increased without a corresponding increase in current assets, *viz.*, debtors, stocks, etc., greater productive efficiency and/or improved selling prices are indicated.

(6) If profits are gradually increased with a corresponding increase in debtors, stocks, etc., an increased turnover is indicated.

(7) If work-in-progress and stocks are subject to wide fluctuations the existence of large contracts requiring lengthy periods for completion is indicated.

(8) If fixed assets are increasing in value without a

corresponding increase in profits, inadequate provision for depreciation and over-valuation of fixed assets is indicated.

(9) If creditors are gradually exceeding debtors, without a corresponding increase in stocks, over-trading is indicated where profits are maintained, whereas a possibility of compulsory liquidation is indicated where profits are non-existent.

The above examples of the more usual deductions cannot be applied without modification to every individual concern, as consideration must be given to any circumstances peculiar to the business under review.

Company Auditors.

APPOINTMENT. The Companies Act, 1948, contains provisions for the compulsory appointment of an auditor to a public or private limited company. Under normal circumstances the appointment is made by the members of the company in annual general meeting, and Section 159 provides that the auditor so appointed is to hold office from the conclusion of that annual general meeting until the conclusion of the next annual general meeting, and at any annual general meeting a retiring auditor, however appointed, will be re-appointed without any resolution being passed unless :—

(a) he is not qualified for re-appointment (see page 430) ; or

(b) a resolution has been passed at that meeting appointing somebody instead of him or providing expressly that he shall not be re-appointed ; or

(c) he has given the company notice in writing of his unwillingness to be re-appointed.

Thus an auditor of a company once appointed will continue to act in that capacity except in the circumstances set out in (a) to (c) above.

Where no auditor is appointed or re-appointed at an annual general meeting, the Board of Trade may appoint a person to fill the vacancy and the company must, within one week of the Board's power to appoint an auditor becoming exercisable, give the Board notice of that fact. Certain conditions must be fulfilled before a new auditor can be appointed, and Section 161 provides that :—

(a) Special notice (see below) is required for a resolution at an annual general meeting (i) appointing as auditor a person other than a retiring auditor ; or (ii) providing expressly that a retiring auditor shall not be re-appointed.

(b) A copy of such an intended resolution must be sent to the retiring auditor forthwith.

(c) When notice is given of such an intended resolution the retiring auditor may make representations in writing to the company and request their notification to members of the company. Thereupon the company must state the fact that representations have been received in any notice of the resolution and send a copy of the representations to every member of the company to whom notice of the meeting is sent, unless they are received too late for it to do so.

(d) When a copy of the representations is not sent as required under (c) above, the auditor may (without prejudice to his right to be heard orally at the meeting) require that the representations shall be read out at the meeting.

A special notice of an intended resolution to be effective must be given to the company at least twenty-eight days before the date of the meeting, and must be given by the company to its members at least twenty-one days before the meeting. When, however, after notice has been given to the company a meeting is called for a date less than twenty-eight days after the date of the notice, the notice will be deemed to be properly given although not within the prescribed time.

These provisions afford members an effective control over the appointment of auditors, and ensure that the retiring auditor shall be properly notified of the intention to appoint a new auditor and enable him to state a case (i.e., make representations) against a new appointment. On the other hand, the modification of the requirements of a special notice where a meeting is called for a date earlier than twenty-eight days after the notice has been received prevents the directors of a company upsetting the otherwise valid notice of intention to appoint a new auditor, because they wish to retain the services of a retiring auditor.

Section 159 also provides that the first auditor of a company may be appointed by the directors at any time before the first annual general meeting, and an auditor so appointed is to hold office until the conclusion of that meeting. The company in general meeting, however, may remove any such auditor and appoint in his place any other person nominated for appointment by any member of the company, notice of nomination having been given to members of the company not less than fourteen days before the date of the meeting. In such an event the existing auditor is entitled to make representations which must be dealt with by the company as explained in (c) and (d) on page 429.

If the directors fail to exercise their powers to appoint the first auditor of the company, the members in general meeting may do so, and thereupon the said powers of the directors cease.

Furthermore, Section 159 provides that the directors may fill any casual vacancy in the office of auditor, but while such vacancy continues, the surviving or continuing auditor or auditors, if any, may act.

The foregoing provisions govern the appointment of an auditor in special circumstances, but in all other cases the auditor is appointed or re-appointed at the annual general meeting in the manner indicated above.

DISQUALIFICATION FOR APPOINTMENT. Section 161 provides that a person will not be qualified for appointment as auditor of a company unless either :—

(a) He is a member of a body of accountants established in the United Kingdom, and for the time being recognised for this purpose by the Board of Trade,* or

(b) He is for the time being recognised by the Board of Trade *either* as having similar qualifications obtained outside the United Kingdom, *or* as having obtained adequate knowledge and experience in the course of his employment by a member of a body of accountants recognised under (a), *or* as having before 6th August, 1947, practised in Great Britain as an accountant.

The above provisions do not apply in the case of a private company which at the time of the auditor's appointment is an exempt private company (see page 88) ; thus an unqualified person or a member of an unrecognised body of accountants can act as auditor to an exempt private company.

Furthermore, none of the following persons is qualified for appointment as auditor of a company :—

(a) An officer or servant of the company.

(b) A person who is a partner of or in the employment of an officer or servant of the company *except* in the case of an exempt private company.

(c) A body corporate.

An auditor is not deemed to be an officer or servant of a company for the purposes of these provisions.

A person will not be qualified for appointment as auditor of any company if he is disqualified from appointment (under (a) or (b) above) as auditor of that company's holding company or subsidiary company.

These provisions aim at securing the appointment of a competent person to act as auditor and in preventing the appointment of any person otherwise interested in the

---

* The Board of Trade have recently announced that members of the following bodies of accountants are recognised for appointment as auditors—Institute of Chartered Accountants in England and Wales ; Society of Incorporated Accountants ; Institute of Chartered Accountants in Scotland ; Institute of Chartered Accountants in Ireland ; and Association of Certified and Corporate Accountants.

management of the company (*i.e.*, officer or servant) or of any person likely to be influenced by a person so interested.

AUDITOR'S REPORT. The most important duty of an auditor is to report to the members upon the company's accounts as laid before the members in general meeting. Section 162 provides that the auditor must make a report to the members on the accounts examined by him, and on every Balance Sheet, Profit and Loss Account, and all Group Accounts (*i.e.*, Consolidated Balance Sheet and Profit and Loss Account in the case of a holding company—see Chapter IX), laid before the company in general meeting during his tenure of office. The following matters are to be contained in the auditor's report in accordance with the Ninth Schedule to the Act :—

(1) Whether he has obtained all the information and explanations which to the best of his knowledge and belief were necessary for the purpose of his audit.

(2) Whether, in his opinion, proper books of account have been kept by the company, so far as appears from his examination of those books, and proper returns adequate for the purpose of his audit have been received from branches not visited by him.

(3) Whether the company's Balance Sheet and (unless it is framed as a Consolidated Profit and Loss Account) Profit and Loss Account dealt with by the report are in agreement with the books and returns.

(4) Whether, in his opinion and to the best of his information and according to the explanations given to him, the said accounts give the information required by the Companies Act, 1948, in the manner so required and give a true and fair view :—

(*a*) in the case of the Balance Sheet, of the state of the company's affairs as at the end of its financial year ; and

(*b*) in the case of the Profit and Loss Account, of the profit or loss for its financial year.

(5) In the case of a holding company submitting Group Accounts, whether, in his opinion, the Group Accounts have been properly prepared in accordance with the provisions of the Companies Act, 1948, so as to give a true and fair view of the state of affairs and profit or loss of the company and its subsidiaries dealt with thereby, so far as concerns members of the company.

The following is a typical form of auditor's report :—

"I have audited the Balance Sheet dated.......... and the Profit and Loss Account for the year ended ...... as above set forth. I have obtained all the information and explanations which to the best of my knowledge and belief are necessary for the purpose of my audit. In my opinion, proper books of account have been kept by the Company, so far as appears from my examination of those books, *and proper returns adequate for the purpose of my audit have been received from branches not visited by me.* I have examined the Company's Balance Sheet and Profit and Loss Account as above set forth, which are in agreement with the books *and returns.* In my opinion, and to the best of my information and the explanations given me, the said accounts give the information required by the Companies Act, 1948, in the manner so required and give a true and fair view, in the case of the Balance Sheet, of the state of the Company's affairs as at ...... and, in the case of the Profit and Loss Account, of the profit (or loss) for its financial year ended .... *"

In the case of a holding company submitting Group Accounts the following form of report is required (in addition to the report to be attached to the Balance Sheet of the holding company itself as shown above) :—

"In my opinion the Group Accounts above set forth have been properly prepared in accordance with the provisions of the Companies Act, 1948, so as to give a true and fair view of the state of affairs and profit (or loss) of the Company and its subsidiaries dealt with thereby so far as concerns members of the Company."

The auditor's report must be attached to the Balance Sheet to which it relates, and it must be read before the members in general meeting and be open to inspection by any member.

The auditor acts as the agent of the members for the purpose of making his report, and he has certain minimum statutory duties to perform (as indicated in (1) to (5) above), which cannot be restricted in any way. These duties involve the examination of the books and

* The words in italics would be included only in appropriate circumstances.

vouchers of the company, but the extent of this examination will be such as the auditor considers necessary to dispose satisfactorily of the statutory duties imposed on him. Section 162 gives the auditor the right of access to the books and vouchers of the company, and the right to demand from officers of the company such information and explanations as he may require. Where the auditor is not satisfied in regard to any matter upon which he is required to report, *e.g.*, that the Profit and Loss Account and/or Balance Sheet do not show a true and fair view of the company's position, or are not drawn up in accordance with the provisions of the Companies Act, 1948, he may request the directors to amend the accounts if that is all that is required, but he cannot compel them to do so, and if they refuse to comply with his request or some other matter is involved, *e.g.*, proper books of account have not been kept, it will be his duty to refer clearly in his report to the matter concerned in order that the members are made aware of the true position. Such a report is termed a *qualified report*, and it is of the greatest importance that an auditor who is not satisfied that all the statutory requirements have been fulfilled should include a qualification in his report otherwise he may be held to have failed in his duty to the members. The requirement that the Profit and Loss Account and Balance Sheet must show a true and fair view of the profit or loss and state of affairs of the company is very wide and it will be necessary for the auditor to use his knowledge and judgment in determining whether or not the accounts under report fulfil these requirements. Examples of circumstances which necessitate a qualification in an auditor's report include insufficient provision for depreciation of fixed assets ; omission of liabilities from the Balance Sheet ; over-valuation of current assets ; and non-disclosure of material factors affecting the profit or loss shown by the Profit and Loss Account.

ADDITIONAL DUTIES. The other principal duties of an auditor to a company include :—

(1) Inclusion in his report of particulars of directors' salaries, pensions, etc., if not already given in the accounts laid before the members (Section 196).

(2) Inclusion in his report of particulars of loans to officers of the company if not already given in the accounts laid before the members (Section 197).

(3) Report upon past profits and losses, dividends, and assets and liabilities for prospectus purposes (Part II, Fourth Schedule).

(4) Certification of capital receipts and payments in a statutory report (Section 130).

CHAPTER XI

STATUTORY AND SPECIALISED ACCOUNTS

Statutory Undertakings (Double Account System).

The Double Account System which applied to such statutory undertakings as railway companies, electricity companies and gas companies is mainly of historic and academic interest as most of the undertakings which adopted this method of presenting their published accounts have now passed into public ownership as a result of various national-isation schemes. Although the system has largely fallen into disuse it is still adopted by certain undertakings, such as water companies and dock and harbour authorities, and it may be of interest to the student of accounting; for these reasons a concise summary of the main features of the Double Account System is given in this Chapter.

The customary method of compiling a commercial Balance Sheet is to marshal the whole of the assets on one side of the statement, and to arrange the whole of the liabilities and capital on the other side of the statement. The fact that the Balance Sheet is thus drafted as one statement results in this method being termed the " Single Account " System, to distinguish it from the " Double Account " System under which the Balance Sheet is drawn up in two divisions, *viz.* :—

(1) RECEIPTS AND EXPENDITURE ON CAPITAL ACCOUNT, which shows on the *credit* side the amount raised for the purposes of the business (*e.g.*, shares, stock, debentures and debenture stock, together with premiums thereon, less discounts); and on the *debit* side how the amount has been expended on the fixed assets (*e.g.*, land and buildings, fixed plant, rolling stock, etc.); and the balance of capital in hand or over-expended.

436

(2) GENERAL BALANCE SHEET, which sets out the current assets and liabilities, including the stock, debtors, cash, creditors, the depreciation account, and the balances of the Revenue Account and of the Capital Account.

The object of the Double Account System is to show what capital has been raised, and for what purpose it has been expended in the undertaking, rather than to show the present value of the assets at any given date, as is done in accounts prepared on the Single Account System. The books are prepared by double entry, as in the case of the Single Account System, but there is an important difference in respect of the treatment of depreciation, all charges for repairs, renewals and replacements in the Double Account System being charged to revenue, and no special provision being made in the statutory form of account for the assets to be shown at less than original cost. Frequently, however, in practice a Depreciation and Renewals Reserve Fund is raised by means of transfers each year from net revenue, the object being to avoid violent fluctuations in the charge for renewals as between successive years, and to equalise, as far as possible, the yearly charge against profits. The Depreciation Fund (if any) appears on the liabilities side of the General Balance Sheet, while the asset remains at its original cost on the debit side of the Capital Account.

The use of the Double Account System was first prescribed under the Regulation of Railways Act, 1868, and was generally adopted by companies or undertakings whose capital was specifically raised for the acquisition or construction of works of a permanent nature, such as railways, tramways, electricity companies, gasworks and waterworks.

The terms " Trading Account " and " Profit and Loss Account " are not used in connection with the Double Account System, the accounts being described as " Revenue " and " Net Revenue " Accounts respectively. The composition of these accounts varies, but, as a general rule, the Revenue Account includes all items relating to the productive working of the undertaking, and its balance is transferred to the Net Revenue Account, in which are usually charged such items as debenture interest, dividends, transfers to reserve, etc.

RECEIPTS AND EXPENDITURE ON CAPITAL ACCOUNT. This account, more briefly termed the *Capital Account*, is generally in columnar form (as illustrated below), showing, on the credit side, the capital receipts (comprising share capital, stocks, debentures, mortgages and other long term loans, discounts and premiums thereon being deducted and added in total) to the date of the previous Balance Sheet, receipts during the year, and total receipts to date. Capital expenditure (comprising fixed or permanent assets and such preliminary expenses as the promotion of a special Act of Parliament) is shown in a similar manner on the debit side. It is interesting to note that receipts from issues of debentures or debenture stock are included in this account, in contradistinction to the general commercial practice in the case of the Single Account System, where debentures are treated as loans and amounts so raised are kept quite distinct from share capital.

RECEIPTS AND EXPENDITURE ON CAPITAL ACCOUNT
FOR THE YEAR ENDED 31ST DECEMBER, 1955

Details.	Expenditure to 31st Dec., 1954.	Expenditure during Year.	Total.	Details.	Receipts to 31st Dec., 1954.	Receipts during Year.	Total.
	£	£	£		£	£	£

NOTE.—The sides of the Capital Account are usually reversed so that the capital receipts and expenditure appear as in the ledger accounts which they summarise, while, as the General Balance Sheet is prepared in the orthodox form, the balance of the Capital Account is carried down to the same side of the General Balance Sheet.

It sometimes happens that the Capital Account shows that more has been expended on permanent assets than has been received by way of capital ; this indicates that revenue earnings have been utilised in the purchase of fixed assets.

GENERAL BALANCE SHEET. This is the second part of the Balance Sheet prepared under the Double Account System. The balance of the Capital Account is brought into this section, and the current assets and liabilities, reserves and undistributed profits are recorded in the usual Single Account manner.

The difference between the presentation of the accounts of companies operating under the Double Account System and those drawn up under the usual Single Account System is shown in the following illustration.

(1) *Double Account System—*

Dr.		CAPITAL ACCOUNT		Cr.
	£			£
To Fixed Assets (in detail) .	61,500	By Ordinary Stock . . .		50,000
,, Balance	13,500	,, Debentures		25,000
	£75,000			£75,000

Dr.		GENERAL BALANCE SHEET		Cr.
Liabilities.			*Assets.*	
	£			£
Balance of Capital Account .	13,500	Stocks and Stores . . .		19,750
Revenue Account . . .	4,500	Cash at Bank		18,250
Current Liabilities . . .	7,000			
Depreciation Fund . . .	13,000			
	£38,000			£38,000

(2) *Single Account System—*

BALANCE SHEET

	£		£	£
Share Capital—		Fixed Assets (in		
Ordinary Shares . . .	50,000	detail) at cost .	61,500	
Profit and Loss		*Less* Depreciation	13,000	
Account	4,500			48,500
		Stocks and Stores . . .		19,750
	54,500	Cash at Bank		18,250
Debentures.	25,000			
Current Liabilities . . .	7,000			
	£86,500			£86,500

The "Double Account" system of presenting final accounts must not be confused with the "double entry" system of book-keeping; any Balance Sheet prepared from double entry books can be drafted in the double account form or the single account form, as may be desired. Thus the Double Account System does not entail the keeping of any special books, and the general ledger of a company operating under this system will present the same appearance as that of an ordinary "single account" company. The chief importance of the Double Account System is found in the fact that it was formerly specified by Act of Parliament for railways and other concerns in the nature of public utilities. Such undertakings were obliged to present their annual accounts in the exact form prescribed either by the special Act under which they were incorporated or by some general Act applying to all concerns carrying on a certain type of business.

REVENUE ACCOUNTS. The Revenue Account generally shows in debit and credit form the gross trading receipts (credit side) and expenditure (debit side) of the undertaking, followed by the income received from investments and miscellaneous sources, the final balance representing the total net income for the period. In some cases, however, the gross receipts and expenditure of each department are shown in separate schedules, the totals being summarised in the Revenue Account, which is merely a statement not in debit and credit form. The balance of the Revenue Account is carried to the Net Revenue Account in the same way that the balance of the Profit and Loss Account is carried to the Appropriation Account.

The Net Revenue Account commences with the balance brought forward from the previous year; to this is added the balance transferred from the Revenue Account; deductions are then made for debenture interest, preference and guaranteed stock interest and other fixed charges, the net balance remaining representing the amount available for dividend on the ordinary stock. There is, therefore, a certain distinction between a Net Revenue Account and an Appropriation Account, as such fixed charges as debenture interest, in the case of an ordinary trading company, would be debited before the balance of profits is carried down to the Appropriation Account.

DEPRECIATION. Under the Single Account System, assets are usually shown in the Balance Sheet at their present worth on a going concern basis, *i.e.*, at cost less depreciation. In a Balance Sheet compiled on double account lines, however, the object is to show how the capital has been expended and therefore the assets must appear at their original cost, no deduction therefrom being possible. This fact has led to an expression of opinion that would appear to be supported by the form of accounts, *viz.*, that the Double Account System makes no provision for depreciation. The only justification for this statement is the fact that expenditure is retained in the Capital Account at its original value plus additions. But provision for depreciation can be, and in practice is, made by building up substantial Depreciation or Renewal Funds out of revenue, such Funds appearing on the liabilities side of the General Balance Sheet. These Depreciation or Renewal Funds are usually augmented by transfers from revenue in years when repairs expenditure is light and drawn upon in years when repairs expenditure is heavy, so that revenue bears a more or less even charge for this form of expenditure each year.

When the Double Account System was first conceived, it was probably thought that the undertakings by which it would be used were of such a permanent nature that no provision for depreciation, as ordinarily understood, would be necessary. It is interesting to observe how this view has been overruled by considerations of practical accounting and prudent finance. Thus, although the Double Account System has been retained in the *form* of the double Balance Sheet, its *practice* has been brought into close agreement with that of companies operating under the Single Account System.

Probably the most serious argument against the Double Account System is that the cost of an asset may remain in the Capital Account after the asset has ceased to exist. This may be so, but if it is understood that the object of the account is to show *how the original capital has been spent*, and if adequate provision is made for renewals (as indicated above) and for the maintenance of the existing equipment, there would appear to be no objection to retaining an obsolete asset in the Capital Account ; for the present requirements of the undertaking are being met by the existing equipment in respect of which proper charges to revenue have been made. In other words, the retention of the obsolete asset in the books does not in any way undermine the finances of the undertaking, neither does it render the *existing* equipment insufficient. However, the treatment of obsolete capital expenditure may be made to accord with the treatment under the Single Account System, for, where a depreciation fund has been built up in respect of the obsolete asset, a transfer may be made from the fund account to the asset account, and the reduction from the latter shown in italics, with the necessary explanation, in the Capital Account.

It cannot be too strongly emphasised that many of the arguments advanced against the use of the Double Account System are founded upon merely theoretical considerations and although, from that point of view alone, they may be perfectly valid, they may be, and frequently are, negatived in practice by means of prudent accounting. The only really serious criticism appears to be that such matters as the provision for capital wastage are left to the discretion of the directors and that the accepted form of account is such as to encourage any tendency to neglect such precautionary measures.

PRESERVATION OF CAPITAL AND OVERCAPITALISATION. It is important to all commercial concerns that their capital should be kept intact, and this is so whether the Single or Double Account System is in use.

The former system preserves capital by charging each year with an amount to represent the expired capital outlay. The total amount so charged in respect of any one asset should equal the original cost of the asset by the time it falls out of use, so that an equivalent amount of liquid assets is retained in the undertaking. The provision for depreciation in this manner results in the assignment of " values " to the assets in successive Balance Sheets, the " value " representing that part of the original expenditure which is deemed to be unexpired. If the estimate of depreciation is correct, capital is being preserved ; if the rate of expiry has been underestimated, capital is being dissipated by the distribution of profits ; if too much profit has been retained in the business the Balance Sheet will err on the side of caution.

The Double Account System presents an entirely different method of keeping capital intact, in that it demands that the relative services rendered by these public utility undertakings should not be allowed to depreciate. The governing statutes have abandoned the idea of eventual replacement, and in place thereof have recognised that capital may be maintained intact by spending whatever sums may be necessary for this purpose, at the expense of revenue. This practice has led to a criticism which in certain circumstances may be justified, *i.e.*, that, under the Double Account System, the practice of maintaining capital by means of repairs and renewals without making a charge to retain in the business an amount representing the expired portion of the original capital outlay, tends to overcapitalisation. Unless profits are retained in the business, renewals can only be met out of additional capital contributions which must be remunerated by way of interest or dividends, although the contributions will not be represented by additional earning power. It will be realised that this criticism is very pertinent unless depreciation is provided for, or profits are otherwise conserved and not distributed " up to the hilt ".

CAPITAL IMPROVEMENTS. Where replacements of original assets take place, and the new asset represents an improvement on the original asset, the usual method is to charge the estimated present cost of replacement in the original form to revenue, and the balance of the cost of the new asset to capital, while any amount received in respect of the sale of the old asset is credited to revenue and thus decreases the actual charge to be written off. Under the Single Account System, on the other hand, the cost of the original asset will already have been written off by annual charges to revenue (or a Depreciation Provision of an equivalent amount will have been built up) and the whole of the additional cost of replacement will be capital.

EXAMPLE

A water company replaces plant costing £40,000 with new plant costing £75,000, the replacement cost of the old plant in its original form being estimated at £50,000. £8,000 is obtained from the sale of the old plant. Compare the method of recording the replacement in the accounts of the water company with that employed in the case of a company operating under the Single Account System.

METHOD 1 (THE DOUBLE ACCOUNT SYSTEM).

The current replacement cost (less the proceeds of the sale of the old plant) is written off to revenue, the excess expenditure being capitalised as an improvement, viz.—

Plant Account	.	.	.	Dr.	£25,000	
Revenue Account	.	.	.	Dr.	50,000	
To Cash .	.	.	.	.		£75,000
Cash .	.	.	.	.	Dr.	£8,000	
To Revenue Account	.	.	.		£8,000

Thus the Plant Account will appear as £65,000 (i.e., £40,000 plus £25,000). The effect of this treatment is to capitalise the improvement only.

METHOD 2 (THE SINGLE ACCOUNT SYSTEM).

Assuming that a Depreciation Provision of £32,000 (i.e., original cost less scrap value) has been built up, this and the £8,000 received will be used to eliminate the old asset thus—

Depreciation Provision	.	.	Dr.	£32,000	
Cash .	.	.	.	.	Dr.	8,000	
To Plant Account	.	.	.		£40,000

and the whole of the £75,000 spent on the new plant will be capitalised—

Plant Account	.	.	.	Dr.	£75,000	
To Cash .	.	.	.		£75,000

There are certain classes of undertakings which are required to prepare and publish accounts in statutory form and others which, on account of their specialised nature, find it desirable to prepare accounts in a more specialised form than is necessary in the case of the normal trading concern. Some of these undertakings have been considered already in this Chapter under the heading " Double Account System " and the special features of the published accounts

Single and Double Account Systems Contrasted.

	Single Account System.	Double Account System.
Form of Account . .	Balance Sheet is a single statement.	Balance Sheet divided into two parts to show how capital has been disbursed and how the balance is represented by current assets and liabilities.
Valuation of Assets .	(a) Fixed assets—present worth represented by cost less depreciation. (b) Current assets—cost or realisable value, whichever is lower.	(a) Fixed assets—at cost, no attempt being made to assign a present worth. (b) As under Single Account System.
Depreciation	Charged against revenue year by year and deducted from the asset to which it relates in the Balance Sheet.	May be provided for by means of funds, but no deduction from the asset is permitted.
Renewals	Capitalised if the old asset has been written off by depreciation.	Charged to revenue (but suitable transfers may be made to or from Renewals Fund to equalise the annual debits to revenue).
Computation of Profits .	Necessary to provide for capital wastage.	Form of account makes the usual form of provision for capital wastage impossible (but see Depreciation above).
Revenue or Capital . .	Revenue — all maintenance and administration expenses. Capital—expenditure on acquisition of assets.	Revenue—as for single account, also all expenditure on renewals of *existing* equipment. Capital—cost of new equipment.
Improvements . . .	Improvement value is usually capitalised.	Subject to modified treatment (see page 443).
Defects	Fails to show the history of capital expenditure.	Tends to over-capitalisation in certain circumstances.

of some of the remaining important classes of undertakings will now be considered in the following paragraphs.

Assurance and Insurance Companies.

The distinction between " Assurance " and " Insurance " is that the former term relates to assurance against an event which will happen, *e.g.*, death of a person, and is practically confined to life assurance business, whereas the latter term represents an insurance against a risk which may or may not take place, *e.g.*, fire, burglary, accident, etc. Most insurance companies transact both classes of business in consideration of the payment of a premium against the risk insured as evidenced by the policy.

The ordinary principles of double entry book-keeping apply to the accounts of assurance and insurance companies but the published accounts must be compiled in the manner prescribed by the Assurance Companies Act, 1909 (as amended by the Assurance Companies Act, 1946) as explained below. These companies (other than " Mutual Companies " formed by the policyholders themselves) are also subject to the provisions of the Companies Act, 1948, with regard to disclosure in published accounts but, where a copy of the Profit and Loss Account and Balance Sheet is deposited with the Board of Trade, the company is exempt from certain provisions of the Act.*

Companies transacting more than one class of business are required to maintain separate " funds ", which are respectively regarded as the property of the policyholders of the appropriate class : thus it is not permissible, for example, to draw on the Life Assurance Fund to meet fire claims. The only exception to this rule is that the funds relating to fire and accident insurance may be merged if desired. It is not essential for the investments of the company to be earmarked for any particular fund, although many companies do in fact adopt this procedure in respect of life assurance business. Frequently, the transactions in respect of life assurance are kept distinct from other business transacted

* The exceptions for assurance companies are contained in Paragraph 24, Part II, Eighth Schedule to the Act (see Appendix I).

by the company so that a separate Balance Sheet may be issued for the life assurance department.

The accounts to be prepared at the end of each financial year are prescribed by the First, Second and Third Schedules to the Assurance Companies Act, 1909, and consist of :—

(1) REVENUE ACCOUNT * for each class of business transacted, showing on the left-hand side—

(a) The Assurance (or Insurance) Fund at the commencement of the year ;

(b) The premium and other income for the year ; and

(c) Deficiency or losses transferred to Profit and Loss Account ;

and on the right-hand side—

(a) Losses (including claims) and expenses chargeable against income ;

REVENUE ACCOUNT OF THE WATCHDOG INSURANCE CO., LTD.

FOR THE YEAR ENDING 31ST DECEMBER, 1955, IN RESPECT OF LIFE ASSURANCE BUSINESS

	£		£
Amount of Life Assurance Fund at the beginning of the year	8,013,000	Claims under Policies paid and outstanding :— By Death	635,000
Premiums	1,112,000	By Maturity . . .	240,000
Consideration for Annuities Granted . . .	75,000	Surrenders, including Surrenders of Bonus . .	24,000
£		Annuities	29,000
Interest, Dividends and Rents . . 670,000		Bonuses in Cash . . .	9,000
		Bonuses in Reduction of Premiums	2,500
Less Income Tax thereon . 285,000		Commission.	28,500
	385,000	Expenses of Management .	75,000
Other Receipts (to be specified)	—	Other Payments (to be specified)	—
		Amount of Life Assurance Fund at the end of the year	8,542,000
	£9,585,000		£9,585,000

* In the preparation of the Revenue Accounts the location of items is reversed and the " Dr." and " Cr." signs and the prefixes " To " and " By " are omitted, *i.e.*, income and gains are shown on the left-hand side and expenses and losses on the right-hand side of the account.

(b) Surplus or realised profits transferred to Profit and Loss Account ; and

(c) The Assurance (or Insurance) Fund at the end of the year.

The profits of a Life Assurance Company can be ascertained only by actuarial valuation (see page 452) and thus the balance of the Revenue Account does not represent profit or loss, but merely the amount of the assets available for the purpose of that fund.

REVENUE ACCOUNT OF THE WATCHDOG INSURANCE CO., LTD.

FOR THE YEAR ENDING 31ST DECEMBER, 1955, IN RESPECT OF FIRE INSURANCE BUSINESS

	£		£
Amount of Fire Insurance Fund at the beginning of the year :—		Claims under Policies paid and outstanding. . .	803,600
£		Commission.	200,000
Reserve for Unexpired		Expenses of Management .	350,000
Risks . 600,000		Contributions to Fire Brigades	13,000
Additional Reserve (if		Other Payments (to be specified)	—
any) . . 48,000		Profit Realised, transferred to Profit and Loss Account	261,000
	648,000		
Premiums	1,600,000		
Interest, Dividends and		Amount of Fire Insurance Fund at the end of the year :—	
Rents . . 68,700		£	
Less Income Tax thereon . 29,100		Reserve for Unexpired	
	39,600	Risks . 640,000	
Other Receipts (to be specified)	—	Additional Reserve (if any) . . 20,000	
			660,000
	£2,287,600		£2,287,600

The profit or loss in respect of fire insurance business (and of accident and other classes of business, for which the form of Revenue Account follows closely the above example) is ascertained after carrying forward as a reserve for unexpired risks a substantial percentage—in the above example, 40 per cent.—of the premium income for the year. The balance of the Revenue Account, after making this adjustment, is transferred to the general Profit and Loss Account as the profit or loss for the year on that particular class of business.

(2) PROFIT AND LOSS ACCOUNT, where more than one class of business is transacted, incorporating the profits or losses transferred from the Revenue Accounts and showing the final unappropriated surplus or deficiency. As in the case of the Revenue Account the sides of the Profit and Loss Account are reversed, thus income not otherwise dealt with and profits transferred from the various Revenue Accounts are shown on the left-hand side, while losses realised as shown in the Revenue Accounts, dividends and bonuses paid to shareholders, and other payments and expenses not chargeable to Revenue Accounts, are included on the right-hand side.

PROFIT AND LOSS ACCOUNT OF THE WATCHDOG INSURANCE CO., LTD.

FOR THE YEAR ENDING 31ST DECEMBER, 1955

		£		£
Balance of last year's account		325,000	Dividends and Bonuses to Shareholders	110,000
	£		Remuneration of Directors.	15,500
Interest and Dividends not carried to			Expenses not charged to other accounts . . .	9,500
other accounts	86,500		Losses Realised :—	
Less Income Tax			Marine Insurance Account	8,000
thereon . .	37,000		Other Payments :—	
		49,500	Income Tax paid and provided for . . .	130,000
Profits Realised :—			Balance as per Balance	
Fire Insurance			Sheet	452,700
Account .	261,000			
Accident Insurance Account	90,000			
		351,000		
Other Receipts :—				
Transfer Fees		200		
		£725,700		£725,700

A company transacting only one class of business is not required to prepare a Profit and Loss Account in addition to its Revenue Account. If the Profit and Loss Account

Q

THE WATCHDOG

BALANCE SHEET ON THE

	£	£
Share Capital :—		
Authorised and Subscribed, 500,000 Ordinary Shares of £5 each, £1 per share paid up . .		500,000
Reserves :—		
Share Premium Account	80,000	
General Reserve	209,000	
Reserve for Depreciation of Investments . . .	100,000	
Profit and Loss Account	452,700	
		841,700
		1,341,700
Insurance Funds per Revenue Accounts :—		
Life Assurance Fund	8,542,000	
Annuity Fund	300,000	
Fire Insurance Fund	660,000	
Accident Insurance Fund	380,000	
Marine Insurance Fund	200,000	
Sinking Fund and Capital Redemption Fund .	102,800	
Other Funds (if any) (to be specified) . . .	—	
		10,184,800
Current Liabilities and Provisions :—		
Claims Admitted but not paid—		
Life Assurance	200,000	
Fire Insurance	230,000	
	430,000	
Annuities due and unpaid	200	
Other Sums owing by the Company—		
Unclaimed Dividends	3,800	
Bills Payable	17,000	
Outstanding Commission and Other Charges :—		
Life Account	9,000	
Fire Account	15,000	
Accident Account	3,000	
Provision for Current Taxation	45,000	
Provision for Final Dividend (net)	97,000	
		620,000
		£12,146,500

NOTE.—In practice additional columns are included to show

INSURANCE CO., LTD.

31ST DECEMBER, 1955

	£	£
Mortgages :—		
Property within the United Kingdom. . . .	500,000	
Property out of the United Kingdom	400,000	
		900,000
Loans :—		
[These are classified under six headings and a representative selection is given.]		
Loans on Life Interests	75,000	
Loans on Stocks and Shares	60,000	
Loans on Company's Policies within their Surrender Values	400,000	
		535,000
Investments :—		
[These are classified under eighteen headings and a representative selection is given.]		
Deposit with the High Court	20,000	
(Securities to be specified)		
British Government Securities	5,570,000	
Municipal and County Securities, United Kingdom	1,760,000	
Foreign Government Securities	500,000	
Debentures and Debenture Stocks. . . .	772,500	
Ordinary Stocks	90,000	
		8,712,500
Current Assets :—		
Agents' Balances.	620,000	
Outstanding Premiums	370,000	
Outstanding Interest and Dividends . . .	35,000	
Cash in Hand and at Bank	974,000	
Other Assets (to be specified)	—	
		1,999,000
		£12,146,500

the corresponding figures for the preceding financial year.

is dispensed with, the additional items normally included therein, may be shown under " Other Receipts " and " Other Payments " in the Revenue Account.

(3) BALANCE SHEET, the statutory form of which follows accepted commercial practice, the credit balances appearing on the left-hand side and the debit balances on the right-hand side. The various items are usually grouped under the following general headings :—

Liabilities :

(a) Share Capital and Reserves (including balance on Profit and Loss Account).

(b) Funds (*i.e.*, balances on Revenue Accounts).

(c) Outstanding Claims.

(d) Other sums owing by the Company.

Assets :

(a) Mortgages (two classes).

(b) Loans (six classes).

(c) Investments (eighteen classes).

(d) Cash and other " liquid " assets.

(e) Sums owing to the Company.

The ascertainment of the profits or losses of life assurance business is achieved by an actuarial valuation of the assets and liabilities of the Life Assurance Fund. Under Section 5, Assurance Companies Act, 1909, this valuation must take place at least once in every five years, and is thus known as the *Quinquennial Valuation*, although in practice many companies have a more frequent valuation for internal purposes.

A statement is drawn up, by reference to actuarial tables, to show the total liability of the company in respect of policies in force, *less* the present value of the total premiums (excluding the " loading " for expenses of management) receivable under the policies, and this net liability is carried to the

left-hand side of a statutory form of account known as the
Valuation Balance Sheet. On the right-hand side of the
Valuation Balance Sheet appears the amount of the Life
Assurance Fund, and the difference between these two
amounts represents the surplus or deficiency as the case
may be, as illustrated in the following example :—

VALUATION BALANCE SHEET OF THE WATCHDOG INSURANCE CO., LTD.

Dr.		AS AT 31ST DECEMBER, 1955		Cr.
	£			£
To Net Liability under Life Assurance and Annuity Transactions	7,217,000	By Life Assurance and Annuity Funds .		8,542,000
„ Surplus (if any) . .	1,325,000	„ Deficiency (if any) .		—
	£8,542,000			£8,542,000

The surplus revealed by the Valuation Balance Sheet
will be dealt with according to the constitution of the company : a common practice is to transfer one-fifth of it each
year to the General Profit and Loss Account.

Banking Companies.

In recording the transactions of a banking concern, the
ordinary rules of double entry book-keeping apply, but owing
to the special nature of the transactions it is necessary that
the banker should be able to ascertain the position of a
customer's account at any time of the day. Accordingly
the " slip system " of posting is used, transactions being
entered direct into the ledger from the debit and credit
slips (cheques, paying-in slips and debit and credit notes)
concerned.

The published Profit and Loss Account and Balance
Sheet are drawn up on the usual commercial lines and disclosure is governed by the provisions of the Companies Act,
1948, subject to certain exemptions applicable to banking
companies.* Briefly, the effect of the exemption provisions

* The exceptions for banking companies are contained in Paragraph 23, Part II,
Eighth Schedule, Companies Act, 1948 (see Appendix I).

is that the following information alone need be disclosed in order to comply with the requirements of the Companies Act, 1948 :—

PROFIT AND LOSS ACCOUNT.

(1) Dividends paid and proposed.

(2) Remuneration of auditors (unless fixed by the company in general meeting).

(3) Whether or not the amount of dividends is subject to taxation.

(4) Comparative figures for the previous year.

BALANCE SHEET.

(1) Particulars of share capital, and classification of assets and liabilities.

(2) Preliminary expenses, capital issue expenses, commissions or discounts on shares and debentures.

(3) Distinction between fixed assets and current assets, and method of valuation of fixed assets.

(4) Sub-division of investments, and amount of goodwill, patents and trade marks ; also the aggregate amounts of proposed dividends (net) and loans under Section 54 of the Act.

(5) Whether any liability is secured other than by operation of law.

(6) Particulars of debentures held by a nominee or trustee for the company.

(7) All matters required to appear by way of note to the Balance Sheet (see page 388) other than the market value of quoted investments.

Furthermore, the Act provides that where, in the Balance Sheet of a banking company, capital reserves, revenue reserves or provisions (other than provisions for depreciation, renewals or diminution in value of assets) are not stated separately, any heading stating an amount arrived at after taking into account such a reserve or provision must be so framed or marked as to indicate that fact [e.g., Current,

Deposit and Other Accounts (including Reserves for Contingencies and Taxation)], and the Profit and Loss Account must indicate by appropriate words the manner in which the amount stated for the company's profit or loss has been arrived at (*e.g.*, " By Net Profit after providing for Taxation and after deducting Transfers to Reserves, out of which Reserves provision has been made for diminution in value of assets ").

The requirements of Sections 196 and 197 of the Act with regard to directors' remuneration and loans to officers (including directors) of the company also apply to banking companies.

An example of the published accounts of a banking company is given on pages 456 and 457,* from which it will be noted that the details given in the published form of Profit and Loss Account are considerably curtailed, while the assets in the Balance Sheet are shown in the order of realisability in view of the importance that is attached to the liquid position of such concerns.

A brief explanation is given, in the following paragraphs, of a selection of the items usually appearing in the Balance Sheets of banking companies.

LIABILITIES. The items under this heading are the amounts owing by the bank to its customers and shareholders, together with the undivided balance to the credit of Profit and Loss Account.

Capital Paid Up is the actual amount of money received from shareholders for shares issued to them. It should be noted that most English joint-stock banks have established a " reserve capital " (under Section 60, Companies Act, 1948) by setting aside part of the uncalled capital for use only in the event of the liquidation of the bank, thus materially strengthening the security available for the bank's depositors.

Reserve Fund is an accumulation of undivided profits and

---

* Comparative figures for the previous year have not been included in the example on pages 456 and 457 owing to lack of space.

THE SAFEGUARD

BALANCE

	£	s.	d.
Share Capital Authorised :—			
2,869,079 Shares of £12 each	34,428,948	0	0
2,000,000 Shares of £2 10s. each . . .	5,000,000	0	0
5,771,052 Shares of £1 each	5,771,052	0	0
	£45,200,000	0	0

Share Capital Issued :—

	£	s.	d.			
2,869,079 Shares of £12 each, £2 10s. paid	7,172,697	10	0			
1,921,677 Shares of £2 10s. each, fully paid	4,804,192	10	0			
1,456,078 Shares of £1 each, fully paid	1,456,078	0	0			
				13,432,968	0	0
Reserve Fund (including Share Premium Account, £4,750,000)				13,432,968	0	0
Dividend payable on 1st February, 1956 . . .				664,931	18	4
Balance of Profit and Loss Account, as below . .				869,258	0	2
				28,400,125	18	6

				£	s.	d.
Current, Deposit and other Accounts (including Reserves for Contingencies and Taxation)	376,703,192	19	10			
Balances due to Affiliated Companies .	3,211,806	9	2			
				379,914,999	9	0
Acceptances and Confirmed Credits on account of Customers				19,779,217	16	3
Engagements on account of Customers . . .				17,695,148	8	7

NOTES.—(1) The aggregate amounts paid in respect of the services of Directors were :—

Directors with Executive Duties—£		
Fees	45,000	
Other Emoluments .	18,700	
Pensions . .	2,500	
		66,200
Other Directors—Fees .	10,000	
		£76,200

(2) Provision for United Kingdom Income Tax in respect of profits to date has been reserved in these Accounts.

(3) Foreign currencies have been converted into sterling at the rates ruling on 31st December, 1955

	£445,789,491	12	4

Dr. PROFIT AND LOSS ACCOUNT FOR

	£	s.	d.
To Interim Dividend, less Income Tax, paid 15th July, 1955 .	664,931	18	4
„ Final Dividend, less Income Tax, payable 1st February, 1956	664,931	18	4
„ Reserve Fund	730,000	0	0
„ Balance carried forward to next Account . . .	869,258	0	2
	£2,929,121	16	10

BANK LIMITED
SHEET
DECEMBER, 1955

	£	s.	d.
Current Assets :—			
Coin, Bank Notes and Balances with the Bank of England	46,918,242	13	10
Balances with, and cheques in course of Collection on other Banks in Great Britain and Ireland	28,375,201	16	8
Money at Call and Short Notice	31,670,909	7	8
Bills Discounted	58,783,656	14	11

Investments, less Reserves :—
(including £425,436 5s. 0d. lodged as security for Public
and other Accounts)—

	£	s.	d.			
Securities of, or guaranteed by, the British Government . .	11,798,351	5	8			
British Dominion and Colonial Government Securities and British Corporation Stocks . .	719,353	11	0			
Other Quoted Investments .	411,185	13	7			
	12,928,890	10	3			
Unquoted Investments (including £500,000 Tax Reserve Certificates)	1,800,000	0	0			
				14,728,890	10	3
Advances to Customers and other Accounts . . .				217,374,230	1	1
				397,851,131	4	5

	£	s.	d.			
Fixed Assets :—						
Investments in Affiliated Companies at cost, less amounts written off . .	7,286,109	10	1			
Bank Premises at cost, less amounts written off	3,177,884	13	0			
				10,463,994	3	1
Liabilities of Customers for Acceptances, Confirmed Credits and Engagements				37,474,366	4	10
				£445,789,491	12	4

THE YEAR ENDED 31ST DECEMBER, 1955   *Cr.*

	£	s.	d.
By Balance from last Account	969,460	0	9
„ Net Profit for the year ended 31st December, 1955, full provision having been made for Rebate, Expenses, Bad and Doubtful Debts, Contingencies and Taxation .	1,959,661	16	1
	£2,929,121	16	10

Q*

of appropriations specially made to provide against unforeseen contingencies of any kind.

Current, etc., Accounts. This is the total amount owing by the bank to its customers and correspondents for deposits of all kinds, on current or deposit account.

Acceptances, etc., on behalf of Customers. Under this heading is entered the total amount of the bank's liability on its signature as endorser or acceptor of bills on behalf of its customers and agents. As the bank is able to fall back on its customers if necessary, a corresponding entry appears on the assets side.

ASSETS. On this side appear the values of the cash, investments and property held by the bank against its liabilities. The assets are always arranged in order of realisability, so that customers and others interested in the concern can estimate the strength and stability of the bank at a glance by observing the proportion of liquid assets maintained by the management.

Cash in hand represents the amount of cash, including coin and notes, held by the bank at its head office and branches, and also the balance of the bank's account at the Bank of England, which is treated as cash. No profit is earned on this item.

Money at Call and Short Notice is surplus money lent by the bank to bill brokers and stockbrokers at a low rate of interest, withdrawable at call or at very short notice. The money is often lent overnight, from one day to the next, or at seven days' notice. The loans are secured by the deposit with the bank of first-class bills or other securities.

Bills Discounted. This represents the bills of exchange which have been discounted by the bank for its customers, and also the investments of the bank in bills which it has itself purchased in the open market.

Investments are chiefly British and Colonial Government securities, local loans, etc., all of which are held more or less permanently, and interest is earned thereon. The portion of the investments " lodged for public accounts " is specially earmarked as security for the due repayment of public funds lodged with the bank on the deposit and current accounts of Government departments and local authorities.

Advances to Customers. This amount is the total owing to the bank by its customers and agents, on overdrafts and loans, and is secured by deposit of title deeds, share certificates, life policies, etc. Interest is paid at varying rates, and forms the bulk of the bank's profits.

Bank Premises. The value of these is generally included at a much reduced figure, although the premises of many banks are extremely valuable. The buildings are, however, difficult to realise in times of stress.

Building Societies.

Building Societies may be defined as " associations of persons formed for the purpose of raising a fund to be employed in making advances to such of their members as desire to borrow on the security of freehold or leasehold property ". The modern form of building society, *i.e.*, the incorporated society, is not a joint-stock company but a special association governed by the provisions of the Building Societies Acts, 1874 to 1894, and controlled by the Registrar of Friendly Societies.

The members of a building society may be divided into two classes, investors and borrowers, the former supplying the funds from which the latter borrow. The difference between the rates of interest received from borrowers, and the rates paid to investors, forms the margin from which the building society meets establishment expenses and accumulates the large reserves so essential to the success of an undertaking of this nature.

The various methods of keeping the internal records of a building society are beyond the scope of this work but it may be stated that the ordinary principles of double entry book-keeping apply equally to building societies' accounts as to those of general commercial undertakings.

The published accounts of a building society must be presented in the form prescribed by the Chief Registrar of Friendly Societies, the form adopted in practice invariably being that set out in the Schedule to the Building Societies Act, 1894, as amended by subsequent legislation. The current form of annual accounts is made up of eight accounts, the general contents of which are summarised in the following paragraphs :—

(1) SHARES ACCOUNT. This account is, in effect, a summary of the year's transactions in all the accounts in the share ledger, showing on the debit side all withdrawals (including interest withdrawn) and the closing balance due to members and on the credit side subscriptions received, interest due for the year and the commencing balance due to members.

(2) DEPOSITS AND LOANS ACCOUNT. This account is also a summary account of all loans, etc., made *to* the society, distinguishing between (a) deposits and loans made by members and (b) bank loans and overdrafts. Thus the commencing balance due on loans, etc., and all deposits and loans received during the year, together with interest due for the year, are shown on the credit side of the account and withdrawals (including interest withdrawn) and the balance due at the end of the year are shown on the debit side of the account.

(3) MORTGAGES ACCOUNT. This is also a summary account of all loans, etc., made *by* the society, distinguishing as regards advances between (a) mortgages not exceeding £1,000 and (b) mortgages exceeding £1,000. The opening balance due to the society is debited together with amounts advanced on mortgages during the year, interest due for the year, and insurance premiums, survey fees, etc., charged to borrowers, while amounts repaid (including interest), losses on the

realisation of mortgaged properties, together with the closing balance due to the society are credited to the account.

(4) INVESTMENTS ACCOUNT.   This account is a combined summary of the society's various investment accounts and interest and dividends on investment accounts, including profits and losses on investments realised during the year.

(5) PROFIT AND LOSS ACCOUNT.   In this account the management expenses and interest, etc., paid are set off against the interest received and other sundry receipts, thereby showing the net gain or loss of the society on the period's transactions.

(6) APPROPRIATION ACCOUNT.   This account is analogous to the Profit and Loss (Appropriation) Account of a limited company.

The form of Accounts 5 and 6 will be apparent from the example on page 462.

(7) GENERAL RESERVE FUND ACCOUNT.   This account shows the opening and closing reserves, appropriations from Account No. 6, and any other transfers to or from reserves. Three further skeleton accounts, 7(a), 7(b) and 7(c), are also provided, under the general heading " Other Reserve Accounts ", for any further reserves that the society may create.

(8) BALANCE SHEET.   Allowing for differences in detail, this statement is on much the same general lines as the Balance Sheet of a commercial concern.   It will be noted from the example on pages 464 and 465 that the main headings are as follows :—

Liabilities—

(a) Due to Holders of various classes of Shares, including Interest (the different classes must be shown separately, and the total must agree with the closing balance on Account No. 1).

(b) Due to Creditors for Deposits and Loans, distinguishing between (a) Deposits and Loans (other than loans from banks), classified according to notice of withdrawal required, and (b) Loans and Overdrafts

THE HOMESTEAD BUILDING SOCIETY

5. PROFIT AND LOSS ACCOUNT FOR THE YEAR ENDED 31ST MARCH, 1955

Dr.   Cr.

Expenditure.	£	s.	d.	Income.	£	s.	d.
Management Expenses :—				Interest from Borrowers	95,630	4	6
Remuneration of Directors	705	8	5	Interest and Dividends from			
Remuneration of Staff and				Investments	17,211	4	2
Auditors' Fees	5,200	0	0	Bank Interest	292	13	6
Rent, Rates, Insurance,				Rents from Letting of Office			
Heat, Light, Cleaning,				Premises	1,758	19	6
Repairs (Offices)	2,712	7	3	Survey Fees and Expenses	643	12	3
Printing, Stationery and				Other Fees, Fines, Rules and			
Postages	824	16	8	Pass Books	112	17	9
Advertising, Commission and				Commission (Fire, Life, etc.,			
Agency Fees	1,935	2	1	Insurance)	849	14	0
Other Expenses (to be speci-				Other Income (to be speci-			
fied) :—				fied) :—			
Total Management Expenses	11,377	14	5				
Survey Fees and Expenses	760	0	0				
Interest on Deposits and Loans	8,006	10	7				
Income Tax	12,038	14	3				
Profits Tax	4,000	0	0				
Losses on Mortgages as per A/c No. 3							
Losses on Realisation of In-							
vestments as per A/c No. 4	372	18	3				
Depreciation :—							
Investments							
Office Premises, Furniture, etc.	2,913	12	0				
Other Assets							
Other Expenditure (to be specified) :—							
Balance carried down to A/c No. 6	77,029	16	2				
	£116,499	5	8		£116,499	5	8

Dr.   6. APPROPRIATION ACCOUNT.   Cr.

	£	s.	d.		£	s.	d.
Interest, Dividend and Bonus to Shareholders	68,910	2	7	Balance brought forward			
Other Appropriations :—				Balance brought down from A/c No. 5	77,029	16	2
General Reserve	8,119	13	7				
	£77,029	16	2		£77,029	16	2

from Banks (the total must agree with the closing balance on Account No. 2).

(c) Other Liabilities and Contingency Accounts (to be specified).

(d) Reserves (details required of the various reserves).

(e) Balance carried forward as per Account No. 6.

Assets—

(a) Balance due or outstanding on Mortgages, not including prospective interest (the total of this asset must agree with the closing balance on Account No. 3 and considerable detail must be given as will be apparent from a study of the illustration on page 465).

(*b*) Investments (the sub-division of this item follows the sub-division in Account No. 4 and the total of this asset must agree with the closing balance on Account No. 4, while the market value at the date of the Balance Sheet must be shown inset and any accrued interest must also be stated).

(*c*) Other Assets (to be specified).

Separate schedules must also accompany the above accounts, showing certain prescribed particulars relating to mortgages held by the society, that must be included in computing the statutory borrowing limits of the society. In this connection, it should be noted that by the provisions of the Building Societies Act, 1874, such bodies are prevented from borrowing more than two-thirds of the amount for the time being secured to the society by "active" mortgages. The term "active" mortgages is used to denote all mortgages other than those required to be shown in the second and third of the aforementioned schedules. The contents of these schedules, three in number, are indicated by their headings :—

(1) Mortgages where the repayments are not upwards of twelve months in arrear, and the property has not been upwards of twelve months in possession of the society, and where the present debt exceeds £5,000 ;

(2) Property of which the society has been upwards of twelve months in possession ; and

(3) Mortgages where the repayments are upwards of twelve months in arrear, and the property has not been upwards of twelve months in possession of the society.

THE HOMESTEA

8. BALANCE

Liabilities.	£	s.	d.	£	s.	d.
Due to Holders of various classes of Shares, including Interest, viz. :—						
Subscription Shares	514,979	11	8			
Paid-up Shares	1,654,791	1	5			
Total, as per A/c No. 1				2,169,770	13	1
Due to Creditors for Deposits and Loans :—						
Deposits and Loans (other than Loans from Bank) (to be classified according to notice required) :—						
Deposits at one month's notice . .	284,832	8	11			
Total, as per A/c No. 2				284,832	8	11
Loans and Overdrafts from Bank . .	100,000	0	0			
As per A/c No. 2				100,000	0	0
Other Liabilities and Contingency Accounts (to be specified) :—						
Income Tax	7,450	0	0			
Profits Tax	1,500	0	0			
Sundry Expenses Creditors . . .	120	0	0			
Total				9,070	0	0
Reserves :—						
General Reserve	133,119	13	7			
Special Reserve	6,423	8	10			
Total				139,543	2	5
				£2,703,216	4	5

BUILDING SOCIETY

	£	s.	d.
Assets.			
Balance due or outstanding on Mortgages, not including prospective interest, *viz.* :—			
Mortgages from Members where the repayments are not upwards of 12 months in arrear and the property has not been upwards of 12 months in possession of the Society :—			
On 3,778 Mortgages where the debt does not exceed £500	1,075,962	5	8
On 660 Mortgages where the debt exceeds £500 and does not exceed £1,000	482,374	10	2
On 138 Mortgages where the debt exceeds £1,000 and does not exceed £3,000	235,759	13	5
On 18 Mortgages where the debt exceeds £3,000 and does not exceed £5,000	59,817	10	4
On 9 Mortgages where the debt exceeds £5,000, as shown by Part I of the Schedule	187,308	17	2
Total of Mortgages available under Section 14 of the Act of 1894	2,041,222	16	9
(If the Society has any Mortgages from non-members, the like particulars as above are to be given in full for all such Mortgages.)			
Balance as shown in Parts II and III of Schedule, *viz.* :—			
On 2 Mortgages on Property of which the Society has been upwards of 12 months in possession, as shown by Part II of the Schedule (Present amount included in assets).	727	3	8
On 3 Mortgages where the repayments are upwards of 12 months in arrear, and the property has not been upwards of 12 months in possession of the Society, as shown by Part III of the Schedule (Present debt)	200	10	0
Total number of Mortgages = 4,608 Total, as per A/c No. 3	2,042,150	10	5

Investments :—	Market Value at date of Balance Sheet.					
	£	s.	d.	£	s.	d.
British Government Securities	161,500	15	0	154,520	14	1
Colonial and Dominion Securities	203,250	0	0	200,000	0	0
British Municipal and County Securities	149,176	4	9	147,269	10	4
Other Investments (to be specified) :—	—			—		
Interest Accrued				623	14	7

	£	s.	d.
Total, as per A/c No. 4	502,413	19	0
Other Assets (to be specified) :—			
Office Premises, Furniture, etc.	94,206	8	0
Cash at Bank and in Hand	64,445	7	0
	£2,703,216	4	5

Charities.

Charitable institutions are non-profit making concerns and the accounts prepared, which will differ in form according to the nature of the particular charity, usually comprise a Receipts and Payments Account or an Income and Expenditure Account. Where the latter is prepared it will be accompanied by a Balance Sheet. The preparation of Receipts and Payments Accounts and Income and Expenditure Accounts has already been explained in Chapter I.

ENDOWED CHARITIES ACCOUNTS. The Charitable Trusts Act, 1853, provides that, in the case of endowed charities, the trustees must make up accounts annually to the 31st December (or any other appointed day) and that such accounts must show, *inter alia*, the gross income received or accrued due, all balances in hand at the commencement and end of the year and the payments made or outstanding in respect of the year.

Clubs.

The final accounts of a club present no unusual features as they generally comprise a Receipts and Payments Account or, preferably, an Income and Expenditure Account accompanied by a Balance Sheet (see Chapter I).

An effective system of stock control is essential as the greater part of the expenditure may relate to purchases of liquor and tobacco, while ample provision should be made in the annual accounts for the periodical redecoration of the premises. The question of depreciation and renewals of china, glass, plate and linen also calls for particular attention and the appropriate charge to revenue may be determined by annual revaluation of the stocks as in the case of loose tools (see page 257) or, alternatively, the original expenditure may be capitalised and all subsequent expenditure on renewals and replacements charged to revenue.

When a club is registered under the Industrial and Provident Societies Acts, 1893 to 1913, it is required to prepare and file the following annual accounts :—

(1) Cash Account.

(2) Refreshments Account, which is in effect a Trading Account showing the gross profit or loss on the provision of refreshments.

(3) Profit and Loss Account.

(4) Application of Profit Account.

(5) Balance Sheet.

Friendly Societies.

Friendly Societies exist in order to provide various benefits to members in the event of sickness, etc., their funds being drawn from entrance fees and contributions paid by members, payments therefrom being made to members who are entitled to benefits.

The Friendly Societies Act, 1896, provides that every registered society must send to the Registrar of Friendly Societies a return of the receipts and expenditure, funds and effects of the society as audited. The form of return is prescribed by the Chief Registrar of Friendly Societies and separate forms are available for the various classes of societies. For example, the contents of the principal sections of the annual returns of (a) a benevolent society and (b) an investment society may be summarised as follows :—

(a) BENEVOLENT SOCIETY.

(1) *General Account of Income (debit) and Expenditure (credit)*, comprising—

Income—(a) Contributions for Management and Benefits (distinguishing between different types of benefits) ; (b) Donations ; (c) Entrance Fees ; (d) Fines ; (e) Interest on Investments ; (f) Other Income ; and (g) Balance at beginning of year.

Expenditure—(a) Benefits (distinguishing between different types of benefit) ; (b) Interest on Loans ; (c) Expenses (distinguishing between Salaries, Auditors' Fees, Rent, Rates and Taxes,

Printing, Stationery and Postages and Other Expenses) ; (*d*) Depreciation of Investments and Other Assets ; (*e*) Other Expenditure ; and (*f*) Balance at end of year.

(2) *Balance Sheet,* comprising—

Liabilities—(*a*) Amount of Funds (specifying each type of fund separately) ; (*b*) General Reserve for Depreciation ; (*c*) Amount due to Treasurer ; (*d*) Other Liabilities.

Assets—(*a*) Investments (distinguishing between Mortgages on Land and Buildings, Land and Buildings, British Government Securities, British Municipal Securities and Other Securities) ; (*b*) Balance at Post Office Savings Bank ; (*c*) Balance at Trustee Savings Bank ; (*d*) Balance at Joint Stock Bank ; (*e*) Cash in Hands of Treasurer ; (*f*) Cash in Hands of Secretary ; and (*g*) Other Assets.

(*b*) INVESTMENT SOCIETY.

(1) *Revenue Account,* comprising—

Expenditure (debit)—(*a*) Expenses of Management (distinguishing between Directors' Remuneration, Other Salaries and Wages, Advertising, Audit Fee and Other Management Expenses) ; (*b*) Outgoings on Property ; (*c*) Interest on Loans ; (*d*) Loss on Investments Realised ; (*e*) Other Expenditure ; and (*f*) Balance, Profit to Application of Profit Account.

Income (credit)—(*a*) Rents from Land and Buildings ; (*b*) Interest and Dividends on Investments ; (*c*) Bank Interest ; (*d*) Profit on Investments Realised ; (*e*) Entrance Fees ; (*f*) Other Income ; and (*g*) Balance, Loss to Application of Profit Account.

(2) *Application of Profit Account,* comprising—

Debit side—(*a*) Balance of Loss Brought Forward ; (*b*) Balance of Loss from Revenue Account ;

(c) Income Tax; (d) Interest on Members' Shares in Society; (e) Appropriations to Reserves, etc.; and (f) Profit Unappropriated Carried Forward.

Credit side—(a) Balance of Profit Unappropriated Brought Forward; (b) Balance of Profit from Revenue Account; (c) Appropriations from Reserves, etc.; and (d) Balance of Loss Carried Forward.

(3) *Balance Sheet*, comprising—

Liabilities—(a) Issued Share Capital (distinguishing between Ordinary Shares and Preference Shares and indicating nominal and paid-up values); (b) Loans and Interest (distinguishing between Mortgages on Properties, Bank Overdrafts, Other Secured Loans and Other Unsecured Loans and indicating rate of interest); (c) Other Liabilities (distinguishing between Amounts due to Treasurer, Officers and Employees' Guarantee Deposits and Other Liabilities); and (d) Balance of Profit and Reserve (distinguishing between Unappropriated Profit and Reserve Funds).

Assets—(a) Investments (distinguishing between Freehold Land and Buildings, Leasehold Land and Buildings, Mortgages on Land and Buildings, Other Secured Loans, British Government Securities, Dominion, Provincial and Colonial Government Securities, Foreign Government Securities, British Municipal, County and Public Board Stocks, Dominion and Colonial Corporation Stocks, Foreign Corporation Stocks and Other Investments); (b) Land, Buildings, Fixtures, etc.; (c) Other Assets (distinguishing between Balance at Bank, Cash in Hand, Preliminary Expenses, Expenses Prepaid and Other Assets); and (d) Balance of Loss from Application of Profit Account.

Professional Concerns.

In the final accounts of practising doctors, accountants, solicitors and other professional men it is frequently the custom not to take credit for fees accruing, whether accounts have already been rendered or not, until the fees have actually been received in cash, whereas full provision is made for all expenditure, whether paid or not. In other cases, all fees are taken into account as and when the bills are rendered and provision is made at the year-end for all fees accruing in respect of which accounts have not yet been rendered and, as before, full provision is made for all expenditure. In order to ascertain the true results of the practice, the latter method is advisable and it is being adopted more widely by professional men.*

Where fees are included on the cash basis the following alternative accounting procedures may be adopted :—

(a) Credit Fees (or Costs) Account with all fees received and make no entries in the Fees Account for accounts rendered but not paid and fees accrued in respect of which accounts have not yet been rendered.

(b) Credit Fees Account with all accounts rendered plus a conservative valuation of fees accrued but not yet charged to patients, clients, etc., and debit the individual patients, clients, etc., with all accounts rendered and Work-in-Progress Account with all accrued fees. A reserve is then made for all accounts rendered but not paid in cash (Debit Fees Account and bring down as a credit balance on Fees Account) and the reserve is then deducted from the amount shown in the Balance Sheet as due from patients, etc., while the debit balance on Work-in-Progress is deducted from the item " Fees " in the Profit and Loss Account. Alternatively, the Work-in-Progress Account can be dispensed with so that an equivalent amount is brought down as a debit balance on Fees Account.

* The Inland Revenue are inclined to insist upon the inclusion of all fees, whether actually received in cash or not, in accounts submitted for taxation purposes.

Dr.			FEES ACCOUNT			Cr.
1954		£	1954			£
Dec. 31	To Reserve—Accounts Rendered Not Paid c/d	1,245	Jan. 1–Dec. 31	By Sundry Clients—Accounts Rendered		2,750
	„ Profit and Loss Account	1,980	Dec. 31	„ Work-in-Progress c/d		475
		£3,225				£3,225
1955			1955			
Jan. 1	To Work-in-Progress b/d	475	Jan. 1	By Reserve b/d		1,245
Dec. 31	„ Reserve—Accounts Rendered Not Paid c/d	1,635	Jan. 1–Dec. 31	„ Sundry Clients—Accounts Rendered		3,170
	„ Profit and Loss Account	3,095	Dec. 31	„ Work-in-Progress c/d		790
		£5,205				£5,205
1956			1956			
Jan. 1	To Work-in-Progress b/d	790	Jan. 1	By Reserve b/d		1,635

Profit and Loss Account—

				£	£
Year to 31st December, 1954	.	By Fees	. . . .	1,980	
		Less Work-in-Progress	.	475	1,505
Year to 31st December, 1955	.	By Fees	. . . .	3,095	
		Less Work-in-Progress	.	790	2,305

Balance Sheet—

			£
As at 31st December, 1954	.	Amounts due by Clients .	1,245
		Less Reserve . . .	1,245
As at 31st December, 1955	.	Amounts due by Clients .	1,635
		Less Reserve . . .	1,635

Method (b) is recommended in preference to Method (a) and the effect on the final accounts may be illustrated by the example above showing the appropriate entries for the first two years of an accountant's practice.

The preparation of accounts on a cash basis is not in accordance with the accepted principles of the best practice in accounting, and it is suggested that the accounts of professional men should conform with recognised principles by the inclusion of all revenue (including accrued revenue) whether received in cash or not and that, where it is anticipated cash may not be received, the usual provision should be made for bad and doubtful debts.

Disbursements on behalf of clients, patients, etc., are usually recorded in an analysis book and debited to Clients' (or Patients') Disbursements Account. When accounts are rendered, inclusive of disbursements, the appropriate transfer is made from Clients' Disbursements Account to the debit of Fees Account ; thus the balance on the former account will represent disbursements not yet charged to clients, etc.

SOLICITORS' ACCOUNTS. The fiduciary relationship which is usually found to exist between solicitor and client points to the need for a careful and accurate system of accounting. It had been recognised for some time that the best practice was that which kept quite separate accounts of clients' moneys and the solicitor's own moneys and this practice was accordingly followed by most firms. Unfortunately, however, there were cases in which clients' moneys and the solicitor's own moneys had been so intermingled that it was well-nigh impossible to prepare accounts showing how the solicitor stood in relation to his clients. That such a state of affairs could arise in practice was very undesirable and the Solicitors Act, 1933, and the Solicitors' Accounts Rules, 1935, which made it compulsory for every solicitor to keep separate accounts in respect of clients' moneys and those belonging to himself, were designed to remove this possibility. The Solicitors' Accounts Rules, 1935, have been replaced by the Solicitors' Accounts Rules, 1945 (in operation from 1st January, 1945), and the more recent Rules remove certain misunderstandings and ambiguities in the earlier Rules. The principal provisions of the current rules may be summarised as follows :—

(1) *Payments into " Client Account "*. All money received by a solicitor must be paid into his Client Account, unless on immediate receipt it is paid to the client or to someone by his direction or is paid into a separate banking account of the client or of someone named by him. Similarly, money received need not be paid into the Client Account when the client requests that it shall not be done or the amount is received by way of paying a debt due to the

solicitor from his client or to reimburse disbursements or is paid expressly on account of costs
either agreed or in accordance with a bill of costs
or written intimation of the amount of costs due.
Money which may be paid into a Client Account
includes trust money (*i.e.*, money received by a
solicitor-trustee), such amount of the solicitor's own
money as is necessary to open or maintain the
account, money withdrawn by mistake and any
cheque which the solicitor may split but has elected
not to split, *i.e.*, a cheque, part of which should
be paid into Client Account and the balance into
Solicitor's Account.

(2) *Drawings out of " Client Account ".* Money may be
withdrawn from Client Account for a payment to
or on behalf of a client (including a trust), for payment of a debt due to the solicitor from a client
or to reimburse him for disbursements made on
behalf of a client, or for payment of the solicitor's
costs when a bill or written intimation of the amount
has been delivered to the client and the latter has
been notified that the money will be so applied.
In no case can client's or trust money be withdrawn
in excess of the amount standing to the credit of
that particular client or trust.   Furthermore, money
paid in by the solicitor to open or maintain the
account may be withdrawn when no longer required
or money paid in by mistake may be withdrawn.

Payment to a solicitor out of his Client Account
may be made in one of two ways only, either by
a cheque drawn in his favour or by a transfer to
a banking account of the solicitor which is not a
Client Account ; the practice of paying third parties
(*i.e.*, the solicitor's own creditors) by cheque or
transfer from the Client Account is forbidden.

(3) *Books and Accounts.*   A solicitor must keep properly
written up such books and accounts as are necessary
to show all his dealings with clients' or trust money

and to distinguish the money of each separate client or trust. All such books and accounts must be preserved for a minimum period of six years.

The above-mentioned rules are of particular practical importance as Section 1, Solicitors Act, 1941, requires a practising solicitor to deliver annually to the Law Society an accountant's certificate of his compliance with the Solicitors' Accounts Rules.

Apart from slight points of difference regarding the wording of entries and the omission of the prefixes " To " and " By ", the book-keeping of solicitors is based on double entry principles and the final accounts are drawn up in the usual manner subject to slight modifications to ensure complete differentiation between clients' and office moneys.

APPENDIX I

THE COMPANIES ACT, 1948

SECTIONS RELATING TO ACCOUNTS AND AUDIT

53.—Power to pay certain Commissions, and Prohibition of Payment of all other Commissions, Discounts, etc.

(1) It shall be lawful for a company to pay a commission to any person in consideration of his subscribing or agreeing to subscribe, whether absolutely or conditionally, for any shares in the company, or procuring or agreeing to procure subscriptions, whether absolute or conditional, for any shares in the company if—

(a) the payment of the commission is authorised by the articles ; and

(b) the commission paid or agreed to be paid does not exceed ten per cent. of the price at which the shares are issued or the amount or rate authorised by the articles, whichever is the less ; and

(c) the amount or rate per cent. of the commission paid or agreed to be paid is—

　(i) in the case of shares offered to the public for subscription, disclosed in the prospectus ; or

　(ii) in the case of shares not offered to the public for subscription, disclosed in the statement in lieu of prospectus, or in a statement in the prescribed form signed in like manner as a statement in lieu of prospectus and delivered before the payment of the commission to the registrar of companies for registration, and, where a circular or notice, not being a prospectus, inviting subscription for the shares is issued, also disclosed in that circular or notice ; and

(d) the number of shares which persons have agreed for a commission to subscribe absolutely is disclosed in manner aforesaid.

(2) Save as aforesaid, no company shall apply any of its shares or capital money either directly or indirectly in payment of any commission, discount or allowance to any person in consideration of his subscribing or agreeing to subscribe, whether absolutely or conditionally, for any shares in the company, or procuring or agreeing to procure subscriptions, whether absolute or conditional, for any shares in the company, whether the shares or money be so applied by being added to the purchase money of any property acquired by the company or to the contract price of any work to be executed for the company, or the money be paid out of the nominal purchase money or contract price, or otherwise.

(3) Nothing in this section shall affect the power of any company to pay such brokerage as it has heretofore been lawful for a company to pay.

(4) A vendor to, promoter of, or other person who receives payment in money or shares from, a company shall have and shall be deemed always to have had power to apply any part of the money or shares so received in

payment of any commission, the payment of which, if made directly by the company, would have been legal under this section.

(5) If default is made in complying with the provisions of this section relating to the delivery to the registrar of the statement in the prescribed form, the company and every officer of the company who is in default shall be liable to a fine not exceeding twenty-five pounds.

54.—Prohibition of Provision of Financial Assistance by Company for Purchase of, or Subscription for, its Own or its Holding Company's Shares.

(1) Subject as provided in this section, it shall not be lawful for a company to give, whether directly or indirectly, and whether by means of a loan, guarantee, the provision of security or otherwise, any financial assistance for the purpose of or in connection with a purchase or subscription made or to be made by any person of or for any shares in the company, or, where the company is a subsidiary company, in its holding company :

Provided that nothing in this section shall be taken to prohibit—

(a) where the lending of money is part of the ordinary business of a company, the lending of money by the company in the ordinary course of its business ;

(b) the provision by a company, in accordance with any scheme for the time being in force, of money for the purchase of, or subscription for, fully-paid shares in the company or its holding company, being a purchase or subscription by trustees of or for shares to be held by or for the benefit of employees of the company, including any director holding a salaried employment or office in the company ;

(c) the making by a company of loans to persons, other than directors, *bona fide* in the employment of the company with a view to enabling those persons to purchase or subscribe for fully-paid shares in the company or its holding company to be held by themselves by way of beneficial ownership.

(2) If a company acts in contravention of this section, the company and every officer of the company who is in default shall be liable to a fine not exceeding one hundred pounds.

56.—Application of Premiums Received on Issue of Shares.

(1) Where a company issues shares at a premium, whether for cash or otherwise, a sum equal to the aggregate amount or value of the premiums on those shares shall be transferred to an account, to be called " the share premium account ", and the provisions of this Act relating to the reduction of the share capital of a company shall, except as provided in this section, apply as if the share premium account were paid-up share capital of the company.

(2) The share premium account may, notwithstanding anything in the foregoing subsection, be applied by the company in paying up unissued shares of the company to be issued to members of the company as fully paid bonus shares, in writing off—

(a) the preliminary expenses of the company ; or

(b) the expenses of, or the commission paid or discount allowed on, any issue of shares or debentures of the company ;

or in providing for the premium payable on redemption of any redeemable preference shares or of any debentures of the company.

(3) Where a company has before the commencement of this Act issued any shares at a premium, this section shall apply as if the shares had been issued after the commencement of this Act :

Provided that any part of the premiums which has been so applied that it does not at the commencement of this Act form an identifiable part of the company's reserves within the meaning of the Eighth Schedule to this Act shall be disregarded in determining the sum to be included in the share premium account.

57.—Power to Issue Shares at a Discount.

(1) Subject as provided in this section, it shall be lawful for a company to issue at a discount shares in the company of a class already issued :

Provided that—

(a) the issue of the shares at a discount must be authorised by resolution passed in general meeting of the company, and must be sanctioned by the court ;

(b) the resolution must specify the maximum rate of discount at which the shares are to be issued ;

(c) not less than one year must at the date of the issue have elapsed since the date on which the company was entitled to commence business ;

(d) the shares to be issued at a discount must be issued within one month after the date on which the issue is sanctioned by the court or within such extended time as the court may allow.

(2) Where a company has passed a resolution authorising the issue of shares at a discount, it may apply to the court for an order sanctioning the issue, and on any such application the court, if, having regard to all the circumstances of the case, it thinks proper so to do, may make an order sanctioning the issue on such terms and conditions as it thinks fit.

(3) Every prospectus relating to the issue of the shares must contain particulars of the discount allowed on the issue of the shares or of so much of that discount as has not been written off at the date of the issue of the prospectus.

If default is made in complying with this subsection, the company and every officer of the company who is in default shall be liable to a default fine.

58.—Power to Issue Redeemable Preference Shares.

(1) Subject to the provisions of this section, a company limited by shares may, if so authorised by its articles, issue preference shares which are, or at the option of the company are to be liable, to be redeemed :

Provided that—

(a) no such shares shall be redeemed except out of profits of the company which would otherwise be available for dividend or out of the proceeds of a fresh issue of shares made for the purposes of the redemption ;

(b) no such shares shall be redeemed unless they are fully paid ;

(c) the premium, if any, payable on redemption, must have been provided for out of the profits of the company or out of the company's share premium account before the shares are redeemed ;

(d) where any such shares are redeemed otherwise than out of the proceeds of a fresh issue, there shall out of profits which would otherwise have been available for dividend be transferred to a reserve fund, to be called " the capital redemption reserve fund ", a sum equal to the nominal amount of the shares redeemed, and the provisions of this Act relating to the reduction of the share capital of a company shall, except as provided in this section, apply as if the capital redemption reserve fund were paid-up share capital of the company.

(2) Subject to the provisions of this section, the redemption of preference shares thereunder may be effected on such terms and in such manner as may be provided by the articles of the company.

(3) The redemption of preference shares under this section by a company shall not be taken as reducing the amount of the company's authorised share capital.

(4) Where in pursuance of this section a company has redeemed or is about to redeem any preference shares, it shall have power to issue shares up to the nominal amount of the shares redeemed or to be redeemed as if those shares had never been issued, and accordingly the share capital of the company shall not for the purposes of any enactments relating to stamp duty be deemed to be increased by the issue of shares in pursuance of this subsection :

Provided that, where new shares are issued before the redemption of the old shares, the new shares shall not, so far as relates to stamp duty, be deemed to have been issued in pursuance of this subsection unless the old shares are redeemed within one month after the issue of the new shares.

(5) The capital redemption reserve fund may, notwithstanding anything in this section, be applied by the company in paying up unissued shares of the company to be issued to members of the company as fully-paid bonus shares.

60.—Reserve Liability of Limited Company.

A limited company may by special resolution determine that any portion of its share capital which has not been already called up shall not be capable of being called up except in the event and for the purposes of the company being wound up, and thereupon that portion of its share capital shall not be capable of being called up except in the event and for the purposes aforesaid.

65.—Power of Company to Pay Interest out of Capital in Certain Cases.

(1) Where any shares of a company are issued for the purpose of raising money to defray the expenses of the construction of any works or buildings or the provision of any plant which cannot be made profitable for a lengthened period, the company may pay interest on so much of that share capital as is for the time being paid up for the period and subject to the conditions and restrictions in this section mentioned, and may charge the sum so paid by way of interest to capital as part of the cost of construction of the work or building, or the provision of plant :

Provided that—

(a) no such payment shall be made unless it is authorised by the articles or by special resolution ;

(b) no such payment, whether authorised by the articles or by special resolution, shall be made without the previous sanction of the Board of Trade ;

(c) before sanctioning any such payment the Board of Trade may, at the expense of the company, appoint a person to enquire and report to them as to the circumstances of the case, and may, before making the appointment, require the company to give security for the payment of the costs of the enquiry ;

(d) the payment shall be made only for such period as may be determined by the Board of Trade, and that period shall in no case extend beyond the close of the half year next after the half year during which the works or buildings have been actually completed or the plant provided ;

(e) the rate of interest shall in no case exceed four per cent. per annum or such other rate as may for the time being be prescribed by order of the Treasury ;

(f) the payment of the interest shall not operate as a reduction of the amount paid up on the shares in respect of which it is paid ;

(g) nothing in this section shall affect any company to which the Indian Railways Act, 1894, as amended by any subsequent enactment, applies.

(2) The power conferred by this section on the Treasury shall be exercisable by statutory instrument which shall be subject to annulment in pursuance of a resolution of either House of Parliament.

127.—Documents to be Annexed to Annual Return.

(1) Subject to the provisions of this Act, there shall be annexed to the annual return—

(a) a written copy, certified both by a director and by the secretary of the company to be a true copy, of every balance sheet laid before the company in general meeting during the period to which the return relates (including every document required by law to be annexed to the balance sheet) ; and

(b) a copy, certified as aforesaid, of the report of the auditors on, and of the report of the directors accompanying, each such balance sheet ;

and where any such balance sheet or document required by law to be annexed thereto is in a foreign language, there shall be annexed to that balance sheet a translation in English of the balance sheet or document certified in the prescribed manner to be a correct translation.

(2) If any such balance sheet as aforesaid or document required by law to be annexed thereto did not comply with the requirements of the law as in force at the date of the audit with respect to the form of balance sheets or documents aforesaid, as the case may be, there shall be made such additions to and corrections in the copy as would have been required to be made in the balance sheet or document in order to make it comply with the said requirements, and the fact that the copy has been so amended shall be stated thereon.

(3) If a company fails to comply with this section, the company and every officer of the company who is in default shall be liable to a default fine.

For the purposes of this subsection, the expression " officer " shall include any person in accordance with whose directions or instructions the directors of the company are accustomed to act.

128.—Certificates to be Sent by Private Company with Annual Return.

A private company shall send with the annual return required by section one hundred and twenty-four of this Act a certificate signed both by a director and by the secretary of the company that the company has not, since the date of the last return, or, in the case of a first return, since the date of the incorporation of the company, issued any invitation to the public to subscribe for any shares or debentures of the company, and, where the annual return discloses the fact that the number of members of the company exceeds fifty, also a certificate so signed that the excess consists wholly of persons who under paragraph (*b*) of subsection (1) of section twenty-eight of this Act are not to be included in reckoning the number of fifty.

129.—Exemption, in Certain Cases, of Private Companies from the Requirements of Section 127.

(1) A private company shall be excepted from the requirements imposed by section one hundred and twenty-seven of this Act if, but only if,—

> (*a*) the conditions mentioned in the next following subsection are satisfied at the date of the return and have been satisfied at all times since the commencement of this Act ; and

> (*b*) there is sent with the return a certificate, signed by the persons signing the certificates required to be so sent by the last foregoing section, that to the best of their knowledge and belief the said conditions are and have been satisfied as aforesaid :

Provided that if at any time it is shown that the said conditions are then satisfied in the case of any private company, the Board of Trade may on the application of the company's directors direct that, in relation to any subsequent annual returns of the company, it shall not be necessary for the said conditions to have been satisfied before that time, and the certificates sent with those returns shall in that event relate only to the period since that time.

(2) The said conditions are—

> (*a*) that the conditions contained in the Seventh Schedule to this Act are satisfied as to the persons interested in the company's shares and debentures ; and

> (*b*) that the number of persons holding debentures of the company is not more than fifty (joint holders being treated as a single person) ; and

> (*c*) that no body corporate is a director of the company and neither the company nor any of the directors is party or privy to any arrangement whereby the policy of the company is capable of being determined by persons other than the directors, members and debenture holders or trustees for debenture holders.

(3) A prosecution shall not be instituted in England in respect of any failure of a private company to comply with section one hundred and twenty-seven of this Act except by or with the consent of the Board of Trade.

(4) Any reference in this Act to an exempt private company shall be construed as referring to a company with respect to which the conditions mentioned in subsection (2) of this section are satisfied and have been satisfied at all times since the commencement of this Act or since the giving by the Board of Trade of a direction under the proviso to subsection (1) of this section.

(5) References in this section to the said conditions having been satisfied since the commencement of this Act shall, in relation to a company first registered after the commencement of this Act, be construed as referring to the conditions having been satisfied since the company's registration.

147.—Keeping of Books of Account.

(1) Every company shall cause to be kept proper books of account with respect to—

> (*a*) all sums of money received and expended by the company and the matters in respect of which the receipt and expenditure takes place ;

> (*b*) all sales and purchases of goods by the company ;

> (*c*) the assets and liabilities of the company.

(2) For the purposes of the foregoing subsection, proper books of account shall not be deemed to be kept with respect to the matters aforesaid if there are not kept such books as are necessary to give a true and fair view of the state of the company's affairs and to explain its transactions.

(3) The books of account shall be kept at the registered office of the company or at such other place as the directors think fit, and shall at all times be open to inspection by the directors :

Provided that if books of account are kept at a place outside Great Britain there shall be sent to, and kept at a place in, Great Britain and be at all times open to inspection by the directors such accounts and returns with respect to the business dealt with in the books of account so kept as will disclose with reasonable accuracy the financial position of that business at intervals not exceeding six months and will enable to be prepared in accordance with this Act the company's balance sheet, its profit and loss account or income and expenditure account, and any document annexed to any of those documents giving information which is required by this Act and is thereby allowed to be so given.

(4) If any person being a director of a company fails to take all reasonable steps to secure compliance by the company with the requirements of this section, or has by his own wilful act been the cause of any default by the company thereunder, he shall, in respect of each offence, be liable on summary conviction to imprisonment for a term not exceeding six months or to a fine not exceeding two hundred pounds :

Provided that—

(a) in any proceedings against a person in respect of an offence under this section consisting of a failure to take reasonable steps to secure compliance by the company with the requirements of this section, it shall be a defence to prove that he had reasonable ground to believe and did believe that a competent and reliable person was charged with the duty of seeing that those requirements were complied with and was in a position to discharge that duty ; and

(b) a person shall not be sentenced to imprisonment for such an offence unless, in the opinion of the court dealing with the case, the offence was committed wilfully.

148.—Profit and Loss Account and Balance Sheet.

(1) The directors of every company shall at some date not later than eighteen months after the incorporation of the company and subsequently once at least in every calendar year lay before the company in general meeting a profit and loss account or, in the case of a company not trading for profit, an income and expenditure account for the period, in the case of the first account, since the incorporation of the company, and, in any other case, since the preceding account, made up to a date not earlier than the date of the meeting by more than nine months, or, in the case of a company carrying on business or having interests abroad, by more than twelve months :

Provided that the Board of Trade, if for any special reason they think fit so to do, may, in the case of any company, extend the period of eighteen months aforesaid, and in the case of any company and with respect to any year extend the periods of nine and twelve months aforesaid.

(2) The directors shall cause to be made out in every calendar year, and to be laid before the company in general meeting, a balance sheet as at the date to which the profit and loss account or the income and expenditure account, as the case may be, is made up.

R

(3) If any person being a director of a company fails to take all reasonable steps to comply with the provisions of this section, he shall, in respect of each offence, be liable on summary conviction to imprisonment for a term not exceeding six months or to a fine not exceeding two hundred pounds :

Provided that—

(a) in any proceedings against a person in respect of an offence under this section, it shall be a defence to prove that he had reasonable ground to believe and did believe that a competent and reliable person was charged with the duty of seeing that the provisions of this section were complied with and was in a position to discharge that duty ; and

(b) a person shall not be sentenced to imprisonment for such an offence unless, in the opinion of the court dealing with the case, the offence was committed wilfully.

149.—General Provisions as to Contents and Form of Accounts.

(1) Every balance sheet of a company shall give a true and fair view of the state of affairs of the company as at the end of its financial year, and every profit and loss account of a company shall give a true and fair view of the profit or loss of the company for the financial year.

(2) A company's balance sheet and profit and loss account shall comply with the requirements of the Eighth Schedule to this Act, so far as applicable thereto.

(3) Save as expressly provided in the following provisions of this section or in Part III of the said Eighth Schedule, the requirements of the last foregoing subsection and the said Eighth Schedule shall be without prejudice either to the general requirements of subsection (1) of this section or to any other requirements of this Act.

(4) The Board of Trade may, on the application or with the consent of a company's directors, modify in relation to that company any of the requirements of this Act as to the matters to be stated in a company's balance sheet or profit and loss account (except the requirements of subsection (1) of this section) for the purpose of adapting them to the circumstances of the company.

(5) Subsections (1) and (2) of this section shall not apply to a company's profit and loss account if—

(a) the company has subsidiaries ; and

(b) the profit and loss account is framed as a consolidated profit and loss account dealing with all or any of the company's subsidiaries as well as the company and—

(i) complies with the requirements of this Act relating to consolidated profit and loss accounts ; and

(ii) shows how much of the consolidated profit or loss for the financial year is dealt with in the accounts of the company.

(6) If any person being a director of a company fails to take all reasonable steps to secure compliance as respects any accounts laid before the company in general meeting with the provisions of this section and with the other requirements of this Act as to the matters to be stated in accounts, he shall, in respect of each offence, be liable on summary conviction to imprisonment for a term not exceeding six months or to a fine not exceeding two hundred pounds :

Provided that—

(a) in any proceedings against a person in respect of an offence under this section, it shall be a defence to prove that he had reasonable ground to believe and did believe that a competent and reliable person was charged with the duty of seeing that the said provisions or the said other requirements, as the case may be, were complied with and was in a position to discharge that duty; and

(b) a person shall not be sentenced to imprisonment for any such offence unless, in the opinion of the court dealing with the case, the offence was committed wilfully.

(7) For the purposes of this section and the following provisions of this Act, except where the context otherwise requires—

(a) any reference to a balance sheet or profit and loss account shall include any notes thereon or document annexed thereto giving information which is required by this Act and is thereby allowed to be so given; and

(b) any reference to a profit and loss account shall be taken, in the case of a company not trading for profit, as referring to its income and expenditure account, and references to profit or to loss and, if the company has subsidiaries, references to a consolidated profit and loss account shall be construed accordingly.

150.—Obligation to Lay Group Accounts Before Holding Company.

(1) Where at the end of its financial year a company has subsidiaries, accounts or statements (in this Act referred to as " group accounts ") dealing as hereinafter mentioned with the state of affairs and profit or loss of the company and the subsidiaries shall, subject to the next following subsection, be laid before the company in general meeting when the company's own balance sheet and profit and loss account are so laid.

(2) Notwithstanding anything in the foregoing subsection—

(a) group accounts shall not be required where the company is at the end of its financial year the wholly owned subsidiary of another body corporate incorporated in Great Britain; and

(b) group accounts need not deal with a subsidiary of the company if the company's directors are of opinion that—

(i) it is impracticable, or would be of no real value to members of the company, in view of the insignificant amounts involved, or would involve expense or delay out of proportion to the value to members of the company; or

(ii) the result would be misleading, or harmful to the business of the company or any of its subsidiaries; or

(iii) the business of the holding company and that of the subsidiary are so different that they cannot reasonably be treated as a single undertaking;

and, if the directors are of such an opinion about each of the company's subsidiaries, group accounts shall not be required:

Provided that the approval of the Board of Trade shall be required for not dealing in group accounts with a subsidiary on the ground that the result would be harmful or on the ground of the difference between the business of the holding company and that of the subsidiary.

(3) If any person being a director of a company fails to take all reasonable steps to secure compliance as respects the company with the provisions of this section, he shall, in respect of each offence, be liable on summary conviction to imprisonment for a term not exceeding six months or to a fine not exceeding two hundred pounds:

Provided that—

(a) in any proceedings against a person in respect of an offence under this section, it shall be a defence to prove that he had reasonable ground to believe and did believe that a competent and reliable person was charged with the duty of seeing that the requirements of this section were complied with and was in a position to discharge that duty ; and

(b) a person shall not be sentenced to imprisonment for an offence under this section unless, in the opinion of the court dealing with the case, the offence was committed wilfully.

(4) For the purposes of this section a body corporate shall be deemed to be the wholly owned subsidiary of another if it has no members except that other and that other's wholly owned subsidiaries and its or their nominees.

151.—Form of Group Accounts.

(1) Subject to the next following subsection, the group accounts laid before a holding company shall be consolidated accounts comprising—

(a) a consolidated balance sheet dealing with the state of affairs of the company and all the subsidiaries to be dealt with in group accounts ;

(b) a consolidated profit and loss account dealing with the profit or loss of the company and those subsidiaries.

(2) If the company's directors are of opinion that it is better for the purpose—

(a) of presenting the same or equivalent information about the state of affairs and profit or loss of the company and those subsidiaries ; and

(b) of so presenting it that it may be readily appreciated by the company's members ;

the group accounts may be prepared in a form other than that required by the foregoing subsection, and in particular may consist of more than one set of consolidated accounts dealing respectively with the company and one group of subsidiaries and with other groups of subsidiaries or of separate accounts dealing with each of the subsidiaries, or of statements expanding the information about the subsidiaries in the company's own accounts, or any combination of those forms.

(3) The group accounts may be wholly or partly incorporated in the company's own balance sheet and profit and loss account.

152.—Contents of Group Accounts.

(1) The group accounts laid before a company shall give a true and fair view of the state of affairs and profit or loss of the company and the subsidiaries dealt with thereby as a whole, so far as concerns members of the company.

(2) Where the financial year of a subsidiary does not coincide with that of the holding company, the group accounts shall, unless the Board of Trade on the application or with the consent of the holding company's directors otherwise direct, deal with the subsidiary's state of affairs as at the end of its financial year ending with or last before that of the holding company, and with the subsidiary's profit or loss for that financial year.

(3) Without prejudice to subsection (1) of this section, the group accounts, if prepared as consolidated accounts, shall comply with the requirements of the Eighth Schedule to this Act, so far as applicable thereto, and if not so prepared shall give the same or equivalent information :

Provided that the Board of Trade may, on the application or with the consent of a company's directors, modify the said requirements in relation to that company for the purpose of adapting them to the circumstances of the company.

153.—Financial Year of Holding Company and Subsidiary.

(1) A holding company's directors shall secure that except where in their opinion there are good reasons against it, the financial year of each of its subsidiaries shall coincide with the company's own financial year.

(2) Where it appears to the Board of Trade desirable for a holding company or a holding company's subsidiary to extend its financial year so that the subsidiary's financial year may end with that of the holding company, and for that purpose to postpone the submission of the relevant accounts to a general meeting from one calendar year to the next, the Board may on the application or with the consent of the directors of the company whose financial year is to be extended direct that, in the case of that company, the submission of accounts to a general meeting, the holding of an annual general meeting or the making of an annual return shall not be required in the earlier of the said calendar years.

154.—Meaning of " Holding Company " and " Subsidiary ".

(1) For the purposes of this Act, a company shall, subject to the provisions of subsection (3) of this section, be deemed to be a subsidiary of another if, but only if—

(a) that other either—

(i) is a member of it and controls the composition of its board of directors ; or

(ii) holds more than half in nominal value of its equity share capital ; or

(b) the first-mentioned company is a subsidiary of any company which is that other's subsidiary.

(2) For the purposes of the foregoing subsection, the composition of a company's board of directors shall be deemed to be controlled by another company if, but only if, that other company by the exercise of some power exercisable by it without the consent or concurrence of any other person can appoint or remove the holders of all or a majority of the directorships ; but for the purposes of this provision that other company shall be deemed to have power to appoint to a directorship with respect to which any of the following conditions is satisfied, that is to say—

(a) that a person cannot be appointed thereto without the exercise in his favour by that other company of such a power as aforesaid ; or

(b) that a person's appointment thereto follows necessarily from his appointment as director of that other company ; or

(c) that the directorship is held by that other company itself or by a subsidiary of it.

(3) In determining whether one company is a subsidiary of another—

(a) any shares held or power exercisable by that other in a fiduciary capacity shall be treated as not held or exercisable by it ;

(b) subject to the two following paragraphs, any shares held or power exercisable—

(i) by any person as a nominee for that other (except where that other is concerned only in a fiduciary capacity) ; or

(ii) by, or by a nominee for, a subsidiary of that other, not being a subsidiary which is concerned only in a fiduciary capacity ;

shall be treated as held or exercisable by that other ;

(c) any shares held or power exercisable by any person by virtue of the provisions of any debentures of the first-mentioned company or of a trust deed for securing any issue of such debentures shall be disregarded ;

(d) any shares held or power exercisable by, or by a nominee for, that other or its subsidiary (not being held or exercisable as mentioned in the last foregoing paragraph) shall be treated as not held or exercisable by that other if the ordinary business of that other or its subsidiary, as the case may be, includes the lending of money and the shares are held or power is exercisable as aforesaid by way of security only for the purposes of a transaction entered into in the ordinary course of that business.

(4) For the purposes of this Act, a company shall be deemed to be another's holding company if, but only if, that other is its subsidiary.

(5) In this section the expression " company " includes any body corporate, and the expression " equity share capital " means, in relation to a company, its issued share capital excluding any part thereof which, neither as respects dividends nor as respects capital, carries any right to participate beyond a specified amount in a distribution.

155.—Signing of Balance Sheet.

(1) Every balance sheet of a company shall be signed on behalf of the board by two of the directors of the company, or, if there is only one director, by that director.

(2) In the case of a banking company registered after the fifteenth day of August, eighteen hundred and seventy-nine, the balance sheet must be signed by the secretary or manager, if any, and where there are more than three directors of the company by at least three of those directors, and where there are not more than three directors by all the directors.

(3) If any copy of a balance sheet which has not been signed as required by this section is issued, circulated or published, the company and every officer of the company who is in default shall be liable to a fine not exceeding fifty pounds.

156.—Accounts, and Auditors' Report, to be Annexed to Balance Sheet.

(1) The profit and loss account and, so far as not incorporated in the balance sheet or profit and loss account, any group accounts laid before the company in general meeting, shall be annexed to the balance sheet, and the auditors' report shall be attached thereto.

(2) Any accounts so annexed shall be approved by the board of directors before the balance sheet is signed on their behalf.

(3) If any copy of a balance sheet is issued, circulated or published without having annexed thereto a copy of the profit and loss account or any group accounts required by this section to be so annexed, or without having attached thereto a copy of the auditors' report, the company and every officer of the company who is in default shall be liable to a fine not exceeding fifty pounds.

157.—Directors' Report to be Attached to Balance Sheet.

(1) There shall be attached to every balance sheet laid before a company in general meeting a report by the directors with respect to the state of the company's affairs, the amount, if any, which they recommend should be paid by way of dividend, and the amount, if any, which they propose to carry to reserves within the meaning of the Eighth Schedule to this Act.

(2) The said report shall deal, so far as is material for the appreciation of the state of the company's affairs by its members and will not in the directors' opinion be harmful to the business of the company or of any of its subsidiaries, with any change during the financial year in the nature of the company's business, or in the company's subsidiaries, or in the classes of business in which the company has an interest, whether as member of another company or otherwise.

(3) If any person being a director of a company fails to take all reasonable steps to comply with the provisions of subsection (1) of this section, he shall, in respect of each offence, be liable on summary conviction to imprisonment for a term not exceeding six months or to a fine not exceeding two hundred pounds :

Provided that—

(a) in any proceedings against a person in respect of an offence under the said subsection (1), it shall be a defence to prove that he had reasonable ground to believe and did believe that a competent and reliable person was charged with the duty of seeing that the provisions of that subsection were complied with and was in a position to discharge that duty ; and

(b) a person shall not be liable to be sentenced to imprisonment for such an offence unless, in the opinion of the court dealing with the case, the offence was committed wilfully.

158.—Right to Receive Copies of Balance Sheet and Auditors' Report.

(1) A copy of every balance sheet, including every document required by law to be annexed thereto, which is to be laid before a company in general meeting, together with a copy of the auditors' report, shall, not less than twenty-one days before the date of the meeting, be sent to every member of the company (whether he is or is not entitled to receive notices of general meetings of the company), every holder of debentures of the company (whether he is or is not so entitled) and all persons other than members or holders of debentures of the company, being persons so entitled :

Provided that—

(a) in the case of a company not having a share capital this subsection shall not require the sending of a copy of the documents aforesaid to a member of the company who is not entitled to receive notices of general meetings of the company or to a holder of debentures of the company who is not so entitled ;

(b) this subsection shall not require a copy of those documents to be sent—

(i) to a member of the company or a holder of debentures of the company, being in either case a person who is not entitled to receive notices of general meetings of the company and of whose address the company is unaware ;

(ii) to more than one of the joint holders of any shares or debentures none of whom are entitled to receive such notices ; or

(iii) in the case of joint holders of any shares or debentures some of whom are and some of whom are not entitled to receive such notices, to those who are not so entitled ; and

(c) if the copies of the documents aforesaid are sent less than twenty-one days before the date of the meeting, they shall, notwithstanding that fact, be deemed to have been duly sent if it is so agreed by all the members entitled to attend and vote at the meeting.

(2) Any member of a company, whether he is or is not entitled to have sent to him copies of the company's balance sheets, and any holder of debentures of the company, whether he is or is not so entitled, shall be entitled to be furnished on demand without charge with a copy of the last balance sheet of the company, including every document required by law to be annexed thereto, together with a copy of the auditors' report on the balance sheet.

(3) If default is made in complying with subsection (1) of this section, the company and every officer of the company who is in default shall be liable to a fine not exceeding twenty pounds, and if, when any person makes a demand for any document with which he is by virtue of subsection (2) of this section entitled to be furnished, default is made in complying with the demand within seven days after the making thereof, the company and every officer of the company who is in default shall be liable to a default fine, unless it is proved that that person has already made a demand for and been furnished with a copy of the document.

(4) The foregoing provisions of this section shall not have effect in relation to a balance sheet of a private company laid before it before the commencement of this Act, and the right of any person to be furnished with a copy of any such balance sheet and the liability of the company in respect of a failure to satisfy that right shall be the same as they would have been if this Act had not been passed.

159.—Appointment and Remuneration of Auditors.

(1) Every company shall at each annual general meeting appoint an auditor or auditors to hold office from the conclusion of that, until the conclusion of the next, annual general meeting.

(2) At any annual general meeting a retiring auditor, however appointed, shall be reappointed without any resolution being passed unless—

    (a) he is not qualified for reappointment ; or

    (b) a resolution has been passed at that meeting appointing somebody instead of him or providing expressly that he shall not be reappointed ; or

    (c) he has given the company notice in writing of his unwillingness to be reappointed :

Provided that where notice is given of an intended resolution to appoint some person or persons in place of a retiring auditor, and by reason of the death, incapacity or disqualification of that person or of all those persons, as the case may be, the resolution cannot be proceeded with, the retiring auditor shall not be automatically reappointed by virtue of this subsection.

(3) Where at an annual general meeting no auditors are appointed or reappointed, the Board of Trade may appoint a person to fill the vacancy.

(4) The company shall, within one week of the Board's power under the last foregoing subsection becoming exercisable, give them notice of that fact, and, if a company fails to give notice as required by this subsection, the company and every officer of the company who is in default shall be liable to a default fine.

(5) Subject as hereinafter provided, the first auditors of a company may be appointed by the directors at any time before the first annual general meeting, and auditors so appointed shall hold office until the conclusion of that meeting :

Provided that—

    (a) the company may at a general meeting remove any such auditors and appoint in their place any other persons who have been nominated for appointment by any member of the company and of whose nomination notice has been given to the members of the company not less than fourteen days before the date of the meeting ; and

(b) if the directors fail to exercise their powers under this subsection, the company in general meeting may appoint the first auditors, and thereupon the said powers of the directors shall cease.

(6) The directors may fill any casual vacancy in the office of auditor, but while any such vacancy continues, the surviving or continuing auditor or auditors, if any, may act.

(7) The remuneration of the auditors of a company—

(a) in the case of an auditor appointed by the directors or by the Board of Trade, may be fixed by the directors or by the Board, as the case may be ;

(b) subject to the foregoing paragraph, shall be fixed by the company in general meeting or in such manner as the company in general meeting may determine.

For the purposes of this subsection, any sums paid by the company in respect of the auditors' expenses shall be deemed to be included in the expression " remuneration ".

160.—Provisions as to Resolutions Relating to the Appointment and Removal of Auditors.

(1) Special notice shall be required for a resolution at a company's annual general meeting appointing as auditor a person other than a retiring auditor or providing expressly that a retiring auditor shall not be reappointed.

(2) On receipt of notice of such an intended resolution as aforesaid, the company shall forthwith send a copy thereof to the retiring auditor (if any).

(3) Where notice is given of such an intended resolution as aforesaid and the retiring auditor makes with respect to the intended resolution representations in writing to the company (not exceeding a reasonable length) and requests their notification to members of the company, the company shall, unless the representations are received by it too late for it to do so—

(a) in any notice of the resolution given to members of the company, state the fact of the representations having been made ; and

(b) send a copy of the representations to every member of the company to whom notice of the meeting is sent (whether before or after receipt of the representations by the company) ;

and if a copy of the representations is not sent as aforesaid because received too late or because of the company's default, the auditor may (without prejudice to his right to be heard orally) require that the representations shall be read out at the meeting :

Provided that copies of the representations need not be sent out and the representations need not be read out at the meeting if, on the application either of the company or of any other person who claims to be aggrieved, the court is satisfied that the rights conferred by this section are being abused to secure needless publicity for defamatory matter ; and the court may order the company's costs on an application under this section to be paid in whole or in part by the auditor, notwithstanding that he is not a party to the application.

(4) The last foregoing subsection shall apply to a resolution to remove the first auditors by virtue of subsection (5) of the last foregoing section as it applies in relation to a resolution that a retiring auditor shall not be reappointed.

R*

161.—Disqualifications for Appointment as Auditor.

(1) A person shall not be qualified for appointment as auditor of a company unless either—

    (*a*) he is a member of a body of accountants established in the United Kingdom and for the time being recognised for the purposes of this provision by the Board of Trade ; or

    (*b*) he is for the time being authorised by the Board of Trade to be so appointed either as having similar qualifications obtained outside the United Kingdom or as having obtained adequate knowledge and experience in the course of his employment by a member of a body of accountants recognised for the purposes of the foregoing paragraph or as having before the sixth day of August, nineteen hundred and forty-seven, practised in Great Britain as an accountant ;

Provided that this subsection shall not apply in the case of a private company which at the time of the auditor's appointment is an exempt private company.

(2) None of the following persons shall be qualified for appointment as auditor of a company—

    (*a*) an officer or servant of the company ;

    (*b*) a person who is a partner of or in the employment of an officer or servant of the company ;

    (*c*) a body corporate :

Provided that paragraph (*b*) of this subsection shall not apply in the case of a private company which at the time of the auditor's appointment is an exempt private company.

References in this subsection to an officer or servant shall be construed as not including references to an auditor.

(3) A person shall also not be qualified for appointment as auditor of a company if he is, by virtue of the last foregoing subsection, disqualified for appointment as auditor of any other body corporate which is that company's subsidiary or holding company or a subsidiary of that company's holding company, or would be so disqualified if the body corporate were a company.

(4) Notwithstanding anything in the foregoing provisions of this section, a Scottish firm shall be qualified for appointment as auditor of a company if, but only if, all the partners are qualified for appointment as auditor thereof.

(5) Any body corporate which acts as auditor of a company shall be liable to a fine not exceeding one hundred pounds.

162.—Auditors' Report and Right of Access to Books, and to Attend and be Heard at General Meetings.

(1) The auditors shall make a report to the members on the accounts examined by them, and on every balance sheet, every profit and loss account and all group accounts laid before the company in general meeting during their tenure of office, and the report shall contain statements as to the matters mentioned in the Ninth Schedule to this Act.

(2) The auditors' report shall be read before the company in general meeting and shall be open to inspection by any member.

(3) Every auditor of a company shall have a right of access at all times to the books and accounts and vouchers of the company, and shall be entitled to require from the officers of the company such information and explanation as he thinks necessary for the performance of the duties of the auditors.

(4) The auditors of a company shall be entitled to attend any general meeting of the company and to receive all notices of and other communications relating to any general meeting which any member of the company is entitled to receive and to be heard at any general meeting which they attend on any part of the business of the meeting which concerns them as auditors.

163.—Construction of References to Documents Annexed to Accounts.

References in this Act to a document annexed or required to be annexed to a company's accounts or any of them shall not include the directors' report or the auditors' report :

Provided that any information which is required by this Act to be given in accounts, and is thereby allowed to be given in a statement annexed, may be given in the directors' report instead of in the accounts and, if any such information is so given, the report shall be annexed to the accounts and this Act shall apply in relation thereto accordingly, except that the auditors shall report thereon only so far as it gives the said information.

189.—Prohibition of Tax-Free Payments to Directors.

(1) It shall not be lawful for a company to pay a director remuneration (whether as director or otherwise) free of income tax or of income tax other than surtax, or otherwise calculated by reference to or varying with the amount of his income tax or his income tax other than surtax, or to or with the rate or standard rate of income tax, except under a contract which was in force on the eighteenth day of July, nineteen hundred and forty-five, and provides expressly, and not by reference to the articles, for payment of remuneration as aforesaid.

(2) Any provision contained in a company's articles, or in any contract other than such a contract as aforesaid, or in any resolution of a company or a company's directors, for payment to a director of remuneration as aforesaid shall have effect as if it provided for payment, as a gross sum subject to income tax and surtax, of the net sum for which it actually provides.

(3) This section shall not apply to remuneration due before the commencement of this Act or in respect of a period before the commencement of this Act.

190.—Prohibition of Loans to Directors.

(1) It shall not be lawful for a company to make a loan to any person who is its director or a director of its holding company, or to enter into any guarantee or provide any security in connection with a loan made to such a person as aforesaid by any other person :

Provided that nothing in this section shall apply either—

(a) to anything done by a company which is for the time being an exempt private company ; or

(b) to anything done by a subsidiary, where the director is its holding company ; or

(c) subject to the next following subsection, to anything done to provide any such person as aforesaid with funds to meet expenditure incurred or to be incurred by him for the purposes of the company or for the purpose of enabling him properly to perform his duties as an officer of the company ; or

(d) in the case of a company whose ordinary business includes the lending of money or the giving of guarantees in connection with loans made by other persons, to anything done by the company in the ordinary course of that business.

(2) Proviso (c) to the foregoing subsection shall not authorise the making of any loan, or the entering into any guarantee, or the provision of any security, except either—

    (a) with the prior approval of the company given at a general meeting at which the purposes of the expenditure and the amount of the loan or the extent of the guarantee or security, as the case may be, are disclosed ; or

    (b) on condition that, if the approval of the company is not given as aforesaid at or before the next following annual general meeting, the loan shall be repaid or the liability under the guarantee or security shall be discharged, as the case may be, within six months from the conclusion of that meeting.

(3) Where the approval of the company is not given as required by any such condition, the directors authorising the making of the loan, or the entering into the guarantee, or the provision of the security, shall be jointly and severally liable to indemnify the company against any loss arising therefrom.

191.—Approval of Company Requisite for Payment by it to Director for Loss of Office, etc.

It shall not be lawful for a company to make to any director of the company any payment by way of compensation for loss of office, or as consideration for or in connection with his retirement from office, without particulars with respect to the proposed payment (including the amount thereof) being disclosed to members of the company and the proposal being approved by the company.

192.—Approval of Company Requisite for any Payment, in Connection with Transfer of its Property, to Director for Loss of Office, etc.

(1) It is hereby declared that it is not lawful in connection with the transfer of the whole or any part of the undertaking or property of a company for any payment to be made to any director of the company by way of compensation for loss of office, or as consideration for or in connection with his retirement from office, unless particulars with respect to the proposed payment (including the amount thereof) have been disclosed to the members of the company and the proposal approved by the company.

(2) Where a payment which is hereby declared to be illegal is made to a director of the company, the amount received shall be deemed to have been received by him in trust for the company.

196.—Particulars in Accounts of Directors' Salaries, Pensions, etc.

(1) In any accounts of a company laid before it in general meeting, or in a statement annexed thereto, there shall, subject to and in accordance with the provisions of this section, be shown so far as the information is contained in the company's books and papers or the company has the right to obtain it from the persons concerned—

    (a) the aggregate amount of the directors' emoluments ;

    (b) the aggregate amount of directors' or past directors' pensions ; and

    (c) the aggregate amount of any compensation to directors or past directors in respect of loss of office.

(2) The amount to be shown under paragraph (a) of subsection (1) of this section—

    (a) shall include any emoluments paid to or receivable by any person in respect of his services as director of the company or in respect of his services, while director of the company, as director of any sub-sidiary thereof or otherwise in connection with the management of the affairs of the company or any subsidiary thereof; and

(b) shall distinguish between emoluments in respect of services as director, whether of the company or its subsidiary, and other emoluments;

and for the purposes of this section the expression " emoluments ", in relation to a director, includes fees and percentages, any sums paid by way of expenses allowance in so far as those sums are charged to United Kingdom income tax, any contribution paid in respect of him under any pension scheme and the estimated money value of any other benefits received by him otherwise than in cash.

(3) The amount to be shown under paragraph (b) of the said subsection (1)—

(a) shall not include any pension paid or receivable under a pension scheme if the scheme is such that the contributions thereunder are sub-stantially adequate for the maintenance of the scheme, but save as aforesaid shall include any pension paid or receivable in respect of any such services of a director or past director of the company as are mentioned in the last foregoing subsection, whether to or by him or, on his nomination or by virtue of dependence on or other connection with him, to or by any other person; and

(b) shall distinguish between pensions in respect of services as director, whether of the company or its subsidiary, and other pensions;

and for the purposes of this section the expression " pension " includes any superannuation allowance, superannuation gratuity or similar payment, and the expression " pension scheme " means a scheme for the provision of pensions in respect of services as director or otherwise which is maintained in whole or in part by means of contributions, and the expression " contribution " in rela-tion to a pension scheme means any payment (including an insurance premium) paid for the purposes of the scheme by or in respect of persons rendering services in respect of which pensions will or may become payable under the scheme, except that it does not include any payment in respect of two or more persons if the amount paid in respect of each of them is not ascertainable.

(4) The amount to be shown under paragraph (c) of the said subsection (1)—

(a) shall include any sums paid to or receivable by a director or past director by way of compensation for the loss of office as director of the com-pany or for the loss, while director of the company or on or in con-nection with his ceasing to be a director of the company, of any other office in connection with the management of the company's affairs or of any office as director or otherwise in connection with the management of the affairs of any subsidiary thereof; and

(b) shall distinguish between compensation in respect of the office of director, whether of the company or its subsidiary, and compensa-tion in respect of other offices;

and for the purposes of this section references to compensation for loss of office shall include sums paid as consideration for or in connection with a person's retirement from office.

(5) The amounts to be shown under each paragraph of the said subsection (1)—

(a) shall include all relevant sums paid by or receivable from—

(i) the company; and

(ii) the company's subsidiaries; and

(iii) any other person;

except sums to be accounted for to the company or any of its subsidiaries or, by virtue of section one hundred and ninety-three of this Act, to past or present members of the company or any of its subsidiaries or any class of those members ; and

(b) shall distinguish, in the case of the amount to be shown under paragraph (c) of the said subsection (1), between the sums respectively paid by or receivable from the company, the company's subsidiaries and persons other than the company and its subsidiaries.

(6) The amounts to be shown under this section for any financial year shall be the sums receivable in respect of that year, whenever paid, or, in the case of sums not receivable in respect of a period, the sums paid during that year, so, however, that where—

(a) any sums are not shown in the accounts for the relevant financial year on the ground that the person receiving them is liable to account therefor as mentioned in paragraph (a) of the last foregoing subsection, but the liability is thereafter wholly or partly released or is not enforced within a period of two years ; or

(b) any sums paid by way of expenses allowance are charged to United Kingdom income tax after the end of the relevant financial year ;

those sums shall, to the extent to which the liability is released or not enforced or they are charged as aforesaid, as the case may be, be shown in the first accounts in which it is practicable to show them or in a statement annexed thereto, and shall be distinguished from the amounts to be shown therein apart from this provision.

(7) Where it is necessary so to do for the purpose of making any distinction required by this section in any amount to be shown thereunder, the directors may apportion any payments between the matters in respect of which they have been paid or are receivable in such manner as they think appropriate.

(8) If in the case of any accounts the requirements of this section are not complied with, it shall be the duty of the auditors of the company by whom the accounts are examined to include in their report thereon, so far as they are reasonably able to do so, a statement giving the required particulars.

(9) In this section any reference to a company's subsidiary—

(a) in relation to a person who is or was, while a director of the company, a director also, by virtue of the company's nomination, direct or indirect, of any other body corporate, shall, subject to the following paragraph, include that body corporate, whether or not it is or was in fact the company's subsidiary ; and

(b) shall for the purposes of subsections (2) and (3) be taken as referring to a subsidiary at the time the services were rendered, and for the purposes of subsection (4) be taken as referring to a subsidiary immediately before the loss of office as director of the company.

197.—Particulars in Accounts of Loans to Officers, etc.

(1) The accounts which, in pursuance of this Act, are to be laid before every company in general meeting shall, subject to the provisions of this section, contain particulars showing—

(a) the amount of any loans made during the company's financial year to—

(i) any officer of the company ; or

(ii) any person who, after the making of the loan, became during that year an officer of the company ;

by the company or a subsidiary thereof or by any other person under a guarantee from or on a security provided by the company or a subsidiary thereof (including any such loans which were repaid during that year) ; and

(b) the amount of any loans made in manner aforesaid to any such officer or person as aforesaid at any time before the company's financial year and outstanding at the expiration thereof.

(2) The foregoing subsection shall not require the inclusion in accounts of particulars of—

(a) a loan made in the ordinary course of its business by the company or a subsidiary thereof, where the ordinary business of the company or, as the case may be, the subsidiary, includes the lending of money ; or

(b) a loan made by the company or a subsidiary thereof to an employee of the company or subsidiary, as the case may be, if the loan does not exceed two thousand pounds and is certified by the directors of the company or subsidiary, as the case may be, to have been made in accordance with any practice adopted or about to be adopted by the company or subsidiary with respect to loans to its employees ;

not being, in either case, a loan made by the company under a guarantee from or on a security provided by a subsidiary thereof or a loan made by a subsidiary of the company under a guarantee from or on a security provided by the company or any other subsidiary thereof.

(3) If in the case of any such accounts as aforesaid the requirements of this section are not complied with, it shall be the duty of the auditors of the company by whom the accounts are examined to include in their report on the balance sheet of the company, so far as they are reasonably able to do so, a statement giving the required particulars.

(4) References in this section to a subsidiary shall be taken as referring to a subsidiary at the end of the company's financial year (whether or not a subsidiary at the date of the loan).

331.—Liability where Proper Accounts not Kept.

(1) If where a company is wound up it is shown that proper books of account were not kept by the company throughout the period of two years immediately preceding the commencement of the winding up, or the period between the incorporation of the company and the commencement of the winding up, whichever is the shorter, every officer of the company who is in default shall, unless he shows that he acted honestly and that in the circumstances in which the business of the company was carried on the default was excusable, be liable on conviction on indictment to imprisonment for a term not exceeding one year, or on summary conviction to imprisonment for a term not exceeding six months.

(2) For the purposes of this section, proper books of account shall be deemed not to have been kept in the case of any company if there have not been kept such books or accounts as are necessary to exhibit and explain the transactions and financial position of the trade or business of the company, including books containing entries from day to day in sufficient detail of all cash received and cash paid, and, where the trade or business has involved dealings in goods, statements of the annual stocktakings and (except in the case of goods sold by way of ordinary retail trade) of all goods sold and purchased, showing the goods and the buyers and sellers thereof in sufficient detail to enable those goods and those buyers and sellers to be identified.

FOURTH SCHEDULE.

MATTERS TO BE SPECIFIED IN PROSPECTUS AND REPORTS TO BE SET OUT THEREIN.

PART II.

Reports to be Set Out in Prospectus.

19.—(1) A report by the auditors of the company with respect to—

(a) profits and losses and assets and liabilities, in accordance with sub-paragraph (2) or (3) of this paragraph, as the case requires ; and

(b) the rates of the dividends, if any, paid by the company in respect of each class of shares in the company in respect of each of the five financial years immediately preceding the issue of the prospectus, giving particulars of each such class of shares on which such dividends have been paid and particulars of the cases in which no dividends have been paid in respect of any class of shares in respect of any of those years ;

and, if no accounts have been made up in respect of any part of the period of five years ending on a date three months before the issue of the prospectus, containing a statement of that fact.

(2) If the company has no subsidiaries, the report shall—

(a) so far as regards profits and losses, deal with the profits or losses of the company in respect of each of the five financial years immediately preceding the issue of the prospectus ; and

(b) so far as regards assets and liabilities, deal with the assets and liabilities of the company at the last date to which the accounts of the company were made up.

(3) If the company has subsidiaries, the report shall—

(a) so far as regards profits and losses, deal separately with the company's profits or losses as provided by the last foregoing sub-paragraph, and in addition, deal either—

(i) as a whole with the combined profits or losses of its subsidiaries, so far as they concern members of the company ; or

(ii) individually with the profits or losses of each subsidiary, so far as they concern members of the company ;

or, instead of dealing separately with the company's profits or losses deal as a whole with the profits or losses of the company and, so far as they concern members of the company, with the combined profits or losses of its subsidiaries ; and

(b) so far as regards assets and liabilities, deal separately with the company's assets and liabilities as provided by the last foregoing sub-paragraph and, in addition, deal either—

(i) as a whole with the combined assets and liabilities of its subsidiaries, with or without the company's assets and liabilities ; or

(ii) individually with the assets and liabilities of each subsidiary ;

and shall indicate as respects the assets and liabilities of the subsidiaries the allowance to be made for persons other than members of the company.

20. If the proceeds, or any part of the proceeds, of the issue of the shares or debentures are or is to be applied directly or indirectly in the purchase of

any business, a report made by accountants (who shall be named in the prospectus) upon—

    (a) the profits or losses of the business in respect of each of the five financial years immediately preceding the issue of the prospectus ; and

    (b) the assets and liabilities of the business at the last date to which the accounts of the business were made up.

  21.—(1) If—

    (a) the proceeds, or any part of the proceeds, of the issue of the shares or debentures are or is to be applied directly or indirectly in any manner resulting in the acquisition by the company of shares in any other body corporate ; and

    (b) by reason of that acquisition or anything to be done in consequence thereof or in connection therewith that body corporate will become a subsidiary of the company ;

a report made by accountants (who shall be named in the prospectus) upon—

    (i) the profits or losses of the other body corporate in respect of each of the five financial years immediately preceding the issue of the prospectus ; and

    (ii) the assets and liabilities of the other body corporate at the last date to which the accounts of the body corporate were made up.

  (2) The said report shall—

    (a) indicate how the profits or losses of the other body corporate dealt with by the report would, in respect of the shares to be acquired, have concerned members of the company and what allowance would have fallen to be made, in relation to assets and liabilities so dealt with, for holders of other shares, if the company had at all material times held the shares to be acquired ; and

    (b) where the other body corporate has subsidiaries, deal with the profits or losses and the assets and liabilities of the body corporate and its subsidiaries in the manner provided by sub-paragraph (3) of paragraph 19 of this Schedule in relation to the company and its subsidiaries.

PART III.

General Provisions Regarding Reports in Prospectus.

  27. If in the case of a company which has been carrying on business, or of a business which has been carried on for less than five years, the accounts of the company or business have only been made up in respect of four years, three years, two years or one year, Part II of this Schedule shall have effect as if references to four years, three years, two years or one year, as the case may be, were substituted for references to five years.

  28. The expression " financial year " in Part II of this Schedule means the year in respect of which the accounts of the company or of the business, as the case may be, are made up, and where by reason of any alteration of the date on which the financial year of the company or business terminates the accounts of the company or business have been made up for a period greater or less than a year, that greater or less period shall for the purpose of that Part of this Schedule be deemed to be a financial year.

  29. Any report required by Part II of this Schedule shall either indicate by way of note any adjustments as respects the figures of any profits or losses or

assets and liabilities dealt with by the report which appear to the persons making the report necessary or shall make those adjustments and indicate that adjustments have been made.

30. Any report by accountants required by Part II of this Schedule shall be made by accountants qualified under this Act for appointment as auditors of a company which is not an exempt private company and shall not be made by any accountant who is an officer or servant, or a partner of or in the employment of an officer or servant, of the company or of the company's subsidiary or holding company or of a subsidiary of the company's holding company; and for the purposes of this paragraph the expression " officer " shall include a proposed director but not an auditor.

SEVENTH SCHEDULE.

CONDITIONS AS TO INTERESTS IN SHARES AND DEBENTURES OF EXEMPT PRIVATE COMPANY.

Basic Conditions.

1. The basic conditions as to the shares or debentures of the company whose exemption is in question are—

    (a) that no body corporate is the holder of any of the shares or debentures; and

    (b) that no person other than the holder has any interest in any of the shares or debentures;

but these conditions are subject to the exceptions provided for by the following paragraphs of this Schedule.

Exceptions for Normal Dealings of a Business Nature.

2.—(1) The rules contained in the following sub-paragraphs of this paragraph shall apply for the purposes both of the basic conditions and of the exceptions from those conditions.

(2) Where any share or debenture or any interest in any share or debenture is subject to a charge in favour of a banking or finance company by way of security for the purposes of a transaction entered into in the ordinary course of its business as such—

    (a) any interest under the charge, whether of the banking or finance company or a nominee for it, shall be disregarded; and

    (b) if the banking or finance company or its nominee is the holder of the share or debenture, the person entitled to the equity of redemption shall be treated as the holder, whether he has a present right to redeem or not.

(3) Any interest under a contract for the transfer of any share or debenture or of any interest in any share or debenture shall, until execution of an instrument of transfer by the parties, be disregarded unless execution thereof is unreasonably delayed.

(4) Subject to sub-paragraph (2) of this paragraph, on execution of an instrument of transfer of a share or debenture, the transferee and not the transferor shall be treated as the holder, notwithstanding that the transfer requires registration with the company, unless registration is refused.

(5) Any interest of the company itself in any of its shares or debentures, and any lien or charge arising by operation of law and affecting any of the shares or debentures shall be disregarded.

Exceptions for Cases of Death and for Family Settlements.

3.—(1) The basic conditions shall be subject to exceptions for—

(a) any shares or debentures forming part of the estate of a deceased holder thereof, so long as administration of his estate has not been completed ; and

(b) any shares or debentures held by trustees on the trusts of a will or family settlement disposing of the shares or debentures, so long as no body corporate has for the time being any immediate interest under the said trusts other than—

(i) a body corporate established for charitable purposes only and having no right to exercise or control the exercise of any part of the voting power at any general meeting of the company ;

(ii) a body corporate which is a trustee of the said trusts and has such an interest only by way of remuneration for acting as trustee thereof.

(2) For the purposes of this paragraph—

(a) shares or debentures held by trustees on trusts arising on an intestacy shall, if the shares or debentures or an interest therein formed part of the intestate's estate at the time of his death, be treated as if the trusts arose under a will disposing of the shares or debentures ;

(b) the expression " family settlement " means a settlement made either—

(i) in consideration or contemplation of an intended marriage of the settlor or any of the settlor's issue or in pursuance of a contract entered into in consideration or contemplation of any such marriage ; or

(ii) otherwise in favour of any of the following persons, that is to say the settlor, his parents and grandparents, and any other individual who at the date of the settlement is a member of the company or, in the case of a settlement of debentures, a member or debenture holder of the company, and the wife or husband and issue, and the wife or husband of any of the issue, of the settlor, his parents, or any such other individual, and persons taking in the event of a failure of the issue or any class of the issue of any person taking under the settlement ;

(c) the expressions " parent ", " grandparent " and " issue " shall be construed as if the stepchild, adopted child or illegitimate child of any person were that person's child ;

(d) any reference to a wife or husband shall include a former wife or husband and a reputed wife or husband ;

(e) the expression " will " includes any testamentary disposition ;

(f) any reference to a will or family settlement disposing of any share; or debentures shall include a will or family settlement disposing of an interest under another will or family settlement disposing of the shares or debentures.

Exception for Cases of Disability.

4. Where the person entitled to any share or debenture or any interest in any share or debenture is of unsound mind or otherwise under any disability and by reason thereof the share, debenture or interest is vested in an administrator, curator or other person on behalf of the person entitled thereto, then in relation to the share, debenture or interest the person in whom it is so vested and the person entitled thereto shall be treated for the purposes of this Schedule as if they were the same person.

Exception for Trusts for Employees.

5. The basic conditions shall be subject to an exception for any shares or debentures held by trustees for the purposes of a scheme maintained for the benefit of employees of the company, including any director holding a salaried employment or office in the company.

Exception for Shares held by Exempt Private Companies.

6.—(1) The first of the basic conditions shall be subject to an exception for shares held by another private company which is itself an exempt private company :

Provided that this exception shall not apply, if, taking all the following companies together, that is to say—

> (a) the company whose exemption is in question (hereafter in this Schedule referred to as " the relevant company ") ;

> (b) any company holding shares to which this exception has to be applied in determining the relevant company's right to be treated as an exempt private company ; and

> (c) any further company taken into account for the purposes of this proviso in determining the right to be so treated of any company holding any such shares as aforesaid ;

the total number of persons holding shares in those companies is more than fifty, joint shareholders being treated as a single person and the companies themselves and (subject to sub-paragraph (4) of this paragraph) their employees and former employees being disregarded.

(2) Where the relevant company and another company hold shares in each other, the other company shall be treated for the purposes of the foregoing sub-paragraph as an exempt private company if—

> (a) in determining its right to be so treated the exception in that sub-paragraph would apply to the shares in it held by the relevant company, on the assumption that the relevant company was an exempt private company ; and

> (b) in all other respects the other company is entitled to be so treated ;

and where another company's right to be so treated depends on the application to any shares in it of that sub-paragraph, and the application thereof to those shares depends indirectly on the relevant company's right to be so treated, this sub-paragraph shall apply as if those shares were held by the relevant company.

(3) Where by virtue of this paragraph any shares are excepted from the first of the basic conditions, the second of those conditions shall be subject to an exception for any interest in those shares which any person has by virtue of debentures of the company holding those shares, or as trustee of a deed for securing an issue of debentures of that company.

(4) In the proviso to sub-paragraph (1) of this paragraph, the direction that employees and former employees of the companies shall be disregarded in computing the number of shareholders shall not apply to a person holding shares in a company of which he is not for the time being an employee unless, having been formerly in the employment of that company, he held, while in that employment, and has continued after the determination of that employment to hold, shares in that company.

Exception for Banking or Finance Company Providing Capital.

7.—(1) The first of the basic conditions shall be subject to an exception for any shares or debentures held by or by a nominee for a banking or finance company, where the banking or finance company acquired the shares or debentures or its interest therein in the ordinary course of its business as such and by arrangement with the relevant company or its promoters :

Provided that this exception shall not apply if the banking or finance company has the right (or, where there is more than one such company holding shares or debentures to which this exception has to be applied in determining the relevant company's right to be treated as an exempt private company, they have between them the right) to exercise or control the exercise of one fifth or more of the total voting power at any general meeting of the relevant company.

(2) Where by virtue of the foregoing sub-paragraph any shares or debentures are excepted from the first of the basic conditions, the second of those conditions shall be subject to an exception for the banking or finance company itself, where the shares or debentures are held by a nominee for it, and for any interest in those shares or debentures which any person has by virtue of debentures of the banking or finance company or as trustee of a deed for securing an issue of debentures of that company.

Exceptions for Bankruptcies, Liquidations, etc.

8. The basic conditions shall be subject to exceptions for—

(a) any shares or debentures forming part of the assets in a bankruptcy or liquidation of a holder thereof ; and

(b) any shares or debentures held either—

(i) on trusts created for the benefit of his creditors generally by a person having an interest therein ; or

(ii) otherwise for the purposes of any composition or scheme made or approved under any Act by a court or an officer of a court for arranging the affairs of such a person.

Meaning of " Banking or Finance Company ".

9. In this Schedule the expression " banking or finance company " means any body corporate or partnership whose ordinary business includes the business of banking and any other body corporate whose ordinary business includes the business of lending money or of subscribing for shares or debentures, except that it does not include any such other body corporate unless either—

(a) its shares are quoted or dealt in on a recognised stock exchange ; or

(b) it is designated for the purposes of this paragraph by order of the Board of Trade ; or

(c) it is a subsidiary of a body corporate whose shares are so quoted or dealt in or which is so designated.

EIGHTH SCHEDULE.

ACCOUNTS.

PRELIMINARY.

1. Paragraphs 2 to 11 of this Schedule apply to the balance sheet and 12 to 14 to the profit and loss account, and are subject to the exceptions and modifications provided for by Part II of this Schedule in the case of a holding company and by Part III thereof in the case of companies of the classes there mentioned ; and this Schedule has effect in addition to the provisions of sections one hundred and ninety-six and one hundred and ninety-seven of this Act.

PART I.

GENERAL PROVISIONS AS TO BALANCE SHEET AND PROFIT AND LOSS ACCOUNT.

Balance Sheet.

2. The authorised share capital, issued share capital, liabilities and assets shall be summarised, with such particulars as are necessary to disclose the general nature of the assets and liabilities, and there shall be specified—

(*a*) any part of the issued capital that consists of redeemable preference shares, and the earliest date on which the company has power to redeem those shares ;

(*b*) so far as the information is not given in the profit and loss account any share capital on which interest has been paid out of capital during the financial year, and the rate at which interest has been so paid ;

(*c*) the amount of the share premium account ;

(*d*) particulars of any redeemed debentures which the company has power to re-issue.

3. There shall be stated under separate headings, so far as they are not written off—

(*a*) the preliminary expenses ;

(*b*) any expenses incurred in connection with any issue of share capital or debentures ;

(*c*) any sums paid by way of commission in respect of any shares or debentures ;

(*d*) any sums allowed by way of discount in respect of any debentures ; and

(*e*) the amount of the discount allowed on any issue of shares at a discount.

4.—(1) The reserves, provisions, liabilities and fixed and current assets shall be classified under headings appropriate to the company's business :

Provided that—

(*a*) where the amount of any class is not material, it may be included under the same heading as some other class ; and

(*b*) where any assets of one class are not separable from assets of another class, those assets may be included under the same heading.

(2) Fixed assets shall also be distinguished from current assets.

(3) The method or methods used to arrive at the amount of the fixed assets under each heading shall be stated.

5.—(1) The method of arriving at the amount of any fixed asset shall, subject to the next following sub-paragraph, be to take the difference between—

(*a*) its cost or, if it stands in the company's books at a valuation, the amount of the valuation ; and

(*b*) the aggregate amount provided or written off since the date of acquisition or valuation, as the case may be, for depreciation or diminution in value :

and for the purposes of this paragraph the net amount at which any assets stand in the company's books at the commencement of this Act (after deduction of the amounts previously provided or written off for depreciation or diminution in value) shall, if the figures relating to the period before the commencement of this Act cannot be obtained without unreasonable expense or delay, be treated as if it were the amount of a valuation of those assets made at the commencement of this Act and, where any of those assets are sold, the said net amount less the amount of the sales shall be treated as if it were the amount of a valuation so made of the remaining assets.

(2) The foregoing sub-paragraph shall not apply—

(a) to assets for which the figures relating to the period beginning with the commencement of this Act cannot be obtained without unreasonable expense or delay ; or

(b) to assets the replacement of which is provided for wholly or partly—

(i) by making provision for renewals and charging the cost of replacement against the provision so made ; or

(ii) by charging the cost of replacement direct to revenue ; or

(c) to any investments of which the market value (or, in the case of investments not having a market value, their value as estimated by the directors) is shown either as the amount of the investments or by way of note ; or

(d) to goodwill, patents or trade marks.

(3) For the assets under each heading whose amount is arrived at in accordance with sub-paragraph (1) of this paragraph, there shall be shown—

(a) the aggregate of the amounts referred to in paragraph (a) of that sub-paragraph ; and

(b) the aggregate of the amounts referred to in paragraph (b) thereof.

(4) As respects the assets under each heading whose amount is not arrived at in accordance with the said sub-paragraph (1) because their replacement is provided for as mentioned in sub-paragraph (2) (b) of this paragraph, there shall be stated—

(a) the means by which their replacement is provided for ; and

(b) the aggregate amount of the provision (if any) made for renewals and not used.

6. The aggregate amounts respectively of capital reserves, revenue reserves and provisions (other than provisions for depreciation, renewals or diminution in value of assets) shall be stated under separate headings :

Provided that—

(a) this paragraph shall not require a separate statement of any of the said three amounts which is not material ; and

(b) the Board of Trade may direct that it shall not require a separate statement of the amount of provisions where they are satisfied that that is not required in the public interest and would prejudice the company, but subject to the condition that any heading stating an amount arrived at after taking into account a provision (other than as aforesaid) shall be so framed or marked as to indicate that fact.

7.—(1) There shall also be shown (unless it is shown in the profit and loss account or a statement or report annexed thereto, or the amount involved is not material)—

(a) where the amount of the capital reserves, of the revenue reserves or of the provisions (other than provisions for depreciation, renewals or diminution in value of assets) shows an increase as compared with the amount at the end of the immediately preceding financial year, the source from which the amount of the increase has been derived ; and

(*b*) where—

(i) the amount of the capital reserves or of the revenue reserves shows a decrease as compared with the amount at the end of the immediately preceding financial year ; or

(ii) the amount at the end of the immediately preceding financial year of the provisions (other than provisions for depreciation, renewals or diminution in value of assets) exceeded the aggregate of the sums since applied and amounts still retained for the purposes thereof ;

the application of the amounts derived from the difference.

(2) Where the heading showing any of the reserves or provisions aforesaid is divided into sub-headings, this paragraph shall apply to each of the separate amounts shown in the sub-headings instead of applying to the aggregate amount thereof.

8.—(1) There shall be shown under separate headings—

(*a*) the aggregate amounts respectively of the company's trade investments, quoted investments other than trade investments and unquoted investments other than trade investments ;

(*b*) if the amount of the goodwill and of any patents and trademarks or part of that amount is shown as a separate item in or is otherwise ascertainable from the books of the company, or from any contract for the sale or purchase of any property to be acquired by the company, or from any documents in the possession of the company relating to the stamp duty payable in respect of any such contract or the conveyance of any such property, the said amount so shown or ascertained so far as not written off or, as the case may be, the said amount so far as it is so shown or ascertainable and as so shown or ascertained, as the case may be ;

(*c*) the aggregate amount of any outstanding loans made under the authority of provisos (*b*) and (*c*) of subsection (1) of section fifty-four of this Act ;

(*d*) the aggregate amount of bank loans and overdrafts ;

(*e*) the net aggregate amount (after deduction of income tax) which is recommended for distribution by way of dividend.

(2) Nothing in head (*b*) of the foregoing sub-paragraph shall be taken as requiring the amount of the goodwill, patents and trademarks to be stated otherwise than as a single item.

(3) The heading showing the amount of the quoted investments other than trade investments shall be sub-divided, where necessary, to distinguish the investments as respects which there has, and those as respects which there has not, been granted a quotation or permission to deal on a recognised stock exchange.

9. Where any liability of the company is secured otherwise than by operation of law on any assets of the company, the fact that that liability is so secured shall be stated, but it shall not be necessary to specify the assets on which the liability is secured.

10. Where any of the company's debentures are held by a nominee of or trustee for the company, the nominal amount of the debentures and the amount at which they are stated in the books of the company shall be stated.

11.—(1) The matters referred to in the following sub-paragraphs shall be stated by way of note, or in a statement or report annexed, if not otherwise shown.

(2) The number, description and amount of any shares in the company which any person has an option to subscribe for, together with the following particulars of the option, that is to say—

    (a) the period during which it is exercisable ;

    (b) the price to be paid for shares subscribed for under it.

(3) The amount of any arrears of fixed cumulative dividends on the company's shares and the period for which the dividends or, if there is more than one class, each class of them are in arrear, the amount to be stated before deduction of income tax, except that, in the case of tax free dividends, the amount shall be shown free of tax and the fact that it is so shown shall also be stated.

(4) Particulars of any charge on the assets of the company to secure the liabilities of any other person, including, where practicable, the amount secured.

(5) The general nature of any other contingent liabilities not provided for and, where practicable, the aggregate amount or estimated amount of those liabilities, if it is material.

(6) Where practicable the aggregate amount or estimated amount, if it is material, of contracts for capital expenditure, so far as not provided for.

(7) If in the opinion of the directors any of the current assets have not a value, on realisation in the ordinary course of the company's business, at least equal to the amount at which they are stated, the fact that the directors are of that opinion.

(8) The aggregate market value of the company's quoted investments, other than trade investments, where it differs from the amount of the investments as stated, and the stock exchange value of any investments of which the market value is shown (whether separately or not) and is taken as being higher than their stock exchange value.

(9) The basis on which foreign currencies have been converted into sterling, where the amount of the assets or liabilities affected is material.

(10) The basis on which the amount, if any, set aside for United Kingdom income tax is computed.

(11) Except in the case of the first balance sheet laid before the company after the commencement of this Act, the corresponding amounts at the end of the immediately preceding financial year for all items shown in the balance sheet.

Profit and Loss Account.

12.—(1) There shall be shown—

    (a) the amount charged to revenue by way of provision for depreciation, renewals or diminution in value of fixed assets ;

    (b) the amount of the interest on the company's debentures and other fixed loans ;

    (c) the amount of the charge for United Kingdom income tax and other United Kingdom taxation on profits, including, where practicable, as United Kingdom income tax any taxation imposed elsewhere to the extent of the relief, if any, from United Kingdom income tax and distinguishing where practicable between income tax and other taxation ;

(d) the amounts respectively provided for redemption of share capital and for redemption of loans;

(e) the amount, if material, set aside or proposed to be set aside to, or withdrawn from, reserves;

(f) subject to sub-paragraph (2) of this paragraph, the amount, if material, set aside to provisions other than provisions for depreciation, renewals or diminution in value of assets or, as the case may be, the amount, if material, withdrawn from such provisions and not applied for the purposes thereof;

(g) the amount of income from investments, distinguishing between trade investments and other investments;

(h) the aggregate amount of the dividends paid and proposed.

(2) The Board of Trade may direct that a company shall not be obliged to show an amount set aside to provisions in accordance with sub-paragraph (1) (f) of this paragraph, if the Board is satisfied that that is not required in the public interest and would prejudice the company, but subject to the condition that any heading stating an amount arrived at after taking into account the amount set aside as aforesaid shall be so framed or marked as to indicate that fact.

13. If the remuneration of the auditors is not fixed by the company in general meeting, the amount thereof shall be shown under a separate heading, and for the purposes of this paragraph, any sums paid by the company in respect of the auditors' expenses shall be deemed to be included in the expression " remuneration ".

14.—(1) The matters referred to in the following sub-paragraphs shall be stated by way of note, if not otherwise shown.

(2) If depreciation or replacement of fixed assets is provided for by some method other than a depreciation charge or provision for renewals, or is not provided for, the method by which it is provided for or the fact that it is not provided for, as the case may be.

(3) The basis on which the charge for United Kingdom income tax is computed.

(4) Whether or not the amount stated for dividends paid and proposed is for dividends subject to deduction of income tax.

(5) Except in the case of the first profit and loss account laid before the company after the commencement of this Act the corresponding amounts for the immediately preceding financial year for all items shown in the profit and loss account.

(6) Any material respects in which any items shown in the profit and loss account are affected—

(a) by transactions of a sort not usually undertaken by the company or otherwise by circumstances of an exceptional or non-recurrent nature; or

(b) by any change in the basis of accounting.

PART II.

SPECIAL PROVISIONS WHERE THE COMPANY IS A HOLDING OR SUBSIDIARY COMPANY.

Modifications of and Additions to Requirements as to Company's Own Accounts.

15.—(1) This paragraph shall apply where the company is a holding company, whether or not it is itself a subsidiary of another body corporate.

(2) The aggregate amount of assets consisting of shares in, or amounts owing (whether on account of a loan or otherwise) from, the company's subsidiaries, distinguishing shares from indebtedness, shall be set out in the balance sheet separately from all the other assets of the company, and the aggregate amount of indebtedness (whether on account of a loan or otherwise) to the company's subsidiaries shall be so set out separately from all its other liabilities and—

(a) the references in Part I of this Schedule to the company's investments shall not include investments in its subsidiaries required by this paragraph to be separately set out ; and

(b) paragraph 5, sub-paragraph (1) (a) of paragraph 12, and sub-paragraph (2) of paragraph 14 of this Schedule shall not apply in relation to fixed assets consisting of interests in the company's subsidiaries.

(3) There shall be shown by way of note on the balance sheet or in a statement or report annexed thereto the number, description and amount of the shares in and debentures of the company held by its subsidiaries or their nominees, but excluding any of those shares or debentures in the case of which the subsidiary is concerned as personal representative or in the case of which it is concerned as trustee and neither the company nor any subsidiary thereof is beneficially interested under the trust, otherwise than by way of security only for the purposes of a transaction entered into by it in the ordinary course of a business which includes the lending of money.

(4) Where group accounts are not submitted, there shall be annexed to the balance sheet a statement showing—

(a) the reasons why subsidiaries are not dealt with in group accounts;

(b) the net aggregate amount, so far as it concerns members of the holding company and is not dealt with in the company's accounts, of the subsidiaries' profits after deducting the subsidiaries' losses (or *vice versa*)—

(i) for the respective financial years of the subsidiaries ending with or during the financial year of the company ; and

(ii) for their previous financial years since they respectively became the holding company's subsidiary ;

(c) the net aggregate amount of the subsidiaries' profits after deducting the subsidiaries' losses (or *vice versa*)—

(i) for the respective financial years of the subsidiaries ending with or during the financial year of the company ; and

(ii) for their other financial years since they respectively became the holding company's subsidiary ;

so far as those profits are dealt with, or provision is made for those losses, in the company's accounts ;

(d) any qualifications contained in the report of the auditors of the subsidiaries on their accounts for their respective financial years ending as aforesaid, and any note or saving contained in those accounts to call attention to a matter which, apart from the note or saving, would properly have been referred to in such a qualification, in so far as the matter which is the subject of the qualification or note is not covered by the company's own accounts and is material from the point of view of its members ;

or, in so far as the information required by this sub-paragraph is not obtainable, a statement that it is not obtainable :

Provided that the Board of Trade may, on the application or with the consent of the company's directors, direct that in relation to any subsidiary this sub-paragraph shall not apply or shall apply only to such extent as may be provided by the direction.

(5) Paragraphs (b) and (c) of the last foregoing sub-paragraph shall apply only to profits and losses of a subsidiary which may properly be treated in the holding company's accounts as revenue profits or losses, and the profits or losses attributable to any shares in a subsidiary for the time being held by the holding company or any other of its subsidiaries shall not (for that or any other purpose) be treated as aforesaid so far as they are profits or losses for the period before the date on or as from which the shares were acquired by the company or any of its subsidiaries, except that they may in a proper case be so treated where—

(a) the company is itself the subsidiary of another body corporate ; and

(b) the shares were acquired from that body corporate or a subsidiary of it ;

and for the purpose of determining whether any profits or losses are to be treated as profits or losses for the said period the profit or loss for any financial year of the subsidiary may, if it is not practicable to apportion it with reasonable accuracy by reference to the facts, be treated as accruing from day to day during that year and be apportioned accordingly.

(6) Where group accounts are not submitted, there shall be annexed to the balance sheet a statement showing, in relation to the subsidiaries (if any) whose financial years did not end with that of the company—

(a) the reasons why the company's directors consider that the subsidiaries' financial years should not end with that of the company ; and

(b) the dates on which the subsidiaries' financial years ending last before that of the company respectively ended or the earliest and latest of those dates.

16.—(1) The balance sheet of a company which is a subsidiary of another body corporate, whether or not it is itself a holding company, shall show the aggregate amount of its indebtedness to all bodies corporate of which it is a subsidiary or a fellow subsidiary and the aggregate amount of the indebtedness of all such bodies corporate to it, distinguishing in each case between indebtedness in respect of debentures and otherwise.

(2) For the purposes of this paragraph a company shall be deemed to be a fellow subsidiary of another body corporate if both are subsidiaries of the same body corporate but neither is the other's.

Consolidated Accounts of Holding Company and Subsidiaries.

17. Subject to the following paragraphs of this Part of this Schedule, the consolidated balance sheet and profit and loss account shall combine the information contained in the separate balance sheets and profit and loss accounts of the holding company and of the subsidiaries dealt with by the consolidated accounts, but with such adjustments (if any) as the directors of the holding company think necessary.

18. Subject as aforesaid and to Part III of this Schedule, the consolidated accounts shall. in giving the said information, comply, so far as practicable,

with the requirements of this Act as if they were the accounts of an actual company.

19. Sections one hundred and ninety-six and one hundred and ninety-seven of this Act shall not, by virtue of the two last foregoing paragraphs, apply for the purpose of the consolidated accounts.

20. Paragraph 7 of this Schedule shall not apply for the purpose of any consolidated accounts laid before a company with the first balance sheet so laid after the commencement of this Act.

21. In relation to any subsidiaries of the holding company not dealt with by the consolidated accounts—

 (a) sub-paragraphs (2) and (3) of paragraph 15 of this Schedule shall apply for the purpose of those accounts as if those accounts were the accounts of an actual company of which they were subsidiaries ; and

 (b) there shall be annexed the like statement as is required by sub-paragraph (4) of that paragraph where there are no group accounts, but as if references therein to the holding company's accounts were references to the consolidated accounts.

22. In relation to any subsidiaries (whether or not dealt with by the consolidated accounts), whose financial years did not end with that of the company, there shall be annexed the like statement as is required by sub-paragraph (6) of paragraph 15 of this Schedule where there are no group accounts.

PART III.

EXCEPTIONS FOR SPECIAL CLASSES OF COMPANY.

23.—(1) A banking or discount company shall not be subject to the requirements of Part I of this Schedule other than—

 (a) as respects its balance sheet, those of paragraphs 2 and 3, paragraph 4 (so far as it relates to fixed and current assets), paragraph 8 (except sub-paragraph (1) (d)), paragraphs 9 and 10 and paragraph 11 (except sub-paragraph (8)) ; and

 (b) as respects its profit and loss account, those of sub-paragraph (1) (h) of paragraph 12, paragraph 13 and sub-paragraphs (1), (4) and (5) of paragraph 14 ;

but, where in its balance sheet capital reserves, revenue reserves or provisions (other than provisions for depreciation, renewals or diminution in value of assets) are not stated separately, any heading stating an amount arrived at after taking into account such a reserve or provision shall be so framed or marked as to indicate that fact, and its profit and loss account shall indicate by appropriate words the manner in which the amount stated for the company's profit or loss has been arrived at.

(2) The accounts of a banking or discount company shall not be deemed, by reason only of the fact that they do not comply with any requirements of the said Part I from which the company is exempt by virtue of this paragraph, not to give the true and fair view required by this Act.

(3) In this paragraph the expression " banking or discount company " means any company which satisfies the Board of Trade that it ought to be treated for the purposes of this Schedule as a banking company or as a discount company.

24.—(1) In relation to an assurance company within the meaning of the Assurance Companies Acts, 1909 to 1946, which is subject to and complies with the requirements of those Acts as respects the preparation and deposit with the Board of Trade of a balance sheet and profit and loss account, the foregoing paragraph shall apply as it applies in relation to a banking or discount company, and such an assurance company shall also not be subject to the requirements of sub-paragraphs (1) (a) and (3) of paragraph 8 and sub-paragraphs (4) to (7) and sub-paragraph (10) of paragraph 11 of this Schedule :

Provided that the Board of Trade may direct that any such assurance company whose business includes to a substantial extent business other than assurance business shall comply with all the requirements of the said Part I or such of them as may be specified in the direction and shall comply therewith as respects either the whole of its business or such part thereof as may be so specified.

(2) Where an assurance company is entitled to the benefit of this paragraph, then any wholly owned subsidiary thereof shall also be so entitled if its business consists only of business which is complementary to assurance business of the classes carried on by the assurance company.

(3) For the purposes of this paragraph a company shall be deemed to be the wholly owned subsidiary of an assurance company if it has no members except the assurance company and the assurance company's wholly owned subsidiaries and its or their nominees.

25.—(1) A company to which this paragraph applies shall not be subject to the following requirements of this Schedule, that is to say—

(a) as respects its balance sheet, those of paragraph 4 (except so far as the said paragraph relates to fixed and current assets) and paragraphs 5, 6 and 7 ; and

(b) as respects its profit and loss account, those of sub-paragraph (1) (a) (e) and (f) of paragraph 12 ;

but a company taking advantage of this paragraph shall be subject, instead of the said requirements, to any prescribed conditions as respects matters to be stated in its accounts or by way of note thereto and as respects information to be furnished to the Board of Trade or a person authorised by them to require it.

(2) The accounts of a company shall not be deemed, by reason only of the fact that they do not comply with any requirements of Part I of this Schedule from which the company is exempt by virtue of this paragraph, not to give the true and fair view required by this Act.

(3) This paragraph applies to companies of any class prescribed for the purposes thereof, and a class of companies may be so prescribed if it appears to the Board of Trade desirable in the national interest :

Provided that, if the Board of Trade are satisfied that any of the conditions prescribed for the purposes of this paragraph has not been complied with in the case of any company, they may direct that so long as the direction continues in force this paragraph shall not apply to the company.

26. Where a company entitled to the benefit of any provision contained in this Part of this Schedule is a holding company, the reference in Part II of this Schedule to consolidated accounts complying with the requirements of this Act shall, in relation to consolidated accounts of that company, be construed as referring to those requirements in so far only as they apply to the separate accounts of that company.

PART IV.

INTERPRETATION OF SCHEDULE.

27.—(1) For the purposes of this Schedule, unless the context otherwise requires—

(a) the expression " provision " shall, subject to sub-paragraph (2) of this paragraph, mean any amount, written off or retained by way of providing for depreciation, renewals or diminution in value of assets or retained by way of providing for any known liability of which the amount cannot be determined with substantial accuracy ;

(b) the expression " reserve " shall not, subject as aforesaid, include any amount written off or retained by way of providing for depreciation, renewals or diminution in value of assets or retained by way of providing for any known liability ;

(c) the expression " capital reserve " shall not include any amount regarded as free for distribution through the profit and loss account and the expression " revenue reserve " shall mean any reserve other than a capital reserve ;

and in this paragraph the expression " liability " shall include all liabilities in respect of expenditure contracted for and all disputed or contingent liabilities.

(2) Where—

(a) any amount written off or retained by way of providing for depreciation, renewals or diminution in value of assets, not being an amount written off in relation to fixed assets before the commencement of this Act ; or

(b) any amount retained by way of providing for any known liability ;

is in excess of that which in the opinion of the directors is reasonably necessary for the purpose, the excess shall be treated for the purposes of this Schedule as a reserve and not as a provision.

28. For the purposes aforesaid, the expression " quoted investment " means an investment as respects which there has been granted a quotation or permission to deal on a recognised stock exchange, or on any stock exchange of repute outside Great Britain, and the expression " unquoted investment " shall be construed accordingly.

NINTH SCHEDULE.

MATTERS TO BE EXPRESSLY STATED IN AUDITORS' REPORT.

1. Whether they have obtained all the information and explanations which to the best of their knowledge and belief were necessary for the purposes of their audit.

2. Whether, in their opinion, proper books of account have been kept by the company, so far as appears from their examination of those books, and proper returns adequate for the purposes of their audit have been received from branches not visited by them.

3.—(1) Whether the company's balance sheet and (unless it is framed as a consolidated profit and loss account) profit and loss account dealt with by the report are in agreement with the books of account and returns.

(2) Whether, in their ·opinion and to the best of their information and according to the explanations given them, the said accounts give the information required by this Act in the manner so required and give a true and fair view—

(a) in the case of the balance sheet, of the state of the company's affairs as at the end of its financial year ; and

(b) in the case of the profit and loss account, of the profit or loss for its financial year ;

or, as the case may be, give a true and fair view thereof subject to the non-disclosure of any matters (to be indicated in the report) which by virtue of Part III of the Eighth Schedule to this Act are not required to be disclosed.

4. In the case of a holding company submitting group accounts whether, in their opinion, the group accounts have been properly prepared in accordance with the provisions of this Act so as to give a true and fair view of the state of affairs and profit or loss of the company and its subsidiaries dealt with thereby, so far as concerns members of the company, or, as the case may be, so as to give a true and fair view thereof subject to the non-disclosure of any matters (to be indicated in the report) which by virtue of Part III of the Eighth Schedule to this Act are not required to be disclosed.

APPENDIX II

RECOMMENDATIONS ON ACCOUNTING PRINCIPLES

The Council of the Institute of Chartered Accountants has requested the Taxation and Research Committee (previously known as the Taxation and Financial Relations Committee) to consider and make recommendations to it on certain aspects of the accounts of companies, and the Council propose to publish approved recommendations for the information of members.

The Council recognise that the form in which accounts are submitted to shareholders is (subject to compliance with the Companies Acts) a matter within the discretion of directors, but it is hoped that these recommendations will be helpful to members, in advising, in appropriate cases, as to what is regarded as the best practice.

The recommendations published to date which come within the scope of this book are reproduced in this Appendix; it should be borne in mind, however, that as a number of the recommendations were made before 1st July, 1948, they are subject to the provisions of the Companies Act, 1948, which, in many cases, incorporate the recommendations of the Institute. The dates upon which the various recommendations were made, and the dates of any subsequent amendments to the original recommendations, are included in the Appendix, so that, where appropriate, the reader may make a comparison between the recommendations and the statutory provisions of the Act.

I. TAX RESERVE CERTIFICATES.

It is considered that regard should be had to the relevant conditions of issue set forth in the leaflet issued by the Treasury on 22nd December, 1941, namely :—

(a) Certificates can be used for the payment of income tax (except under Schedule E), sur-tax, national defence contribution (later known as profits tax), excess profits tax, and war damage contributions under Part I of the 1941 Act ; but this right is limited to such liabilities falling due not less than two months and not more than two years (subsequently amended to five years) from the date of the certificate ; if so used interest is allowed at 1 per cent. per annum free of tax (subsequently amended to a rate of interest fixed by the Treasury).

(b) They are not transferable (except under the ordinary law on death, bankruptcy, etc.), and consequently cannot be pledged as security.

(c) They may be surrendered after two months against a cash payment but no interest is then allowable.

(d) The appropriation of the amount represented by the certificate for any of the liabilities referred to in (a) above or the surrender against a cash payment is at the option of the holder.

Recommendation.—It is therefore recommended that :—

(1) The amount of tax reserve certificates held should be shown as a separate item in the Balance Sheet and grouped with the current assets.

(2) The 1 per cent. (subsequently amended) per annum allowed on the surrender of the certificates in payment of taxation, etc., should be treated as interest and not as a reduction of the taxation charge.

Note.—It is suggested that accrued interest to the date of the Balance Sheet should not be taken to credit unless the certificates have been surrendered before the Balance Sheet has been signed.

(12*th December*, 1942.)

II. War Damage Contributions, Premiums and Claims. (12*th December*, 1942.)

[This Recommendation is not reproduced as it is no longer of particular practical importance.]

III. The Treatment of Taxation in Accounts.

The incidence of taxation and its effect on profits and on the financial position disclosed by the Balance Sheet, together with the extent to which the Inland Revenue on the one hand and shareholders on the other have participated in profits, are matters which should be made clear to shareholders.

The assessment of liability to national defence contribution (later known as profits tax) and excess profits tax is based on the profits of the accounting period under review. The assessment of liability to income tax is, however, for the fiscal year ending 5th April and is normally based on the profits of a preceding accounting period. The minimum or legal amount to be provided for taxation is thus the aggregate of taxes assessable on these bases, apportioned, as regards income tax, according to the period covered by the accounts under review.

Income tax so apportioned takes no account, however, either of the balance of the liability assessable for the current fiscal year, or of the liability which, in normal circumstances, will arise in respect of profits included in the accounts but not assessable until the following fiscal year. Further, unless provision be made year by year for income tax based on each year's results, the trend of net available profits will not be apparent, and cases will arise where the profits earned in a succeeding period will bear a disproportionate charge for taxation—indeed, they may even be insufficient to meet it.

In the case of principal and subsidiary companies (as defined in the Finance (No. 2) Act, 1939) excess profits tax is assessable on the principal company in respect of the net excess profits of the group. The principal company has, however, the option of recovering from any subsidiary the tax charge relative to the excess profits of such subsidiary or of crediting any subsidiary with the tax benefit arising from the deficiencies of such subsidiary. The charge for taxation in the principal company's accounts thus depends upon the exercise (in whole or in part) of the option to allocate excess profits tax over subsidiaries and may not be appropriate to the profits shown in the principal company's own accounts.

Recommendation.—It is therefore recommended that :—

(1) The charge for income tax should be stated in the accounts, and subject to war-time or other special circumstances, the charge for national defence contribution (later known as profits tax) or excess profits tax should also be stated.

(2) (a) The charge for income tax should be based on the profits earned during the period covered by the accounts.

(b) Where it has been the practice to charge only the minimum or legal liability, then, until full provision has been made for income tax on all profits up to the date of the Balance Sheet, it is desirable where possible to make provision, in addition, for or towards the balance of the liability for the current and following fiscal years. This provision should be shown separately in the Profit and Loss Account.

(c) Whatever method is adopted, the bases (i) of the charge and (ii) of any supplemental provision made for income tax should be disclosed.

(d) Income tax on revenue taxed before receipt should be included as part of the taxation charge for the year and the relative income should be brought to credit gross.

(3) In the case of principal companies it should be indicated whether the provision for excess profits tax is in respect of the group or whether the sum charged has been arrived at after taking into account amounts allocated over subsidiary companies.

(4) Taxation charges may be affected by losses in the current period, deficiencies brought forward or adjustments of taxation in respect of previous periods, the effect of which, if material, should be disclosed. Any provision made in excess of the amount required to cover the estimated future liability on profits earned to date should, if material, be similarly disclosed.

(5) Any provision for (or in excess of) the estimated future liability to income tax in respect of the fiscal year commencing after the date of the Balance Sheet should not be included with current liabilities but should be grouped with reserves or separately stated as a deferred liability and suitably described.

(13th *March*, 1943.)

Note.—The following amendment to Recommendation III was issued in May, 1948, consequent upon the statutory definition of " provision " in the Companies Act, 1947 (now the Companies Act, 1948).

In the opinion of counsel an amount set aside to meet future income tax is not a liability and accordingly cannot be a " provision " under company law; it follows that for the purpose of the Act it is necessarily a reserve. In view of that opinion, Recommendation III requires amendment in the following respects :—

(a) The word " provision " ceases to be applicable to amounts set aside to meet future income tax.

(b) Such amounts should in all cases be classified as reserves and either included with the other reserves or shown as a separate item.

The following statement by the Council was published in *The Accountant* on 12th April, 1947, and reaffirmed in a statement published in *The Accountant* of 11th March, 1950 :—

Initial allowances, deferred repairs and other adjustments affecting the treatment of taxation in accounts :—

Enquiries have been received from members as to the way in which accounts should make clear the extent to which the Profit and Loss Account of a year is affected by the initial allowances under the Income Tax Act, 1945, and the charging of deferred repairs against provisions made in earlier years. The Council is of opinion that this could best be achieved by:—

(1) Maintaining, for accounting purposes, normal methods of depreciation

as set out in Recommendation IX, thus avoiding any distortion of profits before taxation.

(2) Applying the principles dealing with the treatment of taxation in accounts as set out in Recommendation III, to initial allowances, deferred repairs and other allowances and charges arising from recent taxation legislation, *i.e.*, by indicating the effect, if material, of these items on the amount provided for taxation.

The Council is further of opinion that the desirability of transferring to reserve and spreading over a period of years the taxation benefit resulting from initial allowances is a matter of financial policy.

IV. THE TREATMENT IN ACCOUNTS OF INCOME TAX DEDUCTIBLE FROM DIVIDENDS PAYABLE AND ANNUAL CHARGES.

The payment of a dividend to shareholders does not affect the amount of tax payable by a company, the assessment being on the amount of the profits as adjusted for the purposes of income tax.

On the other hand, income tax deducted upon payment of debenture and other interest, royalties and similar annual charges is in effect assessed on a company for collection from the payee.

Recommendation.—It is therefore recommended that :—

(1) (a) Whether dividends are described " less income tax " or " free of income tax " the amounts shown in respect thereof in the accounts should be the net amounts payable.

(b) Where a company continues the practice of providing for dividends gross the narrative should indicate that the distributions are subject to income tax. The taxation charge should be arrived at after taking credit for the tax deductible on payment of the proposed dividends.

(2) Annual charges for debenture and other interest, royalties and similar annual payments should be charged gross.

(*13th March*, 1943.)

V. THE INCLUSION IN ACCOUNTS OF PROPOSED PROFIT APPROPRIATIONS.

Although certain appropriations of profits, including dividends recommended by directors, are subject to subsequent confirmation by shareholders, the inclusion of all appropriations in the accounts shows the amount which will be required for distribution to the shareholders and completes the accounts for the financial year by showing the results of trading and their application in one account. This course avoids the inclusion in the accounts of the next period of appropriations which were set out in the directors' report for the previous period, and have already been dealt with and disposed of. Also, it facilitates the linking up of the accounts from one period to another, the balance carried forward to the following period being clearly shown in the accounts of each year.

Recommendation.—Provision should be made in the books and in the Annual Accounts for proposed profit appropriations, those subject to confirmation by shareholders being so described. Provision for dividends should be shown as a separate item in the Balance Sheet.

(*13th March*, 1943.)

VI. RESERVES AND PROVISIONS.

A true appreciation of the financial position of a company as disclosed by its Balance Sheet may be rendered difficult or even impossible owing to lack of information as to the extent of undisclosed reserves and to insufficient distinction being made between (a) free reserves retained to strengthen the financial position or to meet unknown contingencies ; (b) capital reserves or other reserves not normally regarded as available for distribution as dividend ; (c) provisions for known contingencies ; and (d) provisions for diminution in value of assets in excess of normal or estimated requirements.

The terms " reserves " and " provisions " are commonly regarded as interchangeable. Accounts would be more clearly understood if the term " reserve " were applied only to reserves which are free, and the term " provision " were confined to amounts set aside for specific requirements.

Unless the amounts involved are stated, the trend of profits may be obscured by transferring amounts to or from undisclosed accounts of the nature of free reserves, by charging abnormal provisions or by utilising provisions no longer required.

Recommendation.—It is therefore recommended that :—

(1) The following distinction should be made between reserves which are free and those in the nature of provisions for specific requirements ; the latter should preferably be described as " Provisions " :—

(a) The term " reserve " should be used to denote amounts set aside out of profits and other surpluses which are not designed to meet any liability, contingency, commitment or diminution in value of assets known to exist as at the date of the Balance Sheet.

(b) The term " provision " should be used to denote amounts set aside out of profits or other surpluses to meet :—

(i) specific requirements the amounts whereof can be estimated closely ; and

(ii) specific commitments, known contingencies and diminutions in values of assets existing as at the date of the Balance Sheet where the amounts involved cannot be determined with substantial accuracy.

(2) Reserves, as defined in (1) (a) above, should be disclosed in the Balance Sheet.

The term " Reserve Fund " should only be used where a reserve is specifically represented by readily realisable and earmarked assets.

Where two or more reserves are retentions of distributable profits available for general use in the business and none of them is created in accordance with statutory requirements or in pursuance of any obligation or policy, the subdivision of such reserves under a variety of headings is unnecessary. Capital and other reserves not normally regarded as available for distribution as dividend, should, however, be separated from those of a revenue nature, the latter group to include any undistributed balance, or, by deduction, any adverse balance on Profit and Loss Account.

(3) As a general principle " Provisions " as defined under (1) (b) (ii), should be disclosed in the Balance Sheet under one or more appropriate headings. Only in circumstances where disclosure of the amount of a particular provision would clearly be detrimental to the interests of a company should it be included under another heading, for example " Creditors " ; the fact that such heading includes " Provisions " should then be indicated in the narrative.

Where practicable, fixed assets in existence at the date of the Balance Sheet should be shown at cost, and provisions for depreciation and for diminution in values should appear as separate deductions therefrom.

(4) Subject as in (3) above in regard to provisions the disclosure of which would be detrimental to the interests of a company, where reserves and provisions are created or increased, the amounts involved, if material, and the sources from which they have been created or increased, should

be disclosed in the accounts. In all cases the utilisation of reserves, and of provisions proved to have been redundant, should be disclosed in the accounts.

(23rd October, 1943.)

Note.—The following amendment to Recommendation VI was issued in May, 1948, consequent upon the statutory definition of " provision " in the Companies Act, 1947 (now the Companies Act, 1948).

In the opinion of counsel nothing that does not fall within the definition of " provision " can properly be described as a provision. In view of that opinion the amounts referred to in paragraph (1) (*b*) (i) of Recommendation VI cannot be described as provisions and the Council has made the following new recommendations :—

(*a*) The word " provision " should cease to be used to denote amounts set aside to meet specific requirements the amounts whereof can be estimated closely ; such amounts should be grouped with creditors since they represent liabilities or accruals.

(*b*) Amounts set aside to meet deferred repairs the execution of which is a contractual or statutory obligation (*e.g.*, under the dilapidations clause of a lease) should be treated as liabilities if the amounts can be determined with substantial accuracy and as provisions if the amounts cannot be so determined.

(*c*) Other amounts set aside to meet deferred repairs because they are regarded as charges necessary for the correct computation of profits should be treated as provisions, on the footing that they are closely analogous to amounts provided for renewals (which are specifically required to be treated as provisions) and differ from these in degree rather than in character.

VII. DISCLOSURE OF THE FINANCIAL POSITION AND RESULTS OF SUBSIDIARY COMPANIES IN THE ACCOUNTS OF HOLDING COMPANIES.

Where a company holds a direct or indirect controlling interest in another company or companies (referred to in this memorandum as " subsidiary undertakings ") a true appreciation of the financial position and the trend of results of the group as a whole can be made only if the accounts of the holding company as a separate legal entity take into account or are supplemented by information as to the financial position and results of the subsidiary undertakings.

The following are three methods of disclosing this supplemental information. Each has its own value and limitations. The first and second methods are suitable only in special cases.

Method (1) : To submit copies of the accounts of each of the subsidiary undertakings.

This method is suitable only where it is desired to focus attention on the financial position and earnings of each component of the group. It is impracticable where the companies are numerous and, in all but the simplest cases, the shareholders of the holding company could not obtain a true view of the group as a whole without considerable explanation of inter-company relations.

Method (2) : To submit statements of the consolidated assets and liabilities and of the aggregate earnings of the subsidiary undertakings as distinct from those of the holding company.

This method is of value where it is desired to show the underlying assets which represent the investment of the holding company in its subsidiary undetarkings, or particular groups of them, and also the earnings attributable thereto.

Note.—As regards methods (1) and (2), if the holding company trades extensively with or through its subsidiary undertakings, the disclosed earnings of the subsidiary undertakings may not by themselves be a true criterion of the real value of the holding company's interests in such undertakings ; in such circumstances their value cannot be assessed separately from the value of the group undertaking as a whole.

Method (3) : To submit a Consolidated Balance Sheet and a Consolidated Profit and Loss Account of the holding company and of its subsidiary undertakings treated as one group.

This method is the most suitable for general application.

It must, however, be remembered that a Consolidated Balance Sheet is not a record of the assets and liabilities of a legal entity and that the liabilities of each company in the group are payable only out of its own assets and not out of the combined assets of the group. Also, there may be special cases where it may be impracticable or inappropriate to include the figures of a particular subsidiary undertaking in the consolidation. This applies especially in the case of subsidiary undertakings operating overseas where, apart from the temporary difficulty of enemy occupation, there may be restrictions on exchange.

A Consolidated Profit and Loss Account does not suffer to the same extent from these limitations and, subject to any necessary explanations, the aggregate results of the group as a whole can be stated. Such disclosure is important even if for any reason the publication of a complete Consolidated Balance Sheet is impracticable or inappropriate.

Recommendation.—It is therefore recommended that in the case of every holding company :—

(1) With the published accounts, statements should be submitted in the form of a Consolidated Balance Sheet and Consolidated Profit and Loss Account or in such other form as will enable the shareholders to obtain a clear view of the financial position and earnings of the group as a whole.

(2) Every consolidated statement should indicate :—

(*a*) The nature and measure of control adopted as a basis for the inclusion of subsidiary undertakings.

(*b*) The reasons for the non-inclusion of any subsidiary undertakings which would normally be included on the basis adopted for the group.

(*c*) The procedure adopted in cases where the accounts of subsidiary undertakings are not made up to the same date as the accounts of the holding company.

(*d*) In the case of subsidiary companies operating overseas, if relatively important, the basis taken for the conversion of foreign currencies as affecting assets, liabilities and earnings.

(3) The Consolidated Balance Sheet should exclude inter-company items and should show the combined resources of the group and its liabilities and assets, aggregated under suitable headings. It should distinguish between capital reserves not normally regarded as available for distribution and revenue reserves, including those which would be available for distribution as dividend by the holding company if brought into its accounts. It should also show the interests of outside shareholders in the capital and reserves of the subsidiary undertakings and, under a separate heading, the interests of the group in subsidiary undertakings which have not been consolidated.

(4) The Consolidated Profit and Loss Account, or other information given as to the earnings of the group, should disclose the aggregate results of the group for the period covered by the accounts, after eliminating the

effect of inter-company transactions. It should be in such a form that these aggregate results may readily be reconciled with those shown by the Profit and Loss Account of the holding company, in which should be stated separately the aggregate amount included in respect of subsidiary undertakings whose accounts have not been consolidated. The following, *inter alia*, should be separately stated :—

(a) The aggregate results of any subsidiary undertakings the Balance Sheets of which have not been included in the consolidation.

(b) The portion of the aggregate net results attributable to outside shareholders' interests in the subsidiary undertakings.

(c) The portion of the consolidated net results attributable to the holding company's interest which remains in the accounts of consolidated subsidiary undertakings or the amount by which the dividends from such subsidiary undertakings exceed the holding company's share of their earnings for the period.

(5) Profits earned and losses incurred by subsidiary undertakings prior to the acquisition by the holding company of the shares to which they are attributable should be viewed as being of a capital nature from the standpoint of the holding company. Such pre-acquisition profits (whether received in dividend or not) should therefore not be brought into account as being available for distribution in dividend by the holding company.

(12th February, 1944.)

VIII. Form of Balance Sheet and Profit and Loss Account.

Businesses are so varied in their nature that there must be flexibility in the manner of presenting accounts and a standard form to suit every commercial and industrial undertaking is neither practicable nor desirable. The financial position can, however, be more readily appreciated if the various items in the Balance Sheet are grouped under appropriate headings and a proper view of the trend of the results can be obtained only if certain principles are consistently applied and if profits or losses of an exceptional nature or relating to previous periods are stated separately in the Profit and Loss Account. In both cases, appreciation is facilitated if the comparative figures of the previous period are also given.

Recommendation.—It is therefore recommended that, subject to compliance with statutory requirements, the Balance Sheet and Profit and Loss Account should be presented in conformity with the following general principles :—

Balance Sheet.—(1) The use of general headings for a Balance Sheet, such as " liabilities " and " assets," is inappropriate and unnecessary. The various items, whatever may be their sequence or designation, should, however, be grouped as indicated below under appropriate headings. Additional groups may be necessary in certain cases to show the aggregate liabilities and assets subject to exchange or other restrictions, special funds and other special items, such as deferred revenue expenditure. Where any material part of a company's liabilities or assets is in foreign currency, the basis of conversion to sterling should be disclosed.

Share Capital.—(2) In addition to the authorised and issued amounts of the various classes of capital and the redemption date of any redeemable preference capital, the terms of redemption should be stated. Particulars of any option on unissued capital should also be given. If dividends on cumulative preference capital are in arrear, the gross amounts of dividends in arrear or the date up to which the dividends have been paid should be stated.

Reserves.—(3) The items to be included in this group are amounts set aside out of profits and other surpluses which are not designed to meet any liability, contingency, commitment or diminution in value of assets known to exist as at the date of the Balance Sheet. Capital and other reserves not normally regarded as available for distribution as dividend should be shown separately from those of a revenue nature, the latter group to include any undistributed balance or, by deduction, any adverse balance on Profit and Loss Account.

(4) A sub-total of share capital and reserves should be given to indicate the members' interest in the company.

Debentures, Mortgages and Long-term Liabilities.—(5) In this group should be included debentures, mortgages and other long-term loans or liabilities. Where practicable, the dates and terms of redemption should be stated.

(6) The expression " long-term " is intended to cover liabilities not due for payment until after the lapse of one year from the date of the Balance Sheet.

Amounts owing to Subsidiary Undertakings.—(7) In addition to the aggregate amount owing to subsidiary companies, the aggregate amount owing to sub-subsidiary companies should be disclosed. Such aggregate amounts may be shown under long-term liabilities, current liabilities, or as a separate group, according to their nature.

Current Liabilities and Provisions.—(8) The items in this group should be classified to disclose their nature and amount including, *inter alia*, (a) trade liabilities, bills payable and accrued charges ; (b) bank loans and overdrafts ; (c) other short-term loans ; (d) interest accrued on debentures and long-term liabilities ; (e) provision for current taxation (see Recommendation No. III) ; (f) provisions to meet specific commitments or contingencies where the amounts involved cannot be determined with substantial accuracy (see Recommendation No. VI) ; and (g) provision for proposed dividends.

Commitments for Capital Expenditure.—(9) Where commitments of material amount for capital expenditure exist at the date of the Balance Sheet, these should be indicated in a suitable note.

Contingent Liabilities.—(10) Contingencies on guarantees, bills under discount, partly-paid shares and similar items, should be dealt with by note.

Fixed Assets.—(11) In this group should be shown under separate headings fixed assets such as (a) goodwill, patents and trademarks ; (b) freehold land and buildings ; (c) leaseholds ; (d) plant, machinery and equipment ; (e) investments acquired and intended to be retained for trade purposes.

(12) Where practicable, fixed assets in existence at the date of the Balance Sheet should be shown at cost, and the aggregate of the provisions for depreciation and for diminution in values up to that date should appear as deductions therefrom.

Shares in and Amounts Owing from Subsidiary Undertakings.—(13) In addition to the aggregate amount of shares in, and the aggregate amount owing from, subsidiary companies, which must be stated separately in accordance with the Companies Act, 1929 (now the Companies Act, 1948), the aggregate amount owing from sub-subsidiary companies should also be stated. The aggregate amounts owing from subsidiary and sub-subsidiary companies may be shown under fixed assets, current assets, or as a separate group, according to their nature.

Note.—In the Balance Sheets of subsidiary and of sub-subsidiary companies the aggregate amount of shares in, and the aggregate amounts owing to and from, the ultimate holding company and its subsidiary undertakings should be stated separately.

Current Assets.—(14) In this group should be included such assets as are held for realisation in the ordinary course of business. They should be stated separately in appropriate sequence and normally include : (a) stock-in-trade and work-in-progress ; (b) trade and other debtors, prepayments and bills receivable ; (c) investments held as part of the liquid resources of the company ; (d) tax reserve certificates ; (e) bank balances and cash.

Note.—Debts of material amount not due until after the lapse of one year from the date of the Balance Sheet should be separately grouped and suitably described.

s*

Preliminary and Issue Expenses, etc.—(15) In this group should be included particulars and amounts of expenditure such as preliminary expenses, issue expenses and discount on capital issues not written off.

PROFIT AND LOSS ACCOUNT.—(16) The Profit and Loss Account should be presented in such a form as to give a clear disclosure of the results of the period and the amount available for appropriation, for which purpose it may conveniently be divided into sections.

(17) Such a disclosure implies substantial uniformity in the accounting principles applied as between successive accounting periods, any change of a material nature, such as a variation in the basis of stock valuation or in the method of providing for depreciation or taxation, should be disclosed if its effect distorts the results. The account should disclose any material respects in which it includes extraneous or non-recurrent items or those of an exceptional nature, and should also refer to the omission of any item relative to, or the inclusion of any item not relative to, the results of the period.

(18) However much supplemental detail of the trading results may be given, the following items should be stated separately in addition to those required by statute :—

(a) Income (gross) from investments in subsidiary undertakings.

    Note.—The treatment of income from subsidiary undertakings will depend on the nature of their relations with the holding company and on whether a consolidated profit and loss account is submitted. Where, for any reason, a consolidated profit and loss account is not submitted, income from subsidiary undertakings should be shown separately unless the trading with the holding company is so interlocked that such separate disclosure might create a misleading impression. If a consolidated profit and loss account is submitted, it should disclose, as a minimum, the items referred to below relative to the group as a whole.

(b) Income (gross) from other investments.

(c) Depreciation and amortisation of fixed assets.

(d) Interest charges (gross) on debentures and long-term liabilities.

(e) Credits or charges in respect of provisions, other than those for specific requirements the amounts whereof can be estimated closely. (See Recommendation No. VI.)

(f) National Defence Contribution (now Profits Tax) or Excess Profits Tax, showing separately, if material, credits or charges in respect of earlier periods.

(g) Credits or charges, if material in amount, which are abnormal in nature or relate to previous periods.

(h) Income Tax and the basis thereof, showing separately, if material, credits or charges in respect of earlier periods. (See Recommendation No. III.)

(i) Amounts set aside for redemption of share and loan capital.

(j) Reserves made or withdrawn. (See Recommendation No. VI.)

(k) Dividends paid or proposed, showing under a separate heading those which are subject to confirmation by the shareholders.

(l) Balances brought in and carried forward.

COMPARATIVE FIGURES.—(19) Comparative figures of the previous period (prepared on the same basis as those for the period under review) should be given both in the Balance Sheet and in the Profit and Loss Account.

DISCLOSURE OF INFORMATION.—(20) If directors of a company desire to disclose in their report information which, but for its inclusion in the report, would be required to be disclosed in the accounts, the relative paragraphs in the report should be clearly distinguished from the remainder of the report and specifically referred to in the accounts.

(15th July, 1944.)

IX. DEPRECIATION OF FIXED ASSETS.

Fixed assets, whatever be their nature or the type of business in which they are employed, have the fundamental characteristic that they are held with the object of earning revenue and not for the purpose of sale in the ordinary course of business. The amount at which they are shown in the Balance Sheet does not purport to be their realisable value or their replacement value, but is normally an historical record of their cost less amounts provided in respect of depreciation, amortisation or depletion.

Depreciation represents that part of the cost of a fixed asset to its owner which is not recoverable when the asset is finally put out of use by him. Provision against this loss of capital is an integral cost of conducting the business during the effective commercial life of the asset and is not dependent upon the amount of profit earned.

The assessment of depreciation involves the consideration of three factors : the cost of the asset, which is known, the probable value realisable on ultimate disposal, which can generally be estimated only within fairly wide limits, and the length of time during which the asset will be commercially useful to the undertaking. In most cases, this last factor is not susceptible of precise calculation. Provisions for depreciation are therefore in most cases matters of estimation, based upon the available experience and knowledge, rather than of accurate determination. They require adjustment from time to time in the light of changes in experience and knowledge, including prolongation of useful life due to exceptional maintenance expenditure, curtailment due to excessive use, or obsolescence not allowed for in the original estimate of the commercially useful life of the asset.

There are several methods of apportioning depreciation as between the several financial periods which constitute the anticipated useful life of the asset. Those most commonly employed in industrial and commercial concerns in this country are the straight-line method and the reducing balance method.

Subject to any periodic adjustment which may be necessary, the straight-line method (computed by providing each year a fixed proportion of the cost of the asset) spreads the provision equally over the period of anticipated use. It is used almost universally in the United States of America and Canada and to a large extent in this country. Though other methods may be appropriate in the case of some classes of assets, the balance of informed opinion now favours the straight-line method as being the most suitable for general application.

The reducing balance method which spreads the provision by annual instalments of diminishing amount computed by taking a fixed percentage of the book value of the assets as reduced by previous provisions, is also largely used in this country. It involves relatively heavy charges in the earlier years of the life of an asset and relatively light charges in the later years. In order to provide depreciation under this method within any given period, the percentage applied needs to be from two to three times that applied under the straight-line method. This is a fact not generally realised, the consequence being that rates of depreciation fixed on this basis may tend to be inadequate.

A third method, known as the sinking fund method, which endeavours to take account of anticipated income from funds set aside for depreciation purposes, is not used to any great extent in industrial and commercial concerns, though in public utility undertakings, where special considerations arise, it is frequently met. Under this method, fixed annual instalments are provided and set aside, which with compound interest, will accumulate to the cost of the asset by the end of its useful life. Where the amounts set aside are invested outside the business, the validity of the calculations depends upon the realisation of the anticipated net rate of interest, and each change in tax rates or interest yield involves recalculation.   Where the amounts are retained as additional working capital, the effect is to make a growing charge in the periodic accounts for depreciation, because the fixed periodic instalment has to be supplemented in each period by an amount equivalent to interest on past provisions.   Experience shows that, with the uncertainties inescapable in industrial and commercial enterprises, it is not prudent to place reliance upon the accrual of additional earnings to the extent required.

A fourth method, also not commonly used in industrial and commercial concerns, is the renewals reserve method, under which round sums, not necessarily computed by reference to the useful lives of the assets, and sometimes determined largely by the results of the year's trading, are provided and set aside as general provisions towards meeting the cost of future renewals.   This method does not accord with a strict view of depreciation and may distort the annual charges to revenue.

The different natures of assets involve consideration in deciding on the method of depreciation appropriate in each case.   Unless the methods adopted are applied consistently the usefulness of periodic accounts for the purpose of comparison of one period with another may be vitiated.

Whatever be the method adopted, the periodical revision of depreciation rates and the ascertainment of the residue of cost which has not been covered by depreciation provisions made up to any given date are greatly facilitated by, and often impracticable without, the maintenance of fixed asset registers showing the cost of each asset, the provisions for depreciation made thereon and the basis on which these have been calculated.

Recommendation.—It is therefore recommended that :—

(1) Provision for depreciation, amortisation and depletion of fixed assets should be applied on consistent bases from one period to another.   If additional provisions prove to be necessary, they should be stated separately in the Profit and Loss Account.   Where practicable, fixed assets *in existence at the Balance Sheet date* should normally be shown in the Balance Sheet at cost and the aggregate of the provisions for depreciation, amortisation and depletion should appear as deductions therefrom (see Recommendation VIII).   The extent to which these provisions are being kept liquid will then be ascertainable from the Balance Sheet as a whole.

(2) Such provisions should be computed on the bases mentioned below as being appropriate to the particular class of asset concerned :—

   (a) *Goodwill and Freehold Land.*—Depreciation does not arise through use in the business, except in the case of freehold land acquired for purposes such as are referred to in (d) below.   Amounts set aside to provide for diminution in value do not constitute a normal charge against revenue and should be shown separately in the Profit and Loss Account.

   (b) *Freehold Buildings, Plant and Machinery, Tools and Equipment, Ships, Transport Vehicles and similar assets which are subject to depreciation by reason of their employment in the business.*—Provision for depreciation should, in general, be computed on the straight-line method. Assets of very short effective life, such as loose tools, jigs and patterns, may, however, frequently be dealt with more satisfactorily by other methods such as re-valuation, which in no case should exceed cost.

   (c) *Leaseholds, Patents and other assets which become exhausted by the effluxion of time.*—Provision for amortisation should be made on the straight-line basis, including, in the case of leaseholds, allowance for the estimated cost of dilapidations at the end of the lease or useful life of the asset if shorter. If a leasehold redemption policy is effected with an insurance company, the charge of the annual premiums to Profit and Loss Account provides a satisfactory method of amortisation if supplemented in respect of dilapidations.

(d) *Mines, Oil Wells, Quarries and similar assets of a wasting character which are consumed in the form of basic raw material or where the output is sold as such.*—Provision for depreciation and depletion should be made according to the estimated exhaustion of the asset concerned. In the case of an undertaking formed for the purpose of exploiting this particular class of asset, if the practice is to make no provision this should be made clear in the accounts so that shareholders may realise that dividends are, in part, a return of capital.

(3) Where a method different from that recommended has hitherto been followed and it is not considered practicable or desirable to make a change in the case of assets already in use, it is suggested that the methods recommended should be followed in cases of assets subsequently acquired.

(4) Details of all fixed assets should be kept (preferably in registers specially maintained) to show the cost of each asset, the provision made for its depreciation and the basis of the provisions made.

(5) Amounts set aside out of profits for obsolescence which cannot be foreseen or for a possible increase in the cost of replacement are matters of financial prudence. Neither can be estimated with any degree of accuracy. They are in the nature of reserves and should be treated as such in the accounts.

(12th January, 1945.)

X. The Valuation of Stock-in-Trade.

No particular basis of valuation is suitable for all types of business but, whatever the basis adopted, it should be applied consistently, and the following considerations should be borne in mind :—

(A) Stock-in-Trade is a current asset held for realisation. In the Balance Sheet it is, therefore, usually shown at the lower of cost or market value.

(B) Profit or loss on trading is the difference between the amount for which goods are sold and their cost, including the cost of selling and delivery. The ultimate profit or loss on unsold goods is dependent upon prices ruling at the date of their disposal, but it is essential that provision should be made to cover anticipated losses.

(C) Inconsistency in method may have a very material effect on the valuation of a business based on earning capacity though not necessarily of importance in itself at any Balance Sheet date.

The following interpretations are placed on the terms " cost " and " market value " :—

(a) Cost.—The elements making up cost are (i) the purchase price of goods, stores and, in the case of processed stock, materials used in manufacture ; (ii) direct expenditure incurred in bringing stock-in-trade to its existing condition and location ; and (iii) indirect or overhead expenditure incidental to the class of stock-in-trade concerned.

Whereas the cost of (i) and (ii) can be ascertained with substantial accuracy, (iii)—indirect or overhead expenditure—can only be a matter of calculation. If (iii) is expressed as a percentage of actual production, the amount added to the stock valuation will fluctuate from one period to another according to the volume produced. To avoid distortion of revenue results, in some cases indirect or overhead expenditure is eliminated as an element of cost when valuing stock-in-trade or, alternatively, only that part which represents fixed annual charges is excluded. In other cases, an amount is included which is based on the normal production of the unit concerned.

The following are bases usually adopted in practice for calculating cost :—

(1) " *Unit* " *Cost.*—Upon this basis, each article, batch or parcel is valued at its individual cost. In certain cases, such as bulk stocks, this method is not always capable of application and records, including the allocation of expenses, may become unduly complicated. Further, it may not be practicable to apply the method to partly processed stocks or finished products where the individual units lose their identity.

(2) " *First in, first out.*"—This basis assumes that goods sold or consumed were those which had been longest on hand and that the quantity held in stock represents the latest purchases. It has the effect of valuing unsold stock in a reasonably close relation to replacement price. In certain manufacturing or producing businesses, however, it is difficult to apply accurately through the various stages of manufacture or production.

(3) " *Average* " *Cost.*—This basis entails averaging the book value of stock at the commencement of a period with the cost of goods added during the period after deducting consumption at the average price, the periodical rests for calculating the average being as frequent as possible having regard to the nature of the business. It has the effect of smoothing out distortion of results arising from excessive, and often fortuitous, fluctuations in purchase price and production costs and is particularly suitable to manufacturing businesses where several processes are involved.

The bases referred to above are founded on the principle that " cost " is an historical fact. In some cases, however, their application is unsuitable or impracticable owing to the nature of the business and stock-in-trade is taken at a cost estimated by one of the following methods :—

(4) " *Standard* " *Cost.*—This basis entails valuing stock at a pre-determined or budgeted cost per unit. It is coming more into use, particularly in manufacturing or processing industries where several operations are involved or where goods are produced on mass production lines.

(5) " *Adjusted Selling Price.*"—On this basis, an estimated cost is obtained by pricing stock at current selling prices and deducting an amount equivalent to the normal profit margin and the estimated cost of disposal.

Other methods of stock valuation are the " base stock " method, which retains permanently certain basic stock at a fixed price not exceeding its original cost, and that known as " last in, first out " which is based on the principle that profit or loss on trading is the difference between the price at which goods are sold and their replacement cost. There is, however, only limited application of either of these methods in this country.

(*b*) MARKET VALUE.—The expression " market value " is commonly interpreted as either :—

(i) the price at which it is estimated that the stock can be realised either in its existing condition or as incorporated in the product normally sold after allowing for all expenditure to be incurred before disposal ; or

(ii) the cost of replacing the stock at the accounting date.

In considering the merits of these alternative methods, regard must be had to the purpose for which stock-in-trade is held, namely, to sell either in its existing condition or as incorporated in a manufactured product. The fact that at the time of valuation the goods could have been acquired at a sum less than their cost only indicates that the expected profit is less than it might have been had it been possible to acquire them at the accounting date—a possibility which often does not exist in view of the quantity held and of the fact that in many cases purchases have to be made for later delivery ; the circumstance has not caused a trading loss but only indicates that the ultimate results under other conditions might have been better.

On the other hand, if at the time of the valuation it is clear that selling prices will not cover cost and expenses yet to be incurred before the goods are disposed of, provision is necessary to meet the anticipated loss.

When estimating the amount of the provision required to cover excess of cost over market value, the method employed may be either (i) to consider each article in stock separately, (ii) to group articles in categories having regard to their similarity or interchangeability, or (iii) to consider the aggregate cost of the total stock-in-trade in relation to its aggregate market value.

Recommendation.—It is therefore recommended that :—

(1) The basis of valuation for stock-in-trade should normally be the lower of cost or market value, calculated as in (2) and (3) below.

In certain businesses, such as tea or rubber producing companies and some mining companies, there is a general custom to value stocks of products at the price subsequently realised less only selling costs ; if this basis is adopted, the fact should be clearly indicated in the accounts.

In the case of long-term contracts, the value placed on work-in-progress should have regard to the terms and duration of the contracts. If, after providing for all known contingencies, credit is taken for part of the ultimate profit, this fact should be indicated.

(2) Cost should be calculated on such a basis as will show a fair view of the trend of results of the particular type of business concerned. Indirect or overhead expenditure, if included as part of the cost of partly processed or finished products, should be restricted to such expenditure as has been incurred in bringing the stock-in-trade to its existing condition and location.

Stocks of by-products, the cost of which is unascertainable, should be valued at current selling price (or contracted sale price where applicable) after deducting expenses to be incurred before disposal. The cost of the main product should be reduced accordingly.

(3) Market value should be calculated by reference to the price at which it is estimated that the stock-in-trade can be realised, either in its existing condition or as incorporated in the product normally sold, after allowing for expenditure to be incurred before disposal. In estimating this price, regard should be had to abnormal and obsolete stocks, the trend of the market and the prospects of disposal.

If the value of stock-in-trade is calculated by reference to replacement cost, it should be described in the Balance Sheet as being " at the lower of cost or replacement value," but in no case should it exceed market value as described above.

(4) For the purpose of estimating the amount of the provision required to reduce stock-in-trade below cost, it may properly be valued on the basis of the lower of its aggregate cost or of its aggregate market value. On the other hand, a more prudent and equally proper course is to take each item of stock (or each category group) and value it on the basis of the lower of its own cost or market value.

(5) Where goods have been purchased forward and are not covered by forward sales, provision should be made for the excess, if any, of the purchase price over the market value and should be shown as such in the accounts.

Note.—Where goods have been sold forward and are not covered by stocks and forward purchases, provision should be made for the excess, if any, of the anticipated cost over sales value.

(6) Whatever basis is adopted for ascertaining cost or calculating market value, it should be such as will not distort the view of the real trend of trading results and should be applied consistently regardless of the amount of profits available or losses sustained. Any reduction in stock values which exceeds the provisions embodied in the above recommendations is a reserve and should be shown as such in the accounts.

(15th June, 1945.)

XI. EXCESS PROFITS TAX POST-WAR REFUNDS.

(19th July, 1946.)

[This Recommendation is not reproduced as it is no longer of particular practical importance.]

XII. RISING PRICE LEVELS IN RELATION TO ACCOUNTS.

In periods when rises in price levels are marked, businesses tend to become undercapitalised and the problems thereby created have been increasingly emphasised in recent months in annual reports, chairmen's speeches, the financial press and elsewhere. As stocks of materials are converted into goods and sold and as fixed assets wear out or become obsolete, substantially greater amounts have to be invested in the assets which replace them than were invested in the purchase of those displaced; other working capital requirements likewise increase.

In some businesses the immediate effects of a rise in price levels are more apparent than in others. Those where rapid stock replacement occurs feel the results quickly, and those whose plant and equipment call for immediate or early replacement feel the effect more rapidly than those for which replacement is a long-term problem. But in nearly all businesses the undercapitalisation will be felt sooner or later if the rise in prices is maintained.

The maintenance of the capacity of the business to cope with the physical volume of goods or services previously handled depends to a large extent upon the correction of this undercapitalisation. This can be done either by obtaining new capital from outside sources or by retaining in the business moneys which would otherwise be free for distribution; or by a combination of these methods.

The raising of new capital from outside sources necessarily implies a surrender by the proprietors of a proportion of their equity in the business or the introduction of prior ranking capital. Some fear that the adoption of this method may later involve the drastic pruning of the capital structure, as happened in the case of some companies in the decade which preceded the last war; but the alternative of retaining resources in the business has its difficulties also.

The basis and scale of taxation in force in Great Britain are such that the extent to which profits can be retained in businesses for the purpose of adjusting the undercapitalisation is seriously restricted. The difference between the original monetary cost of stocks sold and the amount realised on the sale in the ordinary course of business is brought into account for taxation purposes; moreover, the allowances for taxation purposes in respect of the fixed assets are restricted to an amount equal to their original monetary cost. Profits are subjected not only to income tax at 9s. in the £, but also to profits tax in the case of corporate bodies and sur-tax in the case of individuals and partnerships. The amounts which might otherwise accrue in the course of trading and become available for meeting increased costs of replacement are thus gravely diminished.

The combined effect of the rise in price levels and the oppressive burden of taxation has led a number of business men and their advisers to question the validity of the methods of profit ascertainment hitherto generally followed by industrial and commercial undertakings. They do not challenge the generally accepted accounting principle that the profit of a period can be ascertained only after providing, by way of charges against revenue, adequate sums for remedying any impairment of the capital of a business which may have occurred in the ordinary course of trading in that period. Opinions differ, however, as to whether capital for this purpose means (a) the money contributed by the proprietors, including profits left by them in the business for financing it, or (b) the power of that sum of money to purchase a particular volume of goods or equipment. Some business men have adopted the latter conception and accordingly maintain the proposition that profit can be stated correctly only if it is ascertained after treating as revenue charges sums sufficient to provide the increased funds necessary for replacing the stocks consumed or sold and for providing an appropriate proportion of the prospective enhanced cost of replacing the fixed assets used up in carrying on the business.

This proposition is at variance with the accounting practice hitherto generally followed of treating as charges to revenue the actual monetary cost of the stocks consumed or sold and depreciation provisions representing the appropriate proportion of the amounts carried in the books for fixed assets (usually their historical cost). Those who maintain the view hitherto accepted, point out that logical application of the method advocated by those who desire a change would require them in ascertaining profit not only to make charges against revenue on new bases in respect of stocks and fixed assets, but also to provide for the diminished purchasing power of cash and other liquid assets to be used in the business. They put forward the criticism that it would be illogical, in ascertaining profit, to treat as a necessary charge the cost of maintaining the purchasing power of money provided by the issue of fixed preference or loan capital, whilst ignoring the corresponding diminution in the obligation, expressed in terms of purchasing power, to the holders of that capital. They emphasise that if the new conception were adopted the holders of preference shares might be deprived of dividends without acquiring any capital benefit. Moreover, they point out, as regards goods consumed or sold, that those who desire the change have not yet been able to devise a satisfactory method, suitable for general use, of applying the principle advocated and, as regards fixed assets, that, owing to improved processes of manufacture, plant which becomes worn out or obsolete is not invariably replaced. Further, they claim that not only is the suggested change wrong in principle, but also that it strikes at the root of sound and objective accounting because of the practical difficulties of assessing the amounts which would be treated as charges to revenue if the new conception were adopted.

Some suggest that apart from the taxation consequences, which are inescapable in the present state of the law, the problem should be met by arranging, so far as fixed assets are concerned, that the amounts (generally their depreciated historical cost) at which they are carried in the books should be written-up to the amounts which it is estimated might have to be paid if they were to be replaced at the present time by identical assets in a comparable state of depreciation. They also suggest that depreciation should thereafter be calculated upon the written-up figures, but there is not unanimity among them as to whether the future annual instalments of depreciation should be calculated so as (a) to amortise over the residue of the effective life of each asset the whole of the gross replacement cost (i.e., the amount which would have to be paid at the present time to acquire similar assets in a new condition) less the provisions for depreciation already made, or (b) only to provide annually one year's proportion of the gross replacement cost based upon the total life of the asset, ignoring the fact that provisions for earlier years were calculated upon smaller capital sums. In the absence of a sufficient fall in prices, the adoption of the latter method would fail to secure the provision of the funds required by the eventual replacement date, but, on the other hand, might be regarded as providing a fair charge against the revenue of each year on the new basis ; it would need to be supplemented out of profits or otherwise in order to provide the necessary funds.

Apart from the question of depreciation, the writing-up of the fixed assets itself involves practical difficulties, including, *inter alia*, those which arise because relative stability of prices on a new level has not yet been attained, the invalidation of comparisons with figures of previous periods and, in many cases, the lack of data on which satisfactory revaluations could be achieved.

In certain European countries assets have been written-up by the use of price indices, with governmental encouragement in the shape of additional taxation allowances; in Great Britain no such benefit is available and the extra sums provided for depreciation, as in the case of other sums provided to meet increased replacement costs, would be treated as disallowable charges for taxation purposes.

The foregoing matters have been the subject of much discussion among business men and their advisers in Great Britain and North America. There is no generally accepted conclusion in either territory as to the way in which the problems should be solved. It is, however, clear that in Great Britain the effects of the rise in prices when combined with the effects of the basis and scale of taxation cannot, unless profits are sufficient, be met by changes in accounting practice; Parliament alone has the power to mitigate these consequences by changes in the tax law.

The majority of businesses maintain their past practices for the ascertainment of profits and set aside out of those profits such additional sums as are found practicable towards meeting the enhanced costs of replacement. The setting aside of profits for this purpose is viewed by their directors as a major requirement when deciding upon the amounts which they can prudently recommend for distribution in dividends. Some boards of directors are so impressed with the importance of emphasising to their shareholders the implications of the matter that they set aside the sums concerned on the basis of a programme designed to provide by instalments, over the period during which the assets are in effective use, the funds which it is expected will be needed for their replacement. The financial effects of such a plan are identical with those of schemes involving a drastic change in the basis of profit ascertainment as outlined in earlier paragraphs, the material difference being that the extra amounts set aside are treated as appropriations of profits instead of as charges made before profits are ascertained.

Owing to the inherent difficulty of determining in advance the prices which may have to be paid in the future for the replacement of assets, it is impracticable to forecast with any precision the additional reserves which will be required. This fact alone is likely to necessitate modification of any plan whereby the actual sums required to effect replacements are provided by instalments over a period of years, either by way of supplementing depreciation charges or by setting up in lieu of depreciation a provision for renewals based on estimated replacement costs. Moreover, the gap between historical and replacement costs might be too big to be bridged in these ways.

The matters mentioned in the foregoing paragraphs have been under close examination by the Council and the advice given in the Council's Recommendations IX and X, issued in 1945, has been re-examined. In Recommendation X the Council emphasised that profit or loss on trading is the difference between the amount for which goods are sold and their historical cost including expenses of sale and delivery; it recommended that for accounting purposes the basis of valuation for stock-in-trade should normally be the historical cost (or, if lower, the market value as defined in the recommendation). In Recommendation IX the Council expressed a similar view with respect to fixed assets when it emphasised that depreciation provisions should be based on cost and stated in paragraph 5 that: " Amounts set aside out of profits for . . . a possible increase in the cost of replacement are matters of financial prudence (and cannot) be estimated with any degree of accuracy. They are in the nature of reserves and should be treated as such in the accounts." The advice thus given on replacement costs was subsequently endorsed from the legal standpoint by counsel whose opinion was taken by the Institute upon the implications of the Companies Act, 1947 (now the Companies Act, 1948).

The Council sees no need to modify the advice which it has already given, but amplifies this advice in the recommendations set out below. It wishes, however, to draw attention to the fact that the funds which can be accumulated by businesses through charging sums against revenue in absorption of the historical cost of goods sold and assets consumed must, if the enhanced levels of prices are maintained, be inadequate to meet the cost of replacing goods and assets which were purchased at substantially lower levels. It is necessary also to recognise that rising prices, coupled with the present basis and scale of taxation, seriously impair the ability of industry and commerce to maintain their volume of trade or services at pre-war levels and make necessary the taking of steps to strengthen their financial resources for this purpose.

It is, therefore, of the greatest importance that directors should be advised to consider, in relation to the circumstances of their company, the effects of the rise in price levels and the relative merits of (a) relying upon the company's ability to raise new capital as and when it may be required for the purpose of meeting enhancements in replacement costs, and (b) the desirability of setting aside and accumulating out of profits such sums for this purpose as may be practicable. In many cases this consideration may be a matter of major importance in determining the amount of profits which, from the standpoint of financial prudence, should be regarded as available for dividend. It should be borne in mind that if carried to extremes the retention of profits might involve the severe curtailment or even cessation of dividends and the imposition of undue burdens upon existing shareholders, including preference shareholders, for the benefit of future holders of the equity shares.

The desirability of informing shareholders, as to the effects of the rise in price levels on their own company's affairs and as to the steps taken or contemplated to meet them, is a matter for consideration by directors. Where an amount set aside out of profits is determined in accordance with a programme designed to provide the necessary funds by instalments over the period during which the assets are in effective use, the information given should indicate the facts.

Recommendation.—The following further recommendations are now made in amplification of Recommendations IX and X—

(1) Any amount set aside to finance replacements (whether of fixed or current assets) at enhanced costs should not be treated as a provision which must be made before profit for the year can be ascertained, but as a transfer to reserve. If such a transfer to reserve is shown in the Profit and Loss Account as a deduction in arriving at the balance for the year, that balance should be described appropriately.

(2) In order to emphasise that as a matter of prudence the amount set aside is, for the time being, regarded by the directors as not available for distribution, it should normally be treated as a specific capital reserve for increased cost of replacement of assets.

(3) For Balance Sheet purposes fixed assets should not, in general, be written-up on the basis of estimated replacement costs, especially in the absence of a measure of stability in the price level.

(14th *January,* 1949.)

XIII. ACCOUNTANTS' REPORTS FOR PROSPECTUSES : FIXED ASSETS AND
    DEPRECIATION.

The report by a company's auditors, which is required for prospectus purposes under the Fourth Schedule to the Companies Act, 1948, must deal with :—

(a) the profits or losses in respect of each of the five financial years imme-
    diately preceding the issue of the prospectus ; and

(b) the assets and liabilities at the last date to which the accounts were
    made up.

Similar reports by accountants are required in respect of any business which
is to be acquired out of the proceeds of an issue. In practice the reports generally deal with profits or losses over a period of ten years in order to comply
with Stock Exchange regulations.

Such reports must either indicate by way of note any adjustments as respects
the figures of profits or losses or assets and liabilities dealt with by the report
which appear necessary to the persons making the report, or must make those
adjustments and indicate that adjustments have been made. Among the
matters which may require adjustment are the treatment of fixed assets and
the depreciation thereof.

The amounts at which fixed assets stand in the books normally depend on
the price levels at the time of acquisition and the depreciation policy adopted
since that time ; they are not usually intended to indicate the current values
of the assets. Frequently, however, a company obtains from an expert a valuation of fixed assets for inclusion in a prospectus. Under existing conditions
such a valuation may be greatly in excess of the amounts at which the assets
stand in the books. In some cases the valuation figures may be adopted for
the purposes of the company's books, but in others they may be used for prospectus purposes only without being incorporated in the books.

Where the valuation is incorporated in the books, depreciation will in future
necessarily be calculated on the valuation figures, resulting in future earnings
being charged with sums which might be considerably in excess of those charged
in the accounts during the period covered by the report. Consequently, a report
dealing with assets and liabilities on the basis of the valuation taken into the
books would mislead intending investors, if the figures stated in the report for
past profits or losses were arrived at after providing for depreciation on amounts
considerably less than the valuation without any indication being given in the
report of the effect of the valuation on future depreciation provisions. Similar
considerations arise in the case of a business acquired, or to be acquired, on
the basis of a valuation of fixed assets greatly in excess of the amounts carried
for such assets in the books of that business at the time of acquisition.

Where, on the other hand, the valuation is used by the directors in the
prospectus for the purpose of indicating the assets cover for the issue, but the
valuation is not incorporated in the books, then depreciation provisions will be
calculated in future on the book amounts, which may be substantially less than
the valuation. In this case, subsequent profits will be ascertained correctly by
reference to depreciation charges based upon the book amounts, but the assets
cover indicated by the directors will not normally be maintained unless, out of
profits earned during the effective life of the assets which are subject to depreciation, reserves are set aside at least equal to the excess of the valuation of those
assets over their book amounts. The same need for reserves arises in the case
of a holding company where a valuation of the fixed assets of subsidiaries is
used by the directors in the prospectus, but is not incorporated in the books
of the subsidiaries. In these cases the creation of the whole or part of the
necessary reserves may be obligatory under the terms of the prospectus if the
issue is one of redeemable preference shares or debentures ; but, whatever may
be the terms of the issue, intending investors may be misled in regard to the

assets covering their subscriptions unless the necessity for retaining profits, up to the amount of the excess, is recognised fully by the directors in their representations in the prospectus as to the profits which they anticipate will be available for future dividends. The context in which the accountants' report appears may thus have a material effect on the conclusions which the intending investor will draw from the prospectus as a whole.

Special considerations arise where the cost to a holding company of shares in its subsidiaries is in excess of the amounts at which the underlying net assets are carried in the books of the subsidiaries. In some cases the profits of the group may not be stated fairly unless they are arrived at after charging depreciation on that part, if any, of the excess which relates to fixed assets. Circumstances of companies differ greatly and each case has to be considered on the facts. Among the matters requiring consideration is the extent to which the excess is attributable to such assets as goodwill or freehold land, which are not generally regarded as subject to depreciation, or to depreciating assets such as leaseholds, buildings, plant and machinery ; the allocation of the excess between the several types of asset will affect the depreciation, if any, which should be provided and, consequently, the profits.

Another important aspect is that of taxation. If the allowances for taxation purposes are materially different from the corresponding provisions made for depreciation, the net profits after deducting depreciation provisions may give a misleading indication of the profits for taxation purposes and consequently of the net amount available for distribution. A similar position may arise where a material part of the assets comprises depreciating assets on which no allowance is obtainable for taxation purposes. Further, where in future the depreciation provisions will be calculated on a valuation which is not applicable for taxation purposes, the written-down amount for taxation purposes (representing the total maximum amount available for future taxation allowances) may be substantially less than the valuation ; where this is so, provisions for depreciation in future will be greater than the allowances for taxation purposes. In circumstances such as the foregoing, the excess of the depreciation provisions is not the whole amount involved ; to set aside the full depreciation provisions required, the company will have to earn not merely the excess over the taxation allowances but such an amount of taxable profit as after deduction of income tax and profits tax will leave a net sum equal to the excess.

The foregoing paragraphs and the recommendations that follow relate to circumstances in which it may frequently be necessary to make adjustments in respect of fixed assets and depreciation, but it must be borne in mind that the circumstances of one company may differ greatly from those of another. It is necessary to take into account the relevant facts of each case before deciding what, if any, adjustments should be made and what matters should be referred to specifically in the accountants' report.

Recommendation.—It is therefore recommended that the following principles should normally be applied in reporting for prospectus purposes :—

(1) If material to the presentation of the figures, the amounts charged for depreciation in the years under review should be stated in the report.

(2) Where there has been a change (whether of rates or by reason of a valuation) in the basis of depreciation during the period covered by the report, the effect of the change should be indicated in the report if the effect is material and cannot be dealt with appropriately in the adjustments made in arriving at the figures shown in the report.

(3) Where the allowances obtained for taxation purposes differ materially from the corresponding charges made for depreciation in arriving at the profits or losses shown in the report :—

(a) If the difference is material in relation to the profits or losses shown, the report should indicate the fact and should state the amount of the difference (or give the relevant amounts) for the last year covered by the report or for such other period as may be appropriate ;

(b) If the allowances obtained are substantially greater than the amounts charged, it is a matter for consideration whether adjustments should be made so as to substitute the amounts of the allowances for the depreciation charged.

(4) Where the amounts chargeable in future for depreciation are materially in excess of the allowances obtainable for taxation purposes (for example, because the assets include assets on which no allowance for taxation is obtainable, or because of a writing-up of assets on a revaluation, or because of the acquisition of a business on terms that the purchase price of depreciating assets is materially in excess of the amount on which allowances for taxation purposes are available to the purchaser):—

(a) The report should indicate the extent of the excess of the depreciation chargeable over the taxation allowances obtainable for the year immediately subsequent to the period covered by the report ;

(b) The report should also indicate that owing to the disallowance for taxation purposes of this excess, the sum required to cover it is the gross amount which after deduction of income tax and profits tax will leave a net amount equal to the excess.

(5) Where a valuation of fixed assets is adopted for the purposes of the books and accounts :—

(a) It is not normally appropriate or practicable, in a report dealing with a period during which there have been material changes in price levels, to make consequential adjustments in the depreciation provisions for past years ;

(b) The report should, however, indicate the approximate future annual provision computed on the basis of the valuation and should give a comparison thereof with the actual provision made in arriving at the profit or loss shown in the report for the last year covered thereby.

(6) Where a valuation of fixed assets is used by the directors in the prospectus in order to indicate the assets cover for the issue, but the valuation is not adopted for the purposes of the books and accounts :—

(a) The report should not include figures based on, or a reference to, a valuation in excess of the amounts standing in the books ;

(b) Before consenting (under Section 40, Companies Act, 1948) to the inclusion of their report in the prospectus, the accountants should either :—

(i) Ascertain from the directors that the directors' estimates of future profits available for dividend, as shown in the prospectus, have been arrived at after appropriate deductions have been made for the profits which it will be necessary to retain as reserves (including profits set aside for the redemption of preference shares or debentures) in order to maintain the assets cover indicated in the prospectus ; or

(ii) If such deductions have not been made, satisfy themselves that the disclosure is sufficient to show how far the directors have taken this factor into account.

(7) In the case of a holding company effect should be given to the foregoing recommendations where either :—

    (*a*) The cost of its shares in subsidiaries is materially in excess of the amount at which the underlying net assets are carried in their books and a material part of the excess relates to fixed assets which are subject to depreciation ; or

    (*b*) There is used in the prospectus a valuation of the fixed assets of the subsidiaries which is materially in excess of the amount at which such assets are carried in their books or (in a case where the valuation has been adopted by the subsidiaries for the purposes of their books and accounts) were so carried immediately prior to their adoption of the valuation.

(8) In the foregoing recommendations references to " allowances for taxation purposes " should normally be interpreted as the annual allowances (other than initial allowances, balancing allowances and similar items) obtained for income tax purposes for the fiscal years of which the financial years are the basis years. In some cases, however, it may be more appropriate to apply the allowances for profits tax purposes. The circumstances of companies differ greatly and each case should be examined on its merits. In order to obtain a fair basis of comparison it may, for example, be necessary in some cases to take into account, whether by way of spreading or otherwise, initial and balancing allowances and charges, particularly in respect of assets which have a short effective life or where the aggregate depreciation charges over a long period are being compared with the corresponding aggregate taxation allowances.

(11th March, 1949.)

XIV. The Form and Contents of Accounts of Estates of Deceased Persons and Similar Trusts.

(12th August, 1949.)

[This Recommendation is not reproduced as it does not relate to the subject matter of this work.]

XV. Accounting in Relation to Changes in the Purchasing Power of Money.

Accounting Based on Historical Cost.—The primary purpose of the annual accounts of a business is to present information to the proprietors, showing how their funds have been utilised and the profits derived from such use. It has long been accepted in accounting practice that a Balance Sheet prepared for this purpose is an historical record and not a statement of current worth. Stated briefly its function is to show in monetary terms the capital, reserves and liabilities of a business at the date as at which it is prepared and the manner in which the total moneys representing them have been distributed over the several types of assets. Similarly a Profit and Loss Account is an historical record. It shows as the profit or loss the difference between the revenue for the period covered by the account and the expenditure chargeable in that period, including charges for the amortisation of capital expenditure. Revenue and expenditure are brought into the account at their recorded monetary amounts. This basis of accounting is frequently described as the historical cost basis and in this statement the expression " monetary profits " is used to denote profits so computed.

An important feature of the historical cost basis of preparing annual accounts is that it reduces to a minimum the extent to which the accounts can be affected by the personal opinions of those responsible for them. For example, the cost of a fixed asset is known so that in calculating depreciation provisions based on that cost the only respects in which estimates enter into the matter are in relation to the probable useful life of the asset and its realisable value, if any, at the end of its life. Depreciation provisions computed on this basis are intended, by making charges against revenue over the useful life of an asset, to amortise the capital expenditure incurred in acquiring it. For this purpose, estimates of current value or of replacement cost do not arise. Again, there are limits within which estimates and opinions can properly operate in relation to stock-in-trade, provided the bases of calculation are sound in principle and used consistently.

The significance of accounts prepared on the basis of historical cost is, however, subject to limitations, not the least of which is that the monetary unit in which accounts are prepared is not a stable unit of measurement. During a period of rising prices a decrease occurs in the purchasing power of cash and bank balances and assets such as debts and investments carrying fixed rates of interest or dividend, but this decrease is not treated as a reduction of business profits ; nor are business profits shown as being increased by the benefit derived from the fall in the burden, expressed in terms of purchasing power, of loans and other liabilities incurred before the rise in prices but payable in currency of diminished purchasing power. Moreover, the monetary cost at which stock-in-trade is charged against revenue is not sufficient, during a period of rising prices, to meet the cost of replacing the same quantity of stock ; and similarly depreciation charges based on the monetary cost of fixed assets will not provide the amount required to meet the cost of replacement of those assets at higher prices if and when they need to be replaced.

Monetary profits do not therefore necessarily reflect an increase or decrease in wealth in terms of purchasing power ; and in times of material change in prices this limitation upon the significance of monetary profits may be very important. It would be a major development in the building up of a coherent and logical structure of accounting principles if the limitations of accounts based on historical cost could be eliminated or reduced by the adoption of new principles, capable of practical application to all kinds of businesses in a manner which would be independent of personal opinion to a degree comparable with the existing principles based on historical cost.

THE MAIN SUGGESTIONS FOR NEW ACCOUNTING PRINCIPLES.—The main suggestions which have so far been made for new accounting principles to overcome the limitations of the historical cost basis may be considered in the following four broad categories :—

The replacement cost method of dealing with fixed assets.

The writing-up of fixed assets.

The current value method of dealing with stock-in-trade and depreciation of fixed assets.

The index method of adjusting accounts to reflect changes in the purchasing power of money.

The Replacement Cost Method of Dealing with Fixed Assets.—The object of the replacement cost method of dealing with fixed assets is to make charges to Profit and Loss Account to provide the amount needed to meet the cost of replacement. Under this method, therefore, provisions for replacement would be charged, instead of depreciation charges designed to amortise the cost of fixed assets over their useful life. The method was followed more extensively in the past than it is to-day, particularly though not exclusively by public utility undertakings.

Considerable uncertainty attaches to the calculations required by the replacement cost method. Unless an asset is to be replaced within a very short period, the replacement cost cannot be estimated with any accuracy and the method therefore leaves wide scope for extremes of personal opinion in determining each year the charge to be made in computing profits. Moreover improved methods of production and new inventions often render existing plant obsolete with the result that when it is replaced the new equipment is of a different character from the old.

In conditions where prices continue to rise, the uncertainty of the method is emphasised because the estimated replacement cost of assets increases year by year. If each year's charge has been calculated on the basis of one year's proportion of the replacement cost estimated at the time of making the calculation, then the aggregate of the amounts so provided will not be sufficient to meet the actual cost of replacement. If in order to meet this difficulty the calculation each year is made on a cumulative basis so as to make up the deficiency in past provisions, the effect would be to place undue burdens upon particular years. On the other hand if the deficiency were not so made good, the amounts shown as profits would not have been arrived at after providing for the replacement of fixed assets. In the latter event, the effect of applying the method would be to show as profits each year amounts which are neither monetary profits nor profits after providing fully for the replacement of fixed assets ; the more persistent the rise in prices the less significance the profits computed in this way would have, because each further rise in prices would increase the deficiency in the past provisions.

In addition to the foregoing difficulties of calculation and treatment, the method involves other considerations which become apparent when replacement occurs. At that point two courses are open, namely either (a) to bring into the Balance Sheet the cost of the new asset, thus maintaining in the Balance Sheet the cost of the fixed assets in current use ; or (b) to charge the cost of the new asset against the accumulated replacement provisions. If the first course is followed the cost of the asset replaced will be charged against the accumulated replacement provisions ; but if prices have been rising these provisions will exceed the amount charged against them and this excess will be treated as a reserve, thus being recognised in the Balance Sheet as part of the proprietorship interest. This involves the inconsistency that the profits of each year during which the provisions are accumulated will be ascertained after deducting amounts which it is known must in due course be recognised as reserves and could become available for distribution to proprietors. Such a reserve would not be disclosed in the Balance Sheet if the second course were followed (namely the charging of the cost of the new asset against the accumulated replacement provisions), because the Balance Sheet would not show the cost of existing assets ; instead it would continue to include the cost of the asset which has been replaced and if this procedure were followed on each successive replacement the amount standing in the Balance Sheet would be the original cost of an asset which may have been replaced many times.

Another consideration arises in a period of falling prices when replacement would cost less than historical cost. If each year's charge is calculated on the basis of one year's proportion of the replacement cost estimated at the time of making the calculation, then the aggregate of the amounts so provided will fall short of the amount required to amortise the cost of the existing assets. It cannot be assumed that there will be reserves against which to charge the deficiency and it would therefore seem that the charge must be to the Profit and Loss Account. The effect of such a charge would be to adjust the aggregate depreciation charges to what they would have been under the historical cost method. The replacement cost method is therefore not capable of application in a period of falling prices, unless an additional charge is made in order to provide for the full amortisation of capital expenditure actually incurred.

The Writing-up of Fixed Assets.—In some countries businesses have been permitted for taxation purposes to write-up fixed assets in accordance with a legally established index and thereafter to charge depreciation on the written-up amounts.

The writing-up of fixed assets has the effect of treating the business as ceasing and starting afresh on a new basis as from the date of writing-up ; and this is why it is in practice considered to be appropriate and desirable in certain special circumstances, such as where a subsidiary is acquired and the assets are written-up to reflect the cost to the acquiring company, or where subscriptions for new capital are invited on the basis of a current valuation of the assets. Apart from such special purposes, the writing-up of assets appears to be suitable only for the readjustment of all Balance Sheets by government action as part of a process of stabilising a currency.

If fixed assets are written up, the subsequent charges for depreciation will be the amounts required to amortise the written-up amounts of the assets over their remaining life. The figures shown as profits for years subsequent to the writing-up will therefore be arrived at after charging depreciation on amounts which are neither the historical cost nor the estimated replacement cost of the fixed assets. If the writing-up were not based on a legally established or generally accepted index there would be wide scope for the factor of personal opinion in so computing depreciation charges. The method also involves an inconsistency similar to that arising under the replacement cost method. At the time of writing-up, the excess of the written-up amount over the historical cost of the assets concerned would be treated in the Balance Sheet as a capital reserve ; later, when the written-up amount has been fully amortised by subsequent depreciation charges, the reserve could become available for distribution to the proprietors although it will never have appeared as profit in the Profit and Loss Account.

The Current Value Method of Dealing with Depreciation and Stock-in-trade.
—The object of the current value method of dealing with depreciation and stock-in-trade is to express charges for consumption of assets in current values and not in terms of the monetary cost of the assets consumed.

Charges for depreciation of fixed assets would not be regarded as the spreading of historical cost or as provisions for future replacement. They would be regarded as a measurement of asset consumption during the year, calculated by applying the depreciation rates to the estimated current value of the fixed assets instead of to their historical cost. Broadly the effect would be that the charges in any particular year for depreciation of fixed assets would be adjusted to approximately what they would have been if the assets had been purchased at prices ruling in that year instead of when they were in fact purchased. Some advocates of this basis of ascertaining profits suggest that the method by which the current value of fixed assets is estimated should be that best suited to the particular type of business ; for example valuation by the company's engineering staff, or current insurance values, or price indices according to the year of purchase. Such a proposal serves to emphasise the dependence of the method upon personal opinion.

In a period of rising prices when current values are greater than historical cost, the depreciation charges calculated on current values would exceed depreciation calculated on historical cost and the method requires this excess to be shown in the Balance Sheet as a capital reserve. This would involve the inconsistency that an amount which is treated as a deduction in computing profits is recognised in the Balance Sheet as forming part of the interest of the proprietors and could even become available for distribution to them in the event of the reserve being regarded as no longer of a capital nature. In a period of falling prices when current values are less than historical cost, the method would not be capable of application unless an additional charge were made to provide for the full amortisation of capital expenditure actually incurred.

As already indicated, the current value method does not purport to be a means of providing for the replacement of fixed assets. If therefore prices continue to rise and it were desired to accumulate the full amount required to replace fixed assets, it would be necessary to set aside additional sums over and above the depreciation charges calculated on current values. These additional sums would be treated in the Profit and Loss Account as transfers to reserve. The total reserve shown in the Balance Sheet under the current value method would then be the same as that which can be achieved under existing accounting principles ; but whereas under existing principles the creation of that reserve would be shown in the Profit and Loss Account as having been made out of profits, under the current value method part of the amount taken to reserve would be treated, as stated in the preceding paragraph, as a charge in arriving at profits.

The current value method also requires charges for consumption of stock-in-trade to have regard to current values rather than to historical cost. Some advocates of the method suggest that the manner of charging consumption in current values should be left open for consideration in the special circumstances of each case but that certain methods of valuing stock-in-trade, namely LIFO (last in, first out), NIFO (next in, first out), base stock and variants of these should be recognised as means of achieving the desired end and that whatever method is adopted should be indicated in the accounts.

In a period of rising prices the effect of charging consumption of stock-in-trade on the basis of current values would be that the difference between the cost of an article and the higher amount for which it could be replaced at the time of its sale would not form part of the profit on the transaction. In a period of falling prices when stock-in-trade could be replaced at less than its historical cost, the current value method could not be applied unless an additional charge were made to cover the excess of the historical cost over the current value. Whether prices are rising or falling, however, the difference between the cost of an article and its current value may often result to a much greater extent from market fluctuations in the prices of particular goods than from any general trend in the purchasing power of money. Such market fluctuations are an ordinary business hazard affecting profit or loss and their incidence on a particular business may be dependent to a considerable extent upon judgment in buying and on management generally, whereas under the current value method the effect of these fluctuations would be excluded in computing profits.

The Index Method of Adjusting Accounts to Reflect Changes in the Purchasing Power of Money.—The object of the index method of adjusting accounts is to eliminate from profits the effect of fluctuations in the purchasing power of money.

The method is not strictly a proposal for a change from accounting based on historical cost ; it is more in the nature of a proposal for adjusting accounts which have been prepared on the basis of historical cost. The ascertainment of profits involves bringing together in one account monetary amounts for transactions which have taken place not only at various times during the period covered by the account but also at various times in other periods, for example, stock-in-trade at the commencement of the period and fixed assets acquired many years earlier. The theory of the index method is that if there has been a change in the purchasing power of money between the time when a transaction was entered into and the date as on which the accounts are prepared, the currency in which the transaction took place was a currency different from that now in use and must be converted into the new currency. For the conversion process an index of purchasing power would be used.

The technique of applying the index method need not present insuperable difficulties if a satisfactory index were available, although there could be considerable complications in respect of businesses with complex capital structures. An important practical consideration would be that in order to enable the index method to be applied as a part of normal accounting procedure, it would be essential for the index to be available in an up-to-date form month by month ; otherwise it would not be available for use as and when required by a particular business for the rapid production of the annual accounts at the normal accounting date. It would seem from the theory underlying the index method that it must apply not merely to transactions effected in earlier years, such as the purchase of fixed assets or stock-in-trade held at the beginning of the accounting period, but also to transactions during the accounting period if during that period there have been material changes in the purchasing power of money.

Unless all items were converted into the " new currency " and not merely selected items such as depreciation of fixed assets and consumption of stock-in-trade, the account would not, in a period of rising prices, reflect the loss in purchasing power arising from the holding of assets such as investments, debtors and bank balances or the gain arising on liabilities of fixed monetary amount. In businesses where such items are material in relation to fixed assets and stock-in-trade it would be inconsistent to ignore such losses and gains and to take into account only those arising on particular types of assets. To do so would not enable the effects of the diminution in the purchasing power of money to be measured so that they can be eliminated in ascertaining profits or losses. Similar considerations arise in a period of falling prices.

Application of the theory underlying the index method would require an index which represents changes in the purchasing power of money and not indices of changes in the prices of particular articles. If an index of purchasing power were not used, it would be necessary to use different indices for various items in the accounts of any one business ; this procedure would be a means of applying the current value method to stock-in-trade and depreciation but it would not measure the effect of changes in the general purchasing power of money which is the object of the index method. The view might be taken that the use of an accurate index of changes in general purchasing power is not important and that any reasonable index could enable the effects of such changes to be measured with sufficient accuracy, provided the same index were used by all businesses. On the other hand, prices do not move uniformly for all articles and commodities, so that the application of a general index to a particular business could well be inappropriate. Moreover the effect on a particular business of changes in the purchasing power of money may be offset by the benefits derived from technical improvements. The whole theory of the index method therefore needs further examination before it could be accepted as a valid method of adjusting accounts prepared on the basis of historical cost.

If it were established that the theory of a general purchasing power of money is valid and a satisfactory index could be prepared, there would remain the important question of the purpose for which the index method is to be applied. If it were used merely as a means of measuring the effects on the affairs of a business of changes in the purchasing power of money, for the purpose of giving this information in statements supplementary to accounts prepared on the basis of historical cost, it might give information which would be of interest to the management and proprietors. If however the index method were accepted as a means of introducing a new conception of profit, it would carry implications which extend far beyond accounting matters.

ECONOMIC AND SOCIAL ISSUES.—The adoption of any new conception of profit, whether based on the replacement cost method, the writing-up of fixed assets, the current value method, or the index method, would raise much wider questions than the computation of business profits. A conception based on the index method would raise the whole question of the effect of changes in the purchasing power of money on rights expressed in monetary terms. Important economic and social issues would then need consideration and some of these would also arise if a conception of profit based on any of the other three methods were adopted. The following are some of the questions which would need consideration :—

    (a) Whether there should be legal recognition of changes in the purchasing power of money so as to adjust legal rights which have been expressed in terms of money ; for example investments in government and other stocks and shares, rents under leases, pensions, insurance policies, debentures and other liabilities, rights under service agreements and profit sharing schemes to incomes which are dependent on or vary with profits, and the relative rights of life tenants and remaindermen.

(b) The determination of prices of goods and services, particularly the question whether a new conception of profit would make it necessary for prices to be raised in order to enable a business to pay a fair return to investors, or indeed to make a profit at all ; in other words whether the effect would be to cause a further fall in the purchasing power of money and thereby aggravate the problem.

(c) The relative position for taxation purposes of different kinds of businesses and of persons having money incomes, including employees and pensioners of businesses. In the United Kingdom the basis and scale of taxation seriously restrict the extent to which monetary profits may be retained in businesses to meet the increased capital requirements imposed by diminution in the purchasing power of money. A new conception of business profits designed to alleviate this situation would raise the question of what is the proper taxable income of other classes of taxpayer ; in a period of rising prices it would relieve businesses of a large amount of taxation and would therefore raise the further question of how the burden of that relief is to be distributed over other taxpayers.

(d) The effect on the raising of capital for business undertakings if such capital is to be raised on the basis that before dividends can be paid the purchasing power of the capital employed in the business must be maintained, as distinct from the existing position under which it is a matter of policy for directors to consider to what extent monetary profits are to be regarded as available for distribution and to what extent it is desirable to retain profits to meet the future requirements of the business.

(e) The position in the event of the purchasing power of money being increased by falling prices, particularly if the effect of a new conception of profit were to be that the contributed capital would cease to be intact.

(f) The position of persons who have acquired investments on the basis of annual accounts or prospectus statements prepared in accordance with existing accounting principles, if the adoption of a new conception of profit would result in dividends, including those on preference capital, whether or not cumulative, being reduced or passed.

These issues affect not merely every business but also every individual and they involve major considerations of general monetary and social policy which go far beyond the question whether one accounting method of computing business profit is more free from limitations than another.

CONCLUSIONS AND RECOMMENDATIONS.—The Council cannot emphasise too strongly that the significance of accounts prepared on the basis of historical cost is subject to limitations, not the least of which is that the monetary unit in which the accounts are prepared is not a stable unit of measurement. In consequence the results shown by accounts prepared on the basis of historical cost are not a measure of increase or decrease in wealth in terms of purchasing power ; nor do the results necessarily represent the amount which can prudently be regarded as available for distribution, having regard to the financial requirements of the business. Similarly the results shown by such accounts are not necessarily suitable for purposes such as price fixing, wage negotiations and taxation, unless in using them for these purposes due regard is paid to the amount of profit which has been retained in the business for its maintenance.

On the other hand the alternatives to historical cost which have so far been suggested appear to have serious defects and their logical application would raise social and economic issues going far beyond the realm of accountancy. The Council is therefore unable to regard any of the suggestions so far made as being acceptable alternatives to the existing accounting principles based on historical cost.

Recommendation.—Unless and until a practicable and generally acceptable alternative is available, the Council recommends that the accounting principles set out below should continue to be applied :—

(a) Historical cost should continue to be the basis on which annual accounts should be prepared and, in consequence, the basis on which profits shown by such accounts are computed.

(b) Any amount set aside out of profits in recognition of the effects which changes in the purchasing power of money have had on the affairs of the business (including any amount to finance the increase in the cost of replacements, whether of fixed or current assets) should be treated as a transfer to reserve and not as a charge in arriving at profits. If such a transfer is shown in the Profit and Loss Account as a deduction in arriving at the balance for the year, that balance should be described appropriately, since it is not the whole of the profits.

(c) In order to emphasise that as a matter of prudence the amount so set aside is, for the time being, regarded by directors as not available for distribution, it should normally be treated as a capital reserve.

(d) For Balance Sheet purposes fixed assets should not (except in special circumstances) be written-up, especially in the absence of monetary stability.

The Council also recommends to members who are directors or officers of companies or who are asked by clients for advice, that they should stress the limitations on the significance of profits computed on the basis of historical cost in periods of material changes in the purchasing power of money ; and that they should draw attention to the desirability of :—

(a) Setting amounts aside from profits to reserve in recognition of the effects which changes in the purchasing power of money have had upon the affairs of the business, particularly their effect on the amount of profit which, as a matter of policy, can prudently be regarded as available for distribution.

(b) Showing in the directors' report or otherwise the effects which changes in the purchasing power of money have had on the affairs of the business, including in particular the financial requirements for its maintenance and the directors' policy for meeting those requirements, either by setting aside to reserve or by raising new capital.

(c) Experimenting with methods of measuring the effects of changes in the purchasing power of money on profits and on financial requirements. If the results of such experiments are published as part of the documents accompanying the annual accounts, the basis used for the calculations and the significance of the figures in relation to the business concerned should be stated clearly.

(30th May, 1952.)

XVI. ACCOUNTANTS' REPORTS FOR PROSPECTUSES : ADJUSTMENTS AND OTHER MATTERS.

Adjustments Generally.—In the preparation of accountants' reports for the purpose of inclusion in prospectuses (which, where appropriate, should be read as including offers for sale and similar documents) it may be necessary to make various adjustments, in addition to giving consideration to the special matters dealt with in Recommendation XIII. The reports required under the Third, Fourth and Fifth Schedules to the Companies Act, 1948, must either indicate by way of note any adjustments as respects the figures of profits or losses or assets and liabilities dealt with by the report which appear necessary to the persons making the report, or must make those adjustments and indicate that adjustments have been made. There is no statutory guidance as to the nature of the adjustments to be made ; the accountants making the report must form their own judgment. Where required by Section 41 (1) of the Act, a signed statement, setting out the adjustments and giving the reasons therefor, must be attached to or endorsed on the copy of the prospectus delivered to the registrar of companies. .

The accountants' report is necessarily confined to past results and does not purport to deal with future prospects. The intending investor is concerned with the future and he will regard the accountants' report, showing the trend of past results, as being submitted to assist him in forming his own assessment of the prospects. It may therefore be necessary, in order that the trend of past profits may be fairly presented having regard to the purposes of the prospectus, either to make appropriate comments thereon or to adjust the figures.

The circumstances in which adjustments to the figures of profits or losses are usually required fall generally under the following headings :—

(a) Where there are material facts which should have been taken into account in preparing the Profit and Loss Accounts for the various years covered by the report if those facts had been known at the time when the accounts were prepared.

(b) Where there have been material sources of revenue or categories of expenditure which are expected not to recur.

(c) Where during the period covered by the report there has been a material change in the accounting principles applied or where accepted accounting principles have not been applied.

In considering whether an adjustment is required it is essential to bear in mind that the accountants' duty is to report on past profits or losses and not to attempt to forecast results in future conditions.

Adjustments or comments may also be necessary in relation to the statement of assets and liabilities shown in the accountants' report. In particular it will be necessary to consider to what extent it is relevant to include notes which appeared on the last Balance Sheet and to consider the appropriate treatment of matters such as the market value of investments, the accumulated amount of profits tax non-distribution relief, and reserves for future income tax. The accountants' report deals with the assets and liabilities as on the last Balance Sheet date ; but the reporting accountants may have knowledge of events subsequent to that date which may have a material bearing on the conclusions which the intending investor may draw from the prospectus and in such cases the accountants will need to consider their report in the light of that knowledge.

Period Covered by the Report.—Apart from the question of adjustments, the period to be covered by the report requires consideration having regard to the importance of presenting a fair view of the trend of results. At present the Stock Exchange, London, requires the report on profits or losses to cover a period of at least ten years instead of the statutory minimum of five years specified in the Companies Act, 1948.

Taxation.—The treatment of taxation in the accountants' report raises some difficulties, particularly at the time of the issue of this Recommendation, as reports will normally cover periods during which the excess profits tax at varying rates (or the alternative national defence contribution) was in force for part of the time, followed by the profits tax at rapidly changing rates with its complication of non-distribution relief and, for 1952 and 1953, the excess profits levy. Until recently the most usual method of treating taxation has been to use three columns showing :—

 (i) Profits before charging United Kingdom taxation;

 (ii) Excess profits tax (or national defence contribution) and profits tax;

 (iii) Profits before deducting income tax (column (i) less column (ii));

but in recent years some accountants have omitted column (iii). More recently, particularly since the Finance Act, 1952, introduced the further complications of the excess profits levy, some accountants have shown only column (1).

For prospectus purposes accountants are required to report " upon " or " with respect to " the profits and are authorised to make such adjustments as appear to them to be necessary. The Council therefore takes the view that the accountants are free to deal with excess profits tax, national defence contribution, profits tax and excess profits levy in whatever manner they think appropriate to the case and that in the absence of exceptional circumstances it is sufficient to show in a single column the profits before charging United Kingdom taxation, notwithstanding legal cases in which the courts may have interpreted the word " profits " in other contexts. It is, however, necessary that the report shall fairly indicate the basis on which the profits are stated and shall be in such a form that a person reading the prospectus can ascertain the trend of profits during the period covered by the report, so that he can consider the past results in forming his own view of the profits which may become available for interest or dividend in future years.

The excess profits tax was charged under legislation which is no longer in operation and which differed greatly from the new excess profits levy ; and the profits tax borne in past years may bear no relation to the current position regarding " distributions " or to the current rates of profits tax. A report which shows profits before charging United Kingdom taxation will therefore normally be more informative and less likely to be misunderstood than one which states for each year the amounts of excess profits tax or national defence contribution and of profits tax. In each case, however, it will be for the accountants to decide on the appropriate treatment of taxation having regard to all the circumstances. It will also be necessary for the accountants to consider whether there are material amounts of expenditure for which no allowance is obtained for taxation purposes and which therefore absorb earnings of the relative gross amount.

The question of profits tax non-distribution relief has been considered in detail in the Council's " Notes on the Treatment of Profits Tax in Accounts ". The conclusions there reached are as follows and the Council takes the same view in relation to the accountants' report dealing with the assets and liabilities at the last date to which the accounts of the company were made up :—

 " (a) In normal circumstances any attempt to estimate the amount of the profits tax liability which might be incurred on a hypothetical future distribution cannot produce any result of sufficient accuracy to be of value or significance.

 " (b) Even if it were possible to compute a significant figure, it is not normally necessary in law to refer in a Balance Sheet to the existence of an accumulated amount of non-distribution relief, because the existence of such an amount does not constitute either a liability or a contingent liability at the Balance Sheet date and any possible liability which may be incurred in the future as a result of future distributions is not an element which in law requires consideration when determining whether a Balance Sheet gives a true and fair view of the state of affairs of the company as on the Balance Sheet date.

 " (c) Nevertheless the Council considers that it may be helpful to shareholders to remind them that if any of the reserves were distributed a part thereof would normally have to be paid away in profits tax instead of being paid to the shareholders. The Council therefore considers that there is much to commend the practice, now being adopted by some companies, of making the Balance Sheet as informative as possible by including an appropriate reference to the existence of an accumulated amount of non-distribution relief. It is a matter for consideration, in the circumstances of each case, whether the suggested reference should specify the accumulated amount of non-distribution relief or should be made in general terms only :—

    (i) If the accumulated amount is stated, care must be taken to ensure that it will not be misleading, having regard to the relationship between that amount and the amount of reserves shown in the Balance Sheet.

    (ii) If the reference is made in general terms only, the following is an example of wording which may be suitable :

       ' The company has been given profits tax non-distribution relief and accordingly a profits tax charge would normally be incurred in the event of a distribution to shareholders out of reserves, including the balance on Profit and Loss Account.' (If Section 31, Finance Act, 1951, applies, the wording would need variation to cover also a reduction or repayment of capital, or a capitalisation of reserves.)

" (d) Apart from the general position dealt with in (a), (b) and (c) above there may be exceptional circumstances, for example where a liquidation is contemplated, which require special treatment in order to indicate as clearly as possible the significance of the non-distribution relief in the exceptional circumstances."

Presentation.—Persons reading the report will more readily understand the significance of the figures if they are stated as simply as possible with a clear indication of the basis on which they have been computed. An indication of the adjustments which have been made, or of the matters to which it is considered necessary to direct attention, can usually be given conveniently in the form of explanatory notes or narrative following a tabulation of the figures.

Context.—The context in which the accountants' report appears may have a material effect on the conclusions which the intending investor will draw from the prospectus as a whole. Under the Companies Act, 1948, a prospectus containing a report by accountants must not be issued unless the accountants have given and not withdrawn their consent to the issue thereof with their report in the form and context in which it is included ; and a statement that they have so given and not withdrawn their consent must appear in the prospectus.

Stock Exchange Requirements.—In addition to the statutory requirements under the Companies Act, there are also requirements of the stock exchanges. In particular, attention is drawn to the following requirements of the Share and Loan Department of the Stock Exchange, London :—

    (a) *Memorandum regarding certificates of profits for purposes of prospectuses, offers for sale and advertised statements.* This memorandum was issued on 3rd November, 1948, and published in *The Accountant* on 13th November, 1948. The memorandum relates to the " written statement signed by the auditors or accountants setting out the adjustments made in the report on the profits and giving the reasons therefor " which is required to be submitted to the Share and Loan Department and to be available for inspection by the public for not less than fourteen days at a place in the City of London.

    (b) *Announcement regarding pre-acquisition profits.* This announcement was reported in *The Accountant* of 4th June, 1949, as follows :

    " In cases where application is made for the quotation of securities

T

of holding companies the department will require to be satisfied that
in arriving at any estimate contained or to be contained in any
prospectus, offer for sale or public advertisement of the profits of
or any dividends to be paid in respect of the first financial year of
the holding company due account has been taken of the fact that
' pre-acquisition profits ' will not be available for distribution."

(c) *Stock-in-trade.* It is the practice of the Share and Loan Department to
ask the question, " Have the reporting accountants satisfied themselves that stock-in-trade and work in progress (if any) have been
properly taken and valued throughout the period covered by this
report ? " A simple affirmative answer to that question would amount
to the assumption by the reporting accountants of a wider responsibility
than they can normally take, particularly if they have not been the
auditors of the company for the whole of the period ; but if the reporting accountants have satisfied themselves in regard to the matters dealt
with below under " Stock-in-trade and Work in Progress " they should
be able to give the requisite confirmation to the Share and Loan
Department.

Special Circumstances.—In considering the recommendations made below it
must be borne in mind that the circumstances of one business may differ greatly
from those of another. Moreover there are some circumstances, particularly
where the report involves subsidiaries or branches operating in the United
Kingdom or overseas, for which it would be inappropriate to attempt to make
any recommendations of general application. In all cases it is necessary to take
into account the relevant facts before deciding what, if any, adjustments should
be made and what matters should be referred to specifically in the accountants'
report.

Recommendations.—It is therefore recommended that the following principles,
which should be read in conjunction with those dealt with in Recommendation
XIII, should normally be applied by members of the Institute who may be called
upon to report for prospectus purposes ; but it must be emphasised that the
reporting accountants should bear in mind the purpose for which their report
is to be used and exercise their own judgment on whether the observations and
adjustments mentioned below would be appropriate in the circumstances of a
particular case.

PROFITS OR LOSSES. *Presentation.*—The figures relating to profits or losses
should be set out in the report in columnar form, accompanied by appropriate
definition of the bases on which the figures have been computed. A figure of
" average profits " should not be stated.

Taxation.—The report should show for each year the profits (as defined in
the report) before charging any United Kingdom taxation on profits. In the
absence of exceptional circumstances, the report need not include figures showing
excess profits tax, national defence contribution, profits tax, or excess profits levy.

If in any particular case the accountants should consider that there are
exceptional circumstances which make it desirable to show the amounts of excess
profits tax, national defence contribution, profits tax and excess profits levy,
it will be for the accountants to decide whether also to show for each year the
profits after deducting those taxes.

Where there are material items of expenditure which are chargeable in
arriving at profits but are not allowable for taxation purposes, the report should
indicate the amount of such expenditure for the last year covered by the report
or for such other period as may be appropriate ; and should also indicate that
the sum required to cover such expenditure is the gross amount which after
deduction of taxation will leave a net amount equal to the expenditure which
is not allowed. (In relation to depreciation of fixed assets this matter is referred
to more specifically in Recommendation XIII.)

Adjustments Generally.—The reporting accountants should make such adjustments to the profits or losses as shown by the accounts as they consider appropriate and the report should state that this has been done. If the amount involved in any adjustment is of special importance in relation to the results disclosed, the nature of the adjustment should be stated. The accountants should consider whether the amount involved in any such adjustment should also be stated.

Adjustments Based on New Information.—In some cases it may be necessary to consider whether adjustments should be made where there are facts which should have been taken into account in preparing the Profit and Loss Accounts for the various years covered by the report if those facts had been known at the time when the accounts were prepared. These adjustments may often consist of a reallocation, between one year and another, of items such as provisions. Where the correct credit or charge for each year concerned can be ascertained with reasonable accuracy at the date of the report, a reallocation may be appropriate if the amounts are material. In particular :—

(a) *Contract Prices.*—Where material amounts of income were provisional in that they were derived from government or other contracts which were subject to cost investigations, or which for other reasons were known at the time of making up the accounts to be liable to subsequent price adjustments, consideration should be given to the question of whether estimates should be adjusted, having regard to the most recent information.

(b) *Deferred Repairs.*—Owing to conditions arising out of the war many businesses have had to defer necessary expenditure on maintenance of their equipment. Where claims have been made for allowances for deferred repairs for excess profits tax purposes, or provisions therefor have been made in the accounts, these should be regarded as prima facie evidence of the existence of deferred maintenance at the relevant dates. The accountants should, where necessary, make adjustments to correct under- or over-provisions at previous Balance Sheet dates.

(c) *Bad or Doubtful Debts.*—Adjustments should not normally be made, in the light of subsequent events, to provisions which were considered to be reasonably necessary in respect of bad or doubtful debts having regard to information available when the accounts of any year were made up. Exceptional cases do arise however where the amounts involved are very material and in such cases it is necessary to consider whether adjustments should be made.

Stock-in-trade and Work in Progress.—The method of valuing stock-in-trade (whether of raw materials, partly finished or finished stocks) should be reviewed and tested in relation to the fair presentation of the trend of profits. Where it is established that the amount included in the accounts at any particular year end should have been materially different a reallocation should be made. Where during the period covered by the report there has been a material change in the basis on which stock-in-trade was valued and it is not practicable to make an adjustment, because the relevant figures are not ascertainable, there should be an appropriate reservation in the report. The taxation implications of any matters arising on stock-in-trade also require consideration.

In some businesses, for example constructional engineers or public works contractors engaged on large contracts on which work may be in progress over a lengthy period, some profit element may have been included in the valuation of work in progress. In other businesses no profit element may have been included until the period in which the contract has been completed. The basis on which the valuation has been made should be examined from the standpoint of seeing how far the practice which has prevailed is consistent with that in force at the time of the report and of deciding whether it would be appropriate to make adjustments so as to apportion the profit over the period of the performance of the contract.

"*Non-recurring*" *Expenditure.*—It may be undesirable to make an adjustment merely because in the period covered by the report there were items of revenue expenditure which it is believed will not recur in the future. In many businesses special expenditure of one kind or another may be incurred from time to time and it will often be inappropriate to eliminate the particular items which arose in the period covered by the report.

Repayment of Loans.—Where a loan of fixed amount is to be repaid out of the proceeds of the issue, or has been repaid out of the proceeds of an issue during the period covered by the report, an adjustment to eliminate or amend the interest charged in each year may be appropriate. If a material adjustment has been made the fact should be stated in the report. In the absence of special circumstances it is inappropriate to make an adjustment for interest where a bank overdraft is to be repaid or reduced out of the proceeds of the issue. Where interest charges on loans or overdrafts are of material amount and no adjustment is made, the report should state the facts and, if several years are affected, this may conveniently be done by showing the relevant interest charges in a separate column in the report.

Changes in Sources of Income.—Where in the period covered by the report there were material changes in the nature of the business or the sources of income, or there have been exceptional receipts, the circumstances of each case will require consideration in deciding whether any adjustment should be made, but regard should be had to the following general principles :—

(a) Where another business has been acquired by means of an issue of share or loan capital it may be appropriate to make an adjustment to include the profits of the acquired business in respect of the years prior to acquisition ; and for this purpose a suitable method may be to show in a separate column the profits which have been so included. (Where a business is to be acquired out of the proceeds of the new issue, a report on the profits of that business must be given in accordance with paragraph 20 of the Fourth Schedule to the Companies Act, 1948.)

(b) Where however another business has been acquired out of existing resources, the profits of such business for the years prior to the acquisition should not in general be included, for the reason, amongst others, that for those years the profits of the acquiring business already include profits derived from the use of the resources which were later used to acquire the further business. Similar considerations apply where the acquired business had sustained losses prior to acquisition ; but there may be circumstances which require different treatment or appropriate comment in the accountants' report, for example where the further business has a record of material losses and it was acquired towards the end of the period covered by the report.

(c) Where a distinct and material section of the business has been discontinued or sold, it would normally be appropriate to show separately, or to make an adjustment to exclude, the profits attributable to that section of the business where ascertainable. Consideration should however be given to the effect of such adjustments on the trend of results shown by the adjusted profits. If losses have been sustained in the discontinued or sold section of the business and an adjustment is made to exclude those losses, the report should indicate that such an adjustment has been made and state the amounts of the losses so excluded. If no adjustment is made to exclude losses and the discontinuance or sale of the section has had a material effect on the trend of results in the later years, the accountants should refer to the matter in their report.

(d) Considerations similar to those mentioned in (a), (b) and (c) above apply in the case of groups of companies where subsidiaries are acquired or disposed of.

Expenditure not Borne in the Past.—There will be cases where items of expenditure to be incurred in the future have not been borne in the past, or have in the past been materially different in amount. In particular, the charge in future for directors' emoluments may differ materially from that in the past. In view of the length of the period covered by the report and the changes which have occurred in the purchasing power of money, it is usually inappropriate to adjust the past profits or losses. The report should however indicate the facts, for example by way of comparison of the emoluments for the last year covered by the report with what those emoluments would have been under the arrangements in force at the time of making the report.

If the amounts involved are material, management remuneration not covered by directors' emoluments should be dealt with in the manner indicated in the preceding paragraph.

Capital Expenditure.—Where an item which has been charged in the accounts has been disallowed for taxation purposes as being capital expenditure, it should not necessarily be adjusted. Moreover no adjustment should be made to write back, as being capital, expenditure which has been charged in the accounts and allowed for taxation purposes, even though some items may be of a kind which might have been regarded as of a capital nature if a different accounting practice had been followed. Where an adjustment is made, it is necessary to consider whether it has a significant effect on the provisions for depreciation.

Expenditure Carried Forward.—Where a material amount of development or similar expenditure is carried forward on the grounds that it is abnormal and has a continuing value to the business, the nature of the expenditure and the manner in which such expenditure has been dealt with in the past or is proposed to be dealt with in the future, together with the reasons for carrying it forward, should be investigated. The treatment in the report will necessarily depend on the circumstances of each case. If necessary, adjustments should be made so as to charge the expenditure against the revenue of the appropriate period. If expenditure is carried forward the report should indicate the nature and amount of the expenditure carried forward at the close of the period covered by the report and, in some cases, should also indicate the period over which it is to be written-off in future years. Adjustment is not usually required for amounts which represent normal annual expenditure on designs and prototypes of the following year's products of companies whose usual practice is to carry forward such expenditure as a charge against the revenue of the following year.

Conversely, the accountants should consider whether the trend of results has been affected materially by charging against profits expenditure of abnormal amount which could properly have been carried forward to a period following that in which it was incurred.

Items not Passed Through the Profit and Loss Account.—Adjustments should be made in respect of any items which affect the Profit and Loss Account but have not been dealt with through that account.

Accounting Principles Applied.—Where in the period covered by the report there has been a material change in the accounting principles applied, or the method of computing profits or losses has in any material respects not been in accordance with accepted accounting principles, the profits or losses should, if practicable, be adjusted so that they are computed in accordance with consistent and accepted principles or, if this cannot be done, the matter should be explained in the report.

Period Covered by the Report.—The reporting accountants should consider whether a report covering the minimum period required by law, or by a stock exchange, presents a fair view of the trend of results having regard to any exceptional circumstances during that period. It may be necessary to extend the period or make appropriate comments.

Other Considerations.—The reporting accountants may have knowledge of events subsequent to the end of the last year covered by their report, or of other special circumstances not dealt with in the foregoing recommendations, which in their opinion have had or may have a material bearing on the statement of past profits or losses, or on the context in which that statement appears. In such circumstances the accountants should consider whether the facts should be stated in their report or whether this is rendered unnecessary by the manner in which the matter has been dealt with elsewhere in the prospectus.

ASSETS AND LIABILITIES. *Presentation.*—The statement of assets and liabilities should be so arranged that the liabilities are deducted from the assets, ending with the proprietorship interest.

Future Income Tax.—The report should make clear whether an amount has been set aside for future income tax and, if so, should specify the amount and the basis on which it has been computed.

Profits Tax Non-distribution Relief.—The report should include an appropriate reference to the existence of an accumulated amount of non-distribution relief. It is a matter for consideration, in the circumstances of each case, whether the reference should specify the accumulated amount or should be made in general terms only :—

(a) If the accumulated amount is stated, care must be taken to ensure that it will not be misleading, having regard to the relationship between that amount and the amount of reserves.

(b) If the reference is made in general terms only, the following is an example of wording which may be suitable :
  " The company has been given profits tax non-distribution relief and accordingly a profits tax charge would normally be incurred in the event of a distribution to shareholders out of reserves, including the balance on Profit and Loss Account." (If Section 31, Finance Act, 1951, applies, the wording would need variation to cover also a reduction or repayment of capital, or a capitalisation of reserves.)

Investments.—Where quoted investments are held the report should state the market value on the Balance Sheet date ; and if the amount standing in the books is greater than the market value on that date, the statement of assets and liabilities should include the market value instead of the book amount.

Balance Sheet Notes.—The report should incorporate all notes (such as those relating to market values, commitments, rates of exchange or arrears of dividends on cumulative preference shares) which appeared on the last Balance Sheet, so far as the notes are material to a proper appreciation of the position at the Balance Sheet date.

Proceeds of the Issue.—The accountants' report deals with the assets and liabilities at the last Balance Sheet date and should therefore not include any addition in respect of the expected proceeds of the issue. This can appropriately be dealt with elsewhere in the prospectus.

Other Considerations.—The reporting accountants may have knowledge of material events subsequent to the last Balance Sheet date, for example where there has been a material fall in the market value of investments or of stock-in-trade. In such cases and where the reporting accountants have knowledge of any other special circumstances, not dealt with in the foregoing recommendations, which in their opinion have had or may have a material bearing on the statement of assets and liabilities, they should consider whether the facts should be stated in their report or whether this is rendered unnecessary by the manner in which the matter has been dealt with elsewhere in the prospectus.

SUBSIDIARIES, BRANCHES AND OVERSEAS BUSINESSES. Where the report involves subsidiaries or branches or overseas businesses, the circumstances are not usually such as to be suitable for the application of any general recommendations. For example, where subsidiaries or branches have different accounting dates it may not be practicable or appropriate to apportion the figures of profits or losses so as to obtain aggregates for a common period and the appropriate treatment will be a matter for the accountants to decide in the circumstances of each case. Similarly, where a material part of the profits is derived from overseas branches or companies it will be for the accountants to decide whether it is desirable to show separately the amount of such profits, or of the overseas taxation thereon, or of both, and the manner of indicating the position where there are material exchange restrictions on the transfer of overseas profits. All these matters and many others which arise in relation to groups and overseas businesses require consideration of the circumstances in each case to ensure that the report will not be misunderstood. In all cases where a matter is material the report should state clearly what has been done.

The accounts of some subsidiaries or branches may have been audited by accountants other than those who are reporting for prospectus purposes and it is then necessary for the reporting accountants to consider in the circumstances of each particular case whether they should examine the books and records of the subsidiaries or branches concerned, for which purpose it may be necessary to employ overseas agents. The reporting accountants should consider the desirability of communicating with the other auditors to ascertain whether they wish to draw attention to any matters which may be relevant to the report required for prospectus purposes.

CONSENT TO THE INCLUSION OF THE REPORT. Before consenting (under Section 40, Companies Act, 1948) to the inclusion of their report in the prospectus, the reporting accountants should have regard particularly to :—

(a) The manner in which the directors, in their statement of estimated current and future profits, deal with figures shown in the accountants' report and with matters to which attention has been drawn in that report.

    Note.—The Share and Loan Department of the Stock Exchange, London, requires the company to furnish the department with an outline of the facts on which the estimate of profits is founded.

(b) Material facts of which they have knowledge in relation to the directors' estimates.

(c) Whether the directors, in any statement of " value " of ordinary shares in terms of net assets, have paid due regard to the restriction imposed by the existence of an accumulated amount of non-distribution relief.

(d) The manner in which any special circumstances have been dealt with in the prospectus, where the accountants have decided that no reference thereto is necessary in their report.

In cases where their report deals with assets and liabilities of a company or business acquired or to be acquired, the reporting accountants should ascertain from the directors that the directors' estimates of future profits available for dividend, as shown in the prospectus, have been arrived at after appropriate deductions have been made in respect of pre-acquisition profits which will not be available to the acquiring company for distribution as dividend.

(13th November, 1953.)

Note.—The series of " Recommendations on Accounting Principles " are published by Messrs. Gee & Co. (Publishers), Limited, in a booklet of pocket size, in loose-leaf form, which facilitates the addition of further recommendations as and when they become available.

APPENDIX III

EXERCISES

Chapter I

1. Set out briefly the matters calling for special attention before closing the books of a business at the termination of any trading period.

2. What various meanings may an entry in a ledger account have ? Deal with both the debit side and the credit side.

3. What system of Book-keeping would you recommend to a trader starting in business ? Explain the various books which should be kept, so as to enable him to ascertain in the shortest time and most reliable manner the results of his business operations.

4. Show the Journal and Ledger entries to record the following :—

   (a) 1954. Jan. 1. Provision for Bad Debts of £860 standing in the books.

   (b) 1954. Dec. 31. Total of Bad Debts Account £1,000.

   (c) do. Adjust the Provision Account so that it may show a provision of 7½ per cent. on the Book Debts, which are £15,000.

   (d) Assume that business has been continued for another twelve months, i.e., up to 31st December, 1955, and that the Bad Debts are then £1,100. Adjust the Provision for Bad Debts, so that it may show a provision of 7½ per cent. on the amount of the Book Debts, which are then found to be £12,674.

5. A trader keeps his books upon the double entry system. At the periodical stocktaking he extracts a Trial Balance from his ledger ; and, after adjusting some errors, finds that the total of the debit balances equals the total of the credit balances. Is this agreement an absolute proof that the books are correct in every respect and that no further errors exist ? Give reasons for your answer. What further tests, if any, would you apply ?

6. Define Double Entry Book-keeping.

7. What are Real, Personal and Nominal Accounts ? Give an example of each.

8. " The net profit made by a business over a certain period may be quickly ascertained by preparing two statements of affairs, one at the beginning and one at the end of the period, and comparing the positions shown thereby. The required information is obtained with much less labour than if accounts are prepared to cover the trading period."

   State whether you consider the above statement a complete justification for ascertaining profits by the first of the two methods mentioned. Support your arguments by appending *pro-forma* examples showing the ascertainment of the profits of a business for the same period by each of these methods.

9. Enumerate the usual adjustments required in the books of account after the agreement of the Trial Balance.

10. In modern practice, the Journal is subdivided into several subsidiary books. Name them and state what advantages are derived from this practice.

11. Discuss the uses and advantages of Columnar Purchases and Sales Day Books.

12. What do you understand by a Bank Reconciliation Statement ? Prepare one with imaginary figures to illustrate your answer.

13. What do you understand by the Imprest System as applied to Petty Cash ? Give a suitable ruling for a Petty Cash Book. Illustrate with six specimen entries.

14. A client banks all cheques received, and pays wages, petty cash and sundry expenses, including his own drawings, out of the ready money takings, sometimes banking some of the latter if not required for cash payments. He pays by cheque for purchases and payments other than those mentioned. Draft a form of Cash Book with imaginary entries illustrating the method you would recommend him to adopt.

15. Having given that the document reproduced below was published by the Social Club, you are required to prepare such accounts as will, in your opinion, correctly reflect the operations of the year 1955 and the position at the end thereof. All investments may be shown at cost.

BALANCE SHEET FOR 1955.

	£		£
Balance in hand, 1st January	140	Cash paid for Food, etc. .	900
Members' Subscriptions		Servants' Wages . . .	655
received	800	New Furniture Purchased	300
Cash received for Meals, etc.	1,184	Purchase of £1,800 Consols	1,190
Interest on Consols. . .	71	Balance in hand, 31st	
Legacy from J. Johnson		December	150
(a deceased member) .	1,000		
	£3,195		£3,195

" The Committee is glad to say that this Balance Sheet shows that a profit of £10 has been earned during the year, but members are reminded that whereas last year £100 was due to suppliers of food there are now £200 unpaid bills under this head. Further, £200 is now due to the Club for unpaid subscriptions against £150 at the end of last year. At the beginning of the year there was a stock of food, etc., valued at £80, but the stock is now £65. The Consols purchased during the year are in addition to those already held (£1,500, costing £1,200). The Committee has decided to form a Servants' Pension Fund and to transfer £600 thereto, earmarking £750 of the Consols held at the beginning of the year to represent the fund. The Club's furniture was valued last year at £500, but the Committee considers that the existing furniture is now worth £700."

(*Note.*—Any question of apportioning the interest on Consols, or of Income Tax thereon, may be ignored.)

Chapter II

16. What are the distinguishing features of (*a*) a Manufacturing Account, (*b*) a Trading Account, and (*c*) a Profit and Loss Account ? Comment upon the usual form in which these accounts are presented.

T*

17. A firm engages in both merchanting and manufacturing. You are required to prepare accounts, showing the profits on the merchanting and manufacturing departments separately, from the following details. You are to assume that any loss of weight is the natural result of the process of manufacture, and you are to show the cost per pound of the manufactured article. Raw material used in manufacture is valued at the average cost of the opening stock and of subsequent purchases.

Stock at beginning :—		Lbs.	£
Raw Materials	. . . .	9,000	580
Finished Goods	. . . .	10,000	625
Purchases of Raw Materials	. . .	120,000	8,020
Works Materials Consumed	. . .		300
Works Wages	. . . .		400
Works Expenses	. . . .		140
Works Depreciation	. . . .		100
Office Expenses :—			
Merchanting	. . . .		150
Manufacturing	. . . .		300
Wages and Commission (Salesmen) :—			
Merchanting	. . . .		75
Manufacturing	. . . .		175
Interest on Capital :—			
Merchanting	. . . .		80
Manufacturing	. . . .		100
Sales :—			
Raw Materials	. . . .	12,000	1,200
Finished Goods	. . . .	72,000	9,000
Waste Products	. . . .	10,000	500
Stock at close :—			
Raw Materials	. . . .	9,600	640
Finished Goods	. . . .	18,000	1,725

18. What is the difference between gross profit and net profit ? Illustrate your answer by means of *pro-forma* Trading and Profit and Loss Accounts applicable to any business with which you are familiar.

19. What principles would you apply when deciding upon the allocation of items of expenditure to Manufacturing, Trading, or Profit and Loss Account ? Illustrate your answer with specimen items, and state how you would deal with items which admit of alternative treatment.

20. How would you deal with stock and work in progress for the purpose of the final accounts of a manufacturer ?

21. A manufacturer seeks your advice with reference to the form of final accounts which would yield him the maximum of useful information as regards his business operations. Give your advice, supplying a *pro-forma* account or accounts.

22. What is the use or importance of Manufacturing and Trading Accounts to the financial accountant and to the cost accountant respectively ?

23. What are the " Elements of Cost " ?

24. What do you understand by the term " overhead expenses " ? Classify the undermentioned items of expenditure under the various headings of overhead expenses :—

Factory Power.
Engineer's Salary.
Rent and Rates.

Bad Debts.
Travellers' Salaries and Commissions.
Discounts on Sales.
Sundry Repairs.
Depreciation of Machinery.

25. Define the following terms : (a) Prime Cost ; (b) Factory Cost ; (c) Cost of Sales ; (d) Factory Profit.

26. The following is a summary of the accounts of the operations of a company for two successive years. You are required to draw up a comparative statement in single column form (with percentages of the various items based on sales) showing how the gross income has been disposed of in each year so that the trend of events may be displayed. You are also required to add notes expressing the conclusions you draw from the amount or movement of any items which appear to you significant.

ACCOUNT OF TRADING AND PROFIT AND LOSS FOR TWO YEARS.

	1954 £	1955 £		1954 £	1955 £
To Cost of Sales	30,000	35,000	By Sales . . .	50,000	60,000
,, Salesmen's			,, Interest Re-		
Salaries .	5,000	4,500	ceived . .	400	500
,, Salesmen's			,, Discounts Re-		
Expenses .	1,200	1,500	ceived . .	500	450
,, Advertising .	1,100	3,000	,, Profit on Sale of		
,, Other Selling			Fixed Assets	100	550
Expenses .	700	1,000			
,, Office Salaries	5,000	8,500			
,, Rent, Heat and					
Light . .	1,200	2,400			
,, Other Office					
Expenses .	800	1,100			
,, Interest Paid.	100	200			
,, Discounts Al-					
lowed . .	400	600			
,, Net Profit .	5,500	3,700			
	£51,000	£61,500		£51,000	£61,500

27. Two manufacturers, A.B. and X.Y., carry on businesses which are identical in all respects, each producing the same single product. For the two years 1954 and 1955 they each show the following results :—

	1954	1955
Actual Output (units)	1,000	1,200
Sales (units)	1,000	1,000
Selling Price (per unit)	£35	£35
Opening Stock (units)	—	—
Closing Stock (units)	—	200
Direct Materials and Labour and Variable		
Factory Overheads (per unit) . . .	£22	£22
Fixed Factory Overheads	£6,000	£6,000
Selling Expenses	£2,500	£2,500

A.B. produced accounts which showed a net profit of £4,500 for both 1954 and 1955. X.Y.'s accounts showed that profits had risen from £4,500 in 1954 to £5,500 in 1955.

Explain why X.Y. seems to have had a better year in 1955 than in 1954 and also a better year than A.B. had in 1955, despite the fact that they both, in both years, had identical sales revenue and costs. Illustrate your explanation by drafting the Revenue Accounts which the two businesses must have produced to show the results described, and comment on the accounting methods adopted by them.

28. *A.B.*, a merchant, is asking his bankers for an overdraft and has submitted Trading Accounts for four years, of which an abstract is given below. As assistant to the bank manager prepare a concise report on these figures.

TRADING ACCOUNTS.

Year to 30th June	1953 £	1954 £	1955 £	1956 £
Opening Stock . .	3,500	6,500	12,000	8,000
Purchases . . .	18,000	22,500	22,500	24,250
	21,500	29,000	34,500	32,250
Closing Stock . .	6,500	12,000	8,000	12,000
	15,000	17,000	26,500	20,250
Sales	20,000	25,000	33,000	27,000
Gross Profit . .	£5,000	£8,000	£6,500	£6,750

29. During 1954 a trader's accounts revealed the fact that the gross profit earned on sales of £10,000 was £5,000 and that the net profit was £2,000. The accounts for 1955 show sales of £12,000, gross profit of £6,000 and net profit of £2,900. What would you infer from these results? What would be the likely result if in 1956 the sales were increased to £15,000 ?

30. Do you consider that a detailed analysis of sales, to show the turnover in each line, is of value to the management of a business ? Give your reasons, and explain in what directions the information revealed is of practical value.

31. It is said that percentages offer the greatest possible opportunity for the drawing of incorrect and erroneous conclusions. Do you agree ? Give reasons.

32. How would you calculate the ratio of stocks to turnover and book debts to turnover ? What are the objects of making these calculations, and of what value are they to the trader ?

33. Wherein lies the importance of an efficient system of stores control ? What procedure would you lay down to provide against wastage of material and pilfering, and to facilitate periodical stocktaking ?

34. In a large factory the annual stocktaking is a considerable undertaking and causes dislocation. Describe a method by which such an annual stocktaking can be dispensed with.

35. What special considerations arise where finished stocks of manufactured goods are valued at current market price which is in excess of cost price ?

Chapter III

36. What are the provisions set forth in the Partnership Act, 1890, with reference to the following :—

(*a*) Interest on Capital ;

(*b*) Advances to the Firm by a Partner ;

    (c) Payments made by a Partner on behalf of the Firm;

    (d) Management of the Business;

    (e) Partners' Salaries;

    (f) Introduction of new Partners;

    (g) Disputes arising from the Partnership ?

37. S. Blundell and R. Dent are in partnership, and the provisions of the Partnership Deed are that each partner shall be allowed 5 per cent. interest on capital, and that profits and losses shall be shared as to four-fifths and one-fifth. On the 1st January, 1955, their capitals were : Blundell, £1,875 ; and Dent, £375. During the year 1955 they made a loss of £535 before providing for interest on capital. Their drawings during the year were : Blundell, £310 ; and Dent, £175.

    Prepare Profit and Loss Account and Capital Accounts as at 31st December, 1955.

38. What are the principal differences between a partnership and a limited company ?

39. The Trading and Profit and Loss Accounts of X, Ltd. for the year 1955 are summarised below. The Company manufactures a standardised vacuum flask which it sells through two Branches A and B at the best prices obtainable. The Manager, John Hotcold, is entitled to a commission, out of the net profit disclosed, equal to 10 per cent. of the net profit of Branch A before charging such commission. For this purpose it is agreed that the Branch net profit shall be ascertained by deducting from Branch sales (i) the prime cost of the flasks sold at the Branch and (ii) one-third of the general expenses.

    You are required to prepare a computation of John Hotcold's commission for the year :—

TRADING AND PROFIT AND LOSS ACCOUNTS FOR THE YEAR 1955.

	£			£
To Stock of Flasks, 1st		By Sales : —		
January (2,400 flasks)	1,800	Branch A. (12,000		
„ Stock of Materials, 1st		flasks)		11,196
January	780	Branch B. (13,400		
„ Materials Purchased	9,132	flasks)		13,250
„ Manufacturing Wages	9,184	„ Stocks of Flasks, 31st		
„ Gross Profit c/d	5,210	December (1,000		
		flasks)		750
		„ Stock of Materials, 31st		
		December		910
	£26,106			£26,106

	£		£
To General Expenses	2,400	By Gross Profit b/d	5,210
„ Net Profit	2,810		
	£5,210		£5,210

40. Explain the meaning of the following terms :—

    (a) Limited Partnership ; (b) Public Company ; (c) Private Company ; and (d) Exempt Private Company.

41. Discuss, with explanatory figures, the usual contents of the Appropriation Account of a company.

42. How should the following items be disclosed in the final accounts of a company :—

    (1) Dividends paid less tax.

    (2) Debenture Interest paid less tax.

    (3) Interest on Investments received less tax.

    (4) Tax Liability on Profits of preceding year.

    (5) Tax Liability on Profits of current year ?

43. The Authorised and Issued Share Capital of Blank, Ltd., is 100,000 Ordinary Shares of £1 each, and 50,000 6 per cent. Preference Shares of £1 each, both fully paid.

    The preference dividend is payable half-yearly on 30th September and 31st March, and during the year to 31st March, 1956, payments were made on the due dates. No dividend has been paid on the Ordinary Shares for some years, and none is proposed.

    Blank, Ltd., has issued £20,000 5 per cent. Debentures. A full year's interest was paid on 30th September, 1955.

    Blank, Ltd., holds certain Ordinary Shares in Vague, Ltd., and on 1st July, 1955, received from Vague, Ltd., a dividend of £575, representing a net amount after deduction of Income Tax.

    The accounts of Blank, Ltd., for the year to 31st March, 1955, were prepared on the assumption that Income Tax, Schedule D, for 1955–56 (based on the profits of the year to 31st March, 1955) would amount to £8,000. This assumption was incorrect, and £8,400 for Income Tax, 1955–56, was paid on 1st January, 1956.

    At 31st March, 1956, it is estimated that Income Tax, Schedule D, for 1956–57 (based on the profits of the year to 31st March, 1956) will amount to £12,000.

    You are required to show the Income Tax Account for the year to 31st March, 1956, in the ledger of Blank, Ltd., showing the transfer to Profit and Loss Account. Show also how any balance at 31st March, 1956, will be set out in the Balance Sheet at that date. The standard rate of Income Tax for 1955–56 was 8s. 6d. in the £.

44. What considerations must be borne in mind when determining the fund divisible among the members of a company, after a redemption of debentures has been made ?

45. Distinguish between capital and revenue losses. How should capital profits be treated for the purposes of the final accounts ?

46. What is the test to be applied before expenditure can legitimately be charged to an account other than the current Revenue Account ?

47. A company has spent £10,000 in installing plant and machinery which has now become unsuitable for needs of production. No depreciation has been written off. How would you recommend that this expenditure should be treated for the purposes of the final accounts ?

48. The accounts of a business show a considerable variation in the percentage of gross profit calculated on sales. Suggest possible causes of such variations.

49. If presented with a set of comparative Trading and Profit and Loss Accounts, to what special points would you direct attention as an aid to the interpretation of the figures ?

50. In what way may past results be said to be a guide to future policy ?

51. If you were consulted by the directors of a manufacturing business who find that, although their business still has a sufficient margin of solvency, it is earning progressively smaller net profits, describe what tests you would apply to the manufacturing and profit and loss account figures in an endeavour to discover the cause of the falling off in profits.

Chapter IV

52. What is a Balance Sheet, and how does it differ from a Profit and Loss Account ?

53. What do you understand by " marshalling " of items in a Balance Sheet ? State carefully what principles you would apply to the process.

54. Indicate the manner in which the following items should be stated in a Balance Sheet :—

> (a) Goodwill, (b) Investments, (c) Leasehold Premises, (d) Mortgage on Leasehold Premises, (e) Profit and Loss Account, (f) Contingent Liability on Bills Receivable Discounted.

55. State carefully to what extent you think it proper to include overheads in the Balance Sheet valuation of stock-in-trade (i.e., work in progress and finished stock) of a firm's own manufacture. What precautions should be taken in computing the actual amount of overheads so to be included ?

56. It is often said that stock-in-trade should be valued for Balance Sheet purposes " at cost or current market price, whichever is the lower ". Discuss the application of this rule to each of the following cases :—

> (1) A manufacturer of carpets.

> (2) An importer of articles recently subjected to a tariff.

> (3) Swiss watches purchased at a price expressed in Swiss francs, there being no similar articles of British manufacture. (Import duties may be ignored.)

> (4) A company formed to purchase sunken warships on the sea-bed with a view to raising and breaking them, afterwards selling the various parts, scrap, etc.

> (5) A second-hand bookseller (dealing in cheap books only) carrying on a very large business.

> (6) A cargo of Chilian nitrate en route to London for sale there on behalf of its owners, a nitrate company.

57. Elementary text-books sometimes state that stock-in-trade and work-in-progress should be valued in Balance Sheets at " cost or market price whichever is lower ". Critics have objected that this statement is far too rough and ready as a guide to practice. You are required to elaborate the matter and to indicate your interpretation of the terms " cost " and " market price ".

58. You are separately advising two manufacturers in the same line of business. A holds a stock of raw material which he bought at £10 per unit. B holds a stock of the same material which he bought at £15 per unit. A purchase on Balance Sheet date could be effected at £12 per unit. Consider whether you should advise for Balance Sheet purposes :—

> (a) Both to value at £10.

(b) Both to value at £12.

(c) A to value at £10 and B at £12, although the goods are identical.

(d) A to value at £10 and B at £15, although the goods are identical.

59. What do you understand by Fixed Assets and Current Assets ? Give examples of each and state the principles upon which these two classes of assets should be valued respectively for Balance Sheet purposes.

60. Examine critically the following statement : " Goodwill arises from the willingness of the purchaser of a business to pay the seller a value in excess of the book value of the net assets as shown by a Balance Sheet at the date of the sale contract. The excess is considered to be goodwill and is so recorded in the books of the purchaser."

61. It has been said that when a company purchases goodwill it acquires nothing but the probability of enjoying a terminable annuity equal to the expected super-profit. If this statement is true, (a) explain clearly what light it throws on the question whether goodwill should be written down, and (b) state, with brief comment, any counter-arguments which occur to you on the question of writing down.

62. " The value of the goodwill of a business naturally fluctuates in sympathy with the commercial success of the undertaking." Comment on this statement, and give your opinion as to whether such fluctuations should be recorded in the books and accounts of the concern.

63. On what basis would investments be valued for Balance Sheet purposes in the following cases :—

(1) Investments held for trade purposes.

(2) Investments representing a reserve fund.

(3) An investment of surplus working capital ?

64. Discuss the relationship between profits and circulating assets.

65. (a) Stock-in-trade is normally valued at cost, unless market price is lower. Explain carefully what you understand by " cost " in the case of (i) the stock of a wholesale trader ; and (ii) a manufacturer's stock of finished goods.

(b) " In certain circumstances it is permissible to value work-in-progress above cost." You are required to state the nature of these circumstances and to explain the principles upon which the addition to cost should be calculated.

(c) State briefly and concisely how you would expect an increase in the tobacco duty to be reflected in (i) the Trading Account ; and (ii) the Balance Sheet of a wholesale tobacconist. You may assume that the volume of trade (in quantity) remains unchanged, and that the increase in the cost of the goods is entirely passed on to the consumer.

66. (a) A certain public institution invests all its surplus funds in " gilt edged " securities. During the course of a year it both buys and sells stocks, sometimes on cum div. and sometimes on ex div. terms. Explain carefully the accounting considerations arising.

(b) The same institution makes a practice of inserting a note on its Balance Sheet stating the current value of its securities. Explain carefully how that current value is computed.

67. State what principles you would adopt, and your reasons for so doing, when allocating the following to Capital and/or Revenue :—

(a) Stock valued at £15,000 destroyed by fire and for which £15,500 was received from the Insurance Company.

(*b*) Structural alterations to buildings.

(*c*) Cost of conversion of gas plant to oil-fuel plant for generation of electricity.

Chapter V

68. What are the chief classifications into which liabilities may be placed ?

69. What is the Capital Account ? Indicate clearly the differences between the Capital Account of a sole trader and of a limited company.

70. Explain the meaning of the following terms :—

Authorised Capital; Issued Capital; Paid-up Capital; Reserve Capital; Mortgage Debentures; Memorandum of Association; Shares; Preference Shares; Cumulative Preference Shares; Redeemable Preference Shares; Deferred Shares.

71. The Ixion Motor Company, Limited, has recently received £1,000 in respect of premiums on the issue of its shares. How should such premiums be dealt with in the published accounts ? For what purpose may the amount be utilised ?

72. Under what circumstances may shares be issued at a discount ?

73. A company issued 25,000 shares of £1 each and called up the full amount. The last two calls of 5s. each on 600 shares not having been paid, the shares were forfeited. Draft the journal entries recording the forfeiture and show how the share capital will subsequently appear in the company's Balance Sheet. On what terms may the shares be reissued ?

74. A limited company has issued £100,000 Debentures bearing interest at 8 per cent. per annum and redeemable at the option of the company at any time on three months' notice at a premium of 5 per cent., and an authorised Share Capital of £450,000 in Ordinary Shares of £1 each, of which 300,000 have been issued and paid up, a dividend at the rate of 12½ per cent. per annum thereon being regularly paid. The company decides to redeem the Debentures, and to issue the remaining 150,000 Shares to its shareholders at 25s. per share. The premiums on shares are to be used in paying the premiums on redemption of debentures, and the balance transferred to Capital Reserve Account.

Give the journal entries recording the transactions, show the position of the Debenture and Share Capital Accounts when the transaction is completed, and state what is the amount of the additional financial resources available to the company by the operation.

75. The National Oxygen Company, Ltd., seeks and obtains from Messrs. Kudos, Ltd., on 1st January, 1954, a loan of £50,000 for two years at 8 per cent. per annum, interest payable half-yearly. The loan is secured by the issue of £58,000 First Mortgage Debentures as collateral security. What do you understand to be the meaning of the term " collateral security ", as used thus ? Draft the entries in the books of The National Oxygen Co., Ltd., recording the transactions during the period, and show how the loan and collateral security should appear in the Balance Sheet.

76. A limited company offers for subscription, on 15th January, 300,000 Ordinary Shares of £1 each at 5s. per share premium, payable as follows :—

On application . . . 2s. 6d. per share
On allotment (24th January). 5s.   ,,   and 2s. 6d. premium
28th February . . . 2s. 6d.   ,,   and 2s. 6d.   ,,
30th April . . . . 10s.   ,,

Applications are received for 432,300 shares. Applications for 32,300 shares are refused, and amounts paid in respect thereof are refunded, leaving applications for 400,000 shares to be dealt with. Of these, 240,000 from present shareholders are accepted in full, and, in respect of the balance, allotment is made *pro rata*. Excess paid on application is carried to the credit of amounts due on allotment, and, thereafter, of first call.

Give the journal entries required to record these transactions.

77. Company *C* issued, on 1st January, 1953, Debentures of nominal amount £12,000 at a discount of 10 per cent. redeemable by equal drawings at the end of each of three years. At the time of issue it placed the discount on the assets side of its Balance Sheet. Reproduce the Discount on Debentures Account balanced at the end of each of the three years showing what you consider the most equitable method of dealing with the discount.

78. Distinguish clearly between each of the following pairs of terms :—

(*a*) Secured liability ; preferential liability.

(*b*) Unsecured liability ; contingent liability.

(*c*) Fixed asset ; current asset.

(*d*) Fixed charge ; floating charge.

79. Indicate the factors which increase or reduce Working Capital in a business, apart from the introduction or withdrawal of cash capital. Set out with imaginary figures how Working Capital could be shown in accounts published for the information of shareholders.

80. In your opinion, is it necessary for the directors of a Limited Company to deal with contingent liabilities when preparing the annual accounts ? If you consider that such an obligation exists, select two liabilities of this nature and show by means of a *pro-forma* Balance Sheet how you would record them.

81. The following are the summarised Balance Sheets of a Company as at 31st December, 1954 and 1955, and the Profit and Loss Account for 1955 :—

BALANCE SHEETS.

	1954 £	1955 £		1954 £	1955 £
Share Capital—			Goodwill . .	100,000	100,000
6% Preference	100,000	100,000	Freehold Works	40,000	40,000
Ordinary. .	50,000	75,000	Plant and Ma-		
7½% Deben-			chinery (*less*		
tures . .	30,000	20,000	depreciation).	75,000	67,500
Current Liabili-			Loose Tools (*less*		
ties—			depreciation).	6,500	5,700
Trade Accounts	23,500	31,600	Furniture, etc.		
Expenses. .	2,900	1,750	(*less* deprecia-		
Bills Payable	7,600	5,800	tion) . . .	3,500	3,250
Income Tax .	6,500	7,400	Stock . . .	18,000	37,700
General Reserve	30,000	40,000	Debtors (*less*		
Profit and Loss			Provision for		
Account . .	15,400	12,600	Bad Debts) .	20,500	31,500
			Bank Balance .	2,400	8,500
	£265,900	£294,150		£265,900	£294,150

PROFIT AND LOSS ACCOUNT

FOR THE YEAR ENDED 31ST DECEMBER, 1955.

	£		£
To Selling Expenses . .	12,600	By Gross Profit . . .	49,600
„ Administration Ex-		„ Sundry Income . .	2,050
penses	8,300		
„ Debenture Interest .	1,500		
„ Depreciation—			
Plant	7,500		
Tools	800		
Furniture . . .	250		
„ Net Profit . . .	20,700		
	£51,650		£51,650
	£		£
To General Reserve . .	10,000	By Net Profit (1955) .	20,700
„ Dividends paid—		„ Balance (1954) . .	15,400
Preference (1955) .	6,000		
Ordinary (1955) .	7,500		
„ Balance c/d . . .	12,600		
	£36,100		£36,100
		By Balance b/d . .	12,600

What was the amount of the Working Capital of the Company at 31st December, 1954 and 1955, respectively ? Explain what has caused the difference between these two figures.

If you were a director of the Company, what comments would you have to make upon these Accounts ? Would you agree to the distribution as dividend of practically the whole of the balance of £12,600 on the Appropriation Account ? Give your reasons.

82. *D* and *S* form a company, Dee and Ess, Ltd., and start a new business. They each subscribe half the capital in Ordinary Shares. On 1st January they buy equipment at a cost of £500, and a stock of goods for £4,500 which is to be kept up and replaced as fast as it is sold. They plan to make a gross profit of 25 per cent. on sales and to allow their customers, on the average, two months' credit. They propose to pay prompt cash for purchases. Sales are expected to be £2,000 a month for the first three months, and thereafter £6,000 a month.

They rent a shop at a rental of £480 per annum, payable monthly in advance. Their other expenses, including their own remuneration, amount to £220 a month, and are incurred and paid evenly throughout each month.

They calculate the minimum amount of capital which will meet their requirements, and issue the necessary shares for cash.

Everything goes according to plan. At the end of the first year, they depreciate the equipment by 20 per cent., provide for a dividend of 40 per cent., and draw up their accounts.

You are required to prepare (*a*) a statement showing how you calculate the company's capital requirements ; and (*b*) the Revenue Account for the first year and the Balance Sheet as at the end of that year.

83. John Houghton owns a merchanting business, which is run by a manager. The accounts for a certain year and the Balance Sheet as at the end of the year are as follows :—

TRADING AND PROFIT AND LOSS ACCOUNTS.

	£			£	£
Opening Stock	6,500	Sales :—			
Purchases	21,000	Cash	4,000		
Gross Profit c/d . . .	3,000	Credit	16,000		
					20,000
		Closing Stock			10,500
	£30,500				£30,500
Depreciation	655	Gross Profit b/d . . .			3,000
Other Expenses . . .	1,045				
Manager's Salary . . .	800				
Net Profit	500				
	£3,000				£3,000

BALANCE SHEET.

	£	£			£
Bank Overdraft. . . .		8,650	Fixed Assets, at cost less		
Trade Creditors . . .		7,000	depreciation		15,250
Capital Account :—			Stock		10,500
Opening Balance	18,600		Debtors		8,000
Profit for Year	500				
	19,100				
Less Drawings	1,000				
		18,100			
		£33,750			£33,750

Houghton is dissatisfied with these results, dismisses the manager and engages a new one. In his first year, the new manager :—

(a) Doubles the rate of stock turnover, calculated on the average of the opening and closing stocks.

(b) Increases the rate of gross profit to sales by one-third.

(c) By careful buying, reduces the stock by £3,000 by the end of the year.

(d) Doubles the ratio of cash to credit sales.

(e) Takes as remuneration 25 per cent. of the net profit remaining after charging all expenses, including his own remuneration. Other expenses, including depreciation, are unchanged from the previous year.

The ratios of trade creditors to stock and of debtors to credit sales are the same at the end of the year as at the beginning, and Houghton's drawings are the same as in the previous year.

You are required to draft the Trading and Profit and Loss Accounts of the business for the new manager's first year and the Balance Sheet at the end of the year, and to comment briefly on any striking changes disclosed by a comparison of the two Balance Sheets.

84. The following is the Balance Sheet of Downgrade, Ltd., at 30th September, 1955.

	£		£
Issued Capital (fully paid)—		Goodwill	2,000
50,000 Ordinary Shares		Freehold Land and Build-	
of £1 each . . .	50,000	ings (at cost) . . .	50,000
40,000 6 per cent.		Plant at cost (£70,000) *less*	
Cumulative Preference		depreciation	43,000
Shares of £1 each . .	40,000	Current Assets	12,000
		Cash and Bank Balances .	500
	90,000	Profit and Loss Account .	25,000
Unsecured Loans . . .	30,000		
Trade Creditors. . . .	12,500		
Note.—The Preference			
Dividend has been paid to			
30th September, 1950, only.			
	£132,500		£132,500

You are required to redraft the above Balance Sheet on the assumption that the following scheme of reconstruction is carried through :—

(a) All the Ordinary Shares are reduced to the denomination of 2s. 0d. per share.

(b) The Preference Shareholders agree to accept two new fully paid Ordinary Shares of 2s. 0d. each for each Preference Share held. In consideration thereof the arrears of dividend are cancelled and the Preference Shares become non-cumulative.

(c) The Land and Buildings are to be revalued at £45,000.

(d) Goodwill is to be written off.

(e) The debit balance on Profit and Loss Account is to be eliminated.

(f) Any balance available is to be transferred to Capital Reserve Account.

(g) The Ordinary Shareholders subscribe in cash at par for 100,000 new Ordinary Shares of 2s. 0d. each.

(h) The holders of Unsecured Loans accept £30,000 7 per cent. Debentures (carrying a floating charge) in satisfaction of their claims.

85. The following are the summarised Balance Sheets of Black, Ltd., and White, Ltd., on 31st December, 1955.

	Black, Ltd.	White, Ltd.		Black, Ltd.	White, Ltd.
	£	£		£	£
Ordinary Share			Plant and		
Capital (£1			Machinery .	45,000	2,500
Shares) . .	50,000	8,000	Balance at		
Profit and Loss			Bank .	15,000	4,000
Account . .	15,000	5,000	Other Assets .	40,000	9,000
Creditors . .	35,000	2,500			
	£100,000	£15,500		£100,000	£15,500

The following arrangements take effect on 1st January, 1956 :—

(i) Black, Ltd., purchases all the Shares in White, Ltd., at a valuation of 22s. 6d. per Share, and satisfies the purchase consideration by the issue of an appropriate number of its own Shares, which were valued for the purpose at 30s. 0d. each.

(ii) All manufacturing is in future to be carried on by Black, Ltd., which therefore purchases the Plant and Machinery of White, Ltd., for £3,000, and draws a cheque in favour of White, Ltd., for this amount.

(iii) Immediately after the transfer of the Shares has been completed, White, Ltd., declares and pays a dividend of £3,000. Ignore Income Tax.

Show the journal entries for the above matters in the books of Black, Ltd., and set out the summarised Balance Sheet of Black, Ltd., after the completion of these arrangements.

86. On 31st December, 1955, an accountant prepared the following summary representing the Balance Sheet of Blank, Ltd. :—

	£		£
Capital (Authorised, Issued		Goodwill	8,000
and Paid up)—		Fixed Assets	15,000
30,000 Ordinary		Current Assets	6,000
Shares of £1 each	30,000	Profit and Loss Account .	11,000
Current Liabilities . . .	10,000		
	£40,000		£40,000

In order to relieve the financial stringency disclosed, the following scheme was agreed to and all the consequent legal technicalities were properly completed :—

(a) The Directors, by resolution dated 31st January, 1956, valued the Goodwill at £6,000.

(b) Messrs. A. & Co., licensed valuers, certified the value of the Fixed Assets as £12,000, by certificate dated 31st January, 1956.

(c) The Profit and Loss Account balance was eliminated.

(d) The Ordinary Shareholders were each given the option of subscribing in respect of each ten shares held either :—

(i) Ten Preference Shares of £1, issued as 15s. paid, against a cash payment of 18s. per Preference Share. These shares were to carry a cumulative dividend of 5 per cent. per annum.

or (ii) One Debenture Bond of £10 at par, all Bonds ranking pari passu as a specific charge on the company's fixed assets and carrying 2 per cent. per annum interest. The company reserved the right to refuse this option if more than 1,000 Bonds were applied for.

(e) Ordinary Shareholders holding 10,000 Shares accepted option (i) and those holding 9,000 Shares accepted option (ii), and all money due was paid. The remaining shareholders refused both options. The nominal capital of the company was increased by £10,000 so as to cover the new preference issue.

(f) Each Ordinary Share was reduced so as to rank as a £1 share, 8s. paid up. Any available balance arising out of the capital reduction was to be carried to Capital Reserve Account.

You are required to produce from the information given the Balance Sheet of Blank, Ltd., immediately after the arrangements were completed.

87. On 31st December, 1955, the summarised Balance Sheet of Ravary's, Ltd., was as follows :—

	£		£
Authorised Capital, £20,000 divided into 10,000 6 per cent. Cumulative Preference Shares of £1 each, and 10,000 Ordinary Shares of £1 each.		Land and Buildings . .	2,000
		Plant and Machinery . .	5,000
		Tools and Utensils . . .	1,000
		Stock.	7,000
		Sundry Debtors. . . .	3,000
Paid-up Capital—		Bills Receivable. . . .	900
6,000 Ordinary Shares .	6,000		
6,000 Preference Shares .	6,000		
	12,000		
Less Profit and Loss Account Dr. Balance .	8,000		
	4,000		
5 per cent. Debentures .	3,000		
Sundry Creditors . . .	5,000		
Bills Payable . . .	3,000		
Bank Overdraft . . .	3,900		
	£18,900		£18,900

It was decided to reconstruct the Company, and for this purpose Ravary's (New), Ltd., was registered with a Capital of £20,000 divided into 8,000 Ordinary Shares of £1 each, and 12,000 7 per cent. Cumulative Preference Shares of £1 each, to take over the assets and liabilities of the old company.

The Debenture-holders in Ravary's, Ltd., agreed to accept Preference Shares in Ravary's (New), Ltd., in exchange for their debentures.

The Preference Shareholders in Ravary's, Ltd., were to receive one Preference Share in Ravary's (New), Ltd., for every three shares held by them in the old company.

The Ordinary Shareholders were to be allotted one Ordinary Share, 15s. 0d. paid, in Ravary's (New), Ltd., in exchange for every four shares held by them in the old company.

The costs of the reconstruction of Ravary's, Ltd., amounting to £500, were paid by the new company. Construct the Balance Sheet of Ravary's (New), Ltd.

88. The summarised Balance Sheet of Downward, Ltd., on 31st March, 1956, is as follows :—

BALANCE SHEET.

	£	£		£	£
Authorised and			Fixed Assets—		
Issued Share			Goodwill . . .	12,500	
Capital—			Freehold Land and		
50,000 Ordinary			Buildings . .	40,000	
Shares of £1			Plant and Ma-		
each, fully paid	50,000		chinery . .	35,000	
30,000 6 per cent.			Fixtures and Fit-		
Cumulative			tings . . .	7,500	
Preference					95,000
Shares of £1			Current Assets—		
each, fully paid	30,000		Stock-in-Trade .	15,000	
		80,000	Debtors . . .	18,000	
					33,000
Sundry Creditors . . .		60,000	Profit and Loss Account .		12,000
		£140,000			£140,000

The following scheme of reconstruction is arranged :—

(i) A new company, Downward (1956), Ltd., is formed to acquire the business of Downward, Ltd., on 1st April, 1956. The Authorised Share Capital of the new company is 120,000 Ordinary Shares of £1 each.

(ii) The Creditors of the old company are to receive 90 per cent. of the amount due to them, to be discharged as to £40,000 in cash, and as to £14,000 by the issue of 14,000 Ordinary Shares of £1 each in the new company.

(iii) The Preference Shareholders in the old company are to receive two Ordinary Shares in the new company for every three Preference Shares in the old company.

(iv) The Ordinary Shareholders in the old company are to receive one Ordinary Share in the new company for every two Ordinary Shares in the old company.

(v) The Freehold Buildings are to be revalued at £45,000.

(vi) The debit balances on Profit and Loss Account and Goodwill are to be eliminated.

(vii) The Stock-in-trade is to be revalued at £9,000.

(viii) Fixtures and Fittings and Debtors are taken at their values in the Balance Sheet of Downward, Ltd.

(ix) The balance of the purchase consideration is to be taken as the value of the Plant and Machinery.

(x) The balance of the Authorised Share Capital of the new company is issued to subscribers for cash.

Prepare the Balance Sheet of Downward (1956), Ltd., on 1st April, 1956, on the assumption that the above arrangements have been completed.

89. The abridged Balance Sheets of a wholesale trading company at 31st December, 1954, and 31st December, 1955, were as follows :—

BALANCE SHEETS.

	1954 £	1955 £		1954 £	1955 £
Share Capital . .	25,000	25,000	Motor Vehicles at cost, less depre-		
Profit and Loss Account . . .	3,000	11,000	ciation . . .	24,000	15,000
Loan (repayable in			Stock at cost .	15,000	25,000
1960) . . .	—	6,000	Trade Debtors. .	15,500	16,000
Bank Overdraft .	6,000	—	Balance at Bank .	—	3,000
Trade Creditors .	20,500	17,000			
	£54,500	£59,000		£54,500	£59,000

You are given the following information :—

(1) All the Motor Vehicles were purchased on 1st January, 1954. Depreciation has been charged at 20 per cent. on the straight line method in both 1954 and 1955. Certain vehicles, which had cost £5,000, were sold on 1st January, 1955, for £4,000.

(2) The Trading Account for 1955 showed that total sales were £154,000, and that the gross profit was £14,000. No wages or other expenses were charged in the Trading Account. The Stock has been built up from £15,000 to £25,000 at an approximately even rate throughout 1955.

You are required :—

(a) to compute the rate of turnover in 1955 ;

(b) to calculate the working capital at 31st December, 1954, and 31st December, 1955 ; and

(c) to set out, in the form of a column of figures, the sources of the increase in working capital during 1955.

90. The following are the Balance Sheets of John Halifax, Ltd., as at 31st December, 1954, and 31st December, 1955 :—

	1954			1955		
	£	£	£	£	£	£
Share Capital			5,000			5,000
Profit and Loss Account :—						
As at 1st January	250			900		
Profit for Year	1,150			2,675		
	1,400			3,575		
Less Dividend	500			—		
		900			3,575	
Mortgage on Building			—			5,000
Trade Creditors		660			1,535	
Bank Overdraft		—			1,010	
			£6,560			£16,120
Freehold Building at cost			—			5,000
Machinery, at cost	2,500			4,750		
Less Depreciation	800			1,025		
		1,700			3,725	
Stock of Raw Materials		610			1,050	
Work-in-Progress		435			1,525	
Stock of Finished Goods		950			1,600	
Trade Debtors		1,320			2,195	
Cash at Bank		1,545			25	
			£6,560			£16,120

A shareholder asks you to explain why, although the profits have more than doubled, the directors are recommending no dividend for 1955.

You are required to draft a short report to the shareholder, answering his query, so far as it is possible to do so from an examination of the above figures. Add a recommendation as to action which might enable the company to resume payment of dividends.

Chapter VI

91. Explain the nature and importance of the accounting distinction between "provisions" and "reserves". Illustrate your answer by examples.

92. Give specific examples of provisions for (*a*) future losses and accrued expenses; (*b*) future expenses; (*c*) equalisation of expenditure; and (*d*) contingencies.

93. Uno Limited is a manufacturing and trading company. For the purposes of its business it purchases the lease of certain land and buildings having twenty years to run. It finances this purchase by raising the necessary money by means of an issue of first mortgage debentures, redeemable at a premium at the time when the lease runs out. The cost of issue of these debentures was £1,000. One year later you are asked to advise the directors with regard to the draft annual accounts. You find that the £1,000 appears as an asset in the Balance Sheet, that the interest on the debentures has been charged to Profit and Loss Account, but that no provision whatever has been made in respect of the obligation to redeem the debentures nor in respect of the effluxion of the lease. Submit your report.

94. In what ways may debentures be redeemed? Discuss the necessity of building up a " fund " for the purpose of redeeming an issue of debentures.

95. In 1936, the *X.Y.Z.* Co., Ltd., offered for subscription, at par, £15,000 of 5 per cent. Debentures, repayable at par on 30th November, 1955. Interest was payable half-yearly, on 31st May and 30th November. The issue was fully subscribed and all expenses in connection therewith were written off out of Revenue during the first five years of the currency of the issue. By the terms of issue the Company agreed to set aside a sum of £488 annually out of profits to form a Sinking Fund for the redemption of the Debenture issue, such sums to be invested in gilt-edged securities, together with any Interest arising therefrom. On 30th November, 1954, the book value of the investments stood at £12,637, and on 1st December, 1954, a further £488 was duly invested. During the year ended 30th November, 1955, the net income arising from the Sinking Fund Investments amounted to £577, which was re-invested as received. At the end of the period a further £488 was appropriated, all the Sinking Fund Investments were sold, realising £14,850, and the Debentures were repaid.

Prepare the following on 30th November, 1955 :—

1. Debenture Account.
2. Sinking Fund Account.
3. Sinking Fund Investments Account.

How do you consider the balances of the two latter accounts should be dealt with after the above transactions have been recorded?

96. A company has issued 40,000 Redeemable Preference Shares of £1 each. The Shares, which were fully paid, became due for redemption on 31st December, 1955. By the terms of the issue, a premium of 2s. 6d. per Share was payable in cash on redemption. To provide, in part, for the redemption, 20,000 Ordinary Shares of £1 each are issued at a premium of 2s. 0d. each, and the balance of the funds required for the redemption are provided out of profits. The company has a General Reserve of £100,000.

You are required to show the entries relating to the redemption in the company's ledger.

97. Distinguish between the uses of the terms " Revenue Reserves " and " Capital Reserves ".

98. What matters should receive consideration in deciding whether a Reserve Fund should be invested inside or outside a business ?

99. Discuss the relative merits of gilt-edged securities and an insurance policy as a means of investment for a Sinking Fund.

100. Give three examples of the manner in which a bank might accumulate reserves not disclosed in the published Balance Sheet.

101. It is a principle of Company Law that the interests of a limited company's creditors should not be injured by a return of the company's capital to the shareholders. How can this principle be reconciled with the power to issue Redeemable Preference Shares ?

Chapter VII

102. What is depreciation ? Discuss the various methods by means of which provision may be made for depreciation in the accounts of a trader.

103. What are the principal factors to be considered in assessing depreciation of industrial plant ? How would you deal with the question of obsolescence ?

104. A company recently formed to carry on the business of general engineers has appointed you as accountant. Engineers have reported that the company's machinery will be renewable over an average period of 20 years, and the board therefore desires you (a) to charge the expenditure on machinery to a Machinery Account in the general ledger, and (b) to charge such annual depreciation thereon as will reduce the account to reasonable scrap values in 20 years on the diminishing balance system. Explain the advice you would tender.

105. Authoritative opinion holds that, wherever possible, the straight-line method of providing for depreciation of fixed assets should be employed. What reasons support such opinion and how far is the adoption of the method likely to benefit business undertakings ?

106. Plant which cost £30,000 5 years ago and was then expected to last 10 years has been depreciated on the straight-line method. It has now become clear that this plant will have to be wholly replaced in 3 years' time at a cost of £40,000. Submit your proposals for dealing with the situation in the annual accounts.

107. Describe the inter-relation of interest and depreciation in the financial accounts of manufacturing companies.

108. A manufacturing company with a large and miscellaneous plant decides to charge all repairs and renewals (including renewals of specific machines) to revenue and to maintain the original plant at cost without depreciating it. Assuming that, in fact, this procedure would keep up the original efficiency of the plant, explain whether you can approve the plan.

109. The Annuity method of allocating depreciation charges between financial periods results in progressively increasing net charges appearing in the

books. Where the Sinking Fund method is used, however, equal annual instalments bring in increasingly large amounts as interest return. Some critics have urged that methods showing results so divergent cannot both be right and that both ought to be distrusted. State your reasoned opinion.

110. Give a specimen ruling of a form of Plant Register, and state concisely how the Register should be worked in conjunction with the general accounting system.

111. What principles would you adopt in providing for depreciation of the following assets ?

(i) Freehold Land ; (ii) Plant and Machinery ; (iii) Leasehold Buildings ; and (iv) a Quarry.

112. A limited company owns certain machinery costing £1,100 which is estimated to have a useful life of 10 years and a residual value of £110. You are required to compare critically alternative proposals to depreciate this asset :—

(a) at the rate of 9 per cent. per annum on original cost ; or

(b) at the rate of 20 per cent. per annum on the diminishing book value, assuming proposal (b) will leave £118 on the books at the end of 10 years.

113. Discuss the suggestion that, in times of rising prices, depreciation should be calculated on estimated replacement costs in place of original costs.

114. A company raised by an issue of debentures at par the sum of £20,000, which sum is expended in the purchase of leasehold premises costing £20,000. The company is required by the terms of the issue to create a Sinking Fund for the redemption of the debentures at the end of 30 years, when the lease expires. Explain the operation of the Sinking Fund, of what it would consist after the redemption of the debentures, and what amounts would appear in the company's Balance Sheet :—

(a) When the £20,000 was raised and expended upon the purchase of the lease.

(b) At the end of the 30 years and before repayment of the debentures.

(c) At the end of the 30 years and after repayment of the debentures.

In these circumstances, what provision do you consider should be made for the depreciation of the lease ? Give your reasons.

115. Writers on obsolescence, considered in its technical sense, have expressed the following views as to the manner in which it should be reflected in accounting : (a) that it can be dealt with by an increase in the percentage rate of depreciation which would otherwise be allowed ; (b) that it should be the subject of a specific charge in the Profit and Loss Account ; (c) that profits should be appropriated to a Reserve against the contingency of obsolescence occurring.

State your views, and under (a) consider the situation which would arise if the relative asset should remain in effective use after its cost has been written off.

116. (a) On 1st January, 1952, Big Flats, Ltd., took a lease to run for exactly three years of a piece of land and paid £249 as a premium. The Company prepares accounts at the end of each calendar year. Reproduce the Lease Account on the footing that the expenditure is written off under the Annuity system over the three years, reckoning 10 per cent. per annum interest and taking the nearest £ throughout. £249 is the present value (at 10 per cent.) of an annuity of £100 payable at the end of each of three years.

(b) Assuming that an investment can be found to return 10 per cent. net per annum, and that £75 invested at the end of each of three years (reckoning interest to the nearest £) produces £249, show by means of ledger accounts how the lease described above can be written off and renewed by taking advantage of this fact.

117. A company buys a new Factory for £100,000 on 1st January. It finances the purchase by issuing £100,000 Debentures redeemable at the end of 50 years.

The Factory is estimated to have a life of 50 years, at the end of which it will have no residual value.

The directors decide to provide in the annual accounts for depreciation of the building by the straight line method, and for redemption of the Debentures. They take out a Debenture Redemption Insurance Policy at an annual premium of £1,850 per annum, payable on 1st January each year, the first premium being paid on the day the factory is purchased. The policy is carried in the books at the total of the premiums paid to date. It matures at the end of 50 years, in the sum of £100,000, and the Debentures are then redeemed.

You are required to show the relevant ledger accounts as they would appear in the company's books in the first and fiftieth years to record the above transactions. Ignore debenture interest, and assume that the estimates of the factory's life and residual value prove right.

118. A company commenced business on 1st January, 1953. At that date its Balance Sheet showed paid-up capital £3,000 and balance at bank £3,000, there being no other balances. On 1st January, 1953, it purchased a lease of certain premises (expiring 31st December, 1955) making at once in cash a single payment £2,400. The board of directors were desirous of providing for the amortisation of the lease and took out a policy of insurance to provide a sum of £2,400 to be paid on 31st December, 1955. The premiums were £750 per annum, payable on 1st January, 1953, 1954 and 1955. It was ascertained in advance that the surrender value of the policy would be :—

	£
On 31st December, 1953	600
On 31st December, 1954	1,600

Apart from these matters the company received (in cash) each year gross profits of £1,500 and paid (in cash) each year expenses of £500. At the end of each year it paid a dividend in cash of £200 (ignore Income Tax).

It was desired to maintain the policy in the books at its surrender value.

You are required

(a) to construct ledger accounts (balanced each year) to reflect all these facts, assuming that the policy money was paid on 31st December, 1955, and that a new lease was purchased for £2,400 on that date. (You should distinguish carefully between Profit and Loss Account and Appropriation Account.)

(b) To reproduce the Balance Sheet at 31st December, 1955, immediately before the third premium fell due.

119. Smith, Jones and Robinson are partners in a manufacturing firm ; the bulk of their machinery was purchased prior to 1939. Depreciation has been provided hitherto by the straight-line method, the annual charge being computed on the basis that the machines have a life of 20 years. At 31st March, 1956, the firm's annual accounts are being prepared